Foundations of speech act theory

Although speech act notions are routinely accorded a role in theoretical discussions of the problem of meaning in linguistics and philosophy, both the extent and the details of that role have not been investigated as deeply as they deserve. The philosophers and linguists responsible for this volume's twenty-two original papers make significant advances toward raising the standards of debate in this research area, and their investigations into the semantic, pragmatic and grammatical foundations of speech act theory will prove invaluable to scholars and postgraduate students of the philosophy of language.

Savas L. Tsohatzidis is Associate Professor of General Linguistics at Aristotle University of Thessaloniki. He also edited *Meanings and Prototypes: Studies in Linguistic Categorization.*

Foundations of speech act theory

Philosophical and linguistic perspectives

Edited by Savas L. Tsohatzidis

London and New York

First published 1994
by Routledge
11 New Fetter Lane, London EC4P 4EE

Simultaneously published in the USA and Canada
by Routledge
29 West 35th Street, New York, NY 10001

Typeset by Solidus (Bristol) Limited

Printed and bound in Great Britain by
T.J. Press (Padstow) Ltd, Padstow, Cornwall

British Library Cataloguing in Publication Data
A catalogue record for this book is available from the British Library

Library of Congress Cataloging in Publication Data
A catalogue record for this book has been requested

ISBN 0-415-09524-7

Contents

List of contributors

William P. Alston, Department of Philosophy, Syracuse University, Syracuse, New York, USA.

Kent Bach, Department of Philosophy, San Francisco State University, San Francisco, California, USA.

Rod Bertolet, Department of Philosophy, Purdue University, West Lafayette, Indiana, USA.

Graham H. Bird, Department of Philosophy, University of Manchester, Manchester, UK.

William Croft, Center for the Study of Language and Information, Stanford University, Stanford, California, USA, and Max Planck Institut für Psycholinguistik, Nijmegen, The Netherlands.

Marcelo Dascal, Department of Philosophy, Tel Aviv University, Tel Aviv, Israel.

Steven Davis, Department of Philosophy, Simon Fraser University, Burnaby, British Columbia, Canada.

Robert M. Harnish, Departments of Philosophy and Linguistics, University of Arizona, Tucson, Arizona, USA.

David Harrah, Department of Philosophy, University of California, Riverside, California, USA.

David Holdcroft, Department of Philosophy, University of Leeds, Leeds, UK.

Jennifer Hornsby, Corpus Christi College, University of Oxford, Oxford, UK.

Asa Kasher, Department of Philosophy, Tel Aviv University, Tel Aviv, Israel.

John T. Kearns, Department of Philosophy, State University of New York at Buffalo, Buffalo, New York, USA.

Arthur Merin, Department of Computational Linguistics, Logic and Philosophy of Language, University of Stuttgart, Stuttgart, and Department of Philosophy, Logic and Theory of Science, University of Munich, Munich, Germany.

Huw Price, School of Philosophy, University of Sydney, Sydney, Australia.

François Récanati, Centre de Recherche en Epistemologie Appliquée, Ecole Polytechnique/Centre National de la Recherche Scientifique, Paris, France.

Jerrold M. Sadock, Department of Linguistics, University of Chicago, Chicago, Illinois, USA.

D.S. Shwayder, Department of Philosophy, University of Illinois at Urbana, Urbana, Illinois, USA.

Charles Travis, Department of Philosophy, University of Stirling, Stirling, UK.

Savas L. Tsohatzidis, Department of Linguistics, Aristotle University of Thessaloniki, Thessaloniki, Greece.

Daniel Vanderveken, Département de Philosophie, Université du Québec à Trois-Rivières, Trois-Rivières, Québec, Canada.

Ways of doing things with words
An introduction

Savas L. Tsohatzidis

Suppose all you know about John is that, in uttering a certain sentence yesterday at 5 p.m., he either *gave permission* to Mary to marry a linguist, or *wished* Mary to marry a linguist, or *asked* whether Mary is going to marry a linguist, or *predicted* that Mary will marry a linguist, or *objected* to Mary's marrying a linguist. Could you validly infer, from this piece of disjunctive knowledge, that, no matter which one of these five things John might have *done* in uttering the sentence, what he would have *meant* in uttering it would be *the same*? You certainly could not. And this suggests that, in order to identify what a speaker *means* in uttering a sentence of his language, it is not enough that you should know which individual he thereby purports to identify (for example, Mary) and which property he thereby purports to, truly or falsely, ascribe to that individual (for example, the property of getting married to a linguist at some point in the future) – to put it more generally, it is not enough that you should know which *proposition* he purports to be expressing in uttering the sentence he utters. What is required, in addition, is that you should know what is the meaning-determining *act* in the context of which he expresses that proposition – whether, for example, he expresses it in the context of an act of giving permission, or in the context of an act of giving a wish, or in the context of an act of asking a question, or in the context of an act of making a prediction, or in the context of an act of raising an objection, and so on.

These are some of the acts that, under the generic name of *illocutionary acts* that was given them by Austin (1962), constitute the primary subject matter of speech act theory. Why should they be deemed worthy of linguistic or philosophical interest? The main reason derives from what has just been said of them – namely, that they appear to be *meaning-determining* acts, in the sense that the identification of what a speaker means in uttering a sentence of his language is not possible, even after the proposition he thereby purports to express has been identified, unless it is further determined which one among the various types of acts of this kind he is engaged in performing by means of his utterance. If this is so, and if the study of what speakers of a natural language mean by uttering sentences of that language is, as it is generally acknowledged to be, a central object of linguistic and philosophical investigation, it is no wonder that the study of illocutionary acts should be acknowledged as an indispensable component of the study of meaning.

However, acknowledging that the study of a certain phenomenon is a necessary component of the study of meaning is a different thing from actually pursuing or actively encouraging the study of that phenomenon, and this difference has been especially marked in the case of the study of illocutionary acts, where the acknowledgement took place in the context of a tradition where the propositional, as opposed to the illocutionary, component of meaning, was for a long time the primary, if not the only, object of analytical concern. Consequently, in spite of the fact that the decades following Austin's (1962) pioneering work have known considerable advances in the study of speech acts – many of them connected with the previous work of some of the contributors to this volume – there are many fundamental questions, concerning both the internal structure of speech act theory and its external relations, that have not been sufficiently intensely investigated. This volume brings together twenty-two original papers that investigate some of these fundamental questions and that, in so doing, significantly raise the standards by which attempted answers to them could be evaluated.

If, as is commonly supposed, linguistic meaning is primarily a property of sentences, the idea, briefly introduced above, that the study of illocutionary acts is a necessary component of the study of linguistic meaning might be resisted by someone along the following lines: 'Granted, knowing what illocutionary act a *speaker* has performed in uttering a sentence of his language is essential for knowing what he meant in uttering that sentence; it is well known, however, that what speakers of a natural language mean by uttering sentences of that language is not always the same as what those sentences *themselves* mean; given, then, that speaker meanings and sentence meanings can diverge, why should the study of illocutionary acts, essential though they may be in understanding speaker meaning, be deemed a necessary component of the study of linguistic meaning?' Briefly, the answer is in two parts. The first is that any suggestions to the effect that there are no necessary connections of any sort between speaker meanings and sentence meanings should, as far as natural languages are concerned, be regarded with extreme scepticism, since their acceptance would necessitate the acceptance of the dubiously intelligible, if not obviously incoherent, view that it is possible for the sentences of a natural language *never* to mean any of the things actually meant by speakers of that language uttering them. The second part is that, given that *some* connection between speaker meanings and sentence meanings should be acknowledged as indispensable, there is no reason to suppose that it would be impossible to reconcile the specification of that connection with the recognition of the fact that, *occasionally*, what a speaker of a natural language means by uttering a sentence of his language is not identical with what that sentence itself would *standardly* be used to mean in that language: just as the fact that a person can, on a particular occasion, use a hammer in order to open a locked door does not invalidate the definition of hammers as tools that, in the population of tool users in which that person belongs, are standardly used for nailing rather than for opening locked doors, so the fact that a speaker can, on a particular occasion, use a sentence of his language in order to mean something different from what that sentence would be taken as meaning in that language, does not invalidate the characterization of that sentence's linguistic meaning in terms of what its utterances would standardly be used to mean by the members of the sentence-using population in which that speaker belongs. In short, sentence meaning and speaker meaning must be connected, unless the power of natural language sentences to regularly mean things that are also meant by speakers of those natural languages was to be counted as a miraculous coincidence; and the fact that standard procedures are occasionally put to non-standard employments should be no more surprising in the case of the linguistic behaviour of a population than it would be in the case in the non-linguistic behaviour of that population.

It is a logical possibility, of course, that, among the various components that presumably conspire in determining what speakers of natural languages mean, the illocutionary component should turn out to be relevant in specifying only what these speakers occasionally mean rather than what they standardly mean. However, there do not appear to be natural languages where this possibility is realized, since reference to illocutionary acts appears to be necessary in specifying not only what speakers of those languages occasionally mean, but also what they standardly mean (and so, what the sentences they utter themselves mean) – to give just one, obvious, example, no one would be counted as a speaker of English if he was unaware of the fact that the sentences 'Is Mary going to marry a linguist?' and 'Mary is going to marry a linguist' mean different things, and no account of that difference would be believable unless it specified that the knowledge in question is, in part, knowledge of the fact that the former, but not the latter, sentence would be standardly usable by a speaker of English in order to *ask* whether (rather than to state that) a certain individual called Mary is going to marry a linguist, whereas the latter, but not the former, sentence would be standardly usable by a speaker of English in order to *state* that (rather than to ask whether) a certain individual called Mary is going to marry a linguist. Reference to illocutionary acts that speakers of natural languages perform, then, seems necessary in specifying not only what they occasionally mean, but also what they standardly mean. And since one cannot decide on a priori grounds that, in all languages, only certain types of illocutionary act will be relevant in characterizing standard speaker meanings (and hence, sentence meanings), whereas certain other types of illocutionary act will only be relevant in characterizing occasional speaker meanings, it seems advisable to approach the various issues concerning the role of illocutionary acts in characterizing either standard speaker meanings or occasional speaker meanings without arbitrary preconceptions on the particular types of such acts that might turn out to be relevant in the one or in the other of these areas.

On at least one familiar conception of the distinction between semantic and pragmatic investigations, standard speaker meanings (and the sentence meanings that would be characterizable in their terms) would be regarded as the object of semantic theory, whereas occasional speaker meanings would be regarded as the object of pragmatic theory. If, therefore, illocutionary acts are equally necessary in characterizing standard speaker meanings and occasional speaker meanings, the issues arising when one considers their role in these two domains would be most profitably regarded as issues of semantic and of pragmatic theory, respectively. Accordingly, the first part of the volume has been devoted to papers predominantly addressing the role of illocutionary acts in characterizing standard speaker meaning, and the relations that, in that role, they have to other determinants of standard speaker meaning, whereas the second part has been devoted to papers predominantly addressing their role in characterizing occasional speaker meaning, as well as the relations that, in that role, they may have to other determinants of occasional speaker meaning. Needless to say, any paper in the first part may have implications on the sorts of issues discussed in the second part, and any one in the second part may make assumptions on the sorts of questions raised in the first part; so, the papers in the two parts should hardly be viewed as necessarily unconnected, and their different allocation would be best regarded as primarily a function of their different emphases. More importantly, the difference between standard and occasional speaker meaning, though quite clear in many cases, tends not to be entirely clear in others; consequently, the treatment of a particular phenomenon as primarily semantic rather than pragmatic, or conversely, should, in some though not in all cases, be viewed as grounded on a conjecture concerning the overall adequacy of the theoretical framework within which it is so treated, rather than on the pretheoretical obviousness of the belief that it should be so treated.

Whether they investigate illocutionary acts in their semantic or in their pragmatic capacities, the papers so far referred to deal with theoretical questions whose rather abstract character does not require them (though, of course, it does not forbid them either) to proceed to detailed descriptions of or hypotheses about the grammatical characteristics of sentences that, in a given natural language or in various natural languages, are used for standard or non-standard performances of given illocutionary acts. And, indeed, the idea that there *should* be correlations between the type of grammatical structure that an utterance exemplifies and the type of illocutionary act that it performs does not appear to have anything logically necessary about it, even when the illocutionary act in question is among those that the utterance standardly, and not just occasionally, performs.

Nevertheless, unless one assumes (as no one assumes nowadays) that regularities in form are totally unconnected with regularities in meaning, one would have the right to be surprised in finding that there are, in fact, no significant correlations of any sort between types of grammatical structure that utterances exemplify and types of illocutionary acts that they standardly perform; and if one did find such correlations, one might envisage to use them not only as the basis for a systematic description of the grammatical embodiment of semantically or pragmatically relevant distinctions, but also as a source of valuable insights concerning the nature of these distinctions. Consequently, the search for such correlations would not be devoid of theoretical interest, and so the third, and final, part of the volume has been devoted to systematic investigations of the grammatical correlates of illocutionary acts, either within a natural language or across natural languages.

So much for some very general assumptions underlying the volume's organization. I will now try to give very brief and obviously oversimplified, but, I hope, not entirely unhelpful, indications on some of the main issues addressed by the papers in the three parts, and on the ways in which the treatments of these issues that they propose are related both to each other and to previous treatments of the same or related issues in the linguistic and philosophical literature.

PART I

Once it is recognized that, in order to know what a sentence means in a natural language, it is necessary to know not only what would traditionally be regarded as the proposition that the sentence standardly expresses in that language, but also what illocutionary act it would standardly be used to perform in that language, there are at least two lines of investigation that one might be interested in pursuing. First, without wishing to dispute that the traditional account of what it would be for a sentence to have a certain propositional content may, at least in its broad outlines, be taken to be correct, one might concentrate one's efforts on finding out how the richer notion of a sentence's performing an illocutionary act should in its turn be elucidated. Second, having ascertained that the attempt to elucidate that latter notion brings to light certain fundamental but hitherto neglected dimensions of linguistic phenomena, one might wish to investigate whether these same dimensions make possible, once recognized, a better understanding not only of the notion of a sentence's being usable for the performance of an illocutionary act, but also of the very notion of a sentence's having a propositional content. In short, one might wish to study the illocutionary aspects of sentence meaning both with and without the further aim of using one's results in order to *revise*, if necessary, orthodox accounts of the propositional aspect of sentence meaning. And since an orthodox account of the propositional aspect of sentence meaning is one that

explicates that aspect of a sentence's meaning by reference to its truth conditions (which may be assumed to be world-relative, but, except when the
sentence contains indexical elements, are assumed not to be context-
relative), this means that one may study the illocutionary aspect of sentence
meaning with or without the further aim of using one's results in order to
revise, if necessary, the various formulations of truth-conditional accounts
of the propositional aspects of sentence meaning. Now, there are linguists
and philosophers who, while acknowledging that the study of illocutionary
acts is a necessary component of the study of sentence meaning, appear to
take it to be impossible that such a study might lead to an account of the
propositional aspect of sentence meaning that would be revisionary in the
above sense. But this is certainly not a logically impossible outcome, and
one of the most interesting features of the first part of the volume is that it
makes it clear that it is in fact possible. For, although some of the papers in
that part develop accounts of illocutionary aspects of sentence meaning
that do not raise (and, given their objectives, do not have to raise) the
question whether a proper treatment of these aspects would necessitate
revisions in truth-conditional conceptions of the propositional aspects of
sentence meaning, many others develop arguments that are specifically
designed to show that a proper understanding of illocutionary acts provides
both the opportunity to realize serious limitations and the means of overcoming certain difficulties of standard truth-conditional accounts of the
propositional content of natural language sentences.

Given the prominence of the truth-conditional paradigm in recent
linguistic and philosophical discussions of the semantics of natural
languages, the distinction between accounts of illocutionary acts that are
revisionary or non-revisionary with respect to their presumed implications
on the proper treatment of propositional content is probably the most
significant distinction to draw when one considers speech act theory from
the viewpoint of what might be called its 'external' relations. But there may
be equally significant distinctions to make from an 'internal' viewpoint as
well – that is, distinctions reflecting fundamental differences in the aims
and methods of proposed analyses of the notion of an illocutionary act,
independently of how these analyses are situated with respect to the
distinction between revisionary and non-revisionary attitudes towards
truth-conditional accounts of propositional content. Probably the most
basic distinction in this regard has to do with the difference between
imposing extensional and intensional criteria of adequacy on one's answer
to the question of what an illocutionary act is – or, to put the matter in a
way that abstracts away from possible differences on the issue of propositional content, between imposing extensional and intensional criteria of
adequacy on one's answer to the question of what it is for a proposition,
however characterized, to be expressed in the context of a performance of
an illocutionary act. An *extensionally* correct answer to that question
would, for example, be a system that would characterize the set of all and

only those possible act-kinds that would intuitively be regarded as illocutionary act-kinds, by taking some among them as primitive and by specifying operations by means of which all the others could be derived from those taken as primitive. And such an answer might well be all that one would want to be given by way of an analysis of the notion of an illocutionary act. But there is a real sense in which someone in possession of such an answer, although knowing which act-kinds are illocutionary act-kinds, and what are the logical relationships between the primitive and the non-primitive ones, might not know what it is in virtue of which they all *are* illocutionary act-kinds – might not know, that is, what is the (non-disjunctive) property that they all share and that accounts for their recognition as members of a natural class. And it is precisely when one would have succeeded in specifying such a unifying property that one would have provided an *intensionally* correct answer to the question as to what an illocutionary act is. Of course, providing either an extensionally or an intensionally adequate answer is no easy matter, and it is not to be expected either that all the proposed answers will be (or will be intended to be) complete, or that they will all use the same conceptual resources in order to reach their common goals. But there can be little doubt about the value of goals themselves, and several papers in the first part of the volume make significant attempts towards reaching them, either completely or partially, both on the extensional and on the intensional side. Consequently, using this 'internal' dimension of variation alongside the 'external' one mentioned earlier seems to be a safe guide in situating some of the theoretically crucial proposals that this part of the volume is offering.

The papers by John Kearns and David Shwayder are clear examples of how far-reaching the proposed revisions of standard truth-conditional accounts of propositional content can be when taking place in a speech act theoretic framework. Both papers are mainly concerned with the content of acts of asserting, which, of all kinds of illocutionary acts, might appear to be the least likely to disturb standard assumptions about the representation of propositional content; they both argue, however, that this appearance is merely the result of the failure to appreciate that propositional contents, when properly understood, are no less *action*-theoretic objects than the illocutionary acts they support (though, of course, action-theoretic objects with their own distinctive characters). In 'Meaning, structure and speech acts', Kearns begins by characterizing certain fundamental relations holding between elements of complex intentional acts (in particular, the relation between a component act and an act of which it is a component, the relation between a character-giving and a character-receiving act, and the relation between an enabling and an enabled act), as well as two linguistically fundamental kinds of acts that may stand in one or more of these relations to each other – namely, acts of identifying and acts of representing. He then shows how the propositional content of an assertion can be perspicuously analysed by reference to these two acts in their various possible structural arrangements, and how such an analysis reveals an important distinction between assertions whose content is purely identificatory and assertions whose content is representational (a distinction that corresponds to the absence or presence of a quantificational substratum in the content of an assertion). He finally argues that the semantics of first-order logical languages in terms of which the truth conditions of natural language sentences are standardly stated is constrained either not to give any account whatsoever of some of the possible contents of natural language assertions that the analysis reveals, or to give an insufficiently discriminating account of some others among them; and he accordingly recommends that the conceptual framework that the analysis installs should be adopted as the basis for an adequate description of the propositional content of natural language sentences, one (but not the only) upshot of which would be an account of those sentence's truth conditions that is far subtler than those taking their inspiration from the semantical analysis of first-order logical languages. In 'A semantics of utterance, formalized', Shwayder begins by drawing a distinction between two kinds of condition on purposeful acts – conditions whose fulfilment guarantees the achievement of their attempted goals ('conditions of success'), and conditions whose fulfilment guarantees their *being* attempts directed towards these goals ('conditions for doing') – and suggests that linguistic acts could not be efficient communicative instruments unless their 'conditions for doing' conventionally required them to incorporate indications concerning the means of fulfilling their 'conditions of success'. He then analyses the propositional content of acts of asserting (whose primary goal he takes to be the transmission of knowledge) as an indication of precisely such means – in particular, as an indication of *procedures* for determining whether the grounds of knowledge claims are satisfied – and he proposes a formalization of the relevant notion of procedure which, he suggests, is adequate to the representation of propositional contents of arbitrary complexity (and may also be viewed as offering a revealing reconstruction of the Fregean notion of sense). He finally contrasts the principles and results of his approach with those characteristic of the model-theoretic reconstruction of the notion of propositional content in truth-conditional semantics, and argues that it is to be preferred both on general philosophical grounds that testify to its greater explanatory power and on the grounds of increased descriptive adequacy as well.

   Though Kearns and Shwayder are able to formulate their critiques of standard truth-conditional accounts of propositional content simply by concentrating on the content of assertions, it would be unlikely that these accounts should not encounter additional difficulties when the content of the many *other* kinds of illocutionary acts is taken into consideration. It is not surprising, then, that the recognition of such additional difficulties is one of the results of attempting to provide an extensionally adequate characterization of the notion of an illocutionary act – a topic that figures prominently in the papers by Daniel Vanderveken and Arthur Merin. In 'A complete formulation of a simple logic of elementary illocutionary acts', Vanderveken presents the fullest proposal to date of an extensionally adequate characterization of the notion of an illocutionary act, in the form of a logical system where all possible non-basic illocutionary acts are presented as products of the recursive application of one or another of a limited number of operations on one or another of a restricted number of formal objects that are held to adequately represent five basic illocutionary acts (those that would be rendered colloquially by the verbs 'assert', 'direct', 'commit', 'declare' and 'express'). The clear statement of important, and hitherto unrecognized, logical relations between various types of illocutionary acts is one significant result that this attempt at an extensionally adequate definition offers. And a no less significant feature of the present realization of that attempt (as opposed to earlier ones by Vanderveken) is its insistence on, and clear formal embodiment of, the idea that the standard truth-conditional account of propositional content cannot capture certain central features of human rationality that are manifested in the performance of illocutionary acts and that determine their logical relationships, unless appropriately enriched in certain ways (specifically, unless propositional identity is defined not just in terms of truth-conditional equivalence, but also in terms of a notion of bilateral strong implication). Vanderveken's paper, then, would have provided, if successful, both an extensionally adequate characterization of the notion of an illocutionary act and a demonstration of the need of transcending, in order to obtain such a characterization, a purely truth-conditional account of the propositional content of natural language sentences. To a considerable extent, a similar dual concern can also be viewed as the main concern of Arthur Merin's 'Algebra of elementary social acts', though his starting point is characteristically different. Unlike Vanderveken's, Merin's choice of basic speech acts – aletheic or deontic claims, concessions or rejections of such claims, and withdrawals or reiterations of such claims – reflects a theoretical commitment to the view that it is as components of *dialogue* that illocutionary acts should best be elucidated. Having presented a mathematical model of dialogue within which these basic speech acts are defined by means of choices of particular values for certain formally specified parameters, Merin is then able to show that definitions of many other speech act kinds are readily obtainable from it – for example, by choosing alternative values for some of the parameters, or by constructing otherwise similar models where some of the parameters remain unspecified. In parallel, Merin shows that the characterizations of speech acts that his framework provides afford precise accounts of a wide variety of semantic phenomena which, though situated at the propositional rather than at the illocutionary level, have long been known or can easily be shown to be intractable within the bounds of standard truth-conditional accounts of the propositional content of natural language sentences. Like

Vanderveken's, then, Merin's paper purports to offer both appropriate bases for constructing an extensionally adequate characterization of illocutionary acts and important insights on the usability of that characterization in overcoming serious difficulties of truth-conditional approaches to propositional meaning.

William Alston and Jennifer Hornsby assume, for their part, that an appropriate characterization of propositional content is in place, and concentrate instead on the project of combining it with an intensionally, and not just extensionally, adequate characterization of the notion of an illocutionary act. In 'Illocutionary acts and linguistic meaning', Alston arrives at that characterization in the context of the most systematic presentation to date of his well-known proposal to identify the notion of a sentence's being meaningful with the notion of that sentence's having a certain illocutionary act potential. He first formulates certain conditions concerning the relations that must obtain between a speaker and a proposition he expresses in order for that speaker to be performing, while expressing that proposition, an illocutionary act, and argues that standard accounts of illocutionary acts fail to respect these conditions. He then proposes a definition of the notion of a speaker's performing an illocutionary act in terms of the notion of that speaker's assuming responsibility for certain states of affairs related to the proposition he expresses, where the notion of a speaker's assuming responsibility for a certain state of affairs related to the proposition he expresses is explicated via the notion of that speaker's conferring on the members of his linguistic community the right to subject him to various forms of *criticism* in the event that that state of affairs turns out not to obtain. Alston finally shows how that definition avoids the problems encountered by previous ones, how it can incorporate a number of interesting refinements, and how, when employed in the analysis of the concept of meaningfulness, it leads to a characterization of that concept that, unlike many others, succeeds in capturing its normative character. The idea that certain relations between speakers and their linguistic communities – rather than some solitary properties of speakers – is at the heart of the notion of an illocutionary act is also central to, though it is differently elucidated in, Hornsby's 'Illocution and its significance'. Hornsby begins by a searching critique of Austin's not entirely felicitous attempts to distinguish illocutionary acts from so-called locutionary ones on the one hand and from so-called perlocutionary ones on the other, offering at the same time a diagnosis of Austin's difficulties. She then uses that diagnosis as the basis of her own definition of illocutionary acts as acts with the distinctive property that it is a sufficient condition of a speaker's performing them that an attempt by that speaker to perform them should cause the speaker's audience to infer that he does perform them – in other words, as acts for which the possibility of a transition from attempted performance to successful performance requires merely, but essentially, the *recognition* of attempted performance. Hornsby then shows how that definition can be used in elucidating a variety of more specific issues in speech act theory, as well as certain apparently unconnected issues in other areas of philosophical concern (for example, the – prominent in contemporary political debates – issue of silencing, which she reconstructs as the issue of refusing to recognize a person's (or group's) illocutionary attempts, and so effectively undercutting that person's (or group's) capacity to ever aspire to successful illocutionary attempts).

There are interesting and important differences between Alston's and Hornsby's definitions, but one central feature that they share is that, by taking the performance of an illocutionary act by a speaker to crucially involve reference to other members of his linguistic community (either as subjects whose recognitional capacities ensure the success of his attempts, or as subjects whose critical capacities circumscribe the domain of his assumed responsibilities), they stand opposed to attempted definitions of the notion of an illocutionary act in which all reference to a speaker's relations to other members of his linguistic community has been erased and only his internal states are counted as constitutive of the meaningful character of his linguistic accomplishments. Attempts of this sort have not been unpopular, and one among them is especially prominent in some of the more recent writings of John Searle (1983, 1986), in particular in his claim that his influential earlier taxonomy of illocutionary acts into the subcategories of assertive, directive, commissive, expressive and declarative acts can be shown to be coextensive with a subcategorization of these acts into acts of expressing one or another of the basic kinds of mental attitudes that an organism is capable of adopting towards a proposition (for example, the attitude of believing it to be true in the case of assertive acts, the attitude of desiring it to become true in the case of directive acts, the attitude of intending to make it true in the case of commissive acts, etc.), and can therefore lead to an intensionally adequate characterization of the notion of a speaker's performing an illocutionary act in terms of the notion of that speaker's expressing one or another of the basic kinds of mental attitudes that it is humanly possible to adopt towards a proposition. The papers by Steven Davis and Savas Tsohatzidis may be viewed as complementary attempts to show that an intensional characterization of illocutionary acts along these lines may not be as unproblematic as its popularity might suggest. In 'Anti-individualism and speech act theory', Davis argues that, suitably adapted, some important kinds of consideration that have been recently employed in order to show that the contents of mental states cannot be individuated without reference to the linguistic and extra-linguistic environments in which the subjects of those states are situated can be independently employed in order to show that the contents of illocutionary acts cannot be individuated without reference to the linguistic and extra-linguistic environments in which the agents of those acts are situated – an argument that suggests that, even if definitions of these acts in terms of such states were forthcoming, it would not follow, as Searle supposes, that an adequate intensional characterization of the former would need no more conceptual resources than those required for an account of the internal states of an organism. In 'The gap between speech acts and mental states', Tsohatzidis argues that none of the arguments that have been used by Searle in order to motivate the claim that there *are* necessary connections between types of illocutionary acts and types of expressed mental states (between, for example, assertions and expressions of belief, directives and expressions of desire, promises and expressions of intentions, etc.) is successful, and, consequently, that no identification of a speaker's capacity to perform illocutionary acts with his capacity to express his mental states would be legitimate, even if it were possible to individuate the contents of either the acts or the states without reference to their subjects' linguistic and extra-linguistic environment. Taken together, then, these two papers would appear to indirectly support an approach to the problem of intensionally characterizing illocutionary acts which would be like Alston's or Hornsby's in assuming that what happens in an individual's private mind cannot, without reference to his community, determine what, in uttering sentences, that individual means.

It would be naive to suppose, of course, that this or the other, wider or narrower, theoretical divergencies to which reference or allusion has been made so far can be expected to be resolved fairly quickly and easily. On the other hand, it would be hard to deny that the discussions within which the divergencies are expressed presuppose a substantive number of agreements on the kinds of problems to be resolved, and provide a number of standards by means of which progress in their resolution could be measured. And if this is so, one might wonder how there have been people who have been able to greet the appearance of speech act theory on the philosophical scene with the firm denial that either it or the wider philo-sophical movement (of so called 'ordinary language' philosophy) within which it emerged might have any systematic contribution to make to the elucidation of problems of meaning in natural language. To the extent that the answer to that question has merely to do with matters of intellectual fashion it would of course be uninteresting in the present context. But the question surely admits of a more interesting interpretation – namely, as a question regarding the plausibility of certain influential arguments that some of these people had put forward in order to justify their denials. The papers by Huw Price, François Récanati and Charles Travis look at some of the most important of these arguments in detail, and argue that they are far less plausible than they have been supposed to be. In 'Semantic minimalism and the Frege point', Price identifies as one of the main theses underlying the original formulation of speech act theory the thesis that many of the apparently fact-stating uses of sentences are not, in reality, fact-stating, and that the recognition of the fact that they are not provides the only basis for a satisfactory semantic analysis of certain words – as it happens, of certain philosophically very important words – occurring in them. He then shows that an influential argument that has been taken to be fatal to that thesis – the argument that the semantic analysis of the words in question in terms of certain non-fact-stating uses of sentences in which they occur is unacceptable because it gives no account of the role of these same words in other sentences with recognizably different uses – is in fact unsuccessful, since a principled account can be provided of the ways in which the occurrence of these words in sentences whose uses do not have to be mentioned in their analysis systematically depends on their occurrence in sentences whose uses do have to be mentioned in their analysis. He finally suggests that the broader claim concerning the non-fact-stating nature of apparently fact-stating utterances could be fruitfully reformulated in terms of a notion of minimal statementhood (itself modelled on recent proposals of minimalist definitions of truth), and that, thus reformulated – that is, as the claim that not all of the sentences that perform minimal acts of stating are sentences performing acts of physical signalling – it would make possible a clearer understanding both of the importance of the speech act theoretic contribution to the study of sense and of the directions in which that contribution could be furthered. In 'Contextualism and anti-contextualism in the philosophy of language', Récanati identifies as another one of the main theses characteristic of the intellectual climate within which speech act theory was initially conceived the thesis that what the utterance of a sentence expresses is, even when the sentence does not contain indexical expressions, in part determined by the context of its utterance. He then shows that the main argument that has been directed (and has been widely accepted as valid) against semantic analyses proposed in the spirit of that thesis – the argument that these analyses ought to be rejected because they multiply senses beyond necessity – is in fact unsuccessful, since it question-beggingly assumes that the only possible source of variability in a sentence's interpretation is the fact that the sentence is ambiguous in its sense rather than the fact that its sense does not determine a unique proposition unless supplied by contextual information (a possibility that on all sides would be agreed to be clearly exemplified by the case of indexical sentences). Récanati accordingly concludes that the contextualist thesis can hardly be taken to have been undermined in principle, and suggests that the choice between contextualist and anti-contextualist treatments of any particular problem area should only be determined by considering their relative merits with respect to that particular problem area. It would be instructive, in view of Récanati's suggestion, to consider a fresh application and defence of the contextualist strategy in a central problem area, and it is such an application and defence that is provided in Charles Travis' 'On being truth-valued', whose primary concern is with the semantic characterization of predicates. A predicate with a stable sense, Travis argues, does not determine a stable set of truth conditions valid for all its occurrences, and so the question as to what truth-valuable proposition, if any, is expressed by a sentence containing it can only be decided by evaluating the circumstances in which the sentence has been uttered – and in particular, the special character of the assertoric speech act in the context of which it has been produced. One consequence of this fact, Travis then notes, is that many propositions expressed in the context of an assertion may, for contingent reasons, be truth-valueless. But this consequence, he urges, should hardly be counted as unwelcome, both because it offers a unifying framework within which other phenomena can be explained as special cases, and because the standard argument against it – namely that it is bound to lead to contradictions – can be shown to be confused (in not respecting, among other things, an important distinction between claims concerning the truth-valuelessness of statements and claims concerning the truth-valuelessness of thoughts).

If, as these last three papers suggest, the arguments that were once thought to support some kind of generalized scepticism about the semantic relevance of speech act theoretic considerations are unsuccessful, and if, as the other eight papers suggest, there are not only very good independent arguments in favour of their semantic relevance but also precise ways of spelling that relevance out (either in the form of fruitfully renewed accounts of propositional content, or in the form of detailed proposals for extensionally and intensionally adequate characterizations of the notion of illocutionary act), then this part of the volume could surely be viewed as making a significant step towards consolidating the position of speech act theory as a component of an overall semantic theory of natural language, at least by placing the burden of proof on someone who would be willing to challenge that position.

PART II

The distinction between what the utterance of a natural language sentence would standardly mean and what it might occasionally mean (which is not, of course, intended to suggest that 'standard' meanings do not manifest themselves on all occasions, but rather that 'occasional' meanings only manifest themselves on a subset of those occasions) is indisputable in certain central cases, and it is the existence of such cases that has given rise to the greater part of pragmatic, as distinct from semantic, investigations. The problems that such investigations must try to solve are of two broad kinds. First – and obviously, given the existence of a large number of unclear cases – they must try to formulate principles by reference to which it could legitimately be decided whether an interpretation that a sentence receives is or is not dictated by its standard meaning (and also principles by reference to which one might distinguish between different *kinds* of non-standard meanings, since, just as there are pretheoretically obvious differences between meanings that are standardly conveyed and meanings that are non-standardly conveyed, there are also pretheoretically obvious differences between various *sorts* of non-standardly conveyed meanings).

Second, they must try to provide an account of the inferential mechanisms that are presumably responsible for the fact that utterances of natural-language sentences *can* be interpreted in ways that are not dictated by their standard meanings (and also an account of the special forms that these mechanisms must be assumed to be taking when generating different kinds of non-standard meanings). These two problems might be called the problem of delimitation and the problem of explanation, respectively. And although it might be granted that one's proposed solution to the delimitation problem will, to some extent, be influenced by one's proposed solution to the explanation problem, it should also be evident that the two problems are different and that the influence in question should never be allowed to be complete: if one's proposed scheme for explaining *how* something may be non-standardly conveyed is taken to completely determine *what* is non-standardly conveyed, there is a very real danger not only that many of the facts that really are in need of explanation may never be in one's view, but also that many of the facts that one takes oneself to be explaining may turn out to be just artefacts of one's explanatory scheme.

The papers in the second part of the volume are, for the most part, concerned either with proposing new approaches or with criticizing older approaches to aspects of the delimitation and the explanation problems, especially in so far as these problems are related to the speech act components of both standard meanings and occasional meanings. And since the work of Paul Grice (1975, 1979, 1989) was the first serious attempt to address the delimitation and the explanation problems in the linguistic and philosophical literature, they all make reference to basic Gricean themes. But since Grice's account of the distinction between standard meanings and occasional meanings, and of the inferential mechanism that is responsible for the derivation of an utterance's occasional meaning on the basis of its presumed standard meaning, was not designed with the intention of being directly incorporated into a theory of speech acts (in fact, Grice's suggestions concern exclusively standard and occasional meanings of acts of assertion, and they do not even attempt to give a general characterization of assertion in speech act terms), there are many different types of more refined questions that the distinction between standard meanings and occasional meanings may be expected to generate when discussed in a sufficiently articulated speech act theoretic framework. Three of these types of question may be usefully distinguished in the present context, the first concerning issues in the analysis propositional content, and the other two issues in the analysis of illocutionary acts. First, one might consider the mode of applicability of the distinction between standard meaning and occasional meaning at the level of propositional content alone – that is, one might examine under what conditions the proposition that a sentence conveys could or could not be analysed as dictated by its standard meaning, even assuming that the kind of illocutionary act that the sentence performs remains fixed in virtue of that standard meaning. Second, one might examine the mode of employment of the opposition between standard meaning and occasional meaning as an opposition yielding a distinction between two different kinds of *tokens* of the same illocutionary act – in other words, one might be interested in the conditions under which an illocutionary act which, when performed by the utterance of a certain form, should be analysed as one whose performance has been dictated by the sentence's standard meaning, must, when performed by means of an utterance of a sentence of a different form, be analysed as one whose performance was not dictated by that sentence's standard meaning (this is the problem usually discussed in the terminology of 'direct' and 'indirect' performances of illocutionary acts). And finally, one might examine the mode of employment of the opposition between standard meaning and occasional meaning as an opposition yielding a distinction between two different kinds of *types* of illocutionary acts – for example, one might wish to explore the possibility that some, though not all, illocutionary act types are such that *all* their tokens are only performable by means of sentences whose standard meaning does not dictate their performance (in other words, whose performance is always a reflection of occasional rather than of standard speaker meaning). Traditionally, it is only the second of these questions that has absorbed the attention of speech act theorists, and it is in the area of attempted answers to that question that the most detailed analytical proposals are to be found. But the equal theoretical interest of the first and the third could hardly be doubted, and some proposals have recently been made in connection with them. The papers in the second part of the volume appropriately reflect this broadening of concerns, by examining or proposing solutions to either the delimitation or the explanation problem in all three of the areas just indicated.

The conditions of application of the distinction between standard meaning and occasional meaning to the propositional content of illocutionary acts is at the centre of Kent Bach's 'Semantic slack: what is said and more'. Bach begins by recalling Grice's formulation of the distinction between standard and occasional meaning in terms of his notions of what is *said* and of what may be conversationally *implicated* by an uttered sentence, and argues that this formulation is inadequate in two respects: first, and more obviously, it fails to do justice to the fact that what is said sometimes does not correspond to anything that was intended to be conveyed, and second, and most importantly, it forces one to treat as conversational implicatures two kinds of conveyed proposition that cannot be legitimately identified with the content of what is, strictly speaking, said, and yet are too closely related to the content of what is strictly speaking said to be legitimately counted as cases of conversational implicature (these are, on the one hand, the propositions obtained by *expanding* in certain syntactically constrained ways the already specified 'minimal proposition' corresponding to what is strictly speaking said, and, on the other hand, the propositions obtained by *completing* in certain conceptually required ways the underspecified 'propositional radicals' corresponding to what is strictly speaking said). Bach then argues that these problems can be solved by, first, modifying the conception of saying so as not to be taken to always correspond to something that is intended to be conveyed, and, second, by recognizing a category of conveyed propositions that are intermediate between those comprising what is strictly speaking said and those comprising what is conversationally implicated (in his proposed terminology, a distinct category of 'implicitures' that comprises the pragmatically conveyed propositions that are either expansions or completions of what is strictly speaking said, and that form the basis of *further* pragmatic inferences leading to what is conversationally implicated). Bach finally argues that his solution is preferable to ones that are implicit or explicit in certain other recent treatments of some of the problems he is investigating, that it provides the means of elucidating and overcoming additional difficulties in the Gricean framework, and that it shows the Austinian notion of a locutionary – as distinct from an illocutionary – act (to which the revised notion of saying closely corresponds) to be of much more theoretical interest than its relative neglect in the speech act theoretic literature would lead one to suppose.

When employed in order to mark a distinction between different kinds of *tokens* of a given illocutionary act, the distinction between standard and occasional meaning leads, as already noted, to the distinction between 'direct' and 'indirect' performances of an illocutionary act (that is, respectively, between those of its performances that are and those of its performances that are not dictated by the standard meaning of the sentence used for its performance). A highly representative, and perhaps the most influential, formulation of that doctrine is the one by Searle (1979), who contends that the 'indirect' performability of illocutionary acts through sentences whose standard meanings do not authenticate their performance is a special case of the general phenomenon of a hearer's inferring what a speaker conversationally implicates by his utterance – an inference that, in cases of illocutionary indirection, involves, according to Searle, two crucial assumptions: first, that the speaker does perform, 'directly', the illocutionary act whose performance *is* authenticated by the standard meaning of the sentence he utters; and second, that this cannot be *the only* illocutionary act he performs, given that he may be presumed to observe, in the conversational context in which he is situated, certain principles of rationality (of the sort postulated in Grice's theory of conversation) whose observance would only be possible if he simultaneously performed an additional (the so-called 'indirect') act as well. The papers by Rod Bertolet, David Holdcroft and Savas Tsohatzidis suggest, each in its own way, that the doctrine of 'directly', and 'indirectly' performable illocutionary acts, at least in its standard, Searlian, version, is of questionable validity. Bertolet's basic claim in 'Are there indirect speech acts?' is that, in central cases where the notion of indirect performance has been invoked, no illocutionary act other than the so-called 'direct' one can legitimately be supposed to have been performed: the postulation of a further 'indirect' act, Bertolet argues, is both open to the conceptual objection that it confuses the notion of something's having a certain property with the notion of something's being treated *as if* it had that property, and to the methodological objection that it is not necessary in order to explain the relevant facts (these facts can all be explained, on Bertolet's proposal, just by supposing that the result of a hearer's employing the Gricean inferential mechanism in the kinds of circumstances considered by Searle is merely the conclusion that the speaker gives oblique information about certain of his mental states, and not the further conclusion than that he actually performs 'indirectly' the acts that would be normally associated with those states). Holdcroft's basic claim in 'Indirect speech acts and propositional content' is, on the other hand, that, in central cases where the notion of an 'indirect' performance of an illocutionary act has been invoked, no illocutionary act other than this allegedly 'indirect' one can legitimately be supposed to have been performed: the postulation of a background 'direct' act, he argues, often depends on empirically questionable assumptions concerning the extent to which formal indicators of illocutionary potential are available, leads to conceptually untenable results when the allegedly co-present 'direct' and 'indirect' acts happen to have conflicting conditions of satisfaction, and is methodologically suspect since it unnecessarily complicates the account of the inferential mechanisms that, in the absence of clear formal indications of illocutionary potential, a hearer can plausibly be supposed to employ in order to determine what illocutionary act the speaker has performed. The arguments that these two papers offer against Searle's doctrine of 'direct' and 'indirect' illocutionary acts might be supposed to proceed from diametrically opposed premises. But they do not have to be supposed to so proceed, especially if one is prepared to agree that the cases of alleged 'indirectness' that justify the criticisms of the first are not of the same sort as the cases of alleged 'indirectness' that justify the criticisms of the second, and conversely. And if this is so, one further consideration that the papers might invite is that the Searlian account of 'direct' and 'indirect' performances of illocutionary acts is problematic not only because it misanalyses several cases of 'indirectness' that it takes to be central, but also because it unjustifiably assumes that the phenomena that the label of 'indirectness' collects are in fact homogeneous. The issue of heterogeneity is also the main theme of Tsohatzidis's 'Speaker meaning, sentence meaning and metaphor', though the heterogeneity under discussion there is one that Searle clearly acknowledges and attempts to account for, since it does not concern the phenomenon of illocutionary 'indirectness' as such, but rather the relation between that phenomenon and the phenomenon of figurativity – a relation that it is important for Searle to be able to elucidate, since both of these phenomena, though intuitively quite different, are, according to him, cases of occasional speaker meaning and analysable in terms of the notion of conversational implicature. Tsohatzidis argues that Searle does not succeed either in his attempt to properly distinguish between different types of figurativity or in his attempt to properly distinguish figurativity on the one hand and illocutionary 'indirectness' on the other, and he further suggests that, at least as far as one central case of figurativity (the case of metaphor) is concerned, Searle's and many other theorists' unargued assumption that it *is* a case of non-standard rather than of standard meaning is actually in conflict with their official tests for determining whether a given conveyed meaning is conveyed standardly or non-standardly. If the arguments of this paper are well taken, then, it would seem that the doctrine of 'direct' and 'indirect' performances of illocutionary acts suffers, in its current form, from rather serious inadequacies in respect of various delimitation problems. And if, as the papers by Bertolet and Holdcroft suggest, it is also poorly equipped to address various explanation problems, it would appear that few of its current features should be left unchallenged in future research.

One idea that probably *will* continue to motivate future research is that pragmatic considerations of conversational rationality of the sort figuring in Grice's account of the derivation of occasional meanings on the basis of standard meanings must *at some point* be integrated with speech act theoretic considerations. But this general idea can be developed in a more or in a less radical way, and the way it is developed in the doctrine of direct and indirect performances of illocutionary acts is in fact the less radical way: pragmatic considerations are there supposed to facilitate the identification of certain tokens of illocutionary act types – namely, those tokens whose realization does not depend on the standard meanings of the utterances used for their performance – but the assumption is that these same illocutionary act types (and, indeed, all illocutionary act types) are *also* tokened in ways that strictly depend on the standard meanings of utterances used in their performance; within this conception, then, it is legitimate to construct a purely semantic theory covering all illocutionary act types by concentrating on tokens of the latter kind, while allowing that a parallel pragmatic theory might be needed in order to explain the occasional appearances of tokens of the former kind. If, however, one is prepared to argue that there are *types* of illocutionary acts whose tokens are all of the former, and not of the latter, kind – in other words, whose performance is always a matter of occasional rather than of standard meaning – then one opts for the more radical view according to which no purely semantic theory covering all illocutionary act types is possible, and that such a theory will have to contain, alongside the semantic, an irreducibly pragmatic component as well. Marcelo Dascal's paper on 'Speech act theory and Gricean pragmatics' offers a series of considerations that would be useful in appreciating the significance that such a split in the theory of illocutionary act types would have – the significance, for example, of the difference between a semantic characterization of an illocutionary

act type in terms of certain constitutive rules and a pragmatic characterization of the same type in terms of certain defeasible presumptions – and
points out that an early (and generally neglected) indication of the possibility of such a split can be detected in the different ways in which Searle
and Grice were trying to formulate their common opposition to certain
ways of appealing to linguistic evidence in offering solutions to philosophical problems. The papers by Graham Bird and Asa Kasher, on the
other hand, review, the one negatively and the other positively, detailed
recent proposals as to how the split should be motivated and systematically
represented. In 'Relevance theory and speech acts', Bird begins by
surveying Sperber and Wilson's (1986) arguments to the effect that only
three illocutionary act types should be regarded as associated with standard
sentence meanings, and that all the rest, to the extent that may be allowed
to have a place in an account of linguistic communication, should be
characterized pragmatically using the resources offered by their theory of
relevance. He then suggests that none of the arguments Sperber and
Wilson use in order to motivate either the distinction between semantically
encoded and non-semantically encoded illocutionary act types, or the
distinction between communicatively significant and communicatively non-
significant illocutionary act types, rests on secure premises, and that some
of them would not in fact support their purported conclusions, even if their
premises were secure. He finally claims that the principles on which the
theory of relevance is constructed do not ensure that its applications will
not be explanatorily empty, both in general and in connection with the
speech act theoretic issues to which Sperber and Wilson have attempted to
apply them. His conclusion is, then, that at least one way of motivating the
distinction between semantically and pragmatically characterizable illocutionary act types should probably be abandoned. This conclusion does
not, of course, entail that there might not be other ways of motivating that
distinction, and one of Kasher's aims in 'Modular speech act theory:
programme and results' is precisely to defend a different way. Kasher
begins by outlining the general requirements that, on now standard conceptions of cognitive science, should be fulfilled by a theoretical representation of any human competence (linguistic or otherwise) as a property of
the mind. He then adopts a particular set of independently confirmed
criteria for answering, within that general framework, the question of the
extent to which the organization of any particular human competence is
modular or non-modular (that is, depends for its exercise on special-
purpose or on general-purpose information-processing capacities of the
mind). And he finally argues, basing himself both on theoretical considerations and on experimental evidence, that the human competence that is
exercised in the performance of illocutionary acts is organized partly in a
modular and partly in a non-modular way (its modular component being
manifested in the ability to perform illocutionary acts of certain basic types
that have close connections with standard sentence meanings and appear to

be endowed both with special principles of organization and with proper neural embodiments, and its non-modular component being manifested in the ability to perform a wide variety of non-basic illocutionary act types for which no obvious connections with standard sentence meanings exist, and which do not appear to be endowed either with special principles of organization or with proper neural embodiments). It seems, then, that research on the possibility of a distinction between pragmatically and semantically construable illocutionary act types can be a source of interesting results of either a positive or a negative nature, and it is not unlikely that it will be as active in the future as research on the possibility of a distinction between pragmatically and semantically guided interpretations of tokens of a given illocutionary act type has been in the past.

There are, of course, many other areas in which considerations that would generally be described as pragmatic might be relevantly conjoined with research on illocutionary acts. For example, the fact that specific linguistic means are optionally, but fairly systematically, used in indicating the purported senders and intended receivers of certain illocutionary acts and their relative statuses, or the discourse topics to which these acts purport to make contributions and the discourse presuppositions under which they purport to make these contributions, is, as David Harrah shows in his paper 'On the vectoring of speech acts', a fact that, properly understood, provides important insights on the kinds of requirements that are standardly expected to be fulfilled by communicative uses of language, and must therefore be captured by any description of these acts that is sensitive to their standard usability as instruments of communication. Even if, however, the pragmatic component of the study of speech acts is primarily taken to concern the apparently narrower issue of the relation between standard and occasional sentence meanings, as is implicitly or explicitly the case with all the other contributions to the second part of the volume, the complexity of the problems involved is formidable. And it is, I think, in the fact that they force us to accept the recognition of that complexity as a prerequisite to any viable solution that the primary value of these contributions lies. For they clearly suggest that, viewed from the viewpoint of either the propositional or the illocutionary component of speech acts, neither the delimitation nor the explanation problems associated with the distinction between standard and occasional meaning will be as simple as many followers of the Gricean or of other pragmatic theories have tended to suppose. And since they often accompany this suggestion with specific proposals as to how some of the complexities might be untangled, their success would tend to support the view that the domain of speech acts is not only a domain where analytical tools deriving from recent pragmatic theory might be fruitfully applied but also a domain that provides excellent opportunities for sharpening many of these analytical tools.

PART III

The capacity of a sentence to be standardly used in the performance of illocutionary acts of a certain kind need not be *structurally* signalled, in the sense that sentences structurally similar to it are not logically compelled to have similar capacities. Nevertheless, the hypothesis that *some* significant correlation might be found to exist between the illocutionary capacities of sentences and their grammatical characteristics is an interesting empirical hypothesis, and the fact that a particular formulation of that hypothesis – generally known as the 'performative hypothesis' – had to be abandoned in the course of the early history of transformational grammar does not show that every formulation of it would be similarly indefensible. There are two distinct types of interest that research aimed at confirming appropriate formulations of such an hypothesis might serve. First, and less radically, one might be interested in finding correlations between grammatical characteristics and illocutionary capacities simply because, once found, these correlations would make possible a simple and predictively powerful formulation of that part of the semantics of natural language sentences that concerns their illocutionary act potential. Second, and more radically, one might be interested in establishing such correlations in order to extract, by considering the relations between them, certain conclusions about the nature of illocutionary acts that would not be available to theoretical analyses of them that ignore the question of their grammatical manifestation, and that might therefore have to be revised in view of sufficiently powerful grammatical evidence. (Someone following the less radical way, for example, might be interested to find that there are correlations between indicative sentences and acts of asserting, imperative sentences and acts of requesting, and interrogative sentences and acts of questioning, but might not envisage that these correlations, important though they are in systematizing the semantic description of the relevant sentence types, are of any relevance to the analysis of the *concepts* of asserting, of requesting, or of questioning. Someone following the more radical way, however, might, apart from ascertaining these same correlations, observe that interrogative sentences are, in many languages, much more similar, structurally speaking, to indicatives than they are similar to imperatives, and use this observation as a basis for claiming that a theoretical analysis of questions as a kind of heavily hedged assertions would be preferable to the standard analysis of them as a kind of requests.) Of course, these two approaches are not in principle incompatible, but they are usually pursued separately, and they are certainly distinct in respect of the range of data that each one would oblige its follower to take into account: sufficiently rich data from a single language at a time would be enough for the less radical approach, but such data would obviously be insufficient to give credibility to the kinds of claims that would be characteristic of the more radical approach, and appeal to cross-linguistic evidence would accordingly be necessary to support them. The three papers comprising the third part of the volume offer examples of both approaches, and of the insights that may be gained by systematically pursuing either one of them.

Robert Harnish's paper on 'Mood, meaning and speech acts' is a monograph-length contribution proposing a full theory of sentential moods (that is, of standard sentence-type/illocutionary act-type correlations) for a particular language. Harnish prefaces the statement of his theory with an extensive critical review of major linguistic and philosophical proposals concerning the analysis of sentential mood, leading to the formulation of certain criteria that any such analysis must satisfy in order to be both theoretically illuminating and capable of being integrated with the analysis of other facets of sentence meaning. He then formulates a theory of the major sentential moods of English which meets the previously formulated criteria of adequacy, and in which each major sentence type is associated, on the one hand, with a condition controlling its compatibility with some, but not with other, types of illocutionary act and, on the other hand, with a condition controlling its compatibility with some, but not with other, types of satisfaction of propositional content. He finally notes certain descriptive and methodological problems that the further development of this theory would have to solve, and outlines the general character of his proposed solutions to these problems.

Harnish's approach does not require that the analysis of illocutionary acts must be checked for its adequacy by reference to, among other things, the grammatical characteristics of their manifestations, and indeed assumes that an appropriate analysis of them is available prior to the investigation of the grammatical make-up of the utterances tokening them. The papers by Jerrold Sadock and William Croft, on the other hand, argue, each in its own way, that a proper understanding of the nature of illocutionary acts must be sensitive to, among other things, known regularities about the details of their grammatical manifestations, and they naturally seek to support their claims by appealing to cross-linguistic evidence. In 'Toward a grammatically realistic typology of speech acts', Sadock begins by reviewing the best-known taxonomies of illocutionary acts in the philo-sophical literature, and emphasizes both the arbitrary character of many of the criteria that they choose as basic, and the unprincipled way in which they often employ their chosen criteria. He then develops the thesis that the most important of the features that, in these taxonomies, are supposed to establish separate categories of illocutionary acts are in fact only rarely manifested separately, and that the vast majority of commonly occurring types of illocutionary acts can and must be analysed as *combinations* of three of these features in varying degrees of comparative prominence. He finally argues that these three features have characteristic, and cross-linguistically regular, grammatical correlates both in their (rare) isolated and in their (common) combined occurrences, and that this typological evidence in their favour makes categorizations of illocutionary acts based on them clearly preferable to the ones inherited from the philosophical tradition, since these latter either represent as fundamentally distinct certain categories of illocutionary acts whose grammatical manifestations are structurally indistinguishable, or represent as essentially similar certain categories of illocutionary acts whose grammatical manifestations are drastically divergent. A similar willingness to make the analysis and categorization of illocutionary acts more sensitive to cross-linguistic evidence regarding their grammatical manifestation is also central to Croft's 'Speech act classification, language typology and cognition'. Croft first establishes a set of criteria that could be used for defining, in as independent a way as possible from semantic or pragmatic considerations, a cross-linguistically valid notion of 'major sentence type'. He then argues that a good deal of available typological evidence shows that the major sentence types thus definable encode illocutionary functions in a way that is markedly different from the one that one would expect if the philosophically inspired analyses and classifications of illocutionary acts were taken as guides – in particular, that certain dimensions of illocutionary act differentiation that are typologically quite prominent are not represented at all in the usual classifications, and that most differentiations that are represented as discrete on the usual classifications are typologically revealed to be clearly continuous. He finally suggests that the picture of illocutionary activities that emerges from the typological evidence could not easily be dismissed as theoretically inessential, since it appears to have a strong cognitive motivation – specifically to represent an application, in the domain of conversational interaction, of quite basic principles of categorization that natural language speakers use in analysing the structure of human activities.

It is not to be expected, of course, that every thesis that these three studies advance would be accepted without further investigation. It would be difficult to deny, however, that they already succeed in making clear which lines of investigation in this area are likely to lead to important results if pursued systematically, and that they thus suggest that the topic of the relation between illocutionary acts and their grammatical manifestations is far more interesting than its relative neglect by both grammarians and speech act theorists would lead one to suppose.

Coming to the conclusion of this brief overview of some of the volume's contributions to the semantic, pragmatic and grammatical analysis of illocutionary acts, I should mention that it has been incomplete not only – and obviously – because it gave no information on the complex and subtle arguments that the contributors have employed in support of their theses, but also because it did not even make reference to all the interesting theses that they have advanced, and to their interconnections. I hope, however, that the indications provided will be helpful as a first entry into the research area that the volume intends to cover, and that, when their study of its contents is complete, readers will have acquired an infinitely richer appreciation of both the problems and the prospects of speech act theory than I have been able to convey here. I would like to thank the contributors for making this collective endeavour intellectually possible, and the staff of the various departments of Routledge, especially Claire L'Enfant, for ensuring the public delivery of its results.

Part I

Speech acts and semantic theory

1 Illocutionary acts and linguistic meaning

William P. Alston

This paper is a presentation of the basic ideas of a book I am hoping to complete soon, with the above title. The central idea of the book is that sentence meaning is illocutionary act potential. The fact that a given sentence has a given meaning *is* the fact that the sentence has the potential, the capacity to be (standardly) used to perform illocutionary acts of a certain type.

This view was, so far as I know, first unveiled in public by myself in Alston (1963) and (1964b). But it has received little development in print since that period. It was embraced by John Searle (1969), but he has done little to spell out a theory of linguistic meaning in these terms.[1] For myself, though I have published a few articles that present pieces of the view (see Alston 1974, 1977), I have, I fear, been too preoccupied with other things to bring the project to completion up to now. This article is by way of a progress report and, I hope, a harbinger of things to come.

SENTENCE MEANING AND ILLOCUTIONARY ACT POTENTIAL

I will begin by elucidating the 'illocutionary-act-potential (IAP) thesis', which I will canonically formulate as follows:

> (I) A sentence's having a given meaning consists in its having a certain illocutionary act potential.

To elucidate this I need to say something about three concepts, (a) sentence meaning, (b) illocutionary act, and (c) potential.

Sentence meaning

I do not intend to be employing any novel, *outré*, or technical concept of the meaning of a sentence. I mean to be working with the concept that is used in giving a semantic description of a language and, in so doing, assigning meanings to various sentences of the language. In view of persistent confusion about language and the semantics thereof, it might be well to make it explicit that I am speaking of the meanings of *sentence types* (sentence-sized units of a *language*), rather than so-called sentence 'tokens' (what is produced by speakers when they use a certain sentence (type)). My concept deals with language, not with speech.[2] Moreover, in speaking of sentence meaning I am concerned with *linguistic* meaning – the meaning possessed by units of language, where a language is an abstract structure that is employed by people in speech – in contrast to 'speaker meaning', what a speaker means by what he said, and in contrast with 'utterance meaning', the meaning to be ascribed to particular utterances or sentence 'tokens', if, indeed, there is a coherent concept of this latter that is distinct from speaker meaning.

It may help if I list a few 'axioms' that I take to 'locate' the concept of sentence meaning on the conceptual map.

> (A1) The fact that a sentence has a certain meaning is what enables it to play a distinctive role (enables it to be used to convey a certain 'message' or 'content') in communication.

(A1) will eventually be further developed by identifying the 'role' and the 'conveyance of a certain message' with the performance of an illocutionary act of a certain sort. As so understood, (A1) is very close to the IAP thesis (I).

> (A2) Knowledge of the meaning of the sentence uttered is the *linguistic* knowledge a hearer needs in order to understand what is being said.

This can be viewed as the same basic idea as (A1) viewed from the standpoint of the hearer rather than the speaker. (A1) says that a sentence's having a certain meaning is what makes it suitable to be used to say suchand-such, and (A2) says that knowing that the sentence has that meaning is (the linguistic part of) what enables a hearer to know that such-and-such is what is being said.

Note the restriction to *linguistic* knowledge. In most cases knowledge of the language is not sufficient for grasping what is being said. If the sentence has more than one meaning, like 'He got a good hand', the hearer will have to use contextual clues to determine which of those meanings is being exploited in this utterance. Moreover the meaning of a sentence usually does not suffice to determine singular reference. To grasp what is being said in an utterance of 'I will like the house when I get used to it', the hearer will have to know the identity of the speaker, the time of utterance, and which house is being referred to. All of this is information over and above what meaning(s) the sentence has in the language.

> (A3) The meaning of a sentence is a function of the meanings of its constituents plus relevant facts about its structure.

This is a fundamental principle of linguistics. I will later turn it on its head to indicate how one moves from sentence meaning to word meaning. (For a word to have a certain meaning is for it to make a distinctive contribution to the meanings of sentences in which it figures.) One might think that I am trying to have it both ways – taking sentence meaning to be derivative from word meaning *and* taking word meaning to be derivative from sentence meaning. Surely I can't get away with that! The way to resolve this puzzle is to distinguish different orders of priority. Word meaning is prior to sentence meaning in the order of the explanation of particular facts (we explain the fact that a particular sentence means what it does by appealing to the meanings of its constituents plus its structure). While sentence meaning is prior to word meaning in the order of conceptual analysis, or explication. We explain the *concept* of word meaning in terms of the contribution a word makes to the meaning of sentences. We find this distinction of orders of priority in many areas. Ultimate physical particles are prior to macro-objects in the order of the explanation of facts: we explain the properties and behaviour of macro-objects in terms of the properties and behaviour of micro-particles. But our concepts of micro-particles are built up on the basis of antecedently grasped concepts of macro-objects, partly by the use of analogies, and partly in terms of the role micro-particles play in theories and explanations of macro-phenomena. Again, in theology God is prior to creatures in the order of explanation – most fundamentally in the explanation of their existing. Whereas our concept of God is derived from our concepts of creatures by analogy.

(A4) The truth conditions of a statement are at least partly determined by the meaning of the sentence used to make that statement.

Where knowing the meaning of the sentence is all that is necessary for determining what statement is made, that determination can be complete. This may be the case with general statements like *Hexagons have six sides.* But where singular reference ('I'm hungry') and multivocality ('Jim is still running') are involved, the semantics of the sentence does not suffice to determine truth conditions, just because it does not suffice for the determination of what is being asserted. But the meaning still plays a major role.

Illocutionary acts

Now for the concept of an *illocutionary act.* This term, due originally to J.L. Austin (1962), is often seriously underexplained for a technical term. The usual practice is to give a list of examples and leave it up to the reader to form an intuitive concept on that basis. That is pretty much what I will do here, though with some supplementary indications. For a pretheoretical demarcation of illocutionary act concepts I rely on our familiar indirect discourse form. We have a large assortment of devices for making explicit *what someone said* (where this is distinguished from what sentence he uttered), the 'content' of the utterance, what 'message' it conveyed. Here is a small sample.

(1) U (utterer) asserted (admitted, replied, insisted ...) that the window was open.
(2) U promised Jones to take him to the meeting.
(3) U asked Smith for a match.
(4) U predicted that the war would be over soon.
(5) U assured Robinson that he had no intention of leaving.
(6) U remarked that grocery prices are rising.
(7) U expressed his intention of becoming a candidate.
(8) U expressed considerable resentment of Jones' behaviour.
(9) U called the batter safe.
(10) U congratulated Smith on his appointment.
(11) U seconded the motion.
(12) U urged Smith to stick with his plan.

Each of these reports involves an action verb – 'insist', 'predict', 'urge', 'congratulate' – followed by a 'content-specifying' phrase. I will follow Searle (1969: 30) in taking the action verb to specify the 'illocutionary force' of the utterance, while the ensuing phrase specifies the 'propositional content'. I want to emphasize that on my conception illocutionary acts include both of these aspects. There is a tendency in many writers on the subject to restrict attention to illocutionary force and to exclude propositional content from the illocutionary act rubric. But if illocutionary acts are the acts reported by typical indirect discourse locutions, then they include the carrying of the propositional content, as well as doing something with a certain illocutionary force.

Many of my readers will be aware that Austin himself characterized the 'rhetic act' ('performance of an act of using ... vocables with a certain more-or-less definite sense and reference' (1962: 95)), which he distinguished from the illocutionary act, in terms of indirect discourse.

> But the rhetic act is the one we report, in the case of assertions, by saying 'He said that the cat was on the mat', 'He said he would go', 'He said I was to go' (his words were 'You are to go'). This is the so-called 'indirect speech'.
>
> (1962: 96–7)

However I cannot see that Austin did a satisfactory job of making the rhetic–illocutionary act distinction.[3] What difference is there between 'He said that the cat was on the mat' and 'He admitted (remarked, insisted, replied ...) that the cat was on the mat', except for degree of specificity? I think we have to say that the examples Austin tended to give of rhetic acts are simply illocutionary acts with very unspecific illocutionary force. Indeed, sometimes they are not so unspecific. Thus one of his contrasts between phatic (roughly uttering a certain sentence) and rhetic acts is: 'He said "Is it in Oxford or Cambridge?"'; He asked whether it was in Oxford or Cambridge' (Austin 1962: 95). But the latter is clearly a full blooded illocutionary act.

Illocutionary act *potential*

Now what about 'potential'? If sentence meaning is to have any chance of being identified with illocutionary act potential, then we cannot accept the position that any sentence can be used to perform any illocutionary act. For a given sentence does not have all possible meanings. But can I not perform any illocutionary act whatever by uttering the sentence 'The sun is shining'? Can I not express my horror at recent events in Bosnia by uttering that sentence, just by deciding that this is the content of my utterance? Well, maybe so and maybe not. I am not required to decide that issue here. The kind of potential that is in question here is what we may call 'standard' or 'regular' potential or usability, the usability the sentence has just by virtue of the constitution of the language, apart from any *ad hoc* decisions, private codes, or anything else that stands outside the structure of the language. The reason the IAP thesis requires that we be thinking of *standard* potential is that the sentence meaning we aim to elucidate by that thesis is *standard meaning*, the meaning the sentence has by virtue of the semantic structure of the language. If there is a sense in which I can do anything I choose, illocution-wise, with a given sentence (perhaps given suitable arrangements), there is a parallel sense in which I can mean anything whatever by a given sentence, again given appropriate arrangements.

COMMUNICATION THEORIES

The IAP theory belongs to a large group of theories of meaning that we may call 'communication theories'. They fall into a single family by virtue of identifying the meaning of a linguistic expression with what enables it to perform a distinctive role in communication, with its 'communicative potential'. This is, in a way, the obverse of (A1). Since a sentence's meaning what it does is what makes it usable for a certain communicative job, why not just identify its meaning with that usability? That is the basic idea of communication theories.

It may be helpful to mention some theses that are often erroneously thought to follow from the claims that language is essentially a device for communication and that the communicative function of language is crucial for understanding language and, in particular, for understanding the semantic aspect of language.

1   Communication is the only function, or the only essential function, of language.
2   Other functions of language are derivative (in the history of the race or of the individual) from the communicative function.
3   Every language is actually used in communication.

(1) is clearly false. Another prominent and important function of language

is the articulation of thought. (2) may be true, but it does not follow from the communicative approach to the understanding of meaning. As for (3) whether it is true depends on how we draw boundaries around 'language'. In any event, that fate of all these views is independent of the basic commitments of communication theory and of the IAP thesis in particular.

Communication theories differ as to the feature of communication they pick as crucial for meaning. Historically the emphasis has been on the fact that communication involves an attempt to produce psychological effects on an addressee – get the latter to believe or know something, to act in a certain way, to adopt or modify attitudes, and so on. Indeed, prior to my paper 'Meaning and use' (1963) the illocutionary aspect of communication was almost completely ignored in theories of meaning. Thus John Locke (1690: Bk II, ch. 2, sect. i ff.) held that communication is a matter of trying to get someone else to realize what ideas the speaker currently has in his or her mind. One achieves this by producing words that are signs of the presence of those ideas, the words having acquired this capacity by virtue of having been regularly used to convey those ideas to a hearer. The meaning of a word is then identified with the ideas of which it is a sign. Mid-twentieth-century updates of Locke are found in the writings of Charles L. Stevenson (1944: ch. 3) and H.P. Grice (1957, 1968, 1969). Neither of these thinkers deal in Lockean ideas, but the emphasis is still on the fact that communication involves impacts on the psyches of hearers. Stevenson identifies the meaning of a linguistic expression with its disposition to produce psychological effects in hearers, the precise effect varying with circumstances. Grice's more complicated view is that what a speaker means by his utterance is a function of what effects the speaker intends to produce in the hearer by means of the hearer's recognition of that intention. The meaning of a sentence is, roughly, a function of what effects utterances of it are regularly used to produce.

Borrowing another term from Austin, we may term the Locke, Stevenson and Grice accounts <u>perlocutionary</u>-act-potential theories. A 'perlocutionary act' is one the application of which to a speaker entails that the speaker's utterance had an effect of a certain sort. Here are a few examples.

(13) U got A (addressee) to believe (know) that it was raining outside.
(14) U got A to give him a ride home.
(15) U frightened A.
(16) U led A to be more favourably disposed toward the candidate.
(17) U irritated A.[4]

Clearly the psychological effect productions on which Locke, Stevenson and Grice concentrate count as perlocutionary acts. Thus, to put their views in our terms, in holding that a sentence's having a certain meaning amounts to its being usable for producing a certain psychological effect in an addressee, they are taking a <u>perlocutionary-act-potential</u> approach to linguistic meaning. This, then, is a clear alternative to the IAP theory within the communication-theory family. What basis can we find for choosing between them?

Let us give the perlocutionary-act-potential theory as much credit as possible. I would not deny that in communication we typically aim at affecting the psychological state of our hearers. And, though I do not really believe this, I am even willing for the sake of argument to admit that to each distinguishable sentence meaning there corresponds a certain type of psychological state such that whenever one utters a sentence with that meaning one does so in order to produce a state of that type in one's addressee. If that were so, we would have at least an extensional equivalence between a given sentence meaning and a given perlocutionary act potential. And this could well encourage someone to adopt a perlocutionary-act-potential theory of sentence meaning. At least it would be the case that S (sentence) means x if, and only if, S is a correct, appropriate, or effective linguistic vehicle to use to produce in one's hearer psychological effect E. But even if this were true, I would not admit the perlocutionary-act-potential theory to be a dangerous rival to the illocutionary-act-potential theory. For it would still be the case that a sentence has a distinctive perlocutionary act potential *only by virtue of* having a distinctive illocutionary act potential. A given sentence meaning determines a particular perlocutionary act potential only through determining an illocutionary act potential. Consider what makes the utterance of the sentence 'The guests have all left' a good way of getting someone to realize that the guests have all left. It is because the rules of the language, together with conventions for using additional contextual information, are such that when U utters that sentence in a certain context, the hearer will, normally, take U to be asserting of some contextually determined guests that they have left the scene of the utterance at the time of the utterance. And unless A has reason to doubt U's sincerity or reliability, he would normally take it that the guests in question had left; the utterance would have carried out its perlocutionary intention. But that perlocutionary aim would not have been accomplished unless the sentence had the appropriate illocutionary act potential. If the sentence U uttered had as its standard illocutionary act potential, <u>asking A to move over</u>, then, in the absence of some special private code or the like, the utterance would not have had a chance of getting A to realize that the guests had left. Hence, even if there is an extensional equivalence between a given sentence meaning and a given perlocutionary act potential, that should be viewed as a consequence of the IAP theory, rather than as a basis for a rival account of what meaning is. And we have arrived at this result after having granted the perlocutionary-act-potential theory more than it deserves. To the best of my knowledge, no version of the theory even attains the kind of extensional equivalence I have been assuming.

It may be felt that illocutionary act potential gets its plausibility as an account of sentence meaning by remaining so close to the latter as to be unilluminating. The sentence 'The door is open' meaning what it does is a matter of its being standardly usable to tell someone, with respect to a certain door, that it is open. But the concept of telling someone that, is too close to the concept of the sentence's meaning to enable us to make any real progress in understanding sentence meaning. If that is all we have to say, we have not progressed significantly beyond our starting point.[5] I agree with this criticism to the extent of acknowledging that as long as we leave illocutionary act concepts in an unelucidated form, the IAP theory is insufficiently explanatory. But this just means that the theory must embody an account of the nature of illocutionary acts – must say what it is to perform an illocutionary act of a certain sort. If we can manage that, we will have made a significant conceptual advance beyond the semantic terms with which we started.

MATCHING ILLOCUTIONARY ACTS

At this point I must deal with some apparent counter-examples to an identification of sentence meaning with illocutionary act potential, examples that will undoubtedly have occurred to many readers.

Sentence meaning can be unqualifiedly identified with illocutionary act potential only if for each distinguishable sentence meaning there is exactly one illocutionary act type for the performance of tokens of which the sentence is thereby fitted, and vice versa. But the world is not that simple. To start with the most obvious points, there are the cases J. L. Austin used to introduce the concept of illocutionary force, those in which a sentence can be used with the same meaning to perform illocutionary acts with different illocutionary forces. Thus one can use the sentence 'It is going to charge', with one and the same meaning, to simply *state* or to *warn* that a particular bull is going to charge (and, we may add, to *admit, conclude*, or *announce* that it is going to charge). Again, by saying 'Shoot her', using it in its most common sense, I may be *urging, advising* or *ordering* someone to shoot her (Austin 1962: 98–101). Clearly the meaning of one's linguistic vehicle cannot be relied on to determine the illocutionary force of one's utterance. Austin took this to show that illocutionary force is something over and above *meaning* 'in the sense in which meaning is equivalent to sense and reference' (1962: 101). But note that in so far as it shows this, a parallel argument shows that propositional content is not determined by sentence meaning either. The sentence I use on a given occasion may not make the propositional content completely explicit either. By saying 'It will' (in answer to a certain question) I may be asserting that a certain bull is going to charge; that the interest rate will go down, or that a certain ladder will hold steady. Given the appropriate stage-setting I can express any propositional content whatever just by saying 'Yes', surely a limiting case of the underdetermination of illocutionary act by sentential meaning.

What is responsible for the underdetermination in all these cases is the familiar fact that given enough contextual clues it is not necessary to use a sentence rich enough to carry all the details of the illocutionary act. This point applies equally, as we have just seen, to the propositional-content and the illocutionary-force aspects of illocutionary acts. But in many cases we can find a sentence a meaning of which does fully and unambiguously determine a given illocutionary act type. Thus the Austinian illocutionary-force ambiguities can be resolved by beefing up the sentence with a 'performative' verb, yielding 'I warn you it's going to charge' or 'I admit it's going to charge.' And my first propositional-content ambiguity can be resolved by replacing 'It will' with 'The bull over there is going to charge' or 'The interest rate will go down.' So far as I can see, the only aspect of illocutionary acts that seems not to be fully determinable by linguistic meaning is reference (meaning by 'meaning' – meaning – rather than Austin's 'sense and reference'). Note that my beefed-up sentences did not make explicit which bull or which interest rate was involved. And it seems that in most cases we have no choice but to rely on various contextual factors to make clear the precise reference of our singular referring terms. Nevertheless, and this is the crucial point I need to make, although often no sentence meaning can fully determine every detail of one's illocutionary act, there will always be, for any sentence meaning, an *illocutionary act type* that is made completely explicit by that meaning, in the sense that if someone seriously and literally utters the sentence with that meaning, then, *just by knowing that*, we know that he intends to be performing an illocutionary act of that type. Because of the various modes of underdetermination already noted, this type will typically be less specific than a full description of the illocutionary act performed, i.e., less specific than the most specific type under which this particular act falls. But it will be true, none the less, that the act performed is of that type. This criterion gives us what we may call the *matching illocutionary act type* for a given sentence meaning – the one that exactly matches that meaning in content. Here are some matching illocutionary types, assuming a familiar meaning for the sentence in each case.

'It will' – asserting of something that it will do something.

'It's going to charge' – asserting of a certain animal that it will charge soon.

'I agree that it is going to charge' – agreeing to the proposition concerning a certain animal that it is going to charge soon.

'Jones' prize bull is going to charge' – asserting of a certain prize bull belonging to a person named 'Jones' that it is going to charge soon.[6]

As these examples indicate, to construct a matching illocutionary act type we need to find just the degree of specificity that is embodied in the sentence meaning in question – with respect to identity of referents, predicative aspects of the propositional content, illocutionary force, and so on. Note that an illocutionary act type can be too poor for the sentence meaning as well as, like our initial examples, too rich. Thus while <u>insisting that Jones' bull is going to charge</u> is 'too rich' for 'It's going to charge', <u>asserting of something that it will do something</u> is 'too poor' for that sentence meaning.

Making use of the conceptual resources developed in this section, we can accommodate putative counter-examples of the sorts we have been considering by complicating the IAP theory as follows. Each sentence meaning can be identified with its *matching* illocutionary act potential – i.e., the potential of the sentence to be used to perform illocutionary acts of the matching illocutionary act type.[7]

THE ANALYSIS OF ILLOCUTIONARY ACTS

So long as we use illocutionary act concepts in the raw, the most we can say about the meaning of 'Please open the door' from an IAP point of view is that the sentence's meaning what it does is a matter of its being usable to request someone to open a certain contextually indicated door. As we noted above, if the IAP theory is to throw more light on the nature of sentence meaning, it will have to be based on an analysis of illocutionary act concepts that brings out, in a revealing way, what it is to perform an illocutionary act of a certain type.

Let us approach this task by noting that in performing any illocutionary act one is asserting, presupposing, and/or implying various propositions. This is obvious for the large group of acts that fall under the *assertive* rubric – stating, agreeing, insisting, admitting, and so on. To admit, agree, or insist that arsenic is poisonous is to assert that arsenic is poisonous. But in other illocutionary acts also, even if one is not explicitly asserting anything to be the case, there are various states of affairs one is presupposing or implying[8] to obtain. Here are a few examples.[9]

(18) U promised A to take him to the meeting that evening.
    (a) It is possible for U to take A to the meeting in question on the evening of the day of utterance.
    (b) U intends to take A to the meeting in question on the evening of the day of utterance.
(19) U declared a certain meeting (M) adjourned.
    (a) M is in session at the time of utterance.
    (b) U has the authority to terminate that meeting.
    (c) Conditions are appropriate for the exercise of that authority.
(20) U ordered A to come to his room.
    (a) A is not in U's room at the time of utterance.
    (b) It is possible for A to come to U's room.
    (c) U is in a position of authority over A.

On this approach to the problem our next job is to bring out what it is to assert, presuppose or imply that something is the case. Since this kind of activity is more overt and explicit in the case of assertion, that will be a good place to start. What is it to assert that it is raining outside, by uttering 'It is raining outside'? What is added when I move from using that sentence to practise pronunciation or to give an example to using it to make that assertion?

Obviously, what is added must somehow involve the proposition that it is raining outside. Otherwise, how could it make my utterance an assertion of that proposition rather than some other? But it does not involve that proposition in any of the ways that might initially strike one. The truth or falsity of that proposition is neither a necessary nor a sufficient condition of my asserting it. I can assert that p whether it is true or false. More generally, the crucial condition cannot be something that obtains independently of the speaker. Whatever turns my utterance into an assertion that p must connect *me* with p; it must be some 'stance' I have or take *vis-à-vis* p. But here too the most obvious suggestions do not work. My *believing* that p is neither necessary nor sufficient. Not necessary, for I may be lying. Not sufficient, for if it were I would constantly be asserting everything I believe!

There are two further reasons for rejecting my belief that p as the crucial addition here; and a consideration of these reasons will further our endeavour to understand the situation.

(a) The condition must be something within U's control.

It must be 'up to me' whether, in uttering the sentence S, I am asserting that p, rather than, say, practising pronunciation. Surely I can move from one to the other at will.[10]

(b) The condition cannot be merely *externally* related to the utterance, so that it merely amounts to the fact that U has the required attitude to p at the moment of utterance.

For whatever the attitude in question, whether belief or something else, it is clear that I might *have* that attitude while using the sentence to test a microphone rather than to make the assertion in question. The condition must relate the *utterance* to the proposition that p in a more intimate way than that.

So what can U do at will to relate his utterance of a suitable sentence to p in such a way as to constitute that utterance an assertion that p? Well, for one thing, he can utter the sentence in order to get A to believe that p or to take up some other propositional attitude to p. This brings us back to perlocutionary acts. We have already seen that perlocutionary act potential does not suffice to elucidate sentence meaning. Now we have to consider the possibility that an *intention* to perform a perlocutionary act of a certain sort is what turns an utterance into the performance of an illocutionary act of a certain sort. Illocutionary act performance is intended perlocutionary act performance. This is the approach to understanding illocutionary act types taken by Stephen R. Schiffer (1972) and by Kent Bach and Robert M. Harnish (1979). Applied to assertions it would go something like this. To assert that p in uttering S is to utter S with the intention of producing in one's audience the activated belief that p, where this intention must satisfy certain further, and very complicated, conditions. I will not go into those further conditions, since I will argue that the account is not sufficient even without those additional requirements. The reason the account does not work is very simple. There are clear cases of asserting that p in which U does not have the intention in question. I may have no hope of your believing what I say but nevertheless assert that p just because I feel obliged to give a truthful answer to a direct question. I may remark that it is very crowded in here just to make conversation and without having the slightest interest in whether I produce an activated belief in you. Asserting that p does not necessarily involve an aim at affecting the belief of one's auditor. This may be its most frequent or most basic perlocutionary use, but it is not its invariable accompaniment. Once more the perlocutionary has failed to deliver what we need.

What next? I believe that we will find something more promising by introducing the notion of a speaker's *taking responsibility* for the obtaining of a state of affairs or the satisfaction of a condition. The suggestion is that asserting, presupposing, or implying that p are all ways of *taking responsibility* for its being the case that p. In particular, to assert that p is to take responsibility for its being the case that p in uttering an appropriate sentence. This is a notion that I introduced (1964a, 1964b) as a way of bringing out how a speaker must be related to the proposition that p in order that this proposition be involved in an illocutionary act he is performing. It is also introduced by Searle in his model analysis of promising (1969: 62), though he does not put the notion in the centre of the picture as I do.

We must be careful to understand 'take responsibility for state of affairs F' here in a rather special way. The idea is not that the speaker acknowledges that he brought F into existence. It is, rather, like the way in which the head of a department or agency takes responsibility for the efficient and orderly conduct of its affairs, including the work done by subordinates. I, the head, am responsible for all this, not in the sense that I have done all the work myself, but in the sense that I am rightly held to blame if the work is not done properly. I am the one who must 'respond' to complaints about that work. It is in this sense that, for example, U takes responsibility for its being the case that A can come to his room in ordering A to come to his room, and U takes responsibility for the meeting currently being in session in declaring the meeting adjourned. In uttering the sentence in question U knowingly lays himself open to complaints, objections, correction, blame, or some such response, in case the conditions in question are not satisfied. He utters the sentence, recognizing that his utterance is out of order, and hence that there is just ground for complaint, in case the conditions in question are not satisfied. Thus we may take the following as explaining 'In uttering S U took responsibility for its being the case that p'.

> (R1) In uttering S, U knowingly takes on a liability to (lays himself open to) censure, reproach, being taken to task, being called to account ... in case of not-p.

On this account, performing an illocutionary act goes beyond mere sentence utterance by virtue of the speaker's engendering what we might call a 'normative' state of affairs – the speaker's being subject to just complaint or censure, in case certain conditions are not satisfied. It is the shift in normative status that is crucial here; it is not that U does something that makes a respondent psychologically able to blame him.[11] What U does is to render such negative reactions *appropriate* or relevant.[12] Moreover, as in other cases this appropriateness is only prima facie. Whether an overt objection or complaint is justified on the whole depends on other factors. If the transgression is minor, and if being upbraided for it would upset me in such a way as to endanger my health or my life, one would not be justified on the whole in censuring me. And even if censure would be justified, the matter may not be important enough to warrant anyone's taking the trouble. Considerations of decorum or social rank may preclude anyone's actually calling me to account. And so on.

Since it is a matter of U's *taking on* this liability, rather than a matter of U's being subject to the liability, willy-nilly, this suggestion satisfies our first constraint (a) that it be up to U whether the crucial condition holds. And it satisfies the second constraint (b), since U takes on the liability *in* issuing the utterance, not just at the same time thereof.

Needless to say, when I speak of U's *knowingly* taking on the liability, I do not imply that this is something U has before his mind at the moment, something he is consciously envisaging. It can be like other things we 'knowingly', deliberately, intentionally do, while our mind is wholly engaged with other concerns. That it is 'knowing' is shown by how U responds to reactions that presuppose that liability. If he readily acknowledges their pertinence, that satisfies my condition.

This account needs sharpening in at least two respects before it is ready to be sent out into the world.

(i) With respect to each of the conditions, c, for which U takes responsibility, we have to recognize that whether U is blameworthy depends not so much on whether it is actually the case that c, but on U's epistemic position *vis-à-vis* c. If c is not the case but U has every reason to suppose it to obtain, then he cannot be rightly called to account, though there is still something defective about his utterance. Contrariwise, if c does obtain, but U has every reason for thinking it does not, he could still be properly upbraided. To illustrate these points, suppose that, as your superior officer in the military I order you to report to my room. Say you are physically unable to do so, though I have ample reason to think you are able. Then I could hardly be called to account for the issuance of the order (provided I withdraw it when I realize the situation). If, on the other hand, you are able to report but I have ample reason to suppose you are not, but issue the order anyway, perhaps in order to cause confusion, then I could properly be taken to task (by someone who knows all the facts), even though all of the conditions for which I take responsibility are satisfied. There are further complexities here into which I will not be able to go in this paper. For present purposes, let's modify each of the conditions in the above lists by prefacing it with 'U has sufficient reason to suppose that ...'.

(ii) I have been using a scatter-shot technique to give an idea of the reactions to which U renders herself rightfully liable (given certain conditions) in her utterance. I have used a variety of terms – 'complain', 'object', 'blame', 'censure', 'upbraid', 'correct', 'reproach', 'take to task', 'call to account'. It would be desirable to have a more unified account, to say what all these have in common. My suggestion is that they are all appropriate reactions to something *impermissible*, something the agent ought not to have done, something that was in violation of a rule. There is a variety of such reactions just because what specific behaviour is appropriate on the whole depends, as we have seen, on further features of the situation. The only thing that binds all these together is the realization or 'perception' on the part of the reactor that the first party has *violated* some rule. Thus the only way to get a non-disjunctive formulation of the crucial condition is to do it in terms of rule violation.

> (R2) U uttered S as subject to a rule that implies that a necessary con-
> dition of U's uttering S (in circumstances like these)[13] is that U
> have sufficient reason to suppose that:

What follows is then a list of conditions like those given above. (Since we have put the qualifier 'have sufficient reason to suppose that' in the coverall prologue, we need not attach it to each condition.) We may take this as an alternative explication of 'U took responsibility for the obtaining of the following conditions', i.e., an alternative to (R1). I take it to be a deeper explication in that it brings out what is behind the phenomenon of 'taking responsibility', namely, recognizing that a sentence is governed by a rule that lays down conditions of permissible utterance. We will see that this notion is what is crucial to the IAP account of sentence meaning.

I hope it is clear that what is said to be necessary for the performance of the illocutionary act of, for example, promising A to take him to the meeting that evening is not that the conditions listed earlier under that rubric actually obtain, but rather that U *take responsibility* for their obtaining , i.e. (using the (R2) explication), that U utter the sentence as subject to a rule that makes her having sufficient reason to suppose those conditions to obtain a necessary condition of *permissible* utterance of the sentence. This leaves open the possibility that one does perform that illocutionary act even though one or another of those conditions does not, in fact, obtain. It leaves us free to recognize that it is possible for me to promise to take you to the meeting this evening even if it is not possible for me to do so and even if I have no intention of taking you. I would, in that case, be promising insincerely, but I would still be making that promise and could still be held to account for doing so. Again, I can declare the meeting adjourned even if the meeting is not, in fact, in session or even if I lack the requisite authority. My doing so would be highly inappropriate, but still I might have done it.

On my view, U's taking responsibility for the satisfaction of various conditions is not only necessary but also sufficient for an utterance's counting as the performance of an illocutionary act of a certain type. I have not attempted to present and defend a complete listing of such conditions for any illocutionary act type, but I have given some (at least partial) examples of such lists in order to convey the general idea. But whatever the composition of such a list, we are faced with a problem when we apply this account to non-assertive illocutionary acts. Go back to our list of conditions for ordering A to come to U's room.

(21) (a) A is not in U's room at the time of utterance.
     (b) It is possible for A to come to U's room.
     (c) U is in a position of authority over A.

On the assumption that this is a complete list, the view would be that an utterance counts as ordering A to come to U's room just in case U issues his utterance as subject to a rule that requires U to have sufficient reason for supposing these conditions to hold. But now consider the assertion of the joint satisfaction of those conditions. Let us take it, as at least a close approximation, that what one takes responsibility for in asserting that p is simply – p.[14] Assertion is a case of limiting simplicity, in which what is essentially taken responsibility for has the same content as the propositional content of the act – that proposition that is expressed in saying what illocutionary act this is.[15] Thus, if one were to assert the joint satisfaction of those conditions, one would be taking responsibility for exactly what one takes responsibility for in issuing the order in question. But then what, on our account, distinguishes the order from the correlated assertion of the satisfaction of the conditions?

The key to resolving this problem is to note that non-assertive illocutionary acts typically involve the production of what we may call a 'conventional effect'.[16] Thus orders engender a (prima facie) obligation on the addressee to do what she or he was ordered to do; promises and contractings engender a (prima facie) obligation on the speaker to do what she or he promised or contracted to do. Declaring a meeting adjourned brings it about that the meeting is no longer in session. Marrying a couple changes their legal status in familiar ways. Calling a runner out at second base alters what the runner can subsequently do, in conformity with the rules of baseball. A simple way of distinguishing the order, promise, or adjourning of the meeting from the correlated assertion would be to make the production of the relevant conventional effect a necessary condition of performing the non-assertive, but not the assertive, illocutionary act. What distinguishes ordering A to come to my room from the joint assertion of conditions (21a), (21b) and (21c), is that the former, but not the latter gives rise to a prima facie obligation on A's part to come to my room.

Though I did think of the matter along these lines for some time, I have now abandoned that approach. Here is the reason. Contrast a case of ordering, promising or performing some official act in which the standard conventional effect is produced, with one in which something goes wrong that inhibits that fulfilment. Contrast a proper christening with one in which the ceremony was performed on the wrong person – one that had already been christened and had received some other name. It seems clear to me that *what is said* by the (would-be) christener – the 'content' or 'message' communicated by the speaker – is the same in both cases. Hence, going by our pretheoretical criterion for illocutionary acts, the same illocutionary act is performed in both cases. But that means that it cannot be a necessary condition of performing the illocutionary act of christening someone that the standard conventional effect has actually been forthcoming.

This means that with illocutionary acts that are standardly directed to the production of conventional effects, many of the most common locutions for specifying them – adjourn the meeting, christen the ship, hire the new employee, nominate the candidate – do not pick out 'pure' illocutionary acts, but rather illocutionary acts of a certain type plus the actual production of the standard conventional effect. In some cases, however, the most standard locution does identify a 'pure' illocutionary act, one that could be performed without bringing about the conventional effect in question. Here are some familiar examples.

(22) Order someone to do something.
(23) Declare the meeting adjourned.
(24) Promise someone to do something.
(25) Pronounce the couple man and wife.

I can have ordered you to do something even if, in fact, I lack the proper authority and hence confer no obligation on you to do it. ('You shouldn't be ordering him around. You don't have the authority.' This charge presupposes that I did order him and should not have done so.) Likewise I could have *pronounced* you man and wife, even though I lack the power to render you married. Where the only common idioms available are those that, like the first group, entail that the conventional effect was actually forthcoming, we can obtain a pure illocutionary act term by prefacing a qualifier such as 'purport to'. Thus we can speak of <u>purporting to hire an</u> <u>employee</u> and <u>purporting to nominate a candidate</u>.

If this is the way the wind blows, we are still faced with the problem of how to distinguish the non-assertive (typically conventional effect generating) illocutionary act from the assertion of the joint satisfaction of the relevant list of conditions. The solution I suggest is that we think of the non-assertive act as involving taking responsibility for still another condition, namely that the speaker by this utterance is generating the appropriate conventional effect. Even though I can pronounce you man and wife without actually bringing it about that you are married, I cannot perform that illocutionary act without, so to say, purporting to bring this about, representing myself as bring this about. And the latter notions are elucidated in this theory in terms of U's taking responsibility for its being the case that U's utterance brings it about that the addressees enter the marital state. By bringing in the relevant conventional effect as something else for which U takes responsibility, rather than as being itself a necessary condition of illocutionary act performance, we accommodate the point that one can, for example, declare a meeting adjourned even though no meeting gets adjourned.

ILLOCUTIONARY ACT POTENTIAL AND MEANING

Given this account of illocutionary acts, what can we say about what gives a sentence a certain illocutionary act potential? As foreshadowed above, our second explication of 'taking responsibility for' the obtaining of a state of affairs, (R2), already contains the seeds of an answer. According to (R2), to take responsibility for its being the case that p, in uttering a sentence, S, is to utter S as subject to a rule that requires it to be the case that p, as a condition of permissible utterance. But, on our account, to perform an illocutionary act of a certain type *is* to take responsibility for the holding of certain conditions (the obtaining of certain states of affairs) in uttering a sentence, S. And, according to (R2), that means that to perform an illocutionary act of a certain type is to utter S as subject to a rule that requires the satisfaction of those conditions for permissible utterance of that sentence. It is hardly a further step at all to say that a sentence, S, is usable to perform illocutionary acts of a certain matching type *iff* S *is* subject to such a rule. That is, what endows S with a certain illocutionary act potential is that it is constitutive of S's status in the language, more specifically its semantic status, to be governed by such a rule. And on the assumption that S's having a certain meaning in the language is a matter of its having a certain illocutionary act potential, we can say that S's having a certain meaning amounts to its being governed by a certain rule of the sort we have been considering, an *illocutionary rule*, as we may call it.

In one way this conclusion is hardly novel. On the contrary, the idea that linguistic meaning is a matter of rules or conventions is deeply entrenched in conventional wisdom. But it would be a strikingly original contribution to put forward an adequate specification of what kind(s) of rules are constitutive of sentence meaning. Previous attempts to do this have been conspicuously unsuccessful.[17] The task bristles with difficulties, and in this brief sketch I can do no more than indicate the general character of my proposals. In order to do anything within that compass I must introduce drastic simplifications. Let us consider a language, or segment thereof, that is much simpler than natural languages in the following respects. (i) Each meaningful linguistic expression has only one meaning. Thus each sentence will have only one matching illocutionary act potential and will be governed by only one set of illocutionary rules. (ii) Reference is tightly controlled by meaning. Each singular referring expression has exactly one referent, the identity of which is determined by its meaning. We may think of these as Russellian proper names, the semantic status of each of which consists in being used as a label for a certain entity.

Working with these limitations we can simply read the illocutionary rule that gives S its meaning off the matching illocutionary act type for S. Let us say that S is 'Close D', where 'D' is a name for a certain door, and let us say that the matching illocutionary act type is <u>ordering A (the addressee) to close D</u>. We can then analyse that illocutionary act type as follows (assuming that the conditions we listed earlier for orders are complete).

(II)   U ordered A to close D in uttering S *iff* U uttered S as subject to a rule that permits the utterance of S by U only if U has sufficient reason to suppose that the following conditions hold:
(a) D is not now closed.
(b) A can close D.
(c) U is in a position of authority over A.

But then the rule subjection to which gives S its matching illocutionary act potential, and hence its meaning, is the following.

(IR1)   S may be uttered by U only if U has sufficient reason to suppose that the following conditions hold:
(a) D is not now closed.
(b) A can close D.
(c) U is in a position of authority over the addressee.

This model indicates how to construct illocutionary rules corresponding to any matching illocutionary act type for which we have this kind of analysis.

When we move to the complexities of actual languages, this model will have to be modified greatly but not abandoned. When dealing with sentences that have more than one meaning we can no longer take the rule that confers one of those meanings to lay down unqualifiedly necessary conditions for permissible utterance, since it is obviously possible to use the sentence, justifiably, in one of the other meanings. Again, when working with singular referring expressions of the sort typical in natural languages – those like 'he', 'the book', 'Jim', each of which can be used with one and the same meaning to pick out many different entities – we have to take the matching illocutionary act type for a sentence like 'Clean off the table' to be of a relatively unspecific sort like <u>ordering someone to clean off a particular contextually indicated table</u>. And there will be additional problems as to how to formulate the rule corresponding to such a type. I will not be able to get into those problems here.

One complication I will discuss, at least briefly, is this. I hinted above that a given sentence can, unexceptionably, be used to do various things other than perform illocutionary acts of one or more matching types (matching its established meanings in the language). It can be used elliptically (asserting that I will go to a certain meeting by saying 'I will'), metaphorically ('Russia has dropped an iron curtain across Europe'), or ironically ('What a beautiful day!', said on an especially gloomy day). A sentence can be used in a derivative way to give examples or to say things in dramatic productions. It can be used in a non-communicative way to practise pronunciation or test a microphone. In all these cases the sentence may be properly used without the satisfaction of what is required by any of the illocutionary rules governing it. What this means is that illocutionary rules have a limited scope. They do not apply to *any* utterances of the sentence, the way traffic rules apply to any movements of the specified sort. They are more like rules of games that apply only in certain spheres of activity. Just as the rule that forbids a tennis player to be between the baseline and the net applies only when that player is serving, not in the further course of the game or when the person is just warming up, so (IR1) applies to utterances of 'Close D' only when one means to be using that sentence to communicate and does not mean to be using it in a metaphorical, ironical or elliptical way. Thus illocutionary rules will have to be limited in their application to some stretches of speech rather than others. It is not clear exactly how to do this, but, as an illustration, the initial clause of IR1 may be enriched somewhat as follows.

> (IR2) S may be uttered by U in the communicative, literal, straightforward use of language only if U has sufficient reason to suppose that the following conditions hold.

One bonus of this additional complication is that it makes clear how the satisfaction of the crucial condition for illocutionary act performance (uttering a sentence *as subject to* a certain rule) can be under U's control. So long as the rule was in its original unrestricted form it looked as if utterances of S either are or are not governed by the rule; the speaker has nothing to say about it. But now we can see an area of U's discretion. Though an individual cannot determine which illocutionary rules are attached to a sentence, S, in the language, she can determine whether a particular utterance of S is within the range of activity in which a certain illocutionary rule applies. For it depends on U's intentions whether she is practising pronunciation, testing a microphone, or making a straightforward literal use of S. This makes it clear how it can be up to the speaker what illocutionary act potential, if any, is being exploited.

I will conclude with just a word about the meaning of subsentential units. The basic idea, as briefly mentioned above, is that a meaning of a word, for example, is to be thought of as a distinctive contribution that word makes to the illocutionary act potential of sentences in which it occurs. It seems intuitively clear that there is a common contribution made by the word 'door' to the illocutionary act potentials of 'Close the door', 'Is the door closed?', 'What a beautiful door!' and 'The door needs painting'. It is a difficult question as to how that distinctive contribution should be characterized, and I cannot enter into that task here. The point I want to emphasize is that the IAP theory shares with many other approaches to meaning the conviction that the key concept in understanding linguistic meaning is the concept of the meanings of sentences, and that we have to understand the meanings of words in terms of the contributions of words to the meanings of sentences. This conviction is prominent in Frege and Davidson and other advocates of a 'truth-conditions' account of meaning. It also plays a major role in Grice's account in terms of the perlocutionary intentions of speakers. The development of this point by the IAP theory is different in many respects from these thinkers, but it shares their insight as to the most effective point of entrance into the thickets of linguistic meaning.

NOTES

1   In addition I have many reservations about the details of his treatment of illocutionary acts. See Alston 1991.
2   That is, the concept of *sentence meaning* has to do with language, not speech. Obviously, the concept of an illocutionary act is a concept of one sort of thing we do in speech. But, in my view, sentence meaning is identified with illocutionary act *potential*, not with illocutionary acts.
3   This is abundantly documented in Searle 1968.
4   For purposes of this paper I use the principle of act individuation advocated by, for example, A.I. Goldman (1970: ch. 1). On this view true attributions of different act predicates (concepts) always determine different actions. Thus, if, in one and the same breath, one utters the sentence 'It's raining outside', tells Jones that it's raining outside, and gets Jones to realize that it is raining outside, we will say that one has thereby performed three different actions, all of which have the same 'bodily movement base'. Whereas on the account of act individuation favoured by, for example, Donald Davidson ('The logical form of action sentences', in Davidson 1980), one would say that there is only one action here, one that can be correctly described in the three ways I specified as well as in many others. I could structure my discussion in terms of either position, but I find Goldman's idiom more convenient.
5   Perhaps a sense of this difficulty has been responsible for the pervasive neglect of illocutionary acts in communication theories of meaning.
6   This last example illustrates the point that even where we use singular referring expressions to secure unique reference, the meaning of our linguistic devices do not suffice by themselves to pick out the referent uniquely.
7   For a fuller presentation of the thesis in this section see Alston 1987.

8 I shall not explicitly distinguish presupposing and implying in this brief treatment.

9 I do not mean to suggest that this is an exhaustive list of what is presupposed or implied by the illocutionary act in question in each case.

10 In saying this I do not mean to claim that nothing more than a simple act of will is required, only that whatever is required is something I can do at will whenever I choose to.

11 From this perspective the earlier suggestions as to the constitution of illocutionary acts failed because they restricted themselves to purely factual features of the situation, whereas what is crucial is the normative status that U assumes.

12 It is not, of course, that any complaint alleging the non-satisfaction of one of the conditions is thereby *justified*. One who lodges such a complaint may be mistaken in supposing the conditions to be unsatisfied. It is rather that such a complaint is *pertinent*, in that *if* the condition is not satisfied, that is a sufficient reason for taking U to task.

13 This parenthetical phrase is inserted in order to handle matters we will not be able to go into in this brief exposition, particularly the fact that sentences often have more than one meaning and hence are subject to more than one such rule.

14 Note that from the perspective of IAP theory, the fashionable idea that the meaning of declarative sentences is given by 'truth conditions' can be viewed as a special case of IAP theory. For in specifying the IAP of an assertion-making sentence, we would specify what the speaker is taking responsibility for in using it to make an assertion. And this will amount to truth conditions for the assertion. (This comment is subject to cavils concerning objections to taking sentences, as opposed to statements or assertions they can be used to make, to have truth conditions; but I cannot get into that here.)

15 A fuller treatment would require going into the various sorts of illocutionary force within what might be called the assertive family – agreeing, admitting, insisting, remarking, etc. These can all be regarded as forms of asserting, since whether I agree that p, admit that p, insist that p, or remark that p, I take responsibility for its being the case that p. The defining feature of assertion is present in acts of all these sorts. But in each case there is something else the speaker takes responsibility for as well – something that differentiates this member of the assertive family from others. It is only *mere* assertion that exhibits the defining feature of the group without additional encumbrances.

16 I am afraid this does not apply to all non-assertive illocutionary acts. It does not hold of 'expressings', like expressing indignation at his behaviour or expressing appreciation for your help. Moreover, it does not help us to distinguish agreeing that p from the assertion of *p plus whatever else one takes responsibility for in agreeing that p*. I will have to forgo discussion of these issues here, restricting myself to the question of how to distinguish conventional-effect-engendering illocutionary acts from correlated assertions.

17 See Alston 1974 for documentation of this charge.

2 Meaning, structure and speech acts

John T. Kearns

MEANINGFUL ACTS RATHER THAN MEANINGFUL EXPRESSIONS

A linguistic act, or speech act, is an intentional, meaningful act performed with an expression or expressions. Even though the word 'speech' suggests saying something out loud, I use the two expressions 'speech act' and 'linguistic act' interchangeably for acts performed with expressions, whether they are out loud, in writing, or 'in one's head'. Both speakers/writers and their audiences (when they understand the speakers/writers) perform linguistic acts.

The fundamental 'linguistic reality' is constituted by the linguistic acts of a language-using community, together with the dispositions and skills of community members for performing such acts. This understanding of language and speech acts requires that the fields of syntax, semantics and pragmatics be reconceived. The very ideas of syntax, semantics and pragmatics as these are expressed in Morris 1938, and 'implemented' in subsequent research deriving from that conceptual framework, are inadequate and incorrect. In this paper, I will present the outlines of new, more adequate conceptions.

In Kearns 1984, I recognized that some changes were needed in our conceptions of linguistic studies, but my attempts to reconceive the studies were unsatisfactory. I did not go far enough in developing new conceptions, instead landing half-way between the current understanding and a really satisfactory one. And the analyses of linguistic acts on which I based my reconceiving were not deep enough. In this paper, I will attempt to go 'all the way' to the more adequate understanding of syntax, semantics and pragmatics.

Linguistic acts are intentional acts performed by language users. An intentional act is characterized by the agent's intention *for* the act; this is what the agent intends for her act to be – what she intends to be doing. Agents commonly realize the intentions for their acts, but they are not always successful. The child who scribbles, intending to write a letter to his grandparents, is unable to realize his intention for his act because he is unable to read and write. An agent must have an intention *for* her intentional act; there is also an intention *of* many intentional acts. An intention of an act is the purpose the agent intends to achieve by performing the act. Even when the agent's intention for her act is realized, the intention of her act may not be.

A linguistic act is a meaningful intentional act. The words used to perform linguistic acts are not meaningful. But words are conventionally associated with certain types of acts and will normally be used to perform those kinds of act. The meaning of someone's linguistic act is her intention *for* the act. Most words are conventionally associated with more than one type of act. The language user's intention determines which particular type of act she performs. And it is common, by a slip of the tongue or carelessness, for a speaker to use the wrong word in performing a linguistic act. She still performs the kind of act she intends, but the expression she uses will probably mislead her audience.

A person might use the expression 'George Washington' to *attend to*, and *identify*, George Washington. *Identifying George Washington* is a particular type of linguistic act. The same person might use 'was the father of our country' to *acknowledge* George Washington to have been the father of the United States. The particular type of meaningful act that a language user performs can be identified without indicating what expressions she uses. Several different expressions might be used to identify George Washington. By a slip of the tongue, a speaker who knows better might even use 'Thomas Jefferson' to identify George Washington (for herself), and then acknowledge him to have been the father of the United States.

Just as it is linguistic acts rather than expressions which are meaningful, so it is (complex) linguistic acts which have semantically important structures. Expressions are spoken utterances or written inscriptions or (probably) neural episodes. They have spatial and temporal and, perhaps, neural structures. These structures are not what are ordinarily conceived to be syntactic structures; they are not the structures that matter for semantic analysis. Semantic structure is constituted by meaningful component acts being combined in characteristic ways.

This understanding of where meaning resides is at odds with conventional understandings of syntax and semantics. Syntax is thought to focus on the structures of expressions, the structures that are important for the semantic meanings of those expressions. On the conventional understanding, a linguistic act would not be an independently meaningful event; and a complex linguistic act would not have a structure that is given to it by the agent who performs it, when she performs it. For it is expressions which are independently meaningful, and theirs are the structures that count. Speech acts would simply be acts displaying the independently meaningful, independently structured expressions. Internal mechanisms in people generate the meaningful structured items, and then production mechanisms turn these into speech or writing. Conventional current research in syntax and semantics is doomed never to get things entirely right, for it is carried out within an inadequate conceptual framework. This leads to explanations of the phenomena we observe which appeal to expressions that we do not observe, and to transformations which they have undergone. In contrast, the present approach recognizes structures of complex speech acts that are often rather involved, but that are always exemplified in surface phenomena.

Although the current conventional conception of syntax and semantics is inadequate, current research is not simply worthless, a waste of time. Studies of language in this century have given a much better understanding, much more knowledge, than was previously available. But when the inadequate conception of language and linguistic phenomena has provided the basis for research leading to genuine advances, the researchers have failed to understand quite what they were up to. Enlightening syntactic research often has a much more semantic character than has been realized. The present account makes it possible to identify the true character of research dealing with language, and provides the resources for properly evaluating the results of such research.

STRUCTURAL RELATIONS

The fundamental semantic feature of a linguistic act is its structure, the proper object of semantic studies. Acts, not expressions, have meanings or are meaningful, but expressions are the bearers of syntactic features. An expression is a syntactic item. Expressions belong to syntactic categories, like the categories of nouns, verbs, noun phrases and adjectives. Word order is a syntactic feature. So are agreement features like gender, number and case. Although syntactic and semantic features do not even charac-terize the same objects, a linguistic act has both a semantic structure and a *syntactic character.* This character is constituted by the expressions used and their syntactic features.

To better explain semantic structure, I will provide some sample analyses of simple linguistic acts. But this requires some preliminary expla-nation of certain features of linguistic acts, and my notation for represent-ing these features. (A fuller account than I will provide here can be found in Kearns 1984.) There are three *structural relations* linking intentional acts, and these three relations provide the basic semantic links between meaningful linguistic acts. A canonical-form sentence for describing inten-tional acts which have purposes is like this:

X does Y in order to obtain/accomplish Z

Here X is the agent, doing Y is the act or action, and to obtain (accom-plish) Z is the purpose. This purpose is the intention *of* doing Y – it is X's intention of Y. The phrase 'in order' will be used exclusively to introduce expressions for purposes, although not all descriptions of acts with purposes will fit into the procrustean form shown above.

The first of the three structural relations is the relation between an act with a purpose and the act 'defined' by that purpose. If Chuck flips the light switch in order to turn on the lights in the room, his flipping is one act, and his turning on the lights is another. Chuck's intention for flipping is <u>to be flipping the switch</u> – to be moving the switch from the 'off' to the 'on' position. His flipping can be done correctly, and not have the desired effect. The lights might be burned out, the electricity might be off, or Chuck might be flipping the wrong switch. But if things go as Chuck intends, his flipping the switch will initiate a causal process which leads to the event of the lights going on.

The purpose for flipping the switch, to turn on the lights, 'defines' the act Chuck performs if his flipping succeeds – the act of turning on the lights. The purpose expression is transformed to yield a description of the subsequent act. The act of turning on the lights is constituted by the flipping, with its purpose, and the causal sequence leading up to, and including, the lights going on. This act is represented as follows:

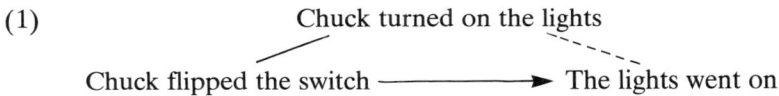

(1)   Chuck turned on the lights

Chuck flipped the switch ——————▶ The lights went on

The arrow represents the process by which Chuck's flipping the switch brings about the lights going on. The act whose purpose 'defines' the turning on is connected by a solid line to the complex act. The lights going on is an event but not an act. This event has no purpose, but is none the less a component of the complex act of turning on the lights. It is connected by a broken line to the (label for the) complex act.

Some complex acts are constituted by intentional components together with causal processes. Others are constituted entirely by component acts. If Leonard steps on Michelle's foot in the darkened theatre, he might apologize by saying 'I did not see you. I am sorry for stepping on your foot.' Each sentence is used to perform a distinct intentional act. The first sentential act explains how he happened to step on Michelle's foot. The second act expresses Leonard's regret. Both sentential acts are performed in order to apologize to Michelle:

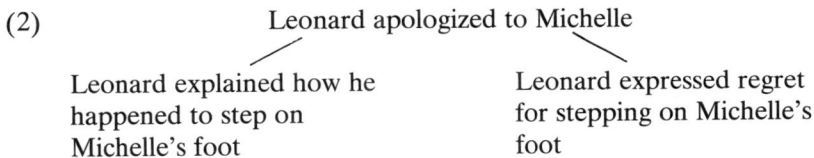

(2)   Leonard apologized to Michelle

Leonard explained how he   Leonard expressed regret
happened to step on   for stepping on Michelle's
Michelle's foot   foot

The complex apology is constituted by the two component acts, with their common purpose.

When Chuck turned on the lights, he did this because he wanted to read the paper, and having the lights on was either necessary (if it was dark) or helpful (if it was not) to his reading. Chuck's act of turning on the lights did not have the purpose <u>to read the paper</u>, because if it did have that purpose, the turning on would be a component of the reading. But the reading is not constituted, in part, by the act of turning on the lights. Turning on the lights prepares for reading, it sets the stage for reading. Turning on the lights is an *enabling* act. Chuck's intention for his act is <u>to turn on the lights, making possible (or facilitating) his reading</u>. He has enabled the reading even if he later chooses not to read, for the turning on the lights is not supposed to bring about the reading. An enabling act is done on purpose, the agent has an intention *for* the act, but it does not have a further purpose – there is no intention *of* the act. However, if act Y is intended to enable act Z, then doing Z is a goal of doing Y. The relation between an enabling act and the act it enables (and is intended to enable) is the second structural relation. It is represented like this, with a broken line:

(3)   Chuck read the paper
                                        ¦
                               Chuck turned on the lights

A more complete diagram is like this:

(4)   Chuck read the paper
                                        ¦
                               Chuck turned on the lights
                          ╱   ╲ ╲ ╲
           Chuck flipped the switch ──────────▶ The lights went on

An intentional act which has a further purpose, or one which is intended to enable (facilitate) a further act, can be done in a special way – it can be given a special character. When Victor turns on the radio in order to bring it about that the weather report is broadcast in the room, he may turn the radio on at a low volume. The reason for performing the act at all may be different from the reason for giving the act its special character. Victor turns on the radio in order to bring the weather report to this room, which will enable him to hear the weather report. But he turns the radio on low in order to not wake up his wife.

It may take no special effort to give an act a special character. The act is just done one way rather than another. But in some cases a separate act is performed to give a character to a further act. Consider Marsha, who sells real estate, and is talking on the phone to Barry, trying to get him to give her the listing for his house. Her talking is an intentional activity, with the purpose of persuading Barry. But recently Marsha attended a lecture by a motivational expert, in which the expert claimed that while talking on the phone, a speaker is more effective if she smiles as she talks. So Marsha deliberately and self-consciously smiles as she talks to Barry – she makes a special effort to smile as she talks. Her smiling is a separate intentional activity, and her intention for the smiling is <u>to smile, giving a more persuasive character to her conversation</u>. In this case, Marsha's reason for smiling is the same as her reason for talking: to persuade Barry to list with Marsha. If X is a basic act, and Y is a character-giving act for X, this is represented either like this:

(5)   (Y +) X

or this:

(6)   X (+ Y)

In Marsha's case, we might use the following diagram:

(7)   (Marsha smiled +) Marsha urged Barry to list with her

The relation between a character-giving act and the act which receives the character is the third structural relation.

The first structural relation is between a component act and the act of which it is a component. It is not a relation between (among) the components of the complex. The third relation is between two components of a complex act, but not two equal components, for the character-giving act depends on the character-receiving act. The relation between an enabling act and the act it enables is between separate acts. Neither is a component of the other. Neither need be a complex intentional act. This might be a reason for choosing some other word than 'structural' as a label for the three kinds of acts, but I can think of no expression that is more suitable. Besides, an enabling and an enabled act are often constituents of what can be considered a single activity, though not a single intentional act.

Ordinarily one thinks of the structure of an object as constituted by relations among its components, and between components and the whole. But a complete account of an object's structure must identify the kinds of component objects linked by the various relations. The three structural relations which link intentional acts are important to intentional linguistic acts. But we also need to understand what kinds of acts get linked by the structural relations.

REPRESENTING

There are many analyses of sentential linguistic acts presented in Kearns 1984, but a high percentage of them are inadequate. The structural relations were correctly identified, but the acts linked by the relations were imperfectly understood. All propositional acts were construed as representing acts constituted by component acts which were themselves representing acts. But representation was misunderstood; two distinct activities were confused with one another. (This same confusion is found in almost all discussions of representing and representation.) Before analysing linguistic acts, I must sketch an adequate account of representing.

We will consider representing where the 'viewer' is consciously aware of an object like a picture or statue, which object is a representation of something further. This is *explicit* representing. If there is such a thing as non-explicit representing, it involves a viewer who is not aware of the representation, but only of what is represented. Explicit representing can be subdivided into (at least) iconic and symbolic representing. In iconic representing, perceptible features of images get 'interpreted' as features of represented objects. In *directly* iconic representing, the features that get interpreted are the same as the represented features, or else they closely resemble those features. Realistic paintings and photographs are directly iconic representations. Indirectly iconic representing involves an element of convention or else an arbitrary assignment. Haloes in paintings are indirectly iconic representations of holiness. The height of a curve in a graph can indirectly iconically represent the number of students getting the grade indirectly iconically represented by the distance from the vertical axis. The discussion here will be exclusively concerned with directly iconic representing, the paradigm of all representing.

Although an image is a representation, representing is not intrinsic to the image. Someone might (in principle) describe an image so completely that the audience could make an exact copy of the image, without mentioning that the image is an image (a representation). And without entailing this either. The image does not represent. *Representing is what some agent does with the image.* To represent is to use an object to become *representationally aware* of a further object or objects, and its (their) features. It is important to distinguish using an image to become representationally aware from simply being (plainly) aware of the image. Any animal that can see can see an image, but it is not clear that all animals with vision can use an image to become representationally aware. For example, my cats seem unable to do this. It is also important to distinguish using an image to become representationally aware of further objects from mistaking an image for what it is an image of. Iconic representations resemble the objects they are used to represent. Confusing a photograph or a mirror image with the real thing is no sign that an animal (or person) is using the image to become representationally aware of objects. When someone does use an image to explicitly represent further objects, she is aware of the difference between the image and the objects of representational awareness.

A picture of a man does not have to be a picture of a particular man. A picture can be used to represent an *arbitrary* man. It probably will not be a picture of a completely arbitrary man. It is more likely to be a picture of an arbitrary blue-eyed man with brown hair, having a variety of other features. A picture can be used to represent some particular objects and some arbitrary objects. We might have a picture of Napoleon on a horse, where Napoleon is, of course, a particular person but the horse is no horse in particular. We might have a picture of particular real objects in a situation that did not occur. And there might be a picture of real objects in an historical situation. Most photographs are like this.

When an agent uses an image to represent, there is no difference between the awareness of arbitrary objects of a kind and the awareness of particular objects. Someone who looks at a picture of Napoleon, knowing him to be Napoleon, has the same kind of representational awareness as the viewer who thinks the picture to be of no particular person. Both are representationally aware of a short man, wearing a cape, etc. Strictly speaking, the objects of representational awareness are always arbitrary objects of various kinds, and arbitrary situations. But as well as using images to be (become) representationally aware of objects, people (agents) use images to *identify* particular objects and particular situations. The person who sees the picture of Napoleon, and knows it to be of Napoleon, uses the picture to identify Napoleon. Even the person who sees the picture and knows that the artist painted a real person, uses the picture to identify Napoleon, though she may not know who Napoleon is or that he is named Napoleon. (She uses the picture to identify the person the artist intended. That person happens to be Napoleon.) The viewer who thinks the painting to be of no one in particular does not use the picture to identify anyone, though she does use it to represent.

Representing is distinct from identifying, though the two are ordinarily conflated. One can use an image – a painting, a photograph, a statue – to represent without identifying. One can use an image to both represent and identify. Someone who uses an image to identify a particular object uses the image to *direct her attention to,* to *attend to,* the object. Her representational awareness of an arbitrary object of a kind is transformed to constitute attending, while the represented features are construed as features of the identified object. In order for someone to use an image to identify a particular object or objects, she needs some independent access to those objects. For it is her intention which determines what objects she identifies. In directly iconic representing, the similarity between the representation (the image) and certain kinds of objects is what allows an agent to use the image to become representationally aware. Similarity is important for iconic representing. But similarity does not account for identifying. One can use a poor likeness to identify a particular object. ('This is a painting of Richard, though it doesn't look much like him.') One can decline to use a good likeness. ('Although this painting looks just like Fran, it is really of her older sister.') To use an image to identify a particular object, the agent must intend that object.

Representational awareness is of arbitrary objects of kinds, not of particular objects. But we commonly speak both of representing particular objects and of representing arbitrary objects. I shall continue to speak this way, but regard such speaking as loose and informal. Strictly speaking, an image can only be used to represent arbitrary objects. As a technical term for talking about an activity that can combine representing and identifying, I will use the verb 'portray'. A person can use a painting to portray Napoleon. Napoleon might be portrayed on a horse that is no horse in particular. Napoleon might also be portrayed on a particular horse. And someone might use a picture to portray an historical event. The picture might (be used to) portray Cornwallis surrendering to George Washington at Yorktown.

Images can be used to simply represent, without identifying anything. They can be used to both represent and identify. In contrast, language provides us with the resources to identify objects without representing or portraying them, though we also use language to represent. We can use expressions like 'Napoleon' and 'George Washington' and 'the capital of New York State' to attend to the particular objects Napoleon, George Washington, and Albany without being representationally aware of either people or cities. We can use 'was the father of his country' to acknowledge George Washington to have been the father of the United States without being representationally aware of anyone or any feature.

THE PURELY IDENTIFYING STAGE OF LANGUAGE USE

A person can notice, can attend to, a present object without saying or thinking any words. She can also use words to simply express her attending to a present object, and to try to get her audience to direct their attention to that object. Once a person has learned to connect certain words to certain objects, she can use the words to attend to, to think about, those objects, whether or not the objects are present. She can attend to them without looking at them (or feeling them, etc.). Having directed her attention to a particular object, she can then apply other (appropriate) words to that object – she uses these other words to acknowledge that object to be one thing or another.

For a simple example, suppose Carol replies to a question about Tom's occupation by saying 'Tom teaches.' She uses the name 'Tom' to attend to, to identify, Tom. Focusing on Tom provides a target whom she can acknowledge to teach. In using 'teaches' for Tom, Carol is performing an act with the force of an assertion. We will represent Carol's acts like this:

(8)   Tom : ⊢ teaches

                                          |
                                        Tom

This is an adaptation of the diagrams illustrated earlier. The acts performed are represented by the words used to perform them. The lower occurrence of 'Tom' represents the act of using 'Tom' to identify Tom. This act enables, by providing a target, Carol's act of using 'teaches' to acknowledge Tom to teach (to be a teacher). In representing linguistic acts, a complete expression will be assembled as one 'moves up' the diagram. Only the lower occurrence of 'Tom' represents an act, the upper occurrence simply repeats the word 'Tom' for the sake of having a complete sentence on the top line. The expression that is actually used to perform an enabled act is flanked by a colon (or two colons, if it is in the middle). The assertion sign '⊢' is prefixed to the acknowledging expression to indicate the force of the acknowledging act.

If, instead of being asked about Tom's occupation, Carol was asked what Tom was doing, she might have replied 'Tom is sleeping.' Carol used 'Tom' to identify Tom, which allowed her to use 'is sleeping' to acknowledge Tom to currently (at that time) be sleeping. She might simply have used 'is sleeping' as a 'unit', to perform a simple intentional (linguistic) act:

(9)   Tom : ⊢ is sleeping
                               |
                               |
                             Tom

However, if Carol spoke more deliberately, she could use 'is' and 'sleeping' to perform separate intentional acts. She might have used 'sleeping' to acknowledge Tom to currently be sleeping, and used 'is' to make explicit the time with which her acknowledging act was concerned:

(10)   Tom : ⊢ (is +) sleeping
                               |
                               |
                             Tom

The auxiliary 'is' is used to give a special, explicit, character to Carol's acknowledging act. The difference between Carol's two ways of using 'is sleeping' would show up in the timing and intonation of Carol's speech acts. In the second case, there might be a very slight pause between 'is' and 'sleeping'. The two statements made with the one sentence would convey the same information and have the same truth conditions. The second structure would be appropriate to contrast what Tom is doing now with his past or future actions, emphasizing the 'presentness' of Tom's sleeping. Even when 'is sleeping' is used as a unit, the presence of the auxiliary 'is' provides a special character to the acknowledging act; but the special character is not due to a distinct intentional act.

In replying to the question about what Tom does, Carol might have said 'Tom is a teacher', rather than making the more abrupt statement 'Tom teaches.' If she had, she might have used 'is a teacher' as a unit:

(11)   Tom : ⊢ is a teacher
                               |
                               |
                             Tom

to acknowledge Tom to be a teacher. But she might also have used 'a teacher' as a unit, and performed a distinct act with 'is':

(12)   Tom : ⊢ (is +) a teacher
                               |
                               |
                             Tom

This would be appropriate to contrast what Tom does at present (what he did at the time of the utterance) with what he did previously. Carol could also use 'is a' as a character-giving unit:

(13)   Tom : ⊢ (is a +) teacher
                                   |
                                   |
                                  Tom

This would show up in her pronouncing 'is a' together, and pausing slightly before she utters 'teacher'. The character-giving act still makes explicit that Carol is acknowledging Tom's teaching to be his current occupation. The 'a' does not make a special contribution, but is present on the basis of a syntactic (a grammatical) requirement. The indefinite article does mark the acknowledging act as being concerned with a discrete individual of a kind rather than with a lump of stuff, but Carol is not concerned with this contrast in making her statement. If we can imagine a reason why she might be concerned with that contrast, we could get Carol performing acts like these:

(14)   Tom : ⊢ is (a +) teacher
                                   |
                                   |
                                  Tom

or these:

(15)   Tom : ⊢ (is +) (a +) teacher
                                   |
                                   |
                                  Tom

In the first case, Carol emphasizes the discrete character but not the present time, in the second case, she emphasizes both.

Although the sentences in the above examples are syntactic wholes, they are not used to perform single (though complex) linguistic acts, for the attending acts enable the acknowledging acts. Only the acknowledging acts are true or false in the strictest sense. However, we will use the word 'statement' to cover the activity of both attending and acknowledging, and grant that statements are true or false in a derivative sense. Strictly speaking, it is Carol's act of acknowledging Tom to be a teacher that is true. Speaking loosely, the statement composed of both her identifying Tom and her acknowledging him to be a teacher is also true.

Someone can use an expression to attend to an object both when there really is an object and when there is none. She can use 'George Washington' to attend to George Washington, and use 'the man in the next room' to attend when no one is in the next room. But she must think a man is there. Only a real object can be identified. The language user identifies George Washington. In using 'the man in the next room,' she attempts to identify a particular man, but she does not succeed. Her attending act fails to be an identifying act.

For someone to use an expression to identify a particular object, she must be connected to that object, and be aware of this connection. In identifying the object, she *exploits* a connection to that object. Everything is connected to everything else by a variety of 'paths'. There are many spatial routes leading from one (presently existing) object to another. There are causal connections. And each person is connected through her experience to objects in the present and the past. Since these objects are themselves connected in various ways to further objects, we are connected to those further objects via our connections to the objects we have experienced. We are connected to objects we have heard about and read about via our hearing and reading, and the authors' intentions and connections. Each person has a great variety of connections to any given object. But in most cases, the person will not know about the object reached by a path. She will not know that different paths lead to the same object. The objects she does know about are reached by paths she knows about. These paths are objective features in the world, which she exploits in identifying objects. When she attends to an object but fails to identify one, she may exploit a path which does not terminate the way she thinks ('the man in the next room'). She may try to exploit a connection that is not there ('Chuck's daughter' – when Chuck has only sons: her connection to Chuck is not continued to link her to a daughter of Chuck's).

When an image is used to identify an object, the identifier must have independent access to the object, which allows him to intend that object. Images are not conventionally tied to particular objects. But language is conventionally used to identify objects. Different language users who identify a single object will exploit different connections to that object. Linguistic conventions determine how particular people will associate particular expressions with particular objects. In using an expression to identify an object, the language user does not need independent access to that object. She exploits connections that conventional practices have led her to associate with the expression she uses. As she acquires more knowledge, she may associate more connections with the expression, so that the expression is associated with a cluster of connections leading to the object.

Not all identifying acts pick out a target for an acknowledging act. Suppose Carol identifies Tom and acknowledges him to be beside Sheila:

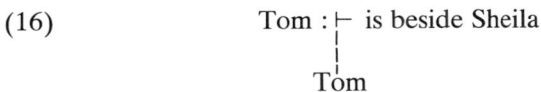

(16)   Tom : ⊢ is beside Sheila
                              |
                              |
                            Tom

This diagram is incomplete, for Carol would not use 'is beside Sheila' as a unit. Carol uses 'Sheila' to identify Sheila. But it is Tom not Sheila who is the focus of Carol's statement, the target of her acknowledging act. Carol identifies Sheila without acknowledging Sheila to be anything. Instead, Carol uses Sheila as a reference point, and then indicates how Tom is situated with respect to Sheila. The act of identifying Sheila, like the act of identifying Tom, enables Carol's acknowledging. But these two acts are not 'equal'. The act of identifying Tom provides a target for the acknowledging act. The expression 'is beside' is not, by itself (with respect to our current conventions), suited for performing an acknowledging act. Identifying Sheila, who serves as a reference point, renders 'is beside' suitable for acknowledging. Only after the expression is suited for this role can there be a question of providing a target. With respect to the acknowledging act, identifying Sheila is prior to identifying Tom. This priority will be indicated as below:

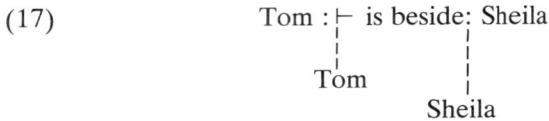

(17)   Tom : ⊢ is beside: Sheila
                         | |
                         | |
                        Tom |
                                        Sheila

The reference point act, which is prior to the target act, is represented at a lower level than the target act.

The structure shown above would be appropriate in addressing an audience who knows where Sheila is, but is looking for Tom. If the audience knows where Tom is and is looking for Sheila, the following structure is more appropriate:

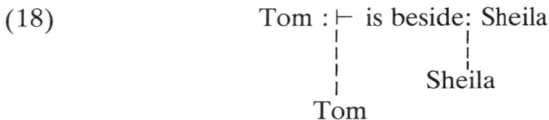

(18)   Tom : ⊢ is beside: Sheila
                         | |
                         | Sheila
                        Tom

(Of course, the speaker could also use a different sentence.)

Reference points can be used for 'locating' objects in other than spatial ways. The sentence 'Tom likes Carol' might be used as follows:

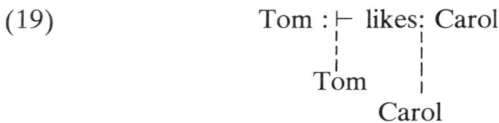

(19)   Tom : ⊢ likes: Carol
                         | |
                         | |
                        Tom |
                                   Carol

Tom is acknowledged to be situated by liking with respect to Carol. The sentence could also be used to acknowledge Carol to be situated by being liked with respect to Tom:

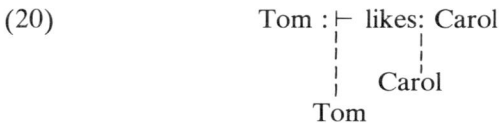

(20)   Tom : ⊢ likes: Carol
                         | |
                         | Carol
                        Tom

Or, finally and somewhat improbably, the pair Tom, Carol can be acknowledged to be a liker–liked pair:

(21)   Tom : ⊢ likes: Carol

                                   | |
                                   | |
                                 Tom   Carol

In this case, there is no reference point, but only a two-membered target. It is somewhat uncommon to perform acts with this structure, but it is not out of the question. If a teacher were contrasting transitive and intransitive verbs, and used 'likes' to illustrate that transitive verbs have a subject and an object, he might perform acts like those represented.

There are both positive and negative acknowledging acts. Carol might deny Tom to be a coach like this:

(22)   Tom : ⊢ is not a coach

                                   |
                                   |
                                 Tom

The word 'not' is added to a positive acknowledging expression to obtain a negative expression. The 'move' from 'is a coach' to 'is not a coach' is an example of a *lexical transformation*. This move is not reflected in speech act structure, but is only a systematic procedure for obtaining one expression from another. A lexical transformation also takes active-voice expressions to passive-voice expressions; another such transformation turns verbs like 'work' ('to work') into nouns like 'worker'.

Someone using an expression to attend to a particular object is trying to identify the object. If she exploits a connection which links her to a real object, she has identified the object. The person who performs an acknowledging act is also trying to perform an identifying act. A correct, or true, acknowledging act is an identifying act. When Carol identifies 'Tom' in the course of stating Tom to be a teacher, her identifying act is preliminary. We might say that she has further identified Tom in correctly acknowledging him to be a teacher. But she has also identified the *situation* of Tom's (currently) being a teacher. A situation is constituted by an object being one thing or another, or by objects being related to one another. Tom's being a teacher is a situation. So is Tom's being beside Sheila. Situations are themselves objects, and ingredients of further situations. Tom's-being-beside-Sheila's preceding Tom's-walking-away-from-Sheila is also a situation – a complex situation containing component situations.

Situations are particular objects. The same situation does not recur. The situation of Tom being beside Sheila on a particular occasion, from one time to another, is different from the situation of Tom's being beside Sheila the next day. A successful acknowledging act involves both criteria which the target satisfies (for being beside, the criteria involve proximity and the orientation of the target's and reference point's bodies) and a connection linking the language user to that particular situation/event.

Consider the following statement about Joan:

(23)   Joan : ⊢ played tennis
                                          |
                                          |
                                        Joan

The acknowledging act does not mean that Joan played tennis at some time or other in the past. Such a statement would require a quantificational use of expressions, which is not 'available' when expressions are used only to attend/identify and to acknowledge/identify. The quantificational use of expressions exceeds the resources of the *purely identifying stage of language use.* The speaker whose statement is represented above is concerned with Joan's activity on a particular occasion. (If he is right, he has identified a particular situation/event of Joan's playing tennis.) The same sentence might be used to make differently organized statements about the same event. Athletic Joan may play several sports; suppose someone has asked what she played yesterday. The speaker might organize his reply like this:

(24)   Joan played : ⊢ tennis
                                          |
                                          |
                                  Joan :played
                                          |
                                          |
                                        Joan

The speaker uses 'Joan' to identify Joan. This enables him to use 'played' to identify the particular situation/event of her playing yesterday. No acknowledging takes place, because it is already understood that Joan was engaged in athletic activity. Attending to the situation/event of Joan's playing yesterday (of Joan's playing tennis yesterday) enables the use of 'tennis' to acknowledge the playing to be tennis playing. A less deliberate speaker might perform the following acts in the same circumstances:

(25)   Joan played : ⊢ tennis
                                          |
                                          |
                                  Joan played

He does not separately attend to Joan, he only focuses on the event of her playing.

Instead of saying simply 'Joan played tennis', the speaker could use the longer sentence 'Joan played tennis yesterday.' There are many more possibilities for organizing acts of using this sentence. In these acts:

(26)   Joan : ⊢ played tennis (+ yesterday)
                                          |
                                          |
                                        Joan

the speaker uses 'yesterday' to identify yesterday, making explicit the day of the event in question, but he does not give any particular emphasis to the day. If he chose to acknowledge both what she played and when she played, he could perform acts like the following:

(27)   Joan played tennis : ⊢ yesterday

                                    Joan : ⊢ played tennis

                                            Joan

The act of acknowledging Joan to have played tennis (yesterday) identifies (or tries to) a situation which is then the target for the 'yesterday'-acknowledging act. If the audience already knew that Joan played tennis on a particular occasion, but was not sure when that occasion was, the speaker might perform these acts:

(28)   Joan played tennis : ⊢ yesterday

                                    Joan :played tennis

                                            Joan

or these:

(29)   Joan played tennis : ⊢ yesterday

                                    Joan played tennis

The difference between merely attending to/identifying the event of Joan's playing tennis and acknowledging Joan to have played tennis is that in the acknowledging case, the language user makes a point of being correct in 'matching' the situation-attending act to the particular object or objects involved. In attending to the situation without performing an acknowledging act, the language user takes for granted the object's being an element of the situation.

In using expressions to attend and acknowledge, and to make explicit certain features of linguistic acts, no representing takes place. The language user is merely identifying, or attempting to, objects and situations, and making clear what he is up to. But expressions can be used to represent. It is characteristic of representing that an object with features (the representation) is used to become representationally aware of arbitrary objects of various kinds. Features of the representation are 'interpreted' as features of the arbitrary objects. When expressions are used to represent, their visible and acoustic features do not get interpreted as features of represented objects. It is intentional, semantic features associated with expressions that get interpreted. The word 'dog' can be used to acknowledge an animal to be a dog. When used in this way, there are criteria that the animal must satisfy to be correctly acknowledged to be a dog. These criteria are intentional features associated with the expression. Once a language user can use 'dog' to acknowledge animals to be dogs, and so can employ the acknowledging criteria associated with the word, he is in a position where he can reflect on what it is to be a dog. This allows him to use 'dog' to represent an arbitrary dog, and to use 'is a dog' to represent an arbitrary object (an arbitrary animal) as a dog.

Symbolic representing initially depends on the purely identifying use of language. For expressions acquire intentional features in being used to perform attending/identifying and acknowledging acts. Once some expressions are used to represent symbolically, new kinds of representing acts performed with new expressions can be introduced. Quantification is possible at the *representational stage of language use*, but not at the purely identifying stage. Linguistic acts performed at the purely identifying stage are linked by two of the three structural relations for intentional acts, the relation between an enabling and an enabled act, and that between a character-giving and a character-receiving act. The third structural relation, the relation between a component act and the complex act 'defined' by the purpose of the component, is characteristic of propositional representing acts. As well as using 'Joan played tennis' to identify Joan and acknowledge her to have played tennis on a particular occasion, the sentence can now be used to portray Joan as playing tennis on some occasion or other in the past:

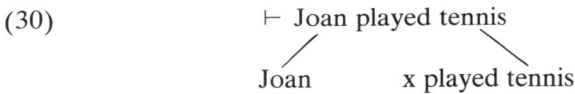

$$(30) \qquad \vdash \text{Joan played tennis}$$
$$\diagup \qquad\qquad \diagdown$$
$$\text{Joan} \qquad \text{x played tennis}$$

The speaker uses 'Joan' to identify Joan, and uses 'played tennis' to represent an arbitrary individual (or person) as playing tennis in the past, both acts being performed in order to portray Joan as playing tennis in the past. (The variable in the diagram is not an expression in the language, but only a feature of the diagram which makes explicit that an arbitrary tennis player is represented.) The speaker both portrays this and accepts the portrayal. This particular representing statement is not very interesting, and it is hard to think of circumstances where it would be appropriate. But this is a kind of statement possible at the representational stage of language use, and not possible before that stage.

At the purely identifying stage of language use, all propositional acts have the form of judgements. One cannot at this stage merely suppose that something is true, and investigate the consequences of the supposition. But one can represent a situation without accepting the representation. One can suppose a representing act – one can represent a situation and suppose that the situation is true. At the identifying stage of language use, truth does not consist in correspondence. Truth is rather a matter of satisfying acknowledging criteria and matching acknowledging acts to preliminary identifying acts. With symbolic representing, truth does consist in correspondence. To accept a representing/portraying act is to accept that things are as the act portrays them.

The use of expressions to represent very much increases the expressive power of language users when compared to what they could say (or think) at the purely identifying stage of language use. But I am not now concerned to explore the two stages of language use. That is undertaken in a much longer work that I am currently preparing. I have given enough information about linguistic acts to allow me to explain how studies of language should be reconceived.

STUDYING LANGUAGE AND LINGUISTIC ACTS

I have been using diagrams in analysing actual and imagined linguistic acts/ activities. These analyses incorporate both semantic and syntactic infor- mation. The diagrams, accompanied by my explanations, have been used to represent various kinds of interrelated speech acts. The linguistic acts/ activities have a semantic structure. But the expressions used to perform the speech acts are syntactic objects possessing syntactic features. These expressions with their features also characterize the speech acts they are used to perform. It is possible to devise purely semantic representations of linguistic acts and activities. A simple example is the following:

(31)   ⊢ An act of acknowledging Tom to be a teacher

        An act of attending to/identifying Tom

The diagram indicates the kinds of acts performed, and their intentional, structural relation. It does not tell us what word Carol used to identify Tom, or what words she used for her acknowledging act. It also fails to indicate the order in which the words used to perform the acts are produced, and whether these words have a certain gender or number or case.

Although the diagram is purely semantic, some semantically important features are not shown. And the diagram does not provide a *fully explicit* representation of that much of the semantic structure that is represented. The diagram does not contain a special notation to indicate that the identifying act provides the target for the acknowledging act, though the label for the acknowledging act makes this clear. The diagram does not indicate the time with which the acknowledging act is concerned. And the diagram does not at all 'spell out' the criteria for being correctly acknowl- edged to be a teacher. For such diagrams to provide adequate represen- tations of semantic structure, they must be accompanied by commentary, and must contain ordinary expressions which are conventionally used to perform acts like those represented (ordinary expressions like 'teacher'). We could reduce the need for commentary and for reliance on natural-language expressions by introducing additional notation to our diagrams; this would make the diagrams more explicit.

But we cannot provide either commentary or notation to obtain a complete representation of semantic structure. For any (attempted) identifying act exploits connections linking the language user to objects in the world. These connections are different for different people. Even when the same language user identifies a single individual on different occasions, the connections she exploits may be different. The connections that are exploited make up part of the semantic structure of an identifying act, for they determine which specific kind of identifying act it is. This much detail cannot be provided by our representations, but is not necessary for a theoretically adequate understanding. It will usually be sufficient to indicate where connections proper to individual language users come in, though to evaluate acts for correctness, we also need to identify their objects. If there are uniform criteria which play a role in determining the connection which is exploited in identifying the act's object, these should be noted in a maximally complete representation of semantic structure. A speaker who uses 'the capital of Illinois' exploits connections peculiar to herself in identifying Illinois. But the further connection between Illinois and Springfield is determined by the acknowledging criteria for 'capital'.

Although we cannot represent semantic structure completely, we can devise representations that are sufficiently complete for understanding linguistic acts. It is easier to obtain maximally complete representations if we provide diagrams plus commentary, and rely on our antecedent understanding of the natural-language expressions that we use, than if we insist on fully explicit representations. It is not 'cheating' to supply commentary and rely on our knowledge of English (or whatever), for in analysing linguistic acts, we do not always want a representation that is as complete and explicit as possible. A representation of a kind of statement only needs to be sufficient for the purpose an analysis is intended to serve. However, in developing a theory rather than making analyses, a system of complete and explicit representations is an appropriate goal.

We can provide entirely semantic representations of linguistic acts/ activities, leaving out such syntactic features as the expressions used, their syntactic categories and features, and the order in which expressions are produced/assembled. This suggests that we develop an abstract semantic theory which is independent of any particular language. If we devise a system which provides representations for everything that it is possible to say, we can then investigate particular languages to determine which possibilities the languages are equipped to realize, and the manners in which they do this. This abstract theory will not belong to linguistics, an empirical study of actual natural languages, but will instead be housed in philosophy, psychology or logic.

However, unless people are equipped with a substantial array of innate ideas or concepts, which I do not believe, there is not much to learn from an abstract semantic theory. People do have innate skills and dispositions which are sufficient for developing and for learning languages. These skills allow people to invent words and use these words to attend to/identify objects, and to acknowledge objects to be this or that. In inventing/ developing language, people both respond to and give shape to their experience and its objects. But which specific meaningful linguistic acts a person performs are determined by the conventions and practices that he or other members of his linguistic community have thought up. Since everyone performs the same general kinds of intentional acts, related by the same structural relations, and everyone inhabits what is more or less the same world, we expect to find massive similarities between the conceptual systems embodied in different languages. But which kinds of meaningful acts can be performed, which concepts are expressed/embodied in a language, can only be determined by investigating existing languages or inventing new ones.

A purely semantic representation of a kind of linguistic act or activity is not a complete or adequate representation of the act/activity. For a statement (or question, command, etc.) has both a semantic structure and a syntactic character (a syntactic character is *not* a syntactic structure). A particular linguistic act/activity is performed with certain expressions, which belong to certain syntactic categories and have certain syntactic features, and these expressions have a definite order. The stuff, or matter, of linguistic acts is sounds or marks or neural episodes. The words used, and their features, constitute the syntactic characters of linguistic acts. The intentional features of component acts, which determine just what kinds of intentional linguistic acts they are, and the structural organization of these component acts also characterize linguistic acts/activities. They constitute semantic structure.

To completely determine a kind of a linguistic act or activity, one must identify both its semantic structure and its syntactic character. Although semantic structure is distinct from syntactic character, it is not appropriate to develop either a purely semantic or a purely syntactic theory of a natural language. The distinct characters do not call for distinct theories. A purely semantic theory would be excessively abstract, omitting much of what is distinctive about a particular natural language. A purely syntactic theory would sin in the opposite direction, omitting the meaningful characters shared by linguistic acts performed with different languages.

Syntactic features and syntactic categories are often identified with an eye to the acts that expressions having the features or belonging to the categories are used to perform. Features like *singular, plural, past tense,* and *future tense,* and categories like *adjective* and *adverb* are *semantically motivated* features and categories; I distinguish them from *brute* features and categories. A brute syntactic feature involves only the shapes, acoustic 'contours', and spatial and temporal organization of written and spoken expressions. If there were a system of rules for obtaining some expressions from others, and this system was formulated solely in terms of brute syntactic features, it would then be a brute syntactic feature of an expression to have been obtained from brutely specified input expressions by applying a definite sequence of rules. An independent, autonomous syntactic theory (a presemantic theory) would characterize well-formed expressions in brute-feature terms. It is conceivable though unlikely that a brute-feature system could be provided for assembling just those sentences of a natural language that are intuitively recognized to be grammatical. But unless the theory were designed with semantic structure in mind, the brute-feature characterizations would have little relation to what we can do with expressions. The vague ideal of intuitive grammaticality is not a very important goal for a theory of a natural language. We have no trouble using sentences, intuitively seen not to be grammatical, to perform meaningful linguistic acts.

Instead of having a syntactic theory or a semantic theory for a natural language, what is wanted is a combined syntactic-semantic theory. This agrees with Montague's remark (in Montague 1974: 210) that syntax and semantics must be developed 'hand in hand'. But how should such a theory be organized? In the twentieth century, rather specialized ideals have been provided for theories of all kinds. Theories should be compositional or 'recursive', having the form of a deductive system. But there are two ways to look at this. A theory can be a set of statements, derived from primitive statements by inferential procedures. The ideal for a syntactic-semantic theory is not axiomatic in this sense. Instead of being an organized body of truths, or theorems, a theory can be a set of constructions. A natural deduction system illustrates this kind of theory, but only if the objects of the system are taken to be proofs (deductions) rather than the results these are used to establish. This type of theory identifies simple items and provides principles for constructing complex ones. The complex constructed objects may either be of interest in their own right – as when they are proofs establishing independently important truths – or they may be representations of some other items of interest. An adequate theory of a natural language should be like this, with its constructions representing kinds of linguistic acts and activities. Such a theory will be generative both in the sense of giving principles for generating (constructing) representations, and in the sense of representing how language users produce (generate) complex linguistic acts and activity.

An adequate syntactic-semantic theory will not have what might be called an 'atomic' or 'atomic-compositional' character. We cannot begin with a number of independent, self-sufficient atoms, and simply provide rules for combining or arranging these atoms. Not all simple acts are capable of being independently performed. An acknowledging act is an enabled act. Whether it is enabled by a perception that was not intended to be an enabling act (as when we acknowledge the animal in front of us to be

a dog), or is made possible by an act intended to be enabling, the acknowledging act is essentially dependent on what enables it. We do not first
perform the acknowledging act, then put it together with other acts.
Similarly, an act performed to provide a special character to another act is
essentially dependent on that other act – the intention *for* the character-
giving act is to give the character.

The principles for constructing representations in a theory of a natural
language should reflect principles for using expressions belonging to
specified (semantically motivated) categories to perform basic acts not
dependent on others. An example of such acts is attending to/identifying
an object. The theory should also indicate principles for using expressions
belonging to specified categories to perform acts depending on other acts,
and principles for combining acts performed with various kinds of expressions to constitute complex acts/activities. The theory must list
syntactic categories and syntactic features, and indicate how these 'show
up'. It must provide syntactic information about kinds of acts – including
principles which determine the syntactic features which are either required
or appropriate for expressions used to perform certain acts. The theory
should incorporate a lexicon identifying syntactic categories of expressions
and providing semantic information about the acts the expressions are used
to perform. It must include an account of lexical transformations and their
semantic 'effects'.

A linguistic theory with maximally complete representations of semantic
structure gives detail often thought to be pragmatic rather than semantic.
This 'pragmatic' character showed up in our earlier analyses. For I found it
convenient to explain different ways of using one sentence by describing
circumstances in which one or another structure is appropriate. For
example, this structure:

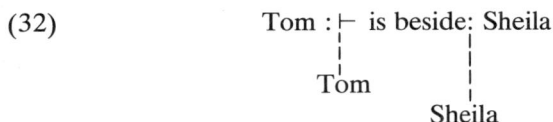

(32)   Tom : ⊢ is beside: Sheila
                          | |
                        Tom |
                                    Sheila

is appropriate when the audience knows where Sheila is but not where Tom
is, and this structure:

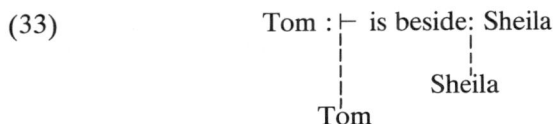

(33)   Tom : ⊢ is beside: Sheila
                          | |
                          | Sheila
                        Tom

is appropriate in the opposite case. The detailed difference between the
two statements is a semantic difference. The fundamental linguistic (and
semantic) reality is constituted by linguistic acts and activities, organized by
the structural relations. But certain semantic structures are better suited

than others for communicating information to a particular audience. The facts of language and language use provide 'space' for a theory of pragmatics which explores the communicating 'jobs' accomplished with detailed semantic structures (and their associated syntactic characters). This theory will also investigate such 'Gricean' phenomena as the deliberate choice of words not conventionally associated with the acts they are used to perform (as in ironic or sarcastic statements), and other deliberate violations of principles governing conversations.

Different statements made with a single sentence often have the same truth conditions. The two statements that can be made with 'Tom is beside Sheila' are like this. So are the 'Joan played tennis'-statements that we considered earlier. Even though the different statements have different detailed semantic structures, we can think of them as having an abstract structure in common. In addition to developing a system of representations for linguistic acts/activities that shows as much semantic structure as possible, we can develop a more abstract system of representations showing semantic structure 'at the level of truth conditions'. One abstract representation would 'fit' those statements made with one sentence that have the same truth conditions, while statements with different truth conditions would receive different representations. The abstract representations would also show syntactic characters associated with statements. If one sentence can be used to make statements having different truth conditions, those different statements might be awarded the same syntactic character. But it is also possible to introduce semantically motivated syntactic features to provide a distinctive syntactic character for each set of truth-conditionally distinct statements made with what superficially seems to be a single sentence.

Most current accounts of both syntax and semantics seem to aim at an abstract level of structure like that associated with truth conditions, rather than at total semantic structure. Although theories of syntax are conceived as dealing with structures of expressions and not acts, the structures assigned to expressions are intended to characterize sentences with respect to (abstractly conceived) statements made with the sentences. And logic is quite explicit about taking semantics to study truth conditions, and about the importance of providing distinct syntactic characters to mark truth-conditionally distinct statements.

Syntactic theories in linguistics are certainly semantically motivated. Otherwise they would have no occasion to assign different structures to a single sentence (to a single sentential string of words). But these theories can be interpreted in different ways. They can be regarded as systems of representations of linguistic acts/activities, showing both semantic structures and syntactic characters at an abstract level. Or they can be conceived as theories of the syntactic characters of abstractly conceived linguistic acts/activities. If the only syntactic features were brute features, then there would be lots of 'so-called' theories of syntax. The first interpretation would be the right interpretation for the allegedly syntactic theories. But allowing ourselves to recognize semantically motivated syntactic categories and syntactic features opens the way to providing a very rich account of the syntactic characters of linguistic acts. For example, from the perspective of brute syntactic features, the phrase 'pretty little girls' school' is a single syntactic item. But if we admit a syntactic relation *modifying*, the one string of words can be used to exemplify different syntactic characters:

(34) (a) pretty [little [girls' school]]
     (b) pretty [[little girls'] school]
     (c) [pretty little] [girls' school]

and so on.

Unless some restriction is placed on what can be counted a syntactic feature, a syntactic counterpart can be provided to every semantic feature. But developing such a rich set of syntactic concepts only camouflages the semantic structures of linguistic acts and activities, and leads to a mis-understanding of the relation between the semantic and the syntactic. For example, the procedures involved in producing representations of syntactic characters are easily mistaken for processes that go on 'inside' language users. Transformations that turn input expressions into different output expressions, that provide for deleting expressions or moving them around, are such procedures. Nothing of the sort takes place in linguistic acts and activities. We do not first say one thing, then convert it into something else. We do not first use an expression to perform a linguistic act, then delete it. Rather than building a complete account of semantic structure into our syntactic concepts, it is more enlightening to develop an explicit account of semantic structure. I propose that what are considered to be syntactic features of expressions be limited to what can be detected by looking or listening. This allows semantically motivated syntactic categories and some semantically motivated syntactic features. We can see and hear the differ-ence between different words, and between 'he' and 'him', between 'boy' and 'boys'. Cases, number and gender are legitimate syntactic features, but modifying relations are not. To say that an adjective modifies a noun is not to make a syntactic statement; it is instead to say how adjective acts are semantically related to noun acts. Similarly, relations between pronouns and their antecedents are semantic rather than syntactic.

If the realm of syntax is limited as I propose, modern theories of syntax in linguistics will become syntactic-semantic theories which provide rep-resentations of both semantic structures and syntactic characters. They are not entirely satisfactory theories, for the representations of semantic struc-ture are neither adequate nor perspicuous. And semantic structure is treated at quite an abstract level. Even if my proposed limitation is not accepted, it must still be conceded that syntactic theories are infected by semantic concerns and concepts. Semantic structure does not grow out of syntactic character; the syntactic characters are introduced to accommodate the intuitively recognized semantic structures.

The linguistic accounts are not 'pitched' at the level of truth conditions (or analogous conditions for questions, commands, etc.). They are directed at a more abstract level, because linguistic accounts group together statements that do not have the same truth conditions. Consider Albert's statement that Sally fell down:

(35)   Sally : ⊢ fell down
                                   ⋮
                                 Sally

Albert identifies Sally, and acknowledges her to have fallen down. But Albert's acknowledging act does not mean that Sally fell down on some occasion or other in the past. Albert's acknowledging act is an attempted identifying act. He acknowledges her to have fallen down on a particular occasion that he intends in performing his acknowledging act, though without specifying which occasion this was. Suppose Sally fell down on two occasions, an hour apart. If Albert witnessed the first fall but not the second, and Bruce witnessed only the second fall, then when each man makes a statement represented by the diagram above, he is making a different claim. Each identifies an event to which he is directly connected via his experience. If Chuck learns about Sally's fall from Albert, then when Chuck makes a Sally-fell-down statement, he exploits an indirect connection in identifying the event. And if David saw Mary fall, but because he was far away mistook her for Sally, and he does not know about Sally's falls, then when he makes a statement represented by the diagram above, his statement is false. His mistake is not 'overcome' by the fact that Sally also fell down – his statement is not correct 'by accident'.

Different statements represented by a single diagram, statements which identify the same components of situations, can have different truth conditions. But these differences are not marked syntactically, as the differences are marked in statements made with these sentences:

(36)   Sally fell down at 10 a.m. yesterday.
(37)   Sally fell down at 11 a.m. yesterday.

From the present perspective, linguistic accounts of syntactic structure are really accounts of semantic structure and syntactic character. These accounts aim at the abstract level of statements having the same syntactic character, whose semantic structures determine the same truth conditions, apart from connections linking linguistic acts to specific situations. The different statements made with 'Sally fell down' do not have exactly the same truth conditions. They do have the same syntactic character. They do have the same truth conditions apart from the different connections which the various language users exploit in identifying falls by Sally. The abstract level at which linguistic theories aim appears to be the level at which syntactic principles 'take effect' for a language like English. From what I have been told, it is not the level at which (all) syntactic principles 'operate' in Japanese, where the focus of a statement is marked syntactically.

Although linguists represent statements at a level only slightly more abstract than the level of truth conditions (they group together statements having the same relatively specific kinds of truth conditions), linguists do not normally attempt to describe the truth conditions of statements (or the analogous conditions for other kinds of sentential acts/activities). Logicians do provide systematic accounts of truth conditions. This is easier in the case of logic than it would be in linguistics, for logicians consider statements at a more abstract level than linguists do. Logicians employ artificial languages in developing their accounts of truth conditions and of deduction. The rules for constructing sentences of these languages are normally formulated in terms of brute syntactic features, but the formulations are clearly guided by a concern for what the various kinds of expression can be used to do. That the logical languages are artificially simple in comparison with natural ones is of great importance in developing logical theories. The logician is normally concerned with certain expressions (and their conventionally associated acts) and certain features of natural languages to the exclusion of others. An artificial language can be designed to incorporate the features of interest, and to omit or simplify the features not being studied. For example, standard logical languages (first-order languages) have no plural forms, no apparatus for marking tenses, etc. It is much easier to use artificial languages to tackle features one or two at a time than it is to give a comprehensive and adequate account for a whole natural language.

It is not entirely accurate to speak of artificial logical *languages* (though I am not proposing to change this usage). The basic linguistic reality is constituted by linguistic acts and activities. Expressions have no 'standing' apart from their use by the community to perform these acts/activities. But no one speaks or writes or thinks the 'languages' of modern logic. We can regard the sentences of artificial languages as instruments that might be used to make statements, and can investigate the kinds of statement that could be made with them. But it makes more sense to regard the sentences as abstract representations of (kinds of) linguistic acts/activities. For example, a first-order sentence 'F(a)' represents a statement constituted by an identifying act and a predicative act having any degree of complexity. (The predicative act is not an acknowledging act, for Tarski-style truth conditions are characteristic of propositional representing acts rather than acknowledging acts.) As representations, logical-language sentences are abstract because they are pitched at the level of truth conditions, they omit many natural-language features, and they are directed toward semantic structure more than syntactic character.

It is common in logic to think of syntax as providing rules for constructing sentences, and of semantics as giving the truth conditions of these sentences. A deductive system then syntactically characterizes semantically distinguished sentences and arguments. But sentences do not have truth conditions or semantic features. The truth conditions are for statements of the kinds represented with the 'sentences'. And arguments are not constituted by syntactic objects. The deductive system codifies techniques for constructing representations of proofs, valid arguments and logically true sentences. When sentences are construed as representations of statements, the 'syntactic' rules give directions for constructing representations. These are representations we can investigate and 'manipulate' to find things out about the kinds of statements they represent.

The sentences of logical languages represent semantic structures associated with the kinds of linguistic acts being studied. They abstract away from the more detailed semantic structures of acts which are not the focus of interest (as when the acts performed in using the predicate 'is a callow youth who inherited a fortune from his grandmother' are represented with 'C( )'). Logical languages represent semantic structure at the level of truth conditions, but give almost no information about syntactic characters. (The languages of logic are not tied to specific natural languages.) These languages are designed so that a uniform statement of truth conditions can be provided for each representation, and no representation is truth-conditionally ambiguous. For a logical language to be unambiguous in this respect is for logical form and grammatical form to coincide.

Because their representations of statements are so abstract, logical languages allow 'neat and tidy' formulations of truth conditions. These formulations are sufficient for exploring semantic, inferential features tied to the kinds of acts represented, but they give little understanding of the truth conditions of natural-language statements. Logical accounts of truth conditions are not *realistic* in the sense of reflecting/explaining the concrete truth conditions of actual statements. In fact, the highly restricted class of statements on which logicians have focused has led to their adopting a too simple paradigm for accounts of truth conditions. The set-theoretic accounts, standard since Tarski, accommodate representing acts performed with predicates, but not acknowledging acts and other acts of attending to/identifying situations. A complete and realistic account of truth conditions for a natural language must be grounded on a comprehensive and thorough understanding of semantic structure. The truth conditions of a statement are what the world must be like if the statement is true, and depend on connections between linguistic acts and objects in the world.

In giving truth conditions for a statement, one should 'follow' the semantic structure of the statement. For example, in a statement like this:

(38)   Sally : ⊢ is asleep
                                   |
                                   |
                                 Sally

the act of using 'Sally' identifies Sally, who is in the world. The act of acknowledging Sally to be asleep is an attempt to identify a particular event of Sally's sleeping. The truth condition for the acknowledging act and, hence, for the statement, is that there be that situation/event. To give (state) the truth conditions is to explain how the basic acts are correlated with objects (when these acts are successful), and which objects the remaining acts are correlated with when the statement is true. An account of truth conditions for a natural language will not employ the interpreting functions found in logic, which subject a language to multiple interpretations. The fundamental attending acts are themselves 'functions' from the world to the objects they identify. Acts which are relevant to truth conditions and which depend on these fundamental acts are like functions from the values yielded by the fundamental acts, or like functions from the fundamental acts themselves.

There are enormous conceptual difficulties in developing a realistic account of truth conditions for the statements of a natural language, and I will not provide an illustration or sample of such an account in this paper. It seems quite difficult to develop an account of situations, one that does not construe them as n-tuples or other set-theoretic constructions. Another difficulty is associated with acknowledging acts. If a speaker performs these acts:

(39) Sally : $\vdash$ fell down

Sally

the speaker has identified Sally as the initial object for a functional account of truth conditions. But he does not simply acknowledge Sally to have fallen down, he acknowledges her to have fallen down on a particular occasion. This acknowledging act is not one that can be correctly performed for Sally on other occasions, or for other people on other occasions. And his act of acknowledging Sally to have fallen on that occasion cannot be performed by other people, because they will not be connected in the same way to her fall. To give a functional account of truth conditions, it is not sufficient to have a 'fell down' function. There must be as many such functions as there are occasions on which someone is in a position to acknowledge a particular person to have fallen down. There cannot simply be one function for each fall that Sally took; for each fall, we need a function for each person in a position to identify that fall. The difficulties in developing a realistic account of truth conditions make the logicians' approach seem pretty attractive. Working at a sufficiently abstract level makes it possible to get by with individuals, n-tuples, sets of individuals and n-tuples, and functions from representations to the individuals, n-tuples, and sets.

The representations in a theory of a natural language should reveal as much semantic structure as possible, and represent syntactic character completely. But there is also room for a system of representations directed to an abstract level of semantic structure or syntactic character. Logical systems represent semantic structure at the level of truth conditions, and pretty much ignore syntactic character. Linguistic theories aim at about the level of truth conditions, but try for a complete account of syntactic character. Someone could also develop a system of representations that is even more abstract than representations at the level of truth conditions. Such a system could be directed toward syntactic characters and the semantic structures associated with them, rather than making semantic structures the primary focus of attention. If what counts as syntactic is understood as I have proposed, the representations of statements would be little different from sentences in which syntactic categories and syntactic features are explicitly marked. Such a system would classify together the different statements made with a sentence like 'Everyone likes someone'. This would provide a shallow, superficial analysis or classification of statements. The realm of the syntactic might be slightly extended from my proposal, without being completely open-ended. This would allow a slightly deeper analysis or classification, perhaps one that distinguishes the two readings of 'Everyone likes someone' without recognizing the different readings of 'Only George hopes he will win'. There is a wide range of levels of abstraction at which a system of representations might aim, but it is not clear why anyone would want to develop such systems. They are theoretically possible but not theoretically interesting.

On the present understanding, the primary linguistic reality is constituted by acts performed with expressions. Since it is these acts which are the 'bearers' of meanings and semantic features, there is no independent and autonomous theory of syntax to provide a foundation for semantic or pragmatic studies. Even if it were (is) possible to devise brute-feature procedures for constructing exactly those sentences which are intuitively seen to be grammatical, this possibility would have little theoretical interest or importance. Sentences are only the vehicles used to perform linguistic acts. Expressions do not determine the semantic structures of acts performed with them. A purely syntactic theory has no interest, though a theory which recognizes enough semantically motivated features can smuggle semantic analyses into an account of syntax. But such an account is either confused or duplicitous. A proper theory for a natural language must explain both the semantic structures and syntactic characters of linguistic acts, correlating the characters with the structures. However, the structures are primary, they are simply marked by syntactic characters.

A proper understanding of language and linguistic acts rules out a separate syntactic theory for a natural language. It also renders an entirely semantic theory of a natural language inappropriate. Such theories are possible. Many logical systems/theories are almost purely semantic. But these theories are suited for dealing with issues/topics common to different languages – such topics as the inferences warranted by certain semantic kinds of statements. The basic theory of a given natural language should provide an inseparable mixture of semantic and syntactic information. There is room for other theories of a natural language besides this basic theory: a theory of pragmatics, a theory of truth conditions, a theory of deduction – of inferences and arguments. These all depend on the basic theory.

3 A semantics of utterance, formalized

D.S. Shwayder

1 PRELIMINARIES

Some fifteen years ago, I had the agreeable opportunity to give a talk, later published under the title of 'A semantics of utterance' (Shwayder 1977). In that paper I sought to adapt some thoughts I had had about the nature of language to the semantic analysis of 'speech acts' or (as I prefer) 'utterance'. My analysis suggested mechanisms for the resolution or 'parsing' of utterances into complementary sememic factors and principles for the association of these into larger complexes. At that time, I was taken by the wishful thought that these ideas just might be serviceable, as a semantics, to linguists interested in lexicography and 'universal grammar' or to those other linguists who might have been curious about a simple mechanism for the 'downward' sememic identification of those tagmemic and morphemic factors of their accustomed and traditional commerce or to 'pragmaticists' curious to see a not so simple 'upward' application of semantic mechanisms to the explanation of usage, especially the figurative adaptation of usage. High aspirations, and no takers so far.

I thought then (and still do) that the factors I had identified and their combinations were quite close to Frege's *Sinn*, with the difference that Frege assigned *Sinn* to words and other expressions and only derivatively to judgements and other utterance kinds. I was already, way back then, appealing to a 'representation' for these 'meanings', and using a crude notational instrumentality for that purpose. This representation seemed to me then, as it still does, to be a kind of formal 'theory of intensions'. I left the paper unburdened of that formalization, for I could not then, even in my wildest fancies, have supposed that self-respecting linguists could find pleasure or instruction in such stuff. My theory of intensions was, however, prefigured in another paper on Fregean *Sinn* (Shwayder 1976).

Latterly, linguists and other theorists of language seem to have become fascinated, I might even say 'obsessed' with theories of intensions. There is a pullulating literature, of which I have but remote notice, dedicated to this style of 'semantics'. I get a distant idea that most of the instrumentalities for this work have been adaptations of Montague Grammar, where Montague

Grammar is itself an offshoot of Tarski's model theory. Model theory has been a boon to mathematics, but I suspect more of a bane to linguistics. I believe that my own 'formalization' qualifies as competition on the field of formal semantics, and I would like to show it off while taking the opportunity to badmouth the opposition.

So, on a more positive note: the aim of this paper is to channel the speculations of the two earlier ones back into a single stream, with the wishful thought that some of this, sketchy as it will be, just might be of some interest to linguists who have survived their exposure to formal philosophy. 'Sketchy' is true: the paper proves nothing; it is meant to be only 'suggestive'. It would take me ages and too many pages to tell a fuller, more metaphysical story, which is in fact in preparation.[1]

2 SEMANTICS IN ACTION

Utterance is nothing if not a kind of *action*, in a familiar if still poorly understood usage of 'action'. As a first step toward specifying that usage, I suggest that action may be characterized as 'meant doing'. More clearly put, there are locutions which afford answers for questions of what a subject meant to do and which then, when ascribed to acts, also provide an answer (there are others)[2] to the question of what the subject did do. I sometimes call such locutions 'specifications of purpose'. When ascribed to acts in response to the 'indexical question' of what a subject meant to do, these specifications of purpose afford an identification of the deed that is, as I believe, 'generic' in an Aristotelian understanding. To call an item a 'meant doing' entails that it was a movement of or resident in the body of a live creature (the 'subject'), and then opens a further question of whether the subject did or did not bring off what it meant to do.

That still says precious little about what *action* is. My chief proposal to that end is that a specification of purpose ascribed to a meant doing entails that some of the movements constituting that doing should have been induced by the subject's *beliefs* that certain conditions were satisfied, where it is further implied that the subject would have failed to bring off what it meant to do if any of those believed 'conditions of success' were not satisfied; so, for example, if the right answer to the question of what I meant to do was to turn on a radio, then, among the conditions of success for that deed were that the box before me was indeed a radio, operative in its switches, transistors and filters, tied into power; if, differently, the right answer were to tune in WILL-FM station, then there would have been additional conditions having to do with the radio's tuning availabilities and the operations of that station. These conditions will of course always be specific to the actual episode, but then, in relation to their formulations, for example, as given above, of *kinds* characteristic of the generic classification conveyed by the specification of purpose.

The condition, that the subject should believe that these various conditions of success for its act are satisfied, is of course not itself a condition of success for its deed. The subject's belief, rather, is a 'truth condition' for the generic identification of the act. I call it a *condition for doing* the act. There are other such conditions for doing implicated by various identifications, generic or otherwise of action, for example, that the subject should be alive. We shall presently and duly take notice of another instance more specific than that.

Utterance, I say, is action, hence meant doing having conditions of success and various conditions for doing. One may well wonder whether it is anything special in its own right. Lots of writers have not seemed to think so. Grice, in his well-known examination of 'non-natural meaning' (Grice 1957), noticed a number of verbal indices suggesting that there is indeed something distinctive here. Utterances are not just any old 'meanings to do' or 'meant doings' but, in a distinctive sense, acts of meaning. Consider:[3] a child kicks a chair. An answer to the action-index question of what he meant to do is 'to kick the chair'. A psychologist could be curious about the *significance* of the deed, and might well ask what 'it meant': was it petulance, spite, misapprehension or just exuberance? Most of us, however, would be puzzled by any further inquiry into what the brat himself 'meant'. Kicking by kids is not a kind of action which ordinarily involves such further wonderings. Contrastingly, a visitor in Britain might wonder what this English child meant in saying of the family car that the bonnet was open. Is it a convertible? We tell him that the child meant that the hood was up. This question of what a subject meant is always appropriate to language – spoken, written or gestural – and also to those adult kicks that are as good (or as bad) as language, for example, under the bridge table. The difference we have noticed is simple and obvious, less telling than Grice's list of comparisons, but I believe sufficient for our purpose. So I submit that the indexical question of what a subject 'meant' (in contradistinction to what it meant to do) can be answered whenever utterance is in the offing, and also elsewhere, in the matter of such other 'conventional behaviours' as ritual and commercial exchange. We recognize language and ritual for what they are, of course: my claim is that our sense of what a subject meant goes with that so far unspecified knowledge and guides the classification. If the question of what a subject meant is not appropriate, then, prima facie, the subject's deed was not linguistic or otherwise 'conventional'. If the question is appropriate, then (unsurprisingly) the deed so far qualifies.

Or does it? There is a difficulty here.

Before coming to that, it will be well first to notice that answers to the 'What did he mean?' question, when appropriate, may be more or less full. A Spaniard says, 'Los pantalones son de lana.' A non-hispanic may be told that the speaker meant that *he thought that the pants were made of wool*, or that *the pants are made of wool* or that *by 'lana'* he meant *wool* or that *by 'pantalones'* he meant *pants*. Any of these could stand as a more or less foreshortened answer to the indexical question.

But now you may wonder, and here is the difficulty: if the Spaniard meant pants, then did he not mean to refer to those pants; and if he meant that the pants are made of wool, did he not mean to say just that; again, if he meant that he thought that the pants were made of wool, did he not mean to express that thought? Conversely, if he meant to say (for example) that the pants were made of wool, it seems he meant that the pants were made of wool. An answer to either question – what the subject meant to do and what he meant – when both are appropriate, provides an equally full answer to the other. If (plausibly) questions were defined by their ranges of answers, it would seem our two indexical questions must be the same, and we would have lost our everyday evidence for the distinctiveness of language.

Well, the two questions are certainly intertwined but still different. The 'meant to do' question, as we earlier observed, invites further inquiry into whether the subject brought off what he meant to do; the simple 'means' question does not. The subject would, for example, have failed in his utterance if there had been no pants on the hook, perhaps because the cloth hanging there had not yet been fashioned into a pair of tubes. Yet the subject still unfailingly meant pants. Meaning unlike meaning-to-do is not the kind of thing one can fail to bring off. Further, we could not determine whether a speaker's utterance succeeded or failed unless we knew what he meant.

It is, I hope, now fairly evident that the answer to the what the subject 'meant' question implicates, not conditions of success for the subject's deed, but *a condition for doing* specific to the fact of utterance and other conventional behaviour.

The aporetic intertwining of answers brings out that this condition for doing, which is characteristic of utterance, is that the subject should, in his action, indicate or 'show' what he means to do. A subject's *meaning* such and such must convey an indication of what that subject means to do.

Now, at last, we are arrived in position to say what the best part of that meaning is: meaning includes an indication of the conditions of success for the subject's action, and we can capture all the rest of that meaning by allowing other conditions to be indicated too. Generally: meaning may be defined by listings of indicatable conditions.

There is lots here to be left unsaid about this 'derivation'. Allow me just a touch of grammar: the 'applications' I envisaged in the earlier paper (Shwayder 1977) all arise from the simple observation that conditions defining what, with tongue in cheek, we may call the total meaning of an utterance may be variously broken down and packaged into separably indicatable 'sememic factors', which I like to call 'uses'. These uses comprise such items as references, predications, attributions and determinations. Indication of some of the conditions defining such a use may require complementation by the indication of other conditions packaged in other uses. Therein, I believe, lies everything syntacticians will ever need for their explanations of complementation (NB, not yet transformation).

I hope that later on you will get some sense of how this works out. For purposes of present illustration, let me register some soft thoughts on two tough cases, those of 'mood indication' ('illocutionary force') and 'act-adverbial modification' (the meanings of 'sentence adverbs').

To deal with either of these sorts of meaning, I must first recollect an Austinian distinction. Utterance usually does but need not always occur in subordination to some other kind of action, for example, communication, persuasion, the organization of knowledge, and so on. From the other side, some of these, for example, communication, may go on unassisted by utterance, as in the lives of dogs and bees. Following Austin, we style as 'perlocutionary' those deeds that proceed 'by utterance', where *what* was done by utterance need not have been. Communication by script or speech is perlocutionary. I get the idea that what some linguists like to call 'pragmatics' is the study of language in its perlocutionary connections.

Mood is problematic partly because, as it seems, there is no utterance not classifiable in 'this way', by mood – as an act of promising, vowing, ordering, commanding, saluting, greeting, requesting, voting, betting, predicting, conjecturing, formulating an hypothesis, naming, defining, expressing an opinion, expressing an intention, depositing money, cheering, and so on. Why is that so, and why is our list of moods open-ended and so unsystematic? Mood, after all, is not all there is to utterance. Determinations of predication, attribution, reference and 'form' cut across determinations of mood. Why, as it seems, should only distinctions in mood be mandatory? The answer is elusive partly because the pattern of mood determination is unclear.

I assume that mood is indeed a feature of the 'meaning' of utterance, one that can be marked to indicate a defining inventory of conditions. The marking is often but not always by use of an expression that incorporates a name for the mood (e.g. 'I vote', 'We conjecture', 'Let us define') but also by use of copulas and by features of word order and intonation.

Now I enter, not an obvious observation, but rather an hypothesis for what these mood-determining conditions are. The conditions indicated in an utterance that contribute to the determination of its mood are ones that facilitate the 'perlocutionary' connection of utterance to our other activities. The conditions that contribute to the determination of predication, etc., do not do that. By this hypothesis, the need for mood is corollary to the plausible thesis that no form of language could exist unless sometime brought into connection with the larger affairs of life. We allow, indeed insist, that any kind of utterance may, in splendid, unsubordinated isolation, be executed in disconnection from these other matters. But surely the isolated occurrence of utterance is the exception from and an attenuation of the richer case.

The evident variety of these 'connecting conditions' accounts for the open-ended and unsystematic appearance of our list of moods.

I once thought that these conditions can be exhaustively if vaguely classified under four headings, as having to do with: (a) the situation, competencies and knowledgeability of the subject; (b) the existence, situation, identity and competencies of addressees or respondents; (c) the existence of 'institutional' arrangements underlain by enabling rules (e.g. games, banking, elections, 'property', 'justice', courses of instruction); and (d) the acquisition, organization and transmission of knowledge. Language, when available, is a natural stand-by in the service of other non-conventional usages underlain by enabling rules and an obvious instrument for organizing and transmitting information and for coping with its absence. No surprise, then, that utterance should be answerable for its success to conditions of these several sorts. All of this is distressingly 'soft' and I have no proper proof, which makes me less sanguine than I once was; I shall none the less continue to use the classification as guide, but warily, in the hope that what follows will confirm the track.

Our analysis of the typical employment of sentence adverbs in act-adverbial usage initially appeals, not 'upward' to perlocutions, but 'downward' to the 'way' in which deeds may be done. Action of any kind may be done quickly or slowly, deliberately or impulsively, politely, deferentially or with regrets. The last three mentioned kinds of modification are 'conventional' in the same understanding as are language, ritual and commercial exchange. In doing any kind of deed politely or deferentially or with regrets, the subject must adapt means calculated to show politeness, deference or regret. Conventions are at hand to enable him to do that, and conditions are indicated by appointed expressions or constructions, for example, that there is a respondent who owns some kind of rank or distinction that the subject lacks.

Linguists will long since have become familiar with transformational interconnections between these two kinds of use – mood indication and act-adverbial modification. Speakers' conventional ways are frequently keyed to their perlocutionary ends. When these connections approach to a pattern, they become explicitly marked (for example) as formal expressions of regret, deference and the like. That shift is apt to be syntactically registered when an itinerant sentence adverb is fixed to a more regular residence in sentences as a mood indicator. Such transformations usually require only the most incidental adaptation in the indication of conditions.

The semantics in action I envisage arises from the idea that *meaning* includes indications of what the subject means to do, supplemented with act-adverbial indications of *how* the meant deed was done. The subject, to secure these 'indications', must adopt means calculated to indicate those various conditions that have figured so largely in the foregoing. Those 'means', of course, are the 'expressions' – words, chiefly, but other sounds too, and other inscriptions, flashes, gestures and also patterns of combination for all of these. We put *meaning* before the word. Other kinds of semantics familiar from the literature – Fregean and model-theoretic alike, whether expounded by logicians or linguists – are moored in their beginnings to words or other expressions, for which they hope to secure meaning by assignment of 'interpretations' to well-formed formulas. The two approaches, from the direction of word meaning to utterance meaning or the reverse, converge. But there are blockages along the road from word to utterance meaning, notably in the matter of explaining the sense of 'token reflexives'. Montague (1974) accepted the challenge under the title of 'pragmatics', which, in his 'other'[4] use of the term, was his name for my kind of enterprise. We will return to that presently. But first . . .

3 FREGEAN SEMANTICS: A SKETCH

Frege's (1892) idea, plausible on its face but also supported by argument, is that an expression will find its appointed object – its *Bedeutung* –, if it does, only by virtue of being pointed, namely of having *Sinn*. Now the expression may or may not actually have a *Bedeutung* but, either way, it must be pointed in the right direction or have *Sinn*. Expressions purged of ambiguity will have one and only one *Sinn* and should have unique *Bedeutung*. So every unequivocal meaningful expression determines a unique *Sinn* and every *Sinn* should determine a unique *Bedeutung*; it follows that every unequivocal, meaningful expression should determine a unique *Bedeutung*. Frege further thought that every meaningful concatenation of meaningful expressions, each having *Sinn*, will have its *Sinn* unequivocally determined by the *Sinn* of its constituents. A meaningful concatenation should also have unique *Bedeutung* and, if it does, that *Bedeutung* will be determined by the *Bedeutungen* of the constituting expressions. If any of the constituent expressions in fact lacks *Bedeutung*, the concatenation also does. Frege's great contribution to logic, achieved with only the most incidental reference to *Sinn*, is part of a theory of the determination of *Bedeutung* by *Bedeutungen*; that kind of 'determination' is also the province of what is sometimes called 'extensional semantics'. Frege left us with no worked-out account of the determination of *Sinn* by *Sinn* or of *Bedeutung* by *Sinn*. Still it is pretty clear what he had in mind.[5] Briefly: there is a one-way or 'functional' determination of *Sinn* by expressions and of *Bedeutung* by *Sinn*, and a one-way determination of the *Sinn* and *Bedeutung* of complex expressions by the *Sinn* and *Bedeutung* of their constituents.

It will now be understood that, for Frege, there cannot be a determination of the *Sinn* of an expression by the *Bedeutung* of that expression or by the *Bedeutungen* of its constituents. Indeed, it is evident, especially in the matter of identities, that expressions with different *Sinn* may have the same appointed *Bedeutungen*. Consequently, for Frege, there is no way by which a theory of intensions (= *Sinn*) can be reduced to a purely extensional semantics.

Frege's doctrine of the determination of *Bedeutung* by *Sinn* is limited to the 'propositional contents' of judgement and the elements of those *Gedanken*. It has no application to judgement itself or to any other indication of mood[6] or to the meanings of sentence adverbs which affect, not the content, but only the 'coloration' of judgement.

Another limitation is more forced and harder to swallow. We have noticed it already. The use of 'this', by virtue of its one regular meaning in English, may be used to find all manner of appointed objects. Frege's analysis would therefore yield false conclusions for 'this' and for other so-called 'token-reflexive' ('indexical', 'demonstrative', 'ostensive') words, had he not providentially dismissed them as being unfit for the exact exposition of thought.

4 MODEL THEORY FOR SEMANTICS

Model-theorizing begins (a) with a disambiguated language (or the presumption of one) for which (b) 'interpretations' or 'models' are found within a domain of identifiable objects, perhaps of mixed 'category', through (c) the assignment of objects to names and free variables and of sets of those objects to predicates. I believe that this method finds its ancestry in those arguments, featured in the writings of Hilbert, for establishing the mutual independence of axioms within groups dished up as 'implicit definitions' of mathematical subject matters. So, to take a crudely formulated example: since some of the axioms of projective geometry are satisfied by, or have as a model, clutches of seven 'points' and seven 'lines', other axioms, having to do with order, that are needed for the characterization of the Euclidean plane are independent of the first cited.

Tarski (1935), in his celebrated definition of *truth* for sentences of first-order formalized theories, implicitly invoked this notion of an interpretation or model. Roughly put: the universal quantification of an open sentence containing a single free variable is true just in case that open sentence is satisfied by all of its models. Montague (1974) and a number of other writers who have used model theory for semantic analysis took original inspiration from a wish to extend Tarski's explanation of truth to modal determinations of *necessity*, in its several varieties. Montague and others (notably including Kripke (1963)) believed that this could be accomplished (still speaking crudely) by allowing the interpretations or models to vary, not over the assignment of objects to free variables (now presumed fixed), but over the assignment of objects to names and sets of objects to predicates.

Here I would like to observe that Tarski's truth definition was conformable to a Fregean account of the determination of *Bedeutung* by *Bedeutungen*, although with truth values and predicate extensions in reversed pride of place. I believe that that is also true of the Montague–Kripke step-beyond, for it seems to me that their model-theorizing could have been taken as providing for the 'extensional' determination of certain sentences, pertaining to so-called second-order systems, that quantify over predicates.

Now, notoriously, conceptions of *necessity* are 'non-extensional' or 'opaque' in Quine's sense (Quine 1953). Montague and others (with mistaken references to Frege) reasonably supposed that determinations of *necessity* are in respect of 'intensions' or *Sinn.* Montague's proposal at this point, if I have understood him, was to treat the *Sinn* of an expression as a *function* from a domain to a set of interpretations, usually a set of subsets of the domain of objects needed for the model structure.

I doubt that that by itself will do the job. The Barwise–Cooper account of generalized quantifiers and determiners (Barwise and Cooper 1981), which is also model-theoretic in character, implicitly explains such 'determiners' as 'all', 'some' and 'the' as names for functions from the extensions of attached predicates to sets of subsets of a presumed domain. Thus the 'some' in 'some man' takes the set of *anthropoi* into the set of all sets that contain an *anthropon.* 'Some', by this, looks to be one of Frege's second-order predicates (*Fuktionnamen*), and the analysis is again conformable to his account of the determination of *Bedeutung* by *Bedeutungen.* So, for example, the sentence 'Some man eats cheese' is true just in case the set of cheese eaters includes a set that members an *anthropon.*

The next and fateful step, retracing if not actually following a suggestion from Wittgenstein's *Tractatus* (Wittgenstein 1921: 4.4 ff.), is to take the domain of these sense-functions to be a range of *possibilities*, pure and simple. In the *Tractatus* set-up, any 'valuation' of a presumed totality of *Elementarsaetze* defines a 'truth possibility' or 'possible world'; the *Sinn* of the *Satz* is then pictured as a pattern of agreement and disagreement with the presumed totality of such possibilities. The *Satz* is necessary just in case it agrees with them all. Montague and Kripke[7] too (if I have understood them) adopted and generalized this explanation of *Satz-Sinn.* The move is breathtaking and gymnastic, but not painless.

A first objection, suggested by one Frege aimed at Hilbertian independence proofs, runs as follows: a sentence properly disambiguated is either true or false and certainly not both. So it cannot be literally 'true' in one possibility and 'false' in another. *Truth in a model* is a notion that either has nothing to do with truth at all or has to be explained in terms of truth literally taken. Frege eventually had to make his peace with those plainly convincing arguments for independence. I do not know what the terms of his capitulation were, but I can imagine he would have eventually been content to concede the variable satisfaction of axiom schemata. But now please observe that there is no service in that way for model-theoretic *semantics.* The various mathematical structures that pass muster as models for an axiom *schema* are all of them equally actual (perhaps because equally noumenal). The sequence of primes is no less 'real' than the sequence of natural numbers. One established case is no more a mere possibility than is any other in the unified world of meta-mathematics.

The main objection of course is that the possibilities needed for model-theoretic semantics are themselves already fully 'intensional', creatures of conception, as even Leibniz once allowed. You are not going to bruise your shins on unactualized possibilities; now, walking more carefully, you conceive that things might have been otherwise with these painful palpabilities.[8] The idea that, by taking possibilities themselves in extension as a domain, we can secure a reduction of *Sinn* through the functional assignment to those possibilities of 'extensional' interpretations for the expressions of a disambiguated language – which is, I think, what model-theoretic semanticists are finally up to – is, well, fraudulent. You are not going to achieve a satisfying explanation of intensions through appealing to items that are already fully intensional. More generally said, and with the alternative in the offing, I think that Leibniz and Frege were right: you cannot take Sense from the one and only world we know by an assignment of expressions to things. That is so precisely because Sense is a provision of indications for getting to the world.

A lesser objection to model-theoretic semantics in both its intensional and extensional phases is that it is insufficiently discriminating. Not everything we say that is true or false is 'about objects', for example, remarks about the weather or the light outside, conveyed maybe by what some linguists have come to call the 'weather "it"' often are not. My own 'system', starting from smudgier stuff, eventually makes provision for referring to identifiable objects in a domain.

Another indiscrimination arises from the model-theoretical semanticist's distinctive brand of 'functional analysis'. Barwise and Cooper concede that clear disparities among 'all', 'every' and 'each' 'cannot be explained purely in terms of the semantics of quantifiers' (1981: 197). I claim that my own 'test-theoretic' semantics handles such matters quite nicely; so, without further ado . . .

5 ROAD-PLAN FOR A 'TEST-THEORETIC' SEMANTICS OF UTTERANCE

I find direction for my theory of intensions and formalized semantics by sighting on a single 'mood' or 'illocutionary force'. Here once again my operations parallel Frege's. His benchmark was *Urteil* ('judgement'); mine, which I call 'assertion', lies close by to his. *Assertion* (in contrast with such moods as *voting, promising, cursing, opining, conjecturing,* and *predicting,* which are 'naturally' realized by use of their own names), while it is meant to cover a broad spread of familiar cases, is factitious and stands in need of explanation. *Assertion* (for me), in other words, is one kind of *saying and meaning what one thinks one knows.* One may opine, or predict or conjecture such and such and then go on to say 'but it may not be so'. But one cannot assert, for example, that she went home and at the same time allow that maybe she didn't. Here are some working specimens, with contrasts in parentheses:

1 Aristotle was twice married (*but not*: Plato was a homosexual, *an 'opinion'*).
2 Crete is an island in the Red Sea (*but not*: Maybe Atlantis was an island off the coast of Spain, *a supposition or 'declaration of possibility'*).
3 There will be a total eclipse of the sun visible from Central Europe on 11 August 1999 (*but not*: There will be a major earthquake in the Bay Area before 1985, *a onetime prediction*).
4 e = 1.6020×10^{-19} columbs (*but not*: Heat is matter in motion, *an hypothesis*).
5 All earthly mountains higher than 8,000 metres are in Asia (*but not*: All birds are warm-blooded, *a generalization*).
6 Pompadour was once the favourite of Louis XV and Barry was later on (*but not*: If Philip II had not reigned for so long, Spain would not have languished, *a conditional*).
7 28 is a perfect number (*but not*: There is no odd perfect number, *a conjecture*).

Assertion has batches of conditions for doing. Here are a few, suggested by our paraphrase of 'assertion' as 'saying and meaning what one thinks one knows to be so'. The 'what' in question is a putative fact identified in relation to a particular formulation. Call it 'F':

(i)   A believes F.
(ii)   A assumes liability for others believing F on the grounds that A told them so.
(iii) A undertakes a 'commitment to the truth' of what he says in that he undertakes to withdraw from asserting F or to correct his assertion in the face of proven falsity or strong contrary evidence, and must acknowledge as criticism that what he said was false, uncertain, unlikely, or did not follow from what was given.
(iv)   A could know facts of sort F (namely, facts classified under F-formulations) in that sense in which I, who do not have absolute pitch, could not, unassisted with instruments or testimony, know the pitch of a note.

More to our concern are those still unspecified 'conditions of success' that define the underlying 'meaning to do'. With an eye on those characteristic kinds of mood-defining conditions noticed in section 2 above, it is fairly evident that *assertion* is not generically limited either by the capabilities of speaker or by the existence and qualifications of respondents. *Knowledge* is the *locus definiens*. Here are three schemata for those conditions of success; they are all needed; each of them is independent of the others; each covers an indefinite diversity, and that consideration emboldens me to think that, as schemata, they may be enough.

First schema

Any assertion indicates as a condition of success that a formulation-specific kind of thing could be known at the time.

Second schema

Any assertion indicates as a condition of success that there exist authorities.

Third schema

Any assertion indicates as a condition of success that there (now) exist specific, sometime applicable procedures of verification and falsification.

The first two schemata are needed, no doubt of that. But it is only the third that feeds into semantics; so I will stick with it. The mentioned 'procedures' are, of course, kinds of action, but specialized to what I call 'tests'. There is lots here better left unsaid about *procedures* and *tests*. Some guiding examples: sniffing to smell, looking to find, watching to notice, probing to touch, pushing to detect displacement, counting to determine how many, titrating, checking a photograph to detect tracks in a bubble-chamber. Now an assertion is successful only if (a) both of the two indicated tests are applicable, where (b) at most one of them is successfully applicable. So it transpires that there are, among the conditions of success indicated in an assertion under the third schema, conditions of applicability or of 'doing' for each of a pair of tests, to which we add as a further condition of success that not both tests be successfully applicable. This overlap among conditions of success for assertion and conditions for the application of tests is a bridge that carries us between assertional utterance, with its various sememic features, and a theory of intensions or formalizable semantics.

'Formalizable', in what way? Every test, I believe, may be represented by (not 'equated with') a pair of sets of occasions – at first entry, a set of occasions on which the test can be applied and, at second entry, a set of occasions on which it can be successfully applied. An occasion is an occasion, namely, an enclosed region of space with its contents at a time. Occasions, note well, are all of them probeable and all of them are equally 'actual'. A test for the presence of an apple on a table will include various locations within which one can reach out and touch the table-top at a given time, and the occasions of successful applicability include that subset of those locations-at-a-time that include an apple. I now leap to a simplification. Let us represent a test, t, by a disjoint pair of sets of occasions, the first for successful applicability and the other for unsuccessful applicability:

$$\langle {}^+\omega_t, {}^-\omega_t \rangle, \text{ where } {}^+\omega_t \cap {}^-\omega_t = 0.$$

Further, a test is applicable just in case

$$^+\omega_t \cup {}^-\omega_t \neq 0.$$

There are of course two such 'representations' for any assertion,

$$\langle {}^+\omega_v, {}^-\omega_v \rangle \text{ and } \langle {}^+\omega_F, {}^-\omega_F \rangle,$$

where, as we have stipulated,

$$^+\omega_v \neq 0 \rightarrow {}^+\omega_F = 0.$$

Tests stand in various relationships, many of which are easily captured (namely 'represented') within this formalism. Commonly, one test is not applicable at all unless another is successfully applicable, for example, we cannot essay to test for the presence of an apple on a table unless we can successfully test for the presence of a table within the indicated environs. The one test 'presupposes' the other. The existence of the table (but surely not of an apple) is a condition of success indicated in the assertion that there is an apple on the table. (It turns out that there are several kinds of presupposition.) We can represent that relationship by saying that the apple verifying test is applicable, namely,

$$^+\omega_{va} \cup {}^-\omega_{va} \neq 0$$

only if the table verifying test is successfully applicable, namely,

$$^+\omega_{vt} \neq 0.$$

I wish I had space to develop what I have only just illustrated,[9] but I must press on to another theme.

The theme runs from the observation that tests may or may not be, not merely applicable *on* occasions, but also applicable *to* something or other, for example, a body, a numerical expression or perhaps even an occasion, namely, a temporally specified region of space with its contents or a 'perspective', as when sighting from a spot in a given direction. *Looking for daylight* just anywhere is not applied to a 'location' in the way in which aiming a photometer is. I will say that the latter but not the former test is *location-applicable.* Now I enter a first grand hypothesis: assertionally-indicated conditions for the applicability of tests are exclusively for tests that are location-applicable. Take a case: you say it is warm out, but that need not be a location-testable assertion true-or-false, for out there it is warm and cold in every degree you can imagine; by way of contrast, saying that it is above 50° down at the weather station is location-testable for both truth and falsity, and I find no reason to question its qualifications for assertionhood.

Location-applicable tests are of *kinds,* each such kind being uniformly applicable to ordered sets of 'comparable' locations. *Subtraction,* for example, is a kind of test that is uniformly applicable to pairs of numerical expressions. I call *subtraction* and every other such *kind* of test a 'proto-criterion'. It is evident that a proto-criterion can be 'represented by' (not 'equated with') a 'triple' of a set of comparable locations, a set of appropriate occasions and a function from ordered n-tuples of the comparable locations to test-representing disjoint pairs of sets of the appropriate occasions. In symbols:

$$PC_1 = \langle \lambda_1, \omega_1, {}^n f_1 \rangle,$$

where

$${}^n f_1(l_1, \ldots l_n) = \langle {}^+\omega, {}^-\omega \rangle, l_1, \ldots l_n \in \lambda_1 \text{ and } {}^+\omega, {}^-\omega \subset \omega_1.$$

Proto-criteria stand in various relationships, for example, $\lambda_2 \subseteq \lambda_1$ (I then say that PC_2 is 'locally dependent on' PC_1) or, again, that $\omega_2 \subseteq \omega_1$ (I then say that PC_2 is 'kinematically uniform with' PC_1) or, again, tests pertaining to a PC_1 may in various ways 'presuppose' tests pertaining to a PC_2.

Behold now my second big 'hypothesis': I believe and can argue that all of the tests whose applicability may be assertionally indicated are of a restricted variety of proto-criterial 'super-kinds', and that the proto-criteria falling thereunder stand in regular relationships of dependence, owing just to their being of one super-kind or another. The nub of this hypothesis is in the claim that conditions on the applicability and successful applicability of any assertionally indicatable test are formulable in terms of a basic inventory of proto-criterial super-kinds. The most fundamental such kind is of tests for existence; I call them 'E's. Examples are reaching into a place to touch something there, displacing an occluder to see the presence of light, reducing a numerical expression to a numeral. All other assertionally indicatable tests are, as I believe, locally dependent upon E's and most of the others also presuppose (successful) E-testing. Two proto-criterial super-kinds of test appear at the next level up, both presupposing E's: 'Feature placing' tests (e.g. for it's being sticky here) are one kind and 'individuations' or Υ's (e.g. displacing a touched something) are the other. Starting at the next level and running across all higher ones are batches of tests for 'predicables' – simple and complex, relational of all orders, sortal of many kinds, homeomeric ('mass terms'), aggregative, and so on. I call all of these Π's. They collectively presuppose (successful) individuation, but then, according to their classifications, have distinguishing test-theoretically exponible features. The other super-kinds of tests I think we need are, in order of increasing dependence, *separations* or tests for immediate distinctness (Δ's), *trackings* or identifications (I's) and, finally A-tests for delimiting regions, for example, sweepings across a table-top or recursions. The test-kinds just named may be submitted to the formalism prefigured earlier, and then actually put into formulas. So, for example, there should be a formula available to designate a test for an existing, individual, distinguishable patch of denim's being blue. (The paired falsification test would be 'disjunction' of other colour tests under the same 'presuppositions'.)

Given a full panoply of E, Υ, Δ, I, A and Π's in any number, we can proceed to definitions of other tests of indefinitely various sorts (e.g. the above alluded to disjunctions), always in terms of the occasions of successful and unsuccessful applicability of their instances. I will not burden this paper with details, which I have found to be sometimes technically challenging.

Now, coming back across the bridge, from testing to utterance: it will always be part of the meaning of an assertion to indicate that a pair of tests are both applicable, to include indications of how the terminal applications go and what the conditions of applicability are. All of this – as much as we need of it, anyway – is, by hypothesis, resolvable into tests of the basic kinds I have named. This representation is abstracted from and stands utterly apart from the words or other expressions by which assertions are conveyed. Still, the test indications correspond to a Fregean *Satz-Sinn*, and our test-theoretic representation yields a theory of the functional determination of *Sinn* by *Sinn* or (if you wish) a theory of intensions. The basic sememic elements in such an account, including some predicables, are represented by basic proto-criteria; the simplest references are represented as individuations. I notice in passing that the pattern of proto-criterial super-kinds determines the *form* of the assertion – a notion that philosophers have patronized and linguists shunned.

Whenever an indicated test is successfully applicable, it determines what corresponds to a Fregean *Bedeutung*. For example, an indication of the applicability of an individuation procedure to a location, presupposing the successful applicability of an existence test to that same location, makes reference to an individual object in that location at question; if the individuation procedure is successfully applicable, then there is an object there, which is the Fregean *Bedeutung* of the expression that conveyed the indication. Again, if either of the indicated procedures is successfully applicable, then the assertion is true or false (as the case may be) and its thus being true or false is the *Bedeutung* of the whole assertion. So here we have, in anticipation, an account of the determination of *Bedeutung* by *Sinn*.

Evidently, the successful applicability of almost any test will be conditioned by the successful applicability of other tests. Here then, in anticipation, are seeds for an account of the determination of *Bedeutung* by *Bedeutungen*, a.k.a. *extensional semantics*.

How, you may wonder, does this differ from model theory? Well (most obviously), meaning, by our proposals, is to be secured, not by a prior selection of referable objects, but rather by indications of procedures for getting to such objects. Some of those underlying procedures do not yet even presuppose the existence of referable objects, for example, existence and individuation procedures do not; indeed, those sorts of tests are implicated in the representation of references to individual objects. Here is one of the places where test theory is more discriminating than model theory. Further discrimination emerges with the use of defined tests. Hear the difference in the descriptions of the tests indicated for the verification of 'All those men are officers' and 'Any of those men are officers': *Exhaustively test for being officers objects selected from the class of men in a delimited region over there* and *Exhaustively test for being both men and officers objects selected from a delimited region over there.*[10]

The road-plan I have charted took direction from our resolution to concentrate on *assertion. Ergo,* we cannot, along this route, secure any direct representation of *assertion* itself, or of any other mood-indication, as a feature of meaning. Act-adverbial modification – Frege's 'coloration' – is similarly inaccessible. So our account of meaning operates within the same limits as would have Frege's. The coverage is still broad. Everything having to do with *reference, predication, attribution, identification, determination, quantification* and *form-determination* can be handled. But now, surely, since those various uses do not change their character when realized in illocutionary settings other than *assertion,* their test-theoretic representations carry over. Here then, in our account, is exposed the authentic face of 'propositions'.

You may now well wonder how this theory of tests is itself to be proven out. Well, in its semantic applications, only by its capacity to account for the actual facts of human representation. Here, as I have claimed, it is at once more discriminating and more accurate than its competitors. But, I must add that, since this account plainly trafficks in the ancient commerce of *existence, individuality, distinctness, identity, generality* and *inherence,* the ultimate validation of my enquiry must finally come from the evidences of a true First Philosophy.

6 CONVERGENCE?

Montague was quick to allow that the orthodox methods of model theory were inadequate to explain the meaning of token reflexives. So he broadened his semantics to comprise occasions of utterance within the basic domain of objects, those occasions replete with speakers, words and the lot; he called that generalization 'pragmatics', in that 'other sense' alluded to in note 4. I myself would be glad to call it 'semantics', and I think linguists should too, for it recalls Bloomfield's (1933) characterization of that study as being of the linguistically distinctive features of situations – an undertaking, he plausibly opined, much too sweeping for mortal investigators. You may sense that Montague's 'pragmatics' and perhaps also what I gather is its successor in the 'situation semantics' of Barwise and Perry (1983) are really very little different from the goods I have been purveying above. There are indeed resemblances, but also differences; and these other doctrines, what I know of them, seem to me to come up short. The two main differences are connected. Montague and his successors still conceive 'interpretation' as a matter of assigning pieces of worlds, real or imagined, to the words we use, whereas, for me, language is always to be thought of as an instrumentality for getting to the world. (My colleague Arthur Melnick goes so far as to think of language as a kind of replacement for those tests, rather in the way that 'ouch's are replacements for screams.) The 'getting to the world' is by way of those indicated tests. It is essential to my scheme that there be this other layer of competency interposed between language and what it is 'about'. So my 'occasions' are not occasions of speech, but rather occasions for applying those tests that are indicated in assertional utterance. This has for one advantage that it enables us to assert statements that lie well outside the time-frame of human existence (for example, about dinosaurs in the cetaceous), for tests may be indicated on an occasion as applicable on other, possibly remote occasions. It matters more in my book that making sense should not be held hostage to accomplished reference of any kind, to objects, occasions or even to words, and this happy circumstance, besides accommodating scepticism and incidentally evading Bloomfield's ban on the study of meaning, obviates bothers over 'opacity' and 'intentional objects'. That is because my 'intensions', taken simply, are 'aspects' of human behaviour and dealt with accordingly, with no presumption that that behaviour ever actually succeeds, and therefore with no need to bring in those objects (*Bedeutungen*) which those intensions would lead us to, if they did succeed.[11]

APPENDIX: FREGE'S PRINCIPLES

1 Every meaningful expression (hereafter, simply 'expression') has a *Sinn* and should have only one *Sinn*. We may therefore stipulate the existence of a function, S (in the usual not in Frege's sense of 'function'), from expressions to *Sinn*.

2 The *Sinn* of a complex expression is determined by the *Sinn* of its constituent expressions. There must be rules of semantical concatenation, and we may accordingly stipulate the existence of a 'concatenation function', K_I, according to which $S(E_1 \hat{\ } E_2) = K_I[S(E_1), S(E_2)]$.

3 Anything may be a *Bedeutungen* – *Gegenstaende* and functions alike, including *Sinn*. On the other hand, lots of things are not *Sinn*: the sun is not, nor is The True.

4 Expressions may or may not have *Bedeutung*. Frege thought that neither 'Odysseus', nor 'die am wenigsten konvergente Reihe' did; and 'der von der Erde am weitesten entfernte Himmelskorper' may not.

5 Expressions which do have a *Bedeutung* should have a unique *Bedeutung*.

6 The rules of an adequate *Begriffsschrift* assure us that every expression pertaining to that notation has a unique *Bedeutung*. The availability of such a *Begriffsschrift* permits us to stipulate the existence of a *Bedeutung* function, *B*, from expressions to things.

7 The *Bedeutung* of a complex expression is uniquely determined by the *Bedeutungen* of the constituent expressions. So here we have another 'concatenation function', K_2, such that $B(E_1 \hat{\ } E_2) = K_2[B(E_1), B(E_2)]$. (E.g. B('It is not the case'$\hat{\ }$'Frege was German') $= K_2[B$('It is not the case'), B('Frege was German')$] = K_2(Neg(\ ),$ The True) = The False.)

8 If an expression, E, lacks a *Bedeutung*, then so too does any complex expression in which E occurs as a constituent. If $B(E_j)$ is undefined, then so too are $B(E_i \hat{\ } E_j)$ and $B(E_j \hat{\ } E_k)$, for all expressions E_i and E_k.

9 Every *Sinn* determines at most a single *Bedeutung*, for any expression that has that *Sinn*. There is therefore a (partial) function, *S*, from *Sinn* to whatever. In an adequate *Begriffsschrift* we try to set things up so that there is a value for every expressible *Sinn*: while *S*('die am wenigsten konvergente Reihe') is undefined in ordinary mathematical German, we should in the *Begriffsschrift* be able to express a corresponding but different *Sinn* for which *S* is defined. (NB, the *Begriffsschrift* must sometimes put new *Sinn* in place of old, which it then leaves untended. The *Begriffsschrift* does not always provide exact translations from the German.)

10 Since different *Sinn* may determine the same *Bedeutung*, there is no inverse function S^{-1} back from *Bedeutungen* to *Sinn*. Some theorists (notably, Wittgenstein in his *Tractatus*) have supposed that some *Sinn* – those of 'basic names' – are determined by their *Bedeutungen*; Frege, so far as I know, never did.

11 Since both the *Sinn* and the *Bedeutung* assigned to an expression might have been differently constituted, neither K_1 nor K_2 have inverses.

NOTES

1 In a work entitled *Statement and Referent*. The first volume has now been published (Shwayder 1992) and I will use it as a source.
2 Throwing darts in the kitchen, I miss the target and hit the cat. One of the things I may be said to have done in this unfortunate incident was to throw for the target (which is also what I meant to do) and another was to crease the poor cat (which I did not mean to do at all).
3 See Shwayder 1992.
4 Other than the earlier mentioned sense in which 'pragmatics' names a kind of

'Gricean' study of perlocutions. Actions merely or purely 'locutionary' are fully pragmatic for Montague and his followers. Montague traced his usage to Morris (1938) and Bar-Hillel (1954).

5   See 'Appendix' for a fuller presentation.

6   Frege's assertion sign was, in the body of his notation, conspicuous for lacking both *Sinn* and *Bedeutung*.

7   In Kripke 1963. The relation whose stipulated features define different modal options are between a designated 'real world', G, and comparable possibilities.

8   David Lewis (1986) contention that every possibility is equally actual relative to itself is an evasion. I will leave it at that.

9   The job is done in 'Appendix D' of Shwayder 1992.

10   'Each S is P' assertions indicate verification by tests of exhaustively coordinately identifying and testing for P individuals selected from a delimited class of S's; corresponding 'Every's, indicate verification by the exhaustive P-testing of individuals selected from a delimited class of identified S's.

11   I am grateful for the chance to present this paper to a meeting of the Linguistics Seminar of the University of Illinois at Urbana.

4 A complete formulation of a simple logic of elementary illocutionary acts

Daniel Vanderveken

In the second half of this century, logicians like Church (1951), Lewis (1918), Carnap (1956), Prior (1967), Cresswell (1975) and Montague (1974) have used the resources of logical formalisms such as proof and model theory in order to formulate philosophical logics like the logic of sense and denotation, modal logic and the logic of time which are important for the purposes of universal grammar. Such logicians have contributed both to the philosophy of language and to the foundations of the syntax and semantics of English and other natural languages. Thus logical formalisms which were originally conceived by Frege, Russell and Tarski for the sole study of formal languages, were successfully used and improved to generate and interpret important fragments of ordinary language.

Like Montague, I think that there is no important theoretical difference between formal and natural languages. However, unlike Montague and Davidson (1984), I do not believe that the formalization of a recursive theory of truth is the single most important objective of semantics. Like Frege (1923), Searle (1969) and Austin (1962), I think that the primary units of meaning in the use and comprehension of language are complete illocutionary acts such as statements, promises and requests, and not isolated propositions (or truth conditions). From a philosophical point of view, such speech acts are intentional actions which are directed at states of affairs in the world. In virtue of their logical form, these speech acts consist of an illocutionary force with a propositional content. They have by nature conditions of success as well as conditions of satisfaction. Moreover, as Searle and I (Searle and Vanderveken 1985) have shown, these two types of succcess and satisfaction conditions are not reducible to the truth conditions of their propositional contents. On this view, the primary objectives of universal grammar are to formalize a theory of success and of satisfaction for illocutionary acts and not only to further develop the theory of truth for propositions.

Until now, formal semantics has been mainly confined to the truth-conditional aspects of meaning and has tended to construe the linguistic competence of speakers as their ability to understand the propositional contents of utterances. Thus formal semantics has been limited to the analysis of expressions like proper names, predicates, connectives and quantifiers whose meaning contributes to the determination of truth conditions. For that reason, most applications of formal semantics to actual natural languages have been restricted to the sole interpretation of declarative sentences expressing assertions. However, logical theories of success and satisfaction are necessary to analyse also the meaning of illocutionary-force markers and performative verbs. They are indispensable to interpret all syntactic types of sentences (imperative, optative, conditional, exclamatory, subjunctive as well as declarative) expressing speech acts with any possible illocutionary force. As I have shown (Vanderveken 1990, 1990–1), the semantic theory of truth advocated by Montague and Davidson for ordinary language is just the special sub-theory for assertive speech acts of the more general theory of satisfaction for speech acts with an arbitrary illocutionary force. On my account, linguistic competence is inseparable from performance: it is essentially the speaker's ability to perform and understand the illocutionary acts which are the meanings of utterances. Moreover, illocutionary logic is needed to formalize the practical and theoretical valid inferences that human beings are able to make in virtue of linguistic competence.

The main purpose of this work is to formulate a complete philosophical logic of elementary acts which is as simple as possible. First, only the basic notions of speech act theory are expressible in the object language of that logic. For example, the propositional contents of the speech acts that are expressible are elementary propositions whose attribute is extensional and truth functions of such propositions. Quantification is limited so as to afford completeness. Moreover, I will analyse here the logical forms of elementary illocutionary acts without worrying about the context dependency of sense and force in ordinary language. Thus all terms of the formal language expressing a force, a proposition or a speech act express the same force, proposition or speech act in all possible contexts of utterance considered in a semantic interpretation. This simplification allows for a simpler formalization of speech act theory that exhibits more clearly and distinctly the fundamental definitions and laws. Moreover such a simple illocutionary logic can be integrated in a general formal semantics of success, satisfaction and truth for ordinary language where sense and force are context dependent. But for that purpose, one must develop a natural generalization of Montague grammar with a richer formal language and logic.

In the first section, I will explain rapidly the principles underlying the formalization. In the second and third sections, I will present the formal object language and the rules of abbreviation of my simple illocutionary logic, IL. The fourth section will define the structure of a standard interpretation for that logic. Finally the fifth section will present a sound axiomatic system, and the last section will enumerate some fundamental valid laws.

PHILOSOPHICAL PRINCIPLES

Natural languages can be learned and spoken by human beings who are intelligent but whose cognitive abilities are restricted. Thus, we can only make a finite number of acts of reference and of predication in an utterance. Consequently, the number of illocutionary acts that we can perform in a context of use of a language is limited. Moreover human speakers are neither omniscient nor perfectly rational in their use and comprehension of language. Although they must be able to distinguish truth from falsehood, competent speakers often understand the propositional contents without knowing *eo ipso* their actual truth value. We can even be inconsistent and assert propositions which are necessarily false. However, as philosophers and cognitive psychologists have pointed out (Cherniak 1986), we are always *minimally consistent* in a sense that still remains to be defined logically. In particular, we know a priori in virtue of competence that certain propositions are necessarily true.

Finally, human speakers are also able to distinguish success from failure as well as satisfaction from non-satisfaction in the use of language. Moreover they are able to make certain practical and theoretical valid inferences in virtue of competence in their attempted performance and understanding of speech acts. Thus they can derive from the hypothesis that some illocutionary acts are successful and satisfied the conclusion that other illocutionary acts are also successful or satisfied. Many such derivations are valid, in the sense that it is not possible for the premises to be successful and satisfied unless the conclusion is also successful or satisfied. In particular, whenever a speaker attempts to perform an illocutionary act, he knows which other illocutionary acts he would also perform in the context of his utterance if his attempt were successful. And a competent hearer also understands that. For example, a speaker who supplicates food and protection knows that he is *eo ipso* requesting food. And the hearer understands that he cannot satisfy the supplication without granting that simpler request. On this view, the *strong illocutionary commitments* of speakers are cognitively realized in their minds. Illocutionary logic must make them decidable in its formalization.

However, it is clear that the inferential abilities of competent speakers are limited. Often we fail to make logically valid inferences in our use of language. In particular, the relation of strict implication that exists between two propositions whenever one has more truth conditions than the other is not cognitively realized in virtue of competence. Thus a speaker can assert the proposition that Paris is a nice city without *eo ipso* asserting the proposition that $2 + 2 = 4$. Fortunately, from the epistemic point of view, each proposition *cognitively implies* some others, in the sense that it is not possible to express that proposition without having in mind the others and without knowing a priori that it cannot be true unless the others are also true. For example, the proposition that Paris is a nice city cognitively implies the proposition that Paris is a city. Because cognitive implication has a psychological reality, it generates systematically illocutionary commitment. Thus whenever a proposition cognitively implies another proposition, it is not possible to assert the first proposition without also asserting the second.

On the basis of these considerations, my formal approach to the semantics of natural language is new under two aspects. First, I impose on formal semantics the development of an *integrated theory of success, satisfaction and truth*. Second, I also impose on the formalization *additional cognitive criteria of adequacy relating to the logical aspects of the psychological reality of linguistic competence*. Like Davidson and Searle, I think that the formalization of semantics must be very constructive and explain the creative and effective mental abilities of competent speakers as well as their intrinsic constitutive cognitive limitations. Until now, most logicians have neglected in their formalisms the cognitive aspects of meaning and understanding. Consequently, some reformulations have to be done in the foundations of logic.

Analysis of propositions

First, speech act theory requires a new *logic of propositions* which is compatible with their expressibility in language use. As Searle pointed out, any proposition that a human being can apprehend is in principle *expressible* in the performance of an illocutionary act. On this account, any adequate analysis of the logical form of propositions in illocutionary logic must satisfy the following *criterion of propositional identity*: when two propositions p and q are identical, it is not possible to perform an illocutionary act of the form F(p) in a context of utterance without also performing in that context the illocutionary act F(q). Thus identical propositions must be intersubstitutible *salva felicitate* in the performance of speech acts. Now, it is clear that propositions with the same truth conditions are *not* intersubstitutible *salva felicitate*. For many assertions with the same truth conditions do not have the same conditions of success. For example, one can assert the proposition that Paris is a city without *eo ipso* asserting the strictly equivalent proposition that Paris is a city and $2 \leq 4$. Consequently, unlike modal and intensional logics, illocutionary logic cannot identify propositions with their truth conditions. In particular, it must distinguish strictly equivalent propositions whose expression requires different acts of reference or of predication.

In *Meaning and Speech Acts* (1990–1), I have formulated a new analysis of the logical form of propositions that takes into account their double nature of senses of sentences and of contents of thought. In that logical analysis, any proposition that is the sense of a sentence in a context of use of a semantic interpretation is also the content of a possible illocutionary act. More recently in (1993), I have developed along these lines a complete minimal natural logic of propositions.

Unlike modal and intensional logics, my new logic describes formally the *structure of constituents* of propositions. It identifies the *finite set of atomic propositions* out of which each proposition is composed. It also analyses *how the senses that are the constituents* of a proposition *are related by predication* in its atomic propositions. On this account, each proposition is a more structured entity than the simple function which associates with each possible context the truth value that it has in the world of that context. Indeed it has a finite number of atomic propositions in addition to truth conditions.

From a logical point of view, an *atomic proposition* is a pair whose first element is the *finite set of senses* that are its propositional constituents. That set of senses contains the *attribute* (the property or relation) that is predicated as well as the *concepts* that serve to refer to objects in the expression of that proposition. As we know, the attribute of an atomic proposition is always predicated *in a certain order* of the objects that fall under its concepts and that predication determines truth conditions. In my logic, the truth conditions of an atomic proposition are formally represented by its second element which is the *set of possible contexts where it is true* given the predication that is made with its constituents. On this view, in virtue of its logical form, the proposition that the king of France does not admire the pope is composed out of a single atomic proposition whose three propositional constituents are the relation of admiration and the two concepts of being the king of France and of being the pope. Thus its first element is the set of these three senses. Moreover, given the order of predication, its second element is the set of all possible contexts where the individual who is the king of France admires the individual who is the pope.

Once all the atomic propositions have been identified, it remains to understand how the truth conditions of the complete proposition are determined from the truth conditions of its atomic propositions. For example, in order to understand entirely the proposition that the king of France does not like the pope, one must understand that it is true if, and only if, its single atomic proposition is false. In modal and intensional logics, the truth conditions of propositions are formally analysed, following Carnap, as functions from possible worlds or contexts into truth values. Even Parry's (1933) logic of analytic implication and Cresswell's (1975) hyperintensional logic, which also aim to analyse the structure of constituents of propositions, have kept the same simple functional explication of truth conditions. On my view, that formal explication is not adequate. Indeed one cannot identify all strictly equivalent propositions which are composed out of the same atomic propositions. For many do not have the same cognitive value and are therefore not intersubstitutible *salva felicitate.* Thus one can assert the proposition that arithmetic is complete without asserting the contradiction that arithmetic is complete and incomplete, even if these two propositions are both impossible and composed out of one and the same atomic proposition predicating completeness of arithmetic. Thus, there is a logical difference in our understanding of the truth conditions of such propositions.

From a cognitive point of view, how do we understand the truth conditions of a proposition from the truth possibilities of its atomic propositions? Like Wittgenstein in the *Tractatus* (1921), I believe that the truth value of a proposition in a world is always a function of the truth values of its atomic propositions in the same world. Thus in order to apprehend completely a proposition, we must apprehend all its atomic propositions and also understand what are the truth possibilities of these atomic propositions that make it true. For example, we understand the elementary proposition that arithmetic is complete in understanding that it is true if, and only if, its unique atomic proposition is true. And that understanding does not contain the knowledge that it is necessarily false. On the contrary, we understand the proposition that arithmetic is complete and incomplete in understanding that it is false no matter what is the truth value of its atomic proposition.

Now, if the truth value of a proposition is indeed a function of the truth values of its atomic propositions, then there is a unique set of truth-value assignments to atomic propositions under which that proposition is true. For example, the proposition that the king of France is rich *and* powerful is true under all truth-value assignments that associate the True to its two atomic propositions. And the proposition that the king of France is rich *or* powerful is true under all truth-value assignments that associate the True to at least one of two atomic propositions. On this account:

> A proposition can be identified logically with the pair containing both the finite set of its atomic propositions and the set of all truth-value assignments to atomic propositions that make it true.

Formally, the set of truth-value assignments to atomic propositions that make a proposition true represents set-theoretically the truth function by the application of which we determine its truth conditions. Incidentally, my truth-functional view of the determination of truth condition is *not extensionalist*. It is compatible with the existence of modal operations on propositions. For such operations create new truth conditions in introducing additional atomic propositions.

Given my new analysis of the logical form of propositions, there is a finer relation of implication that I have called *strong implication*. By definition, a proposition *strongly implies* another one if, and only if, all atomic propositions of the second are atomic propositions of the first and all truth-value assignments to atomic propositions that make the first proposition true also make the second true. As I will argue, strong implication is cognitively realized in virtue of competence. Moreover, given the simple nature of the propositions which are expressible here, strong implication is the only relation of cognitive implication that we need in order to explain illocutionary commitments.

A new logic of illocutionary acts

As Searle and I pointed out (Searle and Vanderveken 1985), a logical theory of success and satisfaction for illocutionary acts can be developed on the basis of a few basic principles that I will now briefly repeat:
First,

> Each illocutionary force can be divided into six types of components which are: an illocutionary point; a mode of achievement of that point; propositional content; preparatory and sincerity conditions; and a degree of strength.

Two forces with the same components are identical because they serve the same linguistic purposes in the use of language.

In the performance of an elementary speech act, the speaker always relates the propositional content to the world so as to determine a direction of fit between words and things. The *illocutionary point* of a force is its principal component: it determines the *direction of fit* of utterances with that force. The four possible directions of fit are:

The words-to-world direction of fit
When the illocutionary act is satisfied, its propositional content fits a state of affairs existing in general independently in the world. All speech acts with the *assertive point*, for example, statements, predictions, testimonies and notifications, have the words-to-world direction of fit. Their point is indeed to represent how things are in the world.

The world-to-words direction of fit
When the illocutionary act is satisfied, the world is transformed to fit its propositional content. All speech acts with the *commissive* and the *directive points*, for example, promises, vows, requests and orders, have the world-to-words direction of fit. Their point is to get the world to be transformed by the future action of the speaker (*commissives*) or of the hearer (*directives*) in order to fit the propositional content.

The double direction of fit
When the illocutionary act is satisfied, the world is transformed by an action of the speaker to fit the propositional content by the fact that the speaker represents it as being so transformed. All speech acts with the *declarative point*, for example, declarations, appointments, definitions and condemnations, have the double direction of fit. Their point is to get the world to fit the propositional content just by saying that the propositional content fits the world.

The empty direction of fit
Sometimes, there is no question of success or failure of fit between

words and things. In that case, the illocutionary act has only the *expressive point*. Its point is simply to express a mental state of the speaker about the state of affairs represented by the propositional content. Examples of expressives are thanks, apologies and laments.

The assertive, commissive, directive, declarative and expressive illocutionary points are the fundamental primitive notions of illocutionary logic. As different points have different conditions of achievement, each point π can be identified with a certain subset of the Cartesian product $I \times U_p$ of the set of I of all possible contexts of utterance and the set U_p of all propositions. By definition, $\langle i, p \rangle \in \pi$ iff the speaker achieves in context i the point π on proposition p.

The *mode of achievement* of a force determines how its illocutionary point must be achieved on the propositional content in the case of a successful performance of an act with that force. For example, the mode of achievement of a command is peremptory: it consists in invoking a position of authority over the hearer. Formally, the mode of achievement μ of an illocutionary point is a function that restricts the conditions of achievement of that point.

The *propositional content conditions* of a force determine the conditions that any proposition must satisfy in each possible context in order to be a possible content of an act with that force in that context. For example, the propositional content of a prediction must be future with respect to the moment of utterance. Formally, a propositional content condition θ is a function from the set I of all contexts into the power set of propositions $\mathscr{P}(U_p)$. Thus $p \in \theta(i)$ if, and only if, p satisfies the propositional content condition θ in context i.

The *preparatory conditions* of a force determine which propositions a speaker would presuppose if he were performing an act with that force in a possible context of utterance. For example, a preparatory condition of a promise is that the future action represented by its content is good for the hearer. Formally, a preparatory condition Σ is a function from $I \times U_p$ which associates with a context i and a proposition p the set of all propositions Q that would be presupposed in the case of a performance of an act of the form $F(p)$ with that preparatory condition in that context.

The *sincerity conditions* of a force determine the modes of the mental states that the speaker would have if he were sincerely performing an act with that force. Formally, it is a set of psychological modes. For example, the sincerity condition of an assertion is the set containing the mode of belief since any speaker who makes an assertion expresses a belief in its propositional content.

Finally, the *degree of strength* of a force measures how strongly the speaker expresses mental states in the performance of a speech act with that force. Formally, it is an integer.

All sets of modes of achievement, propositional content, preparatory and sincerity conditions are Boolean algebras. Thus, for example, there is a *neutral propositional content condition* 1_θ common to all forces which is satisfied by all propositions in all contexts: $1_\theta(i) = U_p$. There is also an *absorbent propositional content condition* 0_θ which is not satisfied by any proposition in any context: $0_\theta(i) = \varnothing$. Only the empty force with impossible conditions of success has that absorbent condition. Moreover, each propositional content condition has a complement. And there is an intersection $\theta_1 \cap \theta_2$ of any two propositional content conditions θ_1 and θ_2: $\theta_1 \cap \theta_2 (i) = \theta_1 (i) \cap \theta_2 (i)$.

Second,

The set of illocutionary forces is recursive.

The *five primitive illocutionary forces* are the simplest possible forces: they have an illocutionary point, no special mode of achievement, a zero degree of strength and only the propositional content, preparatory and sincerity conditions which are determined by their point. These primitive forces are:

1 *the force of assertion* which is named by the performative verb 'assert' and realized in the syntactic type of *declarative sentences*;

2 *the primitive commissive illocutionary force* which is named by the performative verb 'commit';

3 *the primitive directive illocutionary force* which is realized in the type of *imperative sentences*;

4 *the force of declaration* which is expressed in *performative utterances*; and

5 *the primitive expressive illocutionary force* which is realized in the syntactic type of *exclamatory sentences*.

All other illocutionary forces are more *complex*. They can be obtained from the primitives by a finite number of simple operations which consist in restricting the mode of achievement by imposing a new mode, in increasing or decreasing the degree of strength or in adding new propositional, preparatory or sincerity conditions. Thus, the force of request is obtained from the primitive directive by imposing the special mode of achievement which consists in giving option of refusal to the hearer. The force of a yes/no question is obtained from request by adding the propositional content condition that what is asked is a future answer of the hearer. The directive force of a suggestion is obtained from the primitive directive by decreasing the degree of strength. The force of advice is obtained from that of suggestion by adding the preparatory condition that the future action represented by the propositional content is good for the hearer.

From a linguistic point of view, components of force are expressed by modifiers of markers such as the adverbs 'please' and 'alas' in 'Please, help me!' and 'Alas, he was killed'. Such modifiers, when they are combined with a force marker like the imperative or declarative sentential type compose a new marker expressing the complex force obtained by adding the expressed component. Thus, 'please' expresses the polite mode of achievement which consists of giving option of refusal, and 'alas' the sincerity condition that the speaker is sad. Consequently, imperative sentences with 'please' serve to make requests while declarative sentences with 'alas' serve to complain or lament. Some sentential types express complex forces. Thus *interrogative sentences* serve to ask questions which are complex directives. And *optative* and *subjunctive sentences* serve to express respectively the speaker's wish and will.

Third,

> The conditions of success of elementary illocutionary acts are entirely determined by the components of their force and their propositional content.

As is the case for human actions, attempts to perform illocutionary acts can *succeed* or *fail.* Roughly, *a speech act of the form F(p) is performed with success in a context of utterance* if, and only if, in that context, the speaker achieves the illocutionary point of force F on the proposition p with the mode of achievement of F, and p satisfies the propositional content conditions of F with respect to that context of utterance, if the speaker moreover also presupposes in the same context all propositions determined by the preparatory conditions of F for p and if he expresses with the degree of strength of F all mental states of the form m(p) whose psychological mode m belongs to the sincerity conditions of F. For example, a speaker makes a request in a context if, and only if, in that context: first, he makes a linguistic attempt to get the hearer to do an act $\mathscr{A}$ (directive point); second, in this attempt, he gives an option of refusal to the hearer (mode of achievement); third, the propositional content of the utterance is that the hearer will do an act $\mathscr{A}$ (propositional content condition determined by the directive point); fourth, the speaker also presupposes that the hearer is capable of doing that act $\mathscr{A}$ (determined preparatory condition); and finally, he expresses with a normal degree of strength a desire that the hearer do that act (determined sincerity condition).

Fourth,

> The conditions of satisfaction of elementary illocutionary acts are entirely determined by their propositional content and by their direction of fit.

The notion of condition of satisfaction is a generalization of the notion of truth condition that is needed to cover all forces. Just as an assertion is satisfied if it is *true,* a promise is satisfied if it is *kept,* a request if it is *granted,* a command if it is *obeyed,* a question if it is *answered,* and so on. The satisfaction of an illocutionary act F(p) is based on the truth of its propositional content p. When F(p) is satisfied, the proposition p *corresponds to* an existing state of affairs in the world. Moreover, the success of fit between words and things is achieved from the proper direction of fit of the force F. Thus an *illocutionary act with the words-to-world direction of fit is satisfied in a context of utterance* if, and only if, its proportional content is *true* in that context. In such a case, the success of fit between words and things is achieved by the fact that the expressed propositional content matches a state of affairs existing in general independently in the world. On the other hand, *when the illocutionary act has the world-to-words (or the double) direction of fit, it is satisfied in a context* if, and only if, its propositional content is *true* in that context *because* of its performance in that context. Unlike assertive utterances, commissive and directive utterances are self-referential utterances. An assertion is true if, and only if, its propositional content matches an existing state of affairs no matter how that state got into existence. But a promise is kept and a request is granted if, and only if, the speaker or hearer carries out in the world the represented action because of the promise or the request.

THE IDEAL OBJECT LANGUAGE $\mathscr{L}$ OF ILLOCUTIONARY LOGIC IL

The primitive types of $\mathscr{L}$

The primitive types of $\mathscr{L}$ are: ς, r_n (for each natural number n), as well as p, μ, θ, Σ, τ, Ψ and ι.

ς and r_n are the types of *individual concepts* and of *attributes* of degree n; p is the type of *propositions*; μ the type of *illocutionary points* and of *modes of achievement*: θ the type of *propositional content conditions*; Σ the type of *preparatory conditions*; τ the type of *modes of mental states*; Ψ the type of *sincerity conditions*; and ι is the type of *integers*.

The vocabulary of $\mathscr{L}$

The vocabulary of $\mathscr{L}$ contains:

infinitely many *variables*: x_α, x_α^1, x_α^2, ..., y_α, y_α^1, y_α^2, ..., y_α^n, ..., z_α, z_α^1, z_α^2, ..., of each type $\alpha = p$, τ and ι;
infinitely many *constants*: c_α^1, c_α^2, c_α^3, ... of all primitive types α; and
the *logical constants*: 0_ι, 1_ζ, 0_ζ, for each type $\zeta \in \{\mu, \theta, \Sigma, \psi\}$, and π_μ^1, π_μ^2, π_μ^3, π_μ^4, π_μ^5.

A variable of type α ranges over entities of that type while a constant of type α expresses an entity of that type. Thus, constants of type ς express concepts of individuals. Constants of type r_n express attributes (or relations) of degree n. In particular, 0_ι names the *integer zero*, 1_ζ and 0_ζ name respectively the *neutral* and the *absorbent component* of illocutionary force of type ζ. (For example, 1_μ names the neutral mode of achievement.) The logical constants π_μ^1, π_μ^2, π_μ^3, π_μ^4 and π_μ^5 name respectively the *assertive, commissive, directive, declarative* and *expressive illocutionary points.* Finally, if $1 \le k \le 5$, c_ψ^k names the sincerity condition determined by point π_μ^k.

The syncategorematic symbols of $\mathcal{L}$

The syncategorematic symbols of $\mathcal{L}$ are: $*, \forall, \gg, E, \neg, \wedge, ', t, =, \triangleright, \square, (,$ and $)$. They are used as follows.

The rules of formation of IL

The set of terms for atomic propositions

If R_n is a predicate of degree n and $c_1, \ldots, c_n$ are n individual constants of type ς of $\mathcal{L}$, then $R_n (c_1 \ldots c_n)$ is a *term for atomic propositions of $\mathcal{L}$* of the derived type a. $R_n (c_1 \ldots c_n)$ expresses the atomic proposition which is true in a context i if, and only if, the sequence of n individuals which fall in the world of i under the concepts expressed by $c_i, \ldots, c_n$ belongs to the extension in that world of the attribute expressed by R_n.

The set of propositional terms

1   If A_a is a term for an atomic proposition, then (A_a) is a *propositional term of $\mathcal{L}$* (or for short hereafter a p-term). (A_a) expresses the *elementary proposition* which is composed out of the atomic proposition expressed by A_a.
2   Every variable of type p of the vocabulary is also a propositional term.
3   Furthermore, if A_p and B_p are propositional terms, so are $\neg A_p$ and $(A_p \wedge B_p)$. $\neg A_p$ expresses the proposition which is the *negation* of the proposition expressed by A_p. $(A_p \wedge B_p)$ expresses the *conjunction* of the propositions expressed by A_p and B_p.

The set of terms for components of illocutionary force

1   Every constant or variable of a type μ, θ, ψ or ι is a *term for a component of illocutionary force* (or an IFC-term).
2   If A and B are IFC-terms of type ι, then $(A)'$ and $'(A)$ are new IFC-terms of type ι which name respectively the *immediate successor and predecessor of the integer* named by A.
3   If A and B are IFC-terms of the same type ζ, then $(A * B)$ is a new IFC-term of type ζ or $\mathcal{L}$. $(A * B)$ names the *conjunction of the modes of achievement* named by A and B, when A and B are of type μ. $(A * B)$ names the *intersection of the propositional content* conditions

named by A and B, when A and B are of type θ. When A and B are of type Σ or ψ, (A * B) names the *union of the preparatory or sincerity conditions* named by A and B. And finally when A and B are of type ι, (A * B) names the *sum of the integers* named by A and by B.

The set of terms of illocutionary forces

If A_μ, A_θ, A_Σ, A_ψ and A_ι are IFC-terms respectively of type μ, θ, Σ, ψ and ι and $1 \leq k \leq 5$, then $[(A_\mu, A_\theta, A_\Sigma, A_\psi), A_\iota, \pi_\mu^k]$ is *an illocutionary force term* (or for short an IF-term) of $\mathcal{L}$ of the derived type φ (of illocutionary forces).

$[(A_\mu, A_\theta, A_\Sigma, A_\psi), A_\iota, \pi_\mu^k]$ names the *illocutionary force F* which determines the following success conditions:

An elementary speech act with the force F and the propositional content p is *performed* in a context of utterance under an interpretation $\mathcal{R}$ if, and only if, in that context, according to $\mathcal{R}$,

first, the proposition p satisfies the propositional content conditions named by A_θ;

second, the speaker achieves the illocutionary point named by π_μ^k on the proposition p with the mode of achievement named by A_μ;

third, he also presupposes all propositions associated by the preparatory condition named by A_Σ with the propositional content p in that context; and

fourth, he expresses with the degree of strength measured by the integer named by A_ι, all the mental states of the form m(p), whose mode m belongs to the sincerity conditions which are named by A_ψ or determined by the illocutionary point named by π_μ^k.

The set of terms for illocutionary acts

If A_ϕ is an illocutionary force term and A_p is a propositional term, then $A_\phi (A_p)$ is an *illocutionary act term* (or an IA-term) of $\mathcal{L}$ of the derived type Ω (of illocutionary acts). $A_\phi (A_p)$ names the *elementary speech act with the illocutionary force* named A_ϕ *and the propositional content* named by A_p.

Rules of formation of sentences

Sentences about propositions

If A and B are p-terms of IL, then t(A), (≫ A), and (A ▷ B) are *elementary sentences of IL*:

t(A) is true in a context under an interpretation $\mathcal{R}$ if, and only if, the proposition named by A is true in that context under $\mathscr{R}$.

≫ A is true in a context if, and only if, the proposition named by A is presupposed in that context.

$(A \triangleright B)$ means that all atomic propositions of B are also atomic propositions of A.

Sentences about the components of illocutionary acts

If A_p, A_μ, A_θ, A_Σ, A_ψ and A_τ are terms respectively of type p, μ, ϕ, Σ, ψ, and τ, expressions of the form $(A_\mu A_p)$, $(A_\theta A_p)$, $(A_\Sigma A_p B_p)$, $(A_\psi A_\tau)$ and $(E(A_\tau A_p)A_\iota)$ are *elementary sentences* of $\mathscr{S}$:

A sentence of the form $(A_\mu A_p)$ is true in a context under an interpretation $\mathscr{R}$ if, and only if, in that context the speaker achieves according to $\mathscr{R}$ an illocutionary point with the mode of achievement named by A_μ on the proposition named by A_p.

A sentence of the form $(A_\theta A_p)$ is true in a context if, and only if, the proposition named by A_p satisfies in that context the propositional content condition named by A_θ. $(A_\Sigma A_p B_p)$ is true in a context under an interpretation $\mathscr{R}$ if, and only if, the speaker could not perform in that context according to $\mathscr{R}$ an illocutionary act with a force F having the preparatory conditions named by A_Σ and the propositional content named by A_p, without also presupposing the proposition named by B_p.

$(A_\psi A_\tau)$ means that the psychological mode named by A_τ belongs to the sincerity condition named by A_ψ.

Finally, $(E(A_\tau A_p)A_\iota)$ is true in a context under an interpretation $\mathscr{R}$ if, and only if, according to $\mathscr{R}$ the speaker in that context expresses with the degree of strength named by A_ι a mental state of the mode named by A_τ with the propositional content A_p.

Identity sentences

If A and B are terms of the same type, then $(A = B)$ is a sentence of $\mathscr{S}$ which is true in a context of an interpretation $\mathscr{R}$ if, and only if, A and B name the same entitities according to $\mathscr{R}$.

Complex sentences

If A and B are sentences of $\mathscr{S}$, then $\neg A$, $\square A$ and $(A \wedge B)$ are new complex *sentences* of $\mathscr{S}$ which are interpreted as usual: a sentence $\neg A$ is true in a context under an interpretation $\mathscr{R}$ if, and only if, A is false in that context according to $\mathscr{R}$; a sentence $(A \wedge B)$ is true in a context if, and only if, the two sentences A and B are true in that context. And the sentence $\square A$ is true in a context under an interpretation $\mathscr{R}$ if, and only if, A is true in all contexts according to $\mathscr{R}$.

Quantified sentences

If x is a variable and A is a sentence, then $\forall xA$ is a new sentence of $\mathscr{L}$. Such a sentence is true in a context under an interpretation $\mathscr{R}$ if, and only if, all entities that can be values of x in the domain of $\mathscr{R}$ satisfy A in that context.

RULES OF ABBREVIATION

Most fundamental truth-functional, modal, propositional and illocutionary notions which are important for the analysis of elementary speech acts can be derived from the few primitive notions of illocutionary logic IL by using the following rules of abbreviation:

The usual rules for *disjunction* $\vee$, *material implication* $\Rightarrow$, *material equivalence* $\Leftrightarrow$, *strict implication* $\dashv$, *strict equivalence* $\longleftrightarrow$, and *possibility* $\Diamond$.

For example:

$$(A \Rightarrow B) =_{def} \neg (A \wedge \neg B)$$

$$(A \dashv B) =_{df} \Box (A \Rightarrow B)$$

and

$$(A \longleftrightarrow B) =_{def} (A \dashv B) \wedge (B \dashv A).$$

Tautologies
$$TA_p =_{def} A_p = (A_p \Rightarrow A_p)$$
Sentence TA_p means that A_p is a tautology.

Strong implication
$$(A_p \mapsto B_p) =_{def} T(A_p \Rightarrow B_p) \wedge (A_p \rhd B_p)$$

Existential generalization
$$\exists x \, A =_{def} \neg \forall x \, \neg A$$

Unique existential generalization
$$\exists! x \, A =_{def} \exists x \, A \wedge (\forall x' \, ([x'/x] \, A \Rightarrow x' = x)) \text{ as usual.}$$

The primitive illocutionary force of assertion
$$\vdash =_{def} [(1_\mu, 1_\theta, 1_\Sigma, 1_\psi), 0_\iota, \pi^1]$$

The primitive commissive illocutionary force
$$\bot =_{def} [(1_\mu, 1_\theta, 1_\Sigma, 1_\psi), 0_\iota, \pi^2]$$

The primitive directive illocutionary force
$$! =_{def} [(1_\mu, 1_\theta, 1_\Sigma, 1_\psi), 0_\iota, \pi^3]$$

The primitive illocutionary force of declaration
$$\top =_{def} [(1_\mu, 1_\theta, 1_\Sigma, 1_\psi), 0_\iota, \pi^4]$$

The primitive expressive illocutionary force
$$\dashv =_{def} [(1_\mu, 1_\theta, 1_\Sigma, 1_\psi), 0_\iota, \pi^5]$$

The operation of imposing a new mode of achievement on an illocutionary force

$[B_\mu]\,[(A_\mu, A_\theta, A_\Sigma, A_\psi), A_\iota, \pi^k] =_{\text{def}} [((B_\mu * A_\mu), A_\theta, A_\Sigma, A_\psi), A_\iota, \pi^k].$

$[B_\mu]A_\phi$ names the illocutionary force obtained by adding to the force named by A_ϕ the mode of achievement named by B_μ.

The operation of adding a new propositional content condition to an illocutionary force

$[B_\theta]\,[(A_\mu, A_\theta, A_\Sigma, A_\psi), A_\iota, \pi^k] =_{\text{def}} [(A_\mu, (B_\theta * A_\theta), A_\Sigma, A_\psi), A_\iota, \pi^k]$

The operation of adding a new preparatory condition to an illocutionary force

$[B_\Sigma]\,[(A_\mu, A_\theta, A_\Sigma, A_\psi), A_\iota, \pi^k] =_{\text{def}} [(A_\mu, B_\theta, (B_\Sigma * A_\Sigma), A_\psi), A_\iota, \pi^k]$

The operation of adding a new sincerity condition to an illocutionary force

$[B_\psi]\,[(A_\mu, A_\theta, A_\Sigma, A_\psi), A_\iota, \pi^k] =_{\text{def}} [(A_\mu, A_\theta, A_\Sigma, (B_\psi * A_\psi)), A_\iota, \pi^k]$

The operations of increasing and decreasing the degree of strength

$[+1]\,[(A_\mu, A_\theta, A_\Sigma, A_\psi), A_\iota, \pi^k] =_{\text{def}} [(A_\mu, A_\theta, A_\Sigma, A_\psi), (A_\iota)', \pi^k]$
And similarly for $[-1]A_\phi$.

The success value of an illocutionary act

$s([(A_\mu, A_\theta, A_\Sigma, A_\psi), A_\iota, \pi^k]\,(A_p)) =_{\text{def}} \pi^k A_p \wedge A_\mu A_p \wedge A_\theta A_p \wedge \forall x_p$
$(A_\Sigma A_p x_p \Rightarrow \gg x_p) \wedge \forall x_\tau ((A_\psi x_\tau \vee c^k_\psi x_\tau) \Rightarrow E(x_\tau A_p)A_\iota)$

A sentence of form $s(A_\Omega)$ is true in a context if, and only if, the illocutionary act named by A_Ω is *performed* in that context.

The property of having an illocutionary point

$A_\phi \dashv \pi^k =_{\text{def}} \forall x_p (s(A_\phi x_p) \dashv (\pi^k x_p))$

Sentence $A_\phi \dashv \pi^k$ means that the force A_ϕ has the point π^k.

The property of having the words-to-world direction of fit

$\downarrow(A_\phi) =_{\text{def}} (A_\phi \dashv \pi^1)$

The property of having the world-to-words direction of fit

$\uparrow(A_\phi) =_{\text{def}} (A_\phi \dashv \pi^2) \vee (A_\phi \dashv \pi^3) \vee (A_\phi \dashv \pi^4)$

The property of having the double direction of fit

$\updownarrow(A_\phi) =_{\text{def}} (A_\phi \dashv \pi^4)$

The property of having the null or empty direction of fit

$\varnothing(A_\phi) =_{\text{def}} (A_\phi \dashv \pi^5) \wedge \neg\downarrow(A_\phi)) \wedge \neg\uparrow(A_\phi)$

The satisfaction value of an illocutionary act

$t(A_\phi(A_p)) =_{\text{def}} ((\downarrow(A_\phi) \vee \varnothing(A_\phi)) \Rightarrow t(A_p)) \wedge (\uparrow(A_\phi) \Rightarrow$
$(t(A_p) \wedge s(A_\phi(A_p))))$

A sentence of the form $t(A_\phi(A_p))$ is true in a context if, and only if, the speech act named by $A_\phi(A_p)$ is *satisfied* in that context.

The relation of strong illocutionary commitment
$$A_\Omega \rhd B_\Omega =_{\text{def}} (s(A_\Omega) \multimap s(B_\Omega))$$

The sentence $A_\Omega \rhd B_\Omega$ means that it is not possible to perform the speech act A_Ω without also performing the speech act B_Ω.

The relation of being a stronger or identical force
$$A_\phi \rhd B_\phi =_{\text{def}} \forall x_p(A_\phi(x_p) \rhd B_\phi(x_p))$$

Inclusion of conditions of satisfaction
$$(A_\Omega \multimap B_\Omega) =_{\text{def}} t(A_\Omega) \multimap t(B_\Omega)$$

The relation of being two illocutionary acts which are not simultaneously performable
$$(A_\Omega ><_s B_\Omega) =_{\text{def}} s(A_\omega) \multimap \neg s(B_\Omega)$$

The relation of being incompatible illocutionary forces
$$(A_\phi >< B_\phi) =_{\text{def}} \forall x_p(A_\phi(x_p) ><_s B_\phi(x_p))$$

The relation of being two illocutionary acts which are not simultaneously satisfiable
$$(A_\Omega ><_t B_\Omega) =_{\text{def}} (t(A_\Omega) \multimap \neg t(B_\Omega))$$

THE STRUCTURE OF A SEMANTIC INTERPRETATION

The formal semantics for illocutionary logic IL is *model-theoretical*: it specifies how meanings can be assigned to the formulas of its ideal object language in arbitrary *possible interpretations* for that language. In formal semantics, a possible interpretation of a language is called a *model* of all the sentences of that language which are true in all contexts of that interpretation. A possible interpretation fixes arbitrarily the set of individual objects and the set of possible contexts that are considered in that interpretation. All other sets of the domain of that interpretation are then defined from these two basic sets by type-theoretical operations. Although the types of semantic values of formulas must be appropriate, different models with the same domain can interpret differently non-logical constants. However, all these models must respect certain *meaning postulates* in the interpretation of formulas. Such postulates guarantee that the logical constants and syncategorematic expressions have their intended theoretical meaning.

Formally, a *standard possible interpretation* or *model* for $\mathscr{L}$ is an eightuple $\mathscr{M} = \; < \text{I, D, M, U,} \; (\Pi_k), \; >>, \; \mathscr{E}, \; \| \; \| \; >$ where I, D and M are three disjoint non-empty sets, (Π_k) is a family of five functions and U, $>>$, $\mathscr{E}$, and $\| \; \|$ are four functions.

1 I is an arbitrary non-empty set which represents the *set of possible*

contexts of utterance which are considered in the possible interpretation $\mathscr{M}$.

2 D is another non-empty set whose elements represent the *individual objects* which are considered in the interpretation $\mathscr{M}$.

3 M is another arbitrary non-empty set whose elements represent the *psychological modes* which are considered in $\mathscr{M}$.

4 U is a function whose domain is the set of all primitive types of IL. That function associates with each type α the set U_α of all entities which are possible semantic values of terms of type α in the possible interpretation $\mathscr{M}$. For example, U_p is the set of all propositions which are considered in $\mathscr{M}$. By definition:

(a) $U_e = D^I$.
(b) $U_{r_n} = (2^{(D^n)})^I$ where 2 is the set of truth values.
(c) $U_\tau = M$.
(d) If U_a is the set $(\mathscr{P}(U_{r_n} \cup D^I))) \times \mathscr{P}(I)$, then $U_p = \mathscr{P}(U_a) \times \mathscr{P}(2^{U_a})$.
(e) $U_\mu = \mathscr{P}(I \times U_p)$.
(f) $U_\theta = (\mathscr{P}(U_p))^I$
(g) $U_\Sigma = (\mathscr{P}(U_p))^{I \times U_p}$.
(h) $U_\psi = \mathscr{P}(M)$.
(i) U_ι is the set of integers.

The union of all the sets U_α is the *domain* of the possible interpretation $\mathscr{M}$.

Conventions and definitions

If X is an ordered pair, let $id_1(X)$ and $id_2(X)$ be respectively the first and the second term of X. Clearly, if α is an atomic proposition in the possible interpretation $\mathscr{M}$, $id_1(\alpha)$ is the set of propositional constituents of that atomic proposition. And $id_2(\alpha)$ is the set of all contexts where that atomic proposition is true under $\mathscr{M}$.

Similarly, if p is a proposition, $id_1(p)$ represents *the set of atomic propositions* out of which that proposition is composed in the interpretation $\mathscr{M}$. And $id_2(p)$ represents the *set of all truth-value assignments to atomic propositions under which the proposition p is true* according to $\mathscr{M}$.

Thus, the proposition p is *true in a context* i under the interpretation $\mathscr{M}$ if, and only if, there exists at least one assignment $f \in id_2(p)$ such that, for all atomic propositions $\alpha \in id_1(p)$, $f(\alpha) = 1$ if, and only if, $i \in id_2(\alpha)$. And p is *contingent* if, and only if, it is true in some but not all contexts $i \in I$ in $\mathscr{M}$.

By definition, a *tautology* is a proposition p whose second element $id_2(p)$ is the entire set of all truth-value assignments. On the contrary, a *contradiction* is a proposition p such that $id_2(p)$ is the empty set. Finally, a proposition p *strongly implies* another proposition q in $\mathscr{R}$ if, and only if, first, $id_1(q) \subseteq id_1(p)$ and, second, $id_2(p) \subseteq id_2(q)$.

5 Π_1, Π_2, Π_3, Π_4 and Π_5 are five subsets of $I \times U_p$ which represent respectively the *conditions of achievement of the assertive, commissive, directive, declarative and expressive illocutionary points* in the possible interpretation $\mathscr{R}$. Thus, $\langle i, p \rangle \in \Pi_k$ means that the k-th illocutionary point is achieved on the proposition p in the context i according to $\mathscr{R}$.

These five subsets obey the following postulates:

(a) The set $\{p| \langle i, p \rangle \in \Pi_1\}$ of all propositions on which the *assertive illocutionary point* is achieved in a context i under a possible interpretation is *minimally consistent*: it does not contain any contradiction. Moreover, that set is also *closed under strong implication*: if it contains a proposition, it contains also all propositions q which are strongly implied by p. Finally, that set *contains a unique supremum*: whenever it is not empty, it contains a unique proposition which strongly implies all other propositions that it contains.

(b) The set $\{p| \langle i, p \rangle \in \Pi_2\}$ of all propositions on which the commissive illocutionary point is achieved is minimally consistent and contains a unique supremum. Moreover, it is partially closed under strong implication: it contains a proposition p if, and only if, it contains also every non-tautological proposition which is strongly implied by p. And similarly for the set $\{p| \langle i, p \rangle \in \Pi_3\}$ of all propositions on which the *directive illocutionary point* is achieved. Finally, $\Pi_2 \subseteq \Pi_1$.

(c) The set $\{p| \langle i, p \rangle \in \Pi_4\}$ of all propositions on which the *declarative illocutionary point* is achieved in the context i is a set of contingent propositions which are true in that context. If it is not empty, it contains a unique maximal element q that strongly implies all its members. Moreover, $\Pi_4 \subseteq \Pi_1$.

6 $>>$ is a subset of $I \times U_p$. It determines which propositions are presupposed under the possible interpretation $\mathscr{R}$. Thus, $\langle i, p \rangle \in >>$ means that the proposition p is presupposed in the context i according to possible interpretation $\mathscr{R}$. By definition, the set of all propositions $\{p| \langle i, p \rangle \in >>\}$ which are presupposed in a context i under a possible interpretation $\mathscr{R}$ is a proper subset of U_p which is closed under strong implication. Moreover, that set is minimally compatible with the set $\{p| \langle i, p \rangle \in \Pi_1\}$, in the sense that their union is minimally consistent.

7 $\mathscr{E}$ is a subset of $I \times U_\tau \times U_p \times U_\iota$. It determines which mental states are expressed according to the possible interpretation $\mathscr{R}$. Thus, $\langle i, m, p, k \rangle \in \mathscr{E}$ means that the speaker in the context i expresses with the degree of strength measured by the integer k a mental state of the form m(p) in the possible interpretation $\mathscr{R}$. By definition, the set of all modes m such that $\langle i, m, p, k \rangle \in \mathscr{E}$ is a proper subset of M, and the set of all integers $\{k| \langle i, m,$

p, k⟩ ε 𝓔} representing the degrees of strength with which a mental state m(p) is expressed in a context i is an initial segment of integers.

Moreover, ⟨i, p⟩ ∈ Π₅ if, and only if, for some m ∈ M and for some k ∈ Z, ⟨i, m, p, k⟩ ∈ 𝓔 in the possible interpretation 𝓡.

8 Finally, ‖ ‖ is a function which associates with each term A of type α under each possible assignment σ of values to its free variables the entity ‖A‖^σ of $U_α$ which A names under that assignment in the possible interpretation 𝓡. By a possible assignment of values to the free variables of the terms of 𝓛, I mean here any function σ whose domain is the set of all variables of IL and which associates with each variable of type α of IL an entity of the set $U_α$ of the domain of 𝓡.

The evaluation function ‖ ‖ satisfies the following clauses:

(a) For any variable v of type α of 𝓛, ‖v‖^σ = σ(v).
(b) For any constant of type α of 𝓛, ‖c‖^σ ∈ $U_α$. Moreover, if $1 ≤ k ≤ 5$, ‖$c_ψ^k$‖^σ ≠ ∅. Finally, if ⟨i, p⟩ ∈ Π$_k$ then, for all m ∈ ‖$c_ψ^k$‖^σ, there exists an integer n such that ⟨i, m, p, n⟩ ∈ 𝓔.
(c) ‖$R_n(c_1 \ldots c_n)$ ‖^σ = ⟨{‖R_n‖^σ, ‖c_1‖^σ, …, ‖c_n‖^σ}, {j| j ∈ I and ‖R_n‖^σ(j) (⟨‖c_1‖^σ(j), …, ‖c_n‖^σ(j)⟩) = 1}
(d) ‖(A_a)‖^σ = ⟨{‖A_a‖^σ}, {$f ∈ 2^{U_a}$| f(‖A_a‖^σ) = 1}⟩
(e) ‖¬A_p‖^σ = ⟨id₁(‖A_p‖^σ), {f| f ∉ id₂(‖A_p‖^σ)}⟩
(f) ‖$(A_p ∧ B_p)$‖^σ = ⟨(id₁(‖A_p‖^σ) ∪ id₁(‖B_p‖^σ)), (id₂(‖A_p‖^σ) ∩ id₂(‖B_p‖^σ))⟩
(g) ‖$0_ι$‖^σ is the integer zero.
(h) ‖$1_μ$‖^σ = I × U_p and ‖$0_μ$‖^σ = ∅.
(i) ‖$1_θ$‖^σ is the function f ∈ $U_θ$ such that f(i) = U_p, and ‖$0_θ$‖^σ(i) = ∅.
(j) ‖$1_Σ$‖^σ(i, p) = ∅ and ‖$0_Σ$‖^σ is the function f ∈ $U_Σ$ such that f(i, p) = U_p.
(k) ‖$1_ψ$‖^σ = ∅ and ‖$0_ψ$‖^σ = M.
(l) ‖$π^k$‖^σ = Π$_k$.
(m) ‖$A_μ * B_μ$‖^σ = ‖$A_μ$‖^σ ∩ ‖$B_μ$‖^σ.
(n) ‖$A_θ * B_θ$‖^σ is the function f of type θ such that f(i) = ‖$A_θ$‖^σ(i) ∩ ‖$B_θ$‖^σ(i).
(o) ‖$A_Σ * B_Σ$‖^σ is the function f of the type Σ such that f(i, p) = ‖$A_Σ$‖^σ(i, p) ∪ ‖$B_Σ$‖^σ(i, p).
(p) ‖$A_ψ * B_ψ$‖^σ = ‖$A_ψ$‖^σ ∪ ‖$B_ψ$‖^σ
(q) ‖$A_ι * B_ι$‖^σ is the sum of the two integers ‖$A_ι$‖^σ and ‖$B_ι$‖^σ. Moreover, ‖$(A_ι)'$‖^σ and ‖$'(A_ι)$‖^σ are respectively the immediate successor and the immediate predecessor of ‖$A_ι$‖^σ.
(r) ‖$[(A_μ, A_θ, A_Σ, A_ψ), A_ι, π^k]$‖^σ is the function f with domain U_p such that f(p) = ⟨p, 𝓙⟩ where 𝓙 is the subset of I such that i ∈ 𝓙 if, and only if, ⟨i, p⟩ ∈ ‖$A_μ$‖^σ ∩ ‖$π^k$‖^σ, p ∈ ‖$A_θ$‖^σ(i), ‖$A_Σ$‖^σ(i, p) ⊆ {q| ⟨i, q⟩ ∈ >>} and for all m such that m ∈ ‖$A_ψ$‖^σ ∪ ‖$c_ψ^k$‖^σ, ⟨i, m, p, ‖$A_ι$‖^σ⟩ ∈ 𝓔.
(s) If $A_φ$ is an IF-term and A_p is a p-term, ‖$A_φ(A_p)$‖^σ = ‖$A_φ$‖^σ(‖A_p‖^σ).

The truth definition

On the basis of the preceding definitions, a *sentence A of $\mathscr{L}$ is true in a context i under an assignment σ of values of its variables in the interpretation $\mathscr{R}$* under the following conditions:

1 A sentence $t(B_p)$ is true in a context i under σ in $\mathscr{R}$ if, and only if, the proposition $\|B_p\|^\sigma$ is true in i according to $\mathscr{R}$.

2 A sentence $\gg B_p$ is true in a context i under σ in $\mathscr{R}$ if, and only if, $\langle i, \|B_p\|^\sigma \rangle \in {\gg}$.

3 A sentence $(A_p \rhd B_p)$ is true in a context i under σ in $\mathscr{R}$ if, and only if, $\mathrm{id}_1(\|B_p\|^\sigma) \subseteq \mathrm{id}_1(\|A_p\|^\sigma)$.

4 A sentence of the form $(B = C)$ is true in a context i under σ in $\mathscr{R}$ if, and only if, $\|B\|^\sigma = \|C\|^\sigma$.

5 A sentence of the form $(A_\mu A_p)$ is true in a context i under an assignment σ in $\mathscr{R}$ if, and only if, $\langle i, \|A_p\|^\sigma \rangle \in \|A_\mu\|^\sigma$.

6 A sentence of the form $(A_\theta A_p)$ is true in i under σ in $\mathscr{R}$ if, and only if, $\|A_p\|^\sigma \in \|A_\theta\|^\sigma(i)$.

7 A sentence of the form $(A_\Sigma A_p B_p)$ is true in i under σ in $\mathscr{R}$ if, and only if, $\|B_p\|^\sigma \in \|A_\Sigma\|^\sigma(i, \|A_p\|^\sigma)$.

8 A sentence of the form $(A_\psi A_\tau)$ is true in i under σ in $\mathscr{R}$ if, and only if, $\|A_\tau\|^\sigma \in \|A_\psi\|^\sigma$.

9 A sentence of the form $E(A_\tau A_p)A_\iota$ is true in i under σ in $\mathscr{R}$ if, and only if, $\langle i, \|A_\tau\|^\sigma, \|A_p\|^\sigma, \|A_\iota\|^\sigma \rangle \in \mathscr{E}$.

10 A sentence of the form $\neg B$ is true in a context i under σ in $\mathscr{R}$ if, and only if, B is not true in i under σ in $\mathscr{R}$.

11 A sentence of the form $(B_1 \wedge B_2)$ is true in a context i under σ in $\mathscr{R}$ if, and only if, the two sentences B_1 and B_2 are true in that context under σ in $\mathscr{R}$.

12 A sentence of the form $\Box B$ is true in a context i under σ in $\mathscr{R}$ if, and only if, B is true in all contexts $j \in I$ under σ in $\mathscr{R}$.

13 Finally, a sentence of the form $(\forall x)B$ is true in a context i under σ in $\mathscr{R}$ if, and only if, B is true in i under all assignments $\sigma'(x) \neq \sigma(x)$.

Logical truth

A sentence A of $\mathscr{L}$ is *logically true* (or *valid*) (in symbols: $\models A$) if, and only if, it is true in all possible contexts under all assignments in all possible interpretations.

A COMPLETE AXIOMATIC SYSTEM

The illocutionary logic that I have formulated is the extension obtained by adding a richer logic of propositions to the simple logic of illocutionary forces of *Meaning and Speech Acts* (1990–1). These two sub-logics have already been completely axiomatized. There are no propositional terms expressing identity propositions in the new object language. Consequently, we need not formalize here the valid laws of illocutionary commitments that exist between speech acts in virtue of the predications of identity that are made in their propositional contents. Strong implication is the relevant cognitive implication here. Thus the new propositional language just increases the expressive capacities of the logic without requiring non-trivial modifications. It serves to exhibit better the structure of the propositional contents of speech acts. For these reasons, I conjecture that the new illocutionary logic IL is itself also *complete*. I think that all and only its logically true sentences are provable in the following *axiomatic system $\mathscr{S}$*.

The axioms of the formal system $\mathscr{S}$

The axioms of the formal system $\mathscr{S}$ are:

(I)   The axioms of truth functional logic
(II) The axioms of the first-order predicate calculus with identity
(III) The axioms of S5 modal logic
(IV) The axioms of the minimal logic of propositions

> Axiom schema 1: $(A_p \vdash B_p \wedge B_p \vdash A_p) \Leftrightarrow (A_p = B_p)$
> Two propositions which strongly imply each other are identical.

The following axioms for the analysis of atomic propositions
> Axiom schema 2: $A_p \rhd A_p$
> Axiom schema 3: $A_p \rhd B_p \Rightarrow (B_p \rhd C_p \Rightarrow A_p \rhd C_p)$
> Axiom schema 4: $(B_a) \rhd (A_a) \Rightarrow (B_a) = (A_a)$
> Axiom schema 5: $(\neg A_p \rhd A_p) \wedge (A_p \rhd \neg A_p)$
> Axiom schema 6: $(A_p \wedge B_p) \rhd A_p$
> Axiom schema 7: $(A_p \wedge B_p) \rhd B_p$
> Axiom schema 8: $((A_p \rhd B_p) \wedge (A_p \rhd C_p)) \Rightarrow (A_p \rhd (B_p \wedge C_p))$
> Axiom schema 9: $(B_p \wedge C_p) \rhd (A_a) \Rightarrow ((B_p \rhd (A_a)) \vee (C_p \rhd (A_a)))$
> Axiom schema 10: $(A_p \rhd B_p) \Rightarrow \Box(A_p \rhd B_p)$
> Axiom schema 11: $((A_a) = (B_a)) \Rightarrow (t((A_a)) \Leftrightarrow t((B_a)))$
> Axiom schema 12: $((R_n(c_1, \ldots, c_n)) \rhd (R_n'(d_1, \ldots, d_n))) \Rightarrow$
> $\quad ((R_n(e_1, \ldots, e_n))\ (R_n'(e_1, \ldots, e_n)))$
> Axiom schema 13: $((c_1 = d_1) \wedge \ldots \wedge (c_n = d_n)) \Rightarrow$
> $\quad (((R_n(e_1, \ldots, e_n)) \rhd (R_n'(e_1, \ldots, e_n))) \Rightarrow ((R_n(c_1, \ldots, c_n)) \rhd$
> $\quad (R_n'(d_1, \ldots, d_n))))$
> Axiom schema 14: $((R_n(c_1, \ldots, c_n)) \rhd (R_n'(d_1, \ldots, d_n))) \Rightarrow$
> $\quad ((c_i = d_1) \vee \ldots \vee (c_i = d_n))$, where $1 \le i \le n$.
> Axiom schema 15: $\neg((R_n(c_1, \ldots, c_n)) \rhd (R_m(d_1, \ldots, d_m)))$,
> $\quad$ where $n \ne m$.
> Axiom schema 16: $\Box(t((r_n(c_1, \ldots, c_n)) \Leftrightarrow t((R_n(d_1, \ldots, d_n))) \Rightarrow$
> $\quad ((R_n(c_1, \ldots, c_n)) \rhd (R_n(d_1, \ldots, d_n))))$, where $\{c_1, \ldots, c_n\} = \{d_1, \ldots, d_n\}$.

Thus two identical elementary propositions are composed out of the same atomic proposition. A proposition and its negation are composed out of the same atomic propositions. The atomic propositions of a conjunction are the atomic propositions of its conjuncts. A proposition has the same atomic propositions in every context. Two identical elementary propositions have the same propositional constituents. If elementary propositions have attributes of different degrees, they are different. Finally, atomic propositions with the same propositional constituents and truth conditions are identical.

The usual axioms for truth conditions

Axiom schema 17: $t(\neg A_p) \Leftrightarrow \neg t(A_p)$
Axiom schema 18: $t(A_p \wedge B_p) \Leftrightarrow (t(A_p) \wedge t(B_p))$

and finally the following axioms for tautologies

Axiom schema 19: TA_p when A_p is a tautology according to truth tables
Axiom schema 20: $(TA_p \wedge T(A_p \Rightarrow B_p)) \Rightarrow T(B_p)$
Axiom schema 21: $((A_a) = (B_a)) \Rightarrow T(A_p \Leftrightarrow A_p')$,
   where A_p' is obtained from A_p by replacing occurrences of the term (A_a) in A_p by the term (B_a).
Axiom schema 22: $\neg T((A_a^1) \vee \ldots \vee (A_a^n))$, for any $A_a^1, \ldots, A_a^n$.
Axiom schema 23: $\neg T(\neg(A_a^1) \vee \ldots \vee \neg(A_a^n))$, for any $A_a^1, \ldots, A_a^n$.
Axiom schema 24: $T((A_a^1) \vee \ldots \vee (A_a^n) \vee \neg(B_a^1) \vee \ldots \vee \neg(B_a^m))$
   $\Rightarrow (((A_a^1) = (B_a^1)) \vee \ldots \vee ((A_a^1) = (B_a^m)) \vee \ldots \vee ((A_a^n) = (B_a^1)) \vee \ldots \vee ((A_a^n) = (B_a^m)))$, for any $A_a^1, \ldots, A_a^n, B_a^1, \ldots, B_a^m \in L_a$
Axiom schema 25: $T(A_p) \Rightarrow \Box t(A_p)$

All tautologies can be identified by truth tables. Tautologyhood is closed under *modus ponens* and is preserved by the replacement of identical elementary propositions. No elementary proposition can be a tautology or a contradiction. Finally, tautologies are related to the bivalence of their atomic propositions.

(V) The axioms of the additive Abelian group for integers
(VI) The axioms for components of illocutionary forces

Axiom schema 26: $(\forall x_p(A_\zeta x_p \leftrightarrow B_\zeta x_p) \Rightarrow A_\zeta = B_\zeta)$ if $\zeta = \mu$ or θ
Axiom schema 27: $(\forall x_p \forall y_p(A_\Sigma x_p y_p \leftrightarrow B_\Sigma x_p y_p)) \Rightarrow A_\Sigma = B_\Sigma$
Axiom schema 28: $(\forall x_\tau(A_\psi x_\tau \Leftrightarrow B_\psi x_\tau)) \Rightarrow A_\psi = B_\psi$
Axiom schema 29: $(1_\zeta A_p)$ where $\zeta = \mu$ or θ
Axiom schema 30: $\neg\Diamond(0_\zeta A_p)$ where $\zeta = \mu$ or θ
Axiom schema 31: $\neg\Diamond(1_\Sigma A_p B_p)$
Axiom schema 32: $\Box(0_\Sigma A_p B_p)$
Axiom schema 33: $\neg\Diamond 1_\psi A_\tau$

Axiom schema 34: $\Box O_\psi A_\tau$
Axiom schema 35: $(A_\Sigma * B_\Sigma)A_p B_p \Leftrightarrow (A_\Sigma A_p B_p \lor B_\Sigma A_p B_p)$
Axiom schema 36: $(A_\zeta * B_\zeta)A_p \Leftrightarrow (A_\zeta A_p \land B_\zeta A_p)$
   where $= \mu$ or θ
Axiom schema 37: $(A_\psi * B_\psi)A_\tau \Leftrightarrow (A_\psi A_\tau \lor B_\psi A_\tau)$

Axiom schemata 26–34 state the laws of identity for components of illo-cutionary force and fix the logical properties of the neutral and absor-bent components of illocutionary force. Axiom schemata 35–7 determine the nature of conjunctions of modes of achievement, of inter-sections of propositional content conditions and of unions of prepara-tory and sincerity conditions.

(VII)   The axioms for illocutionary points

Axiom schema 38: $(\pi^k A_p \Rightarrow \neg T \neg A_p)$ where $1 \leq k \leq 4$
Axiom schema 39: $(\pi^1 A_p \Rightarrow \exists! x_p \forall y_p (\pi^1 y_p \Leftrightarrow x_p \vdash y_p))$
Axiom schema 40: $(\pi^k A_p \Rightarrow \exists! x_p (\pi^k x_p \land (\forall y_p (\pi^k y_p \Leftrightarrow$
   $(x_p \vdash y_p \land \neg T y_p))))$ where $2 \leq k \leq 3$
Axiom schema 41: $(\pi^4 A_p \Rightarrow \exists! x_p (\pi^4 x_p \land (\forall y_p (\pi^4 y_p \Leftrightarrow$
   $(x_p \vdash y_p \land \neg \Box t(y_p))))$
Axiom 42: $\forall x_p (\pi^4 x_p \Rightarrow t(x_p))$
Axiom 43: $\forall x_p ((\pi^4 x_p \lor \pi^2 x_p) \Rightarrow \pi^1 x_p)$
Axiom schema 44: $(\exists x_\tau c_\psi^k x_\tau) \land ((\pi^k A_p) \dashv \forall x_\tau (c_\psi^k x_\tau \Rightarrow$
   $\exists x_\iota E(x_\tau A_p) x_\iota))$ where $1 \leq k \leq 4$
Axiom schema 45: $\pi^5 A_p \Leftrightarrow \exists x_\tau \exists x_\iota E(x_\tau A_p) x_\iota$

Axiom schema 38 states the law of the minimal consistency of the speaker. Axiom schema 39 asserts that the set of propositions on which the assertive point is achieved is closed under strong implication. It also states the law of foundation for the assertive point. Axiom schemata 40–1 state similar laws for the commissive, directive and declarative points, with the additional requirement of the a posteriority or of the contingency of the propositions on which these points are achieved. Axiom 42 states the truth of the propositional content of a successful declaration. Axiom 43 states the existence of an assertive commitment in the achievement of the declarative or of the commissive illocutionary point. Axiom schema 44 asserts that each illocutionary point determines non-empty sincerity conditions. Finally, Axiom schema 45 states the conditions of achievement of the expressive point.

(VIII) The axioms for presupposition

Axiom 46: $\neg \forall x_p \gg x_p$
Axiom schema 47: $\gg A_p \Rightarrow (A_p \vdash B_p) \Rightarrow \gg B_p)$
Axiom schema 48: $\gg A_p \Rightarrow \neg (\pi^1 \neg A_p)$

The set of presuppositions of a speaker is not the total set of propositions. It is closed under strong implication. There is a law of non-deniability of the preparatory conditions.

(IX) The axioms for psychological expression

Axiom schema 49: $\neg\forall x_\tau E(x_\tau x_p)A_\iota$
Axiom schema 50:
$$E(A_\tau A_p)A_\iota \Rightarrow (\exists x_\iota \neg E(A_\tau A_p)x_\iota \wedge (\exists y_\iota (E(A_\tau A_p)y_\iota \wedge \forall z_\iota (E(A_\tau A_p)z_\iota \Leftrightarrow y_\iota \geq z_\iota))))$$

These axiom schemata state a law of possible sincerity of the speaker, the law of existence of a maximal degree of strength and the transitivity of strength in the expression of mental states.

(X) The axioms for illocutionary forces and acts

Axiom schema 51: $A_\phi = B_\phi \Leftrightarrow \Box(\forall x_p(s(A_\phi x_p) \Leftrightarrow s(B_\phi x_p)))$
Axiom schema 52: $A_\phi A_p = B_\phi B_p \Leftrightarrow (A_p = B_p \wedge (A_\phi A_p) \vartriangleright (B_\phi B_p) \wedge (B_\phi B_p) \vartriangleright (A_\phi A_p))$

These last axiom schemata state the laws of identity for illocutionary forces and elementary speech acts.

The three rules of inference of $\mathscr{S}$

The three rules of inference of $\mathscr{S}$ are:

(I)   The rule of *modus ponens*: From A and (A $\Rightarrow$ B) infer B.
(II) The rule of necessitation: From A infer $\Box$A.
(III) The rule of generalization: From A infer $\forall$xA.

FUNDAMENTAL LAWS OF ILLOCUTIONARY LOGIC

Laws for the components of illocutionary force

The sets of modes of achievement, propositional content, preparatory and sincerity conditions have the logical structure of a *Boolean algebra*. Thus * is idempotent, commutative and associative. There exist neutral and absorbent components of each type. There exists a complement for these types of component. The absorbent components of illocutionary force determine all components: $\models O_\zeta \dashv A_{\zeta'}$, where ζ and $\zeta' \in \{\mu, \theta, \Sigma, \psi\}$. The neutral components are determined by all components. Only the neutral component of forces determines itself.

Finally, the set of degrees of strength is an *Abelian group*.

Laws for illocutionary forces

ANY ILLOCUTIONARY FORCE WITH AN ABSORBENT COMPONENT IS IMPOSS-
IBLE.

THERE EXISTS ONE AND ONLY ONE EMPTY OR IMPOSSIBLE FORCE.

THE LAW OF COMPARATIVE STRENGTH FOR ILLOCUTIONARY FORCES:
Whenever an illocutionary force can be obtained by an application of a
logical operation from another force, they are of *comparative strength*:
either these two forces are identical or one is stronger than the other. Thus:
   THE OPERATION OF ADDING TO AN ILLOCUTIONARY FORCE F A COMPO-
NENT THAT IS ALREADY PART OF IT GENERATES THE SAME FORCE F.

$$\models [A_\zeta]A_\phi = A_\phi \text{ when } \models A_\phi \dashv A_\zeta$$

ANY APPLICATION OF AN OPERATION TO AN IMPOSSIBLE ILLOCU-
TIONARY FORCE GENERATES THE SAME IMPOSSIBLE FORCE.

$$\models \forall x_p \neg \Diamond s(A_\phi(x_p)) \Rightarrow [B]A_\phi = A_\phi$$

THE OPERATIONS WHICH CONSIST IN RESTRICTING THE MODE OF
ACHIEVEMENT, IN INCREASING THE DEGREE OF STRENGTH OR IN ADDING
NEW CONDITIONS ALWAYS GENERATE STRONGER (OR IDENTICAL) ILLOCU-
TIONARY FORCES. ON THE CONTRARY, THE OPERATION WHICH CONSISTS IN
DECREASING THE DEGREE OF STRENGTH GENERATES IDENTICAL OR
WEAKER ILLOCUTIONARY FORCES.

$$\models [A_\zeta]A_\phi \rhd A_\phi, [+1]A_\phi \rhd A_\phi \text{ and } \models A_\phi \rhd [-1]A_\phi$$

The fact that the operations of adding new components or of increasing the
degree of strength generate stronger illocutionary forces is *made visible* on
the surface in the formal language $\mathscr{L}$.

A COMPLETENESS THEOREM FOR THE OPERATIONS ON FORCES:
Any illocutionary force which is stronger than another force can be
obtained from that force by adding a mode of achievement, propositional
content, preparatory or sincerity conditions, or by increasing the degree of
strength.
   If $\models A_\phi \rhd B_\phi$ then, for some A_μ, A_θ, A_Σ, A_ψ and a sequence of n $[+1]$
(where n $\geq$ 0), $\models A_\phi = [A_\mu] [A_\theta] [A_\Sigma] [A_\psi] [+1] \dots [+1] B_\theta$.

COROLLARY 1. ANY ILLOCUTIONARY FORCE WITH A POSITIVE OR ZERO
DEGREE OF STRENGTH IS STRONGER THAN THE PRIMITIVE ILLOCUTIONARY
FORCE WITH ITS ILLOCUTIONARY POINT.

THE ORDER OF APPLICATION OF OPERATIONS ON AN ILLOCUTIONARY
FORCE HAS NO IMPORTANCE.

THE RELATION OF BEING A STRONGER OR IDENTICAL ILLOCUTIONARY FORCE IS A RELATION OF PARTIAL ORDER BETWEEN ILLOCUTIONARY FORCES.
Thus, $\models A_\phi = B_\phi \Leftrightarrow \forall x_p (A_\phi x_p \rhd B_\phi x_p \wedge B_\phi x_p \rhd A_\phi x_p)$.

The set of all possible illocutionary forces of utterances is more logically structured than has been commonly supposed in contemporary philosophy of language.

THE LAW OF MEASURABILITY OF COMPARATIVE STRENGTH:
The relation of comparative strength between forces is *decidable*: one can determine effectively whether $\models A_\phi \rhd B_\phi$.

FORCES WITH COMPLEMENTARY COMPONENTS ARE INCOMPATIBLE.

THE ILLOCUTIONARY FORCE NAMED BY AN IF-TERM CANNOT BE IDENTIFIED WITH A SEXTUPLE CONSISTING OF THE COMPONENTS NAMED BY ITS SIX CONSTITUENT TERMS.

$$\not\models ([(A_\mu, A_\theta, A_\Sigma, A_\psi), A_\iota, \pi^k] = [(B_\mu, B_\theta, B_\Sigma, B_\psi), B_\iota, \pi^n)$$
$$\Leftrightarrow (A_\mu = B_\mu \wedge A_\theta = B_\theta \wedge A_\Sigma = B_\Sigma \wedge A_\psi = B_\psi \wedge A_\iota = B_\iota \wedge \pi^k = \pi^n)$$

Indeed the components of force of different types are not always independent. For example, $\models \top = [\pi^4] \vdash$.

Laws for propositions

UNLIKE STRICT IMPLICATION, STRONG IMPLICATION IS A RELATION OF PARTIAL ORDER. It is reflexive, transitive and anti-symmetric.
   THERE ARE TWO CAUSES OF FAILURE OF STRONG IMPLICATION.
$$\models \neg(A_p \rhd B_p) \Rightarrow \neg(A_p \vdash B_p)$$
$$\models \neg\top(A_p \Rightarrow B_p) \Rightarrow \neg(A_p \vdash B_p)$$
Thus, strong implication is stronger than Parry's analytic implication. Indeed, $\not\models (A_p \dashv B_p) \wedge (A_p \rhd B_p) \Rightarrow A_p = B_p$.

MOST RULES OF ELIMINATION OF NATURAL DEDUCTION GENERATE STRONG IMPLICATION.
   THE LAW OF ELIMINATION OF CONJUNCTION
$\models (A_p \wedge B_p) \vdash A_p$ and $\models (A_p \wedge B_p) \vdash B_p$
   THE LAW OF ELIMINATION OF DISJUNCTION
$\models ((A_p \vdash C_p) \wedge (B_p \vdash C_p)) \Rightarrow (A_p \vee B_p) \vdash C_p$
   THE LAW OF ELIMINATION OF MATERIAL IMPLICATION
$\models (A_p \wedge (A_p \Rightarrow B_p) \vdash B_p$
   THE FAILURE OF THE LAW OF ELIMINATION OF NEGATION
$\not\models (A_p \wedge \neg A_p) \vdash B_p$
Indeed B_p can contain new senses.

THE ONLY RULES OF INTRODUCTION OF NATURAL DEDUCTION WHICH GENERATE STRONG IMPLICATION ARE THOSE IN WHICH THE ATOMIC PROPOSITIONS OF THE CONCLUSIONS ARE ALREADY IN ONE OF THE PREMISES.

THE FAILURE OF THE LAW OF INTRODUCTION OF DISJUNCTION.

$\not\models A_p \vdash (A_p \lor B_p)$ although $\models t(A_p) \dashv t(A_p \lor B_p)$

THE FAILURE OF THE LAW OF CONTRAPOSITION

$\not\models (A_p \vdash B_p) \Rightarrow (\neg B_p \vdash \neg A_p)$

ON THE CONTRARY, THE LAWS OF INTRODUCTION OF NEGATION AND OF CONJUNCTION ARE VALID. Thus,

$\models A_p \vdash B_p \land T(\neg B_p) \Rightarrow (A_p \vdash \neg A_p)$.

A PROPOSITION STRONGLY IMPLIES ALL AND ONLY THE TAUTOLOGIES WHOSE CONTENT IS INCLUDED IN ITS CONTENT:

$\models TB_p \Rightarrow (A_p \vdash B_p \Leftrightarrow A_p \rhd B_p)$

SIMILARLY A CONTRADICTION STRONGLY IMPLIES ALL AND ONLY THE PROPOSITIONS WHOSE CONTENT IS INCLUDED IN ITS CONTENT.

A THEOREM OF FINITENESS FOR STRONG IMPLICATION:
Each proposition only strongly implies finitely many others.

THE RELATION OF STRONG IMPLICATION IS DECIDABLE.
Every speaker who fully understands two propositions knows a priori whether one strongly implies the other. Indeed, when a proposition p strongly implies a proposition q, it is not possible to have in mind all atomic propositions of p without also having in mind those of q. Furthermore, we cannot understand by the application of which truth function the truth conditions of p are determined without understanding *eo ipso* that all truth-value assignments to atomic propositions that make p true also make q true. This is why strong implication is so important in the logical analysis of minimal rationality.

ONE MUST DISTINGUISH TAUTOLOGIES FROM NECESSARY PROPOSITIONS AND CONTRADICTIONS FROM IMPOSSIBLE PROPOSITIONS.
Clearly, few necessarily true propositions are a priori known to be true in virtue of competence as is the case with tautologies. This is why

$\not\models \Box \neg t(A_p) \Rightarrow (A_p \vdash (A_p \land \neg A_p)$

ALL BOOLEAN LAWS OF IDEMPOTENCE, COMMUTATIVITY AND ASSOCIATIVITY OF CONJUNCTION AND DISJUNCTION.

$\models A_p = A_p \land A_p$ and $\models (A_p \land B_p) = (B_p \land A_p)$.

Thus intensional isomorphism is too strong a condition of propositional identity.

Laws for elementary illocutionary acts

THE LAW OF IDENTITY
Two elementary illocutionary acts with the same propositional content and the same conditions of success are identical.

AN ILLOCUTIONARY ACT IS NOT AN ORDERED PAIR CONSISTING OF AN ILLOCUTIONARY FORCE AND OF A PROPOSITIONAL CONTENT.

$$\not\models A_\phi(A_p) = B_\phi(B_p) \Leftrightarrow (A_\phi = B_\phi \wedge A_p = B_p)$$

Indeed, speech acts with the same propositional content and the same conditions of success can have *different forces*. Thus the assertion of a proposition that is past or present with respect to all possible contexts of utterance (for example, the assertion that God has always existed) is also a report on what is represented. But the two forces are different.

THE RELATION OF STRONG ILLOCUTIONARY COMMITMENT BETWEEN ILLOCUTIONARY ACTS IS REFLEXIVE AND TRANSITIVE BUT IS NOT ANTI-SYMMETRIC.

$$\not\models (A_\phi(A_p) \rhd B_\phi(B_p) \wedge B_\phi(B_p) \rhd A_\phi(A_p)) \Rightarrow A_\phi(A_p) = B_\phi(B_p)$$

Indeed there are many different non-performable speech acts.

ILLOCUTIONARY COMMITMENT IS NOT COMPATIBLE WITH STRICT IMPLICATION.

$$\not\models A_p \dashv^3 B_p \Rightarrow A_\phi(A_p) \rhd B_\phi(B_p) \text{ even for the primitives } A_\phi.$$

There are two *cognitive reasons* why the performance of an illocutionary act of the form $F(p_1)$ might not contain the performance of another illocutionary act $F(p_2)$ whose propositional content p_2 is strictly implied by the first proposition p_1. First, it could be possible for competent speakers to express the first proposition without *eo ipso* having in mind the second proposition. When the implied proposition p_2 contains new atomic propositions, its apprehension requires new acts of reference or of predication. Second, the relation of strict implication existing between the two propositions might not be known a priori by speakers in virtue of their linguistic competence. Thus, one can assert the tautology that arithmetic is complete or incomplete without *eo ipso* asserting the necessary proposition that arithmetic is incomplete.

HOWEVER, STRONG ILLOCUTIONARY COMMITMENT IS SYSTEMATICALLY GENERATED BY STRONG IMPLICATION.
ASSERTION IS ENTIRELY COMPATIBLE WITH STRONG IMPLICATION:

$$\models ((A_p \vdash\dashv B_p) \Rightarrow \vdash (A_p) \rhd \vdash (B_p))$$

Any speaker who makes an assertion of a proposition also asserts all propositions strongly implied by that proposition. Indeed, he and the hearer mutually know a priori that this assertion cannot be true unless the others are also true. Thus:

$\models \vdash (A_p \wedge B_p) \vartriangleright \vdash (A_p)$ and $\models \vdash (A_p \wedge B_p) \vartriangleright \vdash (B_p)$

$\models s(\vdash (A_p)) \wedge s(\vdash (B_p)) \dashv s(\vdash (A_p \wedge B_p))$

$\models (A_p \vartriangleright B_p) \dashv \vdash (A_p) \vartriangleright \vdash (A_p \vee B_p)$

$\models (A_p \dashv C_p \wedge B_p \dashv C_p) \Rightarrow \vdash (A_p \vee B_p) \vartriangleright \vdash (C_p)$

$\models (A_p \wedge (A_p \Rightarrow B_p)) \vartriangleright \vdash (B_p)$

THE PRIMITIVE COMMISSIVE AND DIRECTIVE FORCES AND THE FORCE OF DECLARATION ARE PARTIALLY COMPATIBLE WITH STRONG IMPLICATION. If $A_\phi = \perp$ or ! then $\models ((A_p \dashv B_p) \wedge \neg T(B_p)) \Rightarrow A_\phi(A_p) \vartriangleright A_\phi(B_p)$. And $\models ((A_p \dashv B_p) \wedge \neg \Box t(B_p)) \Rightarrow \top(A_p) \vartriangleright \top(B_p)$.

A speaker who performs an illocutionary act F(p) with the aim of establishing a correspondence between language and the world from the world-to-words direction of fit also performs *eo ipso* all illocutionary acts F(q) whose propositional content q is contingent and strongly implied by p.

Unlike assertive speech acts, commissive, directive and declarative speech acts do not commit the speaker to other speech acts of the same type with a tautological propositional content. Indeed, a competent speaker knows a priori that tautologies are true independently of his utterances and that the world cannot be transformed by a human action in order to match such necessary propositions. Thus the directive utterance 'Bring me water and wine!' strongly commits the speaker to the directive 'Bring me wine!' However, that directive does not contain the tautological directive: 'Either bring me or do not bring me wine!'

In the use and comprehension of language, speakers and hearers are able to make certain valid references. Some of these inferences are *theoretical*: their conclusion expresses a speech act with the words-to-world direction of fit. For example, from the assertions that John is in Paris and that if John is in Paris then he is in France, we are able to infer by the so-called *modus ponens* the assertion that John is in France. Other valid inferences that are made in language use are *practical*: their conclusion expresses a speech act with the world-to-words direction of fit. For example, from John's promise to bring a bottle of red or white wine, we are able to derive his promise to bring a bottle of wine.

Laws of preservation of illocutionary commitment

Many laws of illocutionary commitment which are due to strong implication also hold for the complex forces whose special components satisfy the corresponding success conditions. Thus:

$\models (A_\phi(A_p) \vartriangleright B_\phi(B_p) \wedge C_\zeta A_p \dashv C_\zeta B_p) \Rightarrow [C_\zeta] A_\phi(A_p) \vartriangleright [C_\zeta] B_\phi(B_p)$ whenever $\zeta = \theta$ or μ.

$\models (A_\phi(A_p) \vartriangleright B_\phi(B_p) \wedge \forall x_\tau (A_\psi x_\tau \Rightarrow \forall x_\iota (E(x_\tau A_p) x_\iota \dashv E(x_\tau B_p) x_\iota)$
$\Rightarrow [A_\psi] A_\phi(A_p) \vartriangleright [A_\psi] B_\phi(B_p)$

Thus to request help and protection is to request help, because the added polite mode of achievement is also distributive under conjunction.

A LAW OF FOUNDATION FOR STRONG ILLOCUTIONARY COMMITMENT

For any primitive IF-term A_ϕ other than $\dashv$, $\models s(A_\phi A_p) \Rightarrow$
$$\exists x_p(s(A_\phi x_p) \wedge \forall y_p(s(A_\phi y_p) \Rightarrow x_p \vdash y_p))$$

Thus, every assertion that a speaker makes in a context is made by way of a strong assertion whose content strongly implies the content of all other assertions made in that context. And similarly for all other non-expressive primitive forces.

COROLLARY 1. THERE IS A UNIQUE STRONGEST ILLOCUTIONARY ACT IN SUCCESSFUL UTTERANCES WITH A NON-EMPTY DIRECTION OF FIT.

For any primitive IF-term,
$$\models (\neg\emptyset A_\phi \wedge s(A_\phi A_p)) \Rightarrow \exists x_p(s(A_\phi x_p) \wedge \forall y_p(s(A_\phi y_p) \Leftrightarrow A_\phi x_p \rhd A_\phi y_p))$$

COROLLARY 2: A FINITENESS THEOREM

For any illocutionary force F with a non-empty direction of fit, there is only a finite number of speech acts of the form F(p) that a speaker can simultaneously perform in a context. This follows from the finiteness theorem for strong implication.

A LAW OF MINIMAL CONSISTENCY OF THE SPEAKER:
$$\models (\neg\emptyset(A_\phi) \wedge (A_p \vdash B_p)) \Rightarrow \neg\Diamond s(A_\phi(A_p \wedge \neg B_p))$$

Speakers cannot express two propositions which are strongly incompatible with the aim of establishing a correspondence between language and the world from the same direction of fit. Indeed, they know a priori that such linguistic attempts are necessarily condemned to failure. Apparent counter-examples of this law of minimal consistency are non-literal utterance where the speaker means something other than what he says.

COROLLARY: ANOTHER LAW OF ILLOCUTIONARY INCOMPATIBILITY:
$$\models (A_\phi \dashv \pi^k \wedge B_\phi \dashv \pi^n) \Rightarrow ((A_p \vdash \neg B_p) \Rightarrow (A_\phi A_p ><_s B_\phi \neg A_p)),$$
where n and k = 1, 2, or 4

Such speech acts with different directions of fit are incompatible because the responsibility for achieving the success of fit depends on the speaker in the three cases.

THE RATIONALITY OF THE SPEAKER IS NOT IDEAL.
$$\not\models (\uparrow(A_\phi) \vee \downarrow(A_\phi)) \Rightarrow (\neg\Diamond t(A_p) \Rightarrow \neg\Diamond s(A_\phi A_p))$$

The minimal consistency of speakers in their use and comprehension of language is of course weaker than perfect logical consistency. *Speakers can be logically inconsistent in their speech acts.* Thus, speakers can assert necessarily false propositions. They can also make promises that it is impossible to keep. However, in such cases, they do not know a priori in virtue of competence that their utterance is unsatisfiable.

THE SATISFACTION OF AN ILLOCUTIONARY ACT WITH THE WORLD-TO-WORDS DIRECTION OF FIT IMPLIES ITS SUCCESSFUL PERFORMANCE.

$$\models\ \downarrow(A_\phi) \Rightarrow (t(A_\phi A_p) \Rightarrow s(A_\phi A_p))$$

THE LAW OF THE TRUTH OF THE PROPOSITIONAL CONTENT OF A SUCCESSFUL DECLARATION:

$$\models\ \updownarrow(A_\phi) \Rightarrow (s(A_\phi A_p) \Rightarrow t(A_p))$$

By definition, a successful declaration constitutes the performance by the speaker of the course of action represented by its propositional content.

COROLLARY 1. ANY TYPE OF ILLOCUTIONARY ACT CAN BE PERFORMED BY WAY OF A DECLARATION:

$$\models\ (t(B_p) \looparrowleft s(A_\phi A_p)) \Rightarrow (\top B_p \rhd A_\phi A_p)$$

In performative utterances, speakers perform speech acts by way of declaring that they perform them. This is why performative sentences illocutionary entail all other types of sentences.

COROLLARY 2. ANY SUCCESSFUL DECLARATION IS ALSO SATISFIED.

COROLLARY 3. DECLARATIONS ARE SUCCESSFUL IF AND ONLY IF THEY ARE SATISFIED.

ANY DECLARATION CONTAINS AN ASSERTION: $\models\ \top \rhd \vdash$

A speaker who declares that a proposition is true makes that proposition true in virtue of his utterance by asserting that he performs the represented action.

DECLARATIONS ARE THE STRONGEST TYPE OF SPEECH ACT.

Because they have the double direction of fit, declarations are the strongest kind of illocutionary act. From a logical point of view, *all successful declarations are* eo ipso *true, satisfied, sincere and non-defective.* Thus, contrary to what is the case for other speech acts, declarations are self-*guaranteeing utterances.* First, the successful performance of declarations is sufficient to bring about success of fit between language and the world. This is why illocutionary acts of all types can be performed by declaration in performative utterances. But no other type of illocutionary act strongly commits the speaker to declarations. Consequently, the performative hypothesis is false according to illocutionary logic. A sentence is not synonymous with the corresponding performative sentence.

Because declarations are the strongest kind of speech act, it is a mistake to take them as paradigmatic for all illocutionary acts, just as it is a mistake to take performative sentences as paradigmatic forms of expression for illocutionary acts.

ANY ILLOCUTIONARY ACT STRONGLY COMMITS THE SPEAKER TO AN EXPRESSIVE ILLOCUTIONARY ACT.

$$\models\ [(A_\mu, A_\theta, A_\Sigma, A_\psi), A_\iota, \pi^k] \rhd [(A_\mu, A_\theta, A_\Sigma, A_\psi), A_\iota, \pi^5].$$

This law follows from the *neutrality* of the expressive illocutionary point. In the sense in which declarations are the strongest type of illocutionary acts, *expressives are the weakest illocutionary acts.* In the performance of any type of elementary illocutionary act of the form F(p), the speaker expresses propositional attitudes and consequently also performs an expressive illocutionary act. Thus, any type of illocutionary act strongly commits the speaker to expressives. Consequently, any sentence illocutionarily entails the corresponding exclamatory sentence. But the expressive type of illocutionary act does not commit the speaker to any other type. It is a mistake to think that expressives are paradigmatic speech acts.

5 Semantic minimalism and the Frege point

Huw Price

Speech act theory is one of the more lasting products of the linguistic movement in philosophy of the mid-twentieth century. Within philosophy itself the movement's products did not in general prove so durable. Particularly striking in this respect is the perceived fate of what was one of the most characteristic applications of the linguistic turn in philosophy, namely the view that many traditional philosophical problems are such as to yield to an understanding of the distinctive function of a particular part of language. Most typically, the crucial insight was held to be that despite appearances, the function of the part of language in question is not assertoric, or descriptive, and that the traditional problems arose at least in part from a failure to appreciate this point. Thus problems in moral philosophy were thought to yield to an appreciation that moral discourse is expressive rather than descriptive, problems in the philosophy of mind to an understanding of the distinctive role of psychological ascriptions, and so on. The philosophical journals of the 1950s are rich with views like these. (No general term for this approach seems to have become widely accepted at the time. I shall call it 'non-factualism', for what it denies, most characteristically, is the *fact-stating* role of language of a certain kind.)

At the time, many of these non-factualist endeavours drew on the new terminology of speech act theory, taking their lead at least in part from J.L. Austin. It is therefore somewhat ironic that when non-factualism came to be seen as discredited, one of the works responsible was Searle's *Speech Acts*.[1] Non-factualism was thus disowned by the movement from which, at least in part, it drew its inspiration. So it is that while speech act theory prospered outside philosophy, its early pretensions to application within philosophy were reviled or forgotten. Non-factualism was widely thought to have fallen victim to objections urged in the 1960s by Searle, and independently by Peter Geach (who took his inspiration from an argument of Frege's).

Philosophical demise is rarely complete or permanent, however, and non-factualism has been receiving renewed attention more recently, particularly in a relatively new application to the problem of linguistic and psychological content.[2] It would now be easy for a newcomer to fail to notice that for almost a generation the approach was commonly taken to be discredited. It therefore seems worth re-examining the supposedly fatal objection. After all, perhaps non-factualism really is dead, or as dead as a philosophical view can be, and its new devotees simply have not noticed. If not, then it would be nice to know how it managed to recover from what many took to be a mortal blow.

The paper thus begins with a brief reassessment of what I shall call *the Frege argument* (though I shall draw on the versions of the argument advanced by Geach and Searle). One possible outcome of this investigation would be a reaffirmation of the conclusions drawn by Geach and Searle, and thus a return to the status quo *circa* 1965 – perhaps an unexciting result, but a useful one, if the Frege objection succeeds, given non-factualism's current reluctance to lie down. The actual outcome is rather more interesting, however. For one thing the Frege argument turns out to be considerably less powerful than it has been taken to be, so that non-factualism remains a live option. Given the perceived importance of the Frege argument to the 'overthrow' of linguistic philosophy, this conclusion suggests that contemporary philosophy might do well to reconsider. There are many contemporary metaphysical debates which would have looked sterile and misconceived to the linguistic philosophers of the 1950s. Without the Frege argument to fall back on, it would be a brave – or perhaps foolhardy – philosopher who would dismiss out of hand the linguistic point of view.[3]

In the present paper, however, I want to emphasize a different benefit of re-examining the Frege argument. As we shall see, the issues thereby thrown open are ones of fundamental concern in the philosophy of language and the foundations of speech act theory. In hindsight I think it is clear that when speech act theory detached itself from philosophy in the 1960s, a cluster of central issues concerning the nature of assertion, judgement, description, and the like, were left largely unresolved. I hope to show that to re-examine the Frege argument is to reopen these issues in a particularly fruitful way.

The paper is in three main parts. In the first (sections 1 to 4) I argue that the Frege argument is far from conclusive. It imposes certain constraints on the non-factualist, but fails to show that these constraints cannot be satisfied. I shall mention work by some prominent non-factualists that went some way towards showing how their view might meet these constraints. The upshot seems to be that the worst that the non-factualist can be convicted of is a degree of complexity in linguistic theory that factualist views seem to avoid – and for all its unpleasantness, complexity is rarely a fatal complaint.

All the same, the desire to free non-factualism of this complexity motivates the second part of the paper (sections 5 to 7). This part draws on recent interest in what I here call minimal semantics, extending the terminology employed in discussions of so-called minimal theories of truth.[4]

Briefly, I suggest that non-factualists might (a) concede that moral claims (or whatever) are statements in some minimal sense, and use this concession to meet the requirements identified by the Frege argument in the same direct and simple way that is available to a factualist; but (b) reformulate their point about the character of moral claims in such a way that it does not conflict with the proposition that such claims are statements in the minimal sense. The move to a minimal semantics thus enables the non-factualist to sidestep the Frege argument.

I want to suggest that in the process we achieve a fresh and illuminating view of the relationship between truth-conditional semantics and the sort of pragmatic considerations about language often thought to be the proper concern of a theory of force, or speech act theory more generally. As reformulated non-factualism directs our attention to the function of particular parts of discourse. (This functional side of non-factualism is not new, of course; what is new is that it should be clearly divorced from a claim about the *semantic* status of the utterances in question.) The recognition that non-factualism need not be a semantic doctrine then enables us to regard functional pragmatics not as an addition tacked on to deal with the problems of force and tone, but as a complement to the theory of sense whose task is to explain how there come to be uses of language with senses of particular sort – how there come to be utterances with the sense of moral judgements, for example.

True, it is not clear that the reformulated doctrine should really be called non-factualism. As we shall see, it no longer involves the denial that the utterances of some disputed class are factual, or assertoric. Instead it treats these as relatively superficial and uninteresting linguistic categories, over-lying diversity of a different kind. It is this separation of semantic and functional categories which seems to me of most interest to speech act theory. It suggests for example that *assertion* is a very much less fundamental linguistic category than has usually been assumed. At best it is a kind of higher-order category, grouping together some very diverse linguistic activities.

All the same, the question arises as to what these diverse activities have in common, in virtue of which they all come to be part of this single higher-order category. In the third part of the paper (section 8) I conclude by drawing attention to this central issue, an issue which has tended to be overlooked in earlier work. I note that there is a sense in which the issue embodies some of the insights of the Frege argument, and hence that things are not quite so easy for my reconstituted non-factualist as they earlier appeared; but I also note that the issue is not one that the non-factualist's opponents can afford to shirk, so that the dialectical burden of the new issues is evenly spread.

1 THE FREGE–GEACH–SEARLE ARGUMENTS, AND SEARLE'S UNUSED LOOPHOLE

The Frege argument begins by observing that non-factualist accounts characteristically propose an interpretation of just those (*canonical*) sentences or utterances in which constructions of the relevant type – 'It is probable that . . .', 'It is good that . . .', 'It is true that . . .', or whatever – are not part of any clause other than a complete sentence. It is noted that there are many other (*subsidiary*) occurrences of such constructions, and argued that the proposed accounts are unable to deal with at least some of these new cases, though obliged to do so. As Geach says,

> Theories of non-descriptive performances regularly take into account only the use of a term 'P' to call something 'P'; the corroboration theory of truth, for example, considers only the use of 'true' to call a statement true, and the condemnation theory of 'bad' considers only the way it is used to call something bad; predications of 'true' and 'bad' in *if* or *then* clauses, or in the clauses of a disjunction, are just ignored.
>
> One could not write off such uses of the terms as calling for a different explanation from their use to call things true or bad; for that would mean that arguments of the pattern 'if *x* is true (if *w* is bad), then *p*; but *x* is true (*w* is bad); ergo *p*' contained a fallacy of equivocation, whereas in fact they are clearly valid.[5]

Searle's version of the argument is somewhat different, in that he admits a possibility which Geach's appeal to the validity of *modus ponens* would appear to exclude. Searle is objecting to what he calls 'the speech act analysis' of words such as 'good', 'true', 'know' and 'probably', the general form of which he takes to be: 'The word W is used to perform the speech act A.' Searle says that

> any analysis of the meaning of a word (or morpheme) must be consistent with the fact that the same word (or morpheme) can mean the same thing in all the grammatically different kinds of sentences in which it can occur.

For example,

> the word 'true' means or can mean the same thing in interrogatives, indicatives, conditionals, negations, disjunctions, optatives, etc.
>
> (Searle 1969: 137)

However, Searle recognizes that in order to meet this 'condition of adequacy', speech act analysts are

> not committed to the view that every literal utterance of W is a performance of A, but rather [may claim] that utterances which are not performances of the act have to be explained in terms of utterances which are.
>
> (Searle 1969: 138)

Searle thus appears to acknowledge that it need not be said that the contribution the clause makes to the meaning of a conditional in which it occurs as antecedent is identical to the meaning it has when used canonically; but only that the former contribution depends in a rule-governed way (the rule being associated with the conditional form) on the meaning the clause has in the latter case. If Geach's appeal to validity were successful, this view would seem untenable. The validity of *modus ponens* would depend on the meaning of such a clause being invariant between the two contexts.

Having admitted this possibility, however, Searle fails to take advantage of it. He rightly points out that

> the speech act analysts ... need to show ... only ... that literal utterances which are not performances of the act A stand in a relation to performances of A in a way which is purely a function of the way the sentences uttered stand in relation to the standard indicative sentences, in the utterance of which the act is performed.

But he takes this to mean that if such sentences 'are in the past tense, then the act is reported in the past; if they are hypothetical then the act is hypothesized, etc.' He then notes the obvious, namely that 'the speech act analysis of the ... words: "good", "true", "probable", etc. does not satisfy this condition.... "If this is good, then we ought to buy it" is not equivalent to "If I commend this, then we ought to buy it"; "This used to be good" is not equivalent to "I used to commend this"'; and so on. (Searle 1969: 138–9).

Although Searle himself does not canvas other ways in which the meaning of clauses such as 'It is good that p' in various contexts may be systematically related to their meaning when they stand alone, it is clear that if the general objection is to be answered the solution will lie in this direction. However, the argument from *modus ponens* claims to bar the way. Let us test its strength.

2 THE APPEAL TO *MODUS PONENS*

As Geach notes, this argument is due originally to Frege (Frege 1918b, 1960: 129–30), who uses it in arguing that a sentential negation operator cannot be construed as a sign of force; as an indication that a sentence, when uttered, has the force of a denial. Frege's argument is in two parts:

(Fr1)   He notes that a negated sentence may occur as the antecedent of a conditional, where it does not amount to a denial, and concludes that in such a case the negation contributes to the sense of (or thought expressed by) the antecedent.

(Fr2)   He infers from this that if we want to allow that a case of *modus ponens* involving such a conditional is valid, we shall have to allow that the negation does not mark a denial, even when the negated sentence concerned stands alone.

The general principle invoked in (Fr1) is something like this:

Embedded force exclusion (EFE)
Force modifiers cannot occur in embedded contexts.

We shall come back to this, but let us first consider (Fr2). Here the argument might seem to be that the validity of *modus ponens* depends on the meaning of the antecedent clause in the conditional premise being exactly the same as it is when the clause occurs alone (as in the categorical premise). It would follow that because (according to (Fr1)) the negative clause is not a denial in the former context, it is not a denial in the latter. But as Hare points out (Hare 1971: 87) the same argument would show that when the clause stands alone it does not have the force of an assertion; for it lacks this force when used as an antecedent.

A more charitable interpretation is therefore that the argument for (Fr2) depends on the following claim:

Sense identity (SI)
The inference

(1) If not-p then q; not-p; therefore q

is valid only if the second premise has the same sense (or expresses the same thought) as the antecedent of the conditional premise.

If we grant the conclusion of (Fr1) – i.e., that the negation operator has a sense-modifying role in determining the meaning of the conditional premise in (1) – then SI implies that its role in the second premise must also be to modify sense. Thus as (Fr2) claims, the negation operator does not modify force, even in canonical cases.

The function of the appeal to *modus ponens* is therefore to extend the conclusion of (Fr1) to canonical uses of the negation operator (and similarly for such things as modal and ethical operators, in Geach's case). But how is SI to be justified? Not, on the face of it, by Geach's remark that otherwise the inference would contain a fallacy of equivocation. Of course, there are fallacious arguments of the syntactic form 'if p then q; p; therefore q' in which the fallacy turns on the fact that p is used with different senses in each premise. However, to claim bluntly that any argument of this kind is fallacious is just to beg the question (given that both sides agree that (1) is valid). For both sides agree that this claim is incompatible with the view that the two occurrences of 'not-p' in (1) have different senses; but the disagreement is precisely as to which of these incompatible propositions must be given up.

In any case, the use Frege and Geach make of SI depends on the principle EFE. It is EFE which underpins the claim that in the antecedent of a conditional a negation operator modifies sense. But what are the grounds for accepting EFE? Apparently just the observation that in such a context no denial is being made. But this involves the very mistake we noted in the previous section, the loophole for avoiding which is recognized (if not adequately exploited) by Searle. In effect Searle recognizes that in order to make sense of an occurrence of a denial operator in an embedded context, it is not necessary to say that such a subsidiary use has exactly the meaning it has when it stands alone. It is enough that its contribution to the meaning of the containing context should depend on the fact that it does signal a denial, when used canonically. For then there is a clear reason for including a force indicator for denial in the subsidiary positions concerned: in order to show that the clause would have this force, if uttered alone.

We saw that Searle himself does not take advantage of this loophole. But so far we have found nothing in the argument from *modus ponens* that provides an obstacle to others doing so. On the contrary, the appeal to *modus ponens* has to this point depended on the assumption that no such loophole exists.

3 THE ATTRACTIONS OF UNIFORMITY

Frege and Geach do have another argument for SI, however, also appealing to *modus ponens*. Unlike the above argument, this one does not rely on the sub-argument (Fr1). Indeed it offers an independent argument for the conclusion of (Fr1) (i.e., that in the antecedent of a conditional the negation operator modifies sense). This argument begins by noting that we evidently do have identity of sense in

(2)   If p then q; p; therefore q (where p is not negated)

and moreover that this identity of sense is clearly crucial to the validity of the argument form. It then claims that if (1) is to exemplify the same form of inference – as in some sense it surely does – then identity of sense must play the same role. Uniformity seems to require that there be a common account of the conditional form, in the light of which identity of sense plays a constant role in guaranteeing validity. Thus this is an appeal not to a necessary condition for validity as such, but to the need for a uniform explanation of the validity of a class of inferences which evidently have a structural property in common.

Such theoretical uniformity is undoubtedly desirable, but is the only way to achieve it to treat (1) as a special case of (2)? Why not instead treat (1) and (2) as distinct subtypes of a single more general form of inference? It is not obvious that in that case the general criterion for validity would include the required identity of sense. There might rather be some more general condition, which reduced to identity of sense in the special case of (2). In the next section I outline an account of this kind.

4 CONDITIONALS FOR NON-FACTUALISTS

In summary then, the task of a non-factualist who wishes to evade the Frege argument seems to be twofold: first, to find a legitimate account of the significance of a force-modifying construction in a subsidiary clause; and second, to produce a general account of the linguistic function of the 'if ... then ...' construction, such as to enable valid arguments to contain such force modifiers in (at least) the antecedent position. The latter project is best tackled first, for the significance of a subsidiary force modifier will inevitably depend on the nature of the subsidiary context in question. We should not expect a single account, applicable to any and every subsidiary context. The individual accounts will of course have something in common, but this may be nothing more than a common reference to the meaning that the force modifier in question has in a canonical context.

Now in arguing that the utterances of some disputed class are not genuine assertions, non-factualists commonly rely on a distinction between beliefs and others sorts of propositional attitude. With this psychological distinction assumed in place, the non-factualist argues first, that we may characterize assertion as the linguistic expression of belief; and second, that the disputed utterances express some other sort of propositional attitude. Thus Frege's opponent might tell us that negated sentences express disbeliefs rather than beliefs, the emotivist tells us that moral judgements express evaluative attitudes, the probabilistic subjectivist tells us that utterances of the form 'It is probable that p' express the speaker's high degree of confidence that p, and so on.

What concerns us here is not whether this is an adequate route to non-factualism in general, but the fact that by characterizing force in terms of an associated type of propositional attitude, it provides the means to escape the Frege objection. The strategy requires that indicative conditionals themselves be treated non-assertorically. A sincere utterance of 'If p then q' will be said to indicate that a speaker possesses what may be called an 'inferential disposition' – a mental state such that if the speaker were to adopt the mental attitude associated with the utterance 'p', she would be led to adopt the mental attitude associated with 'q'. For example the utterance 'If it is not snowing, then Boris has gone swimming' will be said to express a disposition to move from a state of disbelief that it is snowing, to a belief that Boris has gone swimming.

This suggestion provides a clear sense in which the force-modifying expression makes the same contribution to a canonical utterance, as to a conditional utterance in which it occurs in the antecedent or consequent. In each case it marks the association of the meaning of the whole utterance with a certain kind of propositional attitude: a disbelief, a degree of confidence, an evaluative attitude, or whatever. Other features of the particular occurrence of the expression in question determine first which particular propositional attitude of the given type is involved – its content, in other words – and second, how this propositional attitude stands in relation to the mental state associated with the utterance as a whole. For example in the canonical case for negation (an utterance of the form 'Not-p') the fact that negation is the outermost operator indicates that the mental state associated with the utterance as a whole is just disbelief itself. While in the conditional case, the occurrence of the expression in (say) the antecedent position indicates that possession of the state of disbelief in question is the antecedent condition of the inferential disposition associated with the conditional. (This process of determination may be iterated, if the conditional itself occurs as a component of some larger utterance.)

It is important to distinguish this suggestion from the claim that a conditional *reports* a speaker's possession of such an inferential disposition. If that were so, a conditional utterance would be an assertion about its speaker's state of mind, and would be true or false according to whether the speaker concerned actually had such an inferential disposition. However, the proposal is intended to explain the meaning of the conditional in terms not of its *truth conditions*, but its *subjective assertibility conditions* – i.e., in terms of the state of the speaker that normally licenses its correct use. (The term subjective assertibility condition is being used in the sense involved in saying that the normal condition for the correct use of a statement p is that one believes that p. To say this is not to say that in asserting p one asserts that one believes that p.[6])

The above proposal is similar to, though perhaps a little more psychologically explicit than, one made by Hare in answer to the Frege objection. Hare puts the common central insight rather nicely, saying that we know the meaning of the conditional 'if we know how to do modus ponens'. In other words, the crucial thing is that we are in a position to affirm 'If p then q' 'if we know that if we are in a position to affirm [p], we can go on to affirm [q]' (Hare 1971: 87). Thus to say 'If not-p then q' is to indicate (though not to say) that one's state of mind is such that if one were to deny that p, one would affirm (or be prepared to affirm) that q. The correctness of the inference (1) thus amounts to the fact that (1) is the very inference a readiness to make which is signalled by the conditional premise; and of course the same may be said about (2). In both cases the correctness of the inference is thus analytic: the standard use of the conditional is just such as to license *modus ponens*. Moreover, the role of the force-modifying negation operator in the antecedent of the conditional is now clear. It helps to specify the nature of the circumstances in which the speaker indicates that she would be prepared to affirm the consequent – namely those circumstances in which she would be prepared to deny that p.

In Hare's form or mine, this account is of course only a beginning. Much work would need to be done to show that the notion of an inferential disposition leads to a satisfactory account of ordinary language indicative conditionals, and of simple logical inferences in which they occur. And even if the account works for conditionals, it needs to be extended to the many other subsidiary contexts in which (what the non-factualist regards as) force-modifying operators may occur. For each such context we need a principle which links the general linguistic function of the context itself to the working hypothesis about operators in question, namely that their independent use is to signal a non-assertoric force of some kind. Even as it stands, however, the suggested account of conditionals does serve to establish a crucial general point. To paraphrase Hare (who is concerned with the moral case, of course, see Hare 1971: 93):

> The fact that sentences containing negation cannot be described without qualification as assertions, but have to be explained in terms of the more complex speech act of denial, is no bar to the appearance of negation in contexts where denial is not taking place, provided that the relation of these contexts to those in which it is taking place can be explained.

Hare's is not the only attempt in the literature to offer an account of conditionals with non-assertoric antecedents and consequents. I have already mentioned that of Michael Dummett (see note 6). Simon Blackburn also addresses the problem, again with the intention of defending a form of ethical non-factualism against the Frege argument. His suggestion is that

(3) If it is good that p then it is good that q

is itself an evaluative remark: roughly, it expresses a speaker's approval of the disposition (or as Blackburn calls it the 'moral sensibility') to approve of q, given that one approves of p.[7] Like Hare's theory and mine, this account has the crucial feature that it makes the significance of an embedded force modifier *dependent on* but not *identical to* the significance it has in a canonical context. That said, however, it seems to me that Blackburn's account is less plausible than the approach sketched above. It has the disadvantage that it does not give us a single unified account of conditional utterances, from which the required account of conditionals with embedded moral clauses falls out as a special case – conditionals in general are not expressions of moral sensibility. I suspect that Blackburn has confused two notions of endorsement, the first the semantic endorsement we give to any proposition when we assent to it, and the second the peculiarly moral endorsement we give to an act or state of affairs of which we approve. It is arguable that assent always involves an evaluative or normative element. To assent to a proposition is to take it to be right, correct, true. But this simply means that assent to an ethical proposition involves two sorts of evaluative attitude. To agree that war is evil is to take the proposition 'War is evil' to be correct, to endorse it in that sense; and it is also to express one's disapproval of war. With these notions of endorsement kept distinct, however, there seems no reason to say that accepting a moral conditional necessarily involves anything more than semantic endorsement. It need not itself express a moral attitude, even though it may indicate a certain structure of dependencies between the speaker's moral and non-moral attitudes. 'If all war is evil then the Gulf War was evil' is merely a logical truth.[8]

5 THE MINIMAL TURN

Thus it seems that the Frege argument is less powerful than it appeared to be. It certainly is not watertight, and considerable work has been done towards showing how its weaknesses may be exploited. All the same, there does seem to be at least one charge that will survive these ingenious attempts to evade the Frege argument. Even if they succeed, it will be at the cost of considerable theoretical complexity. It is doubtful whether this counts as an argument against the views that require this expenditure, but it is a valid expression of regret – regret that we cannot have the simplicity of the standard account. If only we could justly retain familiar platitudes about validity, truth-functional connectives, and the like, without cutting ourselves off from the insights of non-factualism.

Well, perhaps we may. An optimistic hint is to be found in recent interest in minimalist notions of truth. At one point in his recent book on minimal theories of truth, Paul Horwich notes that such a notion of truth is not incompatible with such meta-ethical positions as emotivism, provided of course that the emotivist does not insist on trying to characterize her view of moral judgements in terms of truth; for in this case the minimal notion will not bear the weight.[9]

In the present case, this suggests that we might extend the minimalist notion of truth to a minimalist notion of statementhood. A (minimal) statement will simply be any utterance of which it makes sense to say that it is (minimally) true – in other words, in effect, any sentence which provides a well-formed substitution into the context 'It is true that p'. Now surely emotivists and other non-factualists cannot have been denying that certain classes of indicative sentences are statements in this minimal syntactic sense; they had some stronger thesis in mind (albeit perhaps a thesis they would have couched in terms of a stronger notion of truth). So there is evidently room for a simple compromise in response to the Frege argument. If the Fregean will concede that the ordinary platitudes about validity, truth-functional connectives and the like may appeal to nothing more than a minimal notion of truth, then the non-factualist will be entitled to endorse these platitudes at face value, and will not have to embark on the evasive manoeuvres whose complexity gave us cause for regret.

Both sides may resist this compromise on the grounds that they find the minimal notions of truth and statementhood unattractive. As noted, the non-factualist may want to characterize her position in terms of a stronger notion of truth; while the Fregean may feel that the minimal notion is inadequate for the purposes of logical and semantic theory, including that of accounting for the validity of inferences such as *modus ponens*. I do not want to try to address these concerns directly in this paper.[10] Instead I want to sketch the form that non-factualism might take if it endorses this compromise, and thus to show indirectly that the compromise is one that it might happily live with. I also want to indicate some of the character of the minimalist semantic theory which would accompany the compromise – in particular, to indicate some respects in which it differs from orthodox Fregean semantics.

6 FACTS AND LINGUISTIC FUNCTIONS

Suppose that we accept that moral judgements are minimally descriptive, meaning by this that they can be said to be minimally true and false. How might we then formulate a non-factualist doctrine concerning such judgements?

We might appeal to psychology, saying that moral claims do not express beliefs, but rather evaluative attitudes. The immediate trouble with this is that our minimal notion of statementhood will bring with it a minimal notion of belief: a minimal belief will be simply the sort of propositional attitude expressed in a minimal statement. So we need a substantial belief–evaluative attitude distinction. It would be better to talk of a special kind of belief, here using belief in its minimal sense. The resulting position would then amount to the psychological equivalent of the following view.

Let us begin with the platitude that language serves many different functions. It is easy to agree on this, but more difficult to decide how to carve things up – what the various functions of language actually are, or indeed what is meant by a function in this context. It is very tempting to think that one of the main functions of language, perhaps indeed the primary one, is that of description, or the making of factual claims. I want to urge that we resist this temptation, and instead regard this particular functional category as an artificial one, imposed by the structure of language itself. I want to suggest that its apparent unity and cohesiveness is superficial, and overlies considerable diversity. To use an analogy I have appealed to elsewhere, I want to suggest that the functional category of description is like that of manual tasks. What manual functions have in common is essentially that they are all performed or capable of being performed by hand – from a biological point of view the right thing to say is not that the hand has evolved to perform tasks of a single functional category, but that the functional category consists of a diverse assortment of tasks which happen to be thrown together in virtue of the fact that all are or can be performed by that accident of evolution, the human hand.

I shall use the term 'minimal description' for any utterance which is capable of being minimally true or false. The suggestion is thus that within the class of minimal descriptions, we may find subclasses of utterances serving a range of different linguistic functions. (These subclasses will overlap, of course, when subsentential constructions serving different functions are combined in a single utterance.)

Let us now suppose that one of the functions served by some minimal descriptions is that typified by ordinary and (perhaps more contentiously) scientific description of the physical world. Crudely, we might say that the function of this part of language is to signal the presence of certain conditions in the physical environment of a speaker. There would be a number of problems if we tried to make this more precise. For one thing, it would be hard to resist the slide into the semantic language of facts, states of affairs, and so on, which would soon lead us back to the very position from which we are attempting to distance ourselves, namely that the function concerned is that of minimal descriptions as a whole. For another thing, the limits of the 'physical' are ill-defined in a number of relevant ways. Do we count such things as dispositions, for example, or does their modal character already exclude them?

Precision will not be critical, however. The important thing is that the non-factualist should be able to mark some distinction between the function of (say) moral discourse, on the one hand, and the function or cluster of functions of at least a significant part of non-moral discourse, on the other. It will simplify things to assume that there is a single well-defined linguistic task with respect to which this contrast may be drawn – let us call it the task of physical signalling, or natural description – but the thesis could quite well be formulated in more general terms.

Given this simplifying assumption, we thus have a distinction between the semantic (or perhaps better, syntactic) notion of minimal description, and the functional notion of natural description (or physical signalling). My suggestion is then that the non-factualists' central thesis may be thought of as the claim that in certain cases we systematically confuse minimal descriptions for natural descriptions. Moral judgements (or whatever) are minimal descriptions, but are not natural descriptions. Rather they serve some quite distinct linguistic function.

To what extent is this suggestion compatible with the sorts of things that non-factualists typically say? In one sense an emphasis on misconstrual of linguistic function is a core component of any non-factualist thesis. Before all else, non-factualism is the doctrine that utterances of a certain kind are systematically misconstrued (with significant philosophical consequences). However, the functional point is usually put in terms of semantic categories – a fact-stating–non-fact-stating distinction, or something of the kind. In other words the relevant functional divide is thought of in semantic terms. But on the present account the non-factualist's point becomes purely functional, the semantics on both sides of the distinction being agreed to be of the minimal sort. However, it seems to me that this shift makes surprisingly little difference to the philosophical force of the non-factualist move – the relevant philosophical consequences are much the same. A naturalistic reduction of moral properties is ruled inappropriate for the standard reason, for example (namely that it misconstrues the linguistic role of moral judgement).

Let us see how this goes in a little more detail. Consider emotivism. The emotivist typically says that moral claims express evaluative attitudes rather than beliefs. This is compatible with the suggested gloss so long as we make a distinction between minimal belief and natural belief, paralleling that between minimal description and natural description (physical signalling). For then the emotivist may be seen as making the point that moral claims express evaluative attitudes, and that although these are (of course) minimal beliefs, they are not natural beliefs. (Their function does not lie in matching a subject's mental state to states of the physical environment, as we might put it.) This claim will do the usual work of defusing philosophical concerns about the nature of moral facts. The question as to the real nature of a state of affairs referred to by a description is one that may properly be raised in naturalistic terms if the description concerned is a natural description – in this case it is a matter which may be investigated in scientific terms. But if all we have is a minimal description (or indeed if we are considering a natural description from the minimal semantic standpoint), then such a question involves a kind of category mistake. The only possible answers are the sorts of platitudes associated with the minimal notion of truth.

Let me mention two concerns to which this proposal might give rise. One is that on this view there would seem to be no difference between nonfactualism about moral discourse and a certain form of moral realism, namely the view that although there are moral facts and states of affairs, these are not part of the natural world, and are not reducible to natural or physical facts. (In a similar way, the objection would be that non-factualism about psychological ascriptions could not be distinguished from certain forms of dualism.) I think that this is a very important objection, requiring much more attention to do it justice than I can give it here. Briefly, my view is that the objection tends to backfire, in the sense that its effect is to undermine the credentials of such non-reductive realisms. Against a background of minimal semantics, I think that these positions become impossible to distinguish from the (Wittgensteinian?) form of pluralism which embraces the possibility that language comprises a multiplicity of different kinds of discourse. True, non-factualism is also drawn in this direction, but I think it fares rather better, being able to cash its concern with the different degrees of objectivity of different discourses in other terms.[11]

The second concern is more closely related to the issues with which we began. Non-factualism is often characterized in terms of the neo-Fregean conception of the structure of a theory of meaning. That is, the nonfactualist can often be represented as claiming that a certain sentential construction is mistakenly thought to modify the sense of a sentence in which it appears, whereas in fact it modifies the force. The clearest example is again provided by the denial interpretation of sentential negation, which

Frege himself was attacking in his original presentation of the Frege point.[12] What happens to this appealing characterization of non-factualism, if non-factualism is presented in the way I have suggested? This question deserves a section to itself.

7 SENSE, FORCE AND FUNCTION IN MINIMAL SEMANTICS

The above concern may be focused by the following train of thought. Advocates of minimal truth have emphasized its affinity with Tarskian truth theories, and the truth-theoretic approach to a theory of meaning. (Conversely, the 'minimalism' of the truth-theoretic notion of truth had already been emphasized by writers such as McDowell.[13]) But does not this mean[14] that if non-factualists endorse minimal truth they become factualists? In the resulting theory of meaning utterances of the form 'Not-p' have assertoric force, for example.

The non-factualist's response must be to accept the conclusion but to deny that it has the significance the objector is claiming for it. The crucial point is that on the minimal interpretation the conclusion is not incompatible with the non-factualist's positive theses about the significance of (here) negation. For the non-factualist about negation need not renounce the view that its primary role in language is to provide a universal means of indicating that one is dissenting from some particular proposition; or to put it psychologically, the view that negation is associated with the expression of disbelief. It is just that the non-factualist also now remarks that this activity of denial is the sort of linguistic activity which fruitfully comes to be couched in terms of the minimal notion of truth; and thus becomes an assertion, in the minimal semantic sense.

It is worth noting in passing that this opens the way to a considerably more plausible view of negation than is available to the opposition. In accepting Frege's criticism of the denial interpretation of negation, Geach appreciates that it commits him to the view that disbelief must be thought of as 'belief that not'. He says that

> believing, like seeing, has no polar opposite. . . . The distinction of 'pro' and 'contra', of favourable and unfavourable attitude, has its place only in the realm of appetite, will, and passion, not in that of belief; this shows the error in treating religious beliefs as some sort of favourable attitude toward something.

(Geach 1965: 455)

Setting aside Geach's passing defence of religious factualism, let us consider the effect of this position on our understanding of the meaning of negation. All sides will agree that p and not-p are not jointly acceptable, at least in the sense that there would normally be some serious mistake involved in assenting to both. How is the Fregean to account for this striking feature of negation? The obvious suggestion might seem to be that it results from the fact that in virtue of the truth-functional analysis of negation, p and not-p cannot both be true: if p is true then not-p is not true, and vice versa. As it stands this gets us no further, however, for the original issue simply re-emerges with respect to the pair 'p is true' and 'p is not true' (or 'Not (p is true)'). It might seem to be an improvement to note that if p is true then not-p is false, but this simply avoids one difficulty at the expense of another. It now needs to be explained what it is about truth and falsity in virtue of which one would be ill advised to assent to a pair of propositions so related. It is no use saying simply that in virtue of their opposite truth values the two sentences in question are 'incompatible' or 'inconsistent', for then the question will be why incompatibility itself matters; why the rational speaker should take pains to avoid it, among the utterances to which she assents.

The moral of all this is that the notion of incompatibility involves an intrinsic bipolarity: it takes two to tango exactly out of step, so to speak, and these two must fail to hit it off in a very special way. At some point in the Mind–Language–World triangle, this incompatibility must make its appearance. Philosophers who are sufficiently thick-skinned may be inclined to accept a primitive bipolarity at some point on the Language-to-World side of the triangle; perhaps a primitive opposition between truth and falsity, or a primitive exclusion relation between negative and positive facts. In either case they then have the task of relating this piece of metaphysics to psychological and linguistic practice. In effect, they have to explain how speakers become aware of this relation of incompatibility that obtains in the world, link it to their understanding of negation, and hence display the appropriate caution in avoiding judgements of the form 'p and not-p'.

Things are much simpler if we start at the psychological corner. We do not need negative facts or a mysterious primitive opposition between truth and falsity, but merely an appreciation of the situation we face as creatures whose behaviour is determined, in part, by what we may loosely call commitments – changeable behavioural dispositions of various kinds. The premise in the background here is a very simple one: if a creature is to meet the future with anything more than the tools it was born with, it needs the ability to prepare itself in the light of past experience. Plausibly, it is a feature of any reasonably complex system of behavioural dispositions of this kind that the states concerned may conflict, in the sense that they move their bearer in different behavioural directions. To avoid behavioural chaos, any creature capable of such commitments thus needs to be able to remove commitments from its current store, as well adding new ones. In particular, it needs to be able to spot conflicts before they are manifest in behaviour, and to adjust its commitments accordingly. It needs to be able to *reject* one commitment in the light of another.

This act of rejection is functionally distinct from the simpler act of endorsement (the act of adding a commitment to one's current store). More importantly, its functional relationship to the simpler act embodies the incompatibility we were looking for. (The impossibility of simultaneously rejecting and endorsing a given commitment is much like that of entering and leaving a room at one and the same time.) It follows that if negation is explained as initially a sign of denial, and denial as the linguistic expression of rejection, then we shall have some prospect of explaining just what goes wrong with an attempt to endorse both p and not-p.

In sum, we may say in answer to Geach that although strictly speaking he is right to say that belief is not bipolar, in that we can make sense of commitment without the possibility of its polar opposite, a consideration of the functional role of belief makes it plain that the ability to reject commitments is crucial to all but the simplest believers. In order to be useful, judgement must thus become bipolar – commitments must be rejected as well as endorsed – at a very early stage. And in this we have the beginnings of an explanation of a fact about language that otherwise remains primitive and mysterious, namely the incompatibility of an assertion and its negation – an explanation which turns on the hypothesis that the primary role of negation is to indicate denial, or to express disbelief.[15]

The suggestion is that negation thus begins life as a force modifier, indicating a linguistic move of a different pragmatic significance – a different functional role – to anything in the language so far. Once incorporated, however, utterances with this new significance are appropriately subject to the same operations as those of the old. If this suggestion seems puzzling, the following analogy may be helpful. Negative integers are initially introduced via a quite new operator, which is applied to positive integers to yield mathematical entities of a new kind – entities which are not numbers in the previously recognized sense. The existing operations (addition etc.) extend in a natural way to these new entities, however, with the result that they too come to be thought of as numbers. Adopting the symbolic convention that symbols referring to numbers are of the form '[...]', the ordinary expression '−2' may therefore be parsed more explicitly either as '−[2]' or as '[−2]', depending on whether we have decided to treat the products of the operation denoted by the minus sign as themselves comprising numbers. There is no single correct parsing here, merely alternative ways of representing the same thing. The only substantial question is why it is that −[2] is the sort of thing that may be regarded as a number, in some natural extension of the previous usage – to which the answer lies in the availability of natural extensions of the arithmetical operations to the members of the broader class. (Is there a corresponding question in the semantic case? We shall see below that there is.)

In the case of negation the upshot is that we do not have to make a choice between the view that negation indicates denial (or expresses disbelief) and the view that it indicates an assertion with negative content (or expresses such a belief). We may say both things, so long as we are dealing with a suitably minimal notion of belief. Disbelief or dissent comes first, for it is such a notion, cashed in functional terms, that accounts for the presence and utility of negation in the first place. But given that this expression of disbelief takes the minimal assertoric form, we may think of it as the expression of belief.

Putting it in Fregean terms, we might say that the sense–force boundary is not unique – we may have two (or more) ways to parse a given utterance. 'Not-p' may be thought of both as a denial of the proposition that p and as an assertion of the proposition that not-p. The pragmatic account of the function of denial is not a component of a theory of meaning separate from the theory of sense, but a sub-theory, whose task is to explain how there come to be sentences with senses of a particular sort – how there come to be sentences with the sense of negative judgements, for example.

The two parsings engage with two different aspects of a theory of meaning. The platitude that to know the meaning of a sentence is to know the conditions for its correct use has two importantly different readings (not always properly distinguished). It may be taken to refer to what I earlier called subjective assertibility conditions, so that it amounts to the claim

(4) To know the meaning of 'It is snowing' is to know that it is normally appropriate to say 'It is snowing' only when one believes that it is snowing.

Or it may refer to truth conditions, so that the claim is that it is correct to say 'It is snowing' if, and only if, it is snowing; or, in the more familiar form, that

(5) 'It is snowing' is true iff it is snowing.

These claims are not incompatible, of course, and knowledge of meaning surely involves knowledge of both kinds. (5) has the form we expect of the theorems of a content-specifying truth theory – a systematic specification of the meanings of the sentences of an object language by means of sentences in the home language. As has often been emphasized, this enterprise needs only a thin notion of truth. It therefore applies uniformly to all minimally descriptive parts of the object language.

Principle (4) on the other hand has the resources to cope with the functional perspective, which is crucial to the proposed reformulation of non-factualism. We may say for example that

(6) To know the correct use of 'Not-p' is to know that it is normally appropriate to say 'Not-p' only when one *disbelieves* that p.

Note that this is not incompatible with the following instance of (4):

(7) To know the meaning of 'Not-p' is to know that it is normally appropriate to say 'Not-p' only when one believes that not-p.

Interpreted in terms of minimal belief, (4) is true of all minimal descriptions. But it is (6) which captures what is distinctive about utterances of the form 'Not-p'.

In summary, then, the proposed reformulation of non-factualism encounters no special problems with respect to the goals of a theory of meaning. To the extent that such goals are met by a content-specifying truth theory, the reformulated view coincides with the standard account; while to the extent that such a truth theory needs to be supplemented by theses of the form of (4), this form is flexible enough to accommodate the functional perspective adopted by the reformulated view.

8 CONCLUSION: EXPLAINING ASSERTION

At the beginning of the paper I suggested that the interest in a re-examination of the Frege argument lay not simply in its immediate bearing on the viability of non-factualist approaches to various philosophical topics, but also in the fresh perspective it promised to provide on some neglected issues in the philosophy of language and speech act theory. As we shall see, the latter benefit depends in part on an important qualification concerning the former. The path for non-factualism is not quite as smooth as the above account might suggest; and in its bumps lie the real nuggets for those interested more in language itself than in its philosophical applications.

To recap, I have suggested that non-factualism is best served by a strategic retreat, followed by an advance on new grounds. Non-factualists should concede that they put their view in the wrong way – namely, in semantic terms. What they should have said was that the mistake they opposed was that of reading substantial metaphysical conclusions into semantics. Conceding semantics is no significant loss, for the semantic ice is really too thin to support either party. While the non-factualists' intuitions concerning the distinctive role of (say) moral discourse are best cast in functional rather than semantic terms.

As noted earlier, there is an issue as to whether the resulting position should really be called 'non-factualism'. Non-factualists may be well advised to surrender their banner, as well as their untenable semantic position. In one sense this is a relatively insignificant change. The view retains the resources to combat many of the non-factualist's traditional opponents. In the moral case, for example, it remains opposed not only to the metaphysical realists who would populate the world with mysterious moral facts and properties, but also to those who in fleeing this metaphysical nightmare, turn in preference to eliminativism or naturalistic reductionism. Non-factualists always stood opposed to all these choices, and may continue to do so under this new banner.

All the same, there are some respects in which orthodox non-factualists may be discomforted by the new arrangements. Non-factualists are accustomed to riding with anti-realists, even if in some cases uncomfortably so. Under the new scheme their natural allies are realists, albeit of a non-metaphysical sort. Reconstituted non-factualists will find themselves sympathetic with the minimalist realism of writers such as Wittgenstein, Davidson and Rorty (although as I point out in Price 1992, the reconstituted view improves on these minimalist accounts in one crucial respect, namely that it directs our attention to the issue as to what different parts of language are *for*).

The contemporary writer whose views are closest to those of my reconstituted non-factualist is perhaps Simon Blackburn. Blackburn begins with the Humean idea that we project our attitudes and prejudices on to the world, and so see it as populated by seeming facts of our own construction. He then goes on to argue that such a non-factualist can explain our conversing as if there really were such facts – in other words, that the Humean 'projectivist' is entitled to a notion of truth, and to the other trappings of a realist linguistic practice. Thus projectivism supports 'quasi-realism', as Blackburn calls it.[16] On this view moral discourse (or whatever) is not really factual, but has – and is entitled to – the trappings of factuality.

One aspect of these trappings is the ability to be usefully embedded in conditional contexts, and as we noted in section 4, Blackburn has offered an account of what moral statements are doing in such contexts. We saw that in appealing to second-order evaluative judgements, Blackburn's account could be criticized for absorbing too much of the general character of the conditional form into peculiarities of the moral case. Viewed in the light of our appeal to minimal semantics in answer to the Frege point, Blackburn's approach may also seem unnecessarily complicated. In defence of Blackburn, however, it should be conceded that the quasi-realist programme embodies an insight which is in danger of getting lost in the rush to embrace minimal semantics. Not all linguistic functions are such as to be usefully cast in terms of truth and falsity, however minimally these are conceived. Someone who wants to be pluralist about underlying linguistic functions thus owes us an account of what the truth-bearing form achieves in language, and hence an explanation, case-by-case, as to why various disparate functions should invoke it. In so far as conditionals are associated with the truth-bearing form, for example, we need to be told how the general function of the conditional serves the specific purposes of moral discourse, modal discourse, or whatever.

This may sound like the difficult case-by-case work we tried to avoid in invoking minimal semantics. Have we therefore advanced at all by means of this long detour? It seems to me that from the non-factualist's point of view the situation has improved in one crucial respect: the question as to the general function of the truth-bearing form of language has now been raised as an issue that all sides need to address. Previously, in couching their views in semantic terms, the non-factualists effectively conceded to their opponent the latter's right to an unexamined notion of the genuinely factual (or truth-bearing) use of language. The explanatory onus thus lay almost entirely on the non-factualists' side. The new approach distributes the burden much more fairly. True, the non-factualists' opponents may not have *noticed* that there is a general question to be raised concerning the role of truth-bearing constructions in language; but this is hardly a point against non-factualism. In effect, the point is that the complexity which bothered us at the end of section 4 is not a burden for non-factualism alone. The appeal to semantic minimalism does not evade this complexity, for the difficult explanatory issues remain; but it does ensure that the burden is properly spread, and that all sides take their fair share of the load.

It is here that we find the promised theoretical dividend. In responding to the Frege point in the above terms, the non-factualist draws our attention to the existence of a degree of structural complexity in language that we otherwise might have little reason to notice. Our attention is drawn to the possibility that the apparent uniformity of assertoric or declarative discourse may well mask a multiplicity of different functions. More important-antly still, this model of common form over diverse functions raises the issue as to what the common form is for – what it *does* in the service of these diverse functions. Until the non-factualist pressed a case for diversity, we had little reason not to be satisfied with a very simplistic conception of assertoric discourse – roughly, the view that it serves to make descriptive claims, to 'state the facts' as the speaker believes (or claims to believe) them to be. There are other formulations of this conception, of course, but they all take for granted that what is being at least gestured at is a single reasonably coherent linguistic function. The suggested defence of non-factualism gives us reason to question this assumption. The reconstituted non-factualist will argue that the usual formulations have little or no explanatory value, but simply rehash the same bundle of superficial idioms: 'fact', 'truth', 'reference', 'statement', 'belief', and the rest. A genuinely illuminating account would be one which explained the existence of these concepts and idioms (or at least those of them which are in ordinary use) in terms of their contribution to the functions of language more basically construed. The new non-factualist points out that there is an important sense in which such an account need not be monistic – the same tool may do many jobs.

To conclude, the most central issue to which the above considerations direct our attention seems to me to be this one: *what does assertoric discourse do for us?* It is possible to distinguish a number of sub-issues here. What are the concepts of truth and falsity for? (What function do they serve in the lives of a linguistic community?) What is the significance of the linguistic constructions that apparently depend on truth – conditionals, for example? Again, how does it help us to have them? And is there a category of genuine judgements, as opposed to commitments more generally?[17]

In order to address these issues, it is necessary for us to take a detached explanatory stance towards our own linguistic practice. We need to step back from our familiar concepts and practices in order to be able to see the broader picture, and hence to discern the role that the concepts and practices concerned play in our lives. To a degree this detached perspective comes easily to non-factualists, who are accustomed to arguing that language is misleading at close range. It should also come easily to speech act theorists, for they too are used to dissecting out the hidden functions of language. However, the main point I want to urge is that by and large, neither group has stepped back far enough. Both camps have tended to regard the linguistic categories of assertion, description and the like as part of the bedrock – as a firm foundation on which other work may rest. Hence they have failed to see the importance of subjecting these categories them-selves to explanatory scrutiny. In my view the great theoretical significance of the Frege point is that it directs our attention to these long neglected issues.[18]

NOTES

1   Searle 1969. Searle had earlier presented the argument in question in Searle 1962.
2   See for example Kripke 1982, and Boghossian 1990.
3   For more on these themes see Price 1992.
4   I first heard the term 'minimal truth' from Crispin Wright, who uses it in Wright 1993; it is used in a rather different sense by Horwich (1990). Roughly, Wright means by minimal truth the weakest notion of truth compatible with realism about an area of discourse. He takes this notion to encompass both the dis-quotational and normative aspects of truth, and argues that some but not all areas of discourse employ stronger notions of truth. Horwich on the other hand uses the term more or less as a synonym for the disquotational theory, and devotes his book to arguing that we do not need any stronger notion. For the purposes of this paper it will not matter whether the minimal theory is thought as embodying normativity as well as disquotation (though elsewhere I have sided with Wright in arguing that disquotation does not guarantee normativity, which therefore needs to be accounted for separately; see Price 1988: part II).
5   Geach 1960: 223. The argument is repeated in Geach 1965.
6   For more on this important and often overlooked distinction see for example Hare 1976 and Price 1986. On a related point, Michael Dummett once suggested that 'If p then q' could accommodate non-assertoric antecedents if interpreted along the lines of 'If I were to assent (or commit myself) to p, I would commit myself to q' (see Dummett 1973: 351–4; also Wright 1988: 31–3). However, precisely because it confuses a plausible subjective assertibility condition for a conditional with the *content* of the claim concerned, it is vulner-able to the objection that in saying 'If p then q' one is not (necessarily) speaking about oneself. In the context of a consideration of a non-factualist interpret-ation of probability, this objection to Dummett's proposal was raised by Cohen (1977: 29, n. 19), who notes that if Dummett's reading is to apply to the prob-ability case, there should be a use for a construction

   meaning 'If I were to assert (agree) guardedly that *A*, then I should assert (agree) that *B*.' But that would not be a use paraphrasable by 'If it is probable that *A*, then *B*.' For though it happens to be true that if I were to assert (agree) guardedly that it will be cloudy this afternoon I should also assert (agree) that I am excessively cautious in my weather predictions, it is not true that if clouds are probable then I am excessively cautious.

On the view described above, however, the conditional 'If I were to assert guardedly that A, then I should assert that B' is associated with a disposition to infer from a belief that one has asserted guardedly that A, to a belief that one has asserted (or will assert) that B. There is nothing to prevent someone from holding this disposition, but not a disposition to infer from a belief that it is probable that A to a belief that B; and it is the latter disposition which this view associates with the conditional 'If it is probable that A, then B'. (Cohen makes the further point that on Dummett's reading there would be no obvious use for 'If it is probable that A, then I should prefer not to assert guardedly that A'; whereas there is such a use, along the same lines as 'Even if it is true that A, I would prefer not to say so'. The present view handles this in much the same way.)

7 See particularly Blackburn 1971, 1984.
8 Blackburn returns to the issue of conditionals with moral antecedents in Blackburn 1988. He there distinguishes two possible approaches to the problem, one ('slow-track quasi-realism') in keeping with his own earlier approach, and one ('fast-track quasi-realism') more similar to the approach suggested below. He argues that the two approaches are less dissimilar than they appear at first sight. I agree, but suspect that what the fast track yields when localized to the moral case is not Blackburn's version of the slow track but something closer to Hare's.
9 Horwich 1990: 87–8. A similar train of thought has sometimes been used as an argument against non-factualism; see for example McDowell 1981 and Wiggins 1976.
10 In Price 1988: ch. 2, I argue at length that non-factualism cannot be satisfactorily grounded on a notion of truth; while Horwich 1990 responds to the claim that the minimal notion of truth is inadequate for various theoretical purposes.
11 See Price 1992, and Price 1988, part II; also Wright 1988, 1993.
12 It may seem odd to speak of the denial interpretation of negation as an example of non-factualism. As Lloyd Humberstone puts it (in correspondence), 'there seems to be a striking discontinuity between the traditional fare of ... non-factualism, and the force-based treatment of negation. No one has ever advanced a non-factualist thesis with respect to negative statements.' It is true that some versions of non-factualism would have had trouble incorporating the denial view of negation. A position characterized in terms of possession of truth conditions will have its work cut out to maintain that not-p is not simply true when p is false and false when p is true, for example. The grouping of the denial view with other forms of non-factualism looks much more natural if couched in terms of a Fregean force–sense distinction, however – the common claim being that certain utterances lack assertoric force. It seems to me that Humberstone's 'discontinuity' is really a matter of degree, the relevant variable being the ease with which truth and falsity are extended to utterances having the non-assertoric force in question. In the case of negation the bipolarity of truth and falsity guarantees that the extension is very easy indeed.
13 See particularly McDowell 1981.
14 As in effect McDowell 1981: 229, n. 9, suggests.
15 For more on the advantages and complexities of this, see Price 1990. However, the present account (in terms of the need for a procedure for rejecting commit-

ments) now seems to me both simpler and more forceful than the corresponding argument in my earlier paper.

16 See in particular Blackburn 1984.

17 This last issue is central to the dispute between my view (see Price 1988, 1992) and that of Blackburn. In Blackburn's terms, I am someone who extends the quasi-realist project 'all the way down'. Blackburn's difficulty seems to me to be that non-global quasi-realism is in danger of being self-refuting: the better the quasi-realist does locally, the less reason there will be not to 'go global'.

18 I am very grateful for comments from Simon Blackburn, Daniel Stoljar, Lloyd Humberstone and Michael McDermott, and also for the assistance of participants in seminars at Monash University and University of New South Wales.

6 Contextualism and anti-contextualism in the philosophy of language

François Récanati

In the middle of this century so-called 'ordinary-language philosophers' – most prominently Ludwig Wittgenstein, John Austin and Peter Strawson – put forward a new, 'pragmatic' picture of language which stood in sharp contrast to the picture that had been dominant since the beginnings of analytic philosophy. Half a century later it is fair to say that the old picture which ordinary-language philosophers were opposing has been to a large extent restored to its position of dominance. To be sure, bits and pieces of the new picture had to be incorporated, and a number of pragmatic phenomena acknowledged and accounted for. But the old picture was not abandoned, as ordinary-language philosophers had urged; it was elaborated rather than eliminated.

In this paper I want to describe the central conflict between the two pictures ('contextualism' and 'anti-contextualism', as I will call them), and the standard argument against contextualism. My conclusion will be that this argument, which is generally considered to have settled the issue, is in fact question begging and should *not* have settled the issue.[1]

*

What is the debate exactly about? The basic question, I think, is whether we may legitimately ascribe truth-conditional content (the property of 'saying' something, of expressing a thought or a proposition) to natural-language sentences, or whether it is only speech acts, utterances in context, that have content. Consider the type of formal language philosophers of the first half of the century were concerned with. In these languages, sentences are given an interpretation that is fixed and does not depend on the context of use. Natural-language sentences, by contrast, express a complete thought (say something definite) only with respect to a context of utterance – in many cases at least. The linguistic meaning which is assigned to them by virtue of the semantic rules of the language does not make them semantically complete, because this linguistic meaning involves variables that have to be contextually instantiated for the utterance to say something definite. This difference between natural language and a certain type of formal language is well known, and no one has ever attempted to deny it. But there is disagreement as to the *importance* of the distinction. Contextualists hold that the difference between the two types of language is all-important; natural-language sentences, according to them, are essentially context-sensitive, and do not have determinate truth conditions. Anti-contextualists, on the other hand, believe that the difference between the two types of language can be abstracted from through a legitimate idealization.

The anti-contextualist idealization is based on the following claim:

> (1) For every statement that can be made using a context-sensitive sentence in a given context, there is an eternal sentence that can be used to make the same statement in any context.

To obtain an eternal sentence from a context-sensitive one, one has only to replace the indexical constituents of the latter by non-indexical constituents with the same semantic value. Owing to (1), the difference between natural languages and the formal languages in which the context of utterance plays no role turns out not to be essential. Using natural language, we could behave so as to abolish the difference – simply by choosing to utter only eternal sentences. The reason why we also (and mainly) use context-sensitive sentences is only that this enables us 'to speak far more concisely than otherwise' (Katz 1977: 20).

Note that (1) is much weaker than another principle of effability, namely (2):

> (2) Every entertainable *thought* may be expressed by means of an eternal sentence the sense of which corresponds exactly to that thought.

Many philosophers have (rightly) argued against (2). For example, Sperber and Wilson write:

> It seems plausible that in our internal language we often fix time and space references not in terms of universal coordinates, but in terms of a private logbook and an ego-centred map; furthermore, most kinds of reference – to people and events for instance – can be fixed in terms of these private time and space coordinates. Thoughts which contain such private references could not be *encoded* in natural languages but could only be incompletely represented.
>
> (Sperber and Wilson 1986: 192)

(1) is not subject to this criticism. (1) says only that every *statement* can be made using an eternal sentence, not that every *thought* can be literally expressed by an eternal sentence. Now, a statement may be *of* an object, in the sense that it may be about a certain object without involving a particular mode of presentation of that object. Such a *de re* statement corresponds to a *class* of thoughts, each involving a particular (and, perhaps, private) mode of presentation of the object referred to. The fact that, in the thought, there are private modes of presentation attached to the objects

referred to implies that there are thoughts that cannot be totally and adequately represented by means of eternal sentences, but does not imply that there are *statements* that cannot be made by means of eternal sentences: statements are public objects at a more abstract level than thoughts, and as such do not contain private modes of presentation.

The contextualist denies (1), if only because he does not really believe that there are eternal sentences. Various arguments can be given in support of this denial. Let me mention some of these arguments:

(a) It may be argued that there cannot be *reference* without a context – that not only indexical expressions ('I', 'this') and incomplete definite descriptions ('the table', 'the president'), but also proper names and complete definite descriptions are referentially context-dependent. As for proper names, they may be construed as a variety of indexicals (Cohen 1980). This view I personally find more attractive than the alternative, standard view. On the indexical view, the same proper name – say, 'Aristotle' – may refer to different individuals in different contexts; on the standard view proper names are individuated (in part) by their bearers and cannot change their reference while remaining the 'same' proper name. The standard view entails that proper names are part of the language in a very strong sense: mastery of the language requires knowing, for every proper name, who or what the bearer of that name is. This seems to me much too strong. I agree that one does not know what is said by an utterance in which a proper name occurs unless one knows who or what the bearer of the name is, but this does not entail that mastery of the *language* (i.e. systematic knowledge of the meaning of sentence *types*) requires this piece of knowledge. Knowing who or what the bearer of a name is is like knowing who the speaker is: one may have to know this in order to know what is said by means of an utterance, yet this piece of knowledge is extra-linguistic – contextual – rather than linguistic. What is linguistic is only the rule which says that 'I' refers to the speaker, or that a proper name refers to its bearer.[2]

As for complete definite descriptions, there are two lines of argument. One may attempt to show that, in so far as they involve spatio-temporal coordinates, they necessarily involve indexicals or proper names (to fix the origin of the spatio-temporal coordinates); or one may attempt to show that the reference of a definite description always depends on the 'domain of discourse' (Récanati 1987) or 'mental space' (Fauconnier 1985) with respect to which it is intended to be evaluated. Think of the following case: John wrongly believes that Bush is the president of the United States. Knowing that Bush is in the next room, I say: 'If he goes in the next room, John will be surprised to meet the president of the United States.' Here the description 'The president of the United States' refers to Bush rather than to the actual president (Clinton) because it is intended to be interpreted with respect to a world, namely John's belief-world, in which Bush is the president of the United States. (A simpler but more controversial example has John himself straightforwardly and sincerely saying 'The president of the United States is in the next room' and thereby referring to Bush.) On this account, even the reference of a *complete* definite description (like 'The president of the United States in 1993') is context-dependent, since (i) it depends on the domain of discourse with respect to which the description is to be interpreted; and (ii) the domain of discourse itself is context-dependent.

(b) It may be argued that *predication*, in many cases, requires a context, because of what has been called the open texture of most empirical concepts (Waismann 1951). On this view, the meaning of a great number of predicative expressions is not a 'definition' that determines their conditions of application. The latter may change from context to context, as they are underdetermined at the linguistic level. The expressions in question are typically used in talking about 'ordinary' situations, and with respect to these situations they have certain conditions of application; but if one considers extraordinary situations it is not clear in advance what exactly the conditions of application of the expression will be with respect to them (Austin 1979: 67–9; see also Travis 1975, 1981, 1985, 1989; and Searle 1978, 1980, 1983). This will depend on what is considered relevant in the context of utterance.

One may accept these arguments, and still hold that there are eternal sentences. After all, a sentence such as 'Some triangles are equilateral' involves neither reference to particular objects nor empirical properties. What arguments (a) and (b) seem to imply is only that there are some important types of statement that cannot be made by means of eternal sentences. However, it is possible to go further and claim that even a sentence such as 'Some triangles are equilateral' is not an eternal sentence, for at least three reasons:

(c) It may be argued that *quantification* always requires a context. When I say 'Everybody went to Paris', there is an implicit reference to a domain of quantification (everybody in a certain group, everybody in the universe, and so on). This domain must be contextually specified, even if it is the 'universal' domain, as in 'Some triangles are equilateral.' After all, this sentence might be used, quite literally, to say that some triangles *in a relevant set* (e.g. some of the triangles on the blackboard) are equilateral: the universal interpretation is only one contextual interpretation among many others.[3] To be sure, the domain may also be explicitly described in the sentence, but when it is so described the description itself may refer to different domains of quantification depending on the 'domain of discourse' with respect to which it is intended to be interpreted (see above). It follows that no quantificational sentence is eternal.

(d) Even though 'equilateral' is a one-criterion word that has a clear definition, still it makes different contributions to the truth conditions of the utterance where it occurs depending on the 'standards of precision' that are considered relevant in the context of utterance (Lewis 1979). Remember Austin's famous example: 'France is hexagonal.' This sentence will sometimes be considered as true and sometimes as false, depending on the context of utterance ('Good enough for a top-ranking general,' Austin says, 'but not for a geographer') (Austin 1962: 143). It follows that the truth conditions of the utterance depend on the context. The same thing holds in the case of 'Some triangles are equilateral.' The same triangles – for example those on the blackboard – will be considered 'equilateral' or not equilateral depending on the standards of precision that are contextually relevant. It follows that even the conditions of application of 'equilateral' are contextually variable.

(e) *Tense* is known to be indexical. An eternal sentence must therefore be tenseless. But are there tenseless sentences? Anti-contextualist philosophers claim that there is a 'tenseless present', as in 'Snow is white' or 'Some triangles are equilateral.' Does this mean that the 'present tense' is semantically ambiguous between a temporal and a non-temporal (tenseless) reading? To claim that the present is semantically ambiguous would violate the methodological principle Grice called 'Modified Occam's Razor': *Senses are not to be multiplied beyond necessity.* Other theories, which do not posit a semantic ambiguity, are preferable, but they entail that a sentence in the (so-called) 'tenseless present' is not an eternal sentence: the tenseless present interpretation, according to these theories, is highly context-dependent. Again, it follows that 'Some triangles are equilateral' is not an eternal sentence.

I am fully aware that these arguments are controversial; in every case, I take it, a reply is available to the anti-contextualist. Moreover, not all arguments in the list are equally important as far as the contextualism/anti-contextualism debate is concerned. What the contextualist must ultimately show is that there *could not be* eternal sentences, and this conclusion is served – if at all – only by a subset of the above arguments (the arguments pertaining to domains of discourse, open texture and standards of precision). Be that as it may I will not go into the details of the controversy here, for I merely wanted to stress that there *is* room for a controversy. Why, then, is the debate considered as more or less settled? In the 1950s contextualism was taken for granted; nowadays it is considered as refuted. Why? What happened that made anti-contextualism look more attractive than contextualism?

What actually happened is that Paul Grice launched a counter-attack on contextualism, a counter-attack which was very successful. But the victory thereby gained over contextualism was undeserved. As I will now try to show, the argument Grice used in his counter-attack was either fallacious or did not constitute a refutation of contextualism.

*

From the anti-contextualist point of view, the 'normal' case is the case in which a sentence expresses a proposition independent of the context of utterance. The cases in which this is not so (indexical sentences) are reducible to the normal case via principle (1): to use an indexical sentence is to rely on contextual features *instead of* using one of the eternal sentences the language provides for saying the same thing. Indexical sentences are used as convenient abbreviations for longer, eternal sentences. This habit of using abbreviated sentences containing indexical elements does not seriously affect the picture of language that emerges from an exclusive study of (putative) eternal sentences. On this picture, sentences express propositions by virtue of their linguistic meaning alone. It follows that:

Parallelism Principle
If a (syntactically complete) sentence can be used in different contexts to say different things (to express different propositions), then the explanation for this contextual variation of content is that the sentence has different linguistic meanings – is semantically ambiguous.

To be sure, another explanation for a contextual variation of content is possible (and actually preferable) when the sentence contains an indexical expression, for indexical sentences express different propositions in different contexts without being semantically ambiguous. But indexicality is taken to be a well-circumscribed phenomenon; on the anti-contextualist view, indexicality is the characteristic property of a finite class of expressions, the members of which are well known: personal pronouns, demonstratives, tenses, some adverbs indicating location in space and time, some predicates such as 'come', etc. If a sentence which expresses different propositions in different contexts does not contain one of these recognizable expressions, or if it contains one but the contextual variation in propositional content seems unrelated to the fact that it contains it, then we may safely use the Parallelism Principle to conclude that the sentence is semantically ambiguous.

The Parallelism Principle is an essential premise in the Gricean argument against contextualism. A second essential premise is what Grice called Modified Occam's Razor, which I have used earlier in this paper:

Modified Occam's Razor
Senses (linguistic meanings) are not to be multiplied beyond necessity.

By virtue of Modified Occam's Razor, the analyst who observes that a sentence has two different interpretations when uttered in different contexts must refrain from considering that this intuitive difference in interpretation reflects a difference in linguistic meaning, i.e. a semantic ambiguity. She must, if possible, ascribe this difference to a property of the context of utterance rather than to an ambiguity in the sentence itself.

Together, Modified Occam's Razor and the Parallelism Principle entail that the analyst must not only refrain from considering that a contextual difference in interpretation reflects a difference in linguistic meaning, but also refrain from considering that it reflects a difference in propositional content, in 'what is said' by the sentence when it is uttered in this or that context. For suppose we take the difference in interpretation to be a difference in propositional content. Then, by virtue of the Parallelism Principle, this difference in content is to be explained in terms of a difference in linguistic meaning (semantic ambiguity); but positing a semantic ambiguity is precisely what Modified Occam's Razor says the analyst should refrain from doing. It follows that the analyst must, if possible, explain the contextual difference in interpretation by a property of the context of utterance, while maintaining that the sentence itself is not ambiguous and that 'what is strictly and literally said' (the propositional content) does not change from one context to the other.

A general solution along these lines has been sketched by Grice. It is based on the notion of conversational implicature. A conversational implicature is something which is communicated by an utterance and therefore belongs to its overall interpretation, but which belongs neither to the linguistic meaning of the sentence uttered nor to what is said by the utterance of this sentence; it is an aspect of interpretation that is *external* to what is said. (Indeed, working out the implicature of an utterance presupposes identifying what this utterance 'says'.) Modified Occam's Razor and the Parallelism Principle lead one to favour an analysis that accounts for a contextual difference in interpretation in terms of conversational implicature, over an account in terms of a variation in propositional content. This is, basically, the Gricean argument against contextualism.

Contextualism holds that what is said depends on the context of utterance. The evidence in favour of contextualism is provided by indefinitely many examples in which the same sentence, which does not seem to be ambiguous, is used in different contexts to say different things. With respect to these examples, the Gricean argues that:

(i) It is not necessary to consider that, in these examples, the sentence actually says different things in different contexts; it is also possible to account for the facts – namely, the intuitive difference between the interpretation of the utterance in one context and its interpretation in another context – in terms of conversational implicature, while maintaining that one and the same thing is said by the utterance whatever the context.

(ii) Given Modified Occam's Razor and the Parallelism Principle, the account in terms of conversational implicature is actually preferable to an account in terms of a contextual variation of propositional content.

This argument is fallacious, because it begs the question. It involves a premise, namely the Parallelism Principle, which a contextualist cannot accept. Certainly, for a contextualist, it is not true, even in general, that a variation of propositional content has to be accounted for in terms of a variation in linguistic meaning. The contextualist holds that the propositional content of an utterance depends on the context and not just on the linguistic meaning of the sentence. It follows that a contextual variation in the propositional content of the utterance does not entail a corresponding variation in the linguistic meaning of the sentence. The Parallelism Principle has therefore to be dropped, but if it is dropped, then Modified Occam's Razor can no longer be used to show that an account in terms of implicature is preferable to an account in terms of a contextual variation in propositional content. Modified Occam's Razor shows that an account in terms of implicature is preferable to an account in terms of *semantic ambiguity,* but an account in terms of contextually variable propositional content can no longer be reduced to an account in terms of semantic ambiguity, once the Parallelism Principle is dropped. I conclude that the Gricean argument succeeds only by begging the question against contextualism.

In actual practice, the Parallelism Principle is not explicitly stated as a premise of the Gricean argument. However, Modified Occam's Razor (or an equivalent principle of economy) is used to support the conclusion that an account in terms of implicature is preferable to an account in terms of content, and I believe that Modified Occam's Razor can be used to that effect *only if* one accepts the Parallelism Principle. So the latter is actually *presupposed* by the Gricean argument.

Let me give examples of actual uses of the Gricean argument. The first example is its use by Grice himself, against Strawson and ordinary-language philosophers. The second example is a now classical use of the Gricean argument against Donnellan's (1966) view of the referential–attributive distinction.

In *Introduction to Logical Theory* (1952), Strawson claims that there is a difference between the logical formula 'p & q' and the natural-language sentence 'p and q': while the former is logically equivalent to 'q & p', the statement made by 'They had a child and got married' is not the same as the statement made by 'They got married and had a child'; in the latter case, Strawson points out, the order of the clauses 'may be relevant ... to the truth-conditions', while the truth conditions of 'p & q' are given by the truth table for '&' and are therefore independent of the order of the clauses (Strawson 1952: 80–1). Whether the order of the clauses is actually relevant to the truth conditions of a given utterance of 'p and q' depends on the context. In Strawson's terminology, there are various 'uses' of 'and' in natural language, corresponding to different truth conditions for 'p and q'. Sometimes a sentence 'p and q' is used to say that p and then q, and sometimes it is used to say something different (e.g. the same thing as 'p & q').

There is no 'rule' fixing the truth conditions of 'p and q' independent of the context, contrary to what happens in the case of 'p & q'.

This is what Strawson says. Now it is commonly believed that Grice refuted Strawson, by means of the following argument:

(i)   Instead of saying that there is a difference between 'p & q' and 'p and q', we may consider that there is no such difference and that the truth conditions of 'p and q' are actually the same as those of 'p & q'. For example, we may consider the temporal implication in 'They got married and had a child' as a conversational implicature, external to what is said, rather than considering it as part of the truth conditions of the utterance in a certain type of context. In this way, we are able to maintain that the truth conditions of 'p and q' are determined by the truth table for '&', independent of the context of utterance.

(ii) By virtue of Modified Occam's Razor, the account in terms of conversational implicature is preferable to the account in terms of a semantic difference between 'p & q' and 'p and q'.

This argument does not work. I accept the first premise, but I reject the second one. By virtue of Modified Occam's Razor, an account in terms of implicature is preferable to an account in terms of *semantic ambiguity* (i.e. to an account that 'multiplies senses beyond necessity'). But Strawson's claim may be construed as an account in terms of context sensitivity rather than ambiguity. The difference between 'p & q' and 'p and q', according to Strawson, is that the truth conditions of the former are determined by the truth table for '&' and do not vary contextually, while the truth conditions of the latter depend on a number of factors and may vary with the context of utterance. Strawson's claim *per se* does not entail that 'and' is semantically ambiguous: this implication holds only if we accept the Parallelism Principle, according to which every contextual difference in propositional content corresponds to a semantic difference in linguistic meaning. But to accept the Parallelism Principle is to beg the question against contextualism.

If premise (ii) is rejected, as it should be, we are left with an argument (consisting of (i) only) which no longer provides a refutation of Strawson's contextualist position. What it provides is merely an alternative to that position. In other words, Grice's argument only shows that examples such as 'They got married and had a child' *can* be handled within an anti-contextualist framework, thanks to the notion of implicature. But it does not show that these examples *must* be so handled. Contrary to what is commonly assumed, Strawson has not been refuted by the Gricean argument. What has been shown is that a contextualist account of examples such as 'p and q' is not mandatory, but such an account is still possible.[4]

Another, more recent example is provided by contemporary discussions of Donnellan's distinction. Many philosophers argue as follows:

(i)   The difference between the referential and the attributive reading of a definite description may be considered not as a difference in the *content* of what is said by means of a sentence where this description occurs, but as a difference in what is pragmatically 'conveyed' by the utterance. Thus, we may consider that the same proposition is expressed on the attributive and the referential readings, and account for the difference by saying that, in the referential reading, a conversational implicature combines with what is strictly and literally said, while there is no such implicature in the attributive reading.

(ii) Given Modified Occam's Razor, this pragmatic account of Donnellan's distinction is to be preferred to Donnellan's own account in terms of a systematic difference of propositional content (of truth conditions).

Again, premise (ii) must be rejected. Modified Occam's Razor provides no reason to reject an account such as Donnellan's, according to which the difference between the referential and the attributive reading of a description is a difference in truth conditions, in propositional content (Donnellan 1966); it only provides a reason to reject an account in terms of semantic ambiguity. To be sure, accounts in terms of contextually variable truth conditions are generally equated with accounts in terms of semantic ambiguity, in accordance with the Parallelism Principle. But Donnellan cannot accept the Parallelism Principle: he holds that the difference between the two readings is a difference in truth-conditional content, but he also says that the referential–attributive distinction is *not* a semantic ambiguity. Clearly, this implies rejecting the Parallelism Principle. But once the Parallelism Principle is rejected, Modified Occam's Razor can no longer be used against Donnellan's position.[5]

*

Let me conclude. There are, in principle, three ways of handling examples in which the utterance of the same sentence has different interpretations depending on the context. One may (a) consider the sentence as semantically ambiguous; or (b) consider that the propositional content (the truth conditions) of the utterance depends on the context; or (c) account for the difference in interpretation by positing a conversational implicature that combines with what is said in some contexts but not others. Modified Occam's Razor provides a reason for avoiding (a) if possible. But how are we to choose between (b) and (c)?

Modified Occam's Razor does not provide an argument against (b), contrary to what is generally assumed. So we really have two possibilities. How to choose between them in a particular case is an open question, a question that has to be answered for the debate between contextualism and anti-contextualism to be settled in a non-question-begging way. Remember the contextualist arguments I mentioned earlier in this paper: they all rely on a certain way of analysing the examples, in conformity to (b), but this may not be the right way of analysing them. For example, it is an open question whether the sentence 'Some triangles are equilateral' can be used literally to say that *some triangles on the blackboard* are equilateral, or whether 'France is hexagonal' can be used literally to say that France is *roughly* hexagonal. (According to some accounts, the sentences in question can be used to make the statements in question only if they are used *non-literally*: see, for example, Bach 1987; and Sperber and Wilson 1986.) These specific questions, or the general question of the criteria that are to be used in a particular case to make a decision in favour of solution (b) or solution (c), I take to be *empirical* questions.[6]

The problem with the anti-contextualist framework is that, in this framework, these questions are not really considered as open questions. In practice, the anti-contextualist presupposes the Parallelism Principle and describes the case *as if* solution (b) was not a genuine possibility; he recognizes the possibility of solution (b) only when the sentence is a standard indexical sentence. This strategy prevents one from seriously dealing with the questions I have just raised. I conclude that, whether or not one believes that there could be eternal sentences, one should at least adhere to a weak form of contextualism, which might be called 'Methodological Contextualism'. Methodological Contextualism says that there is, in principle, a difference between the linguistic meaning of the sentence and what is said by an utterance of the sentence, and a correlative difference between the linguistic meaning of an expression – whatever it is – and the contribution the expression makes to the proposition expressed by the sentence where it occurs. It is only if we assume this weak form of contextualism that we can hope to be some day in a position to settle the contextualism/anti-contextualism debate.[7]

NOTES

1 Ironically, the argument in question was first put forward by Paul Grice, who himself belonged to the group of ordinary-language philosophers and made a very significant contribution to pragmatics. Grice thought, wrongly I believe, that his important distinction between sentence meaning and speaker's meaning constituted an objection to the contextualism professed by his fellow ordinary-language philosophers. More on this below.
2 For a detailed defence of the indexical view of proper names, see Récanati 1993: chs 8–9.
3 Of course this claim is highly controversial. Many will say that the universal interpretation is the only one that is 'literal'. See below, p. 166.
4 For a contextualist account of 'and', see Carston 1988.
5 A full defence of Donnellan's position is offered in Récanati 1993: ch. 15.
6 These questions are addressed in Récanati 1989, 1993.
7 An ancestor of this paper was my contribution to the conference on 'The Analytic Tradition in Philosophy' (Sheffield, 26–8 March 1988); later versions were read in Paris and Saarebrücken.

7   On being truth-valued

Charles Travis

Can we say what is neither true nor false, but might have been, had the world spoken of been suitably different? One might think we cannot; for we cannot get so far as saying what even might be true without thereby saying what in fact is, if not true, then false. Thus Aristotle suggests, in a simple case:

> there cannot be an intermediate between contradictories, but of one subject we must either affirm or deny any one predicate.
>
> (*Metaphysics*, Book IV, Ch. 7, (1011^b 23–4))

So one cannot predicate at all without doing so truly or falsely. He appears to take this to follow from his account of truth and falsity:

> To say of what is that it is not, or of what is not that it is, is false, while to say of what is that it is, and of what is not that it is not, is true; so that he who says of anything that it is, or that it is not, will say either what is true, or what is false.
>
> (Ibid.: 1011^b 25–8)

In fact, though, Aristotle's account states a condition on having a truth value which words may well fail to satisfy: to be truth-valued, words must speak of what is so, saying of something so that things are that way, or that they are otherwise. That points to a way in which much of what has a truth value does that contingently, so how some things which might have been truth-valued, had they succeeded in what they were rightly understood to aim at, have none.

The key point will be: words are truth-valued, if they are, not merely in virtue of their meaning the right sort of thing, or even that plus their having had the right sort of force, but also in virtue of the character of the act of speaking them, and the way that act fits into its surroundings. There is, on the one hand, what their surroundings accomplished for them by way of fixing content, and, on the other, what the world in fact requires surroundings to achieve in this regard. Where these two things fail to match, as they always might, words which might have had a truth value had there been a match may be contingently such that neither such value is correctly assigned them.

Are there things which are neither true nor false? Of course. This pebble and that wok, for example. Are there words which are neither true nor false? Consider the words 'Argle bargle'. Are there *intelligible* words which are neither true nor false? There is 'Excuse me!', for example. If a wok is not an example of something true, it is then an example of something not true. If it is not true, why not say that it is false? Why not declare any status less than truth falsehood? The answer is suggested by Aristotle's definition. If an item is true, that should be because the way things are, or some aspect of the way things are, is the way things are according to that item (if the item is words, then the way those words say things to be). Equally, if an item is false, that should be because the way things are, or some aspect of it, is *not* the way things are according to that item. There is no way things are according to the wok, so no relevant way for the way things are to fail to be.[1] Again, we can state something given which a truth bearer is true, by stating what is so according to that truth bearer. But there is no doing that for a wok; no true 'The wok is true if, and only if, A' which does so. That is as much reason for denying that the wok is false as there is for denying that it is true. In these respects, 'Argle bargle' and 'Excuse me!' are just like a wok. There are two morals so far. First, falsity, just as much as truth, is a semantic notion. To call something false is to pass judgement on how it represents things just as much as to call it true is. Second, just for that reason, being false is not in general the same thing as being not true.

For reasons like the above, claims that there can be no truth-value gaps are generally restricted. What there cannot be according to Aristotle are *predications* which are neither true nor false. According to Michael Dummett, it is *statements* that must be either true or false (1959: 8). For Frege, it is thoughts, if anything, which must be truth-valued. Whether any of these claims is true depends on precisely what predications, or statements, or thoughts, are; on what decides whether something is one, or where one occurs.

There is a natural idea on which what we say could contingently lack truth value. To put it as J.L. Austin might have, the terms we use are designed for use in, or of, particular sorts of cases. When we get far enough away from the cases the terms were designed for, nothing determines how they are to apply, hence, whether they do apply or not. As Wittgenstein said,

> It is only in normal cases that the use of a word is clearly prescribed; we know, are in no doubt, what to say in this or that case. The more abnormal the case, the more doubtful it becomes what we are to say.
>
> (1953: sect. 142)

Here is a simple case to illustrate Austin's view. The example is suggested by a remark of Austin's, though he did not quite use it as I will. The example itself may not be convincing in the sense that not everyone may agree that the case actually fits the description I will give it. What I want to make plausible, though, is that there may be cases with the features I will assign this one. If, contrary to what I think, things actually are neatly decided in this case, it should not be hard to find others where they are not. The case, anyway, is this. We are sitting in Jones' living room with Jones when suddenly, and quite unexpectedly, he dies. A moment later there is a knock at the door. We open and are asked: 'Is Jones at home?'

A series of intuitions. First, *in the situation just described*, neither 'Yes, he is' nor 'No, he isn't' would answer the question correctly. Second, neither would do so since either would misinform. Third, that is so because neither would state truth. Fourth, nor would either state falsehood. For if 'He is' would have stated falsehood, 'It's false that he is' should have stated truth. But if it is false that Jones is at home, then he is *not* at home, and it should have been true to say so, contrary to the third point. Similarly for 'He isn't.' What informs these intuitions?

If one said to the person at the door 'Jones is at home', one would have described Jones as being at home. That counts as saying *something*. But if the intuitions are right, one would have said nothing true, and nothing false. Why? A simple answer is: one would have described Jones as being in a particular condition. In *those* circumstances for describing him, he neither counts as in that condition, nor as not. If that is so, no wonder 'Jones is at home', said *then*, is neither true nor false. But why think it is so?

The answer I suggest is this. There are reasons for counting Jones as at home. There he is in his chair, for example. There are reasons for counting him as not at home. He is dead. One might say that dead people are not – certainly do not live – anywhere, *a fortiori* not at home. I am not speaking here of reasons for believing in the (non-)existence of some further condition which would be Jones' being at home. This is not epistemology. I am speaking of features in virtue of which the situation might count as Jones' being at home (or not); of what might *constitute* his being at home, or not. How do these conflicting reasons weigh against each other?

It would be nice if there were some neat rule: if someone is dead, he is not at home (this might follow from some more general rule – if someone is dead, he is not anywhere); or, equally nice, a rule: if someone is seated upright at his own hearth, dead or alive, then he is at home. As far as I know, though, no facts about the concept of being at home – that is, facts about what *we* are speaking of when we speak of being at home – determine any such rule, at least as in force absolutely. Neither what we *mean* by being at home, nor what 'at home' means, nor any way the way the world is might matter to what being at home is, given what 'at home' means, decides that any such rule is correct (*tout court*). At least I cannot detect any such fact, and do not believe that there are any. In which case, there is no such rule.

Some readers' intuitions may diverge from mine at just this point. Some may think there *is* a tidy absolute rule. What is needed for such readers is either a long study of the semantics of 'at home' or a different case. But I cannot provide a case per reader (I hope), and do not want to digress. So I will use my intuitions to describe the structure of a certain kind of case, and hope that each reader can provide for himself or herself, some case with that structure.

In the absence of a tidy rule, neither the reasons for, nor those against, counting Jones as at home outweigh their conflicting counterparts. So, in the situation at the door, neither count, as opposed to the others, as deciding whether Jones is at home – that, despite the rival considerations, Jones really is at home (or isn't). As one might say, *isostheneia* reigns. Except that, for Pyrrhonians, at least, *isostheneia* is clearly an epistemo-logical notion – an equal balancing of reasons one might have to take something to be true. Whereas what I have in mind here is what might be called *isostheneia* in nature – an equal balancing of everything, known or unknown, that might make Jones fit the concept or fail to. To distinguish this from the Pyrrhonian notion, I will call it 'Austinian *isostheneia*'.

To generalize, we may describe things as being a certain way, and thereby say neither what is true, nor what is false, where, and precisely where, Austinian *isostheneia* obtains. Since it is generally a contingent matter where Austinian *isostheneia* obtains, there may, in this sense, be contingent truth-value gaps – intelligible and meaningful words, properly understood as aiming to say how things are, which, due to lack of co-operation by the world they speak of, are, as a contingent matter, neither true nor false.

There is, though, a case against this idea. There seems to be an alternative, which may be what Aristotle meant to point to in holding that 'there can be no intermediary between contradictories'. The alternative thought would be this. Sometimes, reasons weigh up unambiguously on the side of truth – there are cases, for example, in which Jones just does count as at home, full stop, so that it cannot fail to be true to say so. Where, for whatever reason, words achieve anything short of this, that cannot be truth, so it must be counted as falsehood. There is no third case. Either it is simply true to say 'It's true', or else the relevant item is false. Austinian *isostheneia* would thus represent a particular variety of falsehood. If Aristotle did not mean to suggest this, others have, for example, Michael Dummett (1959). I will refer to this suggestion as 'Aristotle's ploy', though I may be blaming Aristotle unfairly.

This suggested deployment of 'true' and 'false' does not accord well with ordinary usage. From 'It's false that Jones is at home', for example, we usually feel entitled to conclude that Jones is not at home; and that for the reason Aristotle suggests: to say what is false is to say things to be as they are not (or, etc.). But there is a genre of argument which appears to be a powerful consideration in favour of the ploy. The idea of such arguments is this. Suppose that some utterance of 'Jones is at home' says what is neither true nor false. Call what it does say A. Now, if A, then A (or the thought, claim, proposition, etc., that A) is true. Similarly, if not-A, then A is false. But A is not true. Hence, by *modus tolens*, not-A. But, equally, A is not false. So, similarly, not-not-A. So, not-A, and not-not-A, which is a contradiction.

Note that the reason, if any, for saying that the above words are neither true or false, according to the present paper, is that *in the circumstances in which they were produced,* Jones then neither counted as at home, nor as not at home. If A represents the thought that Jones is at home, the present paper *might* seem to be committed to the claim that it sometimes counts as so that neither A, nor not-A, so to the view that some contradictions some-times count as the case. This is a shorter route to absurdity, avoiding appeal to the notion of truth. It also suggests what such detection of absurdity depends on. Which thought, exactly, is 'A' supposed to be? There will be more about that later.

However, arguments of this genre are no mere bagatelle. Contradictions are not so. If the alternative to Aristotle's ploy is to hold that some are, then we had better be grateful for the ploy.

Yet Austinian *isostheneia* may occur, and, with it, contingent absence of truth value. No contradiction follows from it. To see why, we need to examine the relation between language – English words, say – and the thoughts that may be expressed in it. How many thoughts may be expressed in given English words, compatibly with what they mean, and about given objects and times – about Jones, say, in saying him to be at home? To answer that, we must first resist a certain popular picture of the relation. Here is the picture. What words mean, or meant as used, deter-mines what they say, or said, and thereby what they say, or said, to be so, *modulo* a small and definite set of factors. If the words are lexically, or syntactically, ambiguous, then each reading of them does this for whichever instances of them bear that reading, once it is fixed which reading a given instance bears. The factors which must be added to what meaning fixes to determine what is, or was, said are in general no more than such things as the objects, persons, times and places spoken of. Where such a factor is needed for fixing what is said, it is part of the meanings of the relevant words that this is so; that the indicated factor is thus and so; and that the specific value of that factor, or parameter, for a given speaking, is to be determined in such and such way. For example, it is part of the meaning of 'now' that there is a certain something which must be fixed for it to be determined what was said in speaking it, that that something is a time, and, or so it is usually held by adherents of this view, that, for any given speaking, that time is the time of that speaking. This picture of how meaning relates to what is said is, I claim, mistaken. I will explain this, but, space constraints being what they are, I will not here try to prove it.

The fundamental point

I begin with a point which, if granted, is enough. I will then draw a few consequences. The point is this. Take an English sentence. To avoid side issues, make it one suitable for stating, if anything, contingent facts. Choose values for any parameters the popular picture might allow for – objects and times spoken of, etc. If the sentence is ambiguous in English, choose one of its English readings. Then there are a variety of distinct things to be said, each made true by different conditions of things, each of which would be said in one or another instance of the sentence, compatibly with what it means, and with all the above remaining fixed about it. Everything mentioned so far fixes a certain understanding of the sentence – a certain way in which it may be understood. While bearing *that* understanding – while that remains the right way of understanding it – it may still bear any of a variety of further understandings, where what it says, and when it would be true, depends on which of these – if any – it in fact bears.

An example will show what I mean. (Whether it convinces is another story.) Consider the English 'Ice floats.' Take 'ice' to speak of frozen water, as it sometimes does. Now suppose, as may be, that ice sinks in certain substances – glycerine, perhaps, or mineral oil, or ethanol. Ice is certainly more like a lead weight than a helium balloon in air. Many typical speakings of 'Ice floats', rightly understood, are not shown false by such things, since, so understood, they do not say things to be any way things are not if ice so behaves. Many utterances of 'Ice floats' are not to be understood to speak of the behaviour of ice in air. For some speakings, though, some or all of the above does matter. Sam and Pia, for example, may be wondering what will happen if they drop an ice cube in the bowl of glycerine before them. 'Oh, it'll just bob around,' Sam assures Pia, 'After all, ice floats.' If the cube sinks, then what Sam said in 'Ice floats' is false. Sometimes, though not always, to say 'Ice floats' is to make a commitment as to ice's behaviour in liquids, or even fluids, in general. So there is more than one thing to be said in saying 'Ice floats', where those words mean what they do mean in English; more than one thing, that is, each of which is what sometimes would be said in so speaking. As the example makes clear, there are also more than two things. And, I hope to have suggested, if more than n things, then more than n + 1.

Universality

The fundamental phenomenon is not one of special cases. Part of what I mean by this is that 'Ice floats' is not an abnormal English sentence. Given time and imagination enough, I could have constructed a similar example around any other sentence for stating contingent truths. There is also something more. Consider one more example: 'Ed is puce.' Let 'Ed' refer to a certain cat, and the whole to his condition at a certain time. Suppose that, at that time, Ed has just crawled out of a tub of puce dye into which he had fallen. Then that sentence, with those values of its parameters, might state truth. But it also might state falsehood. What would be said in it on some occasions is refuted by the results of a good wash, or the effects of time. Others say no more than what puce paint may make so. So there is a distinction between what the English 'is puce' says, and what some instance of it might say. The contribution to its whole which 'is puce' makes on a speaking – the understanding it then bears – may well fix a set of facts as to when those words, so spoken, would be true, where what 'is puce' *means* does not decide whether those facts hold.

Consider a contribution of 'is puce' on a speaking – one, say, such that if the puce washes off, then what was said is false. Could 'is puce', while making that contribution, contribute to the saying of any of many distinct things? Yes. It matters to the truth of some of these things, but not others, whether Ed's tongue, or liver, or the pads of his feet, are puce, for example. Such things may or may not matter to being puce on an understanding of being that which excludes being dyed. They are thus not decided by the fact of 'is puce' speaking of puce on that understanding of what being puce is. Similarly for an understanding on which being dyed will do for being puce. If Ed jumps from the tub and rolls in red dust, there are both true and false things to be said of him in words which call him puce on *that* understanding of what being puce comes to. And so on, *ad infinitum*.

There is a related, but distinct, point. Suppose Pia says 'Ed is puce', where her words bear some particular understanding, as described above. Now consider the English predicate 'is as Pia said Ed to be', understood to speak of that speaking, and that instance of calling Ed puce. If the fundamental point holds across sublunary English, then it holds for this predicate as well. From which it follows that, whatever content this predicate has, that content is compatible with saying a variety of distinct things.

The English 'is puce' speaks of a certain way for things to be – *puce*. We might also say: it ascribes a certain property – being puce. Using 'property' in that way has consequences. There are some things, in some conditions – Ed, for example – such that, on some occasions, one states truth, and on others, falsehood, in ascribing precisely that property to that thing in that condition. The property of being puce is one which the *same* thing in the *same* condition, considered sometimes, may count as having, considered other times, as lacking. Correspondingly, there are many distinct thoughts, all of a given object, and a given property, all to the effect that that object has that property. Where a property is something our words might speak of, that such and such property was ascribed to such and such object is not enough to decide under what conditions that ascription would be true, nor, as we shall see, that the ascription is truth-valued at all. That fact does not decide which, if any, thought is at issue. Given universality, the point holds of any property our words might specify.

Contingencies

Take a lexico-syntactically ambiguous sentence such as 'Fiona had a little lamb.'[2] It might be used to say something about keeping ovines. It might equally well be used to say something about eating ovine. The status of that sentence in English makes it, as such, indifferent between those possibilities. To say that there are such possibilities is to say that some instances of those words are in fact remarks on ovine eating, others on ovine keeping. If any such thing is ever so, the meanings of the above words alone cannot make it so. The circumstances in which the words were spoken must, somehow or other, decide that that is the understanding which, so spoken, they in fact bear. About that, I assert this fundamental principle: wherever there is a specific such task for circumstances to perform – deciding in favour of some understanding not determined by meaning alone, or choosing between some two such rivals – it is possible for there to be circumstances which fail to perform it.

Consider, for example, 'I am here.' If a speaking of such words says anything, while bearing the understanding the meanings of those words confer, it is something to the effect that someone (presumably a speaker) is someplace. Suppose that, to your surprise, you encounter an instance of those words in a text on set theory – not quoted, nor part of some little story, but out of context, in a discourse otherwise about sets. Given the way sentences occur in texts, and the way texts are produced, there is no fact about who should be where when if that instance of the sentence is to count as true. If there is only one author, one just *might* take it to concern the author – though why not some proof-reader, or typesetter? But where should the author be, and when? Nothing about the way these words occurred makes it so that they bear any of those understandings on which such questions have answers.

Wittgenstein regarded 'I am here' not only as a favourite philosopher's example, but, as usually discussed, as a typical piece of philosophical nonsense. That is because he saw many things to be said in the words, and not that variety philosophers usually fasten on. If we agree that you will call me from La Frite Partout when you arrive, and that I will then come to meet you there (I being close, your arrival time being uncertain), then if, suspecting that I am a dallier, you instead call from your flat before leaving for the Frite, say 'I am here', and hang up, what you thus say is *not* made true by the trivial fact that you are, at the time of your call, at the place of your calling, much less by the fact that you are then in your flat. If that is right, then, in this respect too, we may say: in particular circumstances, *if they are suitable*, those words may say someone to be somewhere; outwith suitable circumstances, they say nothing to be so, and bear none of the indefinitely many understandings on which they would do so. Where there are rival understandings 'Ed is puce' may bear, while speaking of Ed and calling him puce, surroundings *may* fail to confer any of these on the words spoken in them. That may, or may not, matter to whether the words said anything to be so, so to whether they might be true.

What truth requires

Words, to be true, must say of something so, and of no more than that, that that is so. What sort of understanding must words bear in order to achieve that? Suppose that one might say either of two things, one true, one false, in saying all that given words are rightly understood to have said. There are two understandings the words might have borne, on one of which they would be true, on the other false, and they are not correctly understood to bear the one rather than the other. Then those words fail the condition. For there is nothing so such that in saying precisely that to be so one might either state truth or state falsehood. If Ed has fallen in the vat, then one may say, of him, all the English 'Ed is puce' says, speak of just what those words speak of (being puce etc.) and for all that speak either truth or falsehood. So if Ed is in that condition, those English words cannot as such be either true or false.

It does not follow that if words are true, there is no way things *could* be such that if things were that way, one could state truth, and one could state falsehood in saying all those words say. Sometimes, in calling the freshly dyed Ed puce, one says him to be as he is, since there are truths to be told in so describing things. For some such truths, it would be both possible to state truth and to state falsehood in saying Ed to be just as one said him to be in telling that truth – *if* Ed, on emerging from the dye, had rolled in red dust. That does not yet show that the truth in question could not be a truth, given that Ed has not rolled.

There are tasks circumstances conceivably could perform for given words, choosing between conflicting understandings those words might bear, which circumstances may fail to perform without depriving those words of a truth value. If for words to be true is, as Frege suggests, for them to express a thought, then words may express a thought though the understanding they bear is, in principle, further refinable in any of many conflicting ways, each of which imposes a different truth condition, *none* of which is a correct way of understanding those words. If there is some one way for things to be, identifiable as the way given words describe things as being – in the way that meaningful, unambiguous English words may speak of an identifiable way for things to be (puce, for example) – then, though further conceivable refinements on their understanding may impose different truth *conditions*, it is enough if no (relevant) pair of such refinements would impose different truth values; if no two (relevant) understandings those words might have borne, but which their surroundings did not confer on them, would impose different truth values. There are, again, two things to be said of Ed in calling him puce, one of which would have been true, the other false, had he rolled in dust. If Ed did not roll, then that such understandings of words are available, and that in calling Ed puce you are not correctly understood to have said the one of these things rather than the other, does not matter to whether what you said is true.

To be true, words need not bear an understanding which guarantees them a truth value no matter what. Given that, whether given words achieve what they must to be true is, in general, a contingent matter. It is, of course, a contingent matter what understanding their surroundings confer on them. But it is also contingent whether that understanding is refined enough so that on it words would be true (or false). Had Jones lived, then in saying him to be at home one might have stated truth, though nothing about their proper understanding decides whether those words would have been true had Jones died. Whether Jones lived or died is a contingent matter.

Truth and disambiguation

Some philosophers have suggested that English sentences have truth conditions which are statable, and, as a rule, either satisfied or not. Austin, on the other hand, held that:

> it is a fashionable mistake to take as primary '(The sentence) "S" is true (in the English language)'. Here the addition of the words 'in the English language' serves to emphasise that 'sentence' is not being used as equivalent to 'statement', so that it precisely is not what can be true or false (and moreover, 'true in the English language' is a solecism, mis-modelled, presumably, and with deplorable effect, on expressions like 'true in geometry'.)
>
> (1950: 121)

It is clear why Austin should have said this. For, typically, what an English sentence means (or its parts do) leaves it equally open for it to say both true things and false things, and a wide variety of each (each thing on some use or other). If the fact that it may say true things is reason to hold it true, the fact that it may say false things is equal reason to hold it false; which is to say that neither is decisive reason for either thing.[3] So there *is* no decisive reason for holding either thing. When a sentence might say both true and false things, the way the world in fact is cannot count as making it true; for that cannot be how the English sentence, as such, says things to be. If it were, that would leave the sentence impotent to say the false things it can say on some speakings. By parity of reasoning, the way things are cannot be other than what the sentence says to be so. For a sentence in this condition, nothing so or not so can be what it says to be so. There is no such thing as 'what it says to be so'. Given Aristotle's account of falsity, we thus must also deny that the sentence is false.

An English sentence may, on one speaking or another, say any of many things to be so, as a rule, some of these so, and others not. For that to be so, the proper understanding of the sentence as such must make it no more speak of one of these states of affairs than of any other. Whether things are as they are according to the sentence (assuming that there is a way things are according to it) can turn no more on any one of these things being so than on any other. Nor can it turn on the obtaining or not of anything other than something the sentence might, on a use, say to be so. So there can be nothing on the obtaining of which its truth turns. So it cannot have a truth value.

One might apply Aristotle's ploy to English sentences: they do not do all an item need do to be true; hence they are false. That makes at least most English sentences false. It also means rejecting Aristotle's account of truth and falsity. That would be to miss out on Aristotle's insight on the *semantic* nature of falsehood: 'false', like 'true', is a verdict on a way of representing things; on whether the way things are is rightly represented that way. Such questions arise only where there *is* a way things were represented as being.

Words are neither true nor false if, given everything about what it would be for things to be as those words said things to be, there are both true and false things to say in saying things to be that way, both subject to whatever condition on truth those words are properly understood to be subject to. For then the argument applies. If the fact that one could state truth in saying things to be like that gives reason to count the words as true, it cannot be decisive reason. For there is equal reason, provided by the fact that one could also, in doing all of that, state falsehood, to take the words to be false, so not true.

We may now note: it is not only English sentences that may be in the condition just described, but also English sentences on particular speakings of them. If there are both true and false things to say of Ed in calling him puce, where he has been first dyed, and then dusted, the circumstances of some speakings in which Ed was described as being puce may fail to choose between these.

English sentences thus model the following fact. The proper understandings of some words are understandings equally compatible with speaking truth and with speaking falsehood. For that reason, such words are neither true nor false. Such words fail Aristotle's condition on truth *and* on falsehood: they do not speak of what is so, saying that to be so, or saying things to be otherwise. That possibility of failure shows the condition to be substantial. That, I think, is what Austin had in mind in insisting on, not only 'descriptive conventions' fixing what words of a language say, but also

> *Demonstrative* conventions, correlating the words (= statements) with the *historic* situations, etc., to be found in the world.
>
> (1950: 122)

In sublunary affairs, understandings, when they accomplish this, do so as a contingent matter.

We have now arrived at an account of when, and why, Austinian *isostheneia* arises. It arises for particular words – a certain 'Jones is at home', say – just when there are *two* things to be said in those words, one true and one false, and, for all there is to be understood as to what *was* said in them, one might say either of those things in words bearing all of that understanding, in saying just that.

It is now clear why the initial description of Austinian *isostheneia* was as it was. I did not say that there may be items – Jones, say – which neither have nor lack some property, such as being at home;[4] nor that Jones flatly neither counts as at home nor as not; nor that it is flatly neither true nor false that Jones is at home. What I did say was that in *certain surroundings*, in saying Jones (dead in his chair) to be at home, one would neither say what is true nor what is false; and that that is so because *in those surroundings* Jones (dead) neither counts as at home nor as not. The situation at the door was meant as an example of such surroundings. So, I take it, one *might*, in saying Jones to be at home, say what is neither true nor false. Then again, there are many distinct things to be said of Jones in saying that. That is just the point. One *could* speak truth of Jones (dead) in saying him to be at home; for some purposes he so counts. One could similarly speak falsehood. Just that opens up the possibility of doing neither: surroundings may fail to make us count as doing the one rather than the other. Austinian *isostheneia* is thus a feature of particular speakings of words, arising in particular surroundings, and not a feature in general of such things as saying Jones to be at home.

So does Jones count as at home, or not? On some occasions for counting him one way or the other, he does, on others, not. Does he *now* so count? Now we are doing philosophy. Nothing hangs on our counting him in one way or the other. There is nothing we need do differently in either case. That absence of *point* in deciding is enough for the question to lack a true yes/no answer.

A certain line of thought is thus cut off.[5] It might be thought: *we* cannot decide whether words are true or false, where Austinian *isostheneia* obtains; but that is due to ignorance on our part. The facts (must) decide the issue one way or the other. The idea is that the way the world in fact is decides, somehow, what we actually say in saying Jones to be at home; perhaps by deciding what we really speak of in speaking of being at home; and it decides whether what we thus say is actually so. But there are many things we can, in fact, say in saying Jones to be at home, all quite compatibly with the world being the way it is, some true, and some false. The nature of being at home, whatever that may be, does *not* decide in favour of some of these, or against others. What would need to be decided, by facts beyond our ken, is that the surroundings of some given speaking in which Jones was said to be at home in fact choose some one of these things, ruling out any others which differ from it in truth value. What we would be ignorant of is not anything about what being at home is, but rather, which of two quite possible things was said on a given occasion. We would need to suppose, on this line, that the effects of surroundings on the *understandings* that words, in them, bear might lie essentially beyond the abilities of human beings to appreciate such effects. That is an incredible view of understandings. There is, anyway, no reason to suppose that surroundings always are, or must be, so puissant in choosing between different possibilities for understanding.

The present view of truth-valuelessness also cuts off another main line of defence of Aristotle's ploy. Michael Dummett compares statements to commands, which, in point of obligatory consequences, can only be disobeyed or not, as opposed to bets, which may be won, lost, or off if some pre-established condition is not met. The point is to rule out truth-valuelessness in the case of presupposition failure. ('He stopped beating his wife last week', where he never started.) With that point in view, Dummett says,

> A statement, so long as it is not ambiguous or vague, divides all possible states of affairs into just *two* classes. For a given state of affairs, either the statement is used in such a way that a man who asserted it but envisaged that state of affairs as a possibility would be held to have spoken misleadingly, or the assertion of the statement would not be taken as expressing the speaker's exclusion of that possibility. If a state of affairs of the first kind obtains, the statement is false; if all actual states of affairs are of the second kind, it is true. It is thus *prima facie* senseless to say of any statement that in such and such state of affairs it would be neither true nor false.
>
> (1959: 8)

In the sort of case under discussion here, whether a speaker *has*, in saying 'W', excluded the way things in fact are as a possibility, or whether his words envisaged that, is precisely the question that lacks a determinate answer. It is choosing, as what was said, between things to say which exclude that possibility and things to say which do not, that makes Austinian *isostheneia* arise. Presuppositions in the sense in which the existence of a bet may presuppose that the race is actually won, do not figure here. The words under consideration here are not relevantly ambiguous in their language. I think it would be a great misuse of the term to call the statements in question here 'vague'. If one does call them that, though, then *any* statement is liable to turn out to be vague, depending on what the world it makes claims about turns out to be like. Whether words are vague in this sense will not follow from any fact as to the sort of thing they were rightly understood to say.

There are, then, words which say what might have been true, or false, had the world they spoke of been different, but what is, in fact, neither. Such words say *something*. They do such things as calling something puce, or count, on the occasion of their speaking, as doing that. It need not follow that there are truth-valueless thoughts. For to insist that every thought is truth-valued may be to do either of two different things. If we identify a range of items we will count as thoughts, where an item is identifiable as belonging to that range or not independent of whether it has a truth value, we may then assert as a thesis that every item in that range has a truth value. But to say that every thought is truth-valued may also be to insist that nothing counts, or is to count, as a thought unless it has a truth value, no matter what its other credentials may be. It may then be undecidable whether a thought was expressed in given words without first deciding that what the words say is evaluable as to truth. On this reading, words without truth value do not express a thought. That would allow us still to hold on to the idea that every thought is truth-valued.

If every thought has a truth value, that can only be because, whatever else is so of what words express, lacking a truth value itself disqualifies what they express for the status of thought. On that conception of a thought, thoughts admit the possibility of masqueraders: what words express may be indistinguishable from a thought until enough is revealed about the world to show that for what those words say, Austinian *isostheneia* reigns. If we identify thoughts too closely with coherent understandings borne by the right sorts of words, we will deny the possibility of such masqueraders, and must then recognize the possibility of truth-valueless thoughts. This is the route Frege (1892) took in 'On sense and reference'. I do not know that one or the other use of 'thought' is forced on us absolutely. Still, stipulating that thoughts must have truth values may be far from arbitrary.

Whether it is pointful to insist that every thought is truth-valued depends on what we want thoughts to be. Suppose we take it as essential to being a thought, that every thought is one on which such and such is so; that for every thought, there is that which is so according to it. That is enough to give point to the insistence. Consider words 'Today is hot.' In different surroundings, such words speak of different conditions – conditions at Timbuktu on 1 August, or at Nome on 1 December, or at Houston on 15 May, and so on. For them to be true or false, they must speak of some one of these. If they occur in such a way that they are as much about Houston in May as about Nome in December, then there is nothing for their truth to turn on, hence they cannot have a truth value. But equally, in such a case, there is nothing which is so according to them. For if there were, what could it be? Specify it, and that being so or not would make them true. If the words express a thought, what is so according to the words is what is so according to the thought they express. But that means here that they cannot express a thought.

Now, supposing Jones freshly dead, consider words 'Jones is at home.' Speaking of Jones, they might say any of a variety of things. There is a condition which obtains, Jones being in his chair, which they might say to obtain (on some use). There is also a distinct condition which obtains which is otherwise than things would be according to the words in saying something else they might. On some understandings, though, such words lack a truth value, given the way Jones is. Whether things are as they are according to the words on such understandings turns no more on the one sort of condition that obtains than it does on the other. If what the words say fails, in this way, to choose between these conditions, then the words can say neither of these things to be so. In that case, there can be nothing which is so according to the words. In which case, on the present idea of what a thought is, they cannot have expressed a thought.

Had Jones lived, there would have been a condition such words spoke of – depending on whether Jones stayed home or went to the pub, one which would have made them true or false. It would still be so that nothing about the words decides whether they would have been true had Jones died; that had he died, there would have been two conditions for them to speak of, with no reason to take them to speak of the one rather than the other. But with Jones alive, there are no such conditions of things. There is, instead, an identifiable condition – the way Jones is – on which the truth of the words turns. It is just that condition which is missing where Jones has just died. (Again, the importance of Austin's demonstrative conventions.)

How could we say what it is that is so according to a truth-valueless thought to the effect that Jones is at home, made neither true nor false by Jones dead in his chair? The direct way would be 'What is so on that thought is that _____'. The natural way to fill the blank would be: 'What is so on that thought is that Jones is at home.' But what condition of things does this specify? If it does genuinely specify some way for things to be, then 'at home', occurring in it, must speak of what in fact counts as being at home; what one would rightly call that. Given the variation across occasions in precisely what condition 'at home' speaks of, this can only mean: what one would call being at home – what is rightly so called – in the surroundings of producing that particular specification of what is so on that thought.[6]

Suppose, now, that we are speaking from a position of knowledge of Jones' condition, or at least of his recent death. Then there are various things we might call Jones' being at home; various things that might rightly be called that, given that he is dead. Depending on the surroundings in which we speak, we might use the words 'at home' to speak of a condition Jones is in, or to speak of one he is not in. What we cannot do is to use them so as to have the content they would have in expressing the supposed truth-valueless thought. We cannot use them with the content they might have had, spoken in a position of ignorance. For words with that content would not speak of anything which, from the position we enjoy, might be called, or might count as, Jones' being at home. We could not be understood to call Jones, or the condition he is in, anything at all, or even to aim to characterize Jones in any way, in saying what patently fails to choose between conditions Jones is in and ones he is not in. So nor, in doing that, could we be identifying a condition rightly called (in our surroundings) being at home.

In a state of ignorance, words with content which does not make such choices may *seem* to identify what one might call Jones' being at home, so to express, or to specify, a thought. Knowledge makes that impression vanish, for it makes it no longer seem as if there *is* something which is so according to that supposed thought. The knowledge which disallows such impressions is just that which shows that if there were such a thought, it could not be truth-valued. That is reason to deny that there are thoughts without truth value, though the price for that is admitting that, until all relevant facts are in, nothing merely about the way words were to be understood by itself decides whether they expressed a thought or not.

Preserving the idea that all thoughts are truth-valued has several consequences. First, there is a natural thought on which any thought is equivalent, at least in truth value, to any thought that it is true; so that if p is a thought, and 'x' states what is so according to it, then the truth of p entails x, and vice versa. (One might also hold that 'p is true if, and only if, x' always expresses a truth, provided 'p' and 'x' are related as above.) If there were truth-valueless thoughts, this natural idea would be wrong. For if p, so a suitably related 'x', were truth-valueless, then 'p is true' would be false, hence the equivalence would not hold. By denying that there would be thoughts without truth value, we may preserve the idea of the equivalence. For where 'x' lacks a truth value, there is no appropriate thought of which to predicate truth, even falsely. Preserving the equivalence in this way, though, does nothing to remove the possibility that we may say what contingently lacks, or has, truth value.

A second consequence is this. The idea that words might say something – for example, say Jones to be at home – but lack a truth value seemed threatened by an argument to the effect that that idea entails a contradiction. The argument appeals, *inter alia*, to a pattern of inference which looks like this: 'If A, then A is true; A is not true; so not A'. The first item in the sequence is meant to be a principle about truth, the second, a premise that would hold where the referent of 'A' has no truth value. Now, the question is, what is an *instance* of this pattern? Presumably, this might be: 'If Jones is at home, then that remark is true; that remark is not true; so Jones is not at home.' We also need to suppose that that might be an instance even where the initial 'Jones is at home' lacks a truth value. For that is what is meant to make the second premise true.

But valid patterns of inference represent entailment relations, and we may plausibly hold, with Frege, that such relations hold between thoughts. If there are no thoughts without truth value, then the 'instances' of the pattern which might generate contradiction are no genuine instances at all. Another way of making the same point is this. If 'If Jones is at home, then that remark is true' states anything, it is that on a certain supposition, a certain item is true. But from what supposition is this to follow? Where 'Jones is at home' lacks a truth value, that is precisely because it fails to identify any definite condition on which its truth might turn; it fails to distinguish any *one* condition of things, from among a variety of possibilities, as the condition it speaks of. So, in the present context, it identifies no genuine supposition. The corresponding conditional states no fact.

There is an argument which shows that everything within a certain class must have a truth value. (It certainly does not show this for woks or pebbles.) But the argument is an artefact of a particular method of representation, or, equally, a particular conception of a pattern. There is a formalism designed to exhibit relations between items with truth values. What the argument shows is that everything the formalism deals with must have a truth value. That *might* be put by saying that there are no truth-valueless thoughts. For all that, lack of truth value may happen contingently.

This paper has been concerned to raise and answer a question which might be put like this: can there be intelligible words, properly understood to be in the business of stating facts, which are neither true nor false? I have aimed to capture the idea of those references to intelligibility, businesses, etc., by asking: can there be words which are *contingently* neither true nor false – which, though lacking a truth value, would have had one, had the world they spoke of been sufficiently different? For good measure, I have suggested a negative answer to the question whether there are any words about contingent fact which are more than contingently truth-valued.

Discussion of the main question has centred, traditionally, on problems which arise when terms which purport to refer to an object fail to do so: someone says 'Caesar's cat was puce', but, as it happens, Caesar never had a cat. There are those who would count such words false. Some would even go so far as (implausibly) to claim that, if Caesar had no cat, then it is false that Caesar's cat was puce. For Frege, words in the condition just described must count as neither true nor false, and cannot count as saying anything true, or anything false. For, for Frege, such expressions as 'is puce' express a function – one from objects to truth values. Functions take on values for specific arguments, but take on no values other than for some argument. An expression of a function, with a name of an argument in its argument-place names a value of the function – the value it takes for that argument. An expression of a function with anything other than a name of an argument in that place is simply ill formed; it names nothing. If 'is puce' is an expression of a function, then 'Ed is puce' is, if anything, a name of a value of that function for a particular argument – Ed. If 'Caesar's cat is puce' is not that, it is not anything well formed, and certainly cannot stand for a truth value. So, within Frege's framework, it has no truth value.

It is mandatory for Frege to take the above view. But that view leaves open whether to say that 'Caesar's cat is puce' expresses a thought. In 'On sense and reference', Frege introduced thoughts, in effect, by first noting some fine distinctions which need drawing between one understanding and another words might bear, and then assigning thoughts the task of marking these distinctions (in certain central cases). The near equivalence he there imposed between thoughts and coherent understandings made it natural to take it that where intelligible words missed some referent, hence a truth value, they nevertheless expressed a thought. That would mean that there are un-truth-valued thoughts. In that particular work, Frege accepted, or came very near to accepting, that conclusion.

There is, though, a strong consideration against taking thoughts to be expressed in such cases. Consider words 'Caesar was canny.' It is part of the understanding such words are likely to bear, that there is, or is to be supposed to be, some particular individual, and some particular way to be, such that the thought expressed is one on which that individual is that way. Otherwise put, the thought expressed is one whose truth turns precisely on whether that individual is that way. In a case where there is no such individual, there is no such thought. In the absence of conclusive reason to take given words in this condition to express some thought of a sort other than that which, on their proper understanding, they represented them-selves as expressing, such words express no thought at all. I here compress a case which has recently been made in a most convincing way, notably by John McDowell (1986) and Gareth Evans (1982).

I have been concerned here with threats to being truth-valued posed by the sorts of contributions predicates make to what is said in speaking them. That may seem a different matter altogether. I think it is not. What I have argued is that words, to be truth-valued, must satisfy Aristotle's condition, and that the contributions predicates make do not (in general) ensure that they will do that. That is, truth-valued words must succeed in saying of some way things are, that things are, or are not, *that* way. Austin's 'demon-strative conventions' must succeed in connecting words to the way things are – in his words, to historical states of affairs – in such a way that the words are actually responsible for just those things being, or not being, so – and responsible in that very special and particular way which makes it correct to say 'false' when the responsibility is not met, and 'true' when it is. Words, to be true, must succeed in referring to the way things are, or to something so, just as much as certain words, to be true, must succeed in referring to a cat. Whether there is a cat certain words refer to depends, *inter alia*, on the way, on their proper understanding, the right cat, if any, is to be identified. Whether words succeed in speaking of what is so depends on the way their proper understanding provides of identifying what it is, if anything, which they say to be so. What was to be supposed to be a way of identifying a cat may always fail to be that. That kind of failure makes some words refer to nothing. What was to be supposed to be a way of identifying some aspect of the way things are may also always fail, for contingent reasons, to be that. Whether it does depends on what is in fact so, and what not. Where it does, nothing is identifiable as what was said that might be either true or false. Failure of singular reference, I suggest, is a special case in which this more general sort of failure may arise.

Problems of truth-value gaps, I hope to have shown, contain a moral for our conception of 'speech act theory'. There is an unfortunate tendency to equate speech act theory with the study of illocutionary force. That is unfortunate because it encourages an entirely mistaken view which, in the case of truth and falsity, might be put this way: the illocutionary force words are properly understood to have borne – whether they are an assertion, a question, or a command – decides whether they are eligible for truth or falsity; if they are eligible, then their meaning determines what their truth would require. Given that view, it is all too easy to insist that eligible words which fall short of truth must be false. In fact, though, or so I have argued, words depend in very substantial ways on the character of the act of producing them, and of its surroundings, for determining what their truth would require, even given that their proper understanding, and specifically, their force, makes them eligible for truth value. If the words speak of being at home, or floating, or being puce, then their surroundings must show what it would then be reasonable to do with those characterizations of things; how one might reasonably act on such words given that they were taken to be correct; and, hence, what would count, for the purposes to which those words spoke, as being at home, or floating, or being puce. In one direction, the fact that surroundings may always show more or less about this opens up the possibility that meaningful words which are eligible for truth value may contingently fail to be coherently evaluable as having the one truth value as opposed to the other. In another, the fact that there are such tasks for surroundings to accomplish – that the role of surroundings is far from ending with the fixing of some illocutionary force from within some repertoire of possibilities – calls attention to a crucial area speech act theorists might fruitfully study. (Speech act theorists who have been overly influenced by Austin's *How to do Things with Words* might profit from closer attention to his *Sense and Sensibilia*.)

NOTES

1   Not that there could not be a way things are according to a wok. By convention, for example, the wok might be hung by the door to indicate that the restaurant is open. I am assuming that no such thing is so of the woks here in question.
2   Technically, this is an ambiguous surface form of several distinct, but homophonous, sentences. I hope it will not hurt to waive that point for the present.
3   It is not as if we are ignorant of what the sentence says, or that natural facts, if fully revealed might show this to us – as if one might *discover* some day which of the various things we understand 'Ed is puce' to say on various occasions is what it *really* says. On the contrary, we know perfectly well what the sentence

says, and that there are a variety of distinct things to be said in saying *that.*

4   That would be so on some ideas about categories and category mistakes. But I
     am not out either to defend or to refute such ideas.

5   This line has been defended by Williamson 1992.

6   I am not claiming that this is the only possible understanding for 'at home'
     inside a 'that'-clause. I am claiming that it is the only understanding it can have
     where that clause is to be understood to specify some condition which obtains,
     or obtains according to such and such.

8   Illocution and its significance

Jennifer Hornsby

J.L. Austin thought that the study of language had been too much focused on words, and that the study of action had been too much focused on 'ordinary physical actions': he thought that *illocution* had been neglected (Austin 1962). But for all of Austin's stress on illocutionary acts, I think that he failed to appreciate the significance of his own idea. And I think that subsequent writers, having their own agenda, have not understood what underlies it. My aim in what follows is to provide an account of an idea of *illocution* which reveals the use of words to be *communicative* action. In my account, *illocution* occupies the same sort of theoretical role as it does in Austin's and Searle's.[1] But I elucidate it differently.

The true significance of *illocution* is shown when speech act theory is located in a broader, social context; and I think that a correct account of it has repercussions for certain political questions. Here I shall have space to offer only a sketchy account of the connections that I see: I do so in section 2. In section 1, I develop a conception of the divisions between locutionary and illocutionary, and between illocutionary and perlocutionary, which leads to a definition of *illocutionary act*. The definition is matched to a way of thinking about *illocution* which I claim is more satisfactory than Austin's. (I leave it to an Appendix to contrast my account with Searle's.)

Austin struggled with distinctions between acts and actions, and between acts and consequences; and he never settled on a single way of using the term 'act'. In my usage, 'acts' will denote things people do, and 'actions' will be reserved for particular doings (each one of them 'fixed and physical', as Austin put it). This means that the act–action distinction here is a distinction between properties and particulars. The usage is somewhat stipulative, of course.[2] But it accords with Austin's own principal usage: the speech *acts* of his text are the *things* done with words of his title *How to do Things with Words*. And it accords with the principal usage in recent philosophy of action, where *actions* are taken to be *events*. The absence of some definite terminological policy, and in particular the ambiguous use of 'speech act', has been a barrier to clarity about many issues. I hope that a firmer sense of the nature of the problem of 'demarcating the illocutionary' will be gained when 'act' and 'action' are both used unambiguously.[3]

1 ILLOCUTION

1.1 Language and speech acts

When there is an utterance, there is an *action* of someone's. But in the case of any one such action, there will be many things the speaker has done – many *acts* that she has performed. (For example, an action might be someone's doing (at least) these three things: *uttering the sentence 'It's raining', saying that it's raining, reminding Jane to take her umbrella.*) Each speech act corresponds to a sort of action; so that a principled way of organizing speech acts provides a framework into which the occasions on which one or another is done could be fitted so as to provide for full and fully illuminating accounts of speech actions. The classification of speech acts which Austin got started can then be thought of as a means of imposing system on to the actual data of linguistic communication.

Many writers have come to use 'speech act' more or less synonymously with 'illocutionary act'. But since there are theoretically interesting things which are done with words but which cannot be brought under the head of 'illocutionary', a broader conception of *speech act* than theirs is needed.[4] In an attempt to define 'speech act', someone might seek a class of things all and only the members of which are always, or necessarily, done using speech. But in fact there is no such class; for there are many things which are sometimes done by using words and sometimes done otherwise (example: I can warn you that there's a bull by saying 'There's a bull', and I can warn you that there's a bull by silently gesticulating). We might then think of speech acts as things that *may* be done using words. Obviously this gives an extremely permissive conception of a speech act; but it ensures that nothing that could be of interest is omitted from a classification, and an actual account of certain speech acts can reveal what is actually interesting. Austin's main classification of speech acts into types was into locutionary (which incorporates phonetic, phatic and rhetic),[5] illocutionary and perlocutionary. Each of these categories of speech act subsumes some distinctive range of acts such that a person's doing of any one of them is, typically, her using language.

A complete account of the linguistic practice of any community divides into a portion special to their particular language and concerned with the significance of its sounds, and a portion dealing with the uses to which productions of significant sounds are put. I have argued elsewhere (Hornsby 1988) that this division corresponds to Austin's locutionary–illocutionary division: a theory of locution must be a theory for English or for Bulgarian or for whichever language, but a theory of illocution should have the potential to serve any language. When these two portions are thought to provide for an entire account of the use of some language, it will be apparent that some things people do with words are things that an account of language as such cannot be expected to cover. My suggestion –

to be made more precise in what follows – is that the division between illocutionary and perlocutionary marks a distinction between speech acts which are of proprietary concern to an account of language and speech acts which are not.[6]

A conception of the domain of the illocutionary as the domain of language but not of language-specific meaning fits well with Austin's view of it as of especial concern. His warnings against eliding the illocutionary, against allowing it to be swallowed up by either the locutionary or perlocutionary (Austin 1962: 103), were directed against those who believed that one dealt with language when one dealt with linguistic meaning, and that anything else to be said about language use comes into a much more general account of human behaviour: on their account, there is language-specific meaning, and there is action, but nothing, as it were, in between. But despite his emphasis on the illocutionary, and despite his struggles to 'isolate' it, and to taxonomize it, Austin had extraordinarily little to say about it. There is a curious absence from Austin's writings of any interest in the phenomenon of language in general.

An examination of Austin's treatment of the illocutionary–perlocutionary distinction will not only bear out this conception of the illocutionary (as one that he introduced), but also point us in the direction we should look for an understanding of illocution as a general linguistic phenomenon; and it will, incidentally, explain Austin's own lack of interest in such an understanding.

1.2 Austin on the illocutionary–perlocutionary divide

Austin offered many different ways of making out an illocutionary–perlocutionary distinction, of which three stand out. (a) It is a distinction between things done *in* performing a locutionary act and things done *by* performing a locutionary act (ibid.: 108). (This way of thinking about it explains the *il-* and *per-* terminology.) (b) It corresponds to a distinction between what is essentially conventional – illocutionary – and what is not – perlocutionary (ibid.: 121). (c) It corresponds to a distinction between acts which essentially introduce consequences – perlocutionary – and acts which do not – illocutionary (ibid.: 107, 114, 121).

Austin acknowledged that the 'in'/'by' test could not serve as a criterion for the distinction: he said that it was 'at best very slippery' (ibid.: 131). And although he went to considerable lengths to refine the test, what he came up with is unsatisfactory. This is hardly surprising, when one considers that in hosts of cases it is possible to think of someone *both* as having ϕ-d in ψ-ing *and* as having ϕ-d by ψ-ing.[7] The test is inherently flawed.

Yet the test may cast light on Austin's general classificatory scheme. In the case of any particular action, knowing the acts that it was of, it is possible to impose a certain kind of ordering upon those acts and see some as *more basic than* others.[8] Usually the word 'by' is taken to define 'basic', so that it is said, for instance, that where Jane persuaded John to stay indoors by saying how cold it was outside, *saying how cold it was outside* is more basic than *persuading John to stay indoors*. But the ordering of acts for basicness seems not to be exhausted by 'by': 'in' is apt to make finer discriminations between the relative basicness of acts than 'by' does. (For example, our intuition is that *saying 'It's cold'* (phatic) is more basic than *saying that it's cold* (rhetic), and we may find 'She said that it's cold *in* saying "It's cold"' more natural than 'She said that it's cold *by* saying "It's cold"'.) When the word 'in' supplements the word 'by', allowance is made for cases where, so to speak, the distance between two acts in the ordering or basicness is smaller than what would be required for the truth of the relevant 'by'-sentence. Once 'in' is in, Austin's 'in'/'by' test can be set in the context of an ordering of acts in terms of their relative basicness. Perlocutionary acts (done by doing locutionary ones) then come out as less basic acts than illocutionary ones (done in doing locutionary ones).

If a line is to be drawn between il- and per- locutionary, then the idea of relative basicness will not get us very far: it tells us about the dimension on which we have to draw a line, rather than about where to draw it. But it may assist in understanding the curious refinements that Austin made to his test, when he distinguished a number of different senses both of 'in' and of 'by'. He spoke of two 'in the course of' senses of 'in' as well as a conventional sense (ibid.: 127–8); and he spoke of a 'criterial' as well as a 'means-to-end' sense of 'by' (ibid.: 129–30). A single theme surely underlies all these distinctions of 'senses'. When someone has done one thing in or by doing another, then her doing the one thing arises from her doing the other; and we can ask in what kind of way it arises. Suppose she does some particular thing by saying that p. Is it that in the circumstances saying that p quite simply constitutes doing the thing? Or is there a convention that saying that p counts as doing the thing? Or is it that her action of saying that p had certain consequences in virtue of which it is her doing the thing? Austin's different senses of 'in' or 'by' correspond to the different ways in which acts arise from one another – to different species of basicness, that is, including, it seems, at least *simple, conventional, consequential.*[9]

Austin's other main criteria for making the illocutionary–perlocutionary distinction may seem to come into their own now. According to (b), illocutionary acts are 'essentially conventional'; and according to (c), perlocutionary acts 'bring in consequences'. So we might wrap up all three criteria in one package, and say that Austin thought of illocutionary acts as those that are conventionally less basic than locutionary ones, and of perlocutionary acts as those that are consequentially less basic than locutionary ones. But the idea takes us no further if the project is to carve out the illocutionary. For if we hope to use the notion of consequence to separate the perlocutionary from the illocutionary, we shall now have to say that illocutionary acts do not import consequences at all. Yet Austin himself saw that consequences were not out of the picture where illocution is concerned: he thought that warning was an illocutionary act and persuading a perlocutionary one, but he appreciated that just as one's action would have to have had a certain effect on x for one to have persuaded of something, so apparently one's action would have to have had some effect on x for one to have warned her of something. It may be that the consequence which an action is seen to have when it is viewed as of an illocutionary act is less remote from the action than that which it is seen to have when it is viewed as of a perlocutionary act. So we could always say that a perlocutionary act is consequentially less basic than an illocutionary one (just as each is less basic than a locutionary one). But in order to be in a position actually to locate the boundary between illocutionary and perlocutionary, we should then need a way to distinguish between two different kinds of consequences of actions.[10]

This is where convention might be supposed to come in. Austin seems to have allowed that effects are on the scene whether we see someone as doing an illocutionary thing or as doing a perlocutionary thing, but to have thought that the effect a person's action has which is relevant to its being of an illocutionary act is a *conventional* matter. An audience's arriving in a state of having been warned is, in appropriate circumstances, supposedly, a conventional consequence of a speech action, whereas an audience's coming to be persuaded is a consequence but not a conventional one. Well, if we are in the habit of thinking that language use is a conventional matter, then it may seem fitting to employ convention in demarcating the illocutionary. But we need to be careful about our habitual thought. We may remark that it is a matter of convention that sounds have the significance that they do among the populations of speakers who share a language. The remark brings out the 'non-naturalness' of linguistic meaning. But as it stands, it can be a remark about the domain of the locutionary; it tells us nothing at all about how illocutionary acts arise, which is a question about how people can do what they do do in using sounds having the meanings which (perhaps conventionally) they have. When an English speaker uses the words 'There's a bull', then, arguably at least, she relies on the conventional significance round here that those words have in order to get into the open the thought that a bull is present. But what convention could she rely on in order to warn someone that there's a bull by expressing that thought? It is obviously wrong to say that there is a convention that one expresses the thought that something F is present to warn of the presence of something that is F. And a convention pertaining to thoughts about bulls in particular can hardly be in operation. (Exactly how many conventions would one then have to introduce?) No doubt there is a great deal to be said about the exact role of convention in language use.[11] Perhaps conventions determine locutionary acts, and perhaps some speech acts are indeed related to others by conventional basicness. The point here is only that the illocutionary consequences of speaking require no specific conventions beyond those of the locutionary acts which (arguably) they exploit.[12] Whereas we may isolate a particular causal transaction in explaining how one act arose from another where it was consequentially less basic than the other, there is no convention we can isolate in the cases where Austin seems to say that a convention determines one act to arise from another.

It could be that Austin thought that convention serves in defining the illocutionary because of his initial preoccupation with what is actually a very special class of illocutionary acts. Early on in *How to do Things with Words* (1962), Austin confined his attention to such acts as christening ships and getting married, where particular forms of words are used to carry out some ceremonial or ritual procedure. Perhaps his focus on tailored, conventionalized utterances combined with the vague enough idea that language is 'used in conformity with conventions' to make it appear to Austin that convention could characterize the broad notion of illocution that he later sought to explicate.[13] If so, that would explain in turn why Austin had nothing to say about illocution as such: he wrongly thought that convention said it all. But if it is indeed a mistake to accord to convention the role of marking out what is illocutionary, then we will need to know how illocutionary acts arise from locutionary ones. The absence from Austin's writings of any interest in the phenomenon of language is due to his having missed this question, I think.

1.3 Communication and reciprocity

We saw that illocutionary acts require consequences of a sort, but that they require no specific conventions beyond the locutionary ones which (arguably) are presupposed to them. Consider again the particular case. A person who, in suitable circumstances, expresses the thought that a bull is present may do the less basic thing of warning that a bull is present. There is no convention which ensures that expressing this thought gives rise to a warning; and if we want to speak of a consequence that her action must have had to have been a warning, then the only way is to use the same illocutionary term over again – the audience must have been warned. It seems that the speaker relies only on a certain receptiveness on her audience's part for her utterance to work for her as illocutionarily meant: the audience takes her to have done what she meant to. The audience's being warned appears to depend on nothing more than the audience and the speaker being parties of a normal linguistic exchange.

Let us give the name 'reciprocity' to the condition which provides for the particular way, just illustrated, in which one speech act can arise from another, more basic one. When reciprocity obtains between people, they are such as to recognize one another's speech as it is meant to be taken. That there is reciprocity is a fact exactly as ordinary, and exactly as mysterious, as the fact that speakers have the ability not only to voice meaningful thoughts, but also to be heard, by those who share the language, as doing some of the things that they do when they voice them.

Searle was quite explicit about the crucial element of what is going on here, which he illustrated for the speech act of *telling A that p*. 'If I am trying to tell someone something . . . , as soon as he recognizes [that I am trying to tell it to him], I have succeeded . . . Unless he recognizes that I am trying to tell him [it], I do not fully succeed in telling it to him' (Searle 1969: 47). So what a person relies on to tell A something is A's being open to the idea that she might be telling him what in fact she means to tell him: unless A can readily entertain the idea that she might be doing this, A could hardly take her to be doing it;[14] when A does take her so, he is in a state of mind sufficient, with her utterance, for her to have done it. What reciprocity provides for on this account is the success of attempts to do certain speech acts. It allows there to be things that speakers can do simply by being heard as (attempting to and thus) doing them.

If reciprocity replaces convention as the key to illocution, illocution can assume its proper place in an account of language use. Communication by words requires that speakers should produce recognizable sounds: a language, or system of locution, needs to be in place; and an audience must rely upon knowing what thought a speaker is expressing (determined, perhaps, by conventional relations between sounds and thoughts). But communication, which is a relation between people, requires more than common ways of interpreting patterns of sounds: it requires understanding on an audience's part which is attuned, not only to sounds' significance, but also to speakers' attempted performances of acts like telling. Whatever the particular language, it is a condition of its normal successful use – of speakers' intended communicative acts actually being done – that people be sufficiently in harmony, as it were, to provide for recognition of what speakers are up to. Speakers can exploit, in addition to their knowledge of a language, the existence of reciprocity.

1.4 Illocution

When reciprocity is seen to underlie illocution, we understand what is right in thinking of the illocutionary as within the domain of language (though not of language-specific meaning). And we thereby gain a sense of what is meant by saying that illocutionary acts are 'essentially linguistic': some features of speech actions flow from something in the nature of linguistic communication itself, and those features, which are illocutionary ones, constitute the actions as of certain specifically communicative acts.

Allowing ourselves a background of reciprocity, illocutionary acts might be circumscribed thus:

ϕ-ing is an illocutionary act iff a sufficient condition of a person's ϕ-ing that p[15] is that an attempt on her part at ϕ-ing that p causes an audience to take her to be ϕ-ing that p.

Illocutionary acts are characterized here by reference to certain types of effects (or results, or consequences, or upshots[16]) that actions may have. Just as it is sufficient for an action's being someone's killing someone (i.e. its being of the *killing* sort) that it have as effect someone's death, so it is sufficient for an action's being of some sort which is an illocutionary sort that it have as effect an audience's taking it some way. But the relevant effect, where an act is illocutionary, is very special, being the effect of being taken to be of the act that it is (thereby) of.

Illocutionary effects are especially immediate. And we see now why some have found it tempting to say (what Austin vacillated around saying) that only perlocutionary effects are genuine effects. Some philosophers under the influence of Hume will find it difficult to accept that we have an effect at all where illocution is in question: in order to be content to call something an effect of someone's doing something, they will want to be told more about it than that it is a piece of recognition that can only be specified by reference to its cause. Yet there is an obvious sense in which an audience's recognizing what someone who makes sounds is doing is, like anything else that ensues from those sounds' being made, distinct empirically from the making of them. What is special about illocutionary effects is that our concepts for them are just the concepts of the actions whose effects there are. We need a view about causation which, unlike any Humean one, allows for phenomena that partake of reciprocity, and which can accommodate communication in a causal world, which is, in part, a world of interacting persons.[17] Illocutionary acts are constituents of social practices, and they are sustained by the practices of which they are themselves a part. Actions which are of illocutionary acts work (causally) by virtue of that.

We can see now what truth underlies the idea of those who have wanted to equate the notions of *speech act* and *illocutionary act.* 'Speech act' is sometimes supposed to have application whenever there is an action which counts as a genuine piece of language use. Well, where an illocutionary act is in question, there is, as it were, no distance between doing it and doing it intentionally: the effect characteristic of a piece of illocution just is the effect of a successful attempt at it. So assuming that there is an action only when someone does something or other intentionally,[18] we know that when someone does an illocutionary thing, there is an action. Locutionary things are done intentionally as well, of course. But in the illocutionary case, it is the satisfaction of the very condition which ensures that there is an action which ensures also, via reciprocity, that the action has its own communicative point. If we wanted a definition of speech action, we could say that there is a speech action if, and only if, something illocutionary is done in using the words of some language. *Illocution* would then be shown to be the crux of all those actions which are communicative uses of language.[19]

Next we can see why perlocutionary acts can be thought of as outside the province of a study of language as such. Thinking, as we did, of perlocutionary acts as less basic than illocutionary ones, one may have a conception of an episode of speech, and of further things that went on not in the nature of the episode as an episode of speech but because of additional consequences. The idea of an additional consequence is now the idea of a consequence going beyond any that reciprocity could secure.[20] Some perlocutionary acts, such as *persuading*, require language for their performance, and are, to that extent, linguistic acts; but, unlike illocutionary acts, their being performed still relies on more than reciprocity. Even where some type of effect on an audience is the consequence proper to some perlocutionary act, more is required (to have an instance of that act) than simple recognition on the audience's part of what the speaker is up to. (If I am to *persuade* you that Austin was wrong about convention, it is not enough that you should realize that I mean you to come to think that Austin was wrong: to succeed in persuading you, I must avail myself of the power of reason working in you, and not just of the power of a language working for me.) The line between illocutionary and perlocutionary comes between those acts on the one hand which need invoke only reciprocity to have their proper consequences, and those acts on the other hand which invoke either more than reciprocity or something quite else.[21]

1.5 Illocution and performatives

Austin tried to develop an account of illocution in order to further his 'programme of finding a list of explicit performative words'. We have seen that the account he arrived at covered much more ground than the specifically conventionalized utterances he began from. This is not surprising, of course, given that illocutionary performances extend far beyond uses of performative formulae. When people use explicit performatives (and use them outside rituals or ceremonies), they do so, presumably, because their illocutionary attempts might not succeed without the help of a device for making them evident: when there are many things that one might be doing with one's words, one cannot always rely on one's audience to recognize exactly what one is doing, so that one may have recourse to using an explicit performative – to saying what one is doing, that is.

It might seem to require explanation how a speaker could do something simply by saying that she was: utterances of explicit performatives are typically *true*; and the *truth* of what someone says normally requires more than the mere fact of her saying it.[22] But there is an explanation of this when illocutionary acts are thought of as working through reciprocity. Then the speaker of an explicit performative is doing exactly the sort of thing that can be done with words: she is attempting something such that she will actually have done it if she is taken to be doing it. Saying that she is doing it evidently increases her chances of being taken to do it. One has a better chance of getting someone to recognize one's illocutionary intentions if one lets her know that one is warning her by saying that one is, than if one says only that there's a bull in the field.[23] But even so, one relies on the word 'warn''s meaning in one's mouth what it (perhaps conventionally) does, rather than on any convention peculiar to this form of speech. There may be other speech acts (other than warning) which there is hardly ever any chance of doing without the help of some explicit formula. But even where a performative is indispensable, it can be reciprocity's working that enables success.

Performative formulae are missing from the sentences we ordinarily use to do illocutionary things: we normally have no need to make explicit what we are doing, although, presumably, at considerable risk of considerable tedium, we always *could* make it explicit. *Stating*, for instance, is an illocutionary act, but one an explicit formula for whose performance is very seldom needed: for many expressions of some thought p, it seems to be out of the question that you might have gone in for them and not be seen to have stated that p. (What else might you have been up to?) It is no wonder, then, that Austin found that his distinction between constatives and performatives collapsed: it could not survive his recognition that even when we are stating something, we are doing some illocutionary thing.

Since the explicit performative is a device employed when, for one or another reason, the ordinary working of reciprocity might not run smoothly, Austin, by focusing on such a device, prevented himself from seeing reciprocity working smoothly, as it ordinarily does. This meant that even when he turned from the limited category of conventionalized performatives to the kind he came to call 'explicit', he still failed to grasp the full import of his overall idea of particular things in whose nature it is to be done using words. In order to have a clear idea of reciprocity in action, we should look to central cases of illocution which are furthest from Austin's starting point and which interested him least. Examples of central cases include not only stating (or asserting, or saying in the ordinary *oratio obliqua* sense) but also asking, telling to.[24]

1.6 Illocution in practice

In defending the suggested definition of illocutionary act, I note finally how little it requires. (a) It does not require that every doing of an illocutionary act should be a use of language. (b) It offers no guarantee that an audience will actually realize that a speaker does the illocutionary thing that she means to. (c) It does not rule it out that a speaker might do some illocutionary thing even where no one thought that she meant to. Although these three points show how undemanding the definition is, they can in turn be used to reveal how powerful the concept of illocution itself is.

(a) Austin recognized the first point when he said that an illocutionary act 'can be brought off non-verbally' (Austin 1962: 121). He went on to say that 'even then to deserve the name of an illocutionary act, for example a warning, it [sic] must be a conventional non-verbal act'. This seems wrong; you do not need to draw on a convention in order to deploy the gestures and expressions you may use to warn someone of something. Austin seems to have thought that every action which is of some illocutionary act must partake of whatever is essential to illocution, and then been led to error by thinking of convention as the essence of illocution. Thinking instead of reciprocity as its essence, we understand how there can be non-verbal performances of illocutionary acts by seeing the potential for non-verbal uses of the communicative potential (reciprocity) that language exploits.

(b) When the full range of illocutionary acts is considered, it becomes plain that illocutionary attempts may fail. We have seen that people may sometimes use explicit performatives because their illocutionary attempts would not succeed without the help of a device for making them transparent. But if one's illocutionary meaning would sometimes not be conveyed if it were not made explicit, then, very likely, when it is not made explicit, it is sometimes not in fact conveyed. In practice of course, simple misunderstanding of how a speaker was to be taken is not uncommon. But despite this, there has to be some truth in the thought that illocutionary attempts are such as to be successful. It is a condition of the existence of attempts to do illocutionary things that, when all is well, they should be recognizable for what they are. For unless it were normal for such attempts to be seen to be the illocutionary acts that they may in fact be, there would be no reciprocity and there would not then be illocutionary acts to be done.

(c) The third point was that, although the definition says that someone's recognizing that S meant to do an illocutionary thing is sufficient for her doing it, it does not say that it is necessary. And it would certainly be wrong to think of illocutionary acts as things that can only be done with a little help from an audience. Even illocutionary verbs that we may think of as central, such as *stating*, may not take an indirect object for an addressee, suggesting that no audience need be in the picture (though of course statements typically are made *to* someone). And even where there is an intended audience, the speaker may do some illocutionary act although the audience does not latch on to it. In fact we talk with some ambivalence about cases where an illocutionary attempt is not recognized. (There are examples which we might describe either with 'She warned him, but he never realized the danger' or 'She tried in vain to warn him.') When Searle spoke of '*fully* succeeding', he presumably meant cases in which an illocutionary act is performed with recognition of its performance, so that where there is no recognition there is less than 'full success'. 'Unless [my audi-

ence] recognizes ..., I have not fully succeeded in telling him [something]',
he said (Searle 1969: 47).

There is surely something right about thinking that performances of
illocutionary acts in the absence of reciprocity are in some way defective.
For such performances are not such as to further the usual communicative
ends of language. Someone who does an illocutionary act in spite of the
fact that, in the particular case, her action does not have the effect characteristic of such an act, is not fully understood: she is likely, for instance, to
be frustrated in doing any perlocutionary acts she might have intended to
go in for. It is true that, according to this way of looking at things, actual
doings of illocutionary acts may quite often be defective. But it should not
be counted an objection to using reciprocity to demarcate *illocutionary acts*
that this has the consequence that there are defective cases. The claim is
that *reciprocity*, providing as it does for normal performances of certain
acts, is central to the general idea of *illocution*. And the idea of reciprocity
can be essential to the idea of illocution, without the working of reciprocity's being essential to the isolated performance of any illocutionary
act.[25] Illocutionary acts (such as stating or warning) are those things for
which reciprocity suffices – things which, even if they can be done without
anyone's taking them to be done, are such as to be done when an audience
takes them to be. And if you are genuinely to communicate with language,
then reciprocity is what you must rely on: only where reciprocity prevails,
are you fully understood. One might say that 'perfect' illocutionary acts are
done invoking reciprocity.

2 ILLOCUTION'S SIGNIFICANCE

2.1 The example of refusing

'Perfect' illocutionary acts can be peculiarly easy to do. Provided that you
can get the words out, and you have a suitably receptive audience, there
can be no obstacle to your full success. The effect you need to have, which
then constitutes your action as, for example, *stating something*, is an effect
that can be had without any contrivance on your part. No contrivance is
needed where the presence of reciprocity can be relied on; for then the
illocutionary effects, of recognition, which speech actions have, are present
in the social situation which speakers share with their audiences.

Now there is a counterpart to the fact that 'perfect' illocutionary acts can
be peculiarly easy to do: they can be impossible to do. Just as it is more or
less automatic that an attempt at an illocutionary act is fully successful
when certain socially defined conditions obtain; so, when certain conditions do not obtain, there cannot be a fully successful performance.

An example which illustrates this comes from the case of a woman
responding to a man's sexual advances. In the notorious words of Judge

David Wild: 'it is not just a question of saying no'.[26] The judge was in the process of acquitting a man accused of rape; he wanted the court to believe that the woman had meant 'Yes' by *no*. But a different construction can be put upon his words. To do a perfect illocutionary act of refusing, an utterance of the word 'no' is not enough: a woman may mean to refuse, but a condition of her having fully successfully refused – that she be recognized as attempting to refuse – may not be fulfilled.

Of course, as we have seen, there can be an illocutionary act even when, the speaker having not been fully successful in Searle's sense, there is no 'perfect' illocutionary act. And taking the woman's part against the judge, we can say that she *did* refuse, and say this assuming that she was sincere and without thinking about how she was actually taken. The judge, however, wanted to put the woman's sincerity into question. He hoped to create a presumption of this woman's being insincere; and if she had been insincere, then indeed there would not have been a non-defective act of refusal on her part. By creating such a presumption in court, the judge may have made it difficult to anyone there to believe that the woman had refused (even if she had). Where a presumption of a speaker's lack of sincerity is in place, the demands on the audience lapse, and it becomes impossible for a speaker, with however much sincerity she actually utters 'No', to be taken to refuse.

Once reciprocity is in the picture, we see how it is that a non-defective act of refusal makes demands of an audience as well as of a speaker: such an act must not only be attempted, but be taken to be. We see then that if the presumption introduced with 'It's not just a question of saying no' governed the actual circumstances in which a woman said 'No', then in those circumstances it would be impossible for her fully successfully to refuse. A condition of her refusing which is outside her control would be bound to remain unsatisfied.[27]

No doubt it requires some explaining how it could become impossible to do a perfectly good act of refusing even using a word as well suited for refusal as 'no' is. But this could be explained if we believed that a view of women informs the social practices of which our speech actions are a part.[28] The mind-sets and expectations of those with whom we speak are as much a part of the social situation as our utterances themselves. If the situation is such that the reciprocity of attempt and recognition required for the particular illocution is missing, then a woman's potential for participating in illocutionary acts, and thus, in turn, for securing wanted perlocutionary consequences, is diminished.

2.2 Silencing

I think that the potential of members of certain groups to participate in speech acts is what is at issue in some of the debates about free speech. And I shall finish with a notion of *silencing* which makes a connection between these debates and what I have said about illocution.[29] (The topic of free speech itself I leave for another occasion.)

Feminists have claimed that 'women's voices have gone unheard, masked by male power realities incorporated into language';[30] and similar claims have been made about the 'silencing' of other oppressed groups (other than women). I suggest that when power relations are said to be 'incorporated into language', one idea is that the scope and limits of reciprocity have been determined by powerful groups in a community, and determined so as to restrict the illocutionary potential of members of less powerful groups. A group that is said to be 'silenced', then, is one whose members may be thought of as incapacitated as fully successful doers of some illocutionary acts. It is not that they literally cannot be heard, but that they are not in a position fully successfully to do some of the things that others might fully successfully do using speech. Illocutionary things, whose achievement usually consists in nothing more than someone's being heard (literally) in a setting of reciprocity, are things that they cannot do.

The example of sexual refusal has provided a stark and rather special example of a silenced person – of a person deprived, through no fault of her own, of her illocutionary potential. We should need to turn to different sorts of example to show that the phenomenon of silencing could be real and widespread and affect even such acts as stating. It would then be a further question whether, and to what extent, social mechanisms of silencing are actually at work in our own or any other culture, diminishing people's powers of using speech. But others have made the empirical claim that the promulgation of a demeaning view of a group has rendered members of that group relatively powerless parties in communicative exchanges. Here I have wanted only to make such claims intelligible, by connecting the notion of silencing with something fundamental to an understanding of language use.[31]

This is reciprocity. It has a role to play in an account of language use at a point where Austin wrongly supposed the notion of convention would serve; and it is indispensable to a proper appreciation of the phenomenon of communication between human beings, who, except for reciprocity, would not do any of the things they actually do using words.[32]

APPENDIX

Although I have taken over an idea from Searle in characterizing illocution, I have paid no attention to what Searle himself has had to say about illocution. In fact I think that failure to register the distinction between actions and acts has been an obstacle to his finding a correct, general characterization of *illocution*. (It has not been an obstacle to his providing a variety of interesting accounts, of which the account of telling is only one.) I shall attempt to make this out here (A.1). And I add some further comment on telling (A.2).

A.1

Searle is one of the writers who uses 'illocutionary act' as if it were equivalent to 'speech act' (see section 1.1). The usage can make us think that the idea of *speech* is what underlies the idea of illocution so that nothing further needs to be said to bring out what is distinctive of the *illocutionary*. The usage is encouraged by a conflation of actions with acts, which shows up in such remarks as these: 'The production of the sentence token ... is the illocutionary act' (Searle 1965: 222); and 'The minimal units of human communication are speech acts of a type called illocutionary' (Searle and Vanderveken 1985: 1). 'The production' of the first quotation, and 'the unit' of the second, are presumably to be thought of as particulars. But then they should not be identified with acts of any type, illocutionary or other. (In Searle, a link between 'speech act' and 'illocutionary act' is sometimes forged by way of the claim that an intention to communicate something to someone is a necessary condition for the performance of a speech act. Assuming that there is a performance of a speech act if, and only if, there is a speech action, this claim introduces the conception of speech action defined in section 1.5.)

When Searle and Vanderveken say 'A propositional act is an abstraction from the total illocutionary act' (ibid.: 9), they speak as if a total act were some composite thing of which somehow the whole was illocutionary. To understand this, we might think of a speech act as a speech-action-restricted-to-certain-acts-it-was-actually-of – where the acts in question will be the illocutionary ones and all those less basic than it (compare nn. 8 and 9 on Austin's idea of a 'total speech act'). But when 'speech act' is used in this hybrid way, it is not clear that a propositional (i.e. locutionary) act is any more or less an abstraction from a total speech act than an illocutionary act is. Searle and Vanderveken elaborate on the sense in which a propositional act is supposed to be an abstraction when they say that 'a speaker cannot simply express a proposition and do nothing more'. But (a) it is not impossible to express a proposition without doing an illocutionary thing; and (b) an illocutionary act (just like a propositional one) cannot be the only thing that a speaker does (when there is some use of words). Their idea must be that every genuine speech action is of some illocutionary act (see above). That idea accords some priority to illocutionary acts, but cannot reveal what makes illocution fundamental to language use.

Searle and Vanderveken wish to use the notion of what is essentially linguistic to characterize the illocutionary. They say, 'Perlocutionary acts, unlike illocutionary acts, are not essential linguistic.' And they give a reason 'For it is possible to achieve perlocutionary effects without performing any speech act at all' (ibid.: 12). But the reason cannot supply any correct sense in which the illocutionary is essentially linguistic, since (a) some illocutionary things can be done without the use of speech (as we saw in section 1.1); and (b) some perlocutionary things cannot be achieved excepting by using speech (as we saw in section 1.5). Here Searle and Vanderveken seem to take a step backwards from Austin, who would have accepted that there was something right about the 'essentially linguistic' characterization of the illocutionary, but who was careful to note both of points (a) and (b).

In an attempt to home in on illocution, or the essentially linguistic, Searle and Vanderveken follow Austin in using *convention*. They say (ibid.: 12):

> There could not be any convention that such and such an utterance counts as convincing you, or persuading you, or annoying you, or exasperating you, or amusing you.... There can be conventions whereby such and such counts as a statement or counts as informing you.

And they take the possibility of using explicit performatives to show that conventions operate in illocution. But if explicit performatives rely only on words being used as having their ordinary significance, then noting this possibility does not help to characterize the illocutionary; the conventions in question now are only those that are acknowledged in dealing with locution, albeit those attaching to the particular words that denote what are in fact illocutionary acts. (This is not to deny a relation between illocutionary acts and uses of explicit performatives (see section 1.4).)

A.2

I have taken over Searle's account of telling to illustrate illocution, but should note that it may be controversial whether telling is in fact an illocutionary act. Consider: 'One must assert in order to inform or tell, but not *vice versa*; and telling now seems to be the point or purpose of assertion. This classifies telling among what have ... been called per-locutionary acts' (Aldrich 1966: 56). Well, there is no reason to rule out the possibility that a single action could be someone's doing one thing and her doing another thing, where both those things were illocutionary acts; so the fact that someone may assert and tell has no tendency on its own to show that telling is not illocutionary. And we might think that on occasion a person may state that p only because there is no other way to tell someone that p (just as she utters words that mean that p only because that is her only way to state that p): this removes any suggestion of telling's being an ulterior purpose (where ulterior purpose is associated with what is perlocutionary).

Another objection to treating telling as illocutionary may come from someone who thinks (a) that no one is told that p unless he becomes informed that p; and (b) that a piece of recognition cannot make the difference to whether someone comes to be informed that p. Two points may be made in response. (a) It is not obvious that we cannot tell people things that they reject and thus do not become informed of. (The matter is complicated, see Radford 1969. We show an ambivalence about how to use 'tell' which is parallel to that in the case of 'warn' illustrated parenthetically in the text of section 1.4.) (b) Awareness of what a speaker is up to can be part and parcel not only of understanding but also of the actual communication of facts. Thus reciprocity can ground telling, as well as asserting. (The present objection might also be made against Searle's idea that 'there can be conventions whereby such and such counts as informing you' (see above). I find it much easier to see how reciprocity could provide for the passage of information than to see how convention could.)

It is because I find attractive the view that reciprocity allows for the communication of facts that I am happy to move as directly as I do from Searle's account of telling to an account of illocution. Someone who rejected the view and thought that telling was perlocutionary could still accept that we gain the crucial idea of reciprocity from the account of (fully successfully) telling, and so could think that reciprocity works in illocution in much the way that I suggest.

NOTES

1 Searle (1965) and (1969). There are further references in the Appendix.
2 In non-philosophical English, there is no term unambiguously true of what philosophers regularly call actions. In the ordinary way we are not concerned with the sort of generalization that requires the recognition of a class of actions, and each of 'act' and 'action' sometimes plays one, sometimes the other role that I have marked out for 'act' and 'action'. On the other hand, 'thing done', and the 'something' of 'she did something', only ever (outside of philosophy) denote the things that I am calling 'acts'.
3 See Davidson (1971) for the idea of using 'actions' unambiguously to denote events.

Davidson himself, and many who follow him, have recourse to the formal mode in distinguishing acts from actions: he speaks of actions as coming under different *descriptions*. This is an alternative way of making the act–action distinction used here, because for each (new) description of an action, there is something (new) the agent does, i.e. some (new) act which she performs. But resorting to the formal mode has made it seem as though there were no material-mode talk of the things we do. This in turn has made it seem as though when we are not at the level of descriptions, we must be speaking of actions (rather than what we are sometimes actually speaking of, i.e. acts, things that are done). I avoid Davidson's more familiar way of putting it, then, because I think it has perpetuated the confusion of acts with actions.

And Davidson, whose use of 'action' I am following, is not himself consistent. He speaks, for example, of 'primitive actions'. But 'more primitive than' cannot be a relation between actions: when one thing that someone did is more primitive than another thing she did, her doing the one thing (the action, Davidson would agree) is the *same* as her doing the other thing, and thus cannot be related to it by the non-symmetrical 'more primitive than' relation. Davidson's 'more primitive than' is a relation like '*more basic than*', which is a relation between acts that I make use of in section 1.2 below.

4   Mainly these are writers who are not careful to distinguish acts from actions. See the Appendix; and consider a not at all untypical claim such as this: 'The root idea of a perlocutionary act is of an act which when performed by saying something can be redescribed as the performance of an illocutionary act with certain consequences' (Holdcroft 1978: 20). Speaking like this – as if acts could be redescribed – will lead to the identification of what are in fact different acts, and thus will lead, for instance, to the identification of an arbitrary speech act with an arbitrary illocutionary act. What are really redescribed, when various different acts are seen to have been done, are (in my terminology, see nn. 2 and 3) actions.

5   Austin in fact used 'locutionary' in two different ways (my vague 'incorporate' covers both). When he used it in a characterization of the distinction between illocutionary and perlocutionary (on which more below), he always meant by 'locutionary' an act of the sort which he elsewhere called rhetic. For further details, see Hornsby 1988.

6   Thus stated, there is nothing novel about this suggestion. But there is no agreed way of interpreting it: see the Appendix for Searle's interpretation.

7   Here is an example within the realm of speech acts: it seems equally possible to think of a rhetic act (saying that it is green, for example) as done in doing, or as done by doing, a phatic act (saying 'It's green').

8   The term was introduced by Danto; see his 1965. In Danto and others, the confusion of acts with actions has prevented a correct understanding of basicness. (Cp. n. 3 on Davidson on primitiveness.)

A caveat is needed about the use of 'basic' here. Strictly speaking, one should not think of one act as more basic than another *tout court*; at least for certain pairs of acts, there might be an occasion on which someone did one by doing the other, and a different occasion on which someone did that other by doing the one. Strictly, then, 'more basic than' should be defined relative to particular actions. When we are in the domain of speech act theory, however, we find (except for some insignificant exceptions) that where the relation '*more basic than*' obtains between two things done relative to some one action, it obtains also relative to every other action which is someone's doing the one and her doing the other.

9   Compare Goldman on different sorts of 'generation', in his 1970 chapter 2. Goldman himself takes this to be a relation between actions (or 'act-tokens' as he sometimes calls them). But that is because he fails to see that someone's doing one thing can be (the same event as) her doing another.

The idea of the collection of all the acts arising, by whatever means, from the phonetic (most basic) act will give us Austin's notion of a *total* speech act (relative to any particular speech action, cp. n. 8).

10 When Austin spoke of 'a line between an action we do (here an illocution) and its consequences' (1962: 104), he simply helped himself to the idea of an illocution in separating off the perlocutionary – as if the distinction had already been made out.

When Austin speaks of 'importing an arbitrarily long stretch of what might also be called the "consequences" of our act into the nomenclature of the act itself' (1962: 107), the struggles of someone who has not made a distinction between actions and acts are evident. The 'act' which here has consequences is what we are calling an action. 'The nomenclature of the act' then corresponds to various speech acts (because finding new pieces of nomenclature is a matter of coming to see an action as of different acts, cp. n. 3 above).

11 For a scepticism about the role of convention in an account of language which is

more thoroughgoing than that which is registered here, see Davidson 1984: 265–80.

12 Cp. Strawson 1964. Strawson himself introduces an idea deriving from Grice, of what a speaker non-naturally means, at the place in the account where Austin relied upon *convention.*

13 Cp. Warnock 1989, and 1.4 below.

14 I depart from Searle here, saying 'take her to' rather than 'attempt to take her to'. Those who appreciate the virtues of simplicity in this area will understand why I do not wish to see the audience as employing the concept of attempt. (Of course Searle's own account avoids Gricean-style complexity.)

The use by both Searle and me of the concept of attempt in describing even the *speaker's* state of mind might be questioned. My own view (about action generally, now) is that we attempt to do everything that we intentionally do. (The view will not be found acceptable unless one appreciates that it is possible to attempt something without thinking of oneself as attempting it, and possible then in turn for a hearer to recognize that a speaker has done something in witnessing what is actually an attempt at doing it, but without thinking of it as an attempt at doing the thing.)

15 Strictly one should insert here 'for arbitrary p'. The effect of the insertion is to ensure that the definition tells us whether ϕ-*ing* is an illocutionary act, rather than whether, for particular p, ϕ-*ing that p* is. Something will not be shown to be an illocutionary act by finding particular examples where a speaker's attempt at ϕ-ing that p causes an audience to take the speaker to have ϕ-d that p.

16 I do not distinguish between these here. Although the distinctions are important, I hope it will be clear that they cannot serve on their own to draw the illocutionary–perlocutionary distinction.

17 The view about causation is what inspired 'The Logical Connection Argument', supposedly ruling out the possibility that the connection between (say) someone's wanting to annoy x and her annoying x could be causal. The usual response to the Argument is to say that someone's wanting to annoy x can be redescribed, so that any inclination to speak of 'its' logical connection with her annoying x must go away. It is not obvious that the usual response will work as usual in the present case. But it is also not obvious that there is any pressure to make the usual response, excepting as this comes from a questionable Humean view.

18 This criterion is the one that Davidson made famous, though what he said was that an action is an event that is intentional under some description. See n. 3 for an account of my reluctance to put it Davidson's way.

19 And we can then register agreement with some of Searle's ideas: see the Appendix.

20 Since it can be vague (or doubtful) whether reciprocity is working on its own, there is nothing here to ensure that the line between the illocutionary and the perlocutionary is a hard and fast one. (See the Appendix for a doubt about which side of the line 'tell' should come.)

On the present account, the class of perlocutionary acts is heterogeneous, and we should need to make distinctions within it to understand the character of some of the acts that it contains. *Insinuating* and *showing off* (for example) will turn out to be perlocutionary acts, although in Strawson 1964 they are treated as illocutionary acts, albeit special ones. It is a matter for theoretical decision how to use 'illocutionary' at the end of the day: I have been guided by the idea that, seeing what is illocutionary as what is essentially linguistic, we should expect the class of illocutionary acts to be a relatively homogeneous one.

21 The line drawn here marks off the illocutionary from what is less basic than it.

Further refinements would be needed to take account of the fact that more than one chain of consequences may flow from a single action. People with definite conceptions of the perlocutionary may want to introduce such refinements, and to carry out the further work required to circumscribe perlocutionary acts within the class of acts on the 'less-basic-than' side of the line drawn here.

22   The thought here is what led Austin to say that utterances of explicit performatives are not truth-evaluable. See Hornsby 1988 for a more detailed account (and criticism) of what led him there.

23   At least if the circumstances are such that (reciprocity ensures that) it is plausible that one is warning.

24   If it can be agreed that the ordinary *oratio obliqua* 'say' is used in reports of illocutionary acts, then it will become clear how much ground illocution covers. Though there are differences of nuance, I suspect that 'state' and 'assert' can be treated as grander words for what we usually call saying. The reason why theoreticians talk so much about stating and asserting, rather than the plainer 'saying', is that they need to reserve the use of 'say' ('strict and literal saying', as Grice was wont to put it) for the *rhetic* (or *locutionary* – see n. 5) act.

For the idea of 'central' illocutionary acts, see Hornsby 1988. And for an account which shows how *asking* and *telling to* might be accommodated, see Hornsby 1986.

25   Analytical philosophy's obsessive search for ('logically') necessary and sufficient conditions for the application of a concept (as opposed to a search for 'its essence') can then be part of the explanation why the notion of reciprocity has been overlooked. See McDowell 1980, a paper to which I am much indebted.

26   The judge said this during his summing up, reported in *The Sunday Times*, 12 December 1982.

27.   Doubts on the speaker's part about the obtaining of reciprocity could lead to an inability to go in for illocution: if it seemed that there was no point in trying to be taken to have done something, because one was very unlikely to be so taken, that in turn would detract from one's ability sincerely to do the thing.

28   I mean a view according to which women who do not behave with especial modesty or dress with especial circumspection are ready and willing to gratify men's sexual urges, but will feign unwillingness, whether through a pretended decency, or through a desire to excite. If the view were widespread that this is how women conduct themselves, and if it determined a man's expectations, then it is easy to imagine circumstances in which the reciprocity of intention and understanding required for refusal was missing.

The idea that pornography's production and consumption may promote, or perpetuate, such a view is the context for Dworkin's discussion of free speech (see n. 29).

29   Consider Ronald Dworkin: 'Only by characterizing certain ideas as themselves "silencing" ideas – only by supposing that censoring pornography is like stopping people from drowning out other speakers – can [feminists] hope to justify censorship within the constitutional scheme that assigns a pre-eminent place to free speech' (Dworkin 1991: 108). Dworkin thinks that the assimilation is a confusion: the argument of the remainder of this paper shows why it would not be a confusion if pornography were an agent of silencing.

30   See, for example, Olsen 1978. The notion of 'silence' has been put to many uses in feminist theory. I am singling out a use of the verb whose connection with political theory is most immediate.

31   For a treatment of the claim that pornography silences women (cp. n. 28), and a treatment of the case of sexual refusal (in line with my own, but using a different conception of a speech act and drawing attention to different features

of the case), see Langton 1993. This paper is full of important suggestions about the bearing of ideas in the philosophy of language on feminist debate.

32 I assume that the point of locution cannot be understood except by way of illocutionary notions. Opposition to a non-social conception of language's workings is usually based in denial that meanings can be attached to words privately; opposition might be based also in a denial that speech action can get a foothold outside a context of reciprocity.

9 Anti-individualism and speech act theory

Steven Davis

INTRODUCTION

An illocutionary act is an act which a speaker performs in saying something. It can characteristically be made explicit by the use of a performative verb formula. For example, if a speaker says, 'I'll be there' and it is unclear whether it is a promise that has been made the speaker can make it explicit by saying 'I promise that I'll be there.' Many types of illocutionary acts can be attributed to speakers by ascribing to them sentences which contain 'that'-clauses which specify the content of the illocutionary act which the speaker performed.[1] To revert to our example above, we can say about our speaker that she promised that she would be there. In so saying we attribute to the speaker the act of promising by ascribing to her the sentence 'She promised that she would be there' which contains the content clause 'that she would be there'.

Not all illocutionary act types can be ascribed using 'that'-clauses. For example, if our speaker welcomes someone to her home or thanks him for a gift, there is no appropriate ascription which contains a 'that'-clause which ascribes to our speaker the act which she has performed. We do not say 'She thanked that ...' or 'She welcomed that ...'. We can say, then, that these acts have no contents.[2] However, there are other illocutionary acts the ascriptions for which contain no 'that'-clauses, but which have contents. If our speaker begs Oscar to come to the party, this can be attributed to the speaker by using, 'She begged Oscar to come to the party' which does not contain a 'that'-clause. But the absence of a 'that'-clause does not mean that the act has no content. It is, however, not clear what content it contains. I shall return to this in what follows.

One way of distinguishing those illocutionary acts which have contents from those which do not is to distinguish those acts which can be reported by intentional discourse from those that cannot. There are two standard marks of intentional discourse: failure of existential generalization or of substitutivity of coreferential terms. That is, illocutionary-act ascriptions which contain obliquely occurring expressions to which existential generalization or substitution of coextensive terms *salva veritate* does not apply, ascribe intentional illocutionary acts to speakers.[3] Let us take as our first example,

(1) Alice says that Hamlet is the Prince of Denmark.

From (1) neither (2) nor (3) follows:

(2) There is something such that Alice says that it is the Prince of Denmark.
(3) Alice says that Hamlet is Hamlet.

So this marks someone's saying that such and such is the case as an illocutionary act that has content.

In some cases only one of our tests for intentionality applies. Substitutivity, but not existential generalization, applies to ascriptions of acts of promising and begging. Consider

(4) Alice promised to find Hamlet.
(5) Alice begged Oscar to find Hamlet.

Even if Alice does not know that Hamlet is the Prince of Denmark, it still follows that

(6) Alice promised to find the Prince of Denmark.
(7) Alice begged Oscar to find the Prince of Denmark.

There might be some doubt that substitutivity applies to term positions within the scope of 'promise' and 'beg' in reports of promising or begging. But suppose that Alice promises to marry the man with the black hat and unknown to her the man with the black hat is her father. She has tragically, I would think, thereby, promised to marry her father.

It might seem that because coreferential expressions can be substituted in reports of acts of promising and begging that the reports are *de re* and, therefore, that they do not characterize the contents of Alice's acts of promising or begging. If this were the case, the term positions which are open to substitutivity should be open to existential generalization. But they are not. It does not follow from (4) and (5) respectively, that

(8) There is someone such that Alice promised to find him.
(9) There is someone such that Alice begged Oscar to find him.

Both existential generalization and substitutivity of identicals apply to term positions in ascriptions of thanking or welcoming someone. Consider the following:

(10) Alice thanked Oscar for the book.
(11) Alice welcomed Oscar to the party.

Suppose that, unknown to Alice, the book is the prized possession of Oscar and the party is the noisiest affair on the block. (12) and (13) follow from (10), and (14) and (15) from (11):

(12) Alice thanked Oscar for his prized possession.
(13) There is something for which Alice thanked Oscar.
(14) Alice welcomed Oscar to the noisiest affair on the block.
(15) There is something to which Alice welcomed Oscar.

We can say, then, that the illocutionary acts which would be attributed by using (3), (4) and (5) are illocutionary acts that relate a speaker to a content, while uses of (10) and (11) do not so relate illocutionary acts to contents.

Suppose that I believe *de dicto* that the sun sets over Vancouver Island and that I say *de dicto* what I believe, namely that the sun sets over Vancouver Island. It seems that I can have the belief and say what I do, even if there were no sun nor Vancouver Island. Neither my believing or saying, nor what I believe or say, seems to depend upon the existence of anything except me. It appears that they only require that I have certain concepts or notions and the ability to combine them in certain ways. We might think that it follows from this that the conditions of individuation of beliefs and illocutionary acts depend only on an individual's internal states and behaviour and not on objects other than the individual to which he is related or on the practices of his social or linguistic community. One might further hold that a theory of beliefs, illocutionary acts and intentional states in general, can be adequate without making reference to anything other than the individual. Borrowing a term from Burge, we shall call the views about the individuation and explanation of intentional states 'individualist' and theories which presuppose this view 'individualist theories of intentional states' (Burge 1979: 73).

In a series of articles Burge has presented arguments which cut against individualist criteria of individuation of intentional mental states and events.[4] In this paper I shall try to show what consequences Burge's arguments have for individualist criteria of individuation of illocutionary acts.[5] First, I shall lay out two of Burge's arguments against individualist theories of intentional mental states and events; and second, I shall apply these arguments to the illocutionary acts of saying and promising.

TERMINOLOGICAL DISTINCTIONS

Before turning to these arguments it is necessary to introduce some terminology. Following Burge, I shall call the constituents of contents 'notions' (Burge 1979: 75). For example, understanding the notion *arthritis* is to know what arthritis is. There is a connection between terms and notions. A term can be said to express a set of notions. Thus, 'arthritis' expresses the notion *arthritis* and someone who understands 'arthritis' has the notion of arthritis.[6] Expressions, then, can be used to characterize the content of a thought or an illocutionary act. If Alice says, truthfully,

(16) Arthritis is a disease.

we can capture what belief she expresses and what illocutionary act she performs in, respectively:

(17) Alice believes that arthritis is a disease.
(18) Alice said that arthritis is a disease.

In (17) and (18) the 'that'-clause containing 'arthritis' serves to characterize, respectively, the contents of Alice's belief and of her act of saying
and the contents expressed contain the notion of arthritis.

Not all intentional illocutionary act ascriptions have 'that'-clause content
clauses. Let us reconsider (4) and (5). Neither sentence contains in its
surface form a 'that'-clause. (4), however, is synonymous with

(19) Alice promised that she will find Hamlet.

Thus, it is plausible to suppose that the content clause for (4) is 'that Alice
will find Hamlet'.[7]

There does not, however, seem to be an obvious 'that'-clause candidate
for (5). There is no sentence that has a 'that'-clause complement which is
synonymous with (5). The following is not grammatical.

(20) *Alice begged Oscar that he find Hamlet.

A plausible candidate for the content clause for Alice's act of begging is the
open sentence 'x find Hamlet'.[8]

The second bit of terminology I wish to introduce is also adopted from
Burge (1979: 77). I shall speak of *someone's understanding a notion.*
Understanding the notion of arthritis, for example, is knowing what
arthritis is. Now the key to Burge's thought experiments, as we shall see, is
that someone might have a notion which is part of the content of his
thought or illocutionary act while having only partial understanding of the
notion. When someone has partial understanding of a notion, x, we cannot
speak about the person's knowing what x is. I shall also speak of *someone's
conception of x.* For example, someone's conception of arthritis is what the
person takes arthritis to be. This, then, tells us what the person takes the
notion of arthritis to be. But this does not mean that what a person takes
his notion of arthritis to be is in fact what his notion of arthritis is. A person
can have a conception of arthritis, but his conception can be mistaken or
partial and thus, would not have an understanding of his own notion of
arthritis, although he might be said to have a partial understanding of it.
That is, a person is not authoritative about what his notions are which play
a role in characterizing his own beliefs. He can make mistakes in characterizing his own beliefs.

There are two ways in which someone can have a partial understanding
of a notion. The first is one in which a person has a conception of x, but the
conception he has is not sufficient to distinguish what he takes the notion
of x to be from other notions. In a certain sense he has an incomplete
understanding of the notion of x. The second is one in which a person has a

mistaken conception of x and thus, has a partial understanding of the notion of x. Both sorts of partial understanding are employed in Burge's two arguments, the first in his Twin Earth 'water' argument and the second in his 'arthritis' argument. Neither are necessary to the arguments in which they occur. The 'water' argument could appeal to a mistaken conception, while the 'arthritis' argument could appeal to an incomplete understanding.

BURGE'S ARGUMENTS AND THEIR APPLICATION TO SAYING

Let us turn to Burge's arguments, the conclusion of which is that there are cases in which the bodily movements, the dispositions to behaviour and physical internal states of a person, all non-intentionally described, are not sufficient to individuate his intentional mental states. I shall apply these arguments to illocutionary acts and try to show that the internal states and the bodily movements of a speaker are not sufficient for individuating such acts. Burge presents two kinds of arguments, the first of which emphasizes the role played by the objects to which a person is related in individuating his intentional mental states; and the second, the role played by his linguistic community. The first thought experiment is a variation of Putnam's famous Twin Earth argument (Putnam 1975: 139–44).

Let us imagine a speaker of English, whom I shall call 'Oscar', who inhabits earth and who says such things as, 'Water is good to drink', 'Water is the stuff in rivers and lakes', 'Water freezes in the winter and turns into snow and ice', 'Water, when not frozen, is a clear liquid', etc. Oscar does not know, however, that water is H_2O; it is not part of his conception of water, although it is part of the conception of others to whom Oscar defers on scientific matters. Because of this, Oscar's understanding of the notion *water* is incomplete. Despite this, it is clear that he believes that water is good to drink, that water is the stuff in rivers and lakes, etc.

Now let us imagine someone else, Twoscar, on a planet, Twin Earth, which is identical to Earth, described non-intentionally, except that where Earth has water, Twin Earth has XYZ which has the same superficial characteristics as water.[9] It freezes; it is good to drink; it is the stuff in rivers and lakes; etc. Moreover, the language spoken by Twoscar and the members of his linguistic community contains 'water'. Twoscar, then, is identical to Oscar in the history of his stimulation patterns, in his dispositions to behaviour, in his bodily movements and his internal physical states, again described non-intentionally. Thus, Twoscar would utter the same sentences, phonologically and syntactically described, in the same sorts of situations as Oscar. If he were asked what the stuff is in rivers and lakes, he would say, 'Water', etc. Moreover, Twoscar does not know that the stuff he calls 'water' is XYZ. He, too, has partial understanding of the notion which is expressed by 'water' in his language, although there are scientists in Twoscar's community to whom he defers on scientific matters who know that the stuff in rivers and lakes is XYZ. Furthermore, there is no space travel. No one on Twin Earth has had contact with water. Nor has anyone developed a theory that hypothesizes the existence of water on some distant planet on which there is in fact water. Because of the lack of either causal or theoretical connection with water, I think that it is safe to say that no one on Twin Earth has a *notion* of water.

That Oscar's and Twoscar's utterances are phonologically and syntactically type-identical is not sufficient to guarantee sameness of meaning. 'Water' does not mean the same on Earth and Twin Earth, since the extensions of the terms are not the same on the two planets.[10] On Earth the extension of 'water' is water, while on Twin Earth its extension is XYZ. By hypothesis there is no relevant difference in the internal states and events, etc., of Oscar and Twoscar, where these states and events, etc., are described non-intentionally.[11] Hence, the difference in the meanings of the terms on Earth and Twin Earth cannot be accounted for by appealing to anything in the internal states of Oscar and Twoscar. The conclusion Putnam draws from the thought experiment is that meanings are not determined by internal states (Putnam 1975: 135). That is, meanings are not in the head.

The conclusion which Burge draws from the argument is that the beliefs which Oscar and Twoscar would express by uttering,

(21) Water is good to drink.

cannot be individuated by an appeal to the internal physical states, dispositions to behaviour and bodily movements of Oscar and Twoscar which by supposition are the same. Oscar expresses the belief that water is good to drink. But Twoscar has no such belief and thus, we cannot report his belief by saying,

(22) Twoscar believes that water is good to drink.

The reason that Twoscar has no such belief is that he does not have any notion of water, since neither he nor anyone else on Twin Earth has any casual or theoretical connection with it. Burge's point is that we can keep constant the internal states, dispositions to behaviour and bodily movements of two people, vary their external environment and, thereby, change their intentional mental states. Hence, a criterion of individuation for Oscar's and Twoscar's intentional mental states must make reference to things other than Oscar and Twoscar's internal physical states, dispositions to behaviour and bodily movements.

I wish to draw a similar conclusion about the illocutionary acts which Oscar and Twoscar perform. Let us concentrate on their utterances of (21). In uttering (21) Oscar says that water is good to drink, but Twoscar in uttering a token of (21) does not say the same thing. Thus, we cannot report his illocutionary act by saying:

(23) Twoscar said that water is good to drink.

The reason that Twoscar cannot say that water is good to drink in uttering (21) is the same reason that he cannot believe that water is good to drink. He has no notion of water. Consequently, the illocutionary acts which Oscar and Twoscar perform cannot be individuated by what is in their heads or by their bodily movements, because by hypothesis their internal states and bodily movements are type-identical. Thus, a criterion for the illocutionary acts which Oscar and Twoscar perform must make reference to objects external to them.

In Burge's second thought experiment he keeps constant the objects to which a subject is causally related, his dispositions to behaviour, his bodily movements and his internal states, all non-intentionally described, and changes only the linguistic practices of the subject's surrounding community. In the actual situation, Oscar has a number of true beliefs involving the notion of arthritis. He believes that arthritis can be a painful disease, that his uncle has arthritis, that it is better to have arthritis than AIDS, etc. He, also, believes that he has arthritis in his thigh, a belief he gives up when told by his doctor that arthritis cannot occur in the thigh. We can say, then, that Oscar has a mistaken conception of arthritis and because of this, a partial understanding.

Burge, then, describes a counterfactual situation in which Oscar's internal states remain the same. There is no change in the history of his stimulation patterns, in his internal physical states, in his dispositions to behaviour, in his bodily movements and in the causal relations among them. The only difference is that those in his speech community to whom Oscar defers on linguistic matters use 'arthritis' in the way in which Oscar uses it mistakenly in the actual situation. In the counterfactual situation Oscar does not have the thought that he has arthritis in his thigh, for no one in the counterfactual situation has any notion of arthritis. They have a notion of a disease which can occur in the joints and in thighs which is not a notion of arthritis. Thus, Oscar in the actual situation and in the counterfactual situation has different notions which would be expressed by 'arthritis'. In the actual situation Oscar has a notion of arthritis, but in the counterfactual situation he has no such notion. Hence, in the counterfactual situation Oscar would not have any of the arthritis beliefs which are attributed to him in the actual situation, since in the counterfactual situation he lacks the notion of arthritis.[12]

Burge suggests that we could introduce the term 'tharthritis' into English as it is actually spoken which would express the notion that 'arthritis' expresses in the counterfactual situation. We, then, could describe the thought that Oscar has in this situation, namely, the thought that he has tharthritis in his thigh. But the thought that Oscar has in the actual situation, the thought that he has arthritis in his thigh, is not the same as the thought that he has in the counterfactual situation, namely the thought that he has tharthritis in his thigh, for the two thought events do not have the same content, since arthritis is not the same as tharthritis. So Oscar's beliefs are not the same in the actual and counterfactual situations. By hypothesis there has been no change in Oscar's dispositions to behaviour, internal physical states and bodily movements. Consequently, these cannot account for the difference in Oscar's beliefs. The conclusion that Burge draws from the thought experiment is that in individuating Oscar's beliefs, appeal must be made to the linguistic practices of the linguistic community of which he is a part.

A similar conclusion can be drawn about illocutionary acts. Let us imagine that the thought experiment is as Burge described it and that Oscar utters:

(24) I have arthritis in my thigh.

In the actual situation in uttering (24) Oscar says that he has arthritis in his thigh, but in the counterfactual situation Oscar would not have said that he has arthritis in his thigh, because neither he nor anyone else in his speech community has a notion of arthritis. Thus, in this case Oscar's internal states, disposition to behaviour and his bodily movements do not individuate what illocutionary act he performs.

EXTENSION OF BURGE'S ARGUMENTS TO OTHER SPEECH ACTS

It might seem that Burgean-style arguments need not be invoked to show that illocutionary acts like promising, begging and betting cannot be individuated individualistically, since for there to be such acts there must be others with whom a speaker interacts. When I promise Alice that I will find the Holy Grail, beg her to find it or bet her that I will find it, my promising, begging and betting does not depend only on my own existence, but, also, on the existence of Alice. That is, the individuation of acts of promising, begging and betting depends not only on the existence of a speaker, but also on the existence of others. If my promise had been made to Ruth rather than to Alice or my bet made with her rather than with Alice, then I would have performed different illocutionary acts. Hence, we can conclude from this, without invoking Burgean arguments, that the criterion of individuation of illocutionary acts like promising, begging and betting is not individualistic.

Although this is a correct conclusion to draw, I think that Burgean-style arguments have, as well, a role to play with respect to these sorts of illocutionary acts. Let us suppose that we keep fixed not only the internal physical states, dispositions to behaviour, and bodily movements of the speaker, but also the person to whom the illocutionary act is directed, in this case Alice. The question then arises as to whether the individuation of these illocutionary acts depends upon anything else other than the speaker, his internal states, dispositions to behaviour and bodily movements, and Alice. It is here that Burgean-style arguments can be invoked to show that their individuation does depend upon elements other than the speaker and Alice. Twoscar cannot beg Alice to find water by saying to Alice 'I beg you to find water' on Twin Earth. Nor can Oscar promise Alice that he will find a cure for arthritis in saying to Alice, 'I promise you that I shall find a cure for arthritis', in a counterfactual situation in which 'arthritis' is used to refer to an inflammation in the joints and the thighs. The reason is that Twoscar does not have a notion of water, nor Oscar a notion of arthritis.

Burge claims that his 'arthritis' argument has a certain degree of generality and that it does not depend

> on the kind of word 'arthritis' is. We could have used an artefact term, an ordinary natural kind term, a color adjective, a social role term, a term for a historical style, an abstract noun, an action verb, a physical movement verb, or any of various other sorts of words.
>
> (Burge 1979: 79)

I wish to show that the argument can be extended to illocutionary-act verbs and I shall take as my example 'promise'. It might seem obvious that a Burgean-style 'arthritis' argument applies to 'promise', since that there is an act of promising depends on the linguistic practices of a speaker's linguistic community. But I think that it is of interest to consider the application of the argument to 'promise' in some detail, since, as I hope to show, it has implications for the sense in which a speaker in performing an illocutionary act can be said to be following a set of rules.

Let us suppose that Oscar uses 'promise' in sentences such as, 'Ruth has promised to make chicken soup for me', 'Ruth has kept most of her promises', 'I seldom make promises', 'Promising is not merely predicting what one will do', etc. And since Oscar is, by and large, honest we can attribute to him beliefs using 'promise'. He believes that Ruth has promised to make chicken soup for him, that Ruth has kept most of her promises, that he seldom makes promises, that promising is not merely predicting what one will do, etc. One of the necessary conditions which Searle gives for promising is that a speaker intends that an utterance of 'I promise to do A' will place him under an obligation to do A (Searle 1969: 60). Following Searle, let us call this condition the 'essential condition'. Let us suppose further that Oscar does not take this to be a necessary condition for promising: although he thinks that it would be better to keep his promises than not, he does not think that any obligation is involved. Now let us imagine that Oscar says to Ruth:

(25) I promise to meet you at the party.

Let us further suppose that Oscar holds his belief about the essential condition on promising, until he is told by a member of his linguistic community, to whom he defers on linguistic matters, that in promising, one places oneself under an obligation to promise. It might be thought that, before he is told this, in uttering (25) he has not made a promise. The thought is perhaps that promising is like playing chess; you cannot play chess, unless you know the rules. I think, however, that there is a difference between promising and playing chess. In the case of promising, Oscar is, in fact, held responsible for having promised because, as Ruth could claim, he should have known that promising places him under a prima facie obligation. He is, she could correctly argue, an adult speaker of English and as such, should know what 'promise' means. My claim is that despite his not knowing the essential condition for promising, we would regard Oscar as having made a promise. Our reasons for doing so are that he can obviously use 'promise' correctly in a variety of contexts and that since he is an adult speaker of the language, he should know the essential condition for promising. Promising is like the law, rather than like a game. Ignorance is no defence. We are bound by the law and can commit infractions even though we are ignorant of a particular law.

Let us now imagine a counterfactual situation in which nothing changes about Oscar's internal states, dispositions to behaviour, bodily movements, and causal relations with objects in the world, but in which 'promise' is used by members of Oscar's linguistic community with the mistaken conception that Oscar has in the actual situation. Moreover, let us suppose that they do not have another word in their language which is used in the way in which 'promise' is used in the actual situation. I believe that in the counterfactual situation Oscar would not have the beliefs we reported him to have in the actual situation about promising, nor could he, or anyone else, make promises in this situation, since no one has the notion of promising. The conclusion which we can draw from this, a fairly obvious conclusion given the nature of promising, is that an individual act of promising cannot be individuated by reference to the internal states, bodily movements and dispositions to behaviour of a speaker. Rather, reference must be made to the linguistic practices of the speaker's linguistic community. That is, illocutionary acts like promising are not individuated individualistically.

SPEECH ACT COMPETENCE

I think that there is another, perhaps more interesting, conclusion to be drawn from this example. On Searle's view of illocutionary acts and semantics, the rules for promising are part of the lexical entry for 'promise' in a speaker's idiolect. It is the English speaker's knowledge of the meaning of 'promise' and thus, her knowledge of the rules for promising which enables her to promise. The essential condition is one of the conditions which Searle gives as a necessary condition for promising and, formulated as a rule, one of the rules which govern the correct use of 'promise' in the performative formula. Searle does not think that it is necessary for a speaker to have explicit knowledge of the meaning of 'promise' and thereby, the rules for promising to be able to promise. Searle adopts the notion of internalized unconscious rules from Chomsky (Searle 1969: 42) and applies it to speech acts. An agent need not be conscious of the rules for promising for the rules to be in his head; he can have tacit knowledge of them in the same way as he has tacit knowledge of the syntactic rules and parameters of his idiolect. Searle claims that

> the agent's knowing how to do something [in this case perform an illo-cutionary act] may only be adequately explicable on the hypothesis that he knows (has acquired, internalized, learned) a rule to the effect that such and such, even though in an important sense he may not know that he knows the rule or that he does what he does in part because of the rule.
>
> (Searle 1969: 42)

But if I am right about the application of the 'arthritis' argument to 'promise', then Oscar is not following a set of internalized rules, which includes the essential condition for promising, when in uttering (25) he promises Alice to meet her at the party. What we can conclude is that some of the semantic rules governing performative verb phrases are not in the head of individual speakers. We have, then, an extension of Putnam's argument about meanings not being in the head to some of the rules governing the use of illocutionary-act verbs.

The above application of the 'arthritis' argument can be applied to other illocutionary-act verbs, but I shall not pursue this here. Moreover, there are other consequences that Burge's arguments against individualism have for speech act theory. In particular I think that Burge's arguments against one version of the identity theory which identifies mental intentional-state tokens with brain-state tokens can be adapted to show that illocutionary acts cannot be identified with utterance acts. But I shall leave this topic for another time.

NOTES

1   I shall adopt Burge's use of 'attribute' and 'ascribe' in Burge 1979: 75–6.
2   In the case of thanking someone for a gift the speaker presupposes *that* the person has given the speaker a gift. Searle argues that the presupposition is the propositional content of the speaker's act of thanking the gift-giver (Searle 1979: 15–16). I think that it is an open question whether the presupposition is part of the propositional content of the act of thanking someone. But if it is, then Burge-style arguments apply to such acts as well.
3   These conditions are sufficient conditions for an illocutionary-act ascription to be an ascription of *intentional* discourse. They are not sufficient conditions for intentional discourse in general, since they would mark quoted discourse as being intentional.
4   They are to be found in Burge 1979, 1982a, 1982b, 1986a, 1986b. I shall concentrate my attention on the thought experiments that Burge presents in the

first two articles which he uses in his arguments against individualism. There are a number of criticisms of Burge's arguments, none of which I think is successful. See, for example, Searle 1983. I shall not consider these arguments in this paper.

5 Burge (1986a) points out some of the consequences which his arguments against individualist criteria of the individuation of intentional states have for theories about actions.

6 The converse need not be the case, since someone can understand the notion of arthritis without speaking English, and thus, not understand 'arthritis'.

7 There might be a question raised about whether the notion expressed by 'Alice' is part of the content of Alice's act of promising, whether it should be the notion expressed by 'I' indexed to Alice or whether the subject position of the content clause should be left out of the content all together. I shall not try to answer this question here.

8 There are complex problems here which I cannot consider. There might be good reason to take the content clause to be 'that Oscar find Hamlet', since what Alice wants to bring about by her illocutionary act is that Oscar finds Hamlet. The way in which the notion of Oscar is characterized in the expression of the content clause might depend upon how Alice thinks of Oscar in begging him to find Hamlet.

9 There is a slight complication in taking water as the natural kind on which the thought experiment is run. In the actual and the counterfactual situations Oscar's and Twoscar's physical internal states are supposed to be type-identical, but they are not. If there is water on Earth and XYZ on Twin Earth, then their internal physical states cannot be identical, since Oscar's brain contains water as a constituent, while Twoscar's brain contains XYZ. Despite this, I have used 'water' in my description of Burge's thought experiment, since Putnam's original example and subsequent discussions use it.

10 It is assumed here that difference of extension entails difference of meaning, since meaning is supposed to determine extension.

11 In what follows I shall use 'internal states' and 'intentional mental states' which can be expanded to the more accurate and longer 'internal states and events' which is meant to capture such things as brain states and processes, and 'intentional mental states and events' which is meant to include such things as belief states and thought events.

12 Following Burge 1979, I shall use 'actual situation' and 'counterfactual situation' where others might use 'actual world' and 'possible world'. One difference between this thought experiment and the preceding one is that in this thought experiment we have one person, Oscar, and we imagine him in an actual and a counterfactual situation, while in the preceding thought experiment we have two different people, one on Earth and one on an imaginary planet, both of which are thought of as being actual. The first thought experiment could be changed so that there was only one person and that we imagine him on Earth as it is and, then, on Earth as it would be, if it were similar to Twin Earth. Nothing essential would be changed about the thought experiment, were this change made.

10 The gap between speech acts and mental states

Savas L. Tsohatzidis

INTRODUCTION

Suppose that, following John Searle, you have committed yourself to the thesis (call it 'Thesis A') that three of the major categories of illocutionary acts are the categories of assertive, directive and commissive illocutionary acts, roughly characterizable as follows:[1]

(a) An assertive illocutionary act with propositional content p is an act whose speaker presents as actual the state of affairs represented by p. (Examples: asserting that p, claiming that p, predicting that p, informing someone that p, etc.)
(b) A directive illocutionary act with propositional content p is an act whose speaker attempts to make his hearer make actual the state of affairs represented by p. (Examples: asking someone to p, requesting someone to p, ordering someone to p, imploring someone to p, etc.)
(c) A commissive illocutionary act with propositional content p is an act whose speaker commits himself to make actual the state of affairs represented by p. (Examples: undertaking to p, promising to p, threatening to p, accepting to p, etc.)

Suppose further that, again following Searle, you have committed yourself to the thesis (call it 'Thesis B') that the only kinds of things that are *intrinsically*, as opposed to derivatively, meaningful are not linguistic acts like the act of asserting that something is the case, the act of requesting someone to make something the case, or the act of promising to make something the case, but rather *mental states* like the state of believing that something is the case, the state of desiring that someone make something the case, or the state of intending to make something the case.[2]

If you are committed both to Thesis A and to Thesis B, then you would be justified in fearing that a theory of speech acts that recognizes the categories characterized in (a)–(c) as major illocutionary categories would be running the risk of being, at worst, misguided, and, at best, superficial, *unless* it could be shown that there are conceptual connections of some reasonably strong sort between its major categories of illocutionary acts and the major categories of an independently defensible taxonomy of mental states. Presumably for that reason, Searle has, in several of his recent writings, been eager to affirm that the following theses – among others of a similar sort – are all necessarily true.[3]

(i)   For all Ss and all ps, if a speaker S performs an assertive illocutionary act with propositional content p, then S *expresses the belief* that p is the case.

(ii) For all Ss and all ps, if a speaker S performs a directive illocutionary act with propositional content p, then S *expresses the desire* that his/her hearer make p be the case.

(iii) For all Ss and all ps, if a speaker S performs a commissive illocutionary act with propositional content p, then S *expresses the intention* to make p the case.

So far as I know, Searle has offered only one kind of argument in favour of (i)–(iii) and of some other theses of the same kind – namely, that unless these theses were supposed true, one could not explain the oddity of utterances like the following, whose speakers appear to attempt both to perform assertive, directive or commissive illocutionary acts and to dissociate themselves from the expression of the mental states that, according to (i)–(iii), are necessarily connected with the performance of acts of those types.

(1) *I assert, but I don't believe, that you are lazy.
(2) *I request, but I don't want, your help.
(3) *I promise, but I don't intend, to take you to the movies.

It is my purpose in this paper to suggest that this argument is unsuccessful and that, to this extent, Searle's project of integrating his philosophy of language into his philosophy of mind cannot be supposed to be have been successful either.

THE ARGUMENT AND ITS BACKGROUND

Before going any further, it will be important to realize that the conditions specified in (i)–(iii), though obviously related to, neither entail nor are entailed by, the so-called 'sincerity conditions' that Searle's theory of speech acts has, since its early formulation (in Searle 1969), always associated with illocutionary acts of the kinds characterized in (a)–(c): the condition requiring that a speaker performing an assertive illocutionary act should *express* the belief that a certain state of affairs obtains is not the same as the 'sincerity' condition requiring such a speaker to actually *have* the belief that that state of affairs obtains; the condition requiring that a speaker performing a directive illocutionary act should *express* the desire that his hearer make a certain state of affairs obtain is not the same as the 'sincerity' condition requiring such a speaker to actually *have* the desire that his hearer make that state of affairs obtain; and the condition requiring that a speaker performing a commissive illocutionary act should *express* the intention to make a certain state of affairs obtain is not the same as the 'sincerity' condition requiring such a speaker to actually *have* the intention to make that state of affairs obtain. The 'sincerity' conditions just mentioned should certainly be accepted as correct if understood in the right way, namely, as specifying types of mental states which, though not *necessarily* connected with illocutionary acts of the indicated types, are ascribed *by default* to speakers performing acts of those types – that is, are attributed to them as long as there is no evidence against their attribution, and can be consistently withdrawn whenever such evidence becomes available. And it is with this understanding that they have been proposed by Searle, who has always described them as conditions whose non-fulfilment entails not the *non*-performance but merely the 'defective' performance of assertive, directive and commissive illocutionary acts. However, precisely because the 'sincerity' conditions do not represent necessary features of the illocutionary acts in connection with which they have been proposed, they cannot, as they stand, fulfil Searle's larger, and more recent, project of *defining* his major categories of illocutionary acts by reference to the types of mental states that they mention: since one can certainly assert things that one does not really believe, or request things that one does not really want, or promise to do things that one does not really intend to do, it is impossible to correctly define assertions, requests or promises by reference to the actual *possession* of the relevant beliefs, desires or intentions. And it is at just this point that the introduction of additional conditions like those formulated in (i)–(iii) is supposed to prove its worth. For these conditions do purport to reveal necessary connections between types of illocutionary acts and types of mental states, not by saying, as the 'sincerity' conditions do, that one must *have* certain beliefs, desires or intentions in order to perform assertive, directive or commissive illocutionary acts, but only by saying that one must *express* such beliefs, desires or intentions in order to perform such acts – in other words, that one must present oneself *as* having those beliefs, desires or intentions, whether or not one *actually* has them. If, therefore, what these conditions purport to say is in fact true – and if, furthermore, one is prepared to grant that creatures that would altogether lack genuine beliefs, desires or intentions could hardly *pretend* to have genuine beliefs, desires and intentions – the idea of a necessary connection between speech act concepts and mental state concepts would appear to have been vindicated.[4]

Searle's argument to the effect that the conditions specified in (i)–(iii) do in fact hold relies, as already noted, on the oddity of utterances like (1)–(3), and has been expressed many times, among which the following is representative:

An insincere speech act is defective but not necessarily unsuccessful....

Nevertheless, successful performances of illocutionary acts necessarily involve the *expression* of the psychological state specified by the sincerity conditions of that type of act. The fact that the *expression* of the psychological state is internal to the performance of the act is shown by the fact that it is paradoxical to perform an illocution and to deny simultaneously that one has the corresponding psychological state. Thus, one cannot say 'I promise to come but I do not intend to come', 'I order you to leave but I don't want you to leave' ..., etc. The reason for this is that when one performs the speech act one necessarily *expresses* the sincerity condition, and thus to conjoin the performance of the speech act with the denial of the sincerity condition would be to express and to deny the presence of one and the same psychological state.[5]

According to Searle, then, the reason for the oddity of (1) is that it is part of the meaning of 'assert' that whoever asserts that p is the case *expresses* the belief that p is the case (in other words, presents himself *as* having the belief that p is the case), and that, therefore, a person who both asserts that something is the case and indicates that he does not believe it to be the case is a person who incoherently presents himself as both having and not having a certain belief. Similarly, the reason for the oddity of (2) is that it is part of the meaning of 'request' that whoever requests that p be the case *expresses* the desire that p be the case (in other words, presents himself *as* having the desire that p be the case), and that, therefore, a person who both requests something and indicates that he does not want it, is a person who incoherently presents himself as both having and not having a certain desire. Finally, the reason for the oddity of (3) is that it is part of the meaning of 'promise' that whoever promises to make p be the case *expresses* the intention to make p the case (in other words, presents himself *as* having the intention to make p the case), and that, therefore, a person who both promises to do something and indicates that he does not intend to do it is a person who incoherently presents himself as both having and not having a certain intention. In short, the explanation of the oddity of these and similar utterances rests, according to Searle, on the one hand, with the assumption that it is a conceptual truth that a person who asserts, requests or promises something presents himself *as* being in a certain mental state, and, on the other hand, with the assumption that it is incoherent to present oneself as simultaneously being and not being in a given mental state.

There are at least two ways in which one might try to establish that Searle's argument is unsuccessful: first, by showing that, for some among the examples that would be relevant for the evaluation of his thesis, the semantic explanation he offers is, contrary to what he assumes, not the *only* possible explanation (and that an alternative explanation, which would not entitle him to the theoretical conclusions he wants to draw, is also available); second, by showing that, for some others among the examples that would be relevant for the evaluation of his thesis, the semantic explanation he offers is not just non-unique but quite impossible. We shall presently see that both lines of attack prove to be equally efficient.

WHY THE ARGUMENT FAILS

The first problem with Searle's argument is that, in all relevant cases in which his proposed semantic explanation does appear to work, it is certainly not the *only* explanation that works, since an alternative, pragmatic explanation could equally plausibly be constructed (without, however, entitling him to derive any conclusions about necessary connections between types of illocutionary acts and types of mental states). The pragmatic explanation would begin by taking it as a matter of mutual knowledge between interlocutors that, since people are *usually* (though not invariably) expected to believe what they assert, to want what they request, and to intend to carry out what they promise to carry out, a *ceteris paribus* efficient strategy for *deceiving* others about one's beliefs, desires or intentions would be to assert what one does not believe, to request what one does not want, and to promise to do what one does not intend to do. The explanation would then appeal to a further piece of mutual knowledge between interlocutors, to the effect that a strategy to deceive others has, in general, little chance of being successful if the specific means chosen for implementing it make it *transparent* to others that one does have the intention to deceive them. And it would finally account for the oddity of (1), (2) and (3) by describing their speakers as persons who, on the one hand, give the appearance of having deceitful intents, and, on the other hand, seem to have chosen the ideal means for *failing* to fulfil those deceitful intents. The fact that (1) is odd, for example, would be explicable by reference, on the one hand, to the fact that someone who asserts something without believing it, is, in the absence of indications to the contrary, plausibly taken to be someone who wants to *deceive* his addressees about his real beliefs, and, on the other hand, to the fact that someone who wants to successfully deceive his addressees about his real beliefs should – unlike the speaker of (1) – *hide* from his addresses that he wants to deceive them about his real beliefs. Similarly, the oddity of (2) would be explicable by reference, on the one hand, to the fact that someone who requests something without wanting is, in the absence of indications to the contrary, plausibly taken to be someone who wants to *deceive* his addressees about his real desires, and, on the other hand, to the fact that someone who wants to successfully deceive his addressees about his real desires should – unlike the speaker of (2) – *hide* from his addresses that he wants to deceive them about his real desires. Finally, the oddity of (3) would be explicable by reference, on the one hand, to the fact that someone who promises to do something without intending to do it is, in the absence of indications to the contrary, plausibly taken to be someone who wants to *deceive* his addressees about his real intentions, and, on the other hand, to the fact that someone who wants to successfully deceive his addressees about his real intentions should – unlike the speaker of (3) – *hide* from his addresses that he wants to deceive them about his real intentions. In short, the oddity of (1), (2) and (3) would be explicable not by reference to the alleged fact that they violate a *semantic* constraint to the effect that assertions are necessarily expressions of beliefs, requests are necessarily expressions of desires, and promises are necessarily expressions of intentions, but rather to the fact that they violate an obvious pragmatic principle to the effect that if one wants to *deceive* others by asserting something that one does not believe, or by requesting something that one does not want, or by promising something that one does not intend to do, then it would be in one's own interest not to *tell* the intended victims of one's deception that one does not really believe what one asserts, that one does not really want what one requests, or that one does not really intend to do what one promises to do. And given this explanation, of course, the oddity of (1), (2) and (3) could hardly be used as evidence in favour of a *necessary* connection, of the sort Searle is interested in establishing, between expressions of mental states and performances of illocutionary acts.

The second problem with Searle's argument is that, apart from the fact that a pragmatic explanation is available for all relevant cases that his semantic explanation appears to cover, there are further relevant cases which show that the semantic explanation is, in fact, mistaken (whereas the pragmatic one is not). Notice that, since, by definition, you cannot turn a sentence that is semantically odd into a sentence that is not semantically odd *just* by changing the context in which that sentence is uttered, Searle's explanation predicts that utterances of sentences whereby a speaker attempts both to assert something and to deny that he believes it, or both to request something and to deny that he wants it, or both to promise something and to deny that he intends to do it, will not be acceptable in *any* context. But such sentences do appear to be perfectly acceptable in certain kinds of contexts, and these contexts are, furthermore, precisely the ones for which acceptability rather than unacceptability would be predicted on the pragmatic account (since they are contexts in which the utterance of such sentences would be unlikely or impossible to be construed as part of a *deception* plan).

Consider, to take the case of assertion first, the following utterances:

(4) I don't believe he is in pain, but since he says he is, and since his words would be admitted as the best kind of evidence for settling a question of this kind, I assert that he is.

(5) I don't believe he is older than her, but since the documentary evidence, which usually settles questions of this kind, suggests that he is, I assert that he is.

According to Searle's semantic account, what the speakers of these utterances do is, on the one hand, to present themselves as believing that something is the case, and, on the other hand, to present themselves as not believing that that thing is the case. But since it is contradictory to believe and not to believe that something is the case, and since explicit contradictions are not the kinds of things to which one could manifest one's commitment without oddity, these utterances should be exactly as odd as the ones below:

(6) *I don't believe he is in pain, but since he says he is, and since his words would be admitted as the best kind of evidence for settling a question of this kind, I believe that he is.

(7) *I don't believe he is older than her, but since the documentary evidence, which usually settles questions of this kind, suggests that he is, I believe that he is.

The fact is, however, that, though (6) and (7) are indeed very odd, (4) and (5) are not. Consequently, Searle must abandon his general thesis that assertive illocutionary acts with propositional content p are necessarily expressions of the belief that p is the case. Once that thesis is abandoned, of course, it cannot be invoked in order to provide a *semantic* explanation of the oddity of an utterance like (1). On the other hand, the pragmatic explanation previously sketched can easily account for the fact that the combination of a purported assertion with an expression of disbelief in its content is unacceptable in the case of (1) but acceptable in the case of (4) and (5): on that explanation, recognizing (1) as odd depends on the assumption that the usual motive of a speaker who asserts something without believing it is his desire to *deceive* his audience about his beliefs (as well as on the assumption that someone who tries to deceive his audience is unlikely to be successful if he makes it plain to his audience that he does try to deceive them); it follows from that account, then, that a speaker who both asserts something and explicitly indicates that he does not believe it will *not* be in danger of appearing odd *if* it is difficult or impossible to construe him as thereby trying to *deceive* his audience; but this is exactly what happens with the speakers of (4) and (5), who, so far from assuming the capability to deceive *others* about the truth values of the particular propositions that they choose to assert, openly acknowledge that they may be *themselves* the objects of deception with regard to the truth value of these propositions. The pragmatic account, then, explains in a principled way both the unacceptability of (1) and the acceptability of (4) and (5). And since the very existence, let alone the explanation, of such a contrast is problematic on the semantic account, the choice between them is obvious.[6]

Turning from assertions to requests and promises, we find that utterances like those in (8) and (9) invite similar considerations.

(8) I don't want you to do this dirty job, but since you are alone capable of doing it, and since it is tremendously important for the country, I request of you to do it.

(9) I hereby promise to give you by tomorrow night what you claim I

ought to give you by tomorrow night – but since I am sure that, in the meantime, I will prove to you that your claim has been mistaken, it is not my intention to actually fulfil this alleged obligation.

Given Searle's view that requests are necessarily expressions of desires and that promises are necessarily expressions of intentions, it is difficult to imagine how these utterances could *avoid* being odd. In fact, they should be exactly as odd as the following utterances, whose speakers purport to have and not to have a certain desire, and to have and not to have a certain intention, respectively:

(10)   *I don't want you to do this dirty job, but since you are alone capable of doing it, and since it is tremendously important for the country, I want you to do it.

(11)   *I intend to give you by tomorrow night what you claim I ought to give you by tomorrow night – but since I am sure that, in the meantime, I will prove to you that your claim has been mistaken, it is not my intention to actually fulfil this alleged obligation.

It is clear, however, that, though (10) and (11) are indeed odd, (8) and (9) are not. Consequently, Searle's thesis that a speaker's request that p be the case is necessarily an expression of his desire that p be the case, or that a speaker's promise to make p the case is necessarily an expression of his intention to make p the case, must be abandoned. Abandoning them, however, entails abandoning the thesis that the oddity of utterances like (2) and (3) follows from a violation of a *semantic* condition on requests and promises, and must create the suspicion that there are pragmatic reasons why utterances like (2) and (3) are unacceptable whereas utterances like (8) and (9) are not. On the pragmatic account previously sketched, these reasons are clear enough. Recognizing (2) to be odd depends on its hearer's assumption that, in the absence of indications to the contrary, someone who requests something without wanting it can be plausibly taken to be someone who wants to deceive his audience about his desires, as well as on the assumption that someone who wants to successfully deceive his audience about his desires should not – unlike the speaker of (2) – communicate to his audience his deception plan; however, the speaker of (8) does indicate to his hearers that *his* reason for requesting something without wanting it is not his wish to deceive them about his real desires but rather his inability to satisfy his real desires without compromising his obligation to make a request, and his decision to place the fulfilment of that obligation higher than the satisfaction of his personal preferences; and once the presence of deceitful intent is thus defeated as the sole reason why someone should make requests without really wanting them to be carried out, the question as to whether the utterance of (8) is or is not appropriate for implementing a *deception* plan does not have to arise, and the hearers of (8) are consequently under no compulsion to find it in any way odd.

Similarly with the contrast between (3) and (9). The oddity of (3) depends on its hearer's assumption that, in the absence of indications to the contrary, someone who promises to do something without intending to do it must be someone who wants to deceive his audience about his intentions, as well as on the assumption that someone who wants to successfully deceive his audience about his intentions should not – unlike the speaker of (3) – communicate to his audience his deception plan; however, the speaker of (9) does indicate to his hearers that *his* reason for promising something without intending to do it is not his wish to deceive them about his intentions, but rather his wish to assume, by promising, the obligations that they claim he has, while at the same time fully hoping to convince them that they were mistaken in thinking that he actually has those obligations; and once the presence of deceitful intent is thus defeated as the sole reason why the speaker of (9) should promise to do something without intending to do it, the hearers of (9) need neither raise the question of whether (9) is or is not a successful implementation of a *deception* plan, nor, consequently, find any reason why they should judge it to be an unacceptable utterance. The pragmatic account, then, offers a uniform explanation both of the acceptability of (8) and (9) and of the unacceptability of (2) and (3), and has consequently every right to replace the semantic one, which is not even capable of recognizing that there *could* be a contrast in acceptability in this area.

The moral, I submit, is clear: contrary to what conditions (i)–(iii) assert, the expression of a mental state like the state of believing that p is the case, or of desiring that p be the case, or of intending to make p the case, is not a necessary feature of the act of asserting that p is the case, or of requesting that p be the case, or of promising to make p the case. And if the expression of these mental states is not a necessary feature of the performance of these acts, then Searle's proposal to analyse the supposedly 'derived' meaningfulness of illocutionary acts in terms of the supposedly 'intrinsic' meaningfulness of mental states cannot be regarded as a successful proposal. We shall now proceed to a further, and independently interesting, confirmation of that failure.

EXTENDING THE COUNTERARGUMENTS

The Searlian conditions on assertive, directive and commissive illocutionary acts specified in (i)–(iii) presuppose, but are not presupposed by, the initial characterizations of these acts that his theory provides under (a)–(c). Consequently, the failure of conditions (i)–(iii) to qualify as semantic conditions does not automatically entail that the initial characterizations are themselves incorrect – it only entails that, even if they are correct as far as they go, they do not, by Searle's standards, go far enough, since the basic categories of speech act types that they establish do not correlate significantly with the basic categories of mental state types that, according to him, constitute the most fundamental form of meaningfulness. There is, however, a category of speech act types whose members are *directly* characterized, within Searle's theory, as expressions of mental states of a particular kind; if, therefore, that characterization is, as I think it is, open to objections of the same kind as those just raised against conditions (i)–(iii), these objections would entitle us to conclude that Searle has not only failed to establish revealing correlations between an independently motivated taxonomy of basic speech act types and his preferred taxonomy of basic mental state types, but that he cannot even assume that an independently motivated taxonomy of basic speech act types actually exists. The category in question (known as the category of 'expressive' illocutionary acts) is supposed to be the category of acts whose successful performance consists in the expression of *emotional* states of various kinds, and its prototypical members are acts of apologizing, thanking and congratulating, which are supposedly definable by reference to the expression of feelings of regret, gratitude and gladness, respectively. Thus, apologies about a certain state of affairs p are, according to Searle, necessarily expressions of regret (whether real or feigned) about p, thanks about a certain state of affairs p are necessarily expressions of gratitude (whether real or feigned) about p, and congratulations about a certain state of affairs p are necessarily expressions of gladness (whether real or feigned) about p.[7]

What is Searle's reason for thinking that these definitions are in fact correct? It is, obviously, that the supposition that they are correct provides the only possible explanation of the unacceptability of utterances like (12), (13) and (14), whose speakers would be described by him as incoherently presenting themselves as simultaneously having and not having a certain feeling of regret, a certain feeling of gratitude, or a certain feeling of gladness, respectively:

(12) *I apologize for insulting you, but I feel no regret about insulting you.

(13) *I thank you, but I do not feel grateful to you, for your help.

(14) *I congratulate you, but I don't feel pleased about your promotion.

This claim, however, is, just like the analogous claims about assertive, directive and commissive illocutionary acts, open to two kinds of objection. The first objection is that, as far as this data is concerned, Searle's semantic explanation is certainly not the only possible one, since a pragmatic one can just as plausibly be offered: on that explanation, the reason why hearers find (12), (13) and (14) unacceptable is that they assume, on the one hand, that a speaker who thanks without feeling gratitude, or who apologizes without feeling regret, or who congratulates without feeling gladness, may plausibly be supposed, in the absence of indications to the contrary, to be a speaker who wants to deceive his audience about his real feelings, and, on the other hand, that a minimally intelligent speaker who wants to deceive his audience about his real feelings does not, as a rule, reveal to his audience that he does want to deceive them about his real feelings. The second objection is that, although, as far as this data is concerned, the two explanations may seem equally plausible, further relevant data can easily demonstrate that the semantic explanation is in fact mistaken, whereas the pragmatic one is not. Notice, for example, that utterances like those in (15), (16) and (17) are certainly acceptable:

(15) I apologize for doing such a painful thing to you; but since it was the only means of keeping you alive, I neither feel, nor can pretend that I feel, regret about doing it.

(16) Since it is only in order to please me that you have done this, I thank you for doing it; but since I now know how much harm it will cause me, I can neither feel, nor pretend that I feel, gratitude to you for doing it.

(17) Since you wanted that promotion so desperately, I congratulate you on getting it; but I neither feel, nor can pretend that I feel, pleased about your promotion, since I know that it will ruin your health.

Given Searle's definitions, however, these utterances should be as un-acceptable as the ones below, since their speakers would be simultaneously presenting themselves as having and not having a certain feeling of regret, as having and not having a certain feeling of gratitude, and as having and not having a certain feeling of gladness, respectively:

(18)   *I feel regret about doing such a painful thing to you; but since it was the only means of keeping you alive, I neither feel, nor can pretend that I feel, regret about doing it.

(19)   *Since it is only in order to please me that you have done this, I feel gratitude to you for doing it; but since I now know how much harm it will cause me, I can neither feel, nor pretend that I feel, gratitude to you for doing it.

(20)   *Since you wanted that promotion so desperately, I feel pleased about your promotion; but I neither feel, nor can pretend that I feel, pleased about your promotion, since I know that it will ruin your health.

It appears, therefore that no general *semantic* constraint of the sort proposed by Searle can account for the unacceptability of (12), (13) and (14). And it is also clear that, given the pragmatic explanation of the unacceptability of (12)–(14), the acceptability of (15)–(17) is hardly surprising; for, the speakers of these last utterances do provide to their hearers grounds *against* assuming that they are trying to *deceive* them about their feelings (the reason why they apologize, thank and congratulate without feeling regretful, grateful or pleased, is not, they suggest, that they are hypocrites, but rather that the events that provoked their speech acts have turned out to have, or are likely to have, certain consequences in view of which they are unable to either have or express the feelings that would *normally* accompany speech acts of these kinds); and since the hearers are thus prevented from assuming that the speakers of these utterances do have deceitful intents, they can hardly find the utterances unacceptable on the grounds that they are self-defeating means of achieving those deceitful intents. The pragmatic account, in short, can explain both the acceptable and the unacceptable combinations of apologies with expressions of regret, of thanks with expressions of gratitude, and of congratulations with expressions of gladness. And since the semantic account cannot accept, let alone explain, that there can *be* both acceptable and unacceptable combinations of these sorts, it should certainly be rejected. Rejecting it, however, is admitting that there are no necessary connections between apologies and expressions of regret, thanks and expressions of gratitude, or congratulations and expressions of gladness. And since, without such connections, there can be no definitions of apologies, thanks and congratulations in Searle's theory, it seems that his account of so-called 'expressive' illocutionary acts creates even deeper problems for him than his account of assertive, directive and commissive illocutionary acts: not only can he not claim that there is a category of mental state types (namely, the category of emotional state types) with which an independently established category of expressive speech acts can be revealingly correlated, but he cannot even claim that there is an independently established category of expressive speech act types, since the only feature that is supposed to hold together the putative members of the category – namely, that each of them is, of necessity, an *expression* of some emotional state – is not a feature necessarily satisfied even by its reputedly most characteristic members.[8]

CONCLUSION

The conclusion we are now in a position to reach has a significant degree of generality. As is well known, there are, according to Searle, 'five and only five' categories of illocutionary acts:[9] assertives, directives, commissives, expressives and declarations. The last mentioned among these categories may be safely bypassed in the context of the present discussion, since the question of its connections or non-connections with expressed mental states is a question concerning which Searle does not appear to have reached a definitive answer.[10] Concerning the other four major categories, however, Searle is quite clear about their alleged conceptual connections with specific categories of mental states (assertions being, in his view, necessarily expressions of beliefs; directives necessarily expressions of desires; commissives necessarily expressions of intentions; and expressives necessarily expressions of emotions), as well as about the theoretical significance of this alleged fact – namely, that it confirms the idea that the meaningful character of linguistic events is 'derivative' upon the 'intrinsically' meaningful character of mental states. I have tried to show that

Searle's linguistic arguments for the existence of these necessary connections all fail, and that the assumption of a merely *default* connection between types of speech acts and types of mental states – that is, of a connection that licenses the interpretation of such an act as an expression of such a state as long *as there are no indications to the contrary* – suffices for explaining all the linguistic facts that Searle was interested in explaining, as well as many facts that he fails to explain. People who think that default, as opposed to necessary, connections are too loose for their purposes might, of course, seek to devise better arguments than Searle's in favour of his original conclusion – and they would be right in trying to do so, if they felt attracted to Searle's larger project of showing that the non-intrinsically contentful character of linguistic events can be derived from the intrinsically contentful character of mental states, since it is only by establishing necessary rather than default connections between them that derivability claims of this sort could presumably be supported. But if Searle's arguments for the existence of necessary connections fail, I doubt that any others would succeed,[11] and I am, consequently, not optimistic about the prospects of the larger project either.[12]

NOTES

1 See Searle 1975; Searle and Vanderveken 1985: 38–9, 54–6, 60–1, 99–101, 182–205. For the sake of argument, I will assume here that these characterizations are appropriate, though I have argued elsewhere that they present both minor and major defects (Tsohatzidis 1987a, 1993c).

2 For Searle's views on the nature of mental states and their intrinsically contentful character, see Searle 1983. For important criticisms of these views – which I will be ignoring here – see Devitt 1990 and Dennett 1990. On the derivatively – as opposed to intrinsically – contentful character of linguistic acts, see especially Searle 1983: 4–13, 26–9, 160–79, 1986, 1991a.

3 See Searle 1983: 9–10, 174–5, 177–9, 1986, 1991a; Searle and Vanderveken 1985: 54–6, 102–5.

4 Confusingly, Searle sometimes, though not always, uses the term 'sincerity condition' to refer both to the possession and to the mere expression of mental states (see, for example, Searle and Vanderveken 1985: 22), though it is only the first usage, inaugurated in Searle 1969, that is clearly intelligible: a *sincerity* condition on a speech act is, presumably, a condition whose non-satisfaction would make that act *insincere*, and what makes, for example, an assertion insincere is not that its speaker does not *express* a belief in the truth of its content, but rather that he does not *have* this expressed belief. (Indeed, since, on Searle's latest views, assertions are necessarily expressions of belief in their contents, the idea that the mere expression of such a belief would be sufficient to make any assertion *sincere* would have the absurd consequence that it is impossible for any assertion to ever be insincere – a consequence that Searle explicitly rejects.) The occasionally improper use of 'sincerity condition' to refer both to the (properly so-called) sincerity conditions of the earlier (1969) version of Searle's theory of speech acts and to conditions like (i)–(iii), which only appear in later versions, reflects, I suspect, Searle's unwillingness to clearly acknowledge the fact that the earlier version was, unlike the latter ones, quite

unconcerned about the possibility of *defining* illocutionary acts in terms of mental states. For clear and interesting accounts of the nature and significance of this and related differences between the earlier and later versions, see Liedtke 1990, and Apel 1991. See also Harnish 1990.

5 Searle and Vanderveken 1985: 18–19, italics provided. See also Searle and Vanderveken 1985: 91; Searle 1983: 9–10, 1991b.

6 An interesting consequence of the failure of Searle's proposed identification of assertions with expressions of belief is that it not only deprives him of what he regards (Searle and Vanderveken 1985: 91; Searle 1991b: 185–8) as an 'explanation' of so-called 'Moore's Paradox', but also makes it questionable whether such a thing as 'Moore's Paradox' – interpreted as resulting from an allegedly *universal* incompatibility of assertions with expressions of disbelief – actually exists. I welcome this consequence – and am thus opposed both to Searle and to those of his critics (e.g. Malcolm 1991) who propose alternative explanations of the 'paradox' – but will not further comment on this issue here.

7 See Searle 1975; Searle and Vanderveken 1985: 39–40, 58–9, 62, 211–16.

8 For additional problems facing Searle's proposed definitions of so-called 'expressive' illocutionary acts, see Tsohatzidis 1993b.

9 See, for example, Searle 1975, 1986; Searle and Vanderveken 1985: 37.

10 In some places (e.g. Searle 1975: 360) he explicitly denies that declarations are expressions of any mental states, whereas in other places (e.g. Searle 1983: 172; Searle and Vanderveken 1985: 57–8) he categorically affirms that they are.

11 An important contribution to the theory of speech acts that is as strongly committed as Searle's to the idea that illocutionary acts types are in part definable as expressions of mental state types is the one by Bach and Harnish (1979). Indeed, Harnish (1990) claims that the system of speech act analysis presented in Bach and Harnish 1979 serves Searle's purposes better than Searle's own system. And although this might, in some respects, be true, a look at Bach and Harnish's definitions of 'constatives' (Searle's assertives), directives, commissives, and 'acknowledgements' (Searle's expressives) – see Bach and Harnish 1979: 42, 44, 47–8, 49–50, 51 – will easily convince the reader that if the arguments here presented against Searle's definitions are sound, then they are just as forcefully applicable to the relevant parts of Bach and Harnish's definitions as well.

12 Defining types of illocutionary acts by reference to types of mental states *of their speakers* is, of course, different from defining them in terms of types of mental states that their speakers want to produce *in their hearers*. Nothing I have said applies necessarily to every project of this later type – see, for example, Grice 1957, 1969; Schiffer 1972, 1982; Bennett 1976, 1991; Loar 1981 – though it does apply to specific implementations of them (in particular, to those in which the *content* of the mental state that the speaker wants to produce in the hearer concerns a mental state of the speaker himself). However, what appears to be Searle's main objection to *any* project of this kind – namely, that it confuses illocutionary with perlocutionary effects (see Searle 1986: 210) – appears to me question-begging, since the idea that these effects *are* always distinguishable has notoriously resisted clarification (cf. Tsohatzidis 1986).

11 Algebra of elementary social acts

Arthur Merin

Large parts of talking lives are spent doing four things: making *claims* on someone's resources or credulity; *concessions* of such claims; *denials*; and *retractions*. Not all of these need actual talk. In Civil Society, even in its negotiable margins, much is transacted in silence. Nor does all talk appear to be of those four kinds. Some 10^3 to 10^4 of English verbs or phrase types designate usefully distinct ways of doing things with words.[1] Nevertheless, when all is said and done – asked, warned, baptized, etc. – there remains a suspicion: that much of it is, at the very least, defined against the backdrop of those first four.

One might go further. If ability to propose a deal is what makes our Animal political and rational (Smith 1776: ch. 2), then it is these acts, if any, which are the building blocks of reason. Accordingly, and without prejudice to analysis, I shall refer to them as *elementary social acts* (ESAs).

The objective is not philosophical,[2] but rather to offer a framework for posing and investigating a psychological (and linguistic) hypothesis:

> *Sociomorph* representations – structures whose theories have their most natural models in structures of simple social relations and processes – inform the non-superficial, poorly introspectible recursive component of natural languages.[3]

The hypothesis is to help account for diverse data puzzling to theoretical linguistics, including (a) the apparent failures of *and* and *or* to preserve Fregean invariance under changes of act type; (b) 'scalar implicature'; (c) the meanings of *not*; (d) unexplained properties of conditionals, *only*, and German *nur*; (e) 'neg-raising' and 'polarity' phenomena; (f) relations of claims etc. to 'suggestions', 'requests', 'questions' and modal operators; (g) the kinematic semantics of 'honorifics', and (h) that of *yes* and *no*.

1 BASIC DISCOURSE INSTITUTIONS

1.1 Linguistics, psychology, philosophy

Why psychological? For one because linguistics, to the extent that its data are spontaneous native speaker intuitions (SNSIs), is a branch of experimental psychology cum social anthropology. To elicit SNSIs is to conduct a psychological experiment: often crude, but usually with the saving grace of easy replicability. No assumptions about grey matter or 'psychological reality' are needed to fix where it belongs in the first place.

Why does it matter? Because an autonomous theoretical linguistics will happily sit on the fence or, less happily, roll about in the ditch between philosophy and psychology. Every now and then, usually where 'meaning' is involved, there is confusion of objectives; attended by empirical consequences.

In pre- and post-behaviourist psychology, phenomena are often explained by imputing a certain theory T of some aspect of the world to some proper subsystem S of people's minds. That is, S is assumed to condition forms of conduct as if proceeding on such a theory. T may be crude, even unreasonable. But then it does not stand alone. Human conduct all round will be seen as guided by a whole web of theories T' etc., each associated with a different subsystem. Sometimes they will cohere, and sometimes one or more will override another. (Think of visual illusions or superstitions.)

By contrast, philosophy, particularly that of language, tends to give priority to rational reconstruction of theories that are both introspectible and reasonable. Theories a psychologist might well explain, though never justify, as high-level (by-)products of less introspectible and perhaps less reasonable theories.

The question to ask of a psychological theory P, then, is not: is the tacit naive theory T it elicits as a constraint on verbal conduct reasonable? But rather: is the imputation of T reasonably predictive of one's chosen data? Suppose we impute an (interpreted) theory T_1, a structure whose axioms (or 'theory' in the logician's sense) have as a model also a theory TU_1. Suppose, too, it were unreasonable to entertain TU_1 in introspectible life. Imputation of T_1 might still be reasonable. Neither should a theory T_2 be discriminated against simply because there is a theory TR_2 which is reasonable to entertain in introspectible life, and is a model of T_2's axioms. Nor a theory T_3 because it has no obvious models, fair or foul, in introspectible life.

I begin with a simple human-interest story, soon projected on a system of labelled graphs interpreted as automata. Things get progressively more abstract in sections 1.4–1.11. Use of formal notions is never deep; but not wholly dispensable either. Exposition is fairly informal and assumes a rudimentary acquaintance with abstract algebra.

1.2 A simple discourse institution: intuitive outline

The basic assumption is that large parts of natural languages' pragma-semantic structure are informed by representations of a paradigmatic *discourse institution* (DI) and/or of various transformations of it. The DI is built around a pair of actual or virtual persons, call them *Alter* (A) and *Ego* (E), engaged in joint decision-making about an issue, Φ vs $\neg\Phi$. They are a priori neither omnipotent nor omniscient, and are in the business of persuading one another rather than just speaking their minds.

Suppose Ego utters

(1) Give me $5.

or – another language game this:

(2) The bridge is closed.

Coming out of the blue one should most likely classify (1) as a demand and (2) as an assertion. More abstractly, (1) will be a deontic-boulomaic and (2) an epistemic-alethetic *claim*. Let us treat the two cases in parallel. Assuming for now an invariant 'propositional content' represented by an atomic sentence Φ, a familiar-looking format for representing such a claim would be

(3) $CLA_E\Phi$.

It is understood that the addressee is Alter (A) and that (3) is an expression schema of a formal language glossing either a sentence or a term

(4) {Ego claims/A claim by Ego} (of Alter) that Alter {realize/believe} Φ

Here Φ will represent 'A gives E $5' in instance (1) and 'The bridge is closed' in (2), shorn of declarative inflection. Thus, we might interpret (3) as an act-description or directly as the act itself. Either way we shall have to analyse the notion 'act' further. But nothing is presupposed about the means of performing the act. Of course, one such means might well be an 'explicit performative' (EP) which, in a standard schematic format, might go

(5) I claim that {you give me $5/the bridge is closed}.

What ESAs share with EPs regardless of expression is communicators' constitutional authority to perform ESAs under usual circumstances and in turn.

In response to (3), Alter might either *concede* ($CON_A\Phi$) or *deny* ($DEN_A\Phi$) what Ego claimed. In the first case we move from the 'illocutionary' realm of negotiations to motivating 'perlocutionary' effect.

Alter and Ego subscribe to a set of propositions, conventionally deemed mutual knowledge, which represents constraints on their epistemic or deontic *joint commitments* (JCs). If Ego claims (1) the familiar common-sense presumption is that the proposition expressible 'Alter is to give Ego $5' was not JC. If Ego claims (2), then 'The bridge is closed' is not presumed JC. If Alter concedes, then the proposition becomes JC.

What, if anything, either one of them does with that commitment – carry out the action, act in accordance with the belief – is of no further concern. We deal only with the conventional aspect of perlocution (Davis 1979). It is separated here from illocution by the decision-theoretic distinction between negotiation acts each player may perform *unilaterally* and the commitment change, which requires *bilateral* authorization.

More familiar common sense now, and a technical term. Let the near-obsolete verb 'ostend'[4] stand for the join of 'conventionally imply, implicate, show, intimate, take ostensibly for granted'. The imputation or self-imputation $CLA_E\Phi$ ostends that Ego *ceteris paribus prefers* Φ being JC to Φ not being JC. The converse preference is just as plausibly imputable to Alter when Alter, rather than concede, *denies* Φ ($DEN_A\Phi$). In this case Φ does not become JC. But what happens? One of two things, it seems.

Ego may *retract* the claim ($RET_E\Phi$), explicitly or tacitly by convention. In this case Φ does not become JC, nor are things left in dispute. Whether $\neg\Phi$ now becomes JC or whether a non-commital state is the negotiation outcome is, again, a matter of convention. Moreover, a sense of propriety should rule out gratuitous retractions (as indicators of gratuitous claims). Thus, Ego's retraction may only follow upon Alter's denial.

Retraction is the odd act out. It is close to sequential self-contradiction, and in English meta-pragmatic usage one cannot 'retract that Φ', only retract, say 'one's claim that Φ'.

The alternative to retraction is that Ego insists, which for now and for simplicity we identify with a repeat of the claim, $CLA_E\Phi$. On what basis – sheer stubbornness, new evidence, raised incentives – is of no present concern. But the mere question, occasioned by denial and retraction, brings in another familiar aspect. If Ego makes a claim, Ego ostends *dominance* with respect to the issue.

Ego's claim (1) for money is deemed backed by incentives – threats of violence, offers of food or love – deemed sufficient to sway a conceivably reluctant Alter to part with $5. Ego's claim (2) for credence is deemed backed by evidence, sufficient to sway a conceivably incredulous Alter into conceding adoption as a JC of the proposition that the bridge is closed. (And we may identify consent to adopt as JC with personal adoption as professed belief, if not indeed with a disposition to conduct.)

Conversely, Alter's denial $DEN_A\Phi$ ostends dominance the other way: either an ability to force adoption of $\neg\Phi$ or at least an ability to block adoption of Φ. And now Ego's retraction $RET_E\Phi$ would ostend Alter's dominance on the issue. We pick the first convention for the effect of retraction.[5]

What about Ego's initial claim $CLA_E\Phi$ and Alter's conceding response $CON_A\Phi$? A denial indicates a contested claim, hence an agonistic situation. By contrast, acceptance without batting an eyelid does not intuitively license an imputation to Alter of preferences regarding Φ converse or even just complementary to Ego's. Nevertheless, we make a restrictive assumption of strict converse *ceteris paribus* preferences informing this particular DI throughout. This is not implausible, if the issue is indeed an issue.[6]

For lexicological motivation, contrast 'claim' and its imperative and indicative avatars 'demand' and 'assertion' with things like 'suggestion', bland 'statement', 'advice', 'request', 'plea', 'invitation', etc. One may extract a meaning from 'assertion' and 'demand' which presumes that the actor, call her Eve, is pitted against a sceptical or miserly Adam right from the word go. Why else be assertive?

Similarly, the default for 'concession' is of something granted reluctantly and in response to a claim. If Alter concedes $(CON_A\Phi)$ we may now be sure that Ego prefers Φ, Alter prefers $\neg\Phi$; and of one more thing. It is Ego who has taken the *initiative* with $CLA_E\Phi$. Alter's concession $CON_A\Phi$ or denial $DEN_A\Phi$ or Ego's retraction $RET_E\Phi$ (and of course repeated claims) share that assignment of initiative.

What else is there packed into the foursome format? Plainly, that acts are imputed to one of Alter or Ego. The (presently) acting subject of $CLA_E\Phi$ – the person at whose move in the game the claim of Φ is an alternative – is Ego; that of $CON_A\Phi$ is Alter.

Alter would also be the acting subject of an act represented by $CLA_A\Phi$. But if actors in a game are identified with constant preferences, this belongs to a different language game within the same discourse institution. Now Alter prefers (*ceteris paribus* and without further incentive) that Φ be adopted as JC. There is no room for that in a game that allows change of mind in the face of incentives but not a change of heart. And there are two more games: one in which Ego is the one to claim $\neg\Phi$ $(CLA_E\neg\Phi)$ and one in which Alter claims $\neg\Phi$ $(CLA_A\neg\Phi)$.

Call the family of issues generated by a simple binary issue (Φ vs $\neg\Phi$) that might engage two persons (E and A) a *two-by-two issue*. The relationship between its four variants is not unobvious. Already prior to formalization one can see a portable difference between, say, $DEN_A\Phi$ and $CLA_A\neg\Phi$. When Alter denies Φ, Ego is imputed with initiative. When Alter claims $\neg\Phi$, the initiative is Alter's.[7] This difference will hold even for the case where denial implies strict preference for the contradictory.

Formality helps with the bookkeeping, and with showing if and how the books are cooked. We first represent in the DI the *syntagmatic* relations of ESAs, i.e. conceivably admissible sequences of actions and outcomes in language games. Then we treat of their *paradigmatic* relations, which decompose act-descriptions and take account of their syntagmatic relations.

1.3 Joint commitment states

A proposition Φ partitions Alter and Ego's JCSs (Joint Commitment States) into four classes: placidly uncommitted either way ($[?\Phi?]$); committed one way ($[\Phi]$) or the other ($[\neg\Phi]$); or in conflict ($[\#\Phi\#]$).[8]

How do we know there is a conflict? One of Alter and Ego makes a claim for one of Φ and $\neg\Phi$. Who makes the claim, and for which, will depend on influences of no present concern, treated as environmental. We only demand that:

1 no claim is made for something that is already a JC;
2 no conflict arises without a claim being made;
3 a conflict invariably leads to a negotiation and is resolved one way or another if and when the negotiation is concluded (loudly or tacitly, slowly or in a flash);
4 no negotiation about Φ leads (directly) into a $[?\Phi?]$ state;
5 we need not worry about inferential relations to propositions $\Theta \notin \{\Phi, \neg\Phi\}$, which would require a serious theory of non-monotonic theory change to deal with.

The four equivalence classes are represented by states of an automaton $\mathscr{J}$ (see Figure 11.1).[9]

Inputs a^+, e^+, a^-, e^-, represent unilateral changes of heart and mind. They effect transitions to the conflict state $[\#\Phi\#]$ and are associated with *outputs*, respectively, either of abstract symbol strings $(w) \cdot CLA_A\Phi$, $(x) \cdot CLA_E\Phi$, $(y) \cdot CLA_A\neg\Phi$, and $(z) \cdot CLA_E\neg\Phi$ (where ' $\cdot$ ' is concatenation) or of $\acute{a}$, $\acute{e}$, $\grave{a}$, and $\grave{e}$. Depending on taste one may see 'changes of heart and mind' as causes of, or as constructs inferred from, outputs. (Treat w, x, y, z as aliases for the empty string for now and disregard $\acute{a}$, $\acute{e}$, $\grave{a}$, $\grave{e}$. They are needed only later for an alternative scheme.)

Outputs of $\mathscr{J}$ are *inputs* of machine $\mathscr{N}$ (see Figure 11.2, p. 241). The *outputs* of $\mathscr{N}$, which are associated with conclusion of negotiations, are

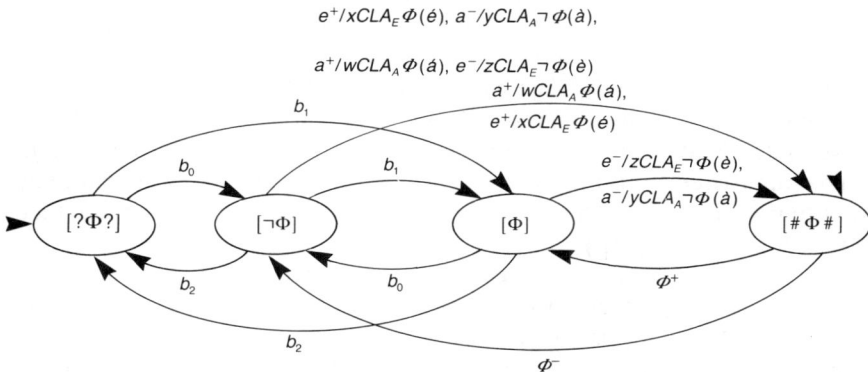

Figure 11.1: Joint commitment states ($\mathscr{J}$)

Notational conventions: Composite labels of form α/β designate α as input and β as output. Simple labels designate inputs. Labels in brackets (α) designate alternate outputs (see text). Arcs with n labels separated by commas expand into n arcs. Double borders indicate intuitively possible 'resting' states.

inputs Φ^+, Φ^- of $\mathscr{J}$.[10] They effect a transition of $\mathscr{J}$ from the conflict state $[\#\Phi\#]$, respectively, to states $[\Phi]$, $[\neg\Phi]$.

Arc labels b_0, b_1, b_2 represent environmental inputs to $\mathscr{J}$. They effect tacit, mutual, *uncontroversial* ('non-issue') transitions of JCS. Example: Alter and Ego see the train coming and see each other seeing it (b_1); Alter and Ego leave the station, and mutually know that they no longer know (or care, or both) whether the train is still there (b_2). Example: Φ becomes an obvious shared goal for perfectly co-operating Alter and Ego where previously $\neg\Phi$ was a shared goal (b_0). Input b_0 is also a cheap *ad hoc* way to get from retraction of a claim to a placid non-commital state.

States of $\mathscr{J}$ are as impersonal and impervious to rhetorical aspects of discourse histories as are the representations of epistemic states favoured by logicians. It is $\mathscr{N}$ which deals with so called rhetorical matters, and the input/output vocabularies are the feedback connection.

1.4 Negotiation states

The machine $\mathscr{N}$ as shown in Figure 11.2 is a composite of several representations, conflated for reasons of space. For the first part of the discussion treat (a) state-labels (e.g. EΦEEE) as arbitrary names (aliases for q_1–q_{16}); (b) upper-case arc labels (e.g. $CLA_A\neg\Phi$) as *inputs*; and (c) disregard broken arcs labelled w, x, y, z and *opdi* and all other lower-case Latin input labels directly on arcs.

The coarse structure of $\mathscr{N}$ is easy to make out. There are 4 similar 4-state sub-automata (one in each corner) corresponding to the 4 cases of a 2-by-2 issue. (Numberings of analogous states are equal mod 4.) Those northeast and northwest are linked directly in one of the alternative schemes (broken lines); similarly those southeast and southwest. The state q_0 [STA/FIN] is initial and final. For now it is 'optical sugar' *qua* final. But *qua* initial it makes $\mathscr{N}$ into a deterministic automaton.

We start in q_0. Suppose Ego claims Φ. Input $CLA_E\Phi$ takes us to q_1. If Alter concedes, described and/or effected by an input symbol $CON_A\Phi$, we move to q_2. Treat @ for now as an alias for the empty symbol string ε. Thus a zero (input-free) transition takes us to the server state q_0, while emitting an output symbol Φ^+. (This symbol is input to $\mathscr{J}$ and takes it from conflict state $[\#\Phi\#]$ to JCS $[\Phi]$.)

Suppose Alter does not concede, but has denied $(DEN_A\Phi)$ the claim. This takes us to q_3. Here two things may happen. Ego can retract with input $RET_E\Phi$, taking us to q_4 whence a zero transition (ε is the empty string) takes us to q_0 with output of symbol Φ^-. (As input to $\mathscr{J}$ it takes $\mathscr{J}$ from state $[\#\Phi\#]$ to state $[\Phi]$.) Alternatively, Ego may insist on the claim $(INS_E\Phi)$, here more simply put as a repeat of $CLA_E\Phi$. This takes us back to q_1. And then any of the options available can follow an arbitrary number of times. (Constraints on, and finer descriptions of, cycles are not of present concern.)

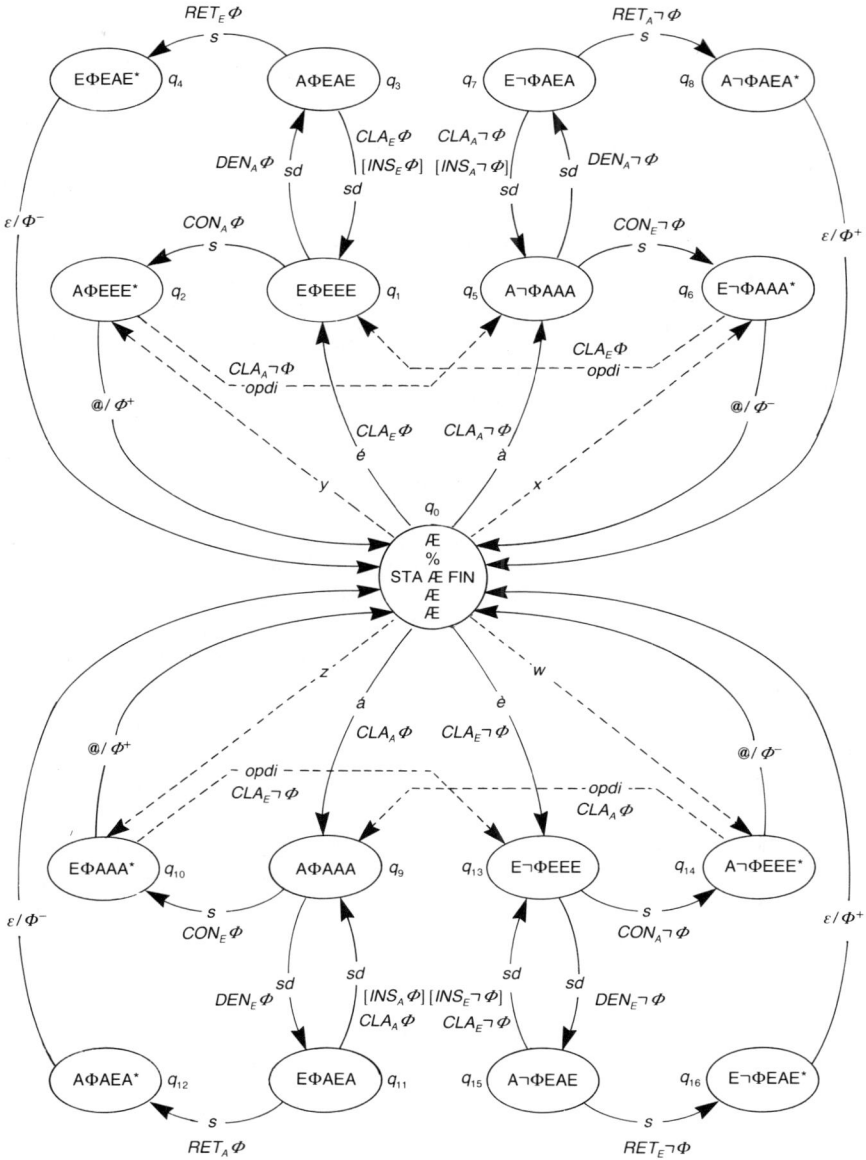

Figure 11.2: Negotiation states (N)

Note: To save space, this diagram conflates several distinct graphs. See text for keys to interpretation.

1.5 A transaction description language

A *transaction* is completed when a final state is reached. We can thus treat N as an acceptor for a formal language L_{TD} of strings over a *transaction description vocabulary* $V_{TD} = \{CLA_E\Phi, \ldots, RET_A \neg \Phi\}$. V_{TD} is defined by the regular expression $V_{TD} := V_{T1} \cdot V_{T2} V_{T3}$ where $V_{T1} = \{CLA, CON, DEN, RET\}$; $V_{T1'} = V_{T1} \cup \{INS\}$, $V_{T2} = \{_E, _A\}$, $V_{T3} = \{\Phi, \neg\Phi\}$ comprise the 'morphemes' of V_{TD}.

The *transaction description language* L_{TD} is the infinite regular language defined by N treated as an acceptor. A sentence of L_{TD} represents a complete transaction. Examples: $CLA_A\neg\Phi \cdot CON_E\neg\Phi$; $CLA_E\Phi \cdot DEN_A\Phi \cdot INS_A\Phi \cdot DEN_A\Phi \cdot INS_A\Phi \cdot DEN_A\Phi \cdot RET_E\Phi$. Non-examples: $CLA_A\neg\Phi$; $CLA_A\neg\Phi \cdot RET_A\neg\Phi$; $DEN_E\Phi \cdot RET_E\Phi$. Complete transactions may thus attain arbitrary finite negotiation length.

1.6 Constant partial function semantics

Each word in V_{TD}, for example $CLA_E\Phi$, labels a transition to just one state. Thus a 'word' denotatum, for example, $|CLA_E\Phi| = CLA_E\Phi$ may be defined as a *constant partial function* (*cpf*) on the set $Q_N = \{q_0, \ldots, q_{16}\}$ of states of N. (A *cpf* on states is a partial *reset*.) Any substring of a sentence of L_{TD} denotes a *cpf* by composition of partial functions. Distinct substrings (including sentences) may denote the same *cpf*. Example: $CLA_E\Phi \cdot DEN_A\Phi \cdot CLA_E\Phi \cdot DEN_A\Phi \cdot CLA_E\Phi \neq CLA_E\Phi$, whereas $|CLA_E\Phi \cdot DEN_A\Phi \cdot CLA_E\Phi \cdot DEN_A\Phi \cdot CLA_E\Phi| = |CLA_E\Phi|$. An explicit performative (EP) would be an intuitive designator of a *cpf* denoted by a substring of length 1 (an 'elementary' *cpf*.)

It is the *syntax* of L_{TD} that represents our intuitions about act-sequences. The *cpf* semantics cannot distinguish among different admissible paths from one state to another. In return it tells what a path amounts to, i.e. what N *qua* memory can tell apart.

1.7 Paradigmatic state semantics for elementary
social acts

The graph establishes a bijection between ESAs (denoted by words of V_{TD}) and target states. This permits association of decision-theoretic properties of ESAs with those states. We interpret each of $Q_{/.} = Q_{/.}\backslash\{q_0\} = \{q_1, \ldots, q_{16}\}$ as a *context* treated as a primitive entity. In the basic DI for the 2-by-2 issue $(\{E, A, \}, \{\Phi, \neg\Phi\})$ each context c is characterized by a 5-tuple:

$$\langle P_S(c), P_O(c), P_P(c), P_D(c), P_I(c) \rangle$$

of binary *parameter* values, where

$P_S(c) \; \varepsilon \; \{E, A\}$: '*acting subject*', (self)-imputed with the act and, intuitively, from whose point of view the ostensible situation is being appraised;

$P_O(c)$ ε $\{\Phi, \neg\Phi\}$: '*issue orientation*', the propositional object of the initial claim;

$P_P(c)$ ε $\{E, A\}$: '*preference*', who (ostensibly) and *ceteris paribus* prefers adoption of $P_O(c)$. Given the assumption of strict and converse preferences, the other person will thus prefer $\neg P_O(c)$. (Below we consider another convention, where $P_P(c)$ is Φ throughout.)

$P_D(c)$ ε $\{E, A\}$: '*dominance*', who (ostensibly) dominates, i.e. here whose preference is ostensibly chosen by a 'social decision function' (SDF) as determining the JCS on the issue. Intuitively, dominance means warrant or overwhelming incentives. P_D incorporates ostensible opportunity costs and tradeoffs against *ceteris paribus* preferences.

$P_I(c)$ ε $\{E, A\}$: '*initiative*', who (ostensibly) has initiated the current transaction in progress by a claim.

Some intuitive motivation for P_P: first, if Alter and Ego are unanimous, there is no issue. If one of them is indifferent there is no issue either. Strict preference factors out the indifference in weak preference. One may object, invoking simple 'information transmission'. But where draw the line between interested and disinterested information? Our hypothetical design default (DD) and a pre-Kantian sense of autonomy are embodied in the pointed question:

(DD) Why ⟨expletive⟩ should I (do or believe that)?

The 'why' itself is of no present concern; virtual or actual agents' concern for it is. As to P_D: that ostensible dominance is all-or-none is not implausible either. (Technically we have a sequence of ostensible *ultimatum games*.)

One will remark that five binary parameters distinguish $2^5 = 32$ contexts. We have only 16. The constraint halving the set is (on present conventions) easily stated: $P_I(c) = P_P(c)$ ('*oeconomicus*'). Persons do not undertake counter-preferential initiatives.

Treating *INS* as a redundant alias for *CLA*, we turn intuitive properties of ESA's into a paradigmatic semantics for *contexts*. A context c is treated as a primitive object, but is sufficiently represented by 5-tuples (see Figure 11.3) labelling states of Figure 11.2. Example: if Ego retracts Φ ($RET_E\Phi$), the ostension (from Ego's point of view) is *inter alia* that Ego *ceteris paribus* prefers Φ, that Ego took the initiative along those lines, and that Alter dominates (hence will turn Alter's preference for $\neg\Phi$ into a JC).[11]

The state q_0 has, so far, no parameter representation. Should we call it a 'context'? Say, the 'zero-context'? As a final state it is a dummy: the starred states in N would do as well by having designated outputs associated with (transitions to) them. As an initial state it serves a more serious purpose (see section 1.11).

	P_S	P_O	P_P	P_D	P_I		P_S	P_O	P_P	P_D	P_I
$CLA_E\Phi$	E	Φ	E	E	E	$CLA_A\Phi$	A	Φ	A	A	A
$CON_E\Phi$	E	Φ	A	A	A	$CON_A\Phi$	A	Φ	E	E	E
$DEN_E\Phi$	E	Φ	A	E	A	$DEN_A\Phi$	A	Φ	E	A	E
$RET_E\Phi$	E	Φ	E	A	E	$RET_A\Phi$	A	Φ	A	E	A
$CLA_E\neg\Phi$	E	$\neg\Phi$	E	E	E	$CLA_A\neg\Phi$	A	$\neg\Phi$	A	A	A
$CON_E\neg\Phi$	E	$\neg\Phi$	A	A	A	$CON_A\neg\Phi$	A	$\neg\Phi$	E	E	E
$DEN_E\neg\Phi$	E	$\neg\Phi$	A	E	A	$DEN_A\neg\Phi$	A	$\neg\Phi$	E	A	E
$RET_E\neg\Phi$	E	$\neg\Phi$	E	A	E	$RET_A\neg\Phi$	A	$\neg\Phi$	A	E	A

Figure 11.3: Elementary social acts and their associated contexts

1.8 Act types

A claim of Φ by Ego is an act. A claim, without further specification, is an *act type*. An act, we might say, is a finest act type.[12] The bijection from fully specified ESAs to contexts offers an economical way of extensional act-typing. We associate act types with subsets of contexts; a partition of contexts is then a typology.[13]

The set $[c°]$ of 16 contexts satisfying $P_I(c) = P_P(c)$ has 2^{16} different subsets. Few of them represent interesting act types; and few partitions of $[c°]$ yield interesting typologies. Among those that do are denotata for V_{T1} (see section 1.6), represented by de-italicized uppercase symbols, and specifiable by (in)equations:

(6) (a) CLA $= \{c \,\varepsilon\, [c°]: P_S(c) = P_D(c) = P_P(c)\}$
    (b) CON $= \{c \,\varepsilon\, [c°]: P_S(c) \neq P_D(c) = P_P(c)\}$
    (c) DEN $= \{c \,\varepsilon\, [c°]: P_S(c) = P_D(c) \neq P_P(c)\}$
    (d) RET $= \{c \,\varepsilon\, [c°]: P_S(c) \neq P_D(c) \neq P_P(c)\}$.

This suggests identifying a notion 'act' with the partition $ACT = \Pi_1 = \{CLA, CON, DEN, RET\}$. Among other intuitively appealing partitions there is Π_2 with elements 'act by $\langle person \rangle$', and Π_3 with elements 'act about $\langle propositional\ object \rangle$'. Thus, a very sparse and obvious compositional semantics for V_{TD} is a semigroup homomorphism $| \ |$ such that, for example, $|CLAE \cdot _E \cdot \Phi| = |CLA| \cap |_E| \cap |\Phi|$. (The set of act types is a lattice under set operations, granted an empty ('null') type.)

Our present typology cannot distinguish claiming from insisting.[14] A more expensive semantics would interpret the morphemes of V_{TD} as binary *relations* on contexts whose intersections are *cpf*s. And then INS would be distinct from CLA. The interest of the simple semantics comes with the idea of context transformations that are total on the set of states, and will thus induce transformations of types.

1.9 A group of context transformations

Let $[c] = [c°] \cup \{c: P_P(c) \neq P_I(c)\}$ be the full set of 2^5 contexts. Let *Trans* : $= \{f_X: X \, \varepsilon \, \{S, O, P, D, I\}\}$ be a set of bijections $f_X: [c] \rightarrow [c]$ such that

(7) $P_X(f_X(c)) \neq P_X(c)$ & $[P_Y \neq P_X \rangle P_Y(f_X(c)) = P_Y(c))]$.

Intuitively, f_X changes context c into context $c' = f_X(c)$ at which P_X has a different value, but which is in all other pertinent respects like c. Since all P_X are binary-valued, each f_X is an involution: $(f_X(f_X(c)) = c$. In the case of $[c°]$, characterized by the constraint $P_P(c) = P_I(c)$, not all parameters can vary independently. Hence $[c°]$ will not be closed under the restrictions to $[c°]$ of every f_X. But composing function saves.

Let T^* be the closure of *Trans* under functional composition. T^* then is the abelian (commutative) group of transformations generated by *Trans*. Notating $(f_X f_Y)(c) := f_X(f_Y(c))$, it is defined by (i) *Trans* $\subset T^*$; (ii) $f_X, f_Y \, \varepsilon \, T^* \rangle f_X f_Y \, \varepsilon \, T^*$ [closure]; (iii) $f_X(f_Y f_Z) = (f_X f_Y)f_Z$ [associativity]; (iv) $f_1 := f_X f_X$ [identity/inverse]; and (v) $f_X f_Y = f_Y f_X$ [commutativity]. T^* has 2^5 elements and is construable as the direct sum $\oplus G_i (i = 1, \ldots, 5)$ of 5 cyclic groups of order 2 (i.e. each G_i isomorphic to $(Z_2, +)$ the integers mod 2 under addition), each generated by a distinct $f_X \, \varepsilon \,$ *Trans*.[15] We now write f_{XY} for $f_X f_Y$, letting (α) denote the group generated by the set α of functions under composition.

Let $T^{°*} := (\{f_X' \mid [c°]: X' \, \varepsilon \, \{O, S, D, PI\}\})$, where the $f_X' \mid [c°]$ are the restrictions to $[c°]$ of the f_X, $X \, \varepsilon \, \{O, S, D, PI\}$ in T^*. (Since $P_I(c) = P_P(c)$ and $f_I(c) \neq f_P(c)$, $[c°]$ is closed under $f_{PI} \mid [c°]$, not under $f_P \mid [c°]$ or $f_I \mid [c°]$.) $T^{°*}$ extends to $(\leq)$ a proper subgroup of T^*.

(8) $T^{°*} := (f_X'[c°]) \leq (f_X: X = O, S, D, PI)$

$T^{°*}$ still affords more freedom to change contexts than the L_{TD} transaction syntax of N with its *cpf* semantics. Hence it can help us investigate further semantic restrictions on transformations implicit in L_{TD}, and means of going beyond them. And by three routes:

1   seeing how act types transform under the action of $T^{°*}$ and finding semantic relations among the elements of V_{TD};
2   looking for partial functions $f_{\leq X'}$ extended by the total functions $f_{X'}$ such that the $f_{\leq X'}$ are (highly context-indexical) *effectors* of ESAs;
3   deriving new DIs subject to rather different restrictions.

1.10 Transformations of act types and the notion 'change in point of view'

What makes a useful act-typology? One criterion is that the corresponding partition Π_1 of $[c°]$ into equivalence classes ('types') have the *substitution property* (is S.P.):[16] i.e. that for all $c, c' \, \varepsilon \, [c]°, f \, \varepsilon \, T^{°*}$

(9) $c \equiv c' \pmod{\Pi_i} \rangle f(c) \equiv f(c') \pmod{\Pi_i}$

That is, suppose subset τ of $[c°]$ is an element of partition Π_i. Any contexts c, c' ε τ are then equivalent, modulo the equivalence relation inducing Π_i. If Π_i is S.P. any $f \varepsilon$ $T^{°*}$ will map c and c' to elements of a single τ' ε Π_i (where $\tau \neq \tau'$ or $\tau = \tau'$, depending on f). That is, f maps 'blocks' of Π_i to 'blocks' of Π_i. We can now define differences.

For any S.P. partition Π_i of $[c°]$ the *difference between two act types* τ, τ' ε Π_i is given by a unique element $f_{\tau - \tau'} = f_{\tau' - \tau}$ of the group $T^{°*}$. We can thus define a group $TT^{°*}$ of transformations $\mathbf{f}_X$ on act types by

(10) $\mathbf{f}_X(\tau) := \{f_X(c) \colon c \varepsilon \tau\}$

Examples: Treat as metalinguistic variables Θ ε $\{\Phi, \neg\Phi\}$ such that $\neg\neg\Theta = \Theta$; ACT ε $\{$CLA, CON, DEN, RET$\}$; H, H', K, K' ε $\{$E, A$\}$ such that H $\neq$ K, H' $\neq$ K'. The graphic schema $\mathbf{f}_X$: TYPE1 $\leftrightarrow$ TYPE2 stands for the proposition $\mathbf{f}_X$(TYPE1) $=$ TYPE2 & $\mathbf{f}_{X-1}$(TYPE2) $\equiv$ $\mathbf{f}_X$(TYPE2) $=$ TYPE1. Each example for an f_X gives (a) a pair of *coarse* types transformed by f_X into one another; and (b) a pair of *finer* types whenever f_X does not preserve all act-type components besides (a).

(11) $\mathbf{f}_O$: ACTΘ $\leftrightarrow$ ACT$\neg\Theta$;

(12) $\mathbf{f}_D$: CLA $\leftrightarrow$ RET; CON $\leftrightarrow$ DEN;

(13) $\mathbf{f}_{PI}$: CLA $\leftrightarrow$ DEN; CON $\leftrightarrow$ RET;

(14) $\mathbf{f}_{PDI}$: CLA $\leftrightarrow$ CON; DEN $\leftrightarrow$ RET;

(15) $\mathbf{f}_S$: CLA $\leftrightarrow$ CON; DEN $\leftrightarrow$ RET;   (a)

         CLA$_H\Theta$ $\leftrightarrow$ CON$_K\Theta$; DEN$_{H'}\Theta$ $\leftrightarrow$ RET$_{K'}\Theta$;   (b)

(16) $\mathbf{f}_{SD}$: CLA $\leftrightarrow$ DEN; CON $\leftrightarrow$ RET;   (a)

         CLA$_H\Theta$ $\leftrightarrow$ DEN$_K\Theta$; CON$_{H'}\Theta$ $\leftrightarrow$ RET$_{K'}\Theta$;   (b)

The actions of $\mathbf{f}_{PDI}$ and $\mathbf{f}_{PI}$ on Π_1 are, respectively, equivalent to those of f_S and f_{SD}. But not on finer types. Thus, unlike $\mathbf{f}_{PDI}$, $\mathbf{f}_S$ does not effect a simple substitution in V_{TD} of, say CON for CLA, but rather of CON_K for CLA_H (where $H \neq K$).

To reconstruct semi-theoretical reflection predicated on free variation of act-descriptions, consider involutive *morphological* transformations μ_j on V_{TD} (see section 1.5). Let μ_1: $ACT_H\Theta$ $\leftrightarrow$ $ACT_K\Theta$ and μ_2: $ACT_H\Theta$ $\leftrightarrow$ $ACT_H\neg\Theta$ ($H \neq K$) be among them. μ_1 would perform a change of person-index in a V_{TD} word, e.g. $CLA_E\Phi$ to $CLA_A\Phi$. Its *semantic* correlate might be expected to be $\mathbf{f}_S$ just as $|\mu_2| = \mathbf{f}_O$. But $\mathbf{f}_S$ $\neq$ $|\mu_1| = \mathbf{f}_{SPDI}$. μ_1 applied to, say, $CLA_E\Phi$ accompanies a change to ostensible conditions under which the same act type (e.g. CLA) would be rationally imputable to (or performable by) the other, here Alter. By contrast, $\mathbf{f}_S$ intuitively corresponds to a *change in point of view*: 'putting yourself in the other's shoes' and facing the same ostensibly objective conditions as before.

Why bother with act-type transformations? Because they are a conceivable design option for the composition of meaning in natural languages. In later applications one might also treat types τ as objects in their own right: elements of a lattice of types *sui generis*, rather than of sets of contexts. (That is, with a lattice homomorphism relating sets τ to objects TYPE.)

1.11 Partial context transformations

Will elements of $T^{\circ *}$ be *effectors* of social acts of just the kind associated with the 'explicit performative' interpretation of language L_{TD}? No. But some related partial transformations of $[c^\circ]$ will be. Let $\text{PFI}([c]^\circ)$ designate the set of *partial injective functions* $[c]^\circ \to [c]^\circ$. On $\text{PFI}([c]^\circ)$ define a binary relation $\leq$ by: $g \leq h \Leftrightarrow g(c) = h(c)$ whenever g is defined for $c \,\varepsilon\, [c]^\circ$. Read $g \leq h$ as 'g is *extended* by h'.

Let Σ_{TE}^+ be the free semigroup over the set $\{o, s, p, d, i\}$ of symbols. Let $[\alpha]$ stand for the string set of permutations of the symbol string α (e.g. $[ab] = \{ab, ba\}$. Let now $V_{TE} \subset \Sigma_{TE}^+$ be the union of string sets $[s]$, $[sd]$, $[opdi]$. Let a map $|\cdot|: V_{TE} \to \text{PFI}([c]^\circ)$ satisfy the condition $|v| \leq f_v \,\varepsilon\, T^{\circ *}$ for $v \,\varepsilon\, V_{TE}, f_v \neq \varnothing$. For example, $|s| \leq f_S$; $|sd| \leq f_{SD}$; $|opdi| \leq f_{OPDI}$. (Since $T^{\circ *}$ is abelian, $f_{OPDI} = f_{DOPI}$, etc., hence $|opdi| = |dopi|$, etc.) Notate $|v|$ as $f_{\leq V}$. Thus

(17) $f_{\leq V} \leq f_V \Leftrightarrow f_{\leq V}(c) = f_V(c)$ whenever $f_{\leq V}(c)$ is defined.

Then words v of V_{TE} denote partial (injective) functions $f_{\leq V}$ on $[c]^\circ$ whose extensions to total (injective) functions f_V on $[c]^\circ$ are elements of $T^{\circ *}$ that generate a subgroup of $T^{\circ *}$. We can extend $|\cdot|$ to an interpretation map defined on a subset of the free semigroup of strings on V_{TE}. They will be proper substrings of a *transaction effector language* $L_{TE'}$ on the vocabulary $V_{TE'} = V_{TE} \cup \{w, x, y, z, @\}$.

Concatenation in the sublanguage L_{TE} on V_{TE} then corresponds to composition of partial functions on the image set $|V_{TE}|$ of V_{TE} under $||$. Augmenting by the identity map on $[c^\circ]$, we get a small category of partial operations on $[c^\circ]$, call it $T^{\circ \sim}$ extending to another, $T^{\circ \sim}$ over $|V_{TE'}|$ whose set of objects is $[c^\circ] \cup \{q_0\}$.

To see how this works, refer back to Figure 11.2 (p. 241): (i) disregard now the arcs marked $\acute{e}$, $\grave{a}$, $\acute{a}$, $\grave{e}$ leaving q_0; (ii) activate the broken arcs (labelled w, x, y, z and *opdi*); (iii) treat lower-case labels (e.g. *sd*, @) on arcs as inputs; and (iv) upper-case labels (e.g. $DEN_E\Phi$) as outputs of $\mathcal{N}$.

The elements of V_{TE} will denote *effectors*, and elements of V_{TD} *descriptors* of elementary social acts. Sentences of L_{TE} will effect transactions described by sentences of L_{TD}. The machine, hence a DI, acts thereby as a *transducer*[17] yielding structural descriptions of acts effected by means that need bear few if any intuitively obvious relations to the effecting inputs.[18] Moreover, if abstract inputs of L_{TE} are seen directly as partial functions on $[c^\circ]$, then L_{TD} strings represent observers' (machine-external) record of actual transaction sequence.

The price is some counterintuitive *ad hoc* features. Return to Alter and Ego. We start again in q_0. Suppose Ego claims Φ. The input is now *xopdi* or, in earlier terms, $xCLA_E\Phi$. It takes us to q_1 on a detour via q_6. Suppose Alter concedes with s (or $CON_A\Phi$). We move to q_2. Alter may immediately turn around to claim $\neg\Phi$ with $CLA_A\neg\Phi$ (abstract input: *opdi*), which takes us to q_5. Or else a conventional interval of time elapses, represented by input symbol @, effecting a transition to q_0 and an output Φ^+ to *J*.

Both detour and alternative look dubious. The first, apart from requiring an extra symbol *x*, makes for a *revanchard* ideology. To make a claim for Φ, Ego enters a negotiation state tantamount to having previously conceded $\neg\Phi$. This is counterintuitive.[19] The option of going back on concessions before they take effect on JCS seems gratuitous, too, unless retractions can be empirically shown to be different or are given a similar privilege (by a map $f_{\leq D}$).

Why *not* go directly to q_1 from q_0? Because q_0 has no interpretation in terms of contexts in $[c°]$; no partial map defined on q_0 would therefore extend to a permutation on $[c°]$. There would no longer be uniform, albeit indexical, denotata for initial (or) ostensibly *revanchard* claims (f_{OPDI}).

To maintain the original act-syntax in transduction with a semantics, one can interpret q_0 as an extra context $c_0 = [\text{Æ}\%\text{ÆÆÆ}]$ where additional parameter values Æ and % represent non-specification. Then *é* denotes a *partial reset* $f_é$ mapping $[\text{Æ}\%\text{ÆÆÆ}]$ to $[\text{EΦEEE}]$, with output $CLA_E\Phi$; analogously for $f_à$ $f_á$ $f_è$. The other $f_{\leq X}$ would remain *partial permutations* of $[c°]$.

This scheme still preserves the act-taxonomy in terms of target states. For certain uses (see Section 2) it is worth retaining. For others, a change is in order. Why? Acts of type CLA are being effected by different kinds of partial functions: $f_{\leq SD}$ for 'insistence' and either $f_{\leq OPDI}$ (after an *ad hoc* detour with *w*, *x*, *y*, *z*) or any one of $f_é$, $f_à$ $f_á$ $f_è$. Thus, relabelling CLA *qua* indexical description of $f_{\leq SD}$ to INS seems attractive. Then insistence would pair with denial as local names for $f_{\leq SD}$, just as concession (CON) and retraction (RET) do for $f_{\leq S}$. If initial claims are, at their most concise, *deictic*, these act types are, as it were, *anaphoric*.

Why bother with partial permutations (and resets)? Because they represent another design option for natural languages.

2 APPLICATIONS AND VARIATIONS

2.1 A semantics for *yes* and *no* (*hai* and *iie*) as responses to non-interrogatives

The DI so far does not represent questions, nor therefore answers to them. But *yes* and *no* also respond to indicatives and imperatives and could therefore do with a denotational semantics.

Suppose Eve claims (1) or (2) ($CLA_E\Phi$) where Φ is 'positive' (cf. Section 2.2). Adam may concede ($CON_A\Phi$) in English by saying *yes*[20] and deny ($DEN_A\Phi$) with *no*. Obvious candidates for denotata of indexicals *yes* and *no* would be $|s|$ and $|sd|$ respectively. But if Eve now retracts ($RET_E\Phi$), doing so with *yes* is odd: *(all) right* would be fine. If Eve insists, i.e. claims again ($CLA_E\Phi$ or $INS_E\Phi$), bare *yes* (best with 'emphatic' prosody) is better than the bare *no* predicted. For Adam to concede ($CON_A\neg\Phi$) Eve's claim of a negative ($CLA_E\neg\Phi$), *no* rather than *yes* is wanted. To deny it ($DEN_A\neg\Phi$), *yes* needs a supplement (e.g. 'it *is*') and is better than *no* with it.

Pope (1973) classifies answers to questions by two binary features: positive/negative [P]/[N], and affirmation/denial [A]/[D] and investigates expressive conflation [–] among the 4 answer types. She notes[21] that English has a [PA–PD, NA–ND] ("H"; 'yes'/'no'), answer system. By contrast, *s* and *sd* would implement her system type [PA–NA, PD–ND] ("I"; 'agree'/'disagree'); and if no language using it existed, one should have to invent it.

Happily, Japanese is a good approximation. As Pope reports, *hai* ('right') is good for conceding either of (i) *Kyoo-wa atu-i des-u ne* ('It's hot today, isn't it') [PA] or (ii) *Kyoo-wa atuku-na-i des-u ne* ('It isn't hot today, is it') [NA]. And *iie* is for denying them [ND, PD], though for (ii) it needs clausal supplementation: *Iie kyoo-wa atu-i des-u.* Suppose this is all there is to *hai* and *iie* and there is no wrinkle on (ii). Then for a suitable format fragment of Japanese, the partial permutation route (section 1.11) would yield:

(18) $|hai| = f_{\leq S}$; $|iie| = f_{\leq SD}$.

Another way of conceptualizing this would be as a relatively 'anaphoric' transformation of act type (sections 1.10, 1.11): for example, as Ego's performance of an act derived from Alter's prior act by application of $\mathbf{f}_S$ or $\mathbf{f}_{SD}$, respectively.

For *yes* and *no*, by contrast, Pope's typing translates most directly into the types of section 1.10, here represented as context sets and with [α] standing for 'type of α'

(19) $[|yes|] = CON\Phi \cup DEN\neg\Phi$; $[|no|] = DEN\Phi \cup CON\neg\Phi$; for 'positive' Φ

Then, kinematically, $|yes|(c) = f_S(c)$ if, and only if, $|no|(c) = f_{SD}(c)$, and $|yes|(c) = f_{SD}(c)$ if, and only if, $|no|(c) = f_S(c)$. That is:

(20) $[|no|] = \mathbf{f}_D([|yes|])$

German *doch* and French *si* (part of a [PA, PD, NA–ND] system "B") are particles for denying negative claims or insisting after denials:

(21) $[|doch|] =_{Ge.} DEN\neg\Phi \cup INS\Phi =_{Fr.} [|si|]$ for 'positive' Φ

They evidently conflate antecedent act types $CLA\neg\Phi$ and $DEN\Phi$, and thus, in a mixed type-transformation representation,

(22) $[|doch|] =_{Ge.} f_{SD}(CLA\neg\Phi \cup DEN\Phi) =_{Fr.} [|si|]$.

Another design option will code assent by some expression type Γ and supply a morpheme constant β such that $\beta\Gamma$ codes denial of whatever Γ concedes. Suppose $|\Gamma| = f_{\leq S}$ in context. Then we might have $|\beta| = g$ where $g(f_{\leq S}) = f_{\leq SD}$; or even simply $|\beta| = f_{\leq D}$. 'Echo'-type answer systems might in parts fit that pattern. Example: Welsh, where Γ is a repeat of the main verb and β would be the special negator *na* (see Sadock and Zwicky 1985: 191). The general principle would then be: *operate on a default act type* to get a marked act type. Here the default would be concession.

Finally, there is the most explicit way of saying *yes* or *no* by *cpf*: for example, by uttering *I (dis)agree with your* ⟨act type⟩ *{that/to}* Θ.

The three broadly distinct ways of saying 'yes' or 'no' – (i) by *cpf*; (ii) partial permutation on contexts amounting to transformation of syntagmatically 'anaphoric' act type; and (iii) transformation of a default act type – suggest at least three broad design options[22] for 'non-truth-conditional' meanings in natural languages that might, in places, induce or be induced by 'truth-conditional' ones. Option (iii) will be further explored next.

2.2 Indirect representation or induction of negation

Consider a DI where preference $P_P(c)$ is always assigned with respect to that Θ of an issue pair $\{\Theta, \neg\Theta\}$ which is expressed unnegated ('positive') in the given natural language. That is, $P_P(c) = H \varepsilon \{E, A\}$ if, and only if, H prefers Θ, regardless of the value $P_O(c) \varepsilon \{\Theta, \neg\Theta\}$. Constraint 'oeconomicus' on P_P and P_I (of Section 1.7) then turns into

(23) $P_P(c) = P_I(c) \Leftrightarrow P_P(f_O(c)) \neq P_I(f_O(c))$.

This new absolutely 'oriented' convention (OC) reflects in a re-labelling of contexts and act-representations. Take Figure 11.3 which represents a 'non-oriented' convention (NC). In acts of type $ACT_H\neg\Phi$, exchange now $P_P(c)$ for $f_P(P_P(c))$. That is, exchange E for A and A for E in the P_P columns of the lower two panels (accordingly in N). Now for instance $CLA_E\neg\Phi = f_{OP}(CLA_E\Phi)$ rather than $f_O(CLA_E\Phi)$.

Next we index act types to the 'subject' parameter. OC now yields a classification, OCS, of act types of grain $ACT\Theta$ by (in)equations *homogeneous* in person-valued parameters. Writing '+' for $P_X(c) = P_S(c)$ and '−' for $P_X(c) \neq P_S(c)$, where $X \varepsilon \{P, D, I\}$, we obtain (Figure 11.4). Example: $RET\neg\Phi$, a retraction of a claim of $\neg\Phi$, has initiative assigned to the actor, but preference for Φ and dominance to the other. Note that OCS correlates *negation* of the propositional object with a change of *preference*

	P	D	I
CLA(Φ)	+	+	+
CON(Φ)	−	−	−
DEN(Φ)	−	+	−
RET(Φ)	+	−	+

OCS

	P	D	I
CLA(¬Φ)	−	+	+
CON(¬Φ)	+	−	−
DEN(¬Φ)	+	+	−
RET(¬Φ)	−	−	+

Figure 11.4: Transformations of default act types

polarity (unlike in the inhomogeneous scheme, derived from NC, where X ε {PI, D, O}).

Consider OCS now in terms of the act-type transformations of section 1.10. Instead of obtaining a claim CLA¬Φ of the negative by a transformation f_O ('negation of content') of the unmarked act type CLAΦ, OCS obtains it by f_P. That is, CLA¬Φ $=_{OCS} f_P$(CLAΦ). (Also DENΦ $=_{OCS} f_{PI}$(CLAΦ), hence DENΦ $=_{OCS} f_I$(CLA¬Φ).) This suggests a hypothesis:

> (IN) Given the constraints of a discourse institution informed by OC, negation in natural languages may induce or be induced by a transformation (on act types or contexts) other than f_O or negation of propositional object.

Change of preference-polarity is a candidate for such a transformation and as an explication of the semi-theoretical notion 'polarity reversal'. Consider first a familiar application.

2.3 Elementary social acts and modal operators

Claim, concession, denial, and retraction have an intuitive image in the traditional 'Aristotelian Square' for modal operators. The conceptual and linguistic link are the deontic categories obligation, permission, prohibition, and exemption. The next step yields necessity, possibility, impossibility and non-necessity.

One way to get from acts to modals is to (i) adopt convention OCS (Figure 11.4); (ii) factor out initiative P_I by a projection yielding, for example, the familiar Fregean identification of DENΦ and CLA¬Φ. Omitting the propositional constant we get a (small, finite) category *Acts* with objects {CLA, CON, DEN, RET} and an abelian group of morphisms generated by {f_P, f_D}. There is also the familiar isomorphic category *Modals* (an 'Aristotelian Square') with objects {NEC, POS, ¬POS, ¬NEC} and its group of morphisms generated by {external negation ($¬_{ex}$), internal negation ($¬_{in}$)} such that $¬_{in} \cdot ¬_{ex} = δ$ (dualization); for example, $δ$ (NEC) = POS = $¬_{in} \cdot ¬_{ex}$ (NEC) = ¬NEC¬.

Now (iii) consider the functor G: *Acts* → *Modals* with the intuitively appealing object map CLA ↦ NEC, CON ↦ POS, DEN ↦ ¬POS, RET ↦

¬NEC. For *G* to be an isomorphism, its morphism map must be $\mathbf{f}_P \mapsto \neg_{in}$, $\mathbf{f}_D \mapsto \neg_{ex}$ such that *G* correlates: (i) *dominance reversal* $\mathbf{f}_D$ with *external negation*; (ii) *preference reversal* $\mathbf{f}_P$ with *internal negation*; (iii) their composition $\mathbf{f}_{PD}$ with *dualization*. And in this transferred sense, since CON = $\mathbf{f}_{PD}$(CLA), claim and concession may be called *dual act types*.

The involution $\mathbf{f}_D$ is not 'negation' of acts.[23] It is merely correlated with negation applying outside a modal operator by a pre- or semi-theoretically appealing isomorphism after suitable abstraction. The appeal can, of course, be motivated. Briefly, it associates, for $\mathbf{f}_D$, (i) deontic necessity – constraint imposition – dominance of the imposer *qua* threat of sanction; (ii) deontic possibility – constraint relaxation – lack of dominance *qua* absence of sanction. And for $\mathbf{f}_P$: the interested imposer's default preference for the constraint imposed, and only grudgingly relaxed with permission. Factoring out interest P_P and substituting $\neg_{in}$ leads to a hybrid form: essentially Anderson's (1956) 'sanction' semantics for deontic logic.

In three-parameter OCS (Figure 11.4), the distinction between DENΦ and CLA¬Φ, is not analogous to that between external and internal negation: CLA¬Φ = $\mathbf{f}_P$(CLAΦ) while DEN(Φ) = $\mathbf{f}_{PI}$(CLAΦ).

Note, however, that OCS is indexed to a single speaker. With the full 4-parameter scheme (NC or OC) an act performed by, say, Ego might well be derived from an act of Alter by application of a type-change operator $\mathbf{f}_X$. (In practice this could amount to the same thing as application of a partial permutation $f_{\leq X}$.) For instance, DEN$_E\Phi$ = $\mathbf{f}_{PI}$(CLA$_E\Phi$) = $\mathbf{f}_{PDI}$(CON$_E\Phi$) = $\mathbf{f}_{SD}$(CLA$_A\Phi$).

2.4 Linguistic reflexes of claim and concession; and 'scalar implicature'

(24) (a) Take an apple and (take) a pear.
     (b) Take an apple or (take) a pear.

(24a) and (24b) may each *inter alia* be interpreted as (i) commands or (ii) permissions, (iii) demands/claims or (iv) concessions. Note that on current, neo-Fregean notions of 'proposition' the 'propositional content' apparently changes between odd- and even-numbered readings (see Kamp 1979; Merin 1992).

Or and *and* appear to denote Boolean 'join' ($\cup$) and 'meet' ($\cap$) on set-theoretic phrase- or clause-denotata in (i) and (iii). Speaker Eve constrains Adam to taking *both* apple and pear in (24a) and *at least one* of the two in (24b). However, in (ii) and (iv), the typical constraints on Adam's conduct are to take (24a) *both, or one, or neither* and (24b) *one or neither*. (We treat 'package deals' of 'both or neither' as inferentially marked cases.) These constraints do not preserve |*and*| = $\cap$, |*or*| = $\cup$; and principled Boolean repair kits are not in sight.

However, one intuition stands out. Suppose there are 'neutral', invariant, addressee-instantiated 'pre-contents' $\alpha = |\Phi \text{ and } \Theta|$, $\beta = |\Phi \text{ or } \Theta|$. Next label (i), (iii) $\text{CLA}_E\Gamma$, and (ii), (iv) $\text{CON}_E\Gamma$, where $\Gamma \varepsilon \{\alpha, \beta\}$. Suppose 'contents' are intensional entities of some kind, weakly orderable by Eve's and Adam's (converse) preferences $\geqq_E$, $\geqq_A$. Then $\text{CLA}_E\Gamma$ claims realization (JC) of a content $\Gamma' \geqq_E \Gamma$ (*at least* Γ) and $\text{CON}_E\Gamma$ concedes realization of a content $\Gamma'' \leqq_A \Gamma$ (*at most* Γ).

The underlying principle is not unreasonable as a default for rational conduct: Eve does not mind getting 'more of' what she claims, but does mind getting 'less'; and does mind giving away 'more of' what she concedes, but does not mind giving away 'less'. And it works the other way, too:

(25) Take my wodget.

will most likely be classed $\text{CON}\Phi$ in a dialect of English where *wodget* means 'wallet', and $\text{CLA}\Phi$ where it means 'garbage'.[24]

Suppose 'content' (i.e. the constraint) is computed on this basis from 'pre-contents'. If *and* designates some form of 'sum', and *or* a non-inclusive 'alternative' (this need not be Boolean XOR) we obtain just the required predictions (see Merin 1992). Indeed, if 'pre-content' and 'content' are of same ontological type, then ESAs *qua* operators are once more akin to *modal operators*.

Finally, consider Adam's likely prior claim or likely subsequent concession to Eve's concession or claim. You now have an explanation of *scalar implicatures* (Horn 1972) attaching variably and defeasibly to Eve's utterances. It will work also for cases 'entailment' will not stretch to, not least among them the late H.P. Grice's (1961) Austinian opener, *It looks red to me*.[25]

This loosely sketched account of speech acts with complex 'content' already exceeds the capabilities of the DIs proposed. But it is a natural extension: from nominal (positive/negative) to ordinal scaling. And the same inventory of operations, for example, the family of f_P, f_{PI} or f_{PDI} operations inducing conversion of preferences, will serve to treat such phenomena in a compositional manner. If the above DI is taken as a basis, the shift from a default claim, to concession (by the same speaker) will be effected by f_{PDI}, which contains f_P as a (non-trivial) factor.[26]

2.5 Negation and De Morgan intuitions without Booleans

Denial is characterizable $\text{DEN} = f_{PI}(\text{CLA}) = f_D(\text{CON})$ for constant actor. Consider now expressions of some semiformal language:

(26) (a) *not*(Φ *or* Θ)
     (b) *not*(Φ *and* Θ)

Suppose that *not* denotes or induces a pair of involutions f_P: Type $\rightarrow$ Type; $g\#$: Pre-Content $\rightarrow$ Pre-Content

(27) $|not| = (\mathbf{f}_{PI}, g\#)$; $|not|(ACT, \Theta) = (\mathbf{f}_{PI}(ACT), \varepsilon\Theta'[\Theta' \neq \Theta])$

where ε is a Hilbert-style choice operator ($\varepsilon x[Qx]$ reads 'some Q') and where $\mathbf{f}_{PI}$ might be just $\mathbf{f}_P$ under certain circumstances. Either will amount to *conversion* of preference relations; and $g\#$ will map the identity relation to *diversity*. In concert they will turn a constraint $[\Gamma' \geqslant_E \Gamma]$ into $[\Gamma' <_E \Gamma]$ (see section 2.4). But given a non-negativity constraint on realizable eventualities, *less than one* of $\{\Phi, \Theta\}$ is none; and *less than both* is one or the other or none, that is:

(28) (a) (*not*Φ *and not*Θ)
      (b) (*not*Φ *or not*Θ)

Thus, intuitions satisfying 'De Morgan's Law' on a Boolean interpretation can be generated without assuming that *and* and *or* denote Boolean intersection and union on propositional content or phrasal abstracts.

In marked cases (classic example: *She didn't take some, she took all*) where $[\Gamma' \leqslant_E \Gamma]$ was the input constraint (e.g. Adam's miserly concession), *not* will yield a constraint $[\Gamma' >_E \Gamma]$; securely so if the input has been prepared as a marked one with *only*. Thus one might suspect something like $|only| = (\mathbf{f}_{PDI}, ID)$. A composite $|not\ only| = (\mathbf{f}_D, g\#)$ would then, at any rate, preserve the default preference attaching to 'claim' while generating diversity from pre-contents. Hence license an inference to a claim for 'more'. For the phenomenology, see Jespersen 1917; for part of the voyage from psychology to logic, consider DIs.

Since operations on types can be derived from operations on contexts, *not* and *only* may well be analysed as denoting (at least in parts), operations on the context of use. Of course, to make this analysis predict in all but rare cases one needs a theory of focus (particularly so for section 2.6). But then, a context need have no less structure than a sentence; so there is no objection in principle to having different action sites on context for one and the same semantically 'polymorphic' expression, distinguished by its focal site within the utterance.

2.6 *If* and *only*, exchanges and polarity phenomena

Consider Robin Lakoff's (1971) example-type of threats and conditional promises, for example:

(29) (a) If you eat any LOXO, I'll {batter you/??give you whatever you like}.
      (b) If you eat some LOXO, I'll {?batter you/give you whatever you like}.

It exhibits alternation between the 'negative polarity item' (NPI) *any* and the 'positive polarity item' (PPI) *some*. There is no apparent negation in the antecedent; a 'negative implicature' (Linebarger 1987) would itself need explaining in (29a); and if there is semantic 'downward entailment' (Ladusaw 1979) it should be there in (29b) as well.

A natural, intuitively pragmatic analysis for (29) is in terms of *exchange proposals* made by speaker Eve to addressee Adam. Schematically for the acceptable versions:

> (a): E *disprefers* antecedent, A *disprefers* consequent
> ⇒ E wishes to *minimize* quantity eaten (antecedent).

> (b): E *prefers* antecedent, A *prefers* consequent
> ⇒ E wishes to *maximize* quantity eaten (antecedent).

But this is what *ceteris paribus* preferences are essentially about. Thus an operation (on the positive default act type) having f_P as a factor would be a candidate for NPI triggerhood, as suggested by the relation between CLA and DEN. Without more detail this is exceedingly vague, and I shall not try to specify.

Still, for the general idea consider *only*.[27] It triggers syntactic inversion in conditionals, e.g.

(30) If Sandy moves {*will Kim/Kim will} jump.

(31) Only if Sandy moves {will Kim/*Kim will} jump.

Semantic tradition will invoke 'underlying negation' or 'reversal of entailment'. But there is no such account (nor any other) for sentence-scope *only* as in

(32) Only, if Sandy moves {*will Kim/Kim will} jump.

Treating *only* as a polymorphic operator with a factor f_P might capture the generalization. In (32), *only* marks the whole conditional as a modest *detraction* from whatever argumentation the preceding utterance pursued. We may thus impute a reversal of preference orientation, indexical to persons.

For (31), suppose that conditionals are represented as *exchange proposals* whatever their content. In this virtual sense they would be *complex social acts* linking, say, Ego's *concession* and Ego's *claim*. Suppose the default act-type sequence for plain *if* is (concession, claim). It is then reversed when the antecedent is modified by *only* to *only if*. (And vice versa, for a marked case.) For motivation of the default in the epistemic-alethic domain, consider a typical dialogue:

(33) Adam: α.
Eve: *If α then β.*

We assume, with obvious indexing, $|\alpha|_A = CLA_A\Phi$. Then $|\alpha|_{Eif}$ (Eve's antecedent) should be the $CON_E\Phi$ part of a deal. Various conventions relating its polarities to $CLA_A\Phi$ are conceivable. The least indexical will proceed from a default source $CLA_E\Phi$ by f_{PDI}. Other options include 'anaphoric' uptake: $CON_E\Phi = f_S(CLA_A\Phi)$. Perhaps the latter route is taken for straightforward 'echo' antecedents.

So much for act-polarity. But *only* also has a frequent reading 'at most' (with a connotation 'less than expected'; see Jespersen 1924: 326). It is accounted for by making two plausible assumptions: (a) 'claim' is the default act-assignment for indicative and imperative utterances; (b) Eve's considerations on 'more of' etc. in section 2.3.

A concession is qualified 'at most'. This is explained if $|only| = f_{PDI}$; and with *only* type-polymorphic (see section 2.5) it should be properly predictive with a theory of focus. Finally, if the default for an *if*-antecedent is 'concession', then the quantitative default 'at least' that comes with an *only if* clause is also closer to getting an explanation.

Consider now German *nur*. As a degree particle it behaves much like *only*, translating readily to 'at most' in all noun-phrase-focus and many verb-phrase-focus contexts. As a modal particle (MP) it is treated as a distinct homophone modulo destressing (see Helbig 1990: 190–9). And there, in imperatives, it forces the marked *concession* assignment. Whereas *Öffne es!* has the same default as 'Open it!', namely 'claim' (demand, command, request),

(34) Öffne es nur!

is virtually synonymous with either of:

(35) Öffne es (nur) ruhig! (*ruhig* lit. 'without anxiety')

MP *ruhig* directly translates the English concession-marker *feel free to*, as in:

(36) Feel free to open it.

The sedimented inference is clear: *without fear of sanction*. By contrast, *nur*, like English *just*, can acquire a menacing tone. Why? It codes concession, by way of preference reversal. But a sanction lies in wait: the tacit consequent of a deal. Our hypothesis must be that MP *nur* is clausal-scope *nur*.

The closest that English *only* comes to MP *nur* is its curious 'optative' use inside conditional antecedents, for example:

(37) If only they would *come* {!/we should be all right}.

(When *they* is more stressed the sentence becomes ambiguous between optative and ordinary-degree reading.) Assume as above that the default act for antecedents is speaker's concession. This attaches speaker's dispreference to them. *Only* (or *nur*), interposed between *if* (or *wenn*) and the antecedent clause proper, again *reverse* this to speaker's *preference*. It is Alter or capricious Fate that should now do the conceding. And the outside *if* together with the -*ed* inflection, ensures that this is not a demand.

2.7 Approximations to suggestion and doubt: applied to neg-raising

Let nonce labels SÜG and DÜB designate act types whose extensions form a partition $\Pi_5 = \{$SÜG, DÜB$\}$ of $[c]°$ where, by convention NC, SÜG := CLA $\cup$ CON $= \{c\!: P_D(c) = P_P(c)\}$; DÜB := DEN $\cup$ RET $= \{c\!: P_D(c) \neq P_P(c)\}$. Π_5 is a *quotient typology*: a coarsening of ACT (Π_1).

Consider, for example, SÜG$_E\Phi$ = $\{$[EΦEEE], [EΦAAA]$\}$ ε τ $\cap$ τ' where τ ε Π_5 and τ' ε Π_2. Ego is acting subject, but the set-valued denotation leaves unspecified the decision-theoretic parameters: whose preference (*cum* initiative) and dominance characterize the context ostended by imputation of SÜG$_E\Phi$.

We might consider SÜG and DÜB as first approximations to *suggestion* and *doubt*, if only because they get closer than do CLA and DEN to disinterestedness. Other approximations[28] are conceivable. And set-valued talk can be rephrased to single-valued by a homomorphism h onto a 'quotient' DI with a state set $Q_{/\,°h}$; SÜG$_E$ (Φ) = $h(\{$[EΦEEE], [EΦAAA]$\})$ ε $Q_{/\,°h}$. One way of interpreting states of $Q_{/\,°h}$ is as formal *linear superpositions* of states in $Q_{/\,°}$, for example, k[EΦEEE] + $(1 - k)$ [EΦAAA] where k ε]0, 1[is a real or rational number. This would admit extensions to 'biased' mixtures where $k \neq \frac{1}{2}$. (For $k = \frac{1}{2}$, rewrite as [EΦÆÆÆ]). The general idea, however, is:

(QDI) Quotienting of DIs is one way of generating new act types that may be natural kinds in naive metapragmatics.

For a less obvious linguistic application consider the widespread phenomenon of 'neg-raising' (NR) exemplified by the seeming equivalence of (a) and (b) in:

(38) (a) I don't {think/believe} that Kim is drunk.
(b) I {think/believe} that Kim isn't drunk.

(39) (a) I don't {want/expect} Kim to be drunk.
(b) I {want/expect} Kim not to be drunk.

Equivalence does not obtain when the matrix verbs are stressed, nor with paradigmatically related verbs *know, assert, admit*, etc. Horn (1978) noted that neg-raisers (which include, for example, *should* and *likely*) tend to be attenuated forms, 'mid-scalar' on their respective epistemic or deontic-boulomaic lexical 'scales'. But a denotational semantics or pragmatics for this construal of NR has not so far been offered. In fact, the status of the 'scales' is none too obvious.

Suppose, then, that 'scales' in question have poles instantiating *claim* and *concession* in their respective substantial domains. The act category of *suggestion* would then stand between them. (Indeed, implementation by formal averages of parameter values would give 'between' its abstract geometric sense.)

Reflective act-type intuitions on (38) and (39) will, if anything, class the (a) forms as 'denials', and the (b) forms as 'assertions of a negative'. The DI framework now offers an explanation which goes beyond observing that NRs δ are somehow self-dual, $\neg\delta\Phi = \delta\neg\Phi$, with respect to negation. For by definition,

(40) $\text{DÜB}_H\Phi = f_D(\text{SÜG}_H\Phi) = f_{PI}(\text{SÜG}_H\Phi).$

The empirical hypothesis: the two ways of getting from $\text{SÜG}_H\Phi$ to $\text{DÜB}_H\Phi$ correspond to different action-sites of the negation morpheme: at the act-designating main clause and in the complement. The distinction by initiative shift would then even account for one of the intuitively felt distinctions between (a) and (b) versions. And the equivalence would not hold for polar types CLA, CON, DEN, RET.

The act category 'suggestion' was noted *inter alia* by Horn as a locus of neg-raisers. Its partial explication in the DI account offers a denotational semantics for taking the apparently circuitous, Austinian route to meaning through (ostensible) speech acts (see Urmson 1952).

2.8 The hard and the soft: requests

Suppose 'dominance' is defined independently of the social decision function (SDF) in terms of resources, opportunity costs, etc. In our familiar DI, call it DI[H] (for 'hard'), the ostensible value of the SDF is deemed to be the preference of the dominant party. Consider now a type DI[S] (for 'soft') where the SDF value is deemed to be the *non*-dominant party's preference, while constraint $P_I(c) = P_P(c)$ (in NC) is retained.

DI[S] models a polite altruistic language game of diffident requests and gracious grants. Its act types might be called request (REQ), grant (GRA), exemption (EXE), plea for exemption (PEX) (the last two for want of a better English term).

Compare, in loose notation, act-sequences in DI[H] with act-sequences in DI[S]:

(41) (a) $\text{CLA}_E\Phi/[E\Phi EEE] - f_{\leq S} \rightarrow \text{CON}_A\Phi/[A\Phi EEE]$
             (claim, concession)
       (b) $\text{REQ}_E\Phi/[E\Phi EAE] - f_{\leq S} \rightarrow \text{GRA}_A\Phi/[A\Phi EAE]$
             (request, grant)

(42) (a) $\text{CLA}_E\Phi/[E\Phi EEE] - f_{\leq SD} \rightarrow \text{DEN}_A\Phi/[A\Phi EAE] - f_{\leq S} \rightarrow$
             $\text{RET}_E\Phi/[E\Phi EAE]$ (claim, denial, retraction)
       (b) $\text{REQ}_E\Phi/[E\Phi EAE] - f_{\leq SD} \rightarrow \text{PEX}_A\Phi/[A\Phi EEE] - f_{\leq S} \rightarrow$
             $\text{EXE}_E\Phi/[E\Phi EEE]$ (request, plea for exemption, exemption)

Note first a peculiar asymmetry of claims [H] and symmetry of requests [S]: to make a *claim* CLA is *ipso facto to claim dominance*.[29] To make a *request* REQ in DI[S] is *ipso facto to offer or concede dominance*.

For Alter faced with a *claim,* the prospect of double loss (issue and status) is *ceteris paribus* a spur to resistance. For Alter faced with a *request,* the prospect of status gain is *ceteris paribus* a spur to compliance. This would make requests efficacious means of getting what one wants (cf. Brown and Levinson 1978). Alter's polite plea for exemption (PEX), if one is made at all, returns the offer. Ego, whose request PEX ever so politely 'denies' should not thereby 'lose face'. Ego is being asked, not told. In return for not getting the grant, Ego is thereby given an opportunity to be magnanimous: to spare Alter compliance with what would have been a claim in DI[H].[30]

How does one get from DI[H] to a partial anti-world DI[S]? Two popular mnemonics suggest themselves. The SDF and thence the paradigmatic semantics of DI[S] is reminiscent of Matthew 5.5: 'Blessed are the meek; for they shall inherit the earth.' But the change to DI[S] also has a syntagmatic correlate.

Compare again the paradigmatic interpretations: $CLA_E\Phi =_H [E\Phi EEE]$ $=_S EXE_E\Phi$; $CON_A\Phi =_H A\Phi EEE =_S PEX_A\Phi$; $DEN_A\Phi =_H A\Phi EAE =_S$ $GRA_A\Phi$; $RET_E\Phi =_H E\Phi EAE =_S REQ_E\Phi$. Use them to refer back to the sub-automaton of N with states $\{q_1, q_2, q_3, q_4\}$ (Figure 11.2, p. 241) and to the sample act-sequences just given. And note the resulting permutation

$$(43) \quad \beta: (q_1, q_2, q_3, q_4) \mapsto (q_4, q_3, q_2, q_1)$$

of contexts c_i (represented by states q_i), reminiscent of Matthew, 20.16: 'So the last shall be first, and the first last.' This route to everyday utopia is representable by a functor F_D from DI[H] to DI[S] which, as it were, permutes states by $[F_D(c)] = [f_D(c)]$ (where $[\alpha]$ is the parametrization type of α) and which preserves the context transformation type ($|s|$, $|sd|$, etc.) of transition arrows.

Is such a functor from 'language game' to 'language game' a mere device for organizing one's theoretical terms, as, one flight down, the group T^* might have seemed? Or does it also furnish likely (components of) denotata of natural language or paralanguage expressions?

Consider 'honorific' features of pronouns, for example, the *tu/vous* distinction described by Brown and Gilman (1960) in terms of 'power' and 'solidarity'. A case can be made (not here) that ostensible, if tacit, changes of convention may occur as a matter of course within ordinary discourse at every turn. How? Wholly asymmetric DIs can be specified equationally, in which one person is Master, the other Slave. Reference could in linguistic practice be made to them. And then the ostensible status equality established by reciprocal, mutual use of honorific *vous* would arise as a time-average, each dialogue partner treated as Master for the time of being spoken to. No speaker, hence neither party, can ostensibly take liberties with the other. Which is as good a definition of social 'formality' as any.

2.9 Yes/no questions, intonation, and *do*

Linguistic common sense, with an eye to Frege (1918a), sees questions as requests to answer. DI[S] and the possibility of asymmetric, mixed DIs suggests a more general hypothesis: what a *request* (as distinct from a claim) is in the deontic-boulomaic domain, a yes/no *question* is in the alethetic-epistemic domain (see Sadock 1974: 111 for a special case). Thus allocation of dominance will essentially differentiate a simple, un-pointed yes/no question from an assertion. Example: consider DI[S] and rewrite REQ to QUE, and GRA to AFF ('affirm'). Then $f_{\leq S}$ will take us from the target state of a 'positive' question to that of an affirmative answer: as a simple *yes* or *hai* would.

There may be more than a chance relation between the resulting pragmatic inversion, at least of dominance relations, and the fact that most known languages code yes/no questions by marked, intuitively inverted speech melody (rising rather than falling); and some, for example, English, even by syntactic 'inversion'.

The hypothesis will not yet explain why positive questions tend, if anywhere, towards doubt (see Anscombre and Ducrot 1981), particularly so when 'pointed' with a stressed auxiliary; and, always, in contrast to 'leading' negative questions. Comparing (a) and (b) of:

(44) (a) Don't penguins fly?
      (b) Don't come in!

(45) (a) Don't you believe it? ⟋
      (b) Don't you believe it! ⟍

it appears that yes/no questions differ from imperatives in ostensible 'preference' default, where *preference* instantiates to *expectation* in questions. Similarly, then, with *do* (noting that *Do come in* with default intonation makes a polite request).[31]

That default would make the most hackneyed of 'indirect speech act' examples, Eve's *Can you pass the salt?*, a direct if tacit *challenge*[32] which Adam is given a chance to rise to and answer ostensibly (and ostensively) by instant supply of evidence. It would also make *Can't you pass the salt?* a much cruder and dangerously counterproductive affair; as indeed it is.

3. CONCLUSION

Section 1 has offered an example of a family of synthetic 'language games' called, for want of a less misleading name, 'discourse institutions'. Section 2 has outlined a wide range of applications in the analysis of natural languages. Sketchily, no doubt; but with enough detail, I think, to illustrate a diversity of design options, starting with choice of parameter transformations and extending to choice and indeed transformations of DI.

That freedom of choice might also spell 'anything goes'. But in fact not

everything goes. The modest algebraic structure employed, besides harden-
ing aspects of might-be 'pragmatics' into kinematic, denotational semantics
(see Scott and Strachey 1971; Davies and Isard 1972; Kamp 1981), also
imposes evident constraints once a particular parametrization is chosen.

Suppose the proposed application turns out to be correct in principle, if
not already in detail. Then it cannot but give empirical bite to a thesis
famously associated with G.H. Mead (1934): that there is less of a difference between certain structures we call mental and those we call social than
either common sense or some austere reactions to it would guess or admit.

NOTES

1 The guess for verbs is Austin's (1962: 150); Ballmer and Brennenstuhl (1981)
   exhibit some 4,800 verb phrases.
2 Cf. Searle (1969, 1975), Searle and Vanderveken (1985), Vanderveken (1990/
   91); for inferential depth, Cohen and Levesque (1990). Hamblin (1971)
   considers the assertoric instance of the foursome in a commitment state change
   setting differing from the present one in most ways, means, and ends. For the
   kind of thing that makes a linguistic theory of speech acts tick, irrespective of
   period-bound explanatory tools, see Sadock (1974: 149, fig. 1). This is close to
   my intended line of business, which cuts across distinctions of mood, might thus
   complement Sadock (1990), and should explicate and extend Ducrot's (1973)
   assertoric argumentation. ESAs are examined with emphasis on imperatives in
   Merin 1991. The present paper derives from a larger MS, 'Descriptors and
   effectors of elementary social acts', prepared for the ESPRIT-DANDI Workshop on Formal Pragmatics, Essex University, September 1991 and a presentation at IBM Research Centre, Stuttgart, March 1992.
3 The 'force dynamics' uncovered in Talmy 1985 would thus constitute a
   (perhaps *the*) complementary *physiomorph* representation system.
4 From Latin *ostendere* 'to show'; see the *OED*. Important now is the kinship to
   'ostensible': non-commital, from the analyst's perspective, about truth or
   warrant. For my part, I prefer not to be committed to the Gricean doctrine that
   comes with 'implicate'. Hence the near-neologism.
5 For binary simplicity. This is psycholinguistics, not philosophy. For models of
   the two alternative policies on retraction, cp. civil procedure in the Law, e.g.
   German *Klagerücknahme* ($271 ZPO) vs *Klageverzicht* ($306 ZPO).
6 All game-theoretical reconstructions of logics are predicated on strict competition. In our DI Alter and Ego are intuitively engaged in a tacit bargaining game
   with incomplete information. They have strictly opposed interests regarding the
   issue Φ ('demand functions'). But the incentives they can muster ('supply
   functions') and therefore their overall opportunity costs (whose minimization
   makes for co-operation) make the game as a whole non-constant-sum (cp.
   Nash 1953).
7 In van der Sandt 1991, denials refer back to prior assertions and 'erase' them
   from context.
8 Cp. Belnap 1977 for the 'single mind' epistemic correlate.
9 A 'sequential machine' or 'automaton' in the mathematical sense is no more
   than two or three sets and one or two functions or relations on them. It is up to
   us what, if any, more concrete empirical interpretations to give them.
10 In this respect *J* and *N* are 'transducers' with partial output functions.
11 ESAs are expressible as EPs true in virtue of utterance. But even so, the

ostensions $P_P(c)$, $P_D(c)$, and even $P_I(c)$ attaching to them are no more than ostensibilia. On the legalistic view, for example, of J.L. Austin, they need not be true, even if the third-person indicative corresponding to the EP indicative is.

12   How fine 'finest' is will be relative to our descriptive resources.

13   Componential analysis of act types ('forces') is as old as analysis of acts. The concise n-tuple format is incidental; not so the choice and use of parameters. Cp. the best known analysis of force (Searle 1969) as, for example, elaborated in Searle and Vanderveken 1985. Its 'preparatory' conditions for assertions ('having evidence') and commands ('authority') are more circumspect instances of P_D. 'Sincerity' conditions have a Janus-faced cousin in P_P, but P_O is unlike the mood-specific 'propositional content' condition. Another 'preparatory condition', that the act not be redundant, is built into the syntax of J.

14   English meta-pragmatic usage restricts use of act-nominals: one can 'make' a claim, concession, denial, even a retraction, but not an insistence. Perhaps this is evidence that the typology is being tacitly adopted for some purposes.

15    $\oplus G_i$ ($i = 1, 2$) yields the Klein 4-group of 'Aristotelian Square' fame, i.e. the symmetry group D_2 of the rectangle.

16   See Hartmanis and Stearns 1966: 38f.

17   Here with a total output function. 'Acceptance' of a string is representable by designated outputs. The unique association of states with ESAs would make intuitive the 'Moore Machine' format, which associates outputs with states rather than edges.

18   One might also specify constraints on definition and composition of L_{TE} string denotata in model-theoretic terms, for example, in terms of partial functions from Times to Contexts.

19   But has a counterpart in current usage of 'defence'. There is no 'Ministry of Attack' nor (now), I believe, a 'War Office'.

20   Though *OK* and *all right* are perhaps better for (1); cp. Sadock and Zwicky 1985: 189.

21   PD refers throughout to DEN¬Φ, not only for English. (Think of 'positive' clausal support added.) Actual systems are never pure, and at least PD always needs open-class supplementation. (For markedness of CLA¬Φ cf. section 2.2.) Sadock and Zwicky (1985: 189) add 'echo' systems. ("H", "I", etc., are Pope's alphabetic labels.)

22   English is "H" by morphology, "I" by intonation, and "B" by tag-deletion (Pope 1973: 486).

23   Nor will it extend non-gratuitously to some operation of 'illocutionary negation' (Searle and Vanderveken 1985) defined on all speech act types. Neither is the mere isomorphism to humdrum group D_2 (see note 15) of any deep significance. But we now have an explication for the view of negation in Lyons (1977: ch. 16.4). Note also that the odd act type out, RET, maps to the poorly lexicalized corner of the Square (see Horn 1972).

24   And no doubt the intermediate case of a friendly suggestion (see section 2.7) where it means **** or the like.

25   See Merin 1991: 695f. for more on 'quantity implicature'.

26   Meaning: $(f_P)^{2n+1}$ for integer n.

27   A trigger of certain NPIs within the verb phrase, for example, *lift a finger, ever*; *only* X (X a noun phrase) as 'subject' will also trigger *at all* or *any* in the predicate verb phrase.

28   For example, by way of DIs where P_I and P_P are independent.

29   We say 'ostend' or 'show' etc. But the claim is there implicitly, and brought out if the ostension is questioned. DIs taking account of this would be Recursive Transition Networks (RTNs) in which the warrant for a claim becomes itself an issue.

30 Languages I am familiar with lack single verbs for PEX and EXE. Perhaps appeal to DI[S] does not really envisage ever so polite denials. The deal – status concession for grant – is being represented as too good to pass up.

31 A DI in which P_1 and P_P may essentially differ might thus be invoked: for example, with $\text{QUE}_E\Theta/[\text{E}\Theta\text{AAE}] - f_{\leq S} \rightarrow \text{AFF}_A\Theta/[\text{A}\Theta\text{AAE}]$. Recalling a proposal for *suggestions* (section 2.6) one might conceive of QUE etc. more generally as linear combinations of type assignments, admitting bias one way or the other (as indicated sometimes by polarity items). This would also address the *gradient* nature of pertinent distinctions coded by prosodic means. (When, for instance, does a question begin to sound 'pointed'?) Again, a map g': $|do| \mapsto |don't|$ with factors $\mathbf{f}_P$ and/or $\mathbf{f}_D$ seems a likely candidate for $|n't|$.

32 Perhaps a better translation of Frege's (1918a) *Aufforderung* than 'request'.

Part II
Speech acts and pragmatic theory

12 Semantic slack
What is said and more

Kent Bach

Like Humpty Dumpty, many philosophers take pride in saying what they mean and meaning what they say. Literalism does have its virtues, like when you are drawing up a contract or programming a computer, but generally we prefer to speak loosely and leave a lot to inference. Language works far more efficiently that way.

TWO KINDS OF LOOSENESS

It helps if you can rely on people not to take you too literally. Imagine a child, upset about a cut finger, whose mother assures him, 'You're not going to die, Peter.' The budding philosopher replies, 'You mean I'm going to live forever, Mom?' Was Mrs Unger stretching the truth? In a way, yes. She could have said, 'You're not going to die from this cut', which would have been more to the point, but she did not. She did not bother saying that because she saw no reason to spell out what she meant. She was not being obscure and she did not expect Peter to be so obtuse. Surely any normal boy would have taken her to mean that he would not die from that cut and would never have considered, at least not consciously, the possibility that what she meant was that he would not die at all. But Peter was annoyingly right: what she meant was not what she said, at least not exactly. She was not speaking literally.

This example illustrates a common but not widely recognized form of non-literality: a sentence can be used non-literally without any of its constituents being so used. Suppose clever Peter had asked his mother, 'When you said I'm not going to die, did you mean it literally?' Mrs Unger, having used each of her words literally, might not see the point of the question. Had she said to him 'You're not going to croak' and he asked if she meant that literally, she would have understood that the use of a particular constituent was in question. *Sentence* non-literality is nothing like metaphor or any other kind of *constituent* non-literality, but it is still a kind of non-literality in its own right (Bach 1987: 71–2). What we call 'loose talk' is often not a matter of using words non-literally, or of using vague or ambiguous words, but simply a matter of leaving words out. So, for example, if you say 'I haven't eaten' you do not include *dinner today* or anything of the sort; if you say 'Everyone must wear a costume' you do not include *who comes to the party*; and if you say 'Tigers have stripes' you do not include *normal*. Using sentences non-literally in this way is so common that we tend neither to be aware of doing it nor to think of it as not literal when others do it. But we do it all the time (as I did just then). Rather than insert extra words into our utterances so as to make fully explicit what we mean, we allow our listeners to read things into what we say. This suggests, at least if what is said is a complete proposition but not the one that is meant, that being inexplicit is a way of not being literal (intuitively we may not think of it as such because no words are being used figuratively).

Consider typical utterances of sentences like the following:

(1) You are not going to die.
(2) I haven't eaten.

In each case, at least once the indexical references and the time of the utterance are fixed, the (literal) meaning[1] of the sentence determines a definite proposition, with a definite truth condition expressible roughly as follows:

(1-TC) The addressee of the utterance of (1) is immortal.
(2-TC) The utterer of (2) has not eaten prior to the time of the utterance.

Each of these determines the *minimal* proposition (Récanati 1989/1991: 102) expressed by the sentence, so-called because it is the proposition which, when compared to whatever the speaker is likely to mean, is linguistically more closely related to the sentence. An utterer of (1) or (2) is likely to be communicating not a minimal proposition but some *expansion* of it. I call this an expansion because what is communicated could have been made explicit with the insertion of an appropriate phrase, such as *from this wound* after *die* or *dinner today* after *eaten*.[2]

Not to be confused with sentence non-literality is another phenomenon, which gained modest recognition in the late 1970s and early 1980s under the labels *semantic generality* (Atlas 1977) and *non-specificity* (Bach 1982) and is more widely known these days as *semantic underdetermination*. Akin to the older notion of sense-generality of words (such as *deep*, *push* and *before*), which lexical semanticists distinguish from homonymy, ambiguity and vagueness (see Atlas 1989: ch. 2), semantic underdetermination is a feature of sentences. An (indicative) sentence is semantically underdeterminate if it fails to express a complete proposition – determine a definite truth condition – even after ambiguity and vagueness are resolved and indexical references (including the time of the utterance) are fixed. Simple examples include utterances of:

(3) Steel isn't strong enough.
(4) Willie almost robbed a bank.

These sentences, though syntactically well formed, are semantically or conceptually incomplete, in the sense that something must be added to the sentence for it to express a complete and determinate proposition. With (3) we need to know strong enough for what (it does not express the weak proposition that steel is not strong enough for something or other). The problem with (4) is due to the word *almost*: what could be communicated is that Willie nearly succeeded at robbing a bank; that he decided against robbing a bank and robbed something else instead; or that he barely refrained from robbing a bank. In these cases what the conventional meaning of the sentence determines is only a fragment of a proposition, or what I call a *propositional radical*; a complete proposition would be expressed only if the sentence were elaborated somehow, so as to produce what I call a *completion* of the proposition. Semantic underdetermination is not a case of (sentence) non-literality because the speaker does mean what he says – it is just that that is not the whole of what he means. What a speaker means must be a complete proposition, but, as will be explained later, in semantic underdetermination the content of what a speaker says is merely a propositional radical.

So we have two distinct phenomena, sentence non-literality and semantic underdetermination, in which what a speaker means is not fully determined by what the sentence means – even if no words are being used figuratively and nothing is being conversationally implicated (no speech act is being performed indirectly). In one case there is a (minimal) proposition expressed by the sentence, but expansion is needed to deliver the more elaborate proposition expressed by the speaker; in the other case, completion is needed just to deliver a proposition. The difference is simply this: with sentence non-literality a minimal proposition is fleshed out; with semantic underdetermination a propositional radical is filled in.

DELIMITING WHAT IS SAID

Both of these phenomena – expansion and completion – have been thought to signal a major oversight in Grice's account of the distinction between what is said and what is implicated. For it seems that pragmatic processes of the same sorts as those involved in conversational implicature, whatever exactly these processes are (here I am not concerned with the adequacy of Grice's or other accounts of these processes), come into play prior to the working out of implicatures. That is, whether or not the hearer takes an utterance literally and directly, he relies on the presumption that the speaker intends his communicative intention to be identifiable under the circumstances (Bach and Harnish 1979: 12–15). He reasons on the supposition that if the speaker cannot plausibly be taken to mean what he says or just what he says, then what the speaker does mean is inferable from what he is saying together with contextual information evident enough to have been expected to be taken into account. A number of philosophers have contended that Grice completely overlooked the fact that inferential processes of essentially the same sorts as those involved in implicature enter into determining what is said. Of course he did recognize that not just linguistic knowledge but certain types of (salient) contextual information play a role in determining what is said. Here he had in mind contextual information relevant to resolving ambiguity and fixing indexical reference (including the time of the utterance), together with the supposition that the speaker's idiolect conforms with standard use of the language (1975/1989: 25). Clearly, then, Grice did recognize a role for pragmatic processes in determining what is said. His critics, noticing that he overlooked what I have been calling expansion and completion, contend that his theory incorrectly counts these phenomena as implicature. They suppose that his conception of saying is too restrictive and that he draws the line between what is said and what is implicated in the wrong place. As I will argue shortly, there is no *line* to be drawn between what is said and what is implicated. Instead, there is considerable middle ground between them.

Sperber and Wilson (1986) as well as Carston (1988) regard expansions and completions as explicit contents of utterances, not as implicatures. However, these phenomena do not fit Grice's conception of what is said, in as much as they are not 'closely [enough] related to the conventional meaning of the ... sentence ... uttered' (Grice 1975/1989: 25). On the other hand, they are too closely related to linguistic meaning to qualify as implicatures. Sperber and Wilson coin the word *explicature* for this in-between category (1986: 182). Why they call it that is not entirely clear. The word *explicature* is supposed to refer to the explicit content of an utterance, but it is a cognate of *explicate*, not *explicit*. And the content of an explicature produced by expansion or completion is not 'explicitly communicated', since part of what is communicated is not expressed. Perhaps this is why Récanati avoids using the term *explicature* in making his case for including expansion and completion (he calls them *strengthening* and *saturation* – 1989/1991: 102) in the category of what is said. Here he is clearly going beyond Grice's 'intuitive understanding of the meaning of [the word] *say*' (1975/1989: 24–5), on which what is said must correspond to 'the elements of [the sentence], their order, and their syntactic character' (1969/1989: 87), but Récanati argues that his extension of Grice's notion is intuitively natural and has the theoretical virtue of not counting expansion (strengthening) and completion (saturation) as cases of implicature.[3]

To some extent the issues here are merely terminological – Grice's 'favored' sense of *say* is stipulative and admittedly 'artificial' (1968/1989: 118) – and, having not confronted the problems of sentence non-literality and semantic underdetermination, he had no occasion to fit the cases of expansion and completion into his scheme. However, two other considerations led Grice to refine the distinction between what is said and what is implicated. First, he distinguished saying from merely 'making as if to say'

(1975/1989: 30), as in irony and metaphor (ibid.: 34), and allowed that making as if to say, like saying, can generate implicatures. Second, he insisted that part of what a speaker means can be closely related to conventional meaning and yet not be part of what is said – it is 'conventionally' rather than conversationally implicated. Leaving these two complications aside for the moment, I grant that Grice did give the impression that he intended the distinction between what is said and what is implicated to be exhaustive. Accordingly, since expansions and completions are not related closely enough to conventional meaning to fall under what is said (in Grice's favoured sense), it does seem that for him they would have to count as implicatures. Sperber and Wilson, Carston and Récanati all find this result unintuitive. I agree with them, though not for their reasons and despite the stipulative character of Grice's distinction. For in my view, what we need in order to maximize intuitive plausibility is more stipulation. Let me explain.

SAYING AND STATING

There are certain peculiarities to Grice's favoured sense of saying. Most notably, for him saying something entails meaning it. This is why Grice uses the locution 'making as if to say' to describe irony, metaphor, etc., since in these cases one does not mean what one appears to be saying. Most of us would describe these more straightforwardly as cases of saying one thing but not meaning that and meaning something else instead. That is what it is to speak non-literally – at least if one does so intentionally. One can also *un*intentionally not say what one means, owing to a slip of the tongue, misusing a word or phrase, or otherwise mis-speaking (Harnish 1976a/1991: 328). Finally, one can say something without meaning anything at all, as in cases of translating, reciting or rehearsing in which one utters a sentence with full understanding and does not just parrot it (recall Austin's distinction between the 'phatic' and the 'rhetic' act), and yet does not use it to communicate. To reckon with these various ways of saying something without meaning it, Grice could have invoked Austin's distinction between locutionary and illocutionary acts, but he did not (he generally avoided the jargon of speech act theory and seemed rather unconcerned with its distinctions). Austin, it may be recalled, defined the locutionary act (specifically the rhetic act) as using certain 'vocables with a certain more-or-less definite sense and reference' (1962: 95). That sounds a lot like Grice's notion of saying, except that for Grice saying something entails meaning it: the verb *say* does not mark a level distinct from the level marked by such illocutionary verbs as *state, tell, ask*, etc., but rather functions as a generic illocutionary verb. It describes any illocutionary act whose content is made explicit. Since virtually all of Grice's examples involve indicative utterances, in practice he uses *say* to mean *explicitly state*. Indeed, the original formulation of his distinction (in Grice 1961) was between stating and implying. Clearly Grice opted for the word *say* in order to widen the scope of his distinction beyond statements.[4]

Considering that he describes non-literal utterances like irony and metaphor not as saying but as making as if to say, it is puzzling that Grice should have assimilated these to implicature. Intuitively, one thinks of implicating as stating or meaning one thing (i.e. saying something in Grice's favoured sense) and meaning something else as well, not as meaning something else instead. Since Grice denies that irony and metaphor are cases of saying in his sense, he should not have described their non-literal contents as implicatures. The same sorts of inference processes are involved as in genuine implicatures, but there is still a big difference between saying one thing and meaning something else as well and meaning something else instead, between speaking indirectly and speaking non-literally (Bach and Harnish 1979: ch. 4). Since implicature is a kind of indirect speech act whereas irony and metaphor are species of non-literal but direct speech acts, the latter should not be classified as implicature. Unfortunately, this is done by both Grice and many of his critics.

So far I have suggested two ways to improve on Grice's taxonomic scheme: replace Grice's distinction between saying (in his favoured sense) and merely making as if to say with the distinction (in indicative cases) between explicitly stating and saying in Austin's locutionary sense; and do not classify non-literality (including sentence non-literality) as implicature. In this way we have a notion of what is said (correlative to the notion of saying) that applies uniformly to three situations: (a) where the speaker means what he says and something else as well (implicature and indirect speech acts generally); (b) where the speaker says one thing and means something else instead (non-literal utterances); and (c) where the speaker says something and does not mean anything. What is said, being closely tied to the (or a) meaning of the uttered sentence, provides the default interpretation of the utterance (at least up to indexicality, ambiguity and underdetermination), the least (as it were) a speaker could mean in using the sentence. And it provides the hearer with the linguistic basis for inferring what, if anything, the speaker means in addition or instead. Next we need to consider how expansion and completion fit into the picture.

IMPLICITURE

In the case of expansion the speaker is using all his words literally but is not using the sentence as a whole literally. Although he could make what he means fully explicit by inserting additional words or phrases into his utterance, he does not. Since part of what he means is implicit, in effect he intends his audience to read those words into his utterance. Of course, what he really intends the audience to do is to figure out the proposition that would be expressed with the embellished sentence, not to construct the sentence itself. The audience is making an inference over propositions, not sentences.[5] Anyway, the resulting proposition is not identical to the proposition being expressed explicitly, since part of it does not correspond to any elements of the uttered sentence. So it is inaccurate to call the resulting proposition the explicit content of the utterance or an explicature. I will instead call it an *impliciture*.[6] I will also apply this term to completions of utterances of semantically underdeterminate sentences.

Implicitures go beyond what is said, but unlike implicatures, which are additional propositions external to what is said, implicitures are built out of what is said. Even when there is no figurative use of words or phrases, as in metaphor, in impliciture, because of sentence non-literality or semantic underdetermination, what the sentence means does not fully determine, even after ambiguities are resolved and indexical references are fixed, what the speaker means. So far as I can tell, the only explanation for the fact that Grice's critics count implicitures as (fully) explicit contents of utterances, or identify them with what is said, is that they uncritically assume, along with Grice, that there is no middle ground between what is said and what is implicated. It is curious to note that Grice himself occasionally alluded to what I am calling impliciture, as when he remarked that it is often 'unnecessary to put in ... qualificatory words' (1978/1989: 44). Although he did describe such cases as implicatures, he appeared to have something distinctive in mind: 'strengthening one's meaning by achieving a superimposed implicature' (1978/1989: 48). By 'strengthening' he appears to have meant increasing the information content of what is said, not adding a whole separate proposition to what was said.[7]

What is involved in completion, which is required whenever the speaker uses a semantically underdeterminate sentence? In completion, what the meaning of the sentence determines is not even a minimal proposition but merely a propositional radical. This suggests that even if the speaker is using his words literally and directly, the hearer must engage in an extra inferential process in order to arrive at *any* proposition. Grice's critics, assuming that what is said must be a proposition, suppose that this extra inference is needed just to determine what is said.[8] They find this conclusion to be so obvious that they do not even consider the alternatives.

What are the alternatives? One could claim that *nothing* is said when a semantically underdeterminate sentence is used, because an impliciture is required to get to a proposition. Underlying such a claim is the idea that a fragment of a proposition, a propositional radical, cannot comprise the full content of what is said. The other alternative is to claim that even though an impliciture is required to get to a proposition, there is still something that qualifies as what is said, whose content is the propositional radical that forms the ground on which the impliciture is worked out.[9] We can reject the first view, according to which nothing is said with a semantically underdeterminate sentence, simply by showing that something *is* said in these cases, straightforwardly ascribable in the usual format of indirect quotation. For example, utterances (3) and (4) can be described as follows:

(3-IQ) S said that steel isn't strong enough.
(4-IQ) S said that Willie almost robbed a bank.

What happens in these cases is that the semantic underdetermination carries over to the *that*-clause in the indirect quotation. So I will opt for the second view. It could be objected that more specification is needed, but needed for what, for specifying what is said or specifying what is meant? I grant that some true utterances of *said-that* sentences do not completely describe what is said,[10] but I deny that ones like (3-IQ) and (4-IQ) must specify more.[11] Perhaps the disagreement here is ultimately terminological: one person's explicature is another one's impliciture.

Be that as it may, impliciture is, on my restrictive notion of what is said, a matter of either fleshing out or filling in what is said. Expansion is the fleshing out of the minimal proposition expressible by an utterance, and completion is the filling in of a propositional radical. I agree with Grice's critics that neither is a case of *implicature*, although both involve essentially the same sort of pragmatic process as in implicature proper, but I see no reason, as they do, to extend the notion of explicit content, of what is said. For me there is inexplicit meaning but no inexplicit saying.

CONVENTIONAL IMPLICATURE?

Grice also disallowed inexplicit saying, but he did recognize a category of explicit non-saying. For there can be elements in what is meant that correspond directly to elements in the sentence uttered but do not enter into what is said. These are *conventional implicatures*, propositions which are merely 'indicated'. Grice's examples of 'problematic elements' are connectives, notably *therefore* (1975/1989: 25 and 1968/1989: 120) and *but* (1969/1989: 88). The connective makes a certain contribution, given by its conventional meaning, to what the speaker means. It indicates a certain relation between the two items it connects, for example, that one is a consequence of the other or that there is a contrast between the two. What Grice denies is that this linguistically specified relation enters into what is said. The implicature that such a relation obtains is a conventional rather than conversational implicature because it is explained not pragmatically but by conventional meaning.

Grice's brief discussions of conventional implicature are intended to narrow down the sense of *say* that he favours because 'I expect it to be of great[est] theoretical utility' (1968/1989: 121). People often suppose (e.g. Carston 1988/1991: 39) that his theoretical motivation for the notion of conventional implicature is to provide for an element of literal content that is not truth conditional. Grice does give this impression when, for example, he denies that an utterance of the sentence

(5) He is an Englishman; he is, therefore, brave.

'would be, strictly speaking, false should the consequence in question fail to hold' (1975/1989: 25–6). In fact, however, the issue in such cases is not truth-conditionality but truth-functionality. All Grice really shows is that the import of connectives like *therefore* and *but* is in a certain way not truth functional. When an utterance of the form p CONJ q implies *p and q* but conveys more than the mere conjunction, there is no way to express its import as a truth function of p and q. After all, the only such truth function *is* conjunction. A truth-functional specification of the import of p CONJ q would require a third clause, an additional conjunct, e.g. to the effect that there is a relation of consequence or contrast between p and q. So, for example, a specification of what was said in the above example would, according to Grice, take the form

(5-GIQ) S said that a certain male is an Englishman, that he is brave, and that being brave is a consequence of being English.

Now if the third conjunct is part of what is said, what is said would contain one more clause than is contained in the sentence used to say it. This further conjunct would not correspond to a clause in that sentence and could not count as part of what is said. For the elements of what is said (in Grice's favoured sense) must correspond to elements in the sentence. The further conjunct, not being such an element, can count only as a conventional implicature.

The trouble with all this is that what is said in utterances of the form p CONJ q, even though they imply *p and q*, does not have to be specified by *p and q*, with or without a third clause. In the above case, for example, there is no reason why the word *therefore* cannot go directly into a two-clause specification of what is said:

(5-IQ) S said that a certain male is an Englishman [and] therefore he is brave.

What is said is true just in case the relevant male is an Englishman and is brave, and being brave is a consequence of being English, but of course what is said is not identical, though it is equivalent, to the explication of its truth condition. To appreciate this, consider an entirely different sort of case. Suppose Tom utters *I regret going home*, thereby saying that he regrets going home. Assume that regretting can be so analysed that what Tom says is true just in case Tom went home, believes he did, and wishes he had not. Did he *say* that? I think not, and I think Grice would think not. A multi-clause analysis of what is said is not identical to what is said (see note 6). It is implied, i.e. entailed but not implicated,[12] by what is said.[13] Of course it is not (conventionally) implicated, since it is not conveyed by the act of saying.

I believe that in Grice's alleged examples of conventional implicature, which all involve non-truth-functional connectives, the specification of what is said can and should include the relevant connective. Grice is led to conventional implicature in each case only because he arbitrarily insists on forcing these specifications into the mould of truth-functional conjunction, whereupon the specification must either include one clause too many or omit the conventional force of the connective.[14] But perhaps the problem is Grice's limited choice of example. Just consider his general diagnosis of what gives rise to conventional implicatures: 'The elements in the conventional meaning of an utterance which are not part of what has been said ... are linked with certain [non-central] speech acts' (1968/1989: 122). Here he gives the example of *moreover*, which is linked with the speech act of adding, an act that requires the performance of a central speech act, like reporting or predicting. Grice does not indicate which non-central speech acts the words *but* and *therefore* are linked to; presumably these are acts of making a contrast and drawing a conclusion (or giving an explanation). However, *moreover* is relevantly different from the two other connectives: unlike *moreover*, *but* and *therefore* signify relationships between the propositions expressed by the clauses they connect. The same is true of various other conjunctions and adverbials not mentioned by Grice, such as *after all, although, anyway, because, despite, even so, for, however, nevertheless, since, so, still, thus* and *yet*. Take the case of *because*, which is linked to the rather central speech act of explaining. In an utterance of:

(6) Because the verdict was unjust, a riot broke out.

What is said is specified by:

(6-IQ) He said that because the verdict was unjust, a riot broke out.

Because is used to express an explanatory relation of some sort between the facts described by the two clauses. But there is another use of *because* that does fit Grice's paradigm. Compare (6) with:

(7) Because you'll find out anyway, your wife is having an affair.

In (7) *because* is not being used to express an explanatory relation between the facts described by the two clauses. Rather, the speaker is using the *because*-clause to explain his speech act of informing the hearer of the fact expressed by the second clause. Accordingly, the hearer cannot plausibly specify what is being said as a conjunction, as in:

(7-IQ) S is saying that because I'll find out anyway, my wife is having an affair.

Grice's diagnosis is correct: specifications of non-central speech acts do not fit comfortably into specifications of what is said. This holds for the following assortment of locutions, at least when used (as they generally are) to perform non-central speech acts:

accordingly, after all, all in all, all things considered, although, anyway, as it were, at any rate, besides, be that as it may, by the way, considering that ..., disregarding ..., even so, finally, first of all, frankly, if I may say so, if you want my opinion, in contrast, in conclusion, in short, in view of the fact that ..., leaving aside ..., loosely speaking, never mind that ..., nevertheless, not to interrupt but, not to mention that, now that you mention it, on the other hand, so to speak, speaking for myself, strictly speaking, taking into account that ..., to be blunt about it, to begin with, to change the subject, to digress, to get back to the subject, to get to the point, to oversimplify, to put it mildly

There is a straightforward explanation of why these locutions do not fit comfortably into specifications of what is said: they are in construction syntactically but not semantically with the clauses they introduce. Syntactically they are sentence adverbials but they function as *illocutionary adverbials* (Bach and Harnish 1979: 219–28), modifying not the main clause but its utterance. The result is as it were a split-level utterance.

I do not believe that we need to resort to the notion of conventional implicature to describe the conventional import of the above locutions, these illocutionary adverbials. Rather, as Grice himself points out, they are used to perform non-central speech acts, such as simplifying, qualifying and concluding. One is not conventionally implying anything in using such a locution; rather, one is providing some sort of gloss or running commentary on one's utterance, for example, concerning its conversational role. So it seems that we can do without the notion of conventional implicature altogether: in Grice's examples of connectives with truth-conditional import, the conventional meaning of the 'problematic element' does enter into what is said; and in the wide assortment of locutions used to perform non-central speech acts, the problematic element does not enter into what is said, but it does not generate a conventional implicature either.

WHAT IS SAID AND NO MORE

Ideally, the notion of saying that is of the greatest theoretical utility should also be intuitively natural. Grice's favoured sense of *say* is too strong in that regard, for it blurs the intuitive distinction between saying something and meaning it. As I explained earlier, a weaker notion accommodates the apparent fact that something is said in the cases of non-literal utterances, non-communicative speech acts, and various sorts of verbal slips. Accordingly, there is much to gain theoretically by enforcing Austin's distinction between locutionary and illocutionary acts, and by reserving the word *say* for locutionary acts instead of using it as a generic illocutionary term. Still, I agree with Grice that on the most useful notion of saying, what is said should be closely related to the conventional meaning of the uttered sentence.[15] In particular, what is said should be determined by the meanings of the elements of the sentence and their syntactic structure – as adjusted for any needed disambiguation or indexical reference fixing, as well as for any elements being used to make running commentary on the utterance. Earlier I argued that the notion of what is said needs no further adjustments in order to handle sentence non-literality or semantic underdetermination. What is needed, rather, is a notion of impliciture to mark the middle ground between what is said (explicit content) and what is implicated. Now I wish to explain and defend this minimalist position.

It should be evident by now that I have been relying on a simple, intuitive test: what is said is specifiable by a *that*-clause embedded in a matrix clause of the form *S said that* ...[16] It would be appropriate to adopt the concurrent perspective of the hearer and take as the canonical form *S is saying* [*to me*] *that*.... Then if, for example, the speaker says,

(8) I like your etchings.

from the hearer's point of view what is being said may be put into the 'HIQ' (hearer's indirect quotation) format, as for example in

(8-HIQ) She is saying that she likes my etchings.

The HIQ format provides the ground on which the hearer, by exploiting mutual contextual information, constructs what the speaker means. In many cases the hearer may have to do some conceptual filling in or fleshing out of what is said before he can even work toward a figurative or oblique interpretation of the utterance. Filling in will be needed if the sentence is semantically underdeterminate, and fleshing out will be needed if the speaker cannot plausibly be supposed to mean just what the sentence means. In fact, both processes can occur within a single utterance, such as *Everybody* [*in my class*] *is coming* [*to my party*].

Let us start with the case of fleshing out, the expansion or qualification of the literally expressed proposition. Notice first that the literally expressed proposition, what Récanati calls the 'minimal proposition expressible by an utterance' (1989/1991: 102), is not necessarily minimal in a logical or informational sense. It is minimal only in the sense that it is the proposition most closely related to the meaning of the sentence. In Récanati's examples,

(9) I have had breakfast.
(10) Everybody went to Paris.

the minimal proposition is either trivially true or wildly false. What a speaker would mean is yielded by 'strengthening' this proposition, for example:

(9-R) I have had breakfast *today*.
(10-R) Everybody *in our group* went to Paris.

In the case of (9), what is meant is a 'richer proposition ... that entails the [minimal] proposition', but this cannot be true of (10) since there the entailment goes the other way. In general, when the minimal proposition is trivially (or otherwise obviously) true, what is meant is logically (or informationally) stronger, whereas when the so-called minimal proposition is wildly (or otherwise obviously) false, what is meant is logically weaker. It seems that what we need here, as illustrated by the above examples, is a notion not of logical strengthening but what might be called *lexical strengthening*: the result of inserting additional words into the sentence.[17]

Lexical strengthening may involve logical strengthening or logical weakening – or neither. In some cases, it does not affect truth conditions at all but simply rules out the implicature of anything logically stronger or weaker, as in:

(11) I have eaten chocolate [*before*].
(12) I haven't [*ever*] had hives.

In a different kind of case, the lexical strengthening involved in the implementation of so-called scalar implicatures, such as:

(13) I don't like you. (i.e. I love you)
(14) I don't believe it. (i.e. I know it)
(15) I don't have three cars. (i.e. I have four)

the implicature is achieved by the *negation* of something weaker. In these cases there is no entailment relation either way. In fact, what is implicated contradicts what is said. It seems that the implicature is mediated by an impliciture involving the insertion of the word *merely*.

Récanati claims on intuitive grounds that what is said when only a 'minimal' proposition is literally expressed is the 'richer' proposition, such as the ones expressed by (9-R) and (10-R) above. People's intuitions seem to favour reporting the richer propositions as what is said, as in:

(9-RIQ) S is saying that he has had breakfast *today*.
(10-RIQ) S is saying that everybody *in his group* went to Paris.

even though material is included that does not correspond to anything in the utterance being reported. But these are untutored intuitions. For one thing, they are insensitive to the distinction between saying and stating (and to the distinction between sentence meaning and speaker meaning), especially in cases of standardization, where the inference from one to the other is short-circuited. People made cognizant of this distinction find that their intuitions change in the direction of Grice's requirement that anything that does not correspond to some element or feature of the uttered sentence is not part of what is said. Then they are in a position to appreciate the difference between what is said, for example, with (9), *I have had breakfast*, and with (9-R), *I have had breakfast today*. They can then understand the point of the question *Do you mean today?* and the non-redundancy of actually using the word *today*, as in (9-R).

Récanati also suggests that intuition resists reporting the minimal proposition as what is said in (9) and (10), purportedly given as follows:

(9-MIQ) S is saying that he has had breakfast *before.*
(10-MIQ) S is saying that everybody *in the world* went to Paris.

Here Récanati is right about the intuitions but wrong to suppose that (9-MIQ) and (10-MIQ) give minimalist reports of what is said in (9) and (10). Rather, they give lexical strengthenings of what is said, albeit ones that are logically equivalent. Besides, in some cases structurally similar to (9) and (10), intuitions favour the minimal propositions as what is said, for example in:

(16) I have had measles.
(17) Everybody is going to die.

So Récanati's account appears to imply that relevant differences in what is said, as between (9) and (16) or between (10) and (17), can depend solely on non-linguistic factors. Also, it is not at all clear how he would account for the possibility, however remote, that in cases like (9) or (10) what the speaker means *is* the minimal proposition, just that and no more. If what is said in that case were not the minimal proposition, what is meant would be *less* than what is said.

Finally, intuitions do not seem to favour Récanati's inflationary conception of what is said in cases where the literally expressed proposition is not all that minimal. In the following cases (adapted from Harnish 1976a):

(18) Jackson squirted the paint on the canvas [*intentionally*].
(19) George squirted the grapefruit juice on the table [*unintentionally*].
(20) Jack and Jill are married [*to each other*].
(21) Mr Jones and Mrs Smith are married [*but not to each other*].
(22) Mr Jones and Mrs Smith are in love [*with each other*].

even though the unuttered (bracketed) material is understood, people are disinclined to include it in the specification of what is said. They appreciate the fact that although what is not uttered is inferable, it is not *there*. All in all, I doubt that there is as much intuitive support for Récanati's inflationary conception of what is said as he imagines. I suspect that what inclines him toward this conception is his assumption that 'genuine cases of non-literality' must be like metaphor (1989/1991: 108), i.e. be figurative, in which case he is arbitrarily excluding sentence non-literality. Be that as it may, I am not disputing the idea that underlies his contention that 'there are pragmatic aspects to what is said' as well as to what is implicated (1989/1991: 116), but in my view these aspects are properly regarded as pertaining to what is implicit in what is said. It is worth noting, by the way, that pragmatic processes are involved even in cases where one means *exactly* what one says. From the hearer's point of view, *not* to read anything into an utterance and to take the (literal) meaning as determining all the speaker means is a matter of contextual interpretation just like (except for being simpler) expanding the utterance.

Now let us take up the question of what is said in the case of semantically underdeterminate sentences. Even though such sentences can express only propositional radicals, their utterance can still be ascribed in the HIQ format without the insertion of additional lexical material (what is left unspecified is given in parentheses):

(23-HIQ) S is saying that she is too tired. (for what?)
(24-HIQ) S is saying that Anacin is better. (than what?)
(25-HIQ) S is saying that she is leaving. (from where?)
(26-HIQ) S is saying that she wants a taxi. (to do what with?)

Suitable *that*-clauses are readily available in these cases simply because they, like the sentences whose utterance they are used to report, do not need to express complete, determinate propositions. In these cases, the lexical insertions and other interpretative manoeuvres needed to deliver a complete proposition do not correspond to anything in the meaning of the constituents of the sentence or in its syntactic structure.

For this reason it would be a mistake to assimilate uses of semantically underdeterminate sentences to the category of elliptical utterances.[18] Utterances are elliptical, strictly speaking, only if the suppressed material is recoverable, at least up to ambiguity, by grammatical means alone, as in tag-questions and such reduced forms as conjunction reduction, verb-phrase ellipsis, and gapping:

(27) Bill is happiest when working.
(28) Bill likes working and so does Bob.
(29) Bill wants pie for dessert and Bob pudding.

Notice that (27) unequivocally entails that Bob is happiest when Bob is working, (28) that Bob likes Bob working, not Bill working, and (29) that Bob wants pudding for dessert. No contextually salient substitutes are allowed. A sentence like (30) can be taken in more than one way:

(30) I know a richer man than Ross Perot. (is or knows?)

but that is because it is syntactically ambiguous – it is not semantically underdeterminate. In all of these cases paraphrases can be given in the HIQ format that spell out the suppressed material:

(27-HIQ) Bill is happiest when *Bill* is working.
(28-HIQ) Bill likes working and *Bob likes* working.
(29-HIQ) Bill wants pie for dessert and Bob *wants* pudding *for dessert.*

and, if necessary, disambiguate, in the case of (30):

(30-HIQ) S is saying that he knows a richer man than Ross Perot
knows.

Since the recovered material corresponds to something in the sentence, though not necessarily to something that is phonologically realized, there is no reason to deny that the paraphrase specifies what is said.[19] This is not the case with reports that include the completion of an utterance of a semantically underdeterminate sentence, for in that case the inserted material is not only unheard, it is not even there syntactically. Linguistically speaking, it is not there to be recovered. For this reason, there is no linguistic basis for including such material in what is said. There is also no need to, since what is said, even if not fully propositional, can go straight into the standard HIQ format, since *that*-clauses can themselves be semantically underdeterminate.

Now it might be objected that if what is said can be a propositional radical, then why should indexical reference be thought to enter into what is said? After all, indexical references, like completions, are determined pragmatically, not semantically.[20] Suppose one utters 'She returned last week' and means that Leona returned to jail some time in the week before the utterance. Then, so the objection goes, in consistency the propositional radical that should count as what was said is not that Leona returned some time in the week before the utterance but that a certain female returned a week before a certain utterance. The use of *certain* turns an indefinite description into a 'definite indefinite' description, indicating that a reference is in the offing. I do not deny that there is a sense in which what is said *is* that a certain female returned a week before a certain utterance, but this is weaker than the sense in question.[21] The objection is that either nothing pragmatic enters into what is said or, in the stronger sense that allows indexical reference to enter in, the filling-in of syntactically unspecified but conceptually mandated semantic slots should enter in as well.

Intuitively, the basis for this objection is that indexicals do not *specify* their referents but merely are used to *indicate* their references. So, for example, in uttering 'She returned last week', one does not really say who returned when. That is true but irrelevant, since *specify* is not the operative sense of *say*. This objection assumes that there is no relevant difference between indexical reference and filling in slots. But there is a relevant difference. Indexical reference fixes the interpretation of an element that occurs in the utterance, be it a pronoun, a demonstrative phrase, a temporal or locational adverb, a tense marker, or just an empty, phonologically null category like PRO. On the other hand, conceptually mandated 'semantic' slots do not occur in semantically underdeterminate sentences at all, not even as empty syntactic categories. Not being sentence constituents, they enter in not at the linguistic level but at the conceptual level. An indexical is there in the sentence.

Moreover, the semantics of indexicals makes essential reference to their utterance (hence Reichenbach's description of them as *token reflexives*). An indexical introduces a variable into the semantic representation of the sentence, and each one has its own semantically specified *referential constraint* on how, in a given context of utterance, it can be used to refer, i.e., on how the variable it introduces acquires a value in a given context of utterance (Bach 1987: 186–92). So, for example, *I* is used to refer to the speaker, *yesterday* to the day before the utterance, *she* to a contextually identifiable female, and *then* to a contextually identifiable time. Note that in most cases, such as the latter two, because of the essential role of the speaker's intention in determining reference, reference is not a well-defined function of context. It is context-relative but not strictly context-dependent (Bach 1987: 186–92).

Still, it might be suggested, just as indexicals introduce variables needing values, so the gaps in propositional radicals introduce slots needing fillers. The trouble with this suggestion is not that it commits the category mistake of treating slots as variables – it could be argued that these slots are conceptual rather than objectual variables – but that it confuses the interpretations assigned to complete syntactic representations with the propositional radicals containing slots generated by conceptual needs. One indication of the difference is the fact that certain transitive verbs can be used optionally without direct objects, whereas others similar in meaning must take objects. Compare *finish* with *complete* or *eat* with *devour*, for example. Despite their semantic similarity, they have distinct syntactic requirements.[22] There is simply no sense in which the slots in propositional radicals have counterparts (syntactic gaps) in the semantically underdeterminate sentences that yield them. For incomplete logical forms can be generated by complete syntactic forms.

All in all, it appears that Grice's linguistic constraint on what is said does not have to be relaxed on account of either sentence non-literality or semantic underdetermination. The standard HIQ format works perfectly well without regard to expansion or completion. The impliciture goes beyond what is said, whether it involves expanding or completing the intended content.

SUMMING UP

We have seen that Grice's distinction between what is said and what is conversationally implicated needs to be modified in various ways. The need for an in-between notion of impliciture is demonstrated by the extensive variety of utterances that require either completing or expanding. For semantic reasons, utterances of semantically underdeterminate sentences require completing; and, for pragmatic reasons, sentence-non-literal utterances, typically of sentences that express propositions that are too obviously true or too obviously false, require expanding. Both cases show the need for a middle ground between the notions of what is said and what is implicated, namely, that which is implicit in what is said. Also, Grice's distinction is not adequate to the case of utterances which contain elements that are not used literally. These should not be assimilated to implicatures, although, like implicitures, they are achieved by means of the same pragmatic processes. As for Grice's notion of saying, it neglects Austin's indispensable distinction between locutionary and illocutionary acts. The notion should be weakened so as not to entail that what is said be part of what is meant. Then, when characterizing non-literal utterances, we can do without Grice's confusing phrase 'making as if to say'. Although not Grice's favoured notion, our weaker, locutionary notion of saying does accord with Grice's sketchily formulated view that what is said should closely correspond to the meaning and form of the uttered sentence. It thereby rules out recent extensions of the notion of what is said or of what is explicit in an utterance. Moreover, it is capable of absorbing some of the cases that Grice classified as conventional implicatures, the rest of which are better construed as collateral speech acts rather than implicatures.[23]

Enough said.

APPENDIX: FURTHER EXAMPLES

There is a greater variety of examples of both semantic underdetermination and of sentence non-literality than was taken up in the text. What follows is an annotated, provisionally categorized list of examples with brief annotations in parentheses. The list could be extended considerably.

Semantic underdetermination

There are various ways in which semantic underdetermination can arise. In the following examples the source or the locus of underdetermination is, where possible, set in small caps. Some of the examples are controversial, being customarily viewed as cases of ambiguity rather than underdetermination, and are offered provisionally.

Referential underdetermination

  indexical, demonstrative

    SHE will be here soon. (which female?)

    THIS guy is dangerous. (what demonstrated guy?)

    THAT is absurd. (what assertion?)

    John went to the store. (when?)

    Bill is STILL complaining. (since when?)

  anaphoric

    Bob told Bill to polish HIS shoes. (Bob's/Bill's)

    Jack and Jill rubbed/massaged THEIR feet. (each other's/respective)

    May I take you HOME? (your place or mine?)

  descriptive anaphors ('sloppy identity')

    The lizard lost his tail, but IT didn't care/grew back. (the lizard/its tail)

    Hillary loves her husband, and SO does Tipper. (loves Tipper's/Hillary's husband).

categorial
> type/token: There are two BEARS in Idaho/the yard.
> act/object: Bill made/accepted the STATEMENT.
> fact/proposition (that-clauses): Bill regretted/imagined THAT he
> went.

Lexical underdetermination (not ambiguity)

LIFT, AGAINST, STRUCTURE, BEFORE, ROUGH, STUFF
PINK Cadillac/dress/paint/grapefruit

Phrasal underdetermination (not syntactic ambiguity)

FAST car/track, HAPPY boy/face/days, HEALTHY body/diet
The cat/the ant crawled UNDER the table. (to get under/while under)
Burt kissed Dolly ON her left cheek/front porch. (where
directed/where done)
TONY'S TEAM is leading the league. (the team Tony owns/plays
for/roots for)
George ALMOST killed the goose. (he refrained/he missed/it survived)

Scope underdetermination

The NUMBER of planets may be EVEN.
A FEW arsonists destroyed MANY buildings. (each/together).
I do NOT BELIEVE that. (disbelieve/have no opinion)

Argumental underdetermination

Mary FINISHED (*COMPLETED)/ARRIVED (*REACHED)/ATE
(*DEVOURED). (what?)
The cow jumped OVER/THROUGH/*TO/*TOWARD. (what?)
VISITOR, VIEWER, USER (of what?) (Cp. He VISITED/*VIEWED/*USED.)
Gentlemen PREFER blondes (to what?)
Marilyn is TOO tall/not short ENOUGH. (for what?)
Mutual knowledge is not RELEVANT. (to what?)
John is READY/LATE/EAGER. (to or for what?)
A mop is NEEDED to dry the floor. (for what?)
(implicit argument: A broom is needed [by x for PRO$_x$] to dry the
floor.)
Gyro believes THAT the inventor of the yo-yo is rich. (Donald
Duncan/whoever invented it)
(in belief ascriptions modes of presentation need not be specified)

Parametric underdetermination

> That lamp is SHORT/CHEAP/OLD. (relative to what?)
> That employee is GOOD/TALENTED/VALUABLE. (in what respect?)
> EVEN cowgirls sing the blues. (in addition to who?)
> Gregor was MERELY a bookkeeper. (as opposed to what?)
> John WANTS a car/a taxi/a sandwich/a woman/a massage/a bath. (to do what with?)
> Jack is IN FRONT OF Jill. (facing/ahead of/nearer than)

> *counterfactuals*
> (unspecified what is assumed fixed, i.e. most similar possible worlds)
> IF Lincoln hadn't gone to the theatre, he wouldn't have been assassinated.

> *explanations*
> (when relevant contrast is unspecified)
> Ross demoted George (rather than Dan) BECAUSE he was responsible.
> Ross demoted George (rather than fire him) BECAUSE he was still needed.

Sentence non-literality

There are various sorts of sentences which, though they express complete propositions, are commonly used to express more specific or elaborate propositions. The difference between the two propositions is not attributable to any particular constituent of the sentence. Except for the last two categories (they seem to require different treatment), what is meant could be made explicit by inserting additional material, as indicated by italics in brackets.

Implicit quantifier domains

> Everyone [*in the class*] is going.
> She had nothing [*appropriate*] to wear.
> The cupboard [*in this house*] is bare.
> Only Bill [*among those in the class*] knows the answer.
> I have always [*since early childhood*] liked spinach.

Implicit qualifications

> All birds can fly [*except ostriches, emus and penguins*].
> I will be there [*at the appointed time*].
> George went to the store [*intentionally*].
> Jack washed the car [*alone*].
> Jack and Jill went up the hill [*together*].

Jack and Jill are married [*to each other*].
... or [*else*] ..., ... and [*then*] ..., ... if [*and only if*] ...

Approximation

There are [*more or less*] 30 students per class.
France is hexagonal [*roughly speaking*].
Berkeley is [*about*] 10 miles from San Francisco.

Precisification

He has [*exactly*] three cars.
He weighs [*exactly*] 198 pounds. (Cp. He weighs 200 pounds.)

Scalar 'implicatures'

It doesn't [*only*] look expensive – it is.
He didn't [*just*] try to climb Half Dome – he did it.
The chef doesn't create [*mere*] meals but works of art.

Metalinguistic negation (Horn 1989: ch. 6)

I didn't trap two mongeese – I trapped two mongooses.
He's not an animal doctor – he's a veterinarian.
I'm not his brother – he's my brother.

Scope shifts (Bach and Harnish 1979: 232)

I only read newspapers. (read newspapers only)
Bill also likes magazines. (likes magazines also)

NOTES

1 The word 'literal' appears in parentheses because 'literal meaning of a sentence' is redundant (cp. 'literal meaning of an utterance'). Accordingly, when I use the phrase 'sentence non-literality' I do not mean that the sentence itself has a non-literal meaning but that the use of the sentence as a whole (in contrast to the use of any of its constituents) is non-literal.

2 When there is a specific form of words, as in many of the examples used later, that signals a sentence-non-literal use, we have what may be called *standardized non-literality* (Bach and Harnish 1979: 224–32; and Bach 1987: 77–85). Like the more commonly recognized phenomenon of *standardized indirection* (Bach and Harnish 1979: 192–219), or what Grice called *generalized conversational implicature* (1975/1989: 37–9), the hearer's inference to what the speaker means is short-circuited, compressed by precedent (though capable of being worked out if necessary), so that the literal content of the utterance may be bypassed. There are quite a few philosophically interesting cases of both

standardized non-literality and standardized indirection. In general, these notions facilitate the process of demarcating (linguistic) meaning from use. Such a demarcation provides an effective antidote to the dread disease *semanticiasis*: multiplying meanings not just beyond necessity but beyond plausibility. Appealing to standardized non-literality helps to defend Russell's theory of descriptions against the 'incomplete description' objection (Bach 1987: 103–8); appealing to standardized indirection helps to show that performatives are ordinary indicative sentences (Bach 1975; Bach and Harnish 1979: 203–9; and Bach and Harnish 1992) and that looking F/being possible/believing that p does not preclude being F/being actual/knowing that p (Grice 1961/1989: 237).

3   Récanati's 'availability' principle, that in what we count as what is said 'we should always try to preserve our pre-theoretic intuitions' (1989/1991: 106) does not, in my view, recognize that our intuitions are insensitive to the distinction between the (locutionary) level of what is said and the illocutionary level of what is stated. The same point applies to his rejection (1993: ch. 13) of what Carston calls the 'linguistic (or grammatical) direction' principle (1988/1991: 38–9), which respects Grice's close correspondence constraint on what is said.

4   Bach and Harnish (1979: 165–72) argue that Grice's distinction, when generalized, is tantamount to the distinction between direct and indirect illocutionary acts. Our later discussion of impliciture, like Grice's implicature, will be limited to indicative cases. Taking up non-indicative cases would introduce some minor complications having to do with how to specify what is said and what is meant. See n. 16.

5   Perhaps I should say *structured* propositions, as read off from semantic representations. At any rate, what I have in mind are more finely individuated than truth conditions.

6   This word is, of course, a cognate not of *implicate* but of *implicit*, whereas the word *explicature* is a cognate not of *explicit* but of *explicate*. Unfortunately, *implicit* has no cognate verb *implicite*.

7   Why does Récanati maintain that this strengthening *is* what is said? Largely on intuitive grounds: the proposition most closely related to the conventional meaning of the sentence, in the cases he considers, is so patently false – or so obviously true – that it could not be what is said. Récanati doubts that anyone, at least anyone other than me, would be willing to acknowledge this 'minimal' proposition as what is said. To which I reply: of course, if your intuitions are insensitive to the distinction between what is said and what is stated or if, like Grice, you intuitively think that saying something requires meaning it, then naturally you will not regard the minimal proposition as the content of what is said. On the other hand, you will thereby be willing to include in what is said elements that do not correspond to elements in the uttered sentence.

8   It is interesting to note that Grice himself, throughout his discussion of saying (1975/1989: 118–22, 1969: 87–8), never commits himself to the position that what is said must be a complete proposition or have a determinate truth condition. Although he schematizes what is said with the notation '*p', where the asterisk is the 'dummy mood indicator' used to take non-indicative utterances into account, nowhere does he stipulate that substitution instances of '*p*' must be propositions. But perhaps that was implicated.

9   Notice that there is an apparent problem for either view, at least on the assumption that *any* (grammatical) sentence can be used literally. For it seems that on either view the use of a semantically underdeterminate sentence cannot, strictly speaking, count as a literal utterance: the speaker cannot mean just what he says. This is vacuously true on the first view, since according to it nothing is said. And on the second view the speaker must mean more than what he says,

since what he means must be a proposition, which a semantically underdeterminate sentence does not express (even with indexical references fixed etc.).
This circumstance suggests that the intuitive definition of literality as meaning
what one says and no more, ignores the case of semantically underdeterminate
sentences. In order to avoid the paradoxical consequence that such sentences
cannot be used literally, it must be modified to allow for meaning not just what
one says but meaning a completion thereof. One does not mean two things in
such a case; rather, a specification of what is meant in terms of what is said does
not completely specify what is meant. See n. 11.

10   For example, if S uttered 'Steel isn't strong enough not to be bent by
      Superman', an utterance of 'S said that something isn't strong enough not to be
      bent by Superman' would incompletely report what S said.
11   Andrew Woodfield points out to me that the mere fact that there are true indi-
      rect quotations like (3-IQ) and (4-IQ) does not show that what is said need not
      be a complete proposition. As he observes, a report of what *S meant* in a case
      like (3) could be made, on analogy with (3-IQ), using

      (3-MIQ)*S* meant that steel isn't strong enough.

(3-MIQ) could be true without completely specifying what S meant – S must
have meant something for which steel is not strong enough. So Woodfield
wonders why, by parity of reasoning, the fact that there are true reports like
(3-MIQ) does not show that what is meant need not be a complete proposition.
However, I was not arguing that the availability of true reports like (3-IQ)
shows that what is said need not be a complete proposition. That is a consequence of the requirement that what is said must closely correspond (in Grice's
sense) with the words used. Rather, I was arguing against the view that *nothing*
is said with a semantically underdeterminate sentence.

12   No philosophical analysis, such as Russell's theory of descriptions, is refuted by
      the fact that the analysans cannot be substituted for the analysandum in specifi-
      cations of what is said.
13   I do not mean to suggest here that what a speaker implicates is never implied by
      what is said.
14   Larry Horn has reminded me of various sorts of expressions not taken up by
      Grice whose use has been thought to yield conventional implicatures: particles
      like *even* and *too*, implicative verbs like *manage* and *fail*, factive verbs like
      forget and *realize*, and clefts (*It was ... who ...*) and pseudoclefts (*What X did
      was ...*). I think that *even* and *too* enter into truth conditions in ways analogous
      to *but* – some sort of contrast is part of the truth-conditional content, and the
      intended contrast is unspecified, as in a case like *Even Bill likes Mary*.
      Karttunen and Peters argue that the embedding *I just noticed that even Bill likes
      Mary* 'does not mean that he has just noticed that other people like Mary or just
      noticed that Bill is the least likely person to do so' (1979: 13). But all this shows
      is that the relation of noticing is not distributive, as illustrated by *I noticed that
      Bill has three cars* (I may have already known that he has two). Horn points out
      that an implicative verb like *manage to* seems to add some sort of adverbial
      content while functioning syntactically like a main verb, but it is not clear to me
      why this should suggest that conventional implicature is involved. The adverbial
      content of such verbs can just enter straightforwardly into the whole truth-
      conditional content of the sentences in which they occur. For example, in *Bill
      managed to finish his homework*, the truth-conditional content includes both
      the finishing and the entailed difficulty. With factive verbs, as in *Bill forgot that
      he had an appointment*, that he had an appointment is part of the
      truth-conditional content of what is said – it is just not part of the content
      of the illocutionary act of assertion. An analogous point applies to cleft and

pseudo-cleft constructions, although their form, like contrastive stress, marks a special, 'illocutional' topic–comment relation (Atlas 1989: 81–91). For a detailed, critical examination of conventional implicature and the related notion of semantic presupposition, see Harnish 1976a.

15 Récanati mentions a 'quotational' notion of saying, which is 'one factor among many that tend to make our intuitions fuzzy and conflicting' (1989/1991: 108), but of course this is not Grice's favoured sense of saying.

16 Although we are focusing on indicative cases, the editor has rightly reminded me that the *said-that* format does not work in certain other cases, such as exclamations, interrogatives and some imperatives (there is in such cases a similar problem of how to specify what is meant). The issue of format for indirect quotation of interrogatives and imperatives is addressed briefly in Bach and Harnish 1979: 25. In any event, the problem with the *said-that* format in certain cases does not in itself show that the locutionary level of analysis does not apply. Indeed, we have seen that the locutionary level is needed to accommodate such phenomena as non-literality and mis-speaking. As for exclamations, like *Hello!*, *Wow!*, and *Egad!*, there does not seem to be any locutionary level, but since such utterances do not seem capable of generating implicitures, we have no reason to worry about them here.

17 To deal with such examples, Récanati has developed the somewhat different notion of 'local strengthening' (1993: ch. 14). I will not take up this notion here, but I believe that it leads to certain difficulties that lexical strengthening avoids.

18 For the same reason it would be a mistake to regard John Perry's (1986) 'unarticulated constituents' as unarticulated constituents of what is said, as in his pet example *It is raining*. Unfortunately, Perry does not distinguish the (locutionary) level of what is said from the illocutionary level of what is stated.

19 I have not discussed the special case of utterances consisting of phrases rather than whole sentences, as in answers to questions. A direct answer to a *wh*-question is a phrase that would fit syntactically in the original site of the *wh*-word in the question. The practice of using just a phrase is so deeply entrenched that the only good reason for using a whole sentence is to make sure that one has understood the question correctly.

20 It could even be objected that since disambiguation is a pragmatic process, what is said should include the propositions (or propositional radicals, as the case may be) determined by *each* of the readings of the sentence. It could be argued that it is only at the level of speaker meaning, i.e. attempting to communicate, that disambiguation enters in. However, this objection ignores the fact that saying something is possible without attempting to communicate anything at all. Saying something (performing a locutionary act) involves more than comprehendingly uttering a meaningful sentence, namely, presenting the hearer with a proposition or propositional radical (more precisely, a 'modified' one expressed in the form '*p') for his consideration, typically though not necessarily as the material on which to work out one's communicative intention. Since the speaker can intend one meaning of the sentence to be in play even if he has no communicative intention, it seems reasonable to restrict what is said to *operative meaning* (Bach and Harnish 1979: 20–3) or what Grice called *applied timeless meaning* (1968/1989: 119).

21 In Bach 1987: 179–82, I opted for this weaker sense, thereby biting the bullet as far as the present objection is concerned.

22 It might be suggested that *finish* and *eat* either lose and then regain their complements during the course of syntactic derivation or that their complements exist all along but only as empty categories. Unfortunately, the first option entails a violation of the Projection Principle, and the second ignores the

requirement that empty categories be syntactically licensed (Chomsky 1986: 93–101).

23 A version of this paper was presented on 31 May 1992 at the Paris Workshop on indexicality and semantic indeterminacy. For comments and suggestions provided there I am indebted to Stephen Neale, John Perry, John Searle and especially François Récanati. I am grateful to Andrew Woodfield for helping me clarify my views on (non-)literality.

13 Relevance theory and speech acts

Graham H. Bird

In the period since Austin, Grice and Searle[1] made their primary contributions to speech act theory two strongly opposed views of that theory have been canvassed. One, following from work initially presented in Searle and Vanderveken's *Foundations of Illocutionary Logic* (1985) and developed in Vanderveken's *Meaning and Speech Acts* (1990–1), has sought to construct a formal theory of such acts which could be accommodated within a system such as Montague Grammar. The other, due initially to Sperber and Wilson's *Relevance* (1986), has argued that there is no room, or need, for a theory of speech acts. On the face of it these two views are strongly opposed, although, as I shall seek to show, that appearance is in part illusory.

Vanderveken's work locates speech act theory quite differently from Wilson and Sperber's Relevance theory. It treats such a theory as an adjunct to a truth-conditional theory of formal semantics, of whatever type, and encourages a view of linguistic theory which has been endorsed by many theorists. That view, with appropriate provisos for phonology and syntax, regards a comprehensive theory of language as consisting of a truth-conditional semantics coupled with a pragmatic theory at least including speech acts. It would certainly be a mistake to suppose that speech act theory *exhausts* all the pragmatic factors which might need to be built into that latter theory. But Austin's picture of a semantic theory (of 'sense' and 'reference') supplemented with a theory of illocutionary force was influential in producing such a dual account of language (see Dummett 1973: ch. 10; McDowell 1977). Vanderveken's work captures that Austinian insight in a formal way, by means of his contrast between a semantics of truth conditions and a semantics of success.

It may seem surprising, therefore, that Sperber and Wilson dismiss speech act theory. They question an assumption expressed by Levinson to the effect that

> Speech acts remain, along with presupposition and implicature, one of the central phenomena that any general pragmatic theory must account for.

> (Levinson 1983: 226)

Sperber and Wilson summarize their own conclusion from such questioning by saying:

> The vast range of data that speech act theorists have been concerned with is of no special interest to pragmatics.
>
> (Sperber and Wilson 1986: 243)

Such a claim might be compatible with Levinson's view so long as Sperber and Wilson allow some place for speech act theory in linguistics (or pragmatics),[2] even though they believe that it has no 'special' role there. But we shall see that their position is in any case unclear in a number of ways, some of which can be outlined in the following theses.

(1a) Speech act theory has no place in linguistics.
(1b) Speech act theory has a restricted role to play in linguistics.

(2a) Speech act theory's restricted role is a matter of its relative unimportance.
(2b) Speech act theory's restricted role is a matter of a necessary limitation on the range of speech acts which deserve to be accommodated within a linguistic theory.

(3a) Speech act theory should be replaced by Relevance theory.
(3b) Relevance theory provides the proper theoretical foundation for the restricted role of speech act theory.

In this paper I want to examine Sperber and Wilson's grounds for preferring Relevance[3] theory to speech act theory in these various ways. I shall try to show that their arguments, even when sound, do not point unequivocally towards any one of these theses. Their primary argument against speech act theory points towards a strong conclusion such as (1a); but the secondary arguments point rather towards (2b) or (3b). Their own discussion raises two kinds of issue which I shall separate. I discuss in the first section their negative criticisms of speech act theory. I look in the second section at the more positive way in which they envisage a role for Relevance theory which either supplements (3b) or replaces (3a) speech act theory.

CRITICISMS OF SPEECH ACT THEORY

The general criticism

In chapter 4, section 10 of *Relevance* Sperber and Wilson outline some of the origins of speech act theory in the work of Austin, Grice and Searle as a preliminary to their criticisms. They place special emphasis on the taxonomy of speech acts and on one link between Gricean implicatures and 'indirect' speech acts. It is true that these aspects have been extensively discussed among speech act theorists, although it is doubtful if they have the central importance which Sperber and Wilson's emphasis implies. But it should be noted that Grice's work had one more fundamental link with speech act theory, through his 'intentional' theory of meaning or communication (Grice 1957, 1969). One way of taking that Gricean theory would be to treat it as an account of a hearer's (H's) recognition of a speaker's (S's) act by means of the former's recognition of the latter's intention. Indeed, as is well known, Searle wrongly assumed that this was the *only* way of construing Grice's theory (Searle 1969: 44–6). Sperber and Wilson themselves accept such a Gricean framework in their own theory, although they emphasize the distinction between the 'communicative' and the 'informative' intention. This perhaps provides a motive for their disregard of such a link. For it is their central objection to speech act theory that the classification of speech acts is not 'part of what is communicated' and so does not play a 'necessary role in comprehension' (Sperber and Wilson 1986: 244). One way of establishing such a claim would be to reject the link between Grice's theory and pragmatic theory, but Sperber and Wilson plainly do not wish to do that.

Instead their argument focuses on an independent analogical objection to treating the classification of speech acts as a necessary part of communication. They say that a speech act classification might be 'invented' to theorize about utterances, or might be developed on the basis of native speakers' own classification of such utterances; but they insist that in neither case does such a classification play a necessary role in communication. Now clearly an invented classification might be vulnerable to such a charge, but it is more difficult to see how a classification derived from native speakers might be so vulnerable. Here, however, Sperber and Wilson make use of their basic criticism, namely that from the analogous fact that tennis players generally *can* classify strokes as volleys, lobs, etc., it does not follow that they *have* to make such classifications in order to play tennis or in order to return shots appropriately.

The general argument is, however, open to a decisive counter. For the plausibility of the tennis analogy rests on the correct belief that tennis players do not have consciously to rehearse to themselves the classifications of shots, still less consciously to deliberate about such a classification, in order to respond appropriately. It might reasonably be said that any player who did preface his responses with such conscious deliberation would be a poor performer. Still it does not follow from such a claim that it is simply unnecessary to grasp or classify the shots in order to respond appropriately. Indeed it is just as implausible to claim that we have to classify consciously as to claim that we do not have to classify at all. A player who draws no distinction between a top-spin and a back-spin lob is just as likely to respond inappropriately to such shots as a conversationalist who fails to distinguish between orders and advice, or between a straightforward and an ironic assertion.

Arguments from analogy tend to be weak and misleading, but I add two points to forestall lines of defence. It is, first, of no use to defend the analogy by insisting that the issue has to do only with the necessity of the link between tennis and shot classification. It might be said that there really is no valid inference from the ability to the necessity to classify shots. But the issue is whether such classification, either in tennis or in conversation, is necessary for a player, and here the issue is bound to be a matter of degree. Just as tennis players come with differing degrees of skill, so conversationalists come with different abilities to respond to utterances. At the limit, a player who could not classify shots at all would be as severely handicapped in his performance as a conversationalist who had no conception of a speech act classification. Such a person might, like an autistic child, be incapable of relating utterances to personal attitudes or relationships, and might with such a handicap be denied to be conducting a genuine conversation. It is worth adding, too, that Sperber and Wilson subsequently modify this general claim since they *are* prepared to accept some limited speech act classifications, such as their Category III acts, as necessary for communication. Although the general analogy points erroneously to a conclusion of type (1a), those subsequent arguments point rather towards the weaker conclusions (2b) or (3b).

That latter point might, second, be reinforced by noting that when we speak of difficulties in communication we more naturally think of difficulties in the way of interpreting utterances pragmatically with respect to their implicatures or speech act classification than of difficulties of a syntactic or semantic sort. Such a point has only intuitive force; it suggests that we reserve room in communication for the ability to comprehend and respond appropriately to conversational utterances in these terms. But this leads to a problem for Sperber and Wilson. For they, too, would not wish to deny that a grasp of the attitudes evinced in utterances forms an essential part of communication. The difference between them and a speech act theorist is not that the latter wishes to include in communication material which Sperber and Wilson wish to exclude; it is rather that they both wish to include such material but to characterize it differently. Sperber and Wilson wish to include certain attitudes on the part of S and H, but do not wish to characterize them in terms of speech act types. Speech act theorists wish to make explicit reference to speech act types, and include in those references appeals to S's and H's attitudes. The point has some importance later, but even at this stage it draws again a distinction between the strong conclusions, (1a) or (3a), and the weaker (1b) and (3b).

The specific criticisms

If, for these reasons, the central criticism of speech act theory is weak, it is possible that the subsidiary arguments are stronger. In those subsidiary arguments Sperber and Wilson classify speech act types under three categories (I, II, and III), and then argue that only one of these categories (III) deserves to be accommodated within a linguistic theory. The three categories can be identified in the following way:

> *Category I.* Speech acts of an 'institutional' kind. (For example, bidding at bridge.)
> *Category II.* Speech acts which are not 'identified as such either by the speaker (S) or the hearer (H)'. (For example, uttering a claim about the future which, with some provisos, will count as a prediction 'without S's ever intending to communicate, or H's ever recovering, the information' that S is making a prediction (Sperber and Wilson 1986: 245).)
> *Category III.* Speech acts of the most general kind, such as 'saying, telling, and asking', which *alone* deserve to be included in a linguistic theory.

The upshot of the discussion of this classification indicates the earlier ambiguity in the conclusion. Clearly if Category III speech acts are included in a linguistic theory, then this would not warrant the strong conclusion (1a). It points instead towards (2b), but still leaves a choice between (3a) or (3b). In this part of their argument Sperber and Wilson adopt positions close to those of Urmson (1977), Warnock (1973) and Cohen (1974) in their criticisms of Austin's theory, and I have published objections to those views which I repeat here in a more pointed form (see Bird 1981a, 1981b). I consider first the rejection of Category I speech acts, then the argument in favour of including Category III, and finally the argument designed to exclude Category II.

Category I

In this first argument Sperber and Wilson echo a point made by Urmson and Warnock, namely that 'institutional' speech acts belong to their various institutions and so do not belong to language (one might say to the 'institution' of language). Thus the speech act of bidding in bridge belongs to the institution of bridge, and so not to language. It should not therefore form part of a theory of language. Such an argument, as it stands, is fallacious. It assumes that some item which belongs to one institution cannot consequently belong to any other. It tacitly legislates that items cannot belong to more than one such institution, although such an assumption is no more plausible in the linguistic context than it would be in the context of gentlemen's clubs. Just as you can belong to a rugby club and to the Athenaeum, so there is no good reason to suppose that words, or word properties, acts or utterances can find a theoretical home in only one institution.

It might be thought that the argument which works so hopelessly for clubs works better for linguistic properties, but although this throws some light on the underlying form of the argument it, too, can be seen to be a mistake. Let us suppose that words in technical contexts, such as law or science, have meanings. Should we be inclined to say that those meanings are of no interest to linguistics because they belong to the non-linguistic institutions of law or science? The underlying suggestion is evidently that what we mean by 'language' is simply what Oxford philosophers used to call 'ordinary (that is, non-technical) language'.[4] It is, of course, open to a linguist to restrict her interest to ordinary features of natural language, but it would still be fallacious to infer from this that meaning itself is confined in that way. Nothing here turns on the difference between a linguistic feature such as meaning and a pragmatic feature such as speech act type.

One final point deserves to be noted in this context. Sperber and Wilson seek to support their view by adding that 'the study of bidding is part of the study of bridge, not of verbal communication' (Sperber and Wilson 1986: 245). Such a claim sits oddly with their later view that to understand the utterance of a bid as such is 'essential to the communication' of that utterance (ibid.), but the additional argument is open to a more serious objection. Of course nobody supposes that linguistics has to encompass the study of bidding strategies in playing bridge; but to 'study bidding' might be to study not the strategy of bidding but the uttering of bids, that is the production and understanding of a bid as such. The argument would be like claiming that we cannot study 'asking', one of their legitimate Category III speech acts, without studying interrogation techniques. There is no good reason to deny so far that the study of the utterance of bids can be included in pragmatics if it also includes the study of asking or asserting.

Category III

The objections to Category III speech acts take two forms. In the first Sperber and Wilson ascribe an assumption to speech act theory with regard to the generic acts of saying, telling and asking, which they then reject. The assumption is that there has to be a direct correlation between these generic acts and syntactic forms such as, respectively, the declarative, imperative and interrogative moods. I shall call this the 'Correlation Thesis'. In the second it is argued that these generic acts can be sharply separated from acts of Categories I and II, and have features which entitle them to be included in a linguistic theory. It is necessary for Category III acts to be distinguished from Categories I and II simply because the latter are not to be included in a linguistic theory. Sperber and Wilson claim that Category III acts are 'genuinely communicative rather than social-institutional' (ibid.: 246), but I have argued already that this does not properly separate Category III acts from those of Category I. For I have suggested that the dichotomy between 'genuinely communicative' and 'social-institutional' is spurious. There are, however, other aspects of this phase of the argument which need to be considered. Since Sperber and Wilson wish to include the generic speech acts of Category III in a linguistic theory, at least within the framework of their own account of Relevance, some of the arguments about that category concern the more positive contribution of their theory, which will be considered in the second section.

The correlation thesis

The initial objection to the treatment of the basic generic speech acts in speech act theory is that it assumes a direct correlation between those generic acts and certain syntactic forms. But that bare point can be dealt with quickly since, so far as I know, no speech act theorist has made that assumption. On the contrary ever since the development of Austin's theories it has been common currency among such theorists that there is no such direct correlation. Even the explicit performative form was recognized to be uttered in a non-performative way in answering such a question as:

　　(1) What do you do at the end of a committee meeting?

by saying:

　　(2) I propose a vote of thanks to the secretary.

In a similar way it was widely recognized that syntactic forms standardly used for one purpose may be deployed for quite different ones. If I find in a questionnaire:

　　(3) Married/Single. Delete whichever is inapplicable.

it will be evident that I am being asked a question, even though the syntactic form is that of an imperative. Sperber and Wilson go on to say that such non-standard uses force the speech act theorist either to 'exclude them as insincere or defective', or alternatively to abandon the 'traditional typology of speech acts' (ibid.: 247). Neither of these claims is true. To regard such cases as 'non-standard' is not to treat them as insincere or defective; and since the 'traditional typology' allowed for their existence, they did not require that typology to be abandoned.

These points seem, indeed, so wide of the mark that some explanation seems to be needed; and such an explanation is not hard to find. Two points might be made. The first is that these claims might rest on a mis-understanding about Searle's theory of speech acts. The second is that Searle's account can be seen to contain a gap, which Relevance theory might be intended to fill. Searle's theory operates in two stages. In the first stage it offers certain necessary and sufficient conditions for the perform-ance of a speech act of type T under standard conditions. In the second stage it ascribes to an illocutionary force indicating device (IFID) used in standard conditions the features listed as its necessary and sufficient con-ditions in the first stage (Searle 1969: 4, 54–6). Searle conceived his own task as attending more to the first than to the second, since he drew a distinction between philosophy and linguistics in which the latter was more concerned with the identification of IFIDs in natural language. His own conception of such IFIDs in English was narrow, though it certainly included explicit performatives and syntactic moods; but he seemed to regard any detailed exploration of such IFIDs as belonging more to linguistics than to philosophy. It may be said that Sperber and Wilson ascribe the Correlation Thesis to such a theory, simply because Searle spent so little time on that linguistic task. Properly understood, however, the two stages in Searle's theory do not commit him to any such view.

Although that diagnosis suggests a way in which such a theory as Searle's might seem to be committed to the Correlation Thesis, it nevertheless points to some gaps in Searle's account. For one thing there is evidently a gap in identifying IFIDs in specific natural languages. A further gap arises if we separate the following three questions:

(i) What are the necessary and sufficient conditions for the performance of a type T speech act?
(ii) How can these conditions be associated with specific IFIDs in natural language L?
(iii) How do Ss and Hs come to understand and ascribe T-type speech acts to utterances?

Searle's theory concentrated on (i). It also acknowledged (ii) without, however, offering any very detailed answers to (ii). But it did not, and did not purport to, answer or acknowledge any question like (iii). Yet it is such a question as (iii) which Sperber and Wilson want to raise and answer. This much is clear from their interest in the way Ss and Hs come to interpret specific utterances in terms of contextual assumptions, shared beliefs, linguistic and encyclopaedic knowledge, ostensive-inferential procedures, and so on. It is implicit in their wish to link Relevance theory to a 'cognitive science' paradigm and to provide a theory which is, as they put it, 'psychologically plausible' (Sperber and Wilson 1986: 170). If this is correct, then it offers a guideline with which to assess Relevance theory and to relate it to a speech act theory such as Searle's. It suggests, for example, that speech act theory and Relevance theory are not rivals, and that perhaps the latter might be used as a complement to the former. It suggests a conclusion close to (3b) such as:

(3c) Relevance theory adds a complementary psychological theory into which speech act theory can be incorporated.

The special status of saying, telling, and asking

In this second part of their argument about Category III acts Sperber and Wilson claim that these generic speech acts *alone*[5] deserve to be accommodated within a linguistic theory, and so are significantly different from acts of categories I and II. For them H's recovery of Category III act types is an essential part of communication. They say:

We ... earlier suggested that the propositional form P of an ordinary assertion is standardly integrated into an assumption schema of the form 'S said that P'.

(Sperber and Wilson 1986: 246)

the recovery of such descriptions [as 'S said that P'] is an essential part of the comprehension process, and the speech acts of saying, telling and asking do not fall into Category II.

(ibid.)

We saw earlier that for Sperber and Wilson Category I acts also form an essential part of the comprehension process, but that they erroneously reject these acts on the ground that they belong to other, social, institutions. If that is an error, then the required differentiation between Category III and Category I acts still has to be made out. Aside from that, however, two other objections can be raised to the argument.

(1) Clearly the central line of the argument is that while Category II acts are *not* essential to comprehension (and this has still to be considered) Category III acts *are* essential. Such a claim is formally ambiguous. Is the claim that all three generic acts are essential to communication, or only that some subgroup, or at least one, is essential? The evidence cited in support of the conclusion is that all known natural languages contain either all three, or some subgroup (Sperber and Wilson 1986: 246), although a more appropriate criterion would be whether it would be *possible* for a natural language to lack all three, or some subgroup.

The claim that every language *has* to contain all three generic types is unsustainable, even if it is true that all known natural languages contain them all. There is no difficulty in constructing a language which, for example, contains only assertions and neither questions nor commands. The descriptive language for chess is such a language. The claim that no language could fail to have *some* basic speech act types is too weak; for it would be satisfied by a language in which the basic act types did not include either saying or telling or asking. Moreover, and following Wittgenstein,[6] it seems difficult to believe that there is even any one generic type which is essential to language. It may be natural to ascribe that kind of primacy to assertion, but such a claim seems too strong.

Perhaps the claim has to be weakened so that no language could fail to contain at least one of these generic speech acts. Even this claim is not obviously correct. Suppose that we consider acts such as promising or warning. Is it evident that such acts have to be subsumed under, or recognized as, one or other of the three generic types? It is of no use to argue that it is unintelligible to imagine an act of promising or warning which was not carried out through some act of saying, or telling, or asking. For all that this establishes, even if it is true, is that acts of promising and warning are also acts of saying, or telling, or asking; it does not establish that promising and warning are subspecies of saying or telling or asking, and on the face of it they are not. To promise is not to assert, even if many acts of promising are made in the form of an assertion. If it is claimed that a language might naturally lack any act of promising or warning, then, as we have seen already, the same is true severally even of the generic acts of saying, telling, and asking.

(2) There is a second difficulty about the primacy given to the three generic acts. Even if it were true that no language could lack all three generic acts, all that this would establish is that these are the basic categories of speech act. But from this it does not follow that linguistic theory has to be restricted to just these types. To draw such an inference would be like arguing that since physics deals with such basic categories of physical objects as gases and fluids, it does not concern itself with hydrogen or water. Perhaps at some point in the descent from such basic categories we shall say that we move from physics to engineering; and similarly at some point in moving from generic to specific speech acts we may see a move from pure to applied linguistics, or from linguistics to psychology or cognitive science. It is problematic in any case how we should draw such a distinction. It is not clear, for example, whether there is a definite line of division to be drawn at all.[7] But since Sperber and Wilson represent their own theory as a part of, or moving towards, psychology or cognitive science it will be difficult for them to insist on such a sharp division.

Category II

Sperber and Wilson reject Category II speech acts, and differentiate them from Category III acts, on the ground that the former are not 'ostensively communicated'. What is ostensively communicated, and so essential to communication in these cases, is a set of assumptions about the utterance which do not involve the classification of the utterance as a Category II act. The argument is illustrated for the case of prediction, of which they say:

> what makes an utterance a prediction is not the fact that the speaker ostensively communicates that she is making a prediction; it is that she ostensively communicates an assumption with a certain property, that of being about a future event at least partly beyond her control.
> (Sperber and Wilson 1986: 245)

There are two related objections to this view. The first is to note that these conditions are not sufficient to make an utterance a prediction. In such utterances as

(4) I intend to take the train to Swindon tomorrow.

or

(5) It might snow next week.

the requirements for prediction are satisfied, but neither is a prediction.[8] (4) is a statement of intention and (5) is about a future event but not a prediction of that event. It might be said that these are trivial points, in that the conditions can easily be revised to accommodate such counter-examples. Of course such revision is both possible and necessary, but it leads to a second and more decisive objection.

For whether such revisions are made or not Sperber and Wilson's claim faces a dilemma. Clearly if the conditions are not sufficient for a speech act of the prediction type, then they will not be conditions which make the utterance a prediction. But if the conditions *are* adequate then the classification is recoverable from the ostensive communication, and then there is no obstacle to the classification's being an essential part of what is ostensively communicated. This dilemma reflects again an ambiguity noted earlier, in which it was unclear whether the intention was to *eliminate* speech act theory (thesis (1a)) or only to *incorporate* it into Relevance theory (thesis (3b) or (3c)). The further question whether such incorporation is possible or desirable will be considered in the second section. For the present, however, the criticisms and dismissal of speech act theory seem both inadequate and ambiguous.

THE POSITIVE THEORY

It was suggested earlier that a theory such as Searle's contains an evident gap. Even if it outlines correctly the necessary and sufficient conditions for a speech act of type T (question (i)) it does not offer any explanation of the way in which Ss and Hs attach these conditions to specific utterances (question (iii)). It does not even, without supplementation, explain how Ss and Hs identify specific IFIDs, although it may be suggested that standard IFIDs, such as explicit performatives, are recognized by any competent speaker who ascribes the associated force as a default position to be queried only in the light of unusual circumstances. Searle's account of IFIDs is, however, perfunctory and narrow. I have attempted to supplement it,[9] as have Sperber and Wilson in their emphasis on irony, metaphor and other stylistic tropes. Even with such additions, however, an explanatory gap still exists either where there is no IFID, or where there are alternative ways of interpreting the utterance. A theory like Searle's provides a formal structure for characterizing speech acts, but it offers no further explanation of the psychological processes which determine the application of that structure. It is that gap which Relevance theory seems designed to fill.

In that case Relevance theory and speech act theory need not conflict. Such a position would be compatible with either thesis (3b) or thesis (3c), and the crucial residual issue would be to decide whether either of those views, or (3a), or some other view, is correct. I shall consider these issues in two stages, asking first whether the Principle of Relevance (PR) has *any* explanatory power, and second whether the illustrative examples throw light on its explanatory role.

The general status of PR

Many commentators have expressed doubts about the role of PR.[10] It suffers undoubtedly from initial ambiguities, many of which Sperber and Wilson have sought to resolve. It relies on an assessment of contextual effect and processing effort which is difficult to determine operationally. And it has been thought to be in danger of collapsing into emptiness. If any of these anxieties were justified, then PR's explanatory power would be in jeopardy.

Sperber and Wilson make it clear that their term 'Relevance' is not to be understood in its colloquial way. PR has to do with the balance of contextual effects over processing effort, so that the greater that balance the more Relevant will be the associated interpretation. They themselves understandably speak often of 'efficiency' rather than Relevance in saying, for example,

> Our claim is that human beings automatically aim at the most efficient information processing possible; this is so whether they are conscious of it or not; in fact the very diverse and shifting conscious interests of individuals result from the pursuit of this permanent aim in changing conditions.
>
> (Sperber and Wilson 1986: 49)

Despite this they also sometimes use 'relevance' as if it were the colloquial term; and they also speak both of 'maximizing' and of 'optimizing' this factor (Sperber and Wilson 1986: 48, 49, 161, 1987: 704, 743, 1988: 152), although it remains uncertain how these are to be distinguished. We might, for example, speak of two interpretations as 'optimal' where the same balance of effect over effort is achieved, even though only one is 'maximal' if it provides greater contextual effects.

Several other important provisos are made about PR. There may be differences between short-term and long-term Relevance, and between different 'levels' of Relevance in specific contexts, such as those of a bar-room conversation or an academic seminar (Sperber and Wilson 1986: 161). Relevance may be defined relative to a context or to an individual. It assumes S's or H's rationality, and its operation is subject to adventitious psychological factors such as alertness (ibid.: 131, 161, 165–6). Sperber and Wilson rightly draw a distinction between the achievement of Relevance and its assumption or presumption in some context. The latter is associated only with its appearing to S or H that certain items are Relevant, even optimally Relevant, to H or S, and not with such a presumption's being accurate (ibid.: ch. 3). They therefore mark this distinction by speaking of the fact of the presumption of Relevance, which is what PR asserts, and its fulfilment, which PR does not guarantee. Nevertheless they also often speak of PR as providing a 'guarantee' on S's part of Relevance to H (ibid.: 49–50).

Perhaps the most important claim made for PR distinguishes it from a Gricean principle of Co-operation. Whereas the latter is a 'norm', PR is by contrast a descriptive, and exceptionless, generalization. Sperber and Wilson say:

> The principle of relevance is a generalisation about ostensive-inferential communication. Communicators and audience need no more know PR to communicate than they need to know the principles of genetics to reproduce. Communicators do not 'follow' PR; and they could not violate it even if they wanted to. PR applies without exception; every act of ostensive communication communicates a presumption of its own relevance.
>
> (ibid.: 162)

Though many of these provisos clarify the role of PR, some queries remain. It remains unclear, for example, how PR can be merely descriptive or non-normative when Sperber and Wilson frequently speak of Ss and Hs being guided in conversation by what they 'should' do according to the principle (Sperber and Wilson 1986: 48–9, 1988: 152). Nor is it clear how that guidance squares with the claimed non-conscious, automatic, operation of PR. Moreover, to assume a background of rationality in appealing to PR is also to invoke a normative element in its operation; and if adventitious factors such as alertness affect whether PR operates or not, then it is hard to see how it can be an exceptionless generalization. All of these points must affect any explanatory role for PR, either with respect to its universal scope or with respect to its status as both non-normative and automatic.

Another set of queries arises from the nature of the presumption involved in PR. It is plausible to suppose that human beings generally aim at efficiency among other things, or what they take to be efficiency, but it is less plausible to suppose that the efficiency they aim at in communication is centred on that of their audience. Sperber and Wilson speak frequently of the operation of PR in terms of S's aiming at an utterance which will be optimally Relevant for H. But although communication is, essentially, *other-directed*, it does not follow that it is *other-centred*. S may naturally have aims in communicating which are other-directed and *self-centred*; nor could it plausibly be maintained that such a posture is in any way non-rational or even non-standard. Cases of that kind, where S manipulates H's attention for S's own benefit might be potential counter-examples to the operation of PR, and if they are not, then the suspicion is that PR is not, after all, open to counter-examples. Sperber and Wilson identify some such cases in talking, for example, of the blackmailer's assumption that the victim can expect, or see, some benefit to himself in the communication, but this manifests the dubious idea that H has some independent benefit to be gained from the exchange, and there is no general reason to suppose that this is always so.

One possible response, suggested already, is that PR marks an 'ideal' situation in which S and H are perfectly rational, properly alert, and even automatically capable of assessing properly their own and their partners' benefits and costs. Such an ideal situation might be extended by requiring adequate or complete information about the situation, and their own and others' beliefs about it. The danger in that case is that if such ideal situations are rare, or even impossible, then a PR which requires them will have its explanatory scope severely restricted. Typically conversations are carried out in less than ideal situations. This will both restrict the explanatory scope of PR and also provide a different direction of interest in accounting for utterances. For such 'imperfect' conversations will be directed as much to querying and clarifying S's and H's responses as to adding information to an already recognized stock of mutual beliefs. Sperber and Wilson sometimes note the hypothesis-forming, and hypothesis-testing character of conversation, but they also lose sight of this through their belief in the determinacy and power of PR itself.[11]

It is worth, therefore, recalling how strong the claims for its explanatory role often are. It is claimed, for example, that

> PR is enough on its own to explain how linguistic structure and background knowledge interact to determine verbal comprehension.
>
> (Sperber and Wilson 1988: 141)

Sperber and Wilson speak also of PR as capable of 'resolving linguistic indeterminacies' (ibid.: 139) and as making it possible 'to derive rich and precise non-demonstrative inferences about the communicator's informative intention' (Sperber and Wilson 1986: 254). For them PR captures the single overriding property which explains how Ss and Hs process information. Such an emphasis on the determinacy of PR's operation conflicts with the model of hypothesis-forming and testing in conversation. It also suggests that PR should be understood as an 'ideal' principle which is scarcely ever satisfied in ordinary contexts, even though it may still usefully function as an idealized explanation.

The residual ambiguities over the content of PR and the variability in claims about its explanatory strength leave uncertainty about its operation. But these handicaps, though potentially serious, would be less serious than a general doubt about the assessment of Relevance itself. If PR were to work adequately, then there should be some way of assessing the required balance of effect over effort. Sperber and Wilson make it clear that they have no way of exactly measuring effects and effort in order to provide such a strict quantitative assessment. Instead they speak of the balance as 'comparative' rather than 'quantitative' (Sperber and Wilson 1986: 79–81, 129–30, 1987: 743). Such a restriction to non-quantitative comparison need not be by itself a decisive handicap; the more serious difficulty arises from the question about how such a comparison is made. We have to recall that the comparison is presumably one which appears to S or H, and not one which might be assessed independently. Or, if it can be assessed independently it may not match the assessments that S and H make, and can then have no explanatory value in determining their own responses to communication.

Even that point understates the dangers in such an account. For there is at least a strong temptation to determine the assessment of the balance, and of the comparison, simply by adverting to the responses which S and H in fact make. The point can be illustrated in terms of a related example which Sperber and Wilson use. In elucidating PR they say

> [It is] ... manifest that people will pay attention to a phenomenon only if it seems relevant to them.

> (Sperber and Wilson 1987: 704)

Such a claim requires that we have some way of assessing the apparent balance of effect over effort which paying attention will bring to the person involved. The temptation is to say that there *must* have been such a balance simply because, after all, the person did pay some attention to the phenomenon. Such a response has the consequence that the appeal to Relevance has no explanatory value. It is to offer, as an *ex ante* explanation, something which is determined *ex post* simply by the given response. The supposed explanatory principle will be in that case not properly independent of what it is supposed to explain. On the contrary the principle will simply, in other terms, express what it is supposed to explain, for there is no independent way of determining the operation of the principle other than what people in fact do.

That PR is in danger of such a fate is to some extent confirmed by other things that Sperber and Wilson say. It is, for example, implicit in their claim that PR is an exceptionless generalization, which we cannot choose to violate even if we wanted to. For this might be interpreted as saying that PR holds come what may; that is, that whatever, *ex post*, H does in response to some utterance it is bound to govern that response. In that case whatever we do in communication will be compatible with PR, but not because PR is a powerful explanatory principle. It gains its exceptionless character, fraudulently, by failing to mark any real distinction between the cases where it does operate and those where it does not. Something similar can be said of their claim that our shifting conscious interests in communication always relate to the permanent underlying ground of Relevance (Sperber and Wilson 1986: 49). For this, too, might be interpreted as claiming that whatever those shifting interests may be, PR can always be adjusted to accommodate them. It is for this reason that some commentators have asked whether Relevance, or efficiency, may not be just one among a whole raft of considerations determining responses in communication.

A similar, related, point can be made about Sperber and Wilson's (1988: 141–2) proof that the correct interpretation of an utterance is the first accessible one consistent with PR, or that there is only one interpretation consistent with PR. For these proofs rest on the assumption that S and H are perfectly rational, have perfect knowledge, and no distractions, in determining that there is only one interpretation consistent with PR. The proof simply builds into the notion of 'consistency with PR' all that is required to demonstrate both that only one interpretation meets the requirements, and that this is the correct interpretation. It does not follow from such proofs that PR is tautologous, although that is a possible danger in such a method. The conclusion might be, as was noted earlier, that PR operates as an ideal which has explanatory value in perfect conditions, much as some scientific principles operate as ideals which are never realized in nature. But although this may throw light on the status of PR, and even modify the dangers of its turning into an empty hypothesis, it does not avoid every potential objection. For even if PR is conceived as an 'ideal' principle, if the ideal circumstances are not generally applicable the specific explanations of utterance interpretation might have to focus more on the divergent factors than on PR itself. Whether that is true cannot be made out just by considering PR on its own, but might be apparent if we examine the specific applications of the principle which Sperber and Wilson consider.

The illustrative examples

Even if PR is vulnerable to these difficulties it might still be true that in practice it can be shown to have some work to do. Sperber and Wilson (1986) illustrate that work in chapter 4 with reference to two examples,[12] although I shall deal with only one. In that primary case they differentiate between four interpretations of the utterance

(6) The bus is leaving.

Such an utterance, in different contexts, might be construed as

(a) a straightforward assertion, a report, of some occurrence;
(b) a metaphorical remark, like 'missing the boat';
(c) an ironic assertion in which the intended content is the denial of what is explicitly said;
(d) a concession, in which S resolves a dispute by admitting an earlier error on her part.

Of these four interpretations (a) and (d) plainly deal directly with speech act classifications. Moreover, (d) involves a classification, uttering a concession, which officially does not figure in Sperber and Wilson's list of recognized generic act types. It was noted earlier that the argument rejecting Category II speech acts, to which concessions naturally belong, was inadequate and its inclusion here seems to confirm that inadequacy. (c) also involves a speech act classification, namely assertion, but not in a straightforward way. Finally (b) is an example of a stylistic trope on which Sperber and Wilson rightly wish to place emphasis.[13]

The explanations offered for the different interpretations are brief (Sperber and Wilson 1986: 248–9) and can be summarized as follows:

(a) Here H 'identifies the propositional form of the utterance and integrates it into the description "S has said that P"'. This first step 'might then provide evidence for the claim that "S believes that P", and, so long as S is trusted, for P itself'.

(b) Here, where there is no bus in sight, and where H is hesitating about joining a group of walkers about to leave, the recovered description 'S has said that P' 'makes manifest that "S believes that if H does not now join the group, it will be too late"'. Again if H trusts S this can be treated as evidence that S's belief is true.

(c) Here the utterance is made in such a way that S dissociates herself from the assertion literally expressed. Then the utterance 'might provide evidence for the belief "S believes that it is absurd to say that the bus is leaving"', and so provides evidence that the bus is not leaving.

(d) Here S's utterance is made in the context of the previous dispute in which S has taken the view that the bus is not leaving. Now, with the palpable evidence that it is leaving she concedes her earlier error.

If we ask whether, or how, PR functions to explain H's selection from these, the initial answer seems to be that PR has no role to play. For certainly in the account given PR is not at any point explicitly mentioned. Of course it would be possible to say, as I noted earlier, that PR is tacitly present and operating simply because these are, *ex hypothesi*, the correct interpretations and it is evidently efficient to have identified them correctly. This would be possible, but fatal to any substantial explanatory role for PR. It would be to use the successful interpretation as a criterion for the operation of PR, instead of deploying PR independently as a genuinely explanatory principle. The promised explanatory use for PR was to explain how H processed utterances, or selected contexts, in order to arrive at an interpretation. To say that H arrives at an interpretation on the ground that what is presented to him 'might provide evidence for' the interpretation neither appeals to PR nor offers any specific explanation of his selection. If there is an explanation to be found in the description of the examples it is one which appeals to the evident circumstances of each case, or to H's beliefs about these circumstances, rather than to PR.

It would be possible, as we have seen, to invoke the notion of an 'ideal' explanation in which PR represents a situation in which S and H are fully rational, perfectly alert, and adequately or completely informed about their mutual beliefs, but this appeal too is open to serious limitations. For one thing its explanatory scope will be restricted in so far as S and H deviate from the ideal. It was suggested earlier that such deviations are the rule rather than the exception. People are usually less than totally rational, alert, and informed in conducting conversations. Indeed it is precisely for those reasons that communication is needed as one way of remedying those defects. Although Sperber and Wilson show some sympathy with this idea that conversations are conducted on an experimental, hypothesis-forming and testing, basis, their claims for PR and its precision work against such a view.

Construed in this way PR is restricted also in terms of the ideal factors which need to be invoked. In the specific interpretations which PR is designed to explain, the crucial factor is H's assessment of the presented evidence. Sperber and Wilson are no doubt right to see communication as a special case of evidence assessment, and so to suggest that the process should be dealt with in that general context in a psychological way. But our assessment of evidence is a highly complex operation and naturally invokes factors such as rationality, expertise, alertness, interests, level of information, to say nothing of distorting prejudices, background convictions, adventitious distractions, and so on. It is not obvious that the Relevance, or efficiency, which PR invokes has any special claim to priority among these items. In noting some of these factors additional to Relevance Sperber and Wilson themselves indicate that PR is not the single, all-encompassing, principle that it is supposed to be. The danger, as we have seen, is that if PR comes to stand generally for such factors whatever they may happen to be, then the principle will collapse into emptiness. To treat even the ideal operation of PR in this way will be to reduce it to a tautology. It will be to reproduce in the worst form the empty construction of the claim that there is only one (correct) interpretation consistent with PR. Such a claim reduces to the view that in an ideal world there is only one possible interpretation for any utterance, where the notion of an ideal world already rules out alternatives such as ambiguity, unclarity, ignorance, and so on. Such an exclusion is not only unrealistic, it is also in danger of explanatory emptiness.

When they introduce the notion of Relevance Sperber and Wilson canvass the possibility that there is no single answer to their question about the way in which we process or select in communication. They nevertheless insist that there is one single property (Sperber and Wilson 1986: 46), namely Relevance, on which such selection depends, and which, through PR, serves to explain our processing and selection practices. The difficulties now noted, however, suggest rather the alternative conclusion, namely that rejection of any single, overriding, principle or property is far more plausible.

CONCLUSION

The discussion in the first section showed that the criticisms of speech act theory were weak. They were generally open to serious, if not decisive, objections, and did not warrant the strong conclusions expressed in theses (1a), (2a), or (3a). What the criticisms pointed to were certain gaps in speech act theory which in principle Relevance theory might fill. Even so there remained ambiguities about how Relevance theory might supplement speech act theory, in terms of theses (3b) or (3c). It was not clear whether Relevance theory might simply be added to speech act theory, as a supplementary theory of the same kind, or whether it was a psychological theory of a different kind into which speech act classifications might be incorporated. Of these alternatives the latter seemed the more appropriate, and the closer to Sperber and Wilson's own claims. In the second section, however, the question was raised whether PR could properly fulfil its explanatory role understood in that latter way. PR was shown to be vulnerable to a number of ambiguities, and some of these cast serious doubt both on its general explanatory role, and on its particular application to utterance interpretation. The most serious danger is that PR, in various ways, collapses into an explanatory emptiness. Even if that danger is evaded, for example by construing PR as an ideal explanatory principle, its power remains limited both by its ideal nature and by the variety of factors which need to be added to, or accommodated within, the notion of Relevance itself. There is room for a psychological supplement to speech act theory, but it is doubtful that PR provides it.

NOTES

1 Austin 1962; Grice 1957, 1989; Searle 1969.
2 I subsequently leave out any explicit reference to 'pragmatics'.
3 I write 'Relevance' with a capital to indicate Sperber and Wilson's intention to use it technically rather than colloquially.
4 The *Shorter Oxford English Dictionary* does not list 'bid' as a bridge term, but does list its use in auctions. It is difficult to see any rationale for treating the auction term as linguistic but not social, while the bridge term is treated as social but not linguistic.
5 Cohen (1974) wanted to include syntactic moods and what he called 'semantic force' in a properly linguistic pragmatics. His account differs somewhat from Sperber and Wilson's.
6 Wittgenstein (1953) outlines a number of fragmentary 'language games' to throw light on aspects of natural language. In at least one of these, the 'builders' language game', there is the suggestion that a language might contain only imperative utterances, and that it would be an error to assume that the language could make sense only if we interpret these utterances as tacitly referring to assertions.
7 There are two points here. One involves the difference between generic and specific speech acts on the same scale. In that case there would be a problem about where, if at all, we draw the line between a 'linguistic' and a 'non-linguistic' speech act. This was one of the anxieties which Cohen (1974)

expressed about Austin's theory. The other involves the difference between contrasting explanations of speech acts; as, say, structurally linguistic or psychological. Sperber and Wilson seem to invoke both kinds of case. I have suggested in Bird (1979, 1981b) that we should not be concerned about the former difference; and my own structural account of speech acts fits into a psychological explanation better than Searle's theory.

8 A short while ago the British Chancellor of the Exchequer was reported to have said: 'The British economy might grow by 1 per cent in 1993; but that's not a prediction.'

9 Bird (1981b). In discussing 'warning' I suggest an account which is both more accurate, and closer to a psychological explanation, than Searle's.

10 See the contributions to the peer review of *Relevance* in *Behavioural and Brain Sciences* 1987, 10, 710–36, and Seuren 1988.

11 This was an aspect of communication which I emphasized in Bird (1974, 1979, 1981b).

12 Other cases are given in *Relevance*; and also in Carston (1988). The examples cited are, however, clearly intended to represent the way in which PR functions.

13 Sperber and Wilson (1986: 223) have another way of discriminating between types of utterance, in accordance with their belief that utterances rarely match the corresponding thoughts exactly, but resemble them in various ways. Although this aspect of their theory is interesting, it is also questionable; but it does not specifically indicate the role of PR, which is the principal interest here.

14 Modular speech act theory
Programme and results

Asa Kasher

MODULAR PRAGMATICS

Modular pragmatics is a research programme. Every research programme is a continuous series of theories that share a conception of objectives, a philosophical 'hard core' and an appropriate methodology. Generative linguistics, as it has been portrayed by Chomsky, is a research programme that has had syntax in its focus.[1] Truth-conditional theories of meaning, as proposed and defended by Davidson, form another research programme, one that has had semantics in its focus.[2] Modular pragmatics is meant to be a research programme that applies to the field of pragmatics the general modular approach to the study of language and cognition, which in turn is a part of the general cognitive approach to the study of the human mind (see Kasher 1991a, 1991b).

According to the cognitive approach to the study of any competence of the human mind, be it vision, imagery, reasoning or natural-language use, the main theoretical objective of such a study is delineation and explanation of that competence within the conceptual framework of cognitive studies.

Within this framework, a human competence is a system of knowledge that is governed by a characteristic set of principles.[3] The system operates as a representation processing device that embodies these principles. This processing device itself is embodied in the human brain.

A delineation and explanation of a competence of the mind, within such a cognitive conceptual framework, takes the form of a theory that answers questions of the following forms:

(C1) What is the domain of competence C?
(C2) What is the system of abstract principles that govern the system of knowledge that constitutes competence C?
(C3) What is the operating system that embodies these principles of competence C and employs them?
(C4) What is the neural embodiment of the abstract principles of competence C and its processing device?

(C5) What is the adjacent system of growth, development or acquisition that enables competence C to arise in a normal person?[4]

Whether a study of pragmatics is a study of a particular human competence or of a certain system of closely related human competences or of some assortment of human competences, a cognitive study of pragmatics is meant to delineate and explain a system or systems of pragmatic knowledge by a theory that answers the questions of these forms, (C1) to (C5), with respect to a particular competence or some particular competences.

If pragmatics is, roughly speaking, the study of language use (see Levinson 1983; Kasher 1977), then cognitive studies of pragmatics, *cognitive pragmatics* for short, is a research programme whose theoretical objectives are delineation and explanation of some system or systems of knowledge of language use, within the conceptual framework of cognitive studies. Theories that are formulated, investigated and improved within this research programme are expected to eventually provide us with adequate answers to questions of the forms (C1) to (C5), about the domain of each system of pragmatic knowledge, its principles, its operation, its embodiments and its arising.

Thus portrayed, cognitive pragmatics shares with other cognitive studies of language as well as with various branches of cognitive science some important features.

First, the conceptual framework pictures every human competence as a *four-tier system of knowledge.* There is a top stratum of abstract principles. Then, the system of abstract principles is embodied in an underlying stratum that operates as a representation-processing device. This device is, in turn, embodied in the brain, the third stratum within this picture. This is a three-tier system that results from the operation of a fourth tier, one that enables the person to reach mature mastery of the competence.

Second, these four-tier systems of knowledge show a most important *top-down independence*: every stratum of the system is independent of the underlying strata. Consider a computer D that runs a program that computes the value of Π to the n-th digit, for any given n. A full understanding of D's competence to compute Π involves a four-tier system of the above-mentioned form. The abstract, mathematical stratum involves the definition of Π and a proof that a certain function correctly specifies, given n, the first n digits of Π. Obviously, this stratum is independent of all the other strata: the flowchart of the program, the underlying electronic system, and the compilation process of the program. Similarly, the flowchart is independent of the structure and operation of the chips of the underlying electronic stratum. In the same vein, the abstract stratum of the human competence of counting and computing is independent of the strata of embodiment in the mind and in the brain. Other human competences, such as language use, reasoning and face recognition, show the same form of top-down independence. Indeed, no bottom-up independence of any stratum of upper strata is expected to appear, since no embodiment of a principle or a device can in any sense be independent of it.[5]

Modular pragmatics is a thread of cognitive pragmatics. It is a research programme of the same theoretical objectives, namely, delineation and explanation of some system or systems of knowledge of language use. However, within the conceptual framework of cognitive pragmatics, which is the general conceptual framework of cognitive studies, modular pragmatics is an attempt to portray the whole spectrum of the human knowledge of language use in terms of systems of knowledge of two types only: *modular* systems and *central* systems.[6] Since the notions of a modular system and of a central system are playing a major role in modular pragmatics, we move now to a brief clarification of each of them.

Traditional views of the mind portrayed it as 'entirely indivisible': 'For, as a matter of fact,' said Descartes,

> when I consider the mind, that is to say, myself inasmuch as I am only a thinking thing, I cannot distinguish in myself any parts ... And the faculties of willing, feeling, conceiving, etc. cannot be properly speaking said to be its parts, for it is one and the same mind which employs itself in willing and in feeling and understanding.
>
> (Descartes 1641: Meditation VI, 196)

A modular approach to the study of the mind portrays the mind as entirely divisible into systems of two types: special faculties, modular systems of knowledge, on the one hand; and general purpose systems, central systems of knowledge, on the other hand.

The notion of *modular system* was explicated by Fodor.[7] Input systems, such as language and vision, are modular on that account, since they possess most or all of certain properties:

(F1) they are domain specific;
(F2) their operation is mandatory;
(F3) there is only limited central access to the representations that they compute;
(F4) they are fast;
(F5) they are 'informationally encapsulated' in the sense of having significantly constrained access to information present in the mind;
(F6) they have outputs that are 'shallow' in the sense of encoding significantly constrained information;
(F7) they are associated with fixed neural architecture;
(F8) they exhibit characteristic and specific breakdown patterns;
(F9) their ontogeny exhibits a characteristic pace and sequencing.

At an early stage of modular pragmatics we showed[8] that:

(MP1) If
       1   by 'pragmatics' we mean a system of knowledge of language use that is reflected in the major facts with respect to:

(i) forces of speech acts;[9]
(ii) perfomatives;
(iii) deixis;
(iv) lexical pragmatical presuppositions;
(v) conversational implicatures;
(vi) politeness principles;[10] and

2   by a 'modular system' we mean a system that satisfies
     conditions (F1) to (F9),

then

pragmatics does not constitute a modular system.

At that stage it was natural to replace the issue of the modularity of pragmatics by a family of issues of the modularity of some components of pragmatics, directly related to phenomena of language use drawn from the list (i) to (vi) or other ones.[11] Although each of these components of pragmatics is related to a feature of language use, each of them is related to what seems to be, in some sense, a separate facet of speech activity in context. There is no reason to assume that they are all mutually dependent on each other or are even closely related parts of one cohesive system. Pragmatic phenomena such as forces of speech acts, deictic expressions and conversational implicatures have each been the subject matter of an apparently independent branch of pragmatics. The question, therefore, naturally arises, whether the apparent mutual independence of these branches of pragmatics is a result of some methodological decision to discuss phenomena in abstraction from their interrelations or whether it is rather a manifestation of an underlying substantive independence of each of the different pragmatic phenomena. Naturally, the issue of the substantive independence of some components of pragmatics can take the form of the problem of the modularity of the related systems of pragmatic knowledge.

However, the relation between the intuitive notion of substantive independence and the technical notion of modularity is at least slightly more complicated than it seems. Whereas conditions (F1) to (F9) of modularity all specify highly interesting features of cognitive systems, not all of these features indicate substantive independence in any ordinary sense of the term. For instance, there is no reason to assume that substantively independent systems of knowledge have to satisfy Fodor's condition (F2) of being 'constrained to apply whenever they can apply' (Fodor 1983: 53), unlike input systems, whose operation is mandatory.

We, therefore, propose that an alternative notion of modularity will be used within cognitive theories when the issue under consideration is that of substantive independence of a competence or a system of knowledge. Let us dub a system of knowledge that satisfies Fodor's conditions (F1) to (F9) an *F-module*, and refer to a system of the proposed alternative type as a *P-module*.

The alternative notion rests on the above-mentioned questions, of forms (C1) to (C5), which a theory has to answer for it to be an adequate delineation and explanation of a competence C of the mind. Intuitively speaking, a competence is shown to be substantively independent when the related questions are answered in a uniquely characterizing way. Accordingly, a P-module will have its independent

(P1) domain;
(P2) theoretic principles;
(P3) information processing;
(P4) neural embodiment;
(P5) acquisition process.

A more accurate specification of conditions (P1) to (P5) of P-modularity will clarify for each of them the relevant sense of independence. Some of the features of F-modularity will play a major role. For instance, conditions (F5), which requires that the system should be informationally encapsulated, and (F6), which requires that the system should produce shallow outputs, form part of a theoretical clarification of (P3). An advanced theory, within the framework of the research programme of modular pragmatics, will rest on such detailed clarification of each of the conditions of P-modularity. On the grounds of such a clarification, one could tackle the problem of whether a certain system of pragmatic knowledge is a P-module or not, as well as more general problems, such as how many pragmatic P-modules are there, and why (see Kasher 1984, 1991a, 1991b). A detailed example will be discussed in the next section.

Central systems are interestingly different from modular ones. According to Fodor's suggestions and arguments, the major distinction is that modular systems are domain specific (P1) and informationally encapsulated (P3), while central systems are domain inspecific and informationally unencapsulated.[12] A system of knowledge for which (P1) and (P3) do not hold, can still have its own theoretical principles, neural embodiment and acquisition process. It is, therefore, reasonable to draw the distinction between these two types of system in terms of conditions (P1) and (P3).

We assume that a central system of knowledge is governed by abstract, general principles that apply to different domains and that its embodiment takes the form of a representation manipulation device that has access to the central store of beliefs held by the person at the time.

Under this notion of a central system of knowledge, it can be shown that:

(MP2)   Conversational implicatures are generated by a central system of pragmatic knowledge.

In an earlier study, we showed that all the Gricean super-maxims and maxims that generate conversational implicatures are derivable from general rationality principles of intentional activity, ones that apply not only to speech but also to painting (see Kasher 1976, 1982). The system of knowledge that governs conversational implicature is, therefore, domain inspecific.

Grice pointed out that different kinds of data are used for the generation of conversational implicatures, including 'the context, linguistic or otherwise, of the utterance' and 'other items of background knowledge'.[13] Consideration of certain types of conversational implicature, such as ironical interpretation of utterances in appropriate contexts (Grice 1989: 34, 53–4), clearly shows that any item of background knowledge can be used in working out an implicature. The system of knowledge that governs conversational implicature is, therefore, also informationally unencapsulated. Thus, this system of pragmatic knowledge is a central one.

MODULAR SPEECH ACT THEORY

Modular speech act theory is that part of modular pragmatics that focuses on speech acts. Accordingly, modular speech act theory is a research programme. Its theoretical objectives are delineation and explanation of some system or systems of knowledge of speech act use, in both production and understanding. Within the conceptual framework of modular cognitive pragmatics, modular speech act theory tries to depict human knowledge of using speech acts in appropriate contexts in terms of modular systems and central ones. In this section we briefly present and discuss a few steps that have been made within this research programme and point out some possible future developments.

Frege's theory of meaning included in addition to *sense* and *reference* two other ingredients, namely, *force* and *tone* (see Dummett 1973, 1981, 1991). The indication of force is an indication of some type of speech act, such as making an assertion, posing a question, issuing a command or expressing a wish. A theory of force, on such an account, is a part of a theory of meaning, but for our present purposes we do not have to commit ourselves to any precisely drawn distinction between semantics and pragmatics. We do, however, adopt the idea that a theory of force has to do with the given variety of types of speech act.

Enumeration of the types of speech act that are performed in English by an appropriate utterance of a first-person singular, present indicative form is a list 'of the order of the third power of 10' by Austin's estimate,[14] but such an enumeration will not have any explanatory power. Taxonomies of speech act types provide us with only quite shallow generalizations, such as 'every speech act is verdictive, exercitive, commissive, behabitive or expositive', to use Austin's classification (Austin 1962: 151). Such classifications are also of no explanatory power.

Within the framework of cognitive pragmatics, the theoretical objective of the research programme is not to specify a family of verbs present in a dictionary that reflects, say, the current usage of certain words in expressions by members of the group of speakers of the cultural entity called, say, Modern British English. Cognitive studies of language do not address cultural entities of the nature of Modern British English, but rather cognitive entities, idiolects that persons have in their minds and brains.[15] Accordingly, cognitive pragmatics does not aim at any enumeration or classification of verbs and correlative speech act types of languages such as Old English or Modern Hebrew, which are cultural entities, but rather at an adequate delineation and explanation of the class of *cognitively possible speech act types*, that is, types of speech act whose existence is compatible with the cognitive constraints that are imposed on human linguistic activity by the human cognitive system or systems of pragmatic knowledge.

A theory of speech act force, within the conceptual framework of cognitive pragmatics, is descriptively adequate and explanatorily powerful, if it shows how the class of the cognitively possible speech act types is delineated in terms of:

(SAT1) a general conception of speech act type as a rule-governed practice whose system of rules satisfies a restricted class of conditions;

(SAT2) a restricted class of cognitively possible basic speech act types; and

(SAT3) a restricted class of basic amplifications of speech act types, that is to say, operations on speech act types (functions) that generate cognitively possible speech act types (systems of rules) when applied to cognitively possible speech act types (systems of rules).

Searle's theory of speech acts (Searle 1969) made several steps towards a general conception of speech act type, as required by (SAT1). The most important contribution of that theory was the deep insight into the nature of the systems of rules that govern speech acts:

(MP3) Human speech acts are governed by systems of rules that are constitutive.[16]

Of a lesser significance has been the classification offered by that theory of the rules that govern speech acts of a particular type. We argued[17] that such systems of rules have a structure that reflects their being systems that govern intentional acts:

(MP4) Human speech acts are governed by systems of rules that specify for each speech act type T:
(i)   the literal *ends* of acts of type T;[18]
(ii) the verbal *means* that may be used for obtaining those ends;
(iii) the conditions that a person has to satisfy in order to play the *role* of the agent of an act of type T;
(iv) the literal *product* of an act of type T.

Preliminary work has also been done in an attempt to delineate the class of basic speech acts. A natural distinction has been drawn between *basic speech acts* and *things done with words*.[19] Roughly speaking, the former are speech acts of types whose knowledge is part of one's knowledge of language itself, whereas the latter are speech acts of types whose knowledge requires more than the knowledge of language. Examples of the latter kind abound: 'I name this ship the *Queen Elizabeth*,' uttered while smashing an appropriate bottle against the stern of the ship, is a famous example. A speaker of any idiolect of English is not required to know *qua* speaker that this is how ships are named. One's knowledge of the practice of naming ships transcends one's knowledge of language, though the practice of ship-naming involves an utterance of an appropriate sentence. We have used an argument that has been put forward by Dummett for other purposes to show that assertion is a basic speech act type. There are reasons to assume that question and command are also basic in the same sense and perhaps requests too.[20] Our working hypothesis is that:

(MP5) Basic speech act types are identifiable by syntactic or intonational features of the relevant sentences.

Work towards delineation of the class of *basic amplifications* of speech act types has been scarce, but some parts of what has been done in Searle's and Vanderveken's more recent works seem useful in this respect (see Searle and Vanderveken 1985; Vanderveken 1990–1). For instance, one component of the suggested analysis of the notion of illocutionary force is *degree of strength* by which a distinction is drawn between similar speech act types such as request and supplication (see Vanderveken 1990–1: vol. I, 119ff.)

Thus far speech act force theory has been sketched within the conceptual framework of cognitive pragmatics. Within the more specific conceptual framework of modular pragmatics, a theory of speech act force will address issues of P-modularity and centrality of related systems of knowledge. There are three different levels on which such issues could arise. On the most general level we have all speech act types under consideration, whether they are basic ones or things done with words. On the least general level we have certain types of speech act under consideration, one at a time.

What seems to us to be the most interesting level on which issues of P-modularity and centrality arise is an intermediate level, where under consideration we have (a) some system of pragmatic knowledge of language use that involves only basic speech act types; and (b) some system of pragmatic knowledge of language use that involves the whole variety of possible speech act types of things done with words, which are not basic speech act types.

The existence of such systems is not self-evident. It is, actually, our hypothesis that:

(MP6) There is a P-modular system of pragmatic knowledge of

language use of basic speech act types.

(MP7)   There is a central system of pragmatic knowledge of language use of things done with words.

We sketch some evidence for parts of these hypotheses.

Evidence for (MP6), the P-modularity hypothesis of the basic speech act system, will take the form of evidence for the independence of this system on one of the above-mentioned levels (P1) to (P5). Evidence for independence on level (P2) of theoretical principles can be found in the philosophical characterization of the class of basic speech act types. Such speech acts are governed, according to (MP3), by constitutive systems of rules. By its very nature, each constitutive system of rules is, in a sense, independent. If the constitutive systems of rules that govern basic speech acts employ only sentences of certain syntactic and intonational properties, as we assume (MP5), then these constitutive systems of rules are also independent of all other constitutive systems of rules, which, in a sense, lends them independence on the level (P2) of theoretical principles.[21]

Some evidence for the independence of the basic speech act system on the level (P4) of neural embodiment has been recently found in a study made within the framework of our Neuropragmatics Project, with Eran Zaidel *et al.*[22] Separate detailed tests, each related to one of the speech act types of assertion, question, command and request, have been administered to appropriate groups of right-handed right brain-damaged and left brain-damaged subjects. Preliminary analysis shows a trend for the latter to perform worse than the former.

Evidence for (MP7), the centrality hypothesis of the system of things done with words, is evidence for the system having general principles, for its being domain-inspecific or for its being informationally unencapsulated.

We assume that the above-mentioned recursive amplifications of speech act types are the principles of this system. Clearly, amplification can take the form of an adding operation, that is, adding to a system of rules that governs speech acts of a certain type yet another rule. Since there do not seem to be any constraints imposed on the content of such added rules, recursive amplification results in domain inspecificity and information unencapsulation.

Evidence for the existence of a system of principles of amplification has been found in another study made within the same framework of the Neuropragmatics Project, with Eran Zaidel *et al.* In a series of cases we have been able to teach a new type of speech act, another one of the things done with words, to subjects of various types of brain damage.

We expect that future studies will shed light on the hypotheses we have put forward, within modular speech act theory, namely (MP5) to (MP7). The combined philosophical and linguistic studies of the related theoretical principles, psychological studies of processing and acquisition, and neuropsychological studies of brain embodiment seem to provide us with an appropriate interdisciplinary setting for a fruitful research programme in pragmatics.

NOTES

1 See Chomsky 1982, 1984; Salkie 1990.
2 See Brandl and Gombocz 1989. The editors of that volume portray Davidson's work as a programme in philosophy of mind.
3 A human competence is held to be a system of knowledge rather than an ability to act. On this use of 'knowledge', see Chomsky 1980.
4 See Chomsky 1988.
5 This explains the interdisciplinary nature of cognitive science, mentioned by Gardner as a characteristic feature of it. See Gardner 1985: 6–7.
6 A third possible type of system, namely, interface ones, will not be presently discussed. See Kasher 1984 and Frazier 1988.
7 Fodor 1983. See also Garfield 1987.
8 Kasher 1984; and the 1991c revised version.
9 By 'force' it will always be meant what is usually called 'illocutionary force'.
10 To be sure, these are at least somewhat imprecise labels of linguistic families of phenomena. In most cases it takes at least a little theory to introduce the very family of facts to be under consideration.
11 As a prime example of the latter, we take 'talk in interaction' as studied by Schegloff and others (Sacks, Schegloff and Jefferson 1974).
12 See Fodor 1983: 101–19, where the notions of isotropic and Quineian systems are also introduced and applied.
13 Grice 1989: 31. In this context we take 'knowledge' to mean belief.
14 Austin 1962: 150; see also the related footnote.
15 For Chomsky's distinction between cognitive *i*-languages and cultural *e*-languages, see Chomsky 1986.
16 The nature of constitutive systems of rules has been analyzed in Searle 1969 and N. Kasher 1978.
17 Kasher 1977. Vanderveken has also used the idea of a recursive analysis, e.g. in his 1990–1, but his theory is couched in terms of those kinds of rule that Searle used in his essay on speech acts (1969), such as 'sincerity' conditions and the like. The cluster of rules or conditions that play a role in a system that governs speech acts of a particular type seems arbitrary, at least in comparison with the following analysis, which is couched in terms of the natural ingredients of intentional activity in general. Many of the details of Searle's and Vanderveken's works are, nevertheless, very useful.
18 Since the same act can serve a series of related ends, a distinction has to be drawn between the ends that a speech act serves in a direct way by the linguistic rules that govern it and other ends. For the former type of ends we use the term 'literal'. See Kasher 1977.
19 Strictly speaking, basic speech acts are also things done with words, but here we mean by 'things done with words' those that are not basic.
20 See Kasher 1981. We are interested in analysing the general conception of speech act as well as the basic speech acts without resorting to communication as an essential ingredient of language, but this part of the philosophical 'hard core' of the present research programme is beyond the scope of this paper. See Kasher 1991a and 1991b. We are aware of some reports that have been made to the effect that some languages do not include one basic speech act or another, but we believe that the alleged linguistic facts can be explained in a

way that is compatible with our tentative identification of some basic speech acts.

21 These systems of rules are as far as we know unique among cognitive systems that have a strong innate ingredient. Constitutive systems abound within various cultural spheres, such as games, morality (see N. Kasher 1978), art (see Kasher 1989), and religion (see Kasher 1980).

22 This project has been supported by grants from the US-Israel Binational Science Foundation (88-00116), The Basic Research Fund of the Israel National Academy of Science and the Humanities (773-92) and Tel-Aviv University. Research has been done by Eran Zaidel (UCLA) and the present author, in collaboration with Dr Rachel Giora, Dr Nahum Soroker and David Graves, as well as Sharon Agam, Tamar Etkes, Gila Batori and Mali Gil.

15 Speech act theory and Gricean pragmatics
Some differences of detail that make a difference

Marcelo Dascal

Two contributions to the philosophy of language have been extremely influential in the development of pragmatics: Searle's speech act theory and Grice's analysis of conversation. The relationship they bear to each other is very close, but not entirely free from conflicts that occasionally emerge. Over the years, I came to suspect that, behind the petty quarrels that often arise between close relatives, there may lie some serious divergences, hampering the harmony of a marriage all pragmaticists wish to be happy and fruitful. Unfortunately, such a wish has led pragmaticists to overlook the import of these divergences. Bringing them to light – I believe – will help to correct some confusions, to improve mutual understanding, and to promote peace in the pragmatic family.

In this paper, I will examine one set of related differences between the two approaches that can – as I will try to show – be traced back to a single source. In the Prolegomena to his William James Lectures on 'Logic and conversation', Grice declares that he is 'in sympathy with the general character of Searle's method' of dealing with a certain problem, but adds that he is 'not entirely happy about the details of his [Searle's] position' (Grice 1989: 15).[1] This divergence 'about the details' – I will argue – amounts in fact to quite different conceptions about the tasks and form of a suitable pragmatic theory, about the division of labour between pragmatics and semantics, and about other issues. It certainly deserves to be examined in detail.

In order to understand the problem that both Searle and Grice address, we must recall their philosophical background. Both of them come from the tradition of 'philosophical analysis' of the 'ordinary language' brand. Within this tradition, philosophically interesting concepts – such as knowledge, reality, goodness, free will – are investigated via the study of the 'logical grammar' of the key terms that ordinarily express them – for example, 'know', 'real', 'good', 'voluntarily'. By examining the conditions under which one can or cannot say, for instance, 'I know my name', 'She has a real job', 'This is a good movie', 'He came voluntarily', one would discover important facts about the meanings of the key terms and thereby of the concepts they express. For example, by noticing that in the phrase 'real job' in the above sentence 'real' is normally understood as marking a contrast between the job referred to and some occupation that is deficient in some respect (for example, in that it is intermittent, unrewarding, has little or no monetary compensation, etc.), and by observing that this is true of many other sentences containing 'real', one concludes that the meaning of the adjective 'real', unlike that of 'blue', has nothing to do with attributing some substantive property to the thing denoted by the noun it modifies; recognition of this fact, in turn, would be an important step towards getting rid of old tangles about the nature of reality. Using this kind of procedure – it was expected – philosophy would acquire a sort of empirical method, based on the analysis of linguistic phenomena, through which traditional philosophical puzzles would either be solved or dissolved.

Searle and Grice, however, questioned the assumptions underlying this method. The method consists in inferring that a certain condition characterizes the *meaning* of a word or phrase from the fact that this condition is required for the appropriate *use* of certain sentences containing that word or phrase. But inappropriateness in the use of a sentence can be due to reasons other than the non-satisfaction of some meaning condition of one of its words or phrases. In particular, these reasons may have to do with general conditions on the use of language, such as the requirement that what one asserts should be informative. Thus, the oddity of saying 'He came voluntarily' in a context where there is no reason to suspect he was dragged or otherwise forced to come could be explained in terms of its uninformativeness: in normal circumstances, it is no news that somebody has control over his actions. In this respect, 'He came voluntarily' (said in the above mentioned context) is just as odd as 'He came wearing a hat' (said in a context where all males wear hats) or even as 'He came' (said in a context where it is obvious to speaker and addressee that he came). But such an oddity does not necessarily reveal features of the meanings of 'wearing a hat', 'came' or 'voluntarily'.

Both Grice and Searle attribute the failure of the analytic philosophers' ('A-philosophers', for short) manoeuvre to their implicit acceptance of the slogan 'Meaning is use'. This slogan, Searle argues, is useless as an analytic tool, because the notion of use is too vague (Searle 1969: 146); it offers 'no way of distinguishing features of the utterance which are due solely to the occurrence of the [analysed] word from features which are due to other characteristics of the sentences or to other extraneous factors altogether' (ibid.: 147). Grice too sees the Wittgensteinian slogan as the culprit and proposes to replace it by the cautionary precept 'be careful not to confuse meaning and use' (Grice 1989: 4). Since the application of this precept requires a distinction between meaning and use, Grice's primary concern is 'to determine how any such distinction ... is to be determined' (ibid.) – a concern shared by Searle, of course (cp. Searle 1969: 154).

Both also agree that to fulfil this task, a *systematic* theory of language is needed (Searle 1969: 149; Grice 1989: 4). Searle believes he has already developed the systematic theory required to handle the phenomena uncovered in the manoeuvre (Searle 1969: 149). Grice, in his characteristic low key, declares that he 'shall be forced to take some tottering steps' (Grice 1989: 4) in the direction of formulating the required theory. Searle's systematic theory is speech act theory. He considers the successful application of the theory to the explanation of the phenomena in question as a confirmation of the theory. Grice's steps lead him to elaborate a number of concepts for the analysis of conversation – such as the Principle of Cooperation, the Maxims, and the notion of implicature. He takes for granted that such concepts can be successfully applied to explain the phenomena uncovered by the A-philosophers' manoeuvre; but he does not endeavour to do so; his concern is rather to apply them to a broader range of phenomena.

Although both Grice and Searle make use of each other's theories and although their purposes are similar, they in fact propose quite different ways of distinguishing and relating meaning and use. As a result, their ways of making these two notions more precise diverge widely and lead in fact to two different ways of conceiving pragmatics, semantics, and their mutual relations. These 'big' differences, I surmise, are already operative in their different ways of handling the philosophical manoeuvre they both criticize. Seen in this light, the divergent orientation of the two projects can be better understood.

Searle's onslaught against the A-philosophers' manoeuvre is blunt: he contends that it is a fallacious move. He analyses three kinds of fallacy of this sort, traces all of them to the lack of a clear distinction between meaning and use, and offers alternative explanations of the data in terms of speech act theory.

The 'naturalistic fallacy fallacy' consists in the claim that 'it is logically impossible for any set of statements of the kind usually called descriptive to entail a statement of the kind usually called evaluative' (Searle 1969: 132). The claim is based on the observation that to pronounce an evaluation (for example, 'This is an Extra Fancy Grade apple') is quite different from asserting that something satisfies the criteria justifying such an evaluation ('This apple has characteristics a, b, and c'). Searle admits the difference, but contends that it is a difference in the *illocutionary force of the utterances* of the two sentences: the former characteristically serves to grade the apple; the latter, to describe it. But from this fact, he argues, one cannot infer that the *proposition* expressed in one of the utterances cannot entail the *proposition* expressed in the other. For 'entailment is a matter of meaning' (Searle 1969: 154), and the meaning of 'Extra Fancy Grade' is fixed, in this case, by the Ministry of Agriculture's definition of this expression in terms of the characteristics a, b, and c; this, in turn, determines the truth conditions of the propositions expressed by the two sentences as well as their logical relations. But their illocutionary forces differ, because, in the first case it is 'a matter of the use of the special terms the sentence contains', namely 'Extra Fancy Grade', which was 'introduced so that apple sorters would have a special term for use in grading apples' (Searle 1969: 154–5). What explains (and corrects) the fallacy in this case, then, is a 'distinction between meaning and use [that] involves a distinction between truth conditions on the one hand and purpose or function on the other' (Searle 1969: 154).

The 'speech act fallacy' consists in explaining the meaning of a word in terms of the fact that its use (in present-tense indicative sentences) characteristically serves to perform a certain speech act. This is a fallacious move because it violates the requirement that if a certain feature belongs to the meaning of an expression, it should be present wherever the expression occurs.[2] Thus, if the condition 'performance of the speech act of commendation' is part of the meaning of 'good', then every (literal) occurrence of 'good' should involve the performance of that act or at least be related to performances of that act

> in a way which is purely a function of the way the sentences uttered stand in relation to the standard indicative sentences, in the utterance of which the act is performed. If they are in the past tense, then the act is reported in the past; if they are hypothetical, then the act is hypothesized, etc.
>
> (Searle 1969: 138)

But this is plainly false, Searle contends, for 'It used to be good' is not equivalent to 'I used to commend it'; 'If that movie is good, then its director deserves the Academy Award' is not equivalent to 'If I commend that movie, then its director deserves the Academy Award'; etc.

Although he rejects the speech act analysis of the meaning of words such as 'good', Searle wants to preserve the intuition that the meaning of such words *is* somehow connected with the performance of specific speech acts. He insists that such a connection is not 'just a contingent fact' (ibid.: 150) but rather 'a matter of conceptual truth' (ibid.: 151) or a 'quasi-necessary truth'.[3] But his explanation of this intuition is quite puzzling. He says that 'good' is a 'grading label', one of a range of terms used for the purpose of performing acts of assessing, grading, evaluating, judging, etc. Furthermore, the assessment it serves to perform is positive, that is, is such that it might be expressed by illocutionary verbs such as 'commend', 'praise', etc. So, 'good' is 'embedded in the institutions' of assessing, grading, evaluating, etc., in a particular way. This is why calling something good is commending. But, Searle contends, to admit *this* is not to say what the meaning of 'good' is, because 'the connection between the meaning of "good" and the performance of the speech act of commendation, *though a necessary one*, is thus a connection at one remove' (Searle 1969: 152; my italics). This is puzzling because the connection is described, in the same paragraph, as both 'quasi-necessary' and 'necessary'. Now, if it is necessary (at whatever number of 'removes'), then it is a matter of meaning, not of use, since 'entailment is a matter of meaning'. If so, the connection with commending does, after all, pertain to the meaning of 'good', contrary to Searle's claim. We will return to this puzzle below.

The 'assertion fallacy' consists in 'confusing the conditions for the performance of the speech act of assertion with the analysis of the meaning of particular words occurring in certain assertions' (Searle 1969: 141). According to Searle, the oddity of *saying*, in ordinary circumstances, things such as 'He came voluntarily' has nothing to do with the concept expressed by 'voluntarily', just as the oddity of saying (in ordinary circumstances) 'He is breathing' has nothing to do with the concept of breathing. Both assertions are odd because, in standard or normal circumstances, their truth is obvious. What they infringe is a condition on 'what it is to make an assertion' (Searle 1969: 144). Speech act theory treats this condition as a *preparatory condition*, shared by the 'information bearing class of speech acts (reports, descriptions, assertions, etc.)'. One of its formulations is: 'it must not be too obviously the case to both S[peaker] and H[earer] that p – if the assertion that p is to be non-defective' (Searle 1969: 149). Since, for Searle, in making an assertion one *implies* the satisfaction of its preparatory conditions, whoever asserts, say, 'He came voluntarily' thereby implies that the context is not normal (for in a normal context the truth of the assertion would be obvious); if this is not the case, then his assertion is defective. The oddity observed by the A-philosopher is thus explained by the disjunction: either the context is not normal or the assertion of p in that context is defective.

Unlike the case of the 'speech act fallacy', there is no intuition about the 'quasi-necessary' connection of a particular word with a speech act to be preserved here. The data are therefore explained quite generally by appeal to one of the *rules* of assertion-making and to a general *presumption* of normality. Notice that, while the former is 'embedded' in the institution of asserting, since it is one of its constitutive rules, the latter is not. It belongs rather to the general background of *any* use of language.[4] As for the non-obviousness condition, Searle acknowledges that

> it runs through so many kinds of illocutionary acts that I think it is not a matter of separate rules for the utterance of particular illocutionary-force indicating devices at all, but rather is a general condition on illocutionary acts ... to the effect that the act is defective if the point to be achieved by the satisfaction of the essential condition is already achieved.

> (Searle 1969: 69)

Nevertheless, he still treats it as a *rule*, albeit a general one, that bears on whether an illocutionary act is *defective* or not. In Grice's system, on the other hand, this 'rule' becomes one of the Maxims (roughly, the Maxim of Quantity).[5] As such, it is, like the condition of normality, a *presumption*, derived from the general presumption of co-operation in communicative behaviour. This difference in status of the non-obviousness (and other) condition(s) is significant, for it marks Searle's preference for treating conditions of use in terms of strict logical relations, as opposed to Grice's tendency to treat them in another way. We shall return to this topic below.

Consider now the puzzle about the quasi-necessary connection between 'good' and the act of commending. What is supposed to explain the quasi-necessary character of the connection and hence the claim that it is not a matter of meaning but of use is the fact that it is mediated by the 'embedding' of an expression in a class of illocutionary 'institutions'. Spelling out the nature of such institutions is the cornerstone of Searle's theory of speech acts. This is done through the enumeration of the *necessary* conditions for performing a specific type of speech act. Such conditions are the *constitutive rules* for the correct performance of the act (Searle 1969: 65ff.). If the act is correctly performed, this *implies* that the rules have been followed, i.e., that the conditions have been satisfied. The institutional facts about speech acts consist, therefore, in a network of *analytic* relations, i.e., *conceptual truths.*[6] But they are not truths about the meanings of particular expressions, except perhaps about the meanings of the *names* of speech acts, such as 'request', 'promise', 'assertion'. For the theory is not about labels or linguistic expressions. It is a general theory about what is required for an act to count as a specific move in the game of speaking, regardless of the particular expressions used in performing the moves or even of the ways different languages provide 'different conventional realizations of the same underlying rule' (Searle 1969: 39).

Now, what does it mean to say that an expression is 'embedded' in the institution that defines a speech act? Presumably, that its *raison d'être* is to be a linguistic realization of (part of) that speech act's constitutive rules. Thus, performative verbs serve primarily as linguistic realizations of illocutionary points; similarly, expressions such as 'amen', 'please', 'hereby', 'His Majesty', 'Extra Fancy Grade', etc., serve primarily as indicators of illocutionary point or of other constitutive aspects of speech acts. If this is the primary function of these words, then to describe their *meanings* without referring to such functions would be grossly inadequate. Consequently, the appeal to the notion of embedding amounts in fact to a (partial) specification of *meaning* in terms of speech act rules, which are supposed to belong to the domain of use.

Thus, although Searle attributes the three fallacies to a lack of a precise distinction between meaning and use, what we discover is that his way of drawing this distinction is neither as steady nor as tight as he might have wanted it to be. Sometimes it is the distinction between truth conditions and illocutionary forces; sometimes, the distinction between the domain of logical relations and the domain of some 'quasi-logical' relations; sometimes it has to do with what is and what is not 'embedded' in the set of institutional conditions required for the performance of speech acts. But it turns out that none of these pairs is exclusively on the side of use or of meaning. Illocutionary acts have satisfaction conditions, which closely parallel truth conditions. These acts and their components are related via entailments and other logical relations, whose elucidation is the job of illocutionary logic. The meanings of certain expressions are characterized in terms of their role in the performance of certain speech acts, to which they are linked either logically or quasi-logically. Illocutionary points, the main components of speech acts, can be units of meaning.

This free interplay between meaning and use should come as no surprise since, ultimately, the difference between them is theoretically otiose for Searle. The immediate reason for this is his adoption of the 'Principle of Expressibility', according to which 'whatever can be meant can be said' (Searle 1969: 19). This principle establishes in fact a one-to-one correspondence between meanings and uses:

> it enables us to equate rules for performing speech acts with rules for uttering certain linguistic elements, since for any possible speech act there is a possible linguistic element *the meaning of which* (given the context of the utterance) is sufficient to determine that its *literal* utterance is a performance of precisely that speech act.
>
> (Searle 1969: 20–1; my italics)

In the light of such an equivalence, the study of speech acts amounts to the study of the meanings of the relevant linguistic elements, and vice versa.

In so far as traditional semantics did not include in its theoretical vocabulary notions such as 'illocutionary point', 'preparatory conditions', etc., it gave only an incomplete semantics of linguistic expressions. What speech act theory does is to enlarge and complete traditional semantics by adding the missing elements. No wonder that it employs the same devices of traditional semantics – necessary and sufficient conditions, analyticity, logically binding rules. It thus *codifies* uses, just as traditional semantics codifies meanings. Furthermore, it purports to be *complete*, in the sense of defining the set of all possible illocutionary acts in terms of a small number of primitives. Such a feat is hailed as a major achievement, for it dispels the 'illusion of limitless uses of language' (Searle 1979: 29) fostered by Wittgenstein and his followers. Instead, speech act theory shows that 'there are rather a limited number of basic things we do with language' (ibid.), all the rest being combinations or variations of these basic things.

There are, however, a number of ways in which the theory is incomplete *qua* theory of use, some of them acknowledged by Searle, others not. In the first place, there are many cases where a speaker does not say exactly what he means. But these, Searle contends, 'are not theoretically essential to linguistic communication' (Searle 1969: 20). They are not essential because the non-literal, ambiguous, or incomplete utterances can *in principle* be paraphrased by their literal, unambiguous, and complete equivalents, which unequivocally *determine* the speech acts performed through the former. Nevertheless, speech act theory *per se* does not have the apparatus necessary for providing the relevant paraphrases. In fact, it borrows this apparatus from Grice's theory, as Searle's treatment of indirect speech acts (Searle 1979: 30–57) and metaphor (ibid.: 76–116) shows. It is as if Grice's theory provided merely a sort of 'transformational' component that relates 'surface' utterances to their 'deep structures', the latter being fully and unambiguously described by the semantics of speech acts.

Second, the theory is incomplete because literal meanings are not really context-free. They depend on an inarticulate Background (Searle 1980) that cannot be made fully explicit. Without this background, even a literal utterance of a sentence is unable to determine unequivocally *precisely* one speech act. But the fact that the background is inarticulate means that it cannot itself be completely represented semantically. Use involves, then, something irreducible to semantics, even to the all encompassing semantics of speech acts.

Third, the theory itself is insufficient for determining whether a given utterance is literal or not. The fact that even perfectly complete, un-ambiguous, and unproblematic sentences can be used indirectly or non-literally requires the existence of some procedure to determine whether *any* of its uses is literal or not. Since only literal utterances correspond to the specification of precisely one speech act, unless such a procedure is avail-able the reduction of use to meaning cannot be achieved. Again, one may borrow for that purpose the apparatus of Grice's theory. But since it would apply, in this case, not only to 'problematic' utterances, but to all utter-ances, its application would touch not the 'surface' but the 'base' com-ponent of the semantics of speech acts. Taken together with the kind of incompleteness due to the role of the Background, this suggests that the formalism or language of the semantics of speech acts is not self-sufficient, in the sense of not offering completely unambiguous representations of meanings.

In his brief remarks on Searle's handling of the A-philosophers' manoeuvre, Grice raises doubts about the precise status of the non-obviousness con-dition for assertions or remarks. Referring to a version of Searle's argument prior to *Speech Acts* (1969), Grice observes that

> Sometimes Searle seems to hold that if the assertibility condition is unfulfilled in the case of a particular utterance, that utterance fails to *be* an assertion; sometimes he seems to hold that, in such a case, it is an assertion which is *out of order*; and sometimes that it is a *pointless* assertion (or remark).

(Grice 1989: 18)

In terms of the later developments of speech act theory, the first alternative corresponds to an *unsuccessful* assertion and the second (as well as perhaps the third, in one of its possible senses) to a *defective* assertion. Now, significantly, Grice picks up the third alternative as the one he considers acceptable: 'the only tenable version of Searle's thesis (which is of course a version to which he subscribes) is that an utterance or remark to the effect that p will be inappropriate if it is pointless' (Grice 1989: 19). 'Indeed [he continues] it would be difficult to disagree with this thesis, and much of what I have to say can be looked upon as a development and extension of the idea contained in it' (ibid.).

The question is, do Searle and Grice subscribe to this thesis *in the same sense*? I think the answer is clearly negative. In *Speech Acts* and later, Searle clearly claims that, in normal contexts, failure to comply with the condition entails defectiveness, i.e., the second, not the third of Grice's alternative readings. And defectiveness is not just a matter of 'inappropriateness', for it has to do with the infringement of one of the constitutive rules of assertion-making. So, Grice's concern, 'lest in accepting this thesis, I be thought to be committing myself to more than I would want to commit myself to' (Grice 1989: 19) is fully justified. What he does not want to be committed to is the view he rightly suspects Searle to hold, namely that

> speech acts of the illocutionary sort [are] conventional acts, the nature of which is to be explained by a specification of the constitutive rules which govern each such act, and on which the possibility of performing the act at all depends.
>
> (ibid.)

Grice opposes this view, for he doubts that 'any *rule* to the effect that a remark should not be made if to make it would be pointless ... would be among the rules the exposition of which would be required to explain the nature of remarking' (ibid.: 20; my italics). Instead, he proposes to account for the inappropriateness in question in terms of 'other features which remarks characteristically have, together perhaps with some more general principles governing communication or even rational behavior' (ibid.).

These principles are, of course, those of his analysis of conversation. The way they might explain the A-philosophers' data is quite different from Searle's way. Typically, these principles generate *suggestions* rather than strictly deductive conclusions. Consequently, such suggestions have no *analytic* force. In short, they do not belong to the realm of *meaning*. And they do not belong to this realm because their generation depends essentially on the intervention of principles of communication that are not part of the meaning of any linguistic expression. Furthermore, such principles function as presumptions, i.e., they are defeasible rules of inference. The inferences they license are, thus, cancellable *without* contradiction, unlike what happens with implications or presuppositions. Treated as a presumption, the rule 'If A asserts that p, then p is not obvious', applied to A's assertion that p (in normal circumstances), does not *entail* that p is in fact not obvious. It only *suggests* that one should proceed on this assumption, unless proven otherwise. Conversely, if such a proof obtains, i.e., if it turns out that p is obvious, this only *suggests* that A may not have in fact asserted that p, rather than proving that his assertion was defective. Whereas in Searle's scheme the defectiveness of the assertion is the obligatory explanation of the obviousness of the remark (given that, *ex hypothesi,* the situation is normal), on the presumptive reading of this rule, other lines of reasoning are open to the addressee: he can inquire whether the presumption holds *in this particular case* (for example, whether A is indeed engaged in co-operative communication), whether it has been deliberately flouted, whether A's assertion is non-obvious in some other way, etc.

Though the suggestions generated through reliance on the communicative maxims are not analytic, they are robust and stable enough to ensure communicative success. In this sense, they offer a natural explanation for the intuition of 'quasi-necessary' connections. Paraphrasing Leibniz, we might say that they incline without necessitating. There is no need to explain this binding force by overburdening the analytic apparatus, the well-behaved domain of logic, which Grice is eager to preserve (see Grice 1989: 22–4). On the other hand, precisely because they are not analytic, they have the necessary flexibility to account for the unpredictable and less well-behaved – though by no means unsystematic – characteristics of language use.

No doubt Searle's speech act theory and Grice's analysis of conversation can complement each other, because each needs the other: Searle's theory because of the kinds of incompleteness mentioned above; Grice's, because the generation of implicatures relies on an initial tentative identification of the utterance meaning, most naturally provided by the semantics of speech acts. But the two theories differ in the kind of understanding they have of what is 'use'. Consequently they suggest quite different models for accounting for use. The difference can be highlighted by a number of oppositions, roughly expressed by means of a few keywords:

Searle	*Grice*
Monological	Dialogical
Formal	Informal
Conventional	Non-conventional
Grammatical model	Non-grammatical model
Constitutive rules	Heuristic rules, presumptions
Implication	Implicature
Semantic	Pragmatic (?)
. . .	. . .

One of the consequences of the adoption by Searle of a particular kind of model is that, for him, phenomena not amenable to treatment in terms of this model are not to be handled as part of a theory of linguistic communication. If such phenomena are at all 'structured', such a structure derives from 'external' principles, alien to the principles of linguistic communication. One such phenomenon is, according to him, conversation (see Searle 1992a). I have criticized this position elsewhere (Dascal 1992), and will not repeat my arguments here. Let me only mention one point in that debate, which acquires an emblematic value in the present context. Searle is certainly right in saying that ' "conversation" does not name a unit of meaning' (Searle 1992b: 143). If this means that conversation cannot be accounted for in terms of the semantic model, I could not agree more. But if this means that 'conversation' does not name a unit of linguistic communication, so that its structure is 'external' to a theory of linguistic communication or use, then Searle's statement simply expresses his own presumption that his is the only possible model for a theory of use.

Speech act theory seeks to treat what it calls 'use' by means of strict rules, which can be formalized into a precise illocutionary logic. It seeks to demonstrate that use can be treated as rigorously as meaning has been; that it is no longer the vague notion used by the A-philosophers; that it is not a matter of an indefinite number of vaguely defined language games. But it may have gone too far in its reduction of use to meaning, thereby proving rather than disproving the slogan it originally opposed. The price of this operation is – as usual – the abandonment of those aspects of the phenomena that do not fit the model and the attempted reduction. Those aspects of use that do not readily fit the institutional mould, the rule-based treatment, are either left to be handled by a complementary theory of use *à la* Grice, or else dumped in the ever present Background. To say that conversation or other aspects of use have no 'intrinsic structure' is to say that they do not fit the kind of structure privileged by Searle. But this does not mean that they have no organization whatsoever. It only means that their principles of organization allow for the open-endedness, the vagueness, the defeasibility that, although not easily codifiable, endow the use of language with a measure of creativity well beyond the rule-based creativity permitted by grammar. To Searle's credit it should be said that, in acknowledging the need for a complementation of his theory, he has at least indicated the need and possibility of another kind of pragmatics.

NOTES

1 Grice's relevant articles are now collected in Grice 1989.
2 Cp. Searle 1969: 137, 152. I have called this requirement the 'Principle of the Invariance of Meaning' (Dascal 1983: 28) and have showed that it is widely used in the philosophy of language and in linguistics. An example of Grice's use of this principle can be found in Grice 1989: 17.
3 Searle 1969: 152. In an earlier paper criticizing Hare's speech act analysis of 'good', Searle argued that, though the act of commendation is not performed in every occasion when 'good' is used, it is 'in the offing' in every such occasion (Searle 1962). This unexplained notion, which is used in that paper to explain the 'non-contingent' character of the connection between 'good' and commending, appears also in *Speech Acts*, in the discussion of another example of the 'speech act fallacy' (Searle

1969: 153). In many respects, the later notion of Background (e.g. Searle 1979: 120ff.) incorporates the earlier notion of 'in the offing', without doing much to clarify it.

4   Presumably it is also part of what Searle later calls the Background. For, to say that 'there are standard or normal situations' (Searle 1969: 144), is not to spell out or articulate what these conditions are in each case.

5   In later versions of speech act theory, another of Grice's Maxims, the Maxim of Quality, is also treated as a preparatory condition: 'the speaker has reasons for the truth of the propositional content' (Vanderveken 1985: 186). Vanderveken also stresses that preparatory conditions are strict *presuppositions* of an illocutionary act, a fact allegedly shown by their non-cancellability and by the consequent parad-oxical character of trying to perform an illocutionary act while at the same time denying its preparatory condition, as in 'You cannot do it but, please, do it!' Sentences such as these are said to be 'linguistically odd' and 'indeed analytically unsuccessful' (Vanderveken 1990–1: vol. I, 115).

6   It should be recalled that Searle (1969: 5ff.) as well as Grice (1989: 196–212) oppose Quine's attempt to eliminate the analytic–synthetic distinction.

16 Are there indirect speech acts?

Rod Bertolet

My purpose in this paper is to explore a sceptical hypothesis about indirect speech acts. The hypothesis is easily stated: there are no indirect speech acts, at least not of the sort that have been prominent in the literature, for example, questions that are also requests. I say that I wish to explore this hypothesis because I am not entirely sure that it is true. I do however think that it deserves to be taken seriously, and I shall outline the argument for thinking this in what follows. The main reason is that the same methodological presumptions that favour what I regard as the most plausible accounts of indirect speech act over their competitors *also* favour taking the sceptical hypothesis seriously.[1] The main evidence in favour of the existence of indirect speech acts, and hence against the sceptical hypothesis, is a well-known set of examples that seem to obviously involve a certain indirectness of communication. It is no part of the sceptical hypothesis to question this point about the indirect conveyance of a message. What I wish to put in doubt is the *explanation* that the various theories of indirect speech acts provide in terms of the performance of a second illocutionary act. Where I wish to begin, then, is with a brief survey of the sorts of examples in question, with as few presumptions about what the proper treatment of these examples is as possible.

SOME FAMILIAR EXAMPLES

At dinner, your companion utters. 'Can you reach the salt?', and you pass the salt to her without pausing to comment on the fact that you can indeed reach it. Later, she utters, 'Are you going to eat those beans?', and you hand them over or reply 'Please, help yourself.' Departing after dinner, you notice undue pressure on your foot and utter 'You're standing on my foot'; your companion removes her foot from yours and apologizes. Here, what is on the face of it a question about one's ability to reach the salt is treated as if it were a request to pass it, what appears to be a question about your intentions with respect to some beans has been treated as if it were a request to be given those beans, and what seems to be a straightforward comment on the placement of someone's foot has been treated as if it were a request to move it.

Qualifiers such as *appears* (to be a question) or *seems* (to be a comment) are called for because, as many have observed, it is no part of the literal meaning of 'Can you reach the salt?' that it has the illocutionary force of a request. Indeed, that such an utterance might be used to make a request seems to be inconsistent with the literal meaning of that sentence, which gives it the force of a question. And yet these utterances are treated as if they were requests, and so perhaps these appearances are misleading.

THE INDIRECT SPEECH ACT ACCOUNT

According to the theory of indirect speech acts, these appearances are indeed genuine, but they are not the whole story. That is, you *have* been asked questions about your ability to reach the salt and intentions regarding a pile of beans, and you have made a comment about the location of her foot, but that is only part of the story, and is indeed the relatively unimportant part. The question about your ability to reach the salt is direct but secondary, serving the primary, indirect speech act of requesting you to pass the salt. Thus, Searle:

> For example, a speaker may utter the sentence 'Can you reach the salt?' and mean it not merely as a question but as a request to pass the salt.
>
> In such cases it is important to emphasize that the utterance is meant as a request; that is, the speaker intends to produce in the hearer the knowledge that a request has been made to him, and he intends to produce this knowledge by means of getting the hearer to recognize his intention to produce it. Such cases, in which the utterance has two illocutionary forces, are to be sharply distinguished from the cases in which, for example, the speaker tells the hearer that he wants him to do something; and then the hearer does it because the speaker wants him to, though no request at all has been made, meant, or understood. The cases we will be discussing are indirect speech acts, cases in which one illocutionary act is performed indirectly by way of performing another.
>
> (Searle 1979: 30–1)

The claims that I wish to question are that (a) the utterance actually has two illocutionary forces; and (b) (this is because) the speaker actually performs two illocutionary acts. It is not so much Searle's account of such alleged facts that I question, as the allegation that they are facts, which is shared by those whose accounts Searle criticizes and those who criticize Searle's own account. What I want to deny is the inference from the fact that the utterances in question are treated *as if* they were requests, to the conclusion that they actually *are* requests, in addition to questions or comments. It will be useful to develop this point just a bit before moving on.

It is often remarked that if one utters 'It's cold in here' to one's butler, the utterance has the force of an order (an order to close the window, perhaps). This may be so, but it is not to say, and I suggest that we should not say, that the utterance *is* an order.[2] In general, x has the force of y (or counts as y, to use another phrase of Searle's) only when x *is not* y.[3] Even in this specialized social situation, while the butler can indeed be expected to treat the utterance *as if it were* an order, this does not entail that the utterance *is* an order. Of course, I have not yet given any argument for this claim. I do think that, intuitively, this is the right thing to say (or, not say), but my argument for this claim is primarily methodological. I do not see any need to postulate a second speech act, or a second illocutionary force to account for what are usually called indirect speech acts. Here, I am in complete agreement with the sort of criticism Searle offers against, for example, Gordon and Lakoff's (1971) conversational postulates, and it will be helpful to next review that criticism, along with objections to the view that sentences such as 'Can you reach the salt?' are ambiguous.

OBJECTIONS TO SEMANTIC ACCOUNTS

Searle notes that his theory does not require that we assume that there are conversational postulates, concealed imperative forces or other ambiguities. He suggests that we can get by with

> a theory of speech acts, certain general principles of cooperative conversation (some of which have been discussed by Grice) and mutually shared factual background information of the speaker and hearer, together with an ability on the part of the hearer to make inferences.
>
> (Searle 1979: 32)

The general point, made more explicit in Searle (1979: 162–79), is that if we can explain the relevant phenomena without appeal to conversational postulates (which are basically Carnapian meaning postulates) or postulated ambiguities, we *should* avoid such semantic complications in our theory. This strategy, which is also critical in Bach and Harnish's rejection of the ambiguity thesis and other approaches (Bach and Harnish 1979: ch. 9), as well as Morgan's (1978) discussion, and inspired by Grice's work on conversational implicature, is one that I wholeheartedly endorse.[4] While the strategy is common enough nowadays, I think it is worthwhile to look at it a little more closely, to make a point that I hope does not seem unduly fussy.

A main vice of the view that sentences standardly used indirectly have meanings additional to their literal ones (the ambiguity thesis) is, according to both Searle, and Bach and Harnish, that it multiplies meanings beyond necessity. But precisely what vice is this? We are usually told that it offends against Occam's Razor.[5] Perhaps most recently, in his quest to avoid the multiplication of unnecessary meanings and semantic ambiguity, Vanderveken claims that his strategy is to use, 'as Grice advises, Occam's Razor' (Vanderveken (1990–1: vol I, 75; he cites Grice 1975). Interestingly, Grice gives no such advice. Grice's own term for the injunction 'Senses are not to be multiplied beyond necessity' is 'Modified Occam's Razor' (1975: 47), and it is clear from the several paragraphs he devotes to the question of what support it might have that he thinks the modification is substantive. Why might this be? I suggest that Occam's Razor bids us to abjure the postulation of *kinds* of things that do not enjoy explanatory value. It's a little hard to defend this claim since our formulations of Occam's Razor are not his; he wrote things that are translated as 'Plurality is not to be posited without necessity' (see Hyman and Walsh 1973: 606). Still, he is most famous for arguing not against redness or roundness, but against universals wholesale, and that is why I think that Grice thinks, and at any rate why I think, that Grice's injunction against the unnecessary proliferation of senses or meanings is a modification of Occam's principle. Those who are already up to their necks in literal meanings will not find Occam's Razor useful in fending off a few more, and the same is true of illocutionary forces. The Razor will, assuming that an ontologically more parsimonious explanation is available, counsel us to forgo Gordon and Lakoff's conversational postulates entirely as idly postulated in the face of the alternative explanation. But this is a rather different point, one that really does ban a *kind* of thing, a conversational postulate. What is at issue regarding the ambiguity thesis is whether to postulate *more than one* sense of an expression to which we have already assigned one such sense. I agree that this is a vice, and one that transgresses theoretical economy, but despite certain similarities it is not the vice against which Occam's Razor proper cuts.[6]

While this qualification is worth mentioning, and frequently overlooked, the main point is indeed that a plausible and motivated theory that avoids ambiguities (or conversational postulates) is to be preferred over one that requires such postulates or ambiguities. This is the strategy that underlies Searle's objections to such theories, and Bach and Harnish's objections to Sadock and others.[7] What I shall suggest is that the same methodological presumptions tell against postulating indirect illocutionary forces and illocutionary acts.

NON-SPEECH ACTS

Let us start with some simple physical acts. Morgan notes that

> If upon being asked my opinion of a spinach soufflé I have been served, I shovel the contents of my plate into the dog's dish, I have rendered my judgement as clearly as if I had said 'It's awful', though less directly.
>
> (Morgan 1978: 265)

While I am not sure that this is less direct than an utterance, it does seem clear that Morgan is right to say that a judgement has been clearly rendered.[8] Presumably, no one would want to claim that Morgan had performed any speech act at all, since he did not speak. Now suppose, to modify an example from the beginning of this paper, that instead of asking your companion whether she is going to finish her beans, you simply gaze longingly at them. This may well serve to make the point that you would like those beans, and get them transferred to your plate. But it will not add up, directly or indirectly, to the illocutionary act of requesting the beans, since illocutionary acts are *speech* acts and your performance has been notably silent. Your imploring gaze may 'have the force of' a request, but it is not one.[9] The relevance of these examples is that they show how we can make our opinions and desires perfectly clear, and get them acknowledged or satisfied, without (I hope) provoking the slightest inclination to say that the non-speaker has actually made any statement or request. My suggestion about so-called indirect speech acts, with one caveat to be noted below (pp. 341–5) is that there is nothing more going on in those examples than in the ones just surveyed, except for the presence of a conversational implicature generated by what the speaker says or asks.

BACK TO SPEECH ACTS

I am inclined to accept what Morgan calls the natural approach to indirect speech acts, which he describes as follows:

> even when I mean to make a *request* in uttering 'Can you pass the salt?', I am using the sentence with its literal meaning of a yes/no question; the fact that, by asking this yes/no question, I can manage to convey what amounts to a request is not a matter of knowledge of English, but a consequence of Grice's maxims, which are, roughly, a set of rules for inferring the intentions behind speech acts, or, from the speaker's view-point, for selecting one's utterances so as to convey one's intentions, by exploiting the maxims. Given that the need for Grice's maxims has already been clearly demonstrated and that we can show how the request nature of 'Can you pass the salt?' is 'calculable', that is, can be derived from Grice's maxims, then Occam's razor dictates that we take this as the correct analysis, lacking strong evidence to the contrary.[10]

As many have noted, one who utters 'Can you pass the salt?' at a dinner table typically cannot be taken to have any real interest in the hearer's competence at salt-passing. What the speaker does have an interest in, and indicates an interest in, is having the salt passed. But how is this indicated? In apparently inquiring about an ability in which he presumably has no interest, the speaker seems to violate either a maxim of quantity by making a conversational contribution greater or less than required, or the maxim of relation enjoining us to be relevant.[11] This indicates that the speaker has some other point to make, which, as we all know, is that he would like to have the salt; the postulation of that desire brings his utterance into conformity with Grice's maxims after all. The postulation of that desire is however *all* that is required to restore the speaker's conversational honour. There is no need to assume, in addition, that the speaker is actually requesting that the salt be passed. The postulation of a second, indirect, illocutionary act of requesting in this case is as idle as the postulation of a request in the case of staring at the beans. It is all right to say that the utterance functions as a request, if this merely means that it is intended and treated *as if it were* a request, but this is not to say that it actually *is* a request. The implicature that the speaker would like to have the salt is all that is required.[12]

Perhaps it would be useful to compare the outline of the inferences Searle thinks the hearer would need to go through to arrive at the correct conclusion with the picture that emerges from the position I am advocating. The first five of the ten steps in his bare-bones reconstruction are as follows:

> *Step 1*: Y has asked me a question as to whether I have the ability to pass the salt (fact about the conversation).
> *Step 2*: I assume that he is cooperating in the conversation and that therefore his utterance has some aim or point (principles of conversational cooperation).
> *Step 3*: The conversational setting is not such as to indicate a theoretical interest in my salt-passing ability (factual background information).
> *Step 4*: Furthermore, he probably already knows that the answer to the question is yes (factual background information). (This step facilities the move to Step 5, but it is not essential.)
> *Step 5*: Therefore, his utterance is probably not just a question. It probably has some ulterior illocutionary point (inference from Steps 1, 2, 3, and 4). What can it be?

> (Searle 1979: 46)

The inference in step 5 seems to be quite unsubstantiated. It is reasonable to infer (and for the speaker to intend that the hearer infer) that the speaker has some ulterior point, but why would this have to be an *illocutionary* point? I cannot see any reason for this qualification (I will consider some alleged linguistic evidence later). The only ulterior point that is required is, again, that the speaker would like to have the salt – a desire that a socially co-operative dinner companion will act to satisfy without being asked.

Were it not for a complication to be discussed in the next section, I would now claim that this is all that goes on with so-called indirect speech acts.

THE ROLE OF CONVENTION OR STANDARDIZATION

Searle observes that stock sentences such as 'Can you reach the salt?' 'seem almost to be conventionally used as indirect' requests (1979: 31), and claims that the hearer 'simply hears it as a request' (ibid.: 46)[13] His explanation is that within the framework of the theory of speech acts and the principles of conversational co-operation that make indirect speech acts possible and intelligible, 'certain forms will tend to become conventionally established as the standard idiomatic forms for indirect speech acts', so that while they retain their literal meanings 'they will acquire conventional uses as, e.g., polite forms for requests' (ibid.: 49). Developing the idea that there can be conventions of language use that are not conventions of meaning, but declining to say that such standard forms are idioms, Morgan suggests that the relevant convention of use is 'To request someone to do such-and-such indirectly, say the sentence "Can you (do such-and-such)?", with its literal sense.'[14] He continues:

> My proposal, then, goes like this: The expression 'Can you . . .' is not an idiom, but has only the obvious literal meaning of a question about the hearer's abilities. One can readily see how the expression could have, via Grice's maxims, the implicature of a request. In fact it has become conventional to use the expression in this way. Thus speakers know not only that 'Can you . . .' has a certain literal meaning (a convention of language); they know also that using 'Can you . . .' is a standard way of indirectly making a request (a convention of usage). Both are involved in a full understanding by the hearer of what is intended in the use of the expression.
>
> (Morgan 1978: 274)

Bach and Harnish think this is on the right track but none the less mistaken, for a number of reasons.[15] Some of the key ones are that if 'there were conventions of use that would allow the speaker to perform the indirect act conventionally and so allow it to be heard as a request only' (recall Searle's claim that one just hears 'Can you pass the salt?' as a request), we could not maintain (a) that 'Can you pass the salt?' is uttered with and as having its apparent literal meaning; (b) that the literal illocutionary act is performed as well as the indirect one; (c) that the act is *indirect* at all.[16] Instead of a genuine convention, they propose a notion of illocutionary standardization to account for (among other things) the way in which the inference that the hearer would have to make initially is short-circuited once a certain form of expression gains common acceptance. It is as follows, where 'MB-ed' stands for 'mutually believed' and 'the CP' for the Gricean co-operative principle (the rest should be obvious):

> *T* is standardly used to *F* in *G* if and only if:
> (i) It is MB-ed in *G* that generally when a member of *G* utters *T*, his illocutionary intent is to *F*, and

(ii) Generally when a member of *G* utters *T* in a context in which it would violate the CP to utter *T* with (merely) its literally determined force, his illocutionary intent is to *F*.[17]

The point is of course to have a way of dealing with the fact that 'Can you pass the salt?' is, unlike 'Are you able to pass the salt?', the sentence that one typically utters when one wants the salt, without falling into the difficulties they see in claiming that this is truly a convention. What is unclear, is why we cannot just say *that* – that this is the, or better a,[18] sentence known to be typically uttered when one wants the salt – without postulating mutual beliefs about illocutionary intentions that strike me as dubious. As I indicated earlier, I think that we can explain the relevant inference without appeal to such.

This, however, supposes that there *is* an inference and hence seems to ignore the intuition that one simply hears the utterance as a request, and the rather plausible point that the inference required when sentences are first used to indicate an interest in the salt is short-circuited eventually, as such uses become more standard. As Morgan puts it, 'the "feel" of an implicature is lacking' (Morgan 1978: 274). I am not clear about what to say about these points. I am not sure that it is correct to say that, psychologically, one just hears it as a request, though certainly one just *treats* it as a request. (In terms of the familiar analogy between words and tools, to say that one uses a screwdriver to hammer in a nail is not to say that one views or 'sees it as' a hammer.) In fact, while it is not entirely decisive, there is some empirical work that suggests that hearers do first compute the literal meaning of the uttered sentence and then go on to infer the so-called indirect request.[19] But in any event, these points can be accommodated with a notion of standardization applicable not to illocutionary forces, but rather to the beliefs and/or desires that lie behind these utterances. For the case at hand, this would be:

'Can you pass the salt?' (T) is standardly used to indicate a desire to have the salt passed in G if, and only if:
(i) It is MB-ed in G that generally when a member of G utters T, he desires to have the salt passed to him; and
(ii) Generally when a member of G utters T in a context when it would violate the CP to utter T with (merely) its literally determined force, he desires to have the salt passed to him.

This seems to me no less plausible than Bach and Harnish's account of illocutionary standardization, and the mutual beliefs it specifies will do just as well to short-circuit the normal process of interpretation. And we can help ourselves to the account Bach and Harnish give of the point that the sentence seems to be used with its customary meaning and force: an utterance of 'Can you pass the salt?' in such circumstances 'is literally an act of asking a question, albeit with obvious insincerity'.[20] While this is somewhat tangential, I am dubious of their extension of this point:

Given the social supposition that it is impolite to impose on people and in particular to tell them to do things, to request indirectly is to 'ask without asking,' or to ask without explicitly asking – that is, by doing something else and letting the request be implied. One is asking, of course, but in such a way that one gives the appearance, albeit transparent, of not asking. Instead, one gives the appearance of posing a question.

(Bach and Harnish 1979: 196)

On their account, however, one does not give the appearance of posing a question, one *does* literally pose a question, although with obvious insincerity. The thought that one might 'ask without asking' seems to be as paradoxical as it sounds; I suggest that these are simply cases in which one lets it be known that one wants something done *without* asking, explicitly or indirectly. It is, I continue to maintain, a mistake to claim that one really is asking, which does not clearly satisfy the demands of politeness anyway.

To return to the main thread about standardization, it is important that even if my doubts about short-circuiting in the 'standard' cases are ill-founded, the notion of illocutionary standardization will not do as a *general* account of so-called indirect speech acts. Consider, in support of this, the nineteen ways of (allegedly) indirectly requesting someone to shut the door Levinson gives, as the beginning of what he contends is an indefinitely long list:

  a. I want you to close the door.
      I'd be much obliged if you'd close the door.
  b. Can you close the door?
      Are you able by any chance to close the door?
  c. Would you close the door?
      Won't you close the door?
  d. Would you mind closing the door?
      Would you be willing to close the door?
  e. You ought to close the door.
      It might help to close the door.
      Hadn't you better close the door?
  f. May I ask you to close the door?
      Would you mind awfully if I was to ask you to close the door?
      I am sorry to have to tell you to please close the door.
  g. Did you forget the door?
      Do us a favour with the door, love.
      How about a bit less breeze?
      Now Johnny, what do big people do when they come in?
      Okay, Johnny, what am I going to say next?

(Levinson 1983: 264–5)

While it is often observed that sentences such as 'Can you pass the salt?'

are more amenable to indirection than ones like 'Are you able to pass the salt?', this should not be taken to show that *only* the typically used sentences are suitable for these purposes. I think Levinson is right to say that there are quite a number of sentences suitable for these purposes (though, of course, I disagree with his claim that 'these purposes' are to indirectly request). And it is surely false that all (or even many) of these meet Bach and Harnish's definition of illocutionary standardization.[21] Thus, even if they are correct about the 'standard' forms, their account will not work for the vast array of other sentences that can be put to the same uses, and hence cannot be a generally correct account of so-called indirect speech acts. Nor, of course, will the Searle–Morgan conventions of usage be of any help with the more creative forms.

For those reasons, I prefer the account I have sketched to those that postulate indirect speech acts. I am officially agnostic about short-circuiting, but the alternative account of standardization I have proposed will accommodate this without the postulation of indirect speech acts. In the last two sections, I will discuss two types of objections, first those based on linguistic evidence, and then the reaction I have often encountered when I have tried out the claim that there are no indirect speech acts, namely, that it is intuitively wrong ('outrageous' might better capture the reaction). But before confronting those matters, I want to briefly consider a different objection, which is that in claiming that the utterer of 'Can you pass the salt?' implicates a desire to have the salt passed, I am in effect granting that there *are* indirect speech acts but just refusing to use a certain label. After all, are Gricean conversational implicatures not just ways of making two statements with the economy of a single utterance?

No, they are not. It has been claimed the implicature generated by someone who utters 'Michael is in Paris or London', namely, that the speaker does not have evidence for saying which of these two cities Michael is in, is from the point of view of speech act theory 'a secondary non-literal assertion'.[22] From the perspective I have on speech act theory, however, this is as serious a mistake as one could make. The mistake is treating such implicatures as an assertion of *any* kind (this is not to deny that they are speech acts). Grice coined the term 'implicature' to do duty for a family of verbs including 'implied', 'suggested', and (least helpfully) 'meant', with the central point being that these are cases in which someone conveys something *without* saying or asserting it. It is, of course, indirect, but not indirect *assertion*. To deny this is, it seems to me, to miss one of the most interesting and important features of the phenomena to which Grice drew our attention. There is an issue between the view I have developed and those which postulate indirect speech acts, whether these are assertions or requests or whatever: it is a genuine metaphysical disagreement. As Searle and Bach and Harnish argue that some have postulated unnecessary meanings or conversational postulates, I have argued that they in turn posit unnecessary illocutionary acts. Speakers have no need to perform second non-literal illocutionary acts to make points that they have already made clear, and we as theorists should not saddle them with such.

A LINGUISTIC OBJECTION

Many of the arguments for indirect speech acts turn on the apparent inter-action between syntax and indirect illocutionary force.[23] I will discuss one of these because it is, I think, representative, and perhaps casts the greatest doubt on the thesis I am defending: the occurrence of 'please' in sentences that I deny are used to make indirect requests. We use sentences such as:

Can you please pass the salt?
Can you pass the salt please?
Will you please pass the salt?
Will you pass the salt please?

commonly enough. The usual claim is that these are directly and literally questions, and indirectly requests, where 'please' modifies the request for the sake of politeness. Further, as Bach and Harnish point out, it seems clear that sentences that are used to ask questions or make statements cannot take 'please'; we do not have either of the following:

*Why do you please pass the salt?
*You never please pass the salt.

(Bach and Harnish 1979: 199)

And this suggests that the first sentences[24] are grammatical *only when* used as requests. (They do not in fact accept this suggestion, but I shall put that point on hold for a moment.) In fact, if the sentence 'Can you pass the salt?' is not used as a request, 'please' would seem to have no business at all entering into it. While one can ask questions politely, it does not seem at all plausible to claim that 'please' indicates *that* (that one is asking a question in a polite fashion) when one utters 'Can you please pass the salt?'

I take this objection to be serious, but I think it can be answered, and I want to borrow two points from those I have thus far been criticizing in order to answer it. These are Bach and Harnish's notion of a paragram-matic fact, and Searle's observation that syntactic phenomena might be explicable by appeal to things other than syntactic elements. Bach and Harnish suggest that sentences such as 'Can you please pass the salt?' are examples of what they call syntactic liberties, 'ungrammatical but perfectly usable sentences that are perfectly acceptable to fluent speakers'.[25] Like the familiar messages on matchbooks and roadsigns, 'Close cover before striking' and 'Slippery when wet', these are not grammatical strings, but they are perfectly serviceable for our communicative purposes. And the same is true for less familiar forms, such as this message that appeared on the door of my office building as I was writing this paper: 'Electrical outages Monday. Scattered electrical outages on receptacles. All lighting will not be affected.' This is certainly interpretable (although the last sentence requires some guesswork). There is no doubt a good bit more to be said about this, but Bach and Harnish are surely right to say that 'A great deal of ordinary language use involves syntactic liberties, everything from answers to questions to newspaper headlines and telegrams' (Bach and Harnish 1979: 231). It seems to me entirely plausible to claim, as they do, that sentences such as 'Can you please pass the salt?' fall into the same category, which undercuts many of the linguistic arguments for ambiguity in such sentences. What it does not do, is explain what 'please' modifies, since, unlike Bach and Harnish, I cannot say that a request is made indirectly when this sentence is uttered.

We can provide such an explanation, however, if we acknowledge and extend Searle's suggestion that the modifier 'frankly' in 'Frankly, you're drunk' modifies the speech act that is performed in uttering that sentence.

> It is not necessary to assume that ['frankly'] also modifies a verb, rather it characterizes the act which the speaker is performing, and that act need not be and in this case is not represented by a verb anywhere in the deep structure of the sentence, since the speaker and hearer already have mutual knowledge of the existence of that act.[26]

While I expect that Searle had only illocutionary acts in mind as the ones being characterized, the more general point is that expressions might well characterize what a speaker is doing, rather than what he is saying, *or* what illocutionary act he may be performing. It is in fact not uncommon to mix speech and other forms of behaviour. A modification of Morgan's example considered earlier might consist of first uttering 'Well, frankly' and then silently shovelling the soufflé into the dog's dish, with the point of the utterance being to indicate that the opinion indicated is one that is frankly rendered. (It certainly is not being frankly *stated.*) Now while I have denied that an utterance of 'Can you please pass the salt?' *is* a request, I have not denied that it *has the force* of a request, so long as 'force' is understood as 'practical effect' rather than 'illocutionary force'. This, plus the fact that it is mutually understood that the hearer will treat the utterance as if it were a request even though it is not one, is I suggest enough to explain the speaker's addition of the word 'please' in the interest of politeness.

I would like to make a final couple of points about appeals to empirical studies before leaving this section. Gazdar claims that there is experimental evidence indicating that hearers are insensitive to the literal meaning of sentences used in so-called indirect speech acts, citing the previously mentioned study by Clark and Lucy (1975), specifically their claim that 'quantitatively, all the sentences behaved according to their conveyed, not their literal, meaning' as one source (Gazdar 1981: 75). They do make this remark in support of the claim to have confirmed the prediction that 'The listener should show evidence that his final representation of a sentence is its intended meaning', but there are two points worth noting here. First, this is not evidence that hearers are *insensitive to* the literal meanings of the sentences in question, and indeed Clark and Lucy claim that their work provides some evidence that hearers do 'construct the literal meaning before the conveyed meaning'.[27] Second, it is surely open to question whether this final representation is really a representation *of the sentence* rather than an interpretation of the *point* of uttering it. So long as this is an open possibility, facts about the 'final interpretation' cannot be used to show that the sentences in question are not uttered and understood as having their literal meanings.

THE INTUITIVE OBJECTION

To many, it just seems *obvious* that the sentence 'Can you pass the salt?' is used to make a request. One prominent philosopher, trying to get me to see that this is a very robust phenomenon that deserves more respect than I am inclined to give it, noted (in correspondence) that anyone who *simply* treats this as a question and responds 'Yes' without passing the salt will be branded as a vapid smartass. I agree, but I see no *linguistic* inappropriateness in such a response: one is simply being socially uncooperative.[28] In fact, as is often observed, the set of possible responses to a 'Can you ...?' sentence is 'just about what one would expect from its literal meaning' (Morgan 1978: 263). A perfectly good response to 'Can you reach that book on the top shelf?' is 'Yes, here you are', *or* just plain 'Yes' with the book being retrieved from the shelf and handed over. There is nothing at all wrong with 'yes' as a verbal response, provided that it is accompanied by the conveyance of the book, or the salt, as the case may be.

The avoidance of the postulation of unnecessary entities, unnecessary, that is, to account for the facts, is a major theme in the arguments that Searle and Bach and Harnish use against their opponents. I have suggested that we do not need to postulate indirect speech acts to account for the phenomena typically *called* indirect speech acts. We may need something like standardization, as characterized by Bach and Harnish, to explain the short-circuiting that 'Can you ...?' formulations seem to exhibit, but this need only involve a standardized way of indicating that one has a certain desire, and not a standardized way of making a request. If I am right in suggesting that we can explain the relevant phenomena without appeal to indirect speech acts, then the same razor, whoever it may be traceable to, enjoins us to forgo them. I cannot see that anything of importance will be lost by doing so.[29]

NOTES

1 The theories I view as the most plausible are those of Searle (1979) and Bach and Harnish (1979); the competitors to which they seem preferable are primarily those of Gordon and Lakoff (1971) and Sadock (1974).

2   See Stampe 1975. While I do not know that he would agree with it, the thrust of the present chapter owes much to Stampe.

3   So for example, in baseball, a ball that bounces over the outfield wall counts as a double, but without some special such rule or convention it would not so count: it is not a double after all. If it were, there would be no need of a special rule declaring that it counts as one. (It can correctly be said to be a ground-rule double, but this is not analogous to being, for example, a line-drive double to left field.) This sort of point is what fuels my doubt about the utility of Searle's constitutive rules, but I do not wish to rely on this further point here.

4   This methodological commitment to explaining as much as possible by appeal to pragmatics, leaving our semantics as uncomplicated as possible, is at the heart of my 1990.

5   So say Searle (1979: 170), and Morgan (1978: 262). Bach and Harnish say that the approach multiplies meanings without necessity without dragging Occam's name into it (1979: 174).

6   I owe this point to Martin Huntley, from discussions some fifteen years ago. He expressed great doubt over whether Grice's modification inherited any plausibility from the original.

7   I must presume familiarity with the details of these objections due to space limitations. Bach and Harnish's criticisms of Searle (1979: 187–91) are somewhat different.

8   Assuming a standard context; I suppose if one were known to reserve the finest fare for one's prizewinning canine the judgement would be equally clear, but rather different.

9   This, even if the actions are produced with the sort of reflexive intensions that figure in Grice's (1957) account of meaning. (In that case, one will have, if Grice is right, *meant that* the soufflé is awful or the beans are desired, but this is because Grice's account is not a theory of *linguistic* meaning, but is much broader.) I hope it is also clear that when we say that the gazing has the force of a request, we do not mean it has the *illocutionary* force of a request.

10   Morgan 1978: 262. Morgan does not endorse this view. I have two qualms about this description of it, the first of which is the already discussed point about the needed modification of Occam's Razor. The other is simply to caution that what *amounts to* a request need not *be* a request, and urge some care in discussing 'the request nature' of 'Can you pass the salt?'

11   It is no doubt a tribute to the vagueness of these categories that it is not clear which maxim is violated; I am inclined to go with relevance.

12   At the other extreme, Vanderveken suggests that the conclusion of the hearer's inferences in such cases 'is always that the speaker means to perform non-literally certain illocutionary acts because their performance is required for the respect of the maxims, given the nature of the literal speech act and the existence of the facts of the conversational background' (1991: 375). I think this is obviously false.

13   I will question whether the second point is correct later.

14   This cannot be quite right; although it works for 'Can you pass the salt?' it fails for 'Can you reach the salt?', which (if it were a request) would be a request for the hearer to pass rather than reach (reach out and touch?) the salt.

15   They discuss Searle's article only, but would presumably raise the same objections against Morgan. There is however an interesting affinity between their claims about short-circuiting what they call the speech act schema and Morgan's notion of a short-circuited implicature.

16   Bach and Harnish 1979: 190–1. They have other objections as well.

17   Bach and Harnish 1979: 195. The point of 'generally' is to accommodate cases in which *T* is simply used literally, as when a physician inquires whether a patient is now able to reach the salt.

18   Searle begins his paper with the example 'Can you reach the salt?', but switches to 'Can you pass the salt?' later in the discussion, and I have done the same here – and indeed both seem pretty common. There are a number of complications that would need to be worked out: see n. 14.

19   See Clark and Lucy 1975; and Clark 1978, for example. Interestingly, latencies are longer for arriving at the 'requestive interpretation' for 'I would love to see the circle coloured blue' than for 'Can you make the circle blue?', but the latencies for the latter are in turn longer than those for the direct 'Please make the circle blue' (Clark and Lucy 1975: 63).

20   Bach and Harnish 1979: 196. This is not *always* true however, as Searle's example 'Can you give me change for a dollar?' (1979: 43) shows.

21   Would one 'just hear these as requests'? One would, I think, just treat them as if they were requests, but that is another matter. I have already expressed my doubts about this psychological claim, but the point is that if it is correct for the non-standard cases, an explanation in terms of what is mutually believed will not be available.

22   Vanderveken 1991: 376. Bach and Harnish think that all of Grice's examples of (particularized) conversational implicatures are clear examples of indirect constatives (1979: 170). Clark sees things the other way around; he remarks in passing that indirect speech acts 'are but one kind' of conversational implicatures (Clark 1979/1991: 225). My own inclination is to resist attempts to subsume implicatures under one of the more familiar categories of illocutionary acts. If this is a mistake, my argument has to be recast so that it charges Searle and Bach and Harnish with postulating the *wrong* illocutionary act, for example, a request rather than an implicature falling into some familiar category. This would, of course, be a significant modification, but it would leave the claim that so-called indirect speech acts have been seriously misconceived in place.

23   See Gordon and Lakoff 1971; Heringer 1972; Sadock 1974; Mittwoch 1976; Gazdar 1980, 1981.

24   They actually only discuss the ones with preverbal 'please'.

25   Bach and Harnish 1979: 199; see also section 10.4.

26   Searle 1979: 167–8. Searle's concern is with the use of such examples to support the performative hypothesis, which postulates a performative verb in the deep structure of such sentences for 'frankly' to modify.

27   Clark and Lucy 1975: 56. In a later paper (Clark 1979), Clark develops a more sophisticated model and declares the one used in Clark and Lucy 1975 too simplistic. None of the very interesting results of this study impugns the point at issue in the text however.

28   Compare Bach and Harnish's discussion of the 'smart-alecky' nature of such responses (1979: 186–7).

29   One would lose the argument Bach and Harnish give in support of the claim that performatives are also statements, since they claim that a performative sentence used performatively 'is used literally, directly to make a statement and indirectly to perform the further speech act of the type (an order, say) named by the performative verb ('order')' (1992: 98). However, there are other routes to the conclusion that performatives are statements; see Stampe 1975. The interesting generalizations Searle explores (1979) can be treated as applicable to ways of *implicating*, and hence preserved.

17 Indirect speech acts and propositional content

David Holdcroft

The topic of indirect speech acts raises a number of important methodological issues for Speech Act Theory (SAT). These focus on the key question of the nature of the link which there must be if SAT is, amongst other things, a theory of the relation between two very different levels of description. The first level is concerned with features of utterances, such as mood and modality, whereas the second with a distinctive class of acts, so-called illocutionary acts. The levels are, of course, quite distinct, yet if the theory is correct it must be possible to give a systematic description of how they are connected. However, as we shall see, it is very difficult to describe that connection.

DIFFICULTIES WITH AUSTIN'S AND SEARLE'S THEORIES

The kind of difficulty there is in giving such a description can be sketched briefly by reference to Austin, the inventor of SAT – though it is, of course, the work of Searle which has been in many respects more influential, particularly in linguistics.

Austin distinguished three different kinds of act that a speaker S can perform when uttering a sentence:

(i) *locutionary act*: the utterance of a sentence with determinate sense and reference;
(ii) *illocutionary act*: the making of a statement, offer, promise, etc. in uttering a sentence, by virtue of the conventional force associated with it (or with its explicit performative paraphrase);
(iii) *perlocutionary act*: the bringing about of effects on the audience by means of uttering the sentence, such effects being special to the circumstances of the utterance.

A key question at this point becomes in virtue of what does an utterance have the force it has; for example, what makes an utterance such as 'I'd be grateful if you'd pass me that book' have the force of a request rather than that of an order or an assertion? Three constraints are I suggest important:

I   An account of an utterance's force should not be exhausted by one of its syntax and semantics; otherwise the illocutionary act would collapse into the locutionary act, and SAT into syntax and semantics.

II Nevertheless, the theory must explain the apparently systematic connections there are between utterances and the forces they have, even though *ex hypothesi* descriptions of the former are quite distinct from ones of the latter.

III If SAT is a distinct theory, the explanations given have to be reasonably specific. If they are not, then the danger of an unsystematic appeal to a heterogeneous set of considerations is evident – which is precisely the sort of objection that Saussure had to attempts to study *parole* systematically.

Attempts to develop SAT suggest that there is considerable tension between these constraints. For in trying to satisfy (II), it is easy to run foul of (I) or (III). Austin's own tentative explanation of illocutionary force illustrates this. His explanation is dominated by the example of so called performative utterances, e.g.,

(1)(a) 'I name this ship the *Queen Elizabeth*' – as uttered when smashing the bottle against the stern.
  (b) 'I bet you sixpence it will rain tomorrow.'

These, he claimed, are not true or false, but have the unusual property that provided they are uttered in the appropriate circumstances, they constitute the performance of the act named by the main verb. In other words, provided (1a) is uttered by the duly appointed person, at the duly appointed place and time, etc., the ship has indeed been named.

However, he argues, the rules governing this conventional procedure are neither syntactic nor semantic. This ensures the satisfaction of constraint (I). Moreover, what Austin says about performatives suggests an answer to (II), namely that an utterance contains elements whose role it is to signal – as opposed to state – what force it has. It is, of course, not always clear what this could be in the case of non-performatives. But Austin suggests that there are other devices which play a role similar to that of a performative prefix, for example, mood, so that '"Shut it, do" resembles the performative "I order you to do it"' (Austin 1962: 73), and the presence of modal auxiliaries, so that '"You must do it" resembles "I order you, advise you, to do it"' (Austin 1962: 74).

However, whilst Austin's description of the conventionally determined circumstances of utterance may be correct for the formulaic examples of performative utterance he cites, his account is overgeneralized, and inapplicable to the utterances involved in ordinary informal communicative situations – that is, to the vast majority. For though I have to use a preordained formula in prescribed circumstances to will and bequeath, I certainly do not have to use a set formula in prescribed circumstances to warn/request/ advise etc. – the variety of ways in which I can do these things is extremely varied. So his answer to (II) is at best incomplete.

At the same time that answer is problematical, since it leaves us without an account of the semantics of

(2) I assert that p.

An utterance of this is not, Austin claimed, true or false, even though one of

(2)(a) He asserted that p

is. So whilst the prefix 'He asserted that ...' does contribute to the truth conditions of (2a), the prefix 'I assert that ...' does not contribute to the truth conditions of (2); its function there is merely to signal that p is asserted. But can there be that kind of difference between the two cases? And is there not a danger on this account that in satisfying constraint (I) we leave ourselves with no intelligible account of the semantics of performatives?

But even if these doubts could be answered, the performative is a poor model on which to base a general account of the connection between an utterance and its illocutionary force, since there are indefinitely many utterances which are not performatives, and many of these simply do not seem to have explicit indicators of their precise force.

Turning to Searle we find a different analysis of an illocutionary act, but one which no more clearly satisfies the constraints (I)–(III) than does Austin's. A key idea in that analysis is that of a set of constitutive rules which an act must satisfy to be of a given type.

Searle analyses illocutionary acts in terms of sets of constitutive conditions of various types as follows (Searle 1969: 66):

Types of illocutionary act

		Request	Assert, state (that), affirm	Question
Types of rule	Propositional content	Future act A of H.	Any proposition p.	Any proposition or propositional function.
	Preparatory	1. H is able to do A. S believes H is able to do A. 2. It is not obvious to both S and H that H will do A in the normal course of events of his own accord.	1. S has evidence (reasons, etc.) for the truth of p. 2. It is not obvious to both S and H that H knows (does not need to be reminded of, etc.) p.	1. S does not know 'the answer', i.e., does not know if the proposition is true, or, in the case of the propositional function, does not know the information needed to complete the proposition truly. 2. It is not obvious to both S and H that H will provide the information at that time without being asked.
	Sincerity	S wants H to do A.	S believes p.	S wants this information.
	Essential	Counts as an attempt to get H to do A.	Counts as an undertaking to the effect that p represents an actual state of affairs.	Counts as an attempt to elicit this information from H.

The propositional content condition, for instance, is a condition on the proposition expressed by the sentence uttered to perform the illocutionary act (IA). Whilst the essential condition, in effect, describes the conventional effect which the performance of the act has on the context: if I promise to do A, then I become committed to doing A; if I assert that p, then I become committed to the truth of p; if I withdraw p, then I am no longer committed to something I once was committed to, etc.[1]

But given the abstractness of the analysis of illocutionary acts, which imports various intentional notions which have no part to play in the analysis of utterances, what reasons could someone have for classifying an utterance as an act of a given kind? Apart from the propositional content condition, the analysis imposes few direct constraints on a sentence uttered to perform a particular act. However, Searle gives – or anyway gave in his 1969 – a general description of what is involved in performing an illocutionary act which, together with the analyses we have been considering, both imposes a very powerful constraint indeed on the sentence uttered to perform a particular act, and gives a very elegant answer to (II).

> The principle is this:
> A sentence X whose literal and serious utterance constitutes an illocutionary act of type K, must contain a device – a so-called IFID (illocutionary force indicating device) – whose semantic role ensures that S is non-deviantly uttered only when conditions constitutive of acts of type K obtain.

For instance, in the case of

(3) I promise to be there,

the IFID is the performative prefix 'I promise that ...', and its semantic role ensures that (3) is non-deviantly uttered only if the conditions constitutive of promising are met. So the way in which Searle tries to meet condition (II) is clear: according to him every sentence contains an IFID whose semantic role is to ensure that a serious and literal utterance of the sentence is an illocutionary act of a specific kind.

Clearly, performative prefixes are one type of IFID on Searle's account; but unless one postulates that all sentences are transformationally derived from performatives, which Searle does not, there must be other types of IFID. However, he is relatively unforthcoming about identifying specific linguistic elements with IFIDs:

> Let us assume for the sake of argument that the general outlines of the Chomsky–Fodor–Katz–Postal account of syntax and semantics are correct. Then it seems to me extremely unlikely that illocutionary act rules would attach directly to elements (formatives, morphemes) generated by the syntactic component, except in a few cases such as the

imperative. In the case of promising, the rules would more likely attach to some output of the combinatorial operations of the semantic component. Part of the answer to this question would depend on whether we can reduce all illocutionary acts to some very small number of basic illocutionary types. If so, it would then seem somewhat more likely that the deep structure of a sentence would have a simple representation of its illocutionary type.

(Searle 1969: 64)

Because he gives so few examples of IFIDs, Searle simply fails to give an account of what features of an utterance determine its force. Moreover, if he is right about the general form such an account must take, then, because of the semantic role allotted to IFIDs in determining the force of a non-deviant use of a sentence, the account threatens to undermine SAT as a distinct part of pragmatics, reducing it in effect to semantics and so violating constraint (I). This is so because on Searle's account it is a matter of meaning that a non-deviant utterance of a sentence has the force it has – so if all IFIDs were like performative prefixes, the mapping of utterances on to forces would be relatively trivial, and there would be very little work left for pragmatics.

This point apart, not only is Searle's theory difficult to evaluate because it largely fails to identify the linguistic items which function as IFIDs, but it is arguably deficient because of the way in which it neglects contextual factors which, though not semantic, nevertheless are partial determinants of force. For instance, it seems obvious that there are important aspects of an utterance's force which cannot be determined by features of it, because they depend on relations in which it stands to other utterances. One has only to consider utterances which constitute replies, objections, illustrations, introductions, etc., to see that it cannot be in virtue of the presence of an IFID that an utterance has one of these dimensions of force.[2] For, ignoring explicit performatives, it is clear that an utterance of one and the same sentence with the same semantic interpretation sometimes constitutes an objection/reply/comment/illustration, etc., and sometimes not. What distinguishes the case in which it does from those in which it does not is not the presence/absence of an IFID, but the contextual relations of the utterance (Holdcroft 1992: 60), and these are not semantic. A further problem is that though, as we shall see, Searle's theory of indirect speech acts acknowledges the importance of contextual features, his core theory allots them no importance at all. So his theory of speech acts is oddly decontextualized (Searle 1992a, b).

As we saw, Searle appeals to IFIDs to satisfy constraint (II); a non-deviant utterance of a sentence has a restricted range of illocutionary forces because of the IFID it contains. However, we argued that if all IFIDs are like performative prefixes, then the explanation is in danger of running foul of constraint (I). Moreover, if all IFIDs were like performative prefixes, then the explanation would entail that every sentence had only one non-deviant use – which is extremely implausible on any account. Clearly, the claim that every sentence contains an IFID would be more plausible if it postulated ones which were less determinate than are performative prefixes; but could there by any such?

Many would argue that there could, and that, for instance, there is a systematic relation between imperatives and directive speech acts which is captured in the following generalization:

(A) If by the serious and literal utterance of an imperative S performs an illocutionary act, it will be one of directive type.

This is in the spirit of the claim, which has been repeatedly made or assumed, that the major sentence types, declarative, imperative and interrogative are associated respectively with assertions, commands and requests, and with questions. But (A) is in a certain respect weaker than that claim, since it does not postulate that an imperative is associated with a command as such, but more generally with acts of directive type. In this respect the view is less at odds with the reported fact that imperatives are rarely used for commanding, but frequently for giving recipes, instructions, suggestions, advice, and so on, than is the view that their (main) use is to command (Ervin-Tripp 1976). Why then is there such an association? It arises, I suggest, because to utter seriously and literally an imperative, in an appropriate context, is at the same time to satisfy the propositional content condition on directives, by mentioning a future act of the hearer; but, as I shall argue later, that does not justify (A).

A similar association between declarative sentences, on the one hand, and representatives and commissives on the other could be suggested:

(B) If by the serious and literal utterance of a declarative S performs an illocutionary act it will be a representative or, in certain cases, either a representative or a commissive.

The rationale would be the same as in the previous case, namely, that the content of a declarative satisfies the propositional content condition on acts of the type in question. It is, of course, true that the connection between an utterance and its force claimed by (A) and (B) is weak; but given that the latter is undetermined by the former, this is hardly an objection to the claim.

So perhaps a sketchy outline of the way in which constraint (II) might be satisfied is as follows:

(C) If a sentence X is uttered seriously and literally, then
  (i) if it is a performative, it has the force determined by the performative prefix;
  (ii) if a declarative, it has the force of a representative or, in certain cases, either a representative or commissive;
  (iii) if an imperative, it has the force of directive, etc.

Arguably, this proposal does not violate (I) since the force of the vast majority of sentences is only partially determined by the sentence uttered, so that a significant role is left to pragmatic factors.

THE PROBLEM OF INDIRECT ACTS

The problem is that there are so many counter-examples to (C) that it is difficult to see why so many people, myself included, should have been tempted to defend it – or indeed, in many cases, rather stronger theses (Holdcroft 1978: 55). Because there are so many counter-examples, I want, in what follows, to concentrate discussion on the declarative counter-examples. They seem to be relatively structured, so that if one cannot deal satisfactorily with them, there would be little hope of dealing with the counter-examples in the other cases – hence the suggestion that they constitute a test case. Here are some examples of declarative counter-examples which can all be used as directives:

(4) (a) I want you to VP.
    (b) I think you have to VP.
    (c) You can (could) VP.
    (d) I wonder whether you would (could) VP.
    (e) You must (have to) VP.
    (f) Officers will wear ties.

Whilst the following can be used as questions, which Searle treats as a species of directive:

(5) (a) I wonder whether p.
    (b) I'd like to know if p.
    (c) You live at 27, Donkey Drive.
    (d) You got home safely.

More examples could be cited; but the main point is clear, declarative utterances can have a considerable variety of forces.

It is possible, as Searle points out, to formulate a generalization about some of the exceptions:

(D) (a) One can perform a directive act by either asserting that one of the preparatory conditions obtains, or by questioning whether it does.
    (b) One can perform a directive by asserting its sincerity condition.
    (c) One can perform a directive by asserting or questioning its propositional content conditions.

(Searle 1979: 72)

Waiving doubts about the idea of a sincerity condition, these generalizations seem correct. However, since utterances of one of the sentences above sometimes have the force of a directive and sometimes that of a representative, the generalizations as such do not determine what force it has in any given case. So, for instance, why do we interpret (4a) as a request in some cases, and as a representative in others?

Searle's answer to this key question makes a distinction between the direct use of (4a), which is determined by its IFID, and its indirect use which can be inferred and is not determined by its IFID. The way in which, according to him, it can be inferred, appeals to Grice's principles of conversation.

An important point that Grice (1975) makes is that, on the assumption that the person with whom we are conversing is collaborating, we try to interpret what he or she says so that it is relevant. If I say that I am out of petrol, and you say that there is a garage around the corner, then I infer that you think that it is open. For if you did not your reply would have been anything but co-operative. It is this idea that Searle's account of indirect speech acts generalizes. If in a particular context the assumption that (7a) has its direct interpretation as a representative cannot be sustained on the assumption that the speaker is co-operative, then what we do is to search for a different interpretation which can be sustained on that assumption.

In an example of the reasoning involved in determining that an utterance of 'Can you pass the salt?' is a request Searle appeals to the generalizations in (E) (Searle 1979: 46–7):

(E)   *Step 1:* X has asked me a question as to whether I have the ability to pass the salt (fact about the conversation).

Step 2: I assume that he is cooperating in the conversation and that therefore his utterance has some aim or point (principles of conversational cooperation).

Step 3: The conversational setting is not such as to indicate a theoretical interest in my salt-passing ability (factual background information).

Step 4: Furthermore, he probably already knows that the answer to the question is yes (factual background information). (This step facilitates the move to Step 5, but is not essential.)

Step 5: Therefore, his utterance is probably not just a question. It probably has some ulterior illocutionary point (inference from Steps 1, 2, 3, and 4). What can it be?

Step 6: A preparatory condition for any directive illocutionary act is the ability of H to perform the act predicated in the propositional content condition (theory of speech acts).

Step 7: Therefore, X has asked me a question the affirmative answer to which would entail that the preparatory condition for requesting me to pass the salt is satisfied (inference from Steps 1 and 6).

Step 8: We are now at dinner and people normally use salt at dinner; they pass it back and forth, try to get others to pass it back and forth, etc. (background information).

Step 9: He has therefore alluded to the satisfaction of a preparatory condition for a request whose obedience conditions it is quite likely he wants me to bring about (inference from Steps 7 and 8).

Step 10: Therefore, in the absence of any other plausible illocutionary point, he is probably requesting me to pass him the salt (inference from Steps 5 and 9).

It is easy to see that an analogous explanation could be given of the interpretation of (4a)–(4d) as requests. This happens in circumstances in which the assumption that all the speaker is doing is performing an act of representative type is inconsistent with the assumption that he or she is co-operating. Moreover, since each of (4a)–(4d) states a felicity condition on a directive, Searle's model explanation can be reduplicated in these cases.

There are of course cases in which the explanation of an indirect speech act could not proceed in that way. Consider:

A: Have a gin and tonic?
B: (who is known to be pregnant) I've read the latest report in the *Lancet*.

Clearly B is refusing A's offer. But her refusal cannot be inferred from the fact that she has asserted a felicity condition of a refusal, for she has done no such thing. Assuming that the latest *Lancet* publicizes the danger to the foetus of alcohol, then one can infer the refusal from the fact that she has given a reason for so doing.[3] Acts of this kind might be called radically indirect, since what is said has no connection with the felicity conditions of the indirect act.

Searle's claim that in such cases one performs one act by means of performing another has been criticized by many as confusing, or even as unintelligible (Leech 1983: 39) However, the idea that there is the same kind of means–end relationship between telling you that I feel cold and asking you to shut the window, as there is between rubbing a match against a matchbox and lighting it does not seem to be in principle wrong. And the oddity of reporting what I did as telling you that I felt cold is readily accounted for by Grice's principles – for to do that, provided that it is obvious that I am cold, is less informative than reporting my primary goal of asking you to shut the window.

The point is crucial for Searle's defence of his version of SAT. For provided that underlying every so-called indirect act there lies a recoverable direct act, then the theory of IFIDs, and with it Searle's way of satisfying (II), is defensible. But if (4a–4d) can be used to request without *inter alia* being used to state something, then the theory and the explanation are indefensible – for in that case declarative sentences can be non-deviantly used to request without asserting anything at all.

But though I think that Searle's theory is defective, it is not because of the unintelligibility in principle of the idea that one act can be performed by performing another one; indeed, this seems to be the right explanation of cases like the one involving B's refusal of a drink discussed above. So in the next section I want to try to do three things: first, describe two difficulties with Searle's theory which point to major defects with it; second, make a number of general points about SAT which follow if I am right; and third, sketch a different and more simple explanation than Searle's.

DIFFICULTIES WITH SEARLE'S SOLUTION

The first difficulty, which suggests that all is not plain sailing, is that in certain cases Searle's theory would require the joint satisfaction of felicity conditions which are meant to be exclusive. Assuming that there is no difficulty in principle with the idea that one can request something by stating something else, which there clearly is not in the case of radically indirect acts, there is a problem with the idea that one can request something which at the same time one asserts to be the case. It is difficult to see, for instance, how one could ask someone to shut a door in the same breath as one informs him that it is shut, for one is trying to get him to bring about something which one represents as actual! The problem is akin to that of expecting someone to shut a door which one believes is already shut.

But what account can Searle then give of 'Officers will wear ties'? If it is uttered to command, then can it consistently also be uttered at the same time to assert something – as his version of the inference theory of indirect speech acts requires? It might perhaps be argued that (4f) is not really indirect, and so that Searle's inference scheme does not apply in this case. The suggestion would be that it is not really indirect because there are two ways of reading it: in the one case 'will' is an auxiliary verb whose role is to mark the future tense; in the other case it is simply a marker of illocutionary force, signalling that a command is being given (see Fraser 1987 on this and modals in general). So (4f) admits of two different readings, and on each of them the act performed is direct. Thus there is no need to suppose that the speaker has to both assert that officers will wear ties and order them to. Such a manoeuvre is perhaps not very plausible; and I think it complicates the theory of IFIDs in ways which Searle should not welcome.[4] But anyway in the case of (5a–5b) it is difficult to see how such a move could be made at all. (5a–5b) are nice examples of what Davidson (1984) calls the autonomy of language, namely, the fact that though a sentence may be best suited for, or even designed for, a certain use, that will not stop it being used in other ways. The use of declaratives as questions, for instance, is often in circumstances in which H is an authority on the topic, so that it is not difficult to see why he should hear what S says as a question. For S cannot really be trying to inform H about a matter on which both S and H know that H is more expert than him; so that his commitment is, as it were, conditional on H's response, unlike the commitment arising from the 'standard' use which is unconditional.

The second difficulty with Searle's position raises a number of issues about his inference schema (E). Recall that it is essential to Searle's argument that the identification of, for instance, the indirect act performed by (4a) involves the prior identification of an assertion – for that saves the thesis about the indicative mood's status as an IFID. Hence, the derivation starts with the assumption that the utterance of (4a) is a representative; this is the default hypothesis so to speak.

But why should it be supposed that the derivation has to start in this way? For it is clear that uttering (4a) is a perfectly orthodox and standardized way of making a request,[5] as Searle acknowledges:

> I am suggesting that *can you, could you, I want you to*, and numerous other forms are conventional ways of making requests (and in that sense it is not incorrect to say that they are idioms), but at the same time they do not have an imperative meaning (and in that sense it would be incorrect to say they are idioms).
>
> (Searle 1979: 76)

The origin of such standardized ways of making a request has, Searle conjectures, to do with politeness. But if uttering (4a) is a standardized way of making a request, then in many contexts the salient hypothesis would surely be that its utterance is a request, and it would be natural to try to corroborate this hypothesis directly.

Suppose that S is in a position of authority and that he has made it clear that he is going to give us instructions. In that case it would be much simpler to try to corroborate the hypothesis that S is requesting us to VP directly without going through Searle's elaborate inference schema:

Background assumptions
(a) S is giving instructions and is in a position to do so.
(b) S has uttered (4a) seriously and literally.
(c) Uttering (4a) is a standardized way of requesting.
(d) S and H know that H can VP.
(e) S is conforming to the Co-operative Principle.

Hypothesis
(i) S is requesting H to VP   ((a) & (c))
Check: Propositional content.   (b)
         Preparatory condition.   (d)
         Sincerity condition.   (e)
         Relevant.   (a)

In other words the inferential process tries to corroborate the most likely hypothesis given the background assumptions, including crucially the conversational goals of the participants. It is true, of course, that there is no reason to suppose that *H* would actually reason in this way, anymore than there is in Searle's, but it is sufficient for my argument, I hope, that he could. For if he could, there is no reason to see the use of (4a) to request as one that is essentially indirect, that has to piggy back on its use to state – so that there is no need, on my proposal, to identify a statement first, in order to identify a request. Hence the proposal does not commit one to the view that an utterance of (4a) is an assertion, however conversationally inappropriate that assumption might be, and what ever else it is.[6]

AN ALTERNATIVE PROPOSAL

One conclusion with important implications for SAT which this points to is that the kind of inferential considerations which Searle invokes to account for the acts which he classes as indirect, should apply equally to the ones he calls direct. Hence, there is no difference in kind between the acts Searle calls direct and the ones he calls indirect – in *both* cases identification involves inferences in an assumed context. Further support for this view rests on the fact we mentioned earlier that whether an utterance is an objection, an illustration, an answer, etc., cannot depend on any intrinsic feature of that utterance, since what is crucial is its relationship to previous utterances.

It also seems clear that attempts to correlate utterances and illocutionary acts by means of generalizations such as (A), (B) and (C) are simplistic. We have seen, for instance, that once contextual factors are taken into consideration in the way they have to be on an inferential account of speech act identification, then it is not even plausible to suppose that the most natural hypothesis to adopt when S utters (4a) is that he is asserting something.[7]

The question remains why generalizations like (B) – indeed often stronger versions which argue that an utterance in the indicative mood labels itself as an assertion – continue to appeal, even to those who adopt an inferential theory of speech acts.

One suggestion would be that this is so because what (B) states in effect is a default value. So the assumption that an utterance of (4a) is an assertion, though defeasible, stands unless defeated. However, this suggestion is, I think, appealing only so long as one supposes that contextual considerations are not intrinsically important, so that in the 'null context' utterances have their default values. But from the perspective of the inferential account of SAT defended here, without a context an utterance cannot have a force at all.

A claim that Davidson makes points in the right direction:

> It is easy to confuse two quite different theses: on the one hand, the (correct) thesis that every utterance of an imperative *labels* itself (truly

or falsely) an order, and the thesis that under 'standard' conditions the utterance of an imperative *is* an order.

(Davidson 1984: 275)

Perhaps the explanation is that sentences in the indicative mood, what I have been calling declaratives, have a syntactic derivation which ensures that when interpreted they form objects of performative verbs of representative type. These are container verbs which take nominalized declaratives as objects; and this, together with the fact that the utterance of a sentence of declarative type satisfies the propositional content condition on representatives, could explain the appeal of (B). The problem is that some declaratives also meet other propositional content conditions, so that they are already quite well adapted for other uses:

(6)   (a) I will be there.
      (b) You will take the 12.40, and change at Doncaster.
      (c) I want you to take the 12.40 and change at Doncaster.

Both (6a) and (6b) directly meet the propositional content condition on speech act types other than representatives, namely, directives, as well as that on representatives. And given the relative vagueness of the specification of the propositional content condition in the case of directives so does (6c). So the fact that they do perhaps contains the germ of an explanation of why declaratives can have such diverse uses.

The way to flesh out this explanation can be seen if one asks why there have to be propositional content conditions on types of speech acts. The answer is, I suggest, that this is so because to be of a certain type an act has to have an appropriate direction of fit, and to have that it has to have a suitable content clause. The first point is uncontroversial; as Searle says:

The members of the assertive class of speech acts ... are supposed in some way to match an independently existing world; and to the extent that they do or fail to do that we say that they are true or false. But the members of the directive class of speech acts ... and the members of the commissive class ... are not supposed to match an independently existing reality but rather are supposed to bring about changes in the world so that the world matches the propositional content of the speech act.

(Searle 1983: 7)

When a speech act is meant to match the world it is said to have the word-to-world direction of fit, and when the world is meant to match the speech act it is said to have the world-to-word direction of fit.

Now for there to be a possible match, and hence a direction of fit, there have to be items to match. Presumably, these are, on the one hand, possible states of affairs, and, on the other, representations of them, which are referentially or indexically linked to them. But the match as such does not determine any direction of fit; if X matches Y, Y matches X, and there is no onus on either to fit the other of the kind required by the notion of a direction of fit. The source of such an onus must depend on something external to X and Y; for example, the fact that X can be manipulated to match Y, or the fact that Y can be constructed to match X, etc. Thus, one might argue that what makes an utterance by a speaker S have the word-to-world fit is not its content p, but the fact that S accepts that if not-p, then there is a compelling reason to retract. On the other hand, what makes an utterance by S have the world-to-words fit is the fact that there is, in the circumstances, no such obligation.[8]

Hence, if an utterance of 'You will be there' is an assertion, and at the appropriate time you are not there, then there is a compelling reason for S to retract; whereas if it is a request, there is no such reason. Perhaps the use of 'You will be there' as an assertion is in some sense primary, because that is what it was 'designed' for. But since it has a content which allows it to have either direction of fit, there is nothing to stop it being used as a request, as well. Moreover, the way in which a direction of fit is determined is no more complicated in the latter case than it is in the former, so that though the former may be in some sense primary, an assertive interpretation is no more direct than is a directive one; which will be more plausible will depend on the context of the utterance. Similarly, for (4a)–(4f); so that given their content clauses, and appropriate contextual assumptions about the speaker's conversational goals, a directive interpretation would often be the natural one (cf. Holdcroft and Smith 1992: 147).

NOTES

1   Two caveats do not affect what follows. First, while both the propositional content condition and the essential condition has a plausible claim to being constitutive, this is not so of the others – I can, for instance refuse a request by pointing out that I am unable to do what is requested. Second, it is difficult to formulate the propositional content condition correctly; the fact that the object of an illocutionary act has a content G, does not mean that the sentence uttered to perform it has the content G – this is clear from the existence of indirect speech acts.

2   The point is clearest for non-performatives. Consider, 'Next, I will talk about p' as part of the opening to a talk, and then occurring in response to the question 'What will you do next?

3   Searle implicity recognizes the existence of types of cases which like this fall outside the scope of (E), but, as far as I can see, does not discuss them. For example,

I have told you until I'm sick that you are *not* to do that.

4   It also does not help Searle, since it precipitates a further difficulty – namely that you cannot treat step 1 of the inference simply as a fact. For we can no longer take it for granted that it is easy to tell whether a sentence is declarative or not, since many surface declaratives will have look-alikes that are not declaratives. So we are going to have to guess which it is; but is our answer not

364   *Foundations of speech act theory*

going to be in part determined by our guess about its likely illocutionary force? So IFIDs will not always help us to identify force, since we will not be able to identify them independently of our identification of force.

5   For an account of standardization, see Bach and Harnish (1979: 193):

> *T* is standardly used to *F* in *G* if and only if:
> (i) It is MB-ed [mutually believed] in *G* that generally when a member of *G* utters *T*, his illocutionary intent is to *F*, and
> (ii) Generally when a member of *G* utters *T* in a context in which it would violate the CP [Co-operative Principle] to utter *T* with (merely) its literally determined force, his illocutionary intent is to *F*.

6   Of course one cannot show that it is not an assertion, but there seems to be no point in assuming that it is or must be. In this connection the pointlessness of the assumption that a question is being asked seems very clear in steps (1)–(5) of Searle's own model derivation. Why not say that it is not a question rather than that it is a question which as such is conversationally inappropriate?

7   Take another example:

> A: Will you promise?
> B: I will be there.

Would it be in any way plausible to treat the hypothesis that B is making a prediction as more salient than the hypothesis that he is making a promise?

8   This sketchy account tries to adapt the interesting and subtle argument of Humberstone 1992 to the case of speech acts.

18 Speaker meaning, sentence meaning and metaphor

Savas L. Tsohatzidis

INTRODUCTION

Two widely held assumptions in contemporary discussions of meaning are, first, that a distinction deserves to be drawn between what sentences of natural languages mean and what speakers of those languages mean by uttering those sentences; and, second, that Grice's theory of conversational implicature (Grice 1975, 1978, 1989) provides an appropriate framework for analysing the various kinds of meaning which are instances of speaker meaning rather than of sentence meaning.

Metaphorical meaning is among the kinds of meaning that those who hold these assumptions (including Grice himself) frequently cite as a kind of meaning which is an instance of speaker meaning rather than of sentence meaning. But since metaphorical meaning can hardly be taken to be a pretheoretically obvious case of meaning that is speaker-based rather than sentence-based – and since there is a considerable number of not obviously flawed theories, both ancient and modern, where the phenomenon of metaphor has been regarded as a semantic rather than as a pragmatic phenomenon[1] – attempts to analyse metaphor within the context of the two assumptions can – and must – be evaluated in at least two ways. First, by considering how well they manage to distinguish metaphor from *other* presumed cases of speaker meaning, assuming that it *is* a case of speaker meaning. And second, by considering how well they motivate their initial assumption that metaphor *is* a case of speaker meaning – in other words, that it *is* a pragmatic rather than a semantic phenomenon. (In what follows, I will be referring to these two questions as the internal and the external question, respectively.)

My purpose in this paper is to examine, from the two perspectives just indicated, John Searle's paper on metaphor (Searle 1979: 76–116), which is one of the best-known attempts to analyse metaphorical meaning as a special case of speaker meaning rather than of sentence meaning, within a broadly Gricean framework. I will argue that Searle's attempt – which, in the respects that are relevant here, is representative of most other pragmatic approaches to metaphor[2] – fails both as an attempt to distinguish metaphor from other presumed cases of speaker meaning, and as an attempt to motivate the assumption that metaphor is in fact a case of speaker meaning. The paper may be viewed, then, as an attempt to suggest that, as far as the linguistically central phenomenon of metaphor is concerned, the widespread tendency to reinterpret as many semantic phenomena as possible in pragmatic terms, may have to be firmly resisted.[3]

THE INTERNAL QUESTION

A speaker speaks *literally*, according to Searle, just in case what *he* means by uttering a sentence is identical with what the sentence he utters *itself* means. (Thus, a speaker who, in saying, 'There are prime numbers', means that there are prime numbers is a speaker who speaks literally, since what he means is identical with what the sentence he utters – namely, the sentence 'There are prime numbers' – itself means.) Cases where what a speaker means by uttering a sentence is not identical with what the sentence he utters itself means come, according to Searle, in two varieties. On the one hand, a speaker who, in uttering a sentence, means *not only* what the sentence he utters itself means but, *in addition*, something else as well is a speaker who speaks *indirectly*. (For example a speaker who, in saying to his hearer, 'Can you tell me the time?', means both that he would like to know whether the hearer can tell him the time *and* that he would like to know what the time is, is a speaker who speaks indirectly, since, although he does mean what the sentence he utters itself means – namely, that he would like to know whether the hearer has the ability to tell him the time – means, in addition, something else that is not meant by the sentence he utters – namely, that he would like to know what the time actually is.) On the other hand, a speaker who, in uttering a sentence, does not mean *at all* what the sentence he utters itself means but something different altogether is a speaker who speaks *figuratively*. (For example, a speaker who, in saying, 'Sally is a block of ice', means that Sally is unemotional, or a speaker who, in saying, 'Sally was very kind to me', means that Sally was very rude to him, are speakers who speak figuratively, since they do not mean at all what the sentences they utter themselves mean – namely, that Sally is a block of ice or that Sally was very kind, respectively – but something else altogether – namely, that Sally is unemotional and that Sally was very rude, respectively.) Finally, a speaker who speaks figuratively – that is to say, a speaker who does not mean at all what the sentence he utters means, but something different altogether – can, according to Searle, be doing the one or the other of two different kinds of things. He may be speaking *ironically*, in which case not only does he not mean at all what the sentence he utters means but means the opposite of what the sentence he utters means; or he may be speaking *metaphorically*, in which case he does not mean at all what the sentence he utters means, but he does not mean the opposite of what the sentence he utters means either. (Thus, a speaker who, in saying, 'You have been very kind to me, Sally', means that Sally has been very rude to him is a speaker who speaks ironically, because not only does he not mean what the sentence he utters means, but means the opposite of what that sentence means – since being rude is the opposite of being kind; whereas a speaker who, in saying 'Sally is a block of ice', means that Sally is unemotional, is a speaker who speaks metaphorically, because, though he does not mean at all what the sentence he utters means, he does not mean the opposite of what that sentence means either – since being a block of ice is not the opposite of being unemotional.)

Let us now assume, as Searle does, that metaphorical meaning *is* exclusively a matter of speaker meaning rather than of sentence meaning (and also that some kind of Gricean account in terms of conversational implicature is available for the explanation of speaker meanings in general and of metaphorical meanings in particular[4]). The internal question to ask about Searle's proposal can them be split into two sub-questions. First, whether it provides a basis for a proper distinction between metaphor and irony. And second, whether it provides a basis for a proper distinction between metaphor and irony, on the one hand, and non-literal but not figurative (that is, indirect) uses of sentences, on the other.

If Searle's way of distinguishing ironical utterances from metaphorical utterances was correct, there would not be any utterances that one could properly describe as *simultaneously* ironical and metaphorical, since saying of an utterance that it is simultaneously ironical and metaphorical is, within Searle's theory, equivalent to saying that what the speaker of that utterance means both is (in view of its ironical character) and is not (in view of its metaphorical character) opposite to what the sentence he utters itself means. But there are certainly utterances that are properly describable as being ironical and metaphorical at the same time. If, for example, I wish to suggest that a certain person that someone has declined to regard as unquestionably ugly, is, in fact, very ugly, I may succeed to do so not only by saying, ironically, 'She is very beautiful indeed!', but also by saying, equally ironically,

(1) She is beauty itself, of course!

But this last utterance would not only be ironical but also metaphorical – as would be any other utterance in which a concrete entity like a person would be identified with an abstract entity like beauty. And since, on Searle's theory, speaking ironically is meaning the opposite of what the sentence one utters means whereas speaking metaphorically is not meaning the opposite of what the sentence one utters means, anyone uttering the metaphorical sentence in (1) ironically would have to be counted as meaning and not meaning at the same time the opposite of what (1) means. Similarly, if I wish to suggest that a person that someone has described as brave is, in fact, not brave at all, I may succeed to do so not only by saying, ironically, 'He is very brave indeed!', but also by saying, equally ironically,

(2) He is a real lion, of course!

But this last utterance would be not only ironical but also metaphorical, as would be any other utterance in which a human being would be presented as belonging to the class of non-human beings. In these and in numerous other cases of the same kind, then, Searle's account would be forced to translate the obviously correct observation that the same utterance can be simultaneously an instance of metaphor and an instance of irony into the incoherent claim that what the speaker of that utterance means both is and is not opposite to what the sentence he utters means. Consequently, Searle's proposed way of distinguishing ironies from metaphors cannot be maintained, even if we grant that the latter are, like the former, mani-festations of speaker meaning rather than of sentence meaning (an assump-tion that the examples just considered already make suspect, since they suggest that metaphorical interpretations are context-free in a way in which ironic interpretations are not: one needs quite specific information about the context in order to determine whether 'She is beauty itself!' or 'He is a real lion!' are meant ironically or non-ironically; but no such information is required in order to determine that they are meant *metaphorically*, and it is, indeed, hard to think of a context in which the metaphors they contain would have *not* been identified and in which they would *still* be counted as acceptable utterances).

Let us now turn to Searle's proposed elucidation of the difference between figurativity and indirection. According to him, what distinguishes an utterer who speaks figuratively from an utterer who speaks indirectly is that, although they both mean certain things that are different from those meant by the sentences they utter, the former does not mean *at all* the thing meant by the sentence he utters, whereas the latter means *in addition* the thing meant by the sentence he utters. If Searle's way of drawing this distinction was correct, then, no utterer would be properly describable as *simultaneously* speaking figuratively and indirectly, since that would mean that this utterer both means and does not mean the thing meant by the sentence he utters. But there certainly are utterers that are properly describable in this way, since their utterances are simultaneously instances of figurativity and indirection. If, for example, I can indirectly suggest to someone that her baby needs a bath by saying to her 'Your baby is full of dirt', I may equally indirectly suggest to her that her baby needs a bath by saying to her,

(3) Your baby has become a piglet.

But the fact that this last utterance can be a vehicle of an indirect sug-gestion hardly prevents it from being a vehicle of metaphor, and it is, in fact, only when its intended metaphorical interpretation has been estab-lished that its indirect force of suggestion can be properly attributed. Similarly, if I can indirectly assert that I find a person called Mary very beautiful by asking, 'Isn't Mary very beautiful?', I can equally indirectly assert that I find that person very beautiful by asking,

(4) Isn't Mary beauty itself?

But the fact that the latter utterance is, just like the former, a possible vehicle of indirection hardly prevents it from being, unlike the former, a vehicle of metaphor, and it is, again, only when its intended metaphorical interpretation has been determined that its indirect force can be properly attributed. Faced with these and numerous other cases of the same sort, however, Searle would be forced to translate the obviously correct observation that a certain utterance is simultaneously an instance of figurativity and an instance of indirection into the absurd claim that its speaker has achieved the impossible task of having meant and of not having meant at the same time what was meant by the sentence he has uttered, since the first of these features is, according to Searle, a necessary feature of indirection, and the second a necessary feature of figurativity. It seems, therefore, that Searle's proposed way of distinguishing between figurativity and indirection is no more successful than his proposed way of distinguishing between the two kinds of figurativity represented by irony and metaphor, respectively. So, the two internal sub-questions that his pragmatic conception of metaphor would have to answer remain unanswered, and we may now proceed to the external question that any such account would have to answer before it could be discussed any further: is there any good reason for supposing that metaphor *is* a matter of speaker meaning rather than of sentence meaning – in other words, that it *is* a pragmatic rather than a semantic phenomenon?

THE EXTERNAL QUESTION

Searle's answer to this question appears to be that it is *obvious* that metaphorical meanings are speaker meanings rather than sentence meanings. But the fact that the question whether a given conveyed meaning is speaker-based rather than sentence-based has obvious answers in certain cases does not entail that it has an obvious answer in every possible case, and this, as noted, is especially clear in the case of metaphor, where many people before and after Searle have regarded as far from obvious the things that he takes to be obvious. It would appear, then, that reference to some independently available criterion would be helpful in settling this fundamental question. And, fortunately for Searle, the Gricean framework within which he operates accepts a widely used criterion – embodied in the so-called 'cancellability test' – which purports to motivate decisions as to whether a given conveyed meaning is speaker-based rather than sentence-based. It appears, however, that Searle has neglected applying the cancellability test before taking his decisions concerning the analysis of metaphor. For, as I will now suggest, application of that test gives, for the vast majority of metaphorical utterances, results that clearly contradict his (and many others') assumption that metaphorical meanings are speaker meanings rather than sentence meanings.

The principle of the cancellability test (whose basic idea comes, again, from Grice (see Grice 1975, 1981, 1989), and which was employed by Searle himself on other occasions, for example, Searle 1979: 30–57) is simple and, I think, sound: If a speaker cannot without oddity deny that, in uttering a given sentence s, he meant a certain thing p, then the fact that he meant p by uttering s can legitimately be taken to be just a function of what s itself means; if on the other hand, a speaker can without oddity deny that, in uttering a given sentence s, he meant a certain thing p, then the fact that he meant p by uttering s cannot legitimately be taken to be just a function of what s itself means. (Thus, the oddity of 'I am a man, but I don't mean to suggest that I am human' shows that, if a speaker who says 'I am a man' is interpreted as meaning, *inter alia*, that he is human, then the legitimacy of that interpretation can be conclusively established by appealing to what the sentence he uttered itself means; on the other hand, the non-oddity of 'I am a man, but I don't mean to suggest that I need a woman' shows that, if a speaker who says 'I am a man' is interpreted as meaning that he needs a woman, the legitimacy of that interpretation cannot be conclusively established by appealing to what the sentence he uttered itself means – though, of course, there might be other, extra-linguistic, reasons in view of which that interpretation could be established as legitimate.)

Now, many of the *non*-metaphorical cases where, for Searle as for many others, a speaker's meaning diverges from a sentence's meaning are easily confirmed to be cases of such divergence by the cancellability test. Thus, the test shows that, if a speaker who says, 'Can you ask Bill to make less noise?', is interpreted as meaning that he wants his hearer to ask Bill to make less noise, then the legitimacy of that interpretation cannot be established by appealing to what the sentence the speaker uttered itself means, since, should the speaker have said something like (5), he would have without oddity denied that this was the interpretation that he intended his utterance to be given.

(5) Can you ask Bill to make less noise? – I don't mean to suggest that I want you to actually ask Bill to make less noise; I simply want to know whether you have the ability to do so.

Similarly, the test shows that, if a speaker who says, 'Why should I ever divorce my wife?', is interpreted as expressing the opinion that there are no reasons why he should divorce his wife, then the legitimacy of that interpretation could not be established by appealing to what the sentence he uttered itself means, since, should the speaker have said something like (6), he would have without oddity denied that this was the interpretation that he intended his utterance to be given:

(6) Why should I ever divorce my wife? – I don't mean to suggest that no reasons could ever be found; I simply want to be told what these reasons are.

What Searle and many others (including Grice) have failed to notice, however, is that, when it is applied to metaphorical utterances, the cancell-ability test gives, in the vast majority of cases (indeed, in *all* cases where the interpretation of the metaphor involves the recognition of a category mistake), results that contradict the thesis that metaphorical meanings are speakers' meanings rather than sentence meanings. Suppose, to adapt one of Searle's favourite examples, that a speaker says, 'My wife Sally is a block of ice', and is thereby interpreted as meaning metaphorically that his wife Sally is, say, unemotional. If this or any other metaphorical interpretation is not part of what the sentence the speaker utters means, then the speaker should be able to cancel without oddity all interpretations of his utterance except the one that is strictly identical to its literal meaning. Suppose, then, that the speaker attempts to block all metaphorical interpretations, by speaking as if Sally is literally a block of ice and nothing else – by saying, for example,

(7) My wife Sally is a block of ice – please put her in the refrigerator before she melts.

This utterance, I submit, would elicit the one or the other of two types of reaction. Either it would be immediately rejected as semantically anom-alous, or it would be accepted as semantically well formed *provided that* the hearer would have managed to interpret the speaker as *still* speaking metaphorically when describing his wife as something that should be put in the refrigerator in order not to melt. But this means that the attempt to cancel without oddity all possible metaphorical interpretations of 'My wife Sally is a block of ice' cannot possibly succeed: either the result will be an utterance that is rejected as odd, or it will be an utterance that is accepted as not odd precisely because the metaphor has *not* been cancelled. And this in turn means that, as far as the cancellability test is concerned, meta-phorical interpretations of uttered sentences must be supposed to be just functions of what the sentences themselves mean rather than functions of what speakers may choose to mean by uttering them. Suppose, to take one more, familiar, example, that the sentence 'Time is money' receives, on a particular occasion of utterance, one of its usual metaphorical interpret-ations. If these interpretations are not determined by what it means but rather by what its speaker has chosen to mean by uttering it, then its speaker should be in a position to block without oddity all metaphorical interpretations of his utterance by going on to speak as if time was, literally, a kind of money and nothing else – by saying, for example,

(8) Time is money – so, how much of your time have you got in your bank?

But this utterance would be either rejected as semantically anomalous or accepted as semantically well formed *provided that* its hearer would have managed to interpret its speaker as *still* speaking metaphorically when describing time as something that can be saved in a bank. This means that the result of the attempt to prevent without oddity the metaphorical interpretation of 'Time is money' will be either an utterance that *is* odd or an utterance whose metaphorical interpretation has *not* been prevented. And since, according to the cancellability test, it is sentence meanings, rather than speaker meanings, that cannot be prevented without oddity, the test's verdict must, as in the previous case, be that the metaphorical meaning of 'Time is money' derives from what *it* means rather than from what any speaker might have chosen to mean by it.

Since the view that metaphor is a matter of speaker meaning rather than of sentence meaning can hardly be regarded as obviously correct, since the cancellability test has been devised precisely in order to help deciding unobvious cases of this kind, and since it is a test that appears both to rest on sound assumptions and to give the expected results in cases where the distinction between speaker meaning and sentence meaning *is* obvious, the only reasonable interpretation of the above results is the interpretation according to which they do in fact show what they appear to show – namely, that metaphors can legitimately be regarded as functions of what sentences themselves mean, rather than as functions of what speakers choose to mean by uttering them. (And if this is so, of course, Searle's previously encountered difficulties in distinguishing metaphorical meaning from what he regards as *other* kinds of cases of *speaker* meaning should hardly appear surprising: for if these other cases *are* cases of speaker meaning whereas metaphors are not, it is no wonder that attempts to distinguish between the former and the latter as special cases of the *same* phenomenon cannot succeed.)

CONCLUSION

My purpose in this paper has been twofold. On the one hand, I have tried to show, that, even if we assume that metaphorical meanings are functions of what speakers, as opposed to sentences, mean, Searle's proposed bases for distinguishing metaphorical meanings from other kinds of speaker meanings are unreliable, since they lead to contradictory statements both in those cases in which an utterance can be simultaneously an instance of metaphor and an instance of irony and in those cases in which an utterance can be simultaneously an instance of figurativity and an instance of indirection. On the other hand, I have tried to show that Searle's assumption that metaphors *are* functions of what speakers, as opposed to sentences, mean, is incorrect, at least when viewed in the light of the test that is most widely accepted as affording a reasoned decision on the question whether a given conveyed meaning is or is not a function of what a sentence, as opposed to a speaker, means.[5] I hope, then, that, if my arguments are well taken, they might be of interest both to those who have been led to suppose that the distinction between speaker meaning and sentence meaning holds the key to the analysis of metaphor, and (for different reasons) to those who have long suspected that metaphor is too fundamental a feature of natural languages to admit of a simple pragmatic, as opposed to a complex semantic, treatment.[6]

NOTES

1   Among many contemporary theories that fit this description, it would suffice to mention, in view of its wide scope and considerable influence, the one put forward in the writings of George Lakoff and Mark Johnson. See Lakoff and Johnson 1980; Lakoff 1987; Johnson 1987. Cp also Lakoff and Turner 1989.

2   And also of some well-known approaches which do not label themselves 'pragmatic', such as Davidson's (1978).

3   I am not, of course, suggesting that no pragmatic reinterpretation of any phenomenon that has been taken to be semantic is ill advised, and have proposed such reinterpretations myself (Tsohatzidis 1990, 1993d). But I do think, and have argued, that many proposed applications of pragmatic notions to explain away semantic perplexities are clearly mistaken (see Tsohatzidis 1987b, 1989, 1992).

4   I will be making this last assumption throughout, but only for the sake of argument. In fact, I believe that the Gricean model of explanation of pragmatic phenomena in terms of the notion of conversational implicature is far from unproblematic (see Tsohatzidis 1993a).

5   For important criticisms of other aspects of Searle's proposal, the reader will profitably consult Cohen 1979 and Cooper 1986. An analysis of metaphor (and related topics) that is directly inspired from Searle, and to which therefore the arguments presented here directly apply, is Vanderveken 1991. These arguments also apply to the pragmatic analysis of metaphor proposed in Fogelin 1989, which, though considerably more sophisticated than – and at certain points justly critical of – Searle's, explictly assumes, like Searle's, the overall correctness of the Gricean approach. A pragmatic analysis of metaphor (and related topics) which is, in important respects, non-Gricean, but which does not avoid what I regard as the central objection to pragmatic accounts, is the one proposed by Sperber and Wilson (1985–6, 1986): in essence, their claim is that the phenomenon of metaphor is of the same kind as the phenomenon of 'loose talk'; but they fail to notice that a speaker who would be interpreted as speaking loosely might without oddity try to cancel this interpretation of his utterance by insisting that he in fact speaks strictly, whereas a speaker who would be interpreted as speaking metaphorically might not without oddity try to cancel this interpretation of his utterance by insisting that he in fact speaks literally; and this, to me at least, is sufficient for concluding not merely that 'loose talk' and metaphor are *not* instances of the same phenomenon, but also that the former is a pragmatic phenomenon whereas the latter is not.

6   I would like to thank my colleague A.-Ph. Christidis, who provided the incentive for, and fruitful observations on, this paper.

19 On the vectoring of speech acts

David Harrah

INTRODUCTION

Most speech acts seem to be focused and directed. They are intended as coming *from* the agent and going *to* the receivers or audience. They are intended to have a certain point, and they are intended to be construed as having a certain point. We shall say here that these speech acts are *vectored.*

Usually the purpose of vectoring is to help the agent by helping others to know what the agent's intentions are. So usually the agent has some objective means for expressing the vector, making it explicit. In the act of speaking, for example, the speaker may use head turning, eye contact, or hand gestures to indicate the intended receivers. In choosing exactly what is to be spoken or written the sender may choose sentences that ostensibly indicate a vector. Examples:

(1) Louise, please carry John's rucksack.
(2) My answer to that question, George, is no.

To mark the distinction between real and ostensible we should say that sentences like (1) and (2) are vector-indicating sentences, but, where this distinction is not relevant, we shall say simply that these sentences are *vectored.*

In this paper we focus on the objective means, and especially on the linguistic means, by which vectoring is expressed. We are concerned in particular with these questions: is there a standard system for expressing vectors in natural language? If so, what is it; and what is its deep rationale? Under what conditions can the audience know that the ostensible vector (the linguistically indicated vector) is the same as the real (the really intended) vector?

SEARCH FOR A PARADIGM CASE

Is there a paradigm case of vectoring, one that can guide our theorizing in a fruitful way? One apparently obvious choice is the case where a small child runs into the street and the child's mother yells

(3) Look out!

Before we could use this case as a guide, however, we should have to analyse it in more detail, articulating a full description of the mother's beliefs, attitudes, and intentions, the child's beliefs, and the physical details of the utterance of (3).

To begin our theorizing we could try to describe the mother-and-child situation in sufficient detail, but then we should have to describe several other apparently simple kinds of paradigm case (involving assertions, questions, replies, and the like), and then abstract from all of these descriptions to formulate a general description of vectoring and vectors. Rather than follow this bottom-up procedure we shall here proceed in a top-down way. We shall choose a relatively complex case as our paradigm of vectoring, analyse it, generalize, construct a model of vectoring, and then relate the model to simpler cases. One reason for choosing this particular case as paradigm is that the vectoring in it is completely transparent.

OUR CHOICE OF PARADIGM

The case that we take as paradigm is the case of the formal memo in a large formal organization. Our exemplar is this:

(4) (a) 21 June 88
(b) To: John West, Chair, Department of Art
(c) From: Clara Clark, Dean, Graduate School
(d) Subject: Bradford Shane, 537–22–0431
(e) Reference: Your memo of 18 June
(f) Assuming that the proposed new programme in Linguistics (hereafter: the programme) is approved by the Academic Senate,
(g) Bradford Shane may enrol in the programme.
(h) How many others wish to enrol?
(i) Please let me know by 30 June.
(j) Clara Clark [i.e., her signature]
(k) copy to: Bradford Shane

Let us suppose that (4) (without the eleven markers '(a)', ..., '(k)') is written on a piece of paper that in California, say, is recognizable by most people as official stationery of the San Diego campus of the University of California. Also suppose that (j) is recognizable as the signature of a Clara Clark.

Exactly what is (4)? Let us use the type–token distinction and say that the token (4) is the piece of paper (the University stationery) with all of (a)–(k) written on it; the token (4–) is the part of the token (4) that has (a)–(i) and (k) on it but not (j); and the type (4–) is the type expressed by (a)–(i) (k) – that is, the type of which (a) – (i), followed by (k), is a token. Thus the token (4–) is a message token, the type (4–) is a message type, and the token (4–) expresses the type (4–). What is the signature (j)? It is a physical object that is attached to the token (4–) to complete the token (4).

Anticipating our later analysis, let us say that, in the type (4–), the string (g)–(i) is the *body* of the message and that (a)–(f) and (k) jointly constitute the *vector part*. Within the latter we may distinguish (a)–(c) and (k) as indicating the intended direction of the message, and (d)–(f) as indicating the intended focus. The rationale for our terminology will become evident below.

TOWARD A THEORY

Now we lay some groundwork for a general theory that will apply not only to (4) but also to a wide variety of other cases. What we offer below is a set of hypotheses concerning what we shall call *standard messages*. Because these messages are expressions in a language L, we must first make clear what we are assuming about L. This we do by formulating some assumptions, LA. Then we present some hypotheses, SMH, concerning the structure and content of standard messages as wholes, followed by some hypotheses, SVH, concerning standard vectors and their components, and later some hypotheses, PH, concerning the presumptions that are the meanings, so to speak, of the components. After presenting all of these hypotheses we shall discuss the deep rationale for the structure of standard messages.

Our hypotheses concerning messages and vectors are formulated not from the point of view of the sender and the sender's intentions but from the point of view of the message, or what the community believes is the normal or standard meaning of the message. For the most part these formulations are set-theoretic and quasi-semantic. Because most of the sets that we refer to are finite, however, a formulation in almost purely syntactical terms can be given.[1]

In much of our discussion below, especially in connection with vectoring, we use the words 'indicate' and 'specify'. In some places the intended meaning may be the same as that of 'denote', in others the same as that of 'express', and in still others the same as that of 'signal'. It is probably best at this stage to think of 'indicate' and 'specify' as primitive terms.

ASSUMPTIONS ABOUT LANGUAGE

Our assumptions about the language L should seem obvious, or at least unobjectionable. Namely:

LA1 The language L has a finite alphabet, and every expression of L is a finite string of letters of this alphabet.

LA2 The syntax of L provides for certain types of expression, including the usual types found in first-order extensional languages. In particular, it has well-defined concepts of variable, constant, term, predicate, formula and declarative sentence. (Here, by 'term' we mean closed term, term without free variables.)

LA3 L has a semantics that includes the usual sort of extensional semantics. In particular, the terms of L denote objects, and the predicates of L have extensions. L has a relation of implication of the usual sort, holding among the declarative sentences of L. Some of the possible interpretations of L are selected as the admissible ones.

LA4 L has a deductive system such that, if x is a declarative sentence, and x is deductively derivable from a set y of declarative sentences, then x is implied by y in the semantic system.

LA5 L might have various types of non-declarative sentence; if so, then it also has a derivation system appropriate for them. (For example, the interrogative (q?) is derivable from the declarative p and the conditional 'If p, then (q?)'.)

LA6 For some types of sentence of L there is a well-defined concept of *wanted reply*. (For example, for each type of interrogative the concept of direct answer is defined, and direct answers count as wanted replies.) The sentences that have wanted replies are the *erotetic sentences* of L. In addition, for each type of sentence of L, there is a well-defined concept of *sufficient reply*.

LA7 Under its admissible interpretations, L can refer to its own expressions and to certain aspects of the communication process. In particular, it has terms that denote standard messages; it can describe the sending and receiving of tokens (or copies of tokens) of standard messages; and it has self-reference. In general, L is adequate for expressing the presumptions of messages, as called for by our hypotheses PH below.[2]

HYPOTHESES ABOUT MESSAGES

To simplify, in all of SMH and SVH below we use 'M' as a variable ranging over standard messages. Unless we give contraindications, each of SMH and SVH is to be understood as prefaced by 'For every standard message M, . . .'

SMH1 M is an expression of L.
SMH2 The concept of standard message is expressible in L.
SMH3 There are terms that denote M under every admissible interpretation of L; and M may contain terms that denote M under every admissible interpretation of L.
SMH4 M consists of a body and a vector part.
SMH5 The body of M is a string of sentences of L.
SMH6 The vector part of M has a direction indicator and a focus indicator.

By SMH1 the message is a linguistic entity rather than, say, a propositional entity expressed by the linguistic one. Likewise for the message body. In contrast, for the moment at least, we make no commitment concerning the vector. We allow it to be a linguistic entity, identical with the vector part of M; but we also allow it to be a propositional or intentional or set-theoretic entity that is expressed by the vector part of M.

SMH7 To the vector part of M there is assigned a set of declarative sentences of L (the *presumptions* of M).
SMH8 The content that is derivable from M is the content that is derivable from (i) the body of M together with (ii) the presumptions of M.
SMH9 R is a *sufficient response* to M if, and only if:

(i) R is the negation of some presumption of M, or
(ii) R is a conjunction $(X_1 \& \ldots \& X_n)$ such that each X_i is a sufficient reply to some erotetic sentence that is derivable from M, and, for every erotetic sentence that is derivable from M, some sufficient reply to it is among the conjuncts X_i.

Loosely speaking, to reply to a message you must either reply completely or deny at least one presumption. This detail is important in connection with the 'assumptions' component of the vector; see below.

HYPOTHESES ABOUT MESSAGE DIRECTION

Next, to formulate out first hypothesis on vectoring, we need some definitions. Here the reader should keep in mind the remarks made above concerning our use of 'indicate' and 'specify'.

D1 A *sender specifier* is a quadruple consisting of:

(i) a linguistic marker FROM that means the same as 'from',
(ii) a name N,
(iii) a two-place predicate S, and
(iv) a term T that denotes a time or time interval.

D2 A *receiver specifier* is a quadruple consisting of

(i)   a linguistic marker TO that means the same as 'to',
(ii) an X that is either a name or a one-place predicate,
(iii) a two-place predicate S, and
(iv) a term T that denotes a time or time interval.

Loosely speaking, (D1) generalizes on (4–c). It specifies a sender by name, specifies (via predicate) a status that the sender has at the time of sending, and specifies the time of sending. (D2) generalizes on (4–b). It allows specification of one receiver (by name) or a class of receivers (by predicate), it specifies a status that the intended receivers will have at the intended time of receiving, and specifies the intended time of receiving. In these definitions, and in (D3)–(D5) below, the one-place predicates specify a class of receivers, and the two-place predicates specify a status that the persons have at the indicated time. Later we shall have more to say about statuses and the role they play in vectoring.

In our exemplar (4) there is only one time indicated – namely, the day denoted by (4–a). Sometimes we want a message to indicate not merely a day but a more specific time, either something as vague as 'morning' or as precise as '0935' or the like. Sometimes we want something less specific than a day, as in 'Christmas [season] 1983' or the like. That is why our definitions allow dating by either times or time intervals.

In (4) the date of the message is clearly intended to be both the time of sending and the intended time of receiving. Occasionally a message indicates two different times, one for the sending and one for the intended receiving, as in:

(5)   To my son, who will be my heir, when you have reached age twenty-one

(6)   To all taxpayers, as patriotic Americans, on Election Day.

Our definitions allow for this sort of double-dating by letting the 'from' part include a sending-time specifier and letting the 'to' part include a receiving-time specifier.

D3   A *routing specifier* is a finite set of finite non-empty sequences Z such that each member of each Z is a finite non-empty set of pairs consisting of

(i)   either a name or one-place predicate; and
(ii) a two-place predicate.

D4   A *distribution specifier* is a 5-tuple consisting of

(i)   a marker DIST that means the same as 'distribution';
(ii) a finite non-empty set of sender specifiers;
(iii) a routing specifier;
(iv) a finite non-empty set of receiver specifiers; and
(v)   a finite set of pairs consisting of (1) a name or one-place predicate and (2) a two-place predicate.

D5 An *exclusion specifier* is a finite set of quadruples as in (D2) except for 'NOT TO' in place of 'TO' and 'not to' in place of 'to'.

SVH1 In the vector part of M the direction indicator indicates a distribution specifier and an exclusion specifier.

Loosely speaking: the distribution specifier must specify a 'from' and a 'to'; it may additionally specify a 'through' (possibly via several parallel channels) and a 'copy to'. The exclusion specifier may specify various restrictions such as 'confidential', 'top secret', 'need-to-know', 'not to be made public until 15 June', 'not to be shown to Smith, ever'.

HYPOTHESES ABOUT MESSAGE FOCUS

D6 A *subject specifier* is a pair consisting of

(i) a marker that means the same as 'subject' ('topic'); and
(ii) a finite set of terms, predicates, and sentences.

D7 A *reference specifier* is a pair consisting of

(i) a marker that means the same as 'thing referred to'; and
(ii) a finite set of triples each of which consists of (1) a finite set of messages; (2) a finite set of expressions of L; and (3) a declarative sentence of L that mentions the sets (1) and (2). ((3) is the *explaining sentence.*)

D8 An *assumption specifier* is a finite set of declarative sentences of L.

SVH2 In the vector part of M the focus indicator indicates a subject specifier, a reference specifier, and an assumption specifier.

Concerning the subject: in (4) the subject, which is specified by (d), is a named individual. (D6) allows this and also allows the specification of a general subject matter, as in

(7) Subject: Graduation requirements

Also, by allowing sentences as well as terms and predicates, (D6) in effect allows the subject to be an assertion, a question, a command, or whatever. The sentence might be in the body of someone else's earlier message, or it might be in the body of the present message. Examples of the latter: the sender discusses a certain question in the body and wants to emphasize this fact, and hence includes an appropriate interrogative in the subject specifier. The author of a newspaper article chooses a declarative sentence from the body and uses that sentence for the headline.

Pragmatically, the subject indicates to the receiver what the sender thinks the message is about, what routines of message processing the receiver should use, and where, as the final step in the message processing, a copy of the message token should be filed. Details of copying and filing are minor but not negligible; see below.

Concerning the reference: loosely speaking, the reference is what the sender is replying to. While the subject is the semantic point of the message, the reference is the communicative point of the message. Normally the reference is a previous message from someone who is now one of the receivers for whom the present message is intended. There are many exceptions, however, as these examples show (and see below, after (PH6)):

(8) Following up on what I said earlier,
(9) In reply to the question asked by your friend,
(10) Anticipating what you are about to say,
(11) – and keep in mind the importance of what I am now telling you –

Concerning the assumptions: in our exemplar (4), (f) specifies two assumptions. These may be expressed by:

(12) 'the programme' abbreviates 'the proposed new programme in Linguistics'
(13) The programme will be approved.

Clearly, (12) is a device for syntactical convenience and thus seems to be semantically vacuous, while (13) seems to be substantive and non-vacuous. Communicatively, however, they have the same status. The receiver of M may reply to M by giving the negation of either (12) or (13); by (SMH9) this counts as a sufficient response to M.

In general, listing a sentence S as an assumption, while keeping it out of the body, indicates to the receiver that the sender wants the receiver to agree that S is to be taken as non-controversial, so that attention can be focused on the body. If the receiver refuses to agree to this, then (by (SMH9)) there need be no further discussion of M.

STANDARD MESSAGE CONTENT

The sender has in mind a certain content and chooses a message M to convey this content; that is, the sender chooses a message M from which the receiver will infer this content. All parties gain if the community adopts a standard logic of messages that specifies for each standard message a standard content – i.e., a logic that effectively specifies for each standard message-expresser X what message M is expressed by X (under standard conditions) and what content may be derived from M (under standard conditions). In this section we sketch one type of standard message logic; later we discuss standard conditions and consider how the receiver may infer that conditions are standard.[3]

First, we must specify the presumptions that attach to the vector. As noted in (SMH7), these are declarative sentences of L, and for each message there should be only finitely many. As noted in (SMH8), the general purpose of the presumptions is to express the semantic content of the vector. Listed below are some hypotheses about the major presumptions. Let us abbreviate 'FROM' by 'Fr' and 'TO' by 'To'. Then, in light of (D1) and (D2), our notation should be clear.

PH1 A sender specifier FrNST brings the presumption that the individual named by N has the status S at time T (i.e., the predicate S is true of N at T).

PH2 A receiver specifier ToXST brings the presumption that the individual named by the name X (or, all of the individuals in the extension of the predicate X) have the status S at time T.

PH3 A sender specifier FrNST, in combination with a receiver specifier ToXST, brings the presumption that roughly

(i)   N at T sends M toward the individuals X;
(ii) the individuals X will receive M at some time during or after T; and
(iii) the individuals indicated (by the routing) for 'through' and 'copy to' will receive M at the appropriate times.

PH4 The exclusion specifier in M brings the presumption that (roughly)

(i) the individuals indicated have the indicated status at the indicated time; and
(ii) none of these individuals will receive M except as allowed by the specifier.

PH5 If L has descriptive terms, then every descriptive term specified by the vector, except those occurring in the expressions called for by (ii) in (D6), brings the presumption that the description is proper.

PH6 A reference specifier brings the presumption that

(i) every message in the sets (1) (see (D7)) is signed and sent by the ostensible sender at the ostensible time; and
(ii) all of the explaining sentences (see (D7)) are true.

We cannot yet impose any more conditions on (D7) or (PH6). The expressions in the sets (2) are somehow relevant to the messages in the sets (1) and relevant to the message that contains the specifier, but we have not yet analysed this sort of relevance. It is very complex. Consider, e.g.:

(14) Your letter as a whole raises some questions.
(15) *Re* his report: I can do better than that.

PH7 The assumption specifier AS in M brings the presumption that every sentence in AS is true.

After determining the presumptions for the vector we establish one or more derivation systems for deriving content from the vector and the body. The essential requirement is that these systems determine, for each type of sentence of L and each standard message M, the set of sentences of that type that are derivable from M. Then we can say that, for each M, under standard conditions, for each sentence that is derivable from M, the sender is committed in the standard way – for example, committed to asserting the declaratives that are derivable from M, asking the interrogatives, commanding the imperatives, and the like.

STANDARD CONDITIONS

There are several conditions that must be met if we are to call a communication situation normal or standard. The one that is most relevant to us here is the condition of the sender's intention: the sender must have standard communicative intentions – i.e. the sender must choose a standard message, send it in the standard way, and intend that it be received and interpreted in the standard way, interpreted by the receiver as having been intended to convey its standard content. The question we focus on now is: when can the receiver reasonably infer that the sender has standard communicative intentions?

The answer comes from sociology. Recall (4), with its various references to status. Clara Clark claims to have the status of being Dean of the Graduate School, and she imputes to John West the status of being Chair of the Department of Art. The important sociological fact here in this example is that California state law controls the use of university materials. Thus, in particular, if someone misuses university stationery, some penalty will apply; and, no matter what the stationery, if someone who is not the Dean claims to be the Dean and claims to take official action, then some penalty will apply. Also, if the person who really is Dean ostensibly takes some official action, but really is only joking, then some penalty will apply. The penalty system is such that, when Californians see something like (4) written on official university stationery, and they recognize (j) as the signature of Clara Clark, and they know that this Clara Clark is the Dean of the Graduate School, then they can reasonably infer that (4) is motivated by standard communicative intentions. That is, (4) is intended in a serious, literal way; in particular the ostensible vectoring expressed by (a)–(f) is, or accurately expresses, the real vectoring intended by Clark.

Let us generalize the analysis. The University of California is an agency of the state of California, so it is protected by state law. Many other organizations that are not state agencies are protected by state law. If John Smith uses the stationery of the Walt Disney Company and falsely claims to be the President of the company, then, depending on what Smith is trying to do, he may be charged with fraud or something worse and then penalized. Let us say that, where there are rules for the proper use of an instrument of communication and penalties for its misuse, the instrument is *protected*. Likewise, where there are rules for proper use of a status claim and penalties for misuse, the status is *protected*. Rules and penalties are relative to social system, so protection is thus relative also. The following are examples of statuses that are effectively protected by the laws of American society: Sheriff of Dade County, resident of Ohio, Treasurer of Ford Motor Company, Medical Doctor licensed to practise in Iowa, wife of, owner of, author of.

The general point is this. Protection is widespread and directly relevant to much of our communication. In a community that has protected instruments of communication and protected statuses, when someone uses a protected instrument and claims a protected status, the audience may reasonably infer that the sender has standard intentions.

One related point: in connection with organizations that have protected instruments and statuses, signatures are effective; that is, the relevant community can effectively recognize the signature as the signature of the signer. This is needed for validation and verification. The act of signing officially initiates the sending process and officially commits the signer to the claim that the signer is the ostensible sender and that the signer is sending the message with standard intentions.

THE RATIONALE OF STANDARD VECTORS

Why do standard messages have standard vectors? Why do standard vectors have the components that they do? Why do they not have other components? Are there any other components that they should have?

Our answer in brief is this. The purpose of the vector is to provide certain kinds of efficiency and civility. Standard vectors provide just the right kinds of efficiency and civility in a very efficient way. They do not need any vector components beyond the ones described in our hypotheses above. We have no proof that establishes this answer to the exclusion of others. What we have is only a likely story. In this section we consider efficiency; in the next we consider civility.

Communication as such does not require vectoring. The sender could simply formulate a message body and then broadcast it worldwide, so to speak, trusting that it would somehow come to the attention of the right audience and then be analysed, interpreted, and used in the right way. Normally, however, the sender has in mind not only a body but also a vector, for either one of two reasons. Either the vector comes first, articulating the essence of the sender's initial communicative intention; or else the body comes first, and the vector then is useful as an efficient means for articulating the intentions about right audience, right analysis, and the like.

Given that the sender has a vector in mind, why include expression of the vector with expression of the message body? One purpose is obvious: it makes for efficiency in transmission, reception, interpretation and use. This efficiency is achieved by the individual components and by the vector as a whole.

The efficiency achieved by the vector as a whole is a general one. Recall the sociology. If the sender sends M via a protected instrument, claims a protected status, and signs in a recognizable way, the audience can infer that the intentions are standard. Then the vector of M can be interpreted in the standard way, the vector of M serves as the vector for all of the speech act sentences in the body of M, and thus those sentences can be interpreted in the standard way.

Expressing a distribution specifier with M makes for the most important kind of efficiency, making objectively clear the sender's intentions about the routing and distribution of M. Expressing the relevant status imputations makes clear the social context for which M is supposed to be meaningful, the social game in which sending M is a move. Expressing the exclusion specifier is the contrapositive; it makes clear who is not to receive M. Why express the sender specifiers? This is to ensure civility, as we explain below.

Expressing a focus for M in general makes for efficiency in message processing. Most languages contain redundancy, most messages contain more than one bit of information, and most bits of information can be filed under more than one category and used in more than one way. Expressing a focus makes clear what is to be selected or emphasized; in general, it makes clear how the sender wants the receiver to analyse and use M.

The subject specifier indicates, out of the total semantic content of the message, what part the receiver should concentrate on, what part might be relevant to the receiver's future interests. The reference specifier indicates, out of the total history of message exchange in the community, which messages are immediately relevant to this one, or to which this one is some kind of response.

The assumption specifier lists sentences that are intended to be non-controversial or at least non-negotiable. The substantive assumptions are intended to articulate background assumptions that are presumably shared by sender and receiver but are needed for analysing the message. Putting these assumptions in the vector, rather than in the body, makes for efficiency in message processing, because (by (SMH9)) either they are all accepted immediately and the analysis continues, or some of them are rejected immediately and the entire message can be rejected immediately. The substantive assumptions are needed for generating the full content of M and thus can be counted as part of the content of M; their being in the vector rather than in the body directs attention away from them and toward the content of the body.

Why do the subject, reference, and assumption specifiers all belong in the message focus? Why does the focus consist of these and only these? Here is a likely story: the sender intends that the message be understood on three dimensions, but the content of each dimension is relatively rich and must be reduced to manageable size via some focus. The focus that the sender intends for the syntactical dimension is expressed by the assumption specifier. The focus that is intended for the semantic dimension is expressed by the subject specifier. The focus for the pragmatic (communicative) dimension is expressed by the reference specifier.

CIVILITY

For our theory of communication we do not need a complete theory of rationality, but we do make one assumption. We assume that rationality in communication involves at least three factors: a desire for success, a respect for logic and a concern for civility.

By civility we do not mean politeness in the usual sense. Rather we mean something akin to a civic sensitivity or civic orientation. It will suffice here to describe it as follows. To be civil in communication is to communicate in such a way that a record can be kept and analysed at will for as long as desired. Civil communication is communication plus a history. If its communication is civil, the community can keep a record of who said what to whom when.

As already noted, one motivation for standard messages with standard vectors is efficiency, and the other is civility. If one uses standard messages, one can be civil in this way: first, choose a standard message. Then choose a message token that is sufficiently durable, sign it, make some durable copies of the signed token, and then send the signed token in conformity with the distribution specifier and the exclusion specifier.

Why does the sender include the sender specifier and sign the token? The sender specifier is the most important factor in civility, the key to keeping a record of who said what. Signing the token validates the sender specifier and provides the basis for verifying the record.

To summarize: suppose that the sender uses a protected instrument of communication, claims a protected status, and signs the token properly. Then, if the message is a standard one (with standard vector), the vector then provides the ground for a public record whereby anyone who examines the signed message token can determine who sent the token and hence who sent the message, when, with what status claims, to whom, and with what understanding about subject matter and communicative point.

OTHER VECTOR COMPONENTS?

According to the analysis outlined above, each standard vector is – loosely speaking – determined by five things: senders, receivers, subject, reference and assumptions. Have we overlooked anything, any kind of item that might be needed in a vector?

Consider the following, which are sometimes found in memos like (4):

(16) Urgent!
(17) Typed by dp
(18) Eyes only!
(19) Retention: two years
(20) Destroy immediately!

All of these concern the message token rather than the message type. Indeed, (16) must be marked on the token in a special way so that the receiver will see it immediately. Do expressions like (16)–(20) introduce a new dimension in vectoring, or call for new components in the vector?

To account for (16)–(20) one might say that what is vectored is the token rather than the type, but there are compelling arguments against this view. For example, the ostensible time of sending is supposed to be the time of signing the (usually one and only) signed token. Other tokens, or copies of the signed token, may be produced at later times, but in them the indicated time is the time of the first signed token. This makes sense only if it is the message type that is vectored, rather than the message tokens.

The direct way to accommodate (16)–(20) is to add them as new components of the vector, or else to lump them together in one new component (call it the *token specifier*). Presumptions attach in the obvious way. For example:

(16′) This message is urgent.
(17′) This message token (the message token signed by the indicated sender at the indicated time) was typed by dp.
(18′) No one will make any copies of any token of this message.
(19′) The intended receiver will retain the received token of this message for at least two years.
(20′) The indicated receiver will immediately destroy every token of this message.

In an alternative treatment we regard (16)–(20) as abbreviations of (16′)–(20′) and add (16′)–(20′) to the routing specifier as a new component of that specifier. The new presumption then is that these sentences are true. The direct treatment sketched above seems to stay closer to the data of observable linguistic forms, but the alternative treatment seems equivalent to it from a logical point of view. Perhaps a compromise is possible: let the vector have a new component – the token specifier – but let it consist of the sentences (16′)–(20′) and any other declarative sentences of L that express the sender's understanding or intentions about the token. We make no claims here about which treatment is best.

PARTIAL VECTORS

According to the analysis presented above, every standard message has a vector with (roughly) five or perhaps six parts. This analysis seems to fit some of the message forms that are used in human communication, but seems not to fit others. Many formal memos seem to lack some of the standard vector components, and of course there are many sentences of natural language that seem to be partially vectored but not fully vectored. Consider the following (where S abbreviates 'Smith will win'):

(21) John, as your friend, I tell you that S.
(22) I tell you, John, as a friend of mine, that S.
(23) Speaking of old friends, S.
(24) Oh, about the election, S.
(25) The answer to that is that S.
(26) It is Smith who will win.
(27) Well, [pause] S.
(28) Assuming that I'm correct about the voting, S.
(29) In the usual sense of 'win', S.

Here is how a vector-theorist looks at (21)–(29). The speaker claims a status in (21) and imputes a status in (22). Each of (23) and (24) specifies a subject. (25) refers directly to a previous utterance; (26) refers indirectly, and in some contexts so does (27). (28) specifies a substantive assumption; (29) specifies a definitional one.

There are two ways to theorize about expressions that seem to be partially vectored. In one way, we say that the sender always has in mind a complete standard vector, but this vector may be expressed in abbreviated form. The sender uses a standard system, adopted by the language community, whereby certain vector components may be deleted or transformed in certain ways according to the sender's needs or communicative style.[4] In the other way of theorizing, we say that in addition to complete standard vectors there are partial standard vectors (or standard partial vectors), and the sender may have one of these in mind and then express it appropriately.

Sometimes a sender wants to send a standard message, with complete vector, with a body that contains partially vectored sentences. In general we think that the vectors of the sentences in the body should cohere with the vector of the message as a whole. Probably the simplest way to define the sort of coherence that we want here is to say that the partials cohere with the complete if the partials are fragments of the complete – provided, of course, that we can first define fragment in a satisfactory way. One obvious alternative is to assign presumptions to the partial vectors and say that those presumptions must be consistent with the presumptions of the complete one. Unfortunately the matter of assigning presumptions to partial vectors will probably not be easy.

PROBLEMS FOR FURTHER RESEARCH

First, fill out and make more precise the theory outlined above. Determine the ontological status of the vector. (Is it intentional? Propositional? Set-theoretic? Linguistic?) If the vector is non-linguistic, determine the rules for expressing the vector. Make more precise the concepts of specification and indication, and relate them to the concepts of classical semantics. Determine the system for abbreviating standard vectors, or a system for constructing partial vectors. Determine precisely the presumptions of vectors and partial vectors.

Second, study the algebra of vectors. Study compositionality and projection rules. Determine the extent to which the components of simple vectors may be combined to form components of complex vectors. There will be some positive results. For example, if V refers to M and V' refers to M' (and both M and M' have actually been sent), then there is a V" that refers to both M and M'. On the other hand, Jones can send two one-sentence messages M and M' and claim the status of sending only one-sentence messages, but Jones cannot combine M and M' and still claim the same status. Conjecture: we shall discover more negative results than positive ones.

Third, determine whether vectors can be generated by some process analogous to the process that generates illocutionary entities according to the theory of Searle and Vanderveken (1985). This question is relevant to both the second problem above and the fourth problem below.

Fourth, construct a plausible theory of learnability for vectoring. How do we learn to construe vector expressions? How do we learn to construct them? Conjecture: because the components of a vector must cohere with the body and with each other, it will be easier to develop a theory of learnability for the theory of complete-but-abbreviatable vectors than for the theory of partial-but-combinable vectors.

Fifth, study the empirical data to determine the class of expressions that are normally construed in terms of standard vectoring, and the class of expressions that are normally construed in terms of other kinds of vectoring. Determine the expressions that can reasonably be construed in terms of standard vectoring. Look for evidence that can help us to decide between the theory of complete-but-abbreviatable vectors and the theory of partial-but-combinable vectors. In all of the empirical work one should consider both synchronic and diachronic studies. Example: study the vectoring of books and manuscripts, from the introductory protocol section of classical Greek manuscripts to the dust jacket and title page and preface of modern books – including this one, of course.

NOTES

1   For a system that provides messages and vectors much like those in the system

described here, but which is defined in almost purely syntactical terms, see Harrah 1985, 1986.

2   For details on extensional languages, see, for example, Gamut 1991. For details on systems like those indicated in LA5–LA7, see Harrah 1985.

3   Our sketch here is incomplete and rather vague; for more details and greater precision, see Harrah 1985.

4   For more on a system of this sort, see Harrah 1986.

Part III

Speech acts and grammatical structure

20 Toward a grammatically realistic typology of speech acts

Jerrold M. Sadock

By setting up a classification of illocutionary forces that had little to do with the theory of speech acts that he was principally concerned with eluci-dating, Austin (1962) established a small but flourishing industry devoted to the taxonomization of the conventional acts that people do in saying things. Austin's five picturesquely named classes – verdictives, exercitives, commissives, behabitives and expositives – have been the subject of much criticism by subsequent taxonomists, the main complaint being that, to the extent that unambiguous criteria are used in characterizing the classes at all, these criteria are *de latero muri*, which is to say, they are unrelated to any of the apparatus that was independently used in the discussion of illocutionary acts in the rest of Austin's work. In his alternative taxonomiz-ation, Searle (1975) improved upon Austin by at least providing a scheme that was not entirely unrelated to the dissection that he provides in *Speech Acts* (Searle 1969).

But there are aspects of Searle's classification, too, that come straight out of the blue. In *Speech Acts* there are only four dimensions in terms of which illocutionary acts are differentiated: the essential condition, prepara-tory conditions, sincerity, and propositional-content conditions.[1] In Searle 1975, however, this list has expanded to an even dozen separate axes that are used to distinguish speech acts, some of which are direct reflections of the conditions in *Speech Acts* (Searle 1969),[2] and some of which are not. Not corresponding to any of the felicity conditions or the corresponding rules of *Speech Acts* are such vague features as 'strength with which the illocutionary point is presented' and such unhelpful characteristics as 'style of performance of the illocutionary act' (used to distinguish acts of announcing from acts of confiding, for example). Searle does, however, state that of the twelve, three dimensions 'seem to me the most important, and I build most of my taxonomy around them' (1975: 348). Two of these – '(illocutionary) point' and 'expressed psychological states' – are directly related to conditions on happy performance from Searle's earlier work, namely the essential condition and the sincerity condition, respectively. The remaining one of the three most important dimensions, which goes by the name of 'direction of fit between words and the world' has no grounding, so far as I can see, in independent considerations of the structure of speech acts.

Even for those parameters that have antecedents in the theory of *Speech Acts*, the determination of the particular values that are allowed seems to me to be a highly arbitrary matter. For example, on the dimension of illocutionary point, which Searle thinks is the single most important, we find five values: the assertive point, the directive point, the commissive point, the expressive point, and the misleadingly named point of declarations, called elsewhere the declarative point. Why we find exactly these points, and not, say, a precative point (for cursing), a lamentative point (for complaints), a suppositive point (for supposing), and so on, I do not know. True, such acts as cursing and supposing seem less mundane, less basic than the five that Searle postulates, but how does Searle know which ones are primitive?

A hint comes from comparing Searle's points to Austin's classes. It is perhaps slightly surprising that Searle recognizes exactly five basic points, the same number as Austin has categories. But it cannot be pure coincidence that there is a clear relationship between the first four of Searle's points and the first four of Austin's categories and that they are presented *in the same order*. The names have been changed, but the innocent have not been protected.

(1) *Austin*   *Searle*
    1 Verdictives   Assertives
    2 Exercitives   Directives
    3 Commissives   Commissives
    4 Behabitives   Expressives
    5 Expositives   Declarations

With the exception of Austin and Searle's fifth category (a big and important exception, to be sure, and one to which I will return directly) the basic illocutionary points of Searle's system seem to be mere refinements of the categories posited on entirely intuitive grounds by Austin. Searle says that his assertive class 'will contain most of Austin's expositives and many of his verdictives as well' (Searle 1975: 355). About the directives he says 'Many of Austin's exercitives are also in this class' (ibid.: 356). With regard to commissives, Searle simply accepts the prior class, writing 'Austin's definition of commissives seems unexceptionable, and I will simply appropriate it' (ibid.). The acts of thanking, apologizing and giving condolences occur on Austin's list of behabitives and are included amongst the expressives by Searle.

The fifth categories, however, differ completely from one author to the other. Austin's category of expositives is almost completely absorbed into Searle's assertives. The latter author's fifth class of declarations is a real puzzler. It includes almost everything that Austin would have classed as a performative, plus other institutionally sanctioned acts that are accomplished by utterances that seem to say that they are accomplished. Searle writes, 'It is the defining characteristic of this class that the ... successful performance guarantees that the propositional content corresponds to the world ... What I am calling declarations were included in the class of performatives' (ibid.: 358). Now in an example such as *I christen this ship the Kneydl*, a successful uttering is a christening. The proposition %I christen this ship the Kneydl%[3] is true just in case the act is successful, and hence this is a Searlean declaration. But if *I christen* is here propositional content, then why are *I state that it is raining*, *I order you to leave*, *I promise to pay you the money*, and *I apologize for stepping on your toe* not all declarations rather than an assertive, a directive, a commissive, and an expressive, as Searle classifies them? I admit to being confused by this treatment, unable to convince myself that the *manner* in which a particular utterance achieves what it does (here by saying that it does what it does) is not entirely independent of the *kind of thing* that it does, that is to say, the 'point' of the utterance.

Besides being *ad hoc* and perhaps partly incoherent, Searle's classificatory system also seems to be highly uneconomical. He posits three important dimensions (point, direction of fit, and expressed psychological state) with five, four, and five values, respectively. Ideally, these parameters would characterize 100 distinct illocutionary types, but in fact, they characterize only the five categories just discussed. Without going into detail, I will simply present the alignment of the values on these three dimensions for the five act types they serve to specify.[4]

(2) | *Point* | *Direction of fit* | *Psychological state* |
| --- | --- | --- |
| assertive | word-to-world | belief |
| directive | world-to-word | desire |
| commissive | world-to-word | intention |
| expressive | none | variable |
| declarative | both | none |

A NEW VIEW

Austin's principal lesson in *How to do Things with Words* is this (Austin 1962: 113):

> whenever I 'say' anything (except perhaps a mere exclamation like 'damn' or 'ouch') I shall be performing both locutionary and illocutionary acts.

This is rendered by Searle (1975) as the formula (3), where 'F' is illocutionary force and 'p' propositional content:

(3) $F(p)$

Searle's formula does indeed give all ordinary utterances both force and meaning, but it amounts to a semantic version of the performative hypothesis. It rigidly separates (what appears to be) a single semanto-pragmatic proposition into (what appear to be) a function and an argument that correspond, respectively, to the illocutionary force and the propositional content. In so doing, it comes to grief over those same pesky utterance types with which Austin began his discussion, and over which numerous subsequent theories have stumbled: the performatives. Thus Searle vacillates, as we have seen, between including the performative prefix in propositional structure (as part of p), which gives rise to the anomalous class of declarations, and excluding it (placing it in F), in which case performatively used sequences like *I promise, I christen*, etc. are outside of the propositional content and hence are counterintuitively treated as not being used with their 'ordinary sense and reference'.

Instead of conceiving these two facets of speech acts as two completely separable parts of a single type of thing (as implied by Searle's formula 'F(p)' and as explicitly assumed by generative semanticists (Lakoff 1977; Sadock 1974)), I would like to explore the idea that these are simultaneous, independent, orthogonal communicative dimensions. On the one hand, then, there is an informational, representational modality to natural language, and on the other, a socially effective modality. If these are conceived of as independent of one another, then there is no oddity in the fact that we may accomplish social ends by representing the world, and nothing paradoxical in the fact that the act of representing the world might be a social end in itself. (Cp. Eilfort and Schiller 1990 for the origins of this idea.)

This interpretation seems very much in line with Austin's summary of his thoughts on speech acts:

> With the constative utterance, we abstract from the illocutionary ... aspects of the speech act, and we concentrate on the locutionary ... With the performative utterance, we attend as much as possible to the illocutionary force of the utterance, and abstract from the dimension of correspondence with the facts.
>
> (Austin 1962: 144–5)

The Searlean recension of Austin does not do justice to this remark, giving equal weight to both types of acts in all sentences. Recognizing the informational and effective aspects of speech as separate dimensions, however, allows us to model the sense of this passage fairly directly: while many, indeed most sorts of utterances have a value in both the informational and effective dimensions, their primary purpose differs; the purpose of the constative – to represent situations, events, and so on – is to be located in the informational dimension; the purpose of performatives – namely, to cause certain socially determined facts to come into existence – is to be found in the effective dimension. But this is not to suggest that the other dimension is absent in either case. The act of representing the world creates a social fact (to be discussed below) and the creation of social facts often requires the representation of past, present, or future states of affairs.

I would like to go one step further, in fact, and suggest that the ordinary act of speech involves *three* distinct and autonomous functional aspects,[5] the third of which has to do with feelings rather than ideas or effects. Acts of speech, I suggest, ordinarily have three separate communicative aspects, namely:

1   an informational, representational aspect (INF) in which conversational negotiations are conducted in terms of propositions that can be judged for accuracy against real or possible worlds;
2   an effective, social aspect (EF) by means of which conventional effects on societally determined features of the world are achieved;
3   an affective, emotive aspect (AF) that is used to give vent to and/or display real or apparent feelings of the speaker.

These three dimensions correspond in a rough way to the propositional content condition, the essential condition, and the sincerity condition of Searle 1969. I do not see them as conditions on the felicitous performance of acts of the second kind mentioned above, however, but rather as distinct and independent conventional facets of human language systems.[6]

The reason for adding the third dimension, the affective component of speech, is to be found in Austin's own observation above to the effect that there are speech acts that seem to have neither locutionary (in my terms 'informational') nor illocutionary (in my terms 'effective') content. When I say 'Ouch!' I merely vent (or at least make a show of venting) an emotion. The act is conventional, of course, in that the phonetics of the pain-expressing speech act vary from language to language (else we would study them in biology, rather than linguistics or philosophy of mind) but that is not the same thing as saying that it is a representational act. Having heard me say 'Ouch!' you might be fairly certain that I might agree with the statement 'That hurt', but you cannot respond 'Liar', or 'You said it', or 'I doubt it', or anything like that. The representation is entirely implied, rather than contained in the utterance. For the same reason, you cannot report such an act by saying 'He said it hurt.' Saying 'Ouch', may likewise imply the desirability of some activity or another on the part of over-hearers, say getting off my toe, or maybe expressing sympathy, but once again, this social effect is implied, rather than contained in the act. Saying 'Ouch' is not the same thing as saying 'Get off my toe', which automatically and conventionally burdens the addressee with the job of getting off the speaker's toe (or suffer unspecified social consequences).

Besides purely emotive acts of speech, there are purely effective acts which involve neither a conventional display of emotion nor a representation of a state of affairs in terms of predicates and arguments. This is sufficient to establish the independence of the effective dimension from the other two. Purely effective acts are fairly common, but have not been much commented on in the literature. Included here are acts accomplished by uttering otherwise meaningless forms such as *hi, bye, amen, ollie ollie oxen free* (and other variants), and so on. These may imply either a representation (for example, 'I recognize you', 'I hope to see you again') or the possession of a particular state of mind (for example, happiness, good wishes), or, more usually, both; but once again, that is not the same as their actually *being* representations or expressions of emotion. If the feeling, let us say, were necessarily expressed as part of the social act of greeting, taking leave, and so on, then such locutions as 'Goodbye and good riddance', could not exist.

Are there pure informational acts? The only candidate for a vehicle of this type that I can think of is the simple declarative sentence, but I cannot convince myself that Austin was wrong in saying that constatives also serve an obligatory, conventional function. I think it is quite possible that every representational act necessarily has either a social or an emotive value, or both. If so, there is an asymmetry between the informational dimension on the one hand and the effective and affective dimensions on the other. Speech acts can be purely effective or purely affective, but they cannot be purely informational. This asymmetry shows up in another way, to which I return below.

Adding the third dimension, we see that there are three basic speech act types (we can no longer call them illocutions) that differ precisely in which of the three basic components is the principal component. There are, in other words, speech acts that are primarily informational – which include the constatives – others that are primarily effective – which include the performatives – and finally acts that are primarily effective. This is not to deny that an act whose primary function is to be located in one of these dimensions has no function on either of the others. Quite the contrary, since, by assumption, the three dimensions are essentially independent. Thus a primarily effective utterance (typically an explicit performative) also represents the world (say, as being one in which the speaker accomplishes the illocutionary act in question) and a primarily informational act, whose principal vector is the constative sentence, does have automatic social consequences, as Austin saw, namely stating, i.e. the placing of a new proposition in the category of pragmatically given, presupposable information, thus burdening all participants in the discourse to accept it as true or to argue against it, or otherwise question its status (cp. Stalnaker 1978; Lewis 1979).

We may also observe that there are acts defined in only two of the dimensions (one of which is primary). Thus we may express interest, curiosity, disbelief, or something along those lines with a grunted 'Huh?'[7] which is clearly devoid of propositional representation of the world. We might reasonably assume that the grunter might alternatively have produced a sentence such as: 'I did not properly assimilate the last remark', but that does not allow the addressee (gruntee?) to respond as if such a representation had been made by saying, for example, 'You're wrong' (i.e. 'You did understand'). Here, I think, the emphasis is clearly on the emotive aspect of the act, though there is a clear obligation placed upon the target of the utterance. Quite automatically, and conventionally, the target of 'Huh?' is socially burdened. He or she must repeat, clarify, or otherwise do what the situation calls for. It is worse than impolite or inconsiderate not to – it is a breach of the social convention instituted by uttering 'Huh?' Such an utterance, then, has both an affective and an effective facet (the latter being primary) but no informational content. Contrasting with this case is a more-or-less informationally bleached form such as 'Beg pardon?' (uttered with question intonation, note) where the social effect is paramount and the association with an emotion (confusion, curiosity or the like) is secondary.

Informational, affective, but non-effective acts are to be found in the otherwise troublesome class of formal exclamations, for example, 'Is it ever expensive!', 'Boy, is it expensive' (McCawley 1973). While the utterer of an exclamation is certainly on record as having a particular view of the world – as representing a certain something as expensive in the examples just discussed – he or she does not make the representation in order to establish some socially defined condition, but rather only in order to vent or display an emotion. Since non-effective acts only incidentally produce social effects, they are among the only acts that do not require an addressee (or potential addressee). They can be uttered to oneself in privacy, without alarming eavesdroppers.

Much more central to the history of speech act theory (too central according to Strawson 1964) are the highly formal utterances that form a part of a religious ceremony, legal proceeding, or game, namely performative and quasi-performative sentences like *I christen* ..., *I bet* ..., *I pronounce* ..., *I bid* ..., *You're fired, I raise you a quarter*. Now the performer of such an act might be expected to have certain thoughts and feelings, but that is just a function of (a) the stereotypical situation in which such acts are performed; and (b) knowledge of general or culturally specific values and goals. In betting that the Bears will win the Superbowl, I do not *display* my belief that the Bears stand a good chance of winning. At most, you may surmise that I have that belief, believing that I (like you) do not want to lose money. I might, however, want to reduce my winnings for tax purposes, or help you out because I feel sorry for you, and so on. In poker, indeed, it is a good idea *not* to display any distinct emotion, or at least not a genuine one. Whether I have certain feelings or not is entirely irrelevant to the felicity of the act. Thus in betting (christening, firing, etc.) one achieves an affect-free social effect and represents the world in a certain way, namely as one in which the act is performed, either by predicating the doing of the act of the speaker (*I resign*) or predicating the result of the act upon its patient (*You're fired*). I think that Austin and Searle were just wrong in assuming a sincerity condition on a par with the one that governs statements, promises, and questions as characterizing Strawsonian conventional performatives. If I say 'I bet the Bears will win, though I sincerely doubt it', I do not in any way weaken the bet. But saying 'The bears will win, though I don't believe that they will', is Moore's paradox.

Let us sum up what we have got, to this point, in the form of a chart of those act types that exist in only one or two of the three dimensions I have assumed. Without prejudice, we may call these 'defective speech acts'.

(4) *Defective speech acts*

	INF	*EF*	*AF*
Ouch!	−	−	+
Hi	−	+	−
Huh?	−	+	+
Boy, it's hot	+	−	+
I bet $5	+	+	−

Now the ordinary act of speech, as I have said repeatedly (if not repetitively), has a value in all three of the principal communicative dimensions: it is a conventional representation of the world; it is conventionally suited to the bringing about of a certain social outcome; and it is a conventional display of a particular emotional state of the speaker. While it may be obvious, I feel that I should point out that these three conventional aspects of the total speech act are independent of the way the natural, artefactual and psychological worlds actually are; representing the world as being a certain way does not make it so; saying something conventionally suited to the secural of certain social effects does not (*pace* Austin) in and of itself bring it about; and a conventional display of a certain emotion is not the same thing as actually having that emotion.

Let me now turn to a number of the kinds of acts that are discussed in the speech act literature and simply ask what their value is in each of these dimensions. Searle (1969) began his discussion of speech acts with a dissection of the act of promising, and so will I.

Regardless of how it is done, an ordinary act of promising involves (a) a representation of the world as one in which a certain voluntary act will be carried out by the speaker; (b) the creation of a social obligation for the speaker to carry out the aforementioned voluntary act; and (c) the expression of the speaker's intention to carry out the said act. The middle feature, the creation of a certain social effect, is definitional. There is an act that we can correctly describe as a promising if, and only if, it results in an obligation upon the speaker to carry out a particular act in the future. Thus a simple 'Okay' will be a promise if it obliges the speaker to do something as when it is a response to 'Will you write me a letter of recommendation?' While the effectual dimension is primary, the representation (either overt or elliptical) is necessary, and the display of the emotion invariable, though it may, of course, be insincere.

Looking at other act types more briefly I will ask: what representation of
the world is made, what conventional effect is achieved, and what attitude
is expressed? The general answers are straightforward and anyone can give
them. The precise wording is not terribly important for present purposes
and is not meant to suggest that these are the only values that exist on these
various dimensions, or even that they are particularly important values.

(5) State
Representation: P (a proposition)
Effect: places P on the record
Affect: expresses speaker's belief in the truth of P

(6) Request
Representation: FUT(P$_a$) (a future act predicated of addressee)
Effect: obligates addressee to do P
Affect: expresses speaker's desire for addressee to P

(7) Promise
Representation: FUT(P$_s$) (a future act predicated of speaker)
Effect: obligates speaker to do P
Affect: expresses speaker's intention to P

(8) Apologize
Representation: PST(P$_{s,u}$) (a past undesirable act of speaker)
Effect: redresses speaker's breach
Affect: expresses speaker's sorrow for having done P

(9) Ask (whether)
Representation: P v ¬P (P a proposition)
Effect: obliges addressee to state P or state ¬P
Affect: expresses speaker's interest in whether P is true or false

(10) Ask (*wh*)
Representation: (∃x)P(x) (P a predicate)
Effect: obliges addressee to state P(C) (C a referring expression)
Affect: expresses speaker's curiosity as to C such that P(C)

(11) Accuse
Representation: PST(P$_{a,u}$) (a past undesirable act of addressee)
Effect: places PST(P) on the record
Affect: expresses speaker's anger at PST(P)

(12) Criticize
Representation: PST(P$_{a,u}$) (a past undesirable act of addressee)
Effect: places BAD(PST(P)) on the record
Affect: expresses speaker's anger at PST(P)

I return now to the asymmetry between the informational dimension and
the others that I mentioned above. The asymmetry shows up also in the
following fact: an effect or affect may be represented, whereas a representation can only be accomplished by representation. Thus it is possible,
within certain limits, to obtain a particular social effect by representing
the actor as carrying out or as having carried out the procedure, or by

representing the affected entity as having suffered the social effect. Let us call the former kind of representations *effector-oriented* representations, and the latter kind *effected-oriented* representations. Thus:

(13) Representations of effect

Act type	*Effector oriented*	*Effected oriented*
State	'I state that ...'	'You are hereby informed that ...'
Request	'I request that ...'	'You must ...'
Promise	'I promise to ...'	'I am committed to ...'
Apologize	'I apologize for ...'	'You have my apologies.'
Ask (whether)	'I ask whether ...'	'You must say whether ...'
Ask (*wh*)	'I ask *wh*...'	'You must say *wh*...'
Accuse	'I accuse you of ...'	'You stand accused of ...'
Greet	'I bid you welcome.'	'You are welcome in my home.'
Congratulate	'I congratulate you.'	'You have my congratulations.'
Condole	'I extend my condolences.'	'You have my condolences.'
Christen	'I christen this child ...'	'This child shall be called ...'
Vote	'Kansas votes for ...'	'Kansas' votes go to ...'

The representational asymmetry also allows for a speaker to express or display a mental attitude by representing him or herself as having certain thoughts or feelings. If the having of such thoughts and feelings is characteristic of a certain effective type, then saying that one has such thoughts and feelings can often achieve the social effect that is normally accompanied by that thought or feeling, as has been frequently noted. This will not work, of course, for those ritualized acts that are not supposed to be accompanied by any particular attitudes. Here are some examples of the representation of an associated affect that can bring about a social effect beyond the representation itself. The last two, lacking an associated affect, can not be accomplished in this way.

(14) Representations of affect

Act type	*Representation of emotive state*
State	'I believe/am convinced that ...'
Request	'I want you to .../wish you would ...'
Promise	'I intend to ...'
Apologize	'I am sorry for ...'
Ask (whether)	'I wonder/am curious as to whether ...'
Ask (*wh*)	'I wonder/am curious as to *wh*...'
Accuse	'I believe/think you ...'
Greet	'I am happy to see you.'
Congratulate	'I am happy for you.'
Condole	'I am sorry for you.'
Christen	—
Vote	—

CONVENTIONALIZATION

In both the categories just adumbrated, i.e. effects achieved by representing the action or its effect, and effects achieved by representing the associated feeling, there are conventionalized and partly conventionalized forms. That is, there are forms where the connection between the representation and the achievement of an extra-representational effect has become conventionalized to the extent that the effective dimension is now primary, and the representation secondary, as with performatives. We can get a rough idea of the extent of conventionalization by finding out whether alternative representations of the same state of affairs succeed as well in accomplishing the social effect. If they do, then there is little conventionalization of form; if they do not, then there is some conventionalization. For example, any representation of the appropriate mental state can function smoothly as an apology (*I feel awful, I'm really upset, I'm truly, truly sorry*). Here, then, the representation itself is primary, the effect achieved only secondarily.[8] If there is conventionalization here, it is what Morgan (1978) has called a 'convention about the language' rather than a 'convention of the language'.

Notice, though, that we say 'Greetings!' but not 'I greet you'; 'You're fired', but not 'I fire you', and so on. Here we are dealing with conventions of the language, conventions that surround not just what is said, but *how* it is said. This is an example where the form is at least somewhat conventionalized and the representation, though clearly present, retreats into the background. Such an utterance is primarily effective, and only secondarily representative. In general, it seems that conventionalizations of the representation of affects is considerably less common than the conventionalization of an effect.

CONCLUSIONS

One of my original motivations for adding yet another taxonomy to the already lengthy list of taxonomies of illocutionary types was that none of the existing ones, and certainly not Austin's or Searle's, had much to do with the systems of speech act distinctions that natural languages actually seem to employ. In every language about which I have enough knowledge to make any claims, there are at least some distinctions as to intended social effect that are manifest in a non-propositional way in the grammar, for example in terms of verbal mood, or word order, or grammatical particles of one kind or another. As Zwicky and I demonstrated (Sadock and Zwicky 1985) most languages make non-propositional distinctions among at least three basic types, clustering around the central features of statement making, question asking, and order giving. One language in our sample, Hidatsa, a Siouan Language, has an imperative-optative type, but no special question form. Since that writing, I have found that the Australian language Nunggubuyu (Heath 1984) has a system of speech act indicators that contains only two members, one for statement making, and one for question posing. Requests, orders, and the like, are handled in this language by asserting future propositions.

Systems such as Austin's and Searle's, with a small number of basic illocutionary types, are insufficient both because they include some distinctions that are rarely if ever explicitly part of a system of sentence types and because they fail to include some that nearly always are. In Austin, there is the distinction between verdictives (used for 'delivering a finding') and expositives (used for the 'expounding of views') which is never, so far as I know, exactly represented in the basic sentence types of any language. In Searle, there is the distinction between declarations and the other types where the distinction is one that by definition cannot form a separate sentence type, since declarations must be carried out by using the assertive type. At the same time, a distinction that is almost invariably present – that between statement making and question asking – is not among the five basic illocutionary types for either Austin or Searle.

When I began this study, it was my hope that the classes of illocutionary acts that seem to be most commonly represented in the sentence-type systems of natural languages would emerge as natural classes in my system. This hope has been largely disappointed because, as I now see things, the sorts of distinctions that Zwicky and I investigated are mostly distinctions that are to be located totally within the effective dimension, only one of three fundamental dimensions that I have proposed.

On the other hand, the primary distinctions that emerge from the view of the structure of speech acts urged here, namely, the distinctions among acts that are primarily representational, primarily effective and primarily affective, are, I believe, to be found in every human language on earth. In all languages there are utterances whose basic purpose it is to represent the world, and this, it seems to me is the special genius of our capacity for speech. But in addition, every language has at least some special forms for establishing automatic social effects, in particular either a type that imposes upon the addressee a requirement for action (i.e. imperatives) or a requirement for representation (i.e. interrogatives), or more commonly both. Most languages also provide a welter of special forms for greeting, thanking, apologizing, and so on. All languages also have special affective forms – exclamations, interjections, expressives, and so on, used for the display of emotion.

Within each of these dimensions there are subtypes, of course. This holds not only for subtypes of social effects of the kind that Zwicky and I studied and which most discussions of speech acts concentrate on, but for the other two dimensions as well. In the Hidatsa language mentioned above, and in a number of other languages, every representation must come with an indication of the warrant for that representation. In Hidatsa, these warrants are encoded in a system of obligatory sentence particles; one of these indicates the mere possibility that the representation is true, another that it is a matter of common knowledge, another that the speaker has heard it from someone else, a fourth that it is a report of the speaker's internal feelings, and yet another that the state of affairs is one for which the speaker has first-hand evidence.

In the realm of affective acts, there are languages that distinguish expressions of pleasure, pain, and so forth, from expressions of the kinaesthetic sense of an event that one has, and there are probably other types as well. In some languages expressives form an elaborate system quite apart from the ordinary representational system (Diffloth 1972, 1976; Schiller 1991).

I will conclude on a negative note, pointing out that I have not offered anything like an explanation for why just these subtypes are to be found within the three major realms of linguistic activity that I have argued for in this chapter. Providing such explanations will demand an examination of the purposes of representational activity, the needs of social institutions that are based on language, and the psychology of human affect. As these tasks go far beyond the purview of linguistic speech act theory, I will leave them to others.

NOTES

1   There are two other sorts of conditions that Searle 1969 mentions as required for the felicitous performance of illocutionary acts, but these seem to apply equally to all kinds of illocutionary acts, and therefore could not serve as a basis of classification. His 'normal input–output conditions' are required for the successful performance of speech acts without regard to category, as are the unnamed conditions regarding the literal use of the language.

2   In Searle and Vanderveken 1985 a somewhat different scheme is used in which the number of dimensions has shrunk to seven. The three basic dimensions discussed here are the same, however.

3   I enclose propositions, as opposed to the sentences that are used to convey them, in percentage signs. Thus when I say 'I am tired' at time t, the expressed proposition, namely AT(t, TIRED(Jerrold Sadock)) is represented as % I am tired%.

4   The class of declarations is bifurcated into a simple class and a class of 'assertive declarations' in Searle 1975. The compound class shares with assertives the expression of a psychological state of belief, but rather than making this system slightly less redundant, the distinction actually produces even more redundancy, since there is now an additional point (that of 'issuing an assertive with the force of a declaration') and an additional direction of fit, word-to-world followed by both. Now the system could characterize one 150 different illocutionary types, but in fact is used to differentiate only 6.

5   These three dimensions were suggested in Sadock 1990, albeit without recognizing quite as explicitly as here the full autonomy of the three components.
    There may be more than three dimensions, but the three discussed here are by far the most important, characterizing most normal utterances in one way or another. As an example of a possible fourth dimension, consider those aspects of utterances that are designed not so much as to effect the social world that human beings construct, but rather the supernatural world of gods, ghosts and goblins. The expression *knock on wood* is one of the few examples in English.

In Eastern European languages such as Yiddish, the number and importance of such expressions makes them hard to overlook. (See Matisoff 1979.)

6   The original motivation for Austin's 'doctrine of infelicities' as a test for types of speech acts is, upon reflection, somewhat unclear. It is somewhat like basing a taxonomy of flying insects on the marks they leave on a windshield.

7   This example was suggested by Hadi Adanali.

8   This is a version of Grice's non-detachability tests for conversational implicature. Thus it is not unreasonable to say that the non-conventionalized representations achieve their social effect by implicature.

21 Mood, meaning and speech acts

Robert M. Harnish

INTRODUCTION

Mood, as it is understood in this work, lies at the intersection of phonology, syntax, semantics and pragmatics. Mood is sentential form with a function. On the form side, sentences are described in terms of syntactic structure (including, occasionally, lexical items) and intonation. On the function side, sentences are described in terms of their literal and direct illocutionary force potential (pragmatics), and the notion of literality involves meaning (at least) what one's sentence means (semantics). The study of mood (again, as here conceived) runs against the grain of much of contemporary linguistics, which is predominately concerned with stating generalizations at a given level (phonological, morphological, syntactic, semantic). The generalizations we will be seeking *relate* these levels, and so will not look at all like traditional linguistic principles. What we are interested in finding are *inferential* principles relating these levels, principles that allow one to infer what someone might have meant (if speaking literally and directly) in uttering something of a given form.

The inferential framework for this study was set up in Bach and Harnish 1979. That study was *schematic* (hence our talk of the speech act schema) as to speaker, hearer, language, speech act and context. The present work expands on Harnish 1983 by deschematizing the theory, i.e. by specifying a language (English) and specific speech acts, properties of speakers and hearers, and aspects of context. The principles developed in this work are intended to contribute to a theory *sufficient* (but not necessary) for accounting for literal and direct linguistic communication. It seems inappropriate at this stage in the history of the subject to spend great effort showing that alternatives are less adequate. It is relatively pointless to compare pieces of insufficient theories, since one theory may handle one aspect of the problem well, but another badly. We will attempt to develop a reasonably comprehensive theory that can then be compared *in toto* with other reasonably comprehensive theories. (For a more extensive discussion see Harnish in preparation.)

We begin by distinguishing verbal mood from sentential mood; verbal mood is an inflectional property of the main verbs whereas sentential mood, following Jespersen 1924, is a form-with-a-function. We lay down broadly Fregean conditions of adequacy on a theory of mood. For instance, the theory should first account for semantic force and content compositionally. Second, it should be specific enough in the information it assigns to sentences to enable speakers to literally and directly communicate what we intuitively suppose them to communicate using these sentences. But third, the information must be general enough that all sentences with the same mood can have the same force potential. And fourth, the theory must not postulate implausible or unintuitive ambiguities in sentences of the various moods. We then distinguish major from minor moods.[1] Intuitively major moods are: (a) highly unrestricted in their productivity; (b) central to communication; (c) high in relative frequency of occurrence; and (d) common to most languages. Examples of the major moods of English are traditionally given as: (1) declarative; (2) imperative; and (3) interrogative (yes/no and *wh*). We survey various semantic theories of mood and we argue that they fail to meet these conditions. We then outline a theory of the major moods for English in terms of compatability conditions between form, force and conditions of fit, and argue that it meets the above conditions of adequacy. The theory raises a number of further issues, some of which we address here, some of which we must postpone.

MOOD

There are two principle conceptions of mood in the literature. The historically first notion of mood is fundamentally an inflectional property of the main verb of a sentence. A sentence then inherits its mood from this verb. We will call this conception 'verbal mood'.

A second, later, conception of mood treats mood basically as a cluster of phonological, syntactic and semantic properties of sentences. We will call this conception 'sentential mood'. Jespersen (1924) for instance, writes:

> Many grammars enumerate the following moods in English, etc.: indicative, subjunctive, imperative, infinitive, and participle. It is however, evident, that infinitives and participles cannot be co-ordinated with the others ... and we shall therefore in this chapter deal with the first three moods only. These are sometimes called fact-mood, thought-mood, and will-mood respectively. But they do not 'express different relations between subject and predicate,' ... It is much more correct to say that they contain attitudes of the mind of the speaker towards the contents of the sentence, though in some cases the choice of a mood is determined not by the attitude of the actual speaker, but by the character of the clause itself and its relation to the main nexus on which it is dependent.
>
> (ibid.: 313)

And Lyons (1968) writes,

> [mood] is best defined in relation to an [unmarked] class of sentences which express simple statements of fact, unqualified with respect to the attitude of the speaker towards what he is saying ... it is customary to refer to the 'unmarked' sentences also (by courtesy, as it were) as being 'in a certain mood'; and the traditional term for this 'unmarked' mood is *indicative* (or *declarative*). Two classes of sentences tend to stand apart from others by virtue of their modality. The first class comprises *imperative* sentences, which do not make statements at all, but express commands or instructions ... *Interrogative* sentences also stand in contrast to declarative sentences ... they may be characterized by additional modalities which indicate the expectations of the speaker.
>
> (ibid.: 303–4)

However, in a more recent work (1977) he retracts his earlier usage,

> It [mood] cannot be identified with either modality or illocutionary force as such ... In traditional usage, 'mood' is applied to such subsets of inflected forms of verbs as are distinguished one from another by means of the terms 'indicative', 'imperative', 'subjunctive', etc.; and we have chosen to respect this usage.
>
> (ibid.: 848)

Lyons does not say what role the verbal notion of mood plays in the theory of language.[2] On the other hand, we will see exactly what role the sentential conception will play. We will follow the tradition of treating mood as a mixed concept by treating it as a *form-with-a-function*.

There is also the compromise position; mood is a verbal inflection indicating the use of the sentence. For instance, Bybee (1985) writes,[3]

> *mood* is a marker on the verb that signals ... what the *speaker* is doing
> with the proposition ... the verb inflection signals a speech act type –
> something the *speaker* is doing with the whole proposition.
>
> (ibid.: 105–6)

More recently, in the Jespersen tradition, Sadock and Zwicky (1985)
characterize a mood (they call it a 'sentence type') in two ways:

1 *Within a language*: a mood is 'a coincidence of grammatical structure
   and conventional (conventionally indicated) conversational use'
   (Sadock and Zwicky 1985: 155). A 'regular association of form and
   speaker's use of sentences' (ibid.: 156). A 'form–use pair' (ibid.: 156).
2 *Across languages*: moods need only have similar uses: 'similar use (but
   possibly different form) in different languages' (ibid.: 156)

Moods also: (a) form a system (ibid.: 158) in the sense that 'the types
are mutually exclusive, no sentence being simultaneously of two different
types' (ibid.: 158–9); and (b) exemplify certain characteristic forms.
However, Sadock and Zwicky's characterization of (a) seems to exclude
the possibility of speech act ambiguous sentences: Sadock and Zwicky note
this, but contend that in the case of, for example, 'How pretty', 'this last
example is not *both* a question *and* an exclamation; rather, it is *either* a
question *or* an exclamation' (ibid.: 195). However, this move takes us to
sentence tokens, not sentence types (in the traditional sense), and it is
sentence types that are the domain of linguistics, and as a sentence type,
these strings are indeed ambiguous. Furthermore, there are cases such as,

(1) (a) Have the missionaries eaten
     (b) Don't you read pornography
     (c) Time flies

where the two forces are correlated with structural differences. For instance
'missionaries' in the question version of (1a) is the subject of 'eaten',
whereas in the order version it is the object of 'eaten'. So the property of
'forming a system' for sentence types is suspect, if it is supposed to be hard
and fast. It is certainly true that such overlap of force is very rare, at least in
English.

We also need to distinguish moods from attitude markers – devices
(particles only?) 'that indicate attitudes, rational and emotional, towards a
proposition' (ibid.: 161). One problem here is that some moods are characterized by Sadock and Zwicky in just this way.[4] Attitude markers are also
said to be (a) not mutually exclusive; (b) embeddable in quotation, where
the attitude is attributed to the person quoted; and (c) such that their
meaning does not deal specifically with speech acts. But in reply we should
note that: (1) sentence types are not mutually exclusive either; and (2) the
meaning of sentence types does not always deal specifically with speech

acts either (think of declaratives and imperatives and the range of speech acts compatible with each).[5]

Conditions of adequacy

The problem facing existing theories is to account for the force (and content) of sentences in the various moods in a way that meets plausible conditions of adequacy. The literature is replete with suggestions.

Survey of conditions of adequacy on a theory of mood

McDowell (1976) suggests that,

> A theory of sense must interact with a theory of force for the language in question. A theory of force would do two things: first, license the identification of linguistic actions, given enough information about them, as performances of propositional acts of specified types (assertion, question, and so on); and second, show how to recover, from a sufficiently full description of an utterance, which may be an utterance of an elliptical or non-indicative sentence, a suitable designation of a suitable indicative sentence. The idea is that a theory of sense and a theory of force, in combination, should enable one to move, from a sufficiently full description of a speaker's utterance, uninterpreted, to a description of his performance as a propositional act of a specified kind with a specified content, that is, a description on the pattern of 'He is asserting that p', 'He is asking whether p', and so on.
>
> (ibid.: 44)

McGinn (1977) proposes that,

> indicatives and nonindicatives share a common core of meaning, and (connectedly) that words, as they recur in sentences of different types, discharge the same semantic function ... a third requirement [is] ... A semantic theory for a natural language will be adequate only if: (i) it serves to 'give the meaning' of every sentence of the language; (ii) it fulfils the first requirement in terms of an assignment of suitable semantic properties to the primitive expressions of the language i.e. it shows how the meaning of an arbitrary sentence depends upon the meanings of its parts, and (iii) it fulfils the second requirement in a systematic and uniform way.
>
> (ibid.: 301–2)

Davidson (1979) suggests that,

> We are now in a position to list the characteristics a satisfactory theory of mood should have. (1) It must show or preserve the relations between indicatives and corresponding sentences in the other moods; it

must, for example, articulate the sense in which 'You will take off your shoes,' 'Take off your shoes,' and 'Will you take off your shoes?' have a common element. (2) It must assign an element of meaning to utterances in a given mood that is not present in utterances in other moods. And this element should connect with the difference in force between assertions, questions and commands in such a way as to explain our intuition of a conventional relation between mood and use.

(ibid.: 14–15)

Lappin (1982) suggests that,

(i) A theory of mood must give a unified and systematic account of the way in which the mood of a sentence interacts with the truth conditional component of its meaning in order to yield a complete interpretation of the sentence. (ii) The theory must exhibit what is particular in the way in which each mood determines the interpretation of the sentences in which it is present.

(ibid.: 559)

Pendlebury (1986) writes,

Two formal constraints are obviously necessary: (a) The value of 'P' should always be recoverable from the value of 'mP', (b) For every sentence-radical 'P', the value of ':P', '?P', and '!P' should differ [where 'mP' is schematic for the specific moods: :P, ?P, !P and ':P is declarative].

(ibid.: 371–2)

From these (and Frege and Grice) we extract and adopt the following conditions of adequacy:

Frege's conditions
(I)   The theory should account for semantic force and content compositionally, in so far as the expression is compositional,
(II)   Non-declaratives are not true or false.
(III)   An unambiguous declarative sentence can be uttered non-assertorically, for example, as a disjunct, or in a joke or a play (*mutatis mutandis* for non-declaratives).

Davidson's conditions[6]
(IV)   The information must be general enough that all sentences with the same mood share relevant aspects of meaning and use, and sentences in different moods can share aspects of meaning and use.
(V)   The theory must assign an element of meaning to utterances in a given mood that is not present in utterances in other moods. And this element should connect with the difference in force between assertions, questions and commands in such a way as to explain our intuition of a conventional relation between mood and use.

McDowell's condition
(VI)   The theory should allow us to infer what act(s) is being directly

performed in the (serious and) literal utterance of expressions (usually sentences) in each mood, given contextual information and definitions of the various illocutionary acts; to infer an illocutionary force (IF) from an utterance act (UA):

(UA) S (seriously and) literally uttered e,
(IF) In (seriously and) literally uttering e, S directly F-ed that p.

Where 'e' is an expression with a mood, 'F' stands of some illocutionary force, and 'p' stands for some propositional content.

Grice's condition

(VII) The theory must not multiply ambiguity, non-literality or indirection beyond necessity.

We turn now to developing a theory of mood meeting these conditions.

A PRELIMINARY ANALYSIS OF THE MAJOR MOODS

The traditional major moods of English are usually given as: indicative/ declarative, imperative, interrogative, subjunctive and optative. We will treat the first three (declarative, imperative and interrogative) as the 'major' moods of English; on the present analysis the subjunctive is not a form-with-a-function in English, and the optative is a minor mood.[7] (These will be discussed briefly in a later section, pp. 439ff.). The distinction between major and minor moods is difficult to draw precisely. Intuitively, a major mood is a form-function-fit correlation which is: (a) unrestricted in its productivity; (b) central in its communicative importance; (c) comparatively high in frequency of occurrence; and (d) does not vary widely from language to language.

Major moods

Analysing mood as form-with-a-function requires a function-independent characterization of form, and this requirement suggests strongly that it be characterized *structurally*. To begin with, let us consider a simple set of sentences which exemplify the relevant moods (the italics indicate emphasis):

(2) ($\vdash$) Declarative: Snow is white.
(!) Imperative: Leave the room!
(Y/N?) Yes/no interrogative:
  (a) Do you like eggplant?
  (b) Snow can be *white*?
(Wh?) *Wh*-interrogative:
  (a) What time is it?
  (b) You saw *what*?

Our problem is how to capture the structural characteristics of these and an unlimited number of other sentences which have the same form–function correlation.

Mood and structure

Although there will be many complications, we will begin with the following first approximation to a structural characterization of the major moods:

> *Mood–Structure*
> $(\vdash)$ NP + Aux + VP
> (!)   (NP) + V2
> (Y/N?)
>   (a)   Aux + NP + VP
>   (b)   NP + Aux +/VP/
> (Wh?)
>   (a)   Wh-x + Aux + (NP) + VP
>   (b)   NP + Aux + [... /Wh-x/ ...]VP

Here are some explications of this notation.[8] Forward slash pairs '/ /' indicate rising intonation. The 'Wh-x' is a questioned element such as 'what x', 'who x', etc. The category 'V2' used in characterizing the imperative mood comes from a system of rules such as:

> S   → NP + Aux + VP
> AUX   → {Tense/Modal} + *do*
> Vn   → [+V, +Aux] Vn − 1

The feature complex [+V, +Aux] can be realized as the auxiliary verbs *have* or *be*. The perfective *have* is strictly subcategorized to require V2 complements; the progressive *be* requires V1 complements; and the passive *be* must be immediately followed by a main verb. The structure for imperative mood (!) allows (and rejects) such imperatives as:

> (3) (a) *Have studied when I get home!: *[have V2 ...]
>   (b) Be studying when I get home!: [be (prog) V1 ...]
>   (c) Be taken to the airport by him!: [be (pass) V ...]
>   (d) Drink your milk!: [V + NP]

What (Mood–Structure) does is pair mood indicators with structural configurations in such a way as to make it intuitively plausible that if a sentence can be analysed in the structural terms, it can then be analysed in the appropriate functional terms.[9] We now correlate form (structurally characterized) with force and content and thus characterize a mood.

Force and content

It has been customary since Frege to analyse sentences into two components.[10] The first part signals the *communicative* or *illocutionary* force (F) potential of the utterance of the sentence, and it indicates whether the utterance is a statement, request, question, promise, warning, etc. The second part signals the *content* (C) of the utterance, and it indicates what the speaker is stating, requesting, asking, promising, warning, etc. So as a first approximation, any inference the hearer makes concerning the speaker's communicative intention (or 'message') will be an inference with a force (F) and a content (C):[11]

Communicative intent:	(F)	(C)
	State	that prices slumped
	Request	him to leave
	Ask	if he likes beans
	Promise	to pay him back
	Warn	him to stay away

Notice, importantly, that there are some intimate connections between force (F) and content (C). In particular the way the world satisfies the content of the utterance depends on the kind of utterance it is:

(4) (a) *Statements* are satisfied when they are *true.*
    (b) *Requests* are satisfied when they are complied *with.*
    (c) *Questions* are satisfied when they are *answered.*

This can be captured by saying that statements have *truth conditions,* requests have *compliance conditions,* and questions have *answerhood conditions.*[12] A hearer does not understand what a speaker is intending to communicate unless the hearer understands which kind of (*satisfaction*) *condition* is associated with the particular use of the sentence uttered.

These conditions reflect what Austin (1953) originally called 'onus of match' and what has come to be known as 'direction of fit':[13]

These differ as fitting a nut with a bolt differs from fitting a bolt with a nut ... which may be called a distinction in point or *onus of match.*

(ibid.: 188)

The declarative mood requires the words to fit the world, whereas the imperative and interrogative mood require the world to (come to) fit the words. What makes a statement such as: 'Snow is white', true is that it fit or match the world in the right way; say by having white and not green snow. True statements report the way the world is, and if the world is not the way the statement claims, the statement is to blame – it is false. But with requests this is not the case – requests do not fit or match the world. Rather, the world (in particular, the hearer or requestee) must fit or match the request – in the way a building is supposed to match its blueprint. A request that is complied with is one where the act of requesting causes the requestee to make the world fit the content of the request. In our example, 'Leave the room' is complied with by the requestee only if the requestee leaves the room, and does so in a virtue of being requested. In general, a hearer who understands a literal and direct utterance will infer something of the form F(C) upon hearing an expression e uttered by the speaker.

The strategies we alluded to earlier have been neutral with respect to such things as which expression is being uttered; what language is being spoken; and what social context it is being spoken in. To get a preliminary idea about how an inferential theory might work, lets look briefly at the simple set of examples given above in (2), and produced in some appropriate context. What is involved in understanding the literal and direct utterance of such sentences? First, it is clear that if a hearer (H) is claimed to understand 'Snow is white', but thought that in uttering it literally and directly S was *requesting* H to make snow white we would say that H did not understand the force of what S was saying. Nor, second, would we think that H understood a literal and direct utterance of 'Do you like eggplant?' if H thought it *answered* by 'Snow is white.' In short, to understand what S is intending to communicate in uttering e literally and directly, H must understand both the *force* and what conditions would satisfy or fit the *content* of the utterance. An adequate pragmatics must correlate sentences with their complete communicative potential:

Declarative: 'Snow is white' is (literally and directly) used to *constate* that snow is white.

Imperative: 'Leave the room!' is (literally and directly) used to *direct* the hearer to leave the room.

Yes/no interrogative: 'Do you like eggplant?' is (literally and directly) used to *ask* if the hearer likes eggplant.

Wh-*interrogative*: 'What time is it?' is (literally and directly) used to *ask* the hearer for the time.

Thus, for current American English, an adequate set of strategies accounting for literal and direct uses of declarative, imperative and interrogative sentences would have to allow the hearer to infer not only what communicative use it had on that occasion, but also its conditions of satisfaction – what would make it true, complied with or answered, as the case may be. As a first approximation, then, an adequate set of strategies might simply be a set of inferences such as the following:

(⊢) *Declarative*: if S utters 'Snow is white', then infer that:
   (i) S is *constating* that snow is white;
   (ii) the constative (statement, etc.) is *true* just in case snow is in fact white.

(!) *Imperative*: if S utters 'Leave the room!', then infer that:

(i) S is *directing* someone to leave the room;
(ii) the request (etc.) is *complied with* just in case that someone leaves the room.
(?) *Yes/no-interrogative*: if S utters 'Do you like eggplant?', then infer that:
   (i) S is *asking* someone if they like eggplant;
   (ii) the question is *answered* just in case that someone tells S whether or not they like eggplant.
(?) Wh-*Interrogative*: if S utters 'What time is it?', then infer that:
   (i) S is *asking* someone what time it is;
   (ii) the question is *answered* just in case someone tells S what time it is.

In the sections that follow we will elaborate, generalize and defend these ideas.

SEMANTICS AND MOOD

Semantics is the study of linguistic meaning – meaning encoded into expressions of a language. What is the semantic contribution of mood? What information is encoded by the form of the moods?

Previous theories

Theories of mood can be taxonomized in a variety of ways. Here we distinguish reductive from non-reductive theories, and within the reductive theories, an autonomous mood-marker approach, a higher-order invariant approach and an uncommitted speech act approach. We will explain these labels as we go along.

Reductive theories

Reductive theories try to reduce non-declaratives semantically to declaratives. One version of such a theory is given by Lewis (1972) who proposed that the (b)-sentences below be derived from the (a)-sentences:

(5) (a) *I direct (order, request, command ...) you* to leave the room
   (b) Leave the room!
(6) (a) *I ask you whether or not* you like eggplant
   (b) Do you like eggplant?
(7) (a) *I ask you* what time it is
   (b) What time is it?

Significantly, declaratives are not derived from performatives:

(8) (a) *I state that* snow is white
   (b) Snow is white.

for the good reason that the performative has different truth conditions; it entails the existence of a stating, but not that snow be white, whereas the simple assertion entails that snow is white but nothing about an assertion.

This proposal meets some of our conditions of adequacy, such as (I), (III), (IV) and (V). But it notoriously fails (II) since it makes non-declaratives true or false, and probably (VI), because it treats performatives as statements and so must make the performative an indirect speech act. Thus, all non-declaratives will constitute indirect speech acts, contrary to condition (VI).[14]

Non-reductive theories: autonomous mood markers

Among non-reductive theories *autonomous mood-marker* treatments characterize each mood as being governed by its own semantics. The problem with this latter approach is how it meets condition (I). For instance, *Stenius (1967)* proposes the following principles for interpreting moods:

> (R3) Produce a sentence in the indicative mood only if its sentence radical is true.
>
> (ibid.: 268)
>
> (R4) React to a sentence in the imperative mood by making the sentence radical true.
>
> (ibid.: 268)
>
> (R5) Answer the question by 'yes' or 'no', according as its sentence radical is true or false.
>
> (ibid.: 273)

How do the semantic contributions of words to the proposition expressed compose with their contribution to the force?

Katz and Postal (1964) propose that,

> special question and imperative morphemes occur in the underlying P[hrase]-markers of questions and imperative sentences.
>
> (ibid.: 74)
>
> We posit an imperative morpheme, *I*, in all and only, underlying P-markers of imperative sentences ... We can assign the sense of 'the speaker requests (asks, demands, insists, etc.) that'.
>
> (ibid.: 76)
>
> The Q morpheme indicates semantically only that the sentence is a question i.e. a paraphrase of an appropriate sentence of the form *I request that you answer* ...
>
> (ibid.: 89)

Again, how does the semantics of I, Q relate to the rest of the sentence?[15]

Sadock and Zwicky (1985) suggest that as a first approximation:

> The declarative is subject to judgments of truth and falsehood. It is used

for making announcements, stating conclusions, making claims, relating stories, and so on. The interrogative elicits a verbal response from the addressee. It is used principly to gain information. The imperative indicates the speaker's desire to influence future events. It is of service in making requests, giving orders, making suggestions, and the like.

(ibid.: 160)

This is of course only a first approximation; declarative sentences can also be used to ask questions ('I would like to know the time') or make requests ('I think you had better leave'), and interrogative sentences can be used to make statements ('Is the pope Catholic?'). These are non-literal or indirect uses of these sentences, but that just shows that the form–function pairing of interest here must be restricted to literal and direct uses. But even restricted to literal and direct uses, these are only rough approximations; consider that 'I would like to influence future events' expresses a desire to influence future events, but is not imperative. And 'Tell me the time!' is used to gain information and elicit a verbal response, but is not interrogative.

Non-reductive theories: higher-order invariants

Other non-reductive accounts try to respect the semantics of each mood, but still find something in common that words can contribute to. This approach does not make non-declaratives true or false, but finds a *higher-order invariant* in all moods such that the semantics of words is their contribution to that semantic value.

Davidson (1979) is perhaps the most radical solution; it certainly is the most obscure. Briefly put, Davidson's idea is to analyse (9a) as (9b):

(9) (a) Put on your hat
    (b) *Mood setter*: My next utterance is imperative
        Indicative core: You will put on your hat

How are we to understand this proposal? Pragmatically,

an utterance of a non-indicative sentence may be decomposed into two distinct speech acts, one the utterance of an indicative sentence, and the other the utterance of a mood-setter. It should not bother us that in fact we do not usually perform these acts one after the other but more or less simultaneously.

(ibid.: 18)

there is the utterance of the non-indicative elements, and there is (perhaps simultaneously) the utterance of the mood-setter. The utterance of a non-indicative is thus always decomposable into the performance of two speech acts.

(ibid.: 18)

Semantically (9b) is wrong because,

I do not want to claim that imperative sentences are two indicative sentences. Rather, we can give the semantics of the utterance of an imperative sentence by considering two specifications of truth conditions, the truth conditions of the utterance of an indicative sentence got by transforming the original imperative, and the truth conditions of the mood-setter. The mood-setter of an utterance of 'Put on your hat' is true if and only if the utterance of the indicative core is imperative in force.

(ibid.: 19)

Syntactically,

the mood setter cannot be any actual sentence of English, since it represents a transformation.

(ibid.: 19)

According to Davidson, this account satisfies his three requirements on an adequate theory:

1   There is an element in common to the moods – the indicative core.
2   Mood is systematically represented by the mood-setter (or its absence in the indicative).
3   Truth theory works here too, and although each sentence is indicative, the combined utterance is not the utterance of a conjunction and so does not have a truth value.

Discussion

This proposal faces a number of *prima facie* objections.

1   Why do performatives have a truth value, but moods, analysed in the same way, do not?
2   Sometimes the utterance of two declaratives is equivalent to the utterance of a conjunction of them; why is this not true in the case of mood?
3   Even if concatenation is not equivalent to conjunction on this analysis of mood, still each sentence should have logical consequences that the non-declarative does in fact not have.
4   In what sense does the mood-setter 'represent a transformation'? What is the mood-setter in a sentence and how would we identify it in another language?[16]
5   What is it for the utterance of the indicative core to be 'imperative in force'? How can we use this concept to analyse the force of imperatives? So does Davidson's analysis really meet his conditions? How does the mood-setter as described 'explain our intuition of a conventional relation between mood and use' (ibid.: 315), since there is no mention of use?

6 Why can we not pick up the (hidden) mood-setter with anaphoric devices (Segal 1991)?
    S: Put on your hat (= My next utterance is imperative. You will put on your hat.)
    H: *No it wasn't, so I won't.

McGinn (1977) wants to satisfy Frege's constraints not by construing non-declaratives as declaratives (*à la* Lewis), but by analysing them into declarative and non-declarative components; a 'mood indicator' and a 'sentence radical'. The latter receives the standard semantic analysis in terms of truth conditions:

> Syntactically, a whole sentence, fit for the performance of complete speech acts, is formed by concatenating a radical with a mood indicator.
> (ibid.: 306)

We can bring out the 'duplexity' of ordinary imperatives, interrogatives and optatives by paraphrasing them as (ibid.: 307):

(10) (a) *Make it the case that* the door is shut.
     (b) *Is it the case that* the door is shut.
     (c) *Would it were the case that* the door is shut.

Notice that the indicative does not receive this treatment, at least not interestingly:

(11) (a) The door is shut.
     (b) *It is true that* the door is shut.

We see an asymmetery here: declaratives appear in the paraphrases of non-declaratives, but not vice versa.[17]
    How can we bring, for example, (10a) into the semantic fold? McGinn (ibid.: 308) sketches two more or less equivalent approaches; the paratactic stemming from Davidson, and the operator.

Paratactic approach[18]
(P) Fulfilled ('Make the case *that*', at t) iff the denotation of *that* is made the case at t.[19]
Operator approach
(O) Fulfilled ('Make it the case that A' at t) iff it is made the case that A is true at t.

The right-hand side of the biconditional gives a truth condition in the normal way.
    Finally, we might generalize this treatment to other moods by invoking, for example,

> a concept of *correctness*, and aim to derive theorems of the form 'S is correct iff p', the truth and fulfillment predicates perhaps being regarded

as restrictions of this general predicate of sentences.

(ibid.: 309)

McGinn does not say what the connection is between sentences (10) and the ordinary (12) i.e. how we get our semantics from (10) to (12).

(12) (a) Shut the door.
(b) Is the door shut?
(c) Would that the door be shut.

Discussion

1 Clause (O) tells us when, for example, (9a) is fulfilled, but is there not more to its meaning than being capable of being fulfilled? How about its use to direct; are questions not also fulfilled in this sense? Do they not mean something different? In discussing a proposal of Dummett's, McGinn argues that,

> it cannot be any feature of the sentence *itself* that confers on its utter-ance the requisite force, or else its utterance would be invariably endowed with that force. Mood, to be sure, conventionally and stan-dardly *signifies* force, but it cannot *guarantee* it. Force is a property of speech acts, mood is a property of sentences.
>
> (ibid.: 303)

And he concludes,

> Mood is a matter of meaning, whereas force is a strictly pragmatic affair ... Having thus carefully distinguished mood from force, we can put the latter aside as semantically irrelevant.
>
> (ibid.: 304)

But is this conclusion warranted? If mood conventionally and standardly signifies force, why can that not be a fact of meaning (semantics) without it *guaranteeing* force? As with, for example, ambiguity, an expression can have a meaning that is not operative on a given occasion. We want our theory to *mark* a connection between mood and force without *guarantee-ing* it.

2 How would one extend (O) (or (P)) to *wh*-questions?[20] Perhaps via answerhood conditions:

> Answered ('Is the door shut', at t) iff H says either that the door is shut at t, or that the door is not shut at t.
> Answered ('What did John shut', at t) iff H says what John shut at t.

We will return to this type of analysis shortly.

Grice (1968) proposed to elucidate the notion of the conventional meaning of an *expression* partly in terms of what a *speaker* would mean in uttering it. In the course of establishing the connection between expressions and speakers Grice used dummy mood indicators '*' to connect the right sentence to the right meaning; roughly: 'When S uttered e, e meant "*p" = $_{df}$ S intended H to recognize what S meant by uttering e, on the basis of H's knowledge that, for S, e has as one of its meanings "*p"',[21] where we 'replace "*" by a specific mood indicator and replace "p" by an indicative sentence. One might then get to *Jones meant that* ⊢ *Smith will go home, Jones meant that !Smith will go home* (which would become: *Jones meant that Smith is to go home)*' (ibid.: 55). We see here the basic idea that the mood of the sentence correlates with, or as we would say constrains, the possible things that can be meant literally in uttering it.

Bach and Harnish (1979) modified Grice's programme and carried it out further. They proposed that each mood (they called it a 'sentence type') correlates a form with a type of saying, and each saying is correlated with conditions of satisfaction and a speech act potential:[22]

Declarative e:
S is saying (to H) at t that ⊢ (... p ...)
S is saying (to H) at t that it is the case that (... p ...)
Imperative e:
S is saying to H at t that !(... p ...)
S is saying to H at t that H is to make it the case that (...p ...)
Yes/no interrogative e:
S is saying to H at t that ?(... p ...)
S is asking H at t (or saying to H at t that H is to tell S) whether or not it is the case that (... p ...)
Wh-*interrogative e*:
S is saying to H at t that ?(... Wh-x p ...)
S is asking H at t (or saying to H at t that H is to tell S) (... Wh-x p ...)
Compatibility Conditions:[23]
  (i)   If S is saying that ⊢(... p ...), S is expressing the belief that p.
  (ii) If *S* is saying that !(... p ...), S is expressing the intention or desire that H make it the case that p.
  (iii) If S is saying that ?(... p ...), S is expressing the intention or desire that H answer S whether or not p.

Our taxonomy of illocutionary acts defines over one hundred acts in terms of expressing attitudes such as belief and desire. In this way the illocutionary force potential (the set of possible types of illocutionary acts) can be defined for each mood in terms of whether or not the act is compatible with the attitude expressed by sentences in each mood.

This proposal is limited in two important ways: first, we say nothing about English or any other actual language. Second, we say nothing concerning the distinctively semantic import of mood.

Lappin (1982) also rejects the Lewis (1972) and Davidson (1979) approaches. He proposes a two part interpretation procedure.[24]

the initial step in interpreting the mood of a sentence is to determine its speech act type in the context of discourse, which a speaker does on the basis of his knowledge of speech act rules. I have argued that the capacity to identify the speech act which the utterance of a sentence performs is only part of what a speaker knows when he understands the mood of the sentence (more properly, the mood of the utterance of the sentence). What is required to complete the analysis of pragmatic mood is a systematic specification of the fulfillment conditions for different speech acts. These conditions are the pragmatic analogue of the truth conditions of declarative sentences.

(ibid.: 566)

Lappin seems to have Searle's constitutive rules in mind for this first step, and he proposes the following fulfilment conditions on the major moods (the numbering is Lappin's):

⊢ [(12)] An utterance of S as an assertion at ti is fulfilled iff S is true at ti.

(ibid.: 567)

![(13)] An utterance of I at ti as a command is fulfilled (obeyed) iff the hearer performs actions which (in part) cause it to be the case that I' is true at tj (i < j) in response to hearing I at ti. (Where I' is the declarative obtained from I by inserting 'you' as the subject of I, and making the necessary changes in the verb and auxiliary of I).

(ibid.)

? [(14)] An utterance of Q as a question at ti is fulfilled (answered) iff the hearer assigns a value (ordered n-tuple of values) to the free variable(s) of Q' at tj (i < j) which either satisfies, or fails to satisfy Q', in response to hearing Q at ti. (Where Q' denotes the open sentence obtained from Q in the following way: If Q is a yes/no interrogative, Q' is an open sentence of the form 'Sq is x' where Sq is a declarative derived from Q by reversing subject–auxiliary inversion and 'x' takes the truth value t or f as its value; if Q is a wh-interrogative, Q' is the open sentence derived from Q by reversing subject–auxiliary inversion and substituting a free variable for each of its wh-phrases).

(ibid.)

How are these supposed to work? Lappin does not illustrate them, but it is instructive to do so.[25] Consider:

(13) (a) Fry eggs!
     (b) Do you fry eggs?
     (c) What do you fry?

[(13')] *Imperative* An utterance of 'Fry eggs!' at ti as a command is fulfilled (obeyed) iff the hearer performs actions which (in part) cause it to be the case that (I′) 'you fry eggs' is true at tj (i < j), in response to hearing I at ti.

Discussion

1 There is no connection between the hearer and 'you' mentioned in I′. Moreover, not all imperatives take 'you' subject, for example, 'Nobody move!' The clause needs to be changed to the hearer or addressee: '... cause it to be the case that the hearer or addressee fries eggs at tj ...'.

2 'in response to hearing I′' is not sufficient; if I say 'Stop!' in such a loud voice that because of an avalanche or a heart attack you stop, you have not 'obeyed' my command. We need to change this clause to something like: '... understanding I was (part of) the hearer's (addressee's) reason for ...'

3 Lappin notes that on his account 'the fulfillment conditions for commands and requests are the same' (ibid.: 568) though commands and not requests involve invoking authority,

> these distinctions between commands and requests will be expressed by the different sets of speech act rules which characterize the necessary and sufficient conditions for performing each speech act.
>
> (ibid.: 568)

But is it just a matter of the speaker's intention (speech act)? Does the hearer not have to comply *because he was ordered* versus *because he was requested*?[26]

4 If [(13)] is an account of what it is for a command performed in uttering I to be fulfilled, then another clause is required for an order, a request, a plea, begging, imploring, etc. How then do we capture the common content on this account? How do we meet our condition of adequacy (IV)?

> [(14′)] *Yes/no question* An utterance of 'Do you fry eggs?' as a question at ti is fulfilled (answered) iff the hearer assigns a truth value to the free variable of (Q′ = Sq is x =) ' "You (do) fry eggs" is x' which either satisfies, or fails to satisfy Q′, in response to hearing Q at ti.
>
> Wh-*question* An utterance of 'What do you fry?' as a question is fulfilled (answered) iff the hearer assigns a value (or ordered n-tuple of values) to the free variable(s) of (Q′ = 'What you (do) fry' =) 'x you (do) fry' at tj (i < j), which either satisfies or fails to satisfy Q′, in response to hearing Q at tj.

Discussion

1 The 'in response to' clause must be replaced for the same reason and in the same way as for the imperative.

2 *Wh*-question: the form of Q′ after the conversion does not take into account *wh*-movement, and we actually need a fragment of a grammar of the language to state the relationship between Q and Q′ correctly.

3 It is obscure what an answer not satisfying Q′ amounts to. In the case of yes/no questions does 'False' or 'No' fail to satisfy Q′? And for *wh*-questions, does something like 'horses' satisfy Q′ above? Are false responses answers? Lappin is not clear on any of this.

4 More generally, there is the question of how Lappin's proposal meets the compositionality condition. As he pointed out in criticizing Stenius,

> it is not clear how the meanings of [mood] operators can combine systematically with the intensions of sentence radicals to generate a composite intension for the entire mood–radical complex.

(ibid.: 563)

Why does the same not apply to Lappin's proposal?

Non-reductive theories: uncommitted speech acts

This approach can trace itself back to some comments of Frege, who says at one point,

> A subordinate clause with 'that' after 'command', 'ask', 'forbid', would appear in direct speech as an imperative. Such a clause has no reference but only a sense. A command, a request are indeed not thoughts, yet they stand on the same level as thoughts.

(1892: 68)

Castaneda also seems to advance such a view in various writings, though it is not completely clear. A recent advocate is Pendlebury.
Pendlebury (1986) makes two arguments against what he calls 'the force treatment' of mood: the idea that,

> mood is merely a conventional (prima facie) indicator of force which has no semantic significance.

(ibid.: 361)

The idea is familiar; declarative, imperative and interrogative sentences (can) share propositional content, but differ in the force with which the proposition is presented:

> the speaker *asserts* that the proposition ... is true, ... he *asks whether* it

is true, and . . . he *directs* his addressee . . . to make it true.

(ibid.: 361)

He then presents his own alternative analysis of the moods.

Arguments against the force treatment

Pendlebury's first argument is that,

> the grammatical mood of a subordinate clause can have semantic significance which cannot be accounted for by the force treatment.

(ibid.: 362)

The semantic significance of mood is brought out by the following pair, where [(5)] may be false when [(6)] is true (ibid.: 363):[27]

> [(5)] Rick thinks he knows that Sam will play it again.
> [(6)] Rick thinks he knows whether Sam will play it again.

Pendlebury wants to trace the difference in meaning to the difference in subordinate clauses,

> this difference in sense seems entirely due to the fact that the subordinate clause in (5) is indicative, while that in (6) is interrogative for there is no other difference between them.

(ibid.: 363)

According to Pendlebury,

> [(14*)] Will Sam play it again?
> (14**) Whether Sam will play it again

are in the same mood – interrogative. It is important for his argument to treat 'that' and 'whether' as part of the subordinate clause, and not as part of a compound verb, for example, 'know that' vs 'know whether', otherwise the difference in meaning could be attributed to that verb. Evidence that subordinate questions are questions is the uniform semantics for all embeddings such as:

> [(8)–(13)] Rick knows when, why, how, what, when . . .

This semantics is given by the principle:[28]

> (K?) '(:a know (?P))' is true iff there is a correct answer '(:Q)' to the question '(?P)' such that '(:a know (:Q))' is true . . . To know why, what, how, who, whether . . . is to know a correct answer to the question headed by that interrogative.

(ibid.: 365–6)

Discussion

Does this show that subordinate clauses are in the various moods?

1 First, there is the obvious fact that (14**), which is said to be in the same mood as [(14*)] cannot be used to ask a question, not even by 'adding' commitment. We will return to this point in discussing his next argument and alternative proposal.

2 Second, given this, how are we to understand his proposed semantics (K?) for embedded interrogatives? That is, what goes in for '(?P)' on the left side of the biconditional cannot always go in on the right side.

3 The difference between [(5)] and [(6)] turns on the difference between the effect of the complementizers 'that' and 'whether (or not)'. The latter allows [(6)] to be true under the condition that Rick thinks Sam will not play it again (where [(5)] does not), which is one answer to the related question [(14*)]. However, this is not sufficient to motivate the conclusion that the complement of 'know' in [(6)] is interrogative in mood. General principles relating parts of sentences to matrix sentences show an entailment relation, but not an analysis. If so, (T!) below,

(T!) '(:a told (!P))' is true iff the addressee makes true (:P) at some later time in response to understanding '(!P)'

would show that in 'I told him to leave', '(him) to leave' is imperative in mood. Or even worse, (L!) below relates the embedded clause to exclamations in sentences such as 'Look at how pretty that bush is!':

(L!) 'Look at (!?P)' is complied with iff there is an exclamation (!?P) such that 'The addressee looks at (!?P)' is true.

Pendlebury hints that he applauds such a consequence, but we need not.

Pendlebury's second argument is that,

> if we subtract, or bracket off, the positive force of an act of asserting, or an act of asking, or an act of ordering, then in each case all we are left with is the mere expression of a proposition ... This seems to me quite wrong. Asserting, asking, and ordering have something in common even when they do not involve the same proposition, namely the commitment which is present when one speaks seriously and for oneself, but absent when, for example, one reads aloud, or quotes, or reports someone else's words.

(ibid.: 368)

The alternative proposal

The idea is that we analyse the force associated with mood as:

(SA) Asserting = expressing a proposition with positive force
Asking = expressing a question with positive force
Ordering = expressing an order with positive force

(ibid.: 368)

Between a positive speech act and the descriptive content of the sentence uttered, there is a third item which the force treatment fails to recognize. And it is *this* item – what I am calling the proposition, the question, or the order – which makes the speech act an act of asserting, or asking, or ordering, as the case may be.

(ibid.: 370)

Discussion

1 We can see that (SA) licenses *addition* as well as subtraction,[29] and that we should get an asking from (14**) by adding positive force. But try as we can, we will not get such a speech act.

2 This thing that is left over at the level of a proposition when commitment is subtracted is extremely obscure. It is not at all clear what it is or does.

3 We can account for the fact that removing commitment does not leave just a proposition by noting that the connection between force and mood does not have to be unconditional; it can involve connections between literal and serious utterances, and forces.

Form, force, fit

We will now try to turn our complaints against previous theories into a positive proposal.

Form and force

What is the connection between form and force? How should we analyse the connection between uttering an expression with the form of a particular mood '*p' and performing some illocutionary act of F*-ing that p? (where '*' is a dummy mood indicator for declarative $\vdash$, imperative !, or interrogative ?, and 'F*' is a dummy force indicator correlated with constating ($\vdash$), directing (!), and questioning (?) respectively, and 'p' is a dummy propositional content indicator). The strongest view, favoured by those attracted to use theories of meaning, is this:

(*:F) If S utters '*p' then S is F*-ing that p.

But (*:F) is too strong; it violates condition III: (a) '*p' may occur as a constituent of a longer expression, say as a disjunct or antecedent of a conditional; (b) S might be joking, reciting poetry, practising elocution, acting in or writing a play, implicating, etc. (see Davidson 1979: 10; McGinn 1977: 303).

Again, following Frege, we might add that 'seriousness' is required,[30]

(serious *:F) If S utters '*p' seriously, then S is F*-ing that p.

Unfortunately we have no analysis of speaking seriously, unless it amounts to meaning something. Even so, we need not mean what we say, and so we need to enforce a closer connection between '*p' and F*-ing.

Another possibility is to treat the expression '*p' as a 'conventional device' for F*-ing that p (see Dummett 1973: 32).

(conventional *:F) '*p' is conventionally used to F* that p.

The advantage here is that one need not always use something in accordance with its conventional use – one might use a coffee cup as a paperweight. But there are serious doubts about such conventions, the most important of which is that they do not seem to exist (see Strawson 1964). As Davidson (1979) notes, we cannot simply add some device to signal a conventional assertion, because, 'every joker, storyteller and actor will immediately take advantage of the strengthened mood to simulate assertion' (ibid.: 13). The connection between the sentence and its actual force is mediated by all sorts of non-linguistic facts.[31]

How about a more circumspect connection somewhere between (serious *:F) and (conventional *:F):

(literal *:F) If S utters '*p' literally (meaning at least what S says), then S is F*-ing that p.

According to (literal *:F), the connection between mood (*p) and force (F*) is mediated by literality – saying something and meaning (at least) it. Since this fact is contextual and extra-linguistic, one could know that an utterance if literal would be, for example, a constative without knowing that it is in fact literally on this occasion an assertion. Finally we will need the notion:

(direct *:F) If S utters '*p' directly, then S is F-ing that p without doing it by doing some other illocutionary act.[32]

We will say that a force F is in the *literal illocutionary force potential* of an expression '*p' just in case in uttering '*p', S could be literally F*-ing that p. And we will say that a force F is in the *direct illocutionary force potential* of an expression '*p' just in case in uttering '*p', S could be directly F*-ing that p. We will say that the *illocutionary force potential* (*simpliciter*) of an expression '*p' is its *literal and direct* illocutionary force potential (IFP):

(IFP) The IFP of '*p' is the set of all forces F such that if S utters '*p' literally, then S could be directly F*-ing that p.

So as far as force goes, mood signals IFP and direction of fit.

Form and fit

We have decided that the form of mood contributes to IFP and direction of fit, but what fits what? Here traditional semantics looms large. It was Frege's idea that the sense of a declarative sentence is the 'thought' or 'proposition' that its truth conditions obtain, and that the semantics of words and phrases is to be given by their contribution to the sense of the sentences in which they occur (see McGinn 1977: 301). This is fine for declarative sentences which have truth conditions, but how about imperatives and interrogatives?[33] Collecting together our discussions of previous proposals we offer as a second approximation, to fill out, Schema S as follows:

(S) e is satisfied iff:

[⊢p] e is satisfied (true) at time t, in context C iff p at t in C.

[!p] e is satisfied (complied with) at t, in C iff the addressee (H) makes it the case that p at t, in C in part because H understands the force of the utterance of e at t′ (< t) in C′.

[Y/Np] e is satisfied (answered) at t in C iff H says that p or not p at t in C in part because H understands the force of the utterance of e at t′ (< t) in C′.[34]

[Whp] e is satisfied (answered) at t in C iff H says what x is such that it makes p(x) true at t in C, in part because H understands the force of the utterance of e at t′ (< t) in C′.

Semantics of mood

Returning now to the semantics of mood, we will say that the semantics of the mood of '*p' is exhausted by characterizing three pieces of information encoded into '*p', namely, (a) the illocutionary force potential (IFP); (b) the direction of fit or satisfaction; and (c) conditions of fit or satisfaction. If this is on the right track it should satisfy our conditions of adequacy, at least at some preliminary level.

Adequacy

1 Words all contribute in their normal way to the sentences in which they occur, because the words themselves do not contribute to mood, only the configuration of these words.[35] So they can contribute what they normally do to satisfaction.

2 Non-declaratives have compliance and answerhood conditions with world-to-word direction of fit, not truth conditions with word-to-world direction of fit.

3 All sentences in all moods can be uttered non-literally or non-seriously

and still retain their meaning and mood, because IFP is defined in terms of literality and directness, which are contextual features, independent of the semantics of the sentence. Expressions can occur as constituents without changing their meaning because force is associated with the utterance of a complete expression, not a constituent – for example, a sentence, not a clause.[36] Frege (1879: 2) proposed the 'horizontal' or 'content' stroke as a formal reconstruction of the idea that something 'combines the symbols following it into a unit'. Hare (1989: 31ff.) proposes a 'sign of completeness' to hold together the constituent parts of the sentence and to mark the complete unit – to show where it begins and ends.[37]

4 The common elements are the IFP and direction of fit. The conditions of satisfaction vary from instance to instance.

5 The IFP determined by mood constrains the class of illocutionary acts being literally and directly performed. Given the context of utterance, the hearer is expected to be able to infer the appropriate force.

6 No unnecessary ambiguity, non-literality or indirection is postulated or entailed by the theory.

7 The theory fulfils this condition by associating each mood with a (literal and direct) illocutionary force potential (via an expressed attitude and the taxonomy of definitions of illocutionary acts), then identifying the actual force as picked out via the speaker's communicative intentions and contextual beliefs. Thus, the theory licenses inferences from (UA) to (IA):

(UA) S (seriously and) literally uttered '*p',
(IA)   In (seriously and) literally uttering '*p', S directly F*-ed that p.

In the next section we will see how this works in more detail.

COMPATIBILITY CONDITIONS

A common defect of illocutionary act semantics, as well as 'message models' or 'code models' of linguistic communication is that they forge too tight a connection between the meaning of the expression being uttered and the communicative intent of the speaker.[38] According to the approach we are following here, the utterance is literal if there is a certain kind of *compatibility* between the form and meaning of the expression and the force and content of the communicative intent one has in uttering it literally and directly. There has to be a certain compatibility between what the sentence means (in the language) and what the speaker means in uttering it. We take up these compatibility relations first for force, then for content.

Form, expressed attitude, force

The inference from form to (illocutionary) force proceeds in two stages; first, there is an inference from form to expressed attitude; then there is an inference from expressed attitude to force. At each stage there are compatibility conditions to be stated.

Form–expressed attitude

These conditions require that the structural description of each mood be correlated in some manner with the proper expressed attitude. A first approximation to such compatibility conditions is given below:

Form–Expressed Attitude Compatibility Conditions (F–EA, CC)
($\vdash$)
Form: NP + Aux + VP
Expressed Attitude: S believes that p.

(!)
Form: (NP) + V2
Expressed Attitude: S desires/intends that H make it the case that p.

(Y/N?)
Form: (i)   Aux + NP + VP
         (ii) NP + Aux + /VP/
Expressed Attitude: S desires that H tell S whether or not it is the case that p.

(Wh?)
Form: (i)   Wh-x + Aux + (NP) + VP
         (ii) NP + Aux + [... Wh-/x/ ...] VP
Expressed Attitude: S desires that H tell S Wh-x such that p(x).

In the case of (Wh?), we will informally read the notation in the expressed attitude as: S desires that H tell S which x it is that satisfies the x slot in p. Thus, 'Who broke the window?' would be compatible with: S desires that H tell S which person x is such that x broke the window.

Expressed attitude–illocutionary force

Since each communicative illocutionary act is analysed by the theory into complex representational attitudes, it is possible to correlate sentence structures with illocutionary acts of the relevant type.[39]

In general, there will be a correlation between the attitude expressed in the utterance of e, and the literal and direct illocutionary act. To be literal the illocutionary act will have to be L-Compatible with the expression uttered. Thus, given the prior correlations established in (F–EA, CC) we can continue the linking as follows:

Expressed Attitude–Illocutionary Force Compatibility Conditions (EA–IF, CC)
($\vdash$)
Expressed Attitude: S believes that p.
Communicative Illocutionary Force: Any act with the belief that p as a necessary condition in its analysis.

(!)
Expressed Attitude: S desires/intends that H make it the case that p.
Communicative Illocutionary Force: Any act with the desire/intention that H make it the case that p as a necessary condition.

(Y/N?)
Expressed Attitude: S desires that H tell S whether or not it is the case that p.
Communicative Illocutionary Force: Any act with the desire that H tell S whether or not it is the case that p as a necessary condition.

(Wh?)
Expressed Attitude: S desires that H tell S Wh-x such that p(x).
Communicative Illocutionary Force: Any act with the desire that H tell S Wh-x such that p(x) as a necessary condition.

It seems clear that the class of communicative illocutionary acts mentioned in the second clause of each of the above compatibility conditions is tantamount to what has traditionally been called the (literal and direct) 'illocutionary force potential' (IFP) of an utterance of an expression e. Given any suitable system of analysis for communicative illocutionary acts it is then possible to say, relative to that taxonomy, which acts fall within the (literal and direct) IFP of the utterance force potential (perhaps not all expressions have such potential). In particular, relative to the taxonomy mentioned above, each expression which has an expressed attitude associated with it by (F–EA, CC) will then have, by (EA–IF, CC), a class of communicative acts as members of its IFP. Thus one could, in principle, run through the variety of illocutionary acts in the taxonomy and the variety of relevant sentences in the language and correlate particular names of particular kinds of acts with each of the sentences.

Thus, for example, saying that (it is the case that) John *will* (future) close the door is L-compatible with only certain constatives and commissives. Saying that H *is to* close the door is L-compatible with only certain directives. Furthermore, considerations involving propositional content (*what* is said) further narrows down the set of L-compatible illocutionary acts. For instance, performing a predictive, but not a retrodictive, is L-compatible with:

(15) Uttering 'John will close the door' and saying that it will be the case that John closes the door,

because a predictive allows for future time reference,[40] but a retrodictive requires past time reference. Also, some commissives are L-compatible with (15) (for instance, acts of swearing that such-and-such is the case), but other commissives are not (for example, acts of surrendering, inviting, bidding and volunteering). Thus, having inferred that S is saying that it will be the case that John closes the door, H is still free (linguistically) to infer that S is performing any one of a number of different illocutionary acts including predicting, guessing, informing, conforming, conceding, assenting, replying, suggesting and guaranteeing. To identify which act S is performing, H needs more information than is available from what S has said.

These remarks hold true, *mutatis mutandis*, for other types of utterance such as (16) and (17) below:

(16) In uttering 'Close the door!' S is saying that H is to close the door.
(17) In uttering 'Did John close the door?' S is asking (or saying that H is to tell S) whether or not John closed the door.

In the case of (16) the acts of requesting, demanding and ordering are L-compatible with what is said, but not acts of stating, prohibiting, promising or congratulating. Likewise with (17); the acts of questioning, querying and inquiring, but virtually no other illocutionary acts named in the taxonomy are L-compatible with S's asking whether or not John closed the door.

Form, locution, fit

The effect we want from our inference principles (whatever they may turn out to be) is a certain 'compatibility' between the mood of the sentence and its functional import such that this correlation contributes to determining (a) its condition of satisfaction; and (b) whether the illocutionary act is literal or not. We begin formulating the compatibility conditions for (a) as follows:

Form–Locution Compatibility Condition (F–L, CC)
($\vdash$)
Form: NP + Aux + VP
Locution: S is saying that $\vdash$ (... p ...); i.e. S is saying that it is the case that (... p ...).

(!)
Form: (NP) + V2
Locution: S is saying that !(... p ...); i.e. S is saying that H is to make it
   the case that (... p ...).

(Y/N?)
Form: (i) Aux + NP + VP
        (ii) NP + Aux + /VP/
Locution: S is asking (or saying that H is to tell S) whether or not it is
   the case that (... p ...).

(Wh?)
Form: (i) Wh-x + Aux + (NP) + VP
        (ii) NP + Aux + [... Wh-/x/ ...]VP
Locution: S is asking (or saying that H is to tell S) (... Wh-x[p(x)]
   ...).[41]

Part of the import of mood is the correlation it establishes between
sentences and various conditions of fit or satisfaction. If a hearer H claimed
to understand 'Snow is white', but thought that in uttering it literally and
directly S was requesting H to make snow white, we would be reluctant to
admit that he understood what S was saying. Furthermore, if H thought
that in literally and directly uttering 'Do you like eggplant?' S was saying
that you like eggplant, we could conclude that H did not understand what
was being communicated. Nor would we think that H understood a literal
and direct utterance of 'Do you like eggplant?' if H thought it was literally
and directly answered by 'Snow is white.' In short, to understand what S is
intending to communicate in uttering e literally and directly, H must understand what conditions would satisfy or fit the content (p) of the act,
assuming it has such conditions.

   If e is declarative, then what is said may be correlated with *truth conditions*. For other sentence types we generalize the notion of satisfaction
and thereby allow a single format of specification for what is said. For
instance, if e is imperative, the that-clause specifying what S says (that
(... p ...)) is not itself imperative but of the form, 'that H is to do A' (or
'that H is to make it the case that p') and so represents a *compliance condition*.

   Interrogative sentences offer two options. On the one hand it could be
argued that sentences like 'What time is it?' do not express propositional
content and their use is to be reported with 'ask' – S asked H what time it
is. On this view interrogative sentences are conventional means for
performing illocutionary acts of just one particular kind, namely asking a
question (see Schiffer 1972: 114ff.). If this is correct, then the locutionary
step ('S said that ...') is simply bypassed in the case of interrogatives, and
indirect quotation will take the form 'S asked ...'. On the other hand it
might be suggested that what is said when S uses an interrogative ex-

pression like 'What time is it?' is: that H is to tell S what time it is (see, for example, Katz 1977: 205 ff.). In general, the form of the report will be: S says that H is to tell S____, where the blank is filled in by some expression determined by e. On this account questions would be a particular case of requests and would be performed normally via the schema. Since either account is compatible with the above programme, in that they both induce answerhood conditions as the type of satisfaction, we can leave this matter unresolved for now.

In short, to understand what S is intending to communicate in uttering e literally and directly, H must understand what conditions would satisfy or fit the content (p) of the locutionary act. Again, as a first approximation to formulating such conditions we will adopt the following:[42]

Locution–Fit Compatibility Conditions (L–F, CC)
($\vdash$)
What S said in saying that $\vdash$ (... p ...) *is true* iff (its content) p is the case.
(Truth condition)

(!)
What S said in saying that !(... p ...) *is complied with* iff H makes (its content) p the case, in part because H understands the force of the utterance. (Compliance condition)

(Y/N?)
What S asked (or said H was to tell S) in asking whether or not ?(... p ...) *is answered* iff H either says that p, or says that Neg-p, in part because H understands the force of the utterance. (Answerhood condition)

(Wh?)
What S asked for (or said H was to tell S) in asking ?(... Wh-x[p(x)] ...) *is answered* iff H tells S Wh-x is such that p(x), in part because H understands the force of the utterance (Answerhood condition)

In sum, we have proposed principles connecting strings of words (sentences) to locutionary functions via their structural descriptions (forms) and their (operative) meaning. And we have connected these forms and locutionary functions (L-functions) with conditions of fit (or satisfaction). Note that it might not be the case that conditions of fit can be read off from operative meaning alone, and that reference back to forms of words or their utterance cannot be avoided.[43] Although we have represented 'what is said' as having conditions of fit, other levels can have them too – for example, the illocutionary level. However, since communicative illocutionary acts are reduced to representational attitudes, conditions of fit at this level are the province of 'psychosemantics', not semantics (see, for instance, Fodor 1987).

Pragmatic rules

A central question in the theory of linguistic communication concerns the nature of the connection between linguistic forms (the publicly observable signals) and their associated (literal and direct) communicative intent. In Bach and Harnish 1979 we schematized a possible answer: the Speech Act Schema (SAS).

Inferring fit and force from form

The theory developed so far has only conditions of compatibility between form, expressed attitude and fit which must obtain if the utterance is to conform to our intuitions of literality; we have said nothing about the *principles of inference* that connect these levels of representation. Although we would like to have a system of inferences fewer in number than the set of levels they relate, it is not obvious that linguistic communication works that way. But if it does, that fact will be revealed only by the development of a pragmatically useful and adequate semantics. In lieu of such a development we can state the inference rules in a brute force fashion, hoping that subsequent insights will enable us to break them up in a theoretically motivated way.

By following the direct and literal strategy of the SAS, the hearer is able to infer the literal and direct illocutionary force potential (IFP) of the utterance of expression e. The connection is forged by a sequence of compatibility conditions on the structure of e, the expressed attitudes, and the Locution–Fit compatibility conditions. Each of these can be converted into a rule of inference from one level to the next, securing that the inference respects the compatibility conditions.

Pragmatic derivations

The above principles can be organized into a canonical form. As with the Speech Act Schema (SAS) in general, this form represents the overall flow of information from utterance to communicative intent – it certainly will not represent the online information processing of a normal hearer, if only because hearers do not wait until the end of an utterance to begin deeper levels of processing.[44]

FURTHER ISSUES

So far we have organized this material in terms of levels of representation, we are now going to organize it by mood. We want to look briefly at each mood and show where some work remains to be done. But before doing that we should mention complications which affect all moods, about which we will have very little to say here.[45] We then turn to each major mood.

Stylistic variation: intonation[46]

Although some intonational features have been coded into the characterization of the moods, there undoubtedly are other facts that have been missed. Here we are hampered by the tradition in prosody studies not to relate intonation contours rigorously to speech act phenomena (see Liberman 1978; Bing 1980).

(Contrastive) stress

Some have suggested that differences in stress constitute a difference in use, and so should be reflected in a pragmatic theory. Consider, for example, the difference in well-formedness of the following two talk exchanges:

(18) S_1: John saw a professor in a red shirt fleeing the scene of the crime

  S_2: No; He saw a CONVICT in red shirt fleeing the scene of the crime.

(19) S_1: (same as above)

  S_2: *No; He saw a convict in a RED shirt fleeing the scene of the crime.

We can agree with the data without agreeing that they affect the theory as stated. In the above example it seems clear that the communicative force and content of each utterance by S_2 is the same, but still acknowledge that they have different *conditions of contextual appropriateness*; it is the relation of the utterances to context that accounts for the above oddity. Basically, as with all forms of stylistic variation, the structure of the sentence can 'package' the content (and perhaps force) in distinct ways appropriate to the history and future of the talk-exchange being participated in.

Stylistic variation: syntax

Next, there are a number of 'stylistic variants' of most sentences in each mood:[47]

Parentheticals
(20) (a) Wouldn't you agree (that) John likes eggplant?

  (b) John, wouldn't you agree, likes eggplant.

  (c) John likes, wouldn't you agree, eggplant?

  (d) John likes eggplant, wouldn't you agree.

Topicalization
(21) (a) John, I really like.

  (b) In three hours, everything is going to double in size.

Stylistic inversion
(22) (a) Into the room stepped an enormous man with a Panama hat.

(b) Hanging on the wall directly opposite us was a picture of Richard Nixon.

Negative Inversion

(23) (a) Not once did his eyes waver from the scene that was developing before him.

(b) Only once in a million years would Nature conspire to produce such a remarkable accident.

(c) At no time did we think that we had a chance of winning.

VP topicalization

(24) (a) They said that they were going to defeat the Red Sox in three games, and defeat them in three games they did.

(b) They said they would be rich, and rich they were.

Ellipsis

(25) (a) (Gapping) Mary hit the hay and John the bottle.

(b) (VP Deletion) The man who didn't leave saw the man who did.

(c) (Comparative deletion) Mary found more counter-examples than John (found).

(d) (Subject–verb Gapping) John ate dinner last night, and breakfast this morning.

Although it would be premature to assert without qualification that these differences are not communicative, it does seem in many cases that the effect of such stylistic variation has more to do with matters of contextual appropriateness than illocutionary force (expressed attitudes and conditions of fit); variants may change the usefulness of the expression from the point of view of prior or expected discourse.

Vocatives

Some sentences have a constituent which is used to attract the attention of the intended audience:

(26) John (Hey, You over there, etc.)

(a) Look out!

(b) What time is it?

(c) The store is closed.

This constituent is not the subject of the sentence, even in the imperative case, since we can have vocatives with subjects:

(27) John, you push and I'll pull.

It is not clear how to deal with vocatives structurally (see Zwicky 1974).

Free fragments

We do not always speak in full, grammatical sentences. Sometimes we choose to utter 'pieces'. We will call these expressions 'free fragments' – free because they can be free-standing contributions to a talk exchange, and fragments because they do at least seem to be fragments of longer sentences. Are these always pieces of full sentences, uttered perhaps because we feel the hearer can infer the rest from context? What are the restrictions, if any, on what can be a free fragment? These are some of the questions we want to take up, but not here and now. Here we are interested in the question: what their uses are, and how to fit them into our analysis of mood.

Yanofsky (1978) noted that there were noun phrases that are well formed, not derivable from full sentences, but usable and often used with the same force as (full) sentences:[48]

[(1)]   Teamwork (exhortation)
[(2)]   My friend (sarcastic)
[(3)]   My lunch (exclamation)
[(4)]   Your move (request the hearer make his move)
[(5)]   The time (request for the time)

Sadock and Zwicky (1985: 187–8) offer noun phrases such as:

[(118)] Some whiskey
[(119)] The goblins
[(120)] Six of the pink ones with sprinkles on top
[(121)] All of you with beards
[(122)] Lord Threshingham
[(123)] A beer, please
[(124)] The left shoulder, please

which can be uttered to convey a request, order, offer, warning, threat etc., and prepositional phrases, such as,

[(125)] Near the window!
[(126)] On the stairs!
[(127)] On to the table!

which can be uttered with directive or exclamatory force. Sadock and Zwicky do not go into the class of expressions that can have such uses. Barton (1990) suggests that the maximal projection of any category X can be a fragment, and proposes that the grammar be generalized to 'equalize the status of sentences and constituents as two classes of structures generated by the grammar' (1990: 208). Thus we find fragments which do the job of all the major (and perhaps minor) moods:

Proto-declaratives
(28)   NP: My friend (sarcastic)

Proto-imperatives
(29) (a) NP: Your move, No Parking
     (b) PP: Off with his head, On with the show
     (c) AP: Dinner
Proto-interrogatives
(30) (a) NP: The time
     (b) VP: Want some coffee
     (c) ??: She like her new job

We will say that forms such as these are moodless, though in may cases they can and will be interpreted as elliptical for sentences of a certain mood. Many if not most free fragments can in principle be extended to sentences of more than one mood:

(31) (a) Here is *dinner. Dinner* is ready (served).
     (b) Come to *dinner*!
     (c) *Dinner* anybody?

There is no obvious reason to assign a free fragment itself to any particular mood.

Stylistic variation and mood

Even though these stylistic variants all have basically a single illocutionary force, there are differences associated with many of them; for instance, topicalizations can be used to focus attention on a certain object, event or state of affairs from many mentioned in the utterance. Should we therefore say that these are differences in use, and so constitute different moods of English? This approach would encode the form–function correlation directly, without recourse to an abstract level of syntactic representation. To take such an approach might certainly be plausible if we were attempting to produce a theory of the identification of mood in real time.

Or should we perhaps move to a more abstract level of syntactic representation wherein these variations are coded into a single level of representation? This second approach would allow us to, for example, subsume elliptical structures under the specifications for full structures. The assumption that the moods are stated in terms of abstract levels of representation is not equivalent to the claim that surface structure is irrelevant. Rather, surface structure is relevant in that it provides the basis for the reconstruction of the canonical abstract form on the basis of which the mood is determined. Implicit here is a somewhat more refined view of the form–function correlation than we have been working with thus far. It assumes that there is a mapping from surface form to underlying form, and from underlying form to function.[49]

A third alternative would be to acknowledge differences in use which are not illocutionary, remain at the surface level of syntactic representation of moods, but define a mood in such a way as to allow for the right kind of variation. The trick, of course, is to say what the 'right kind' of variation is, but we can take heart from other enterprises which have taken partially pretheoretic notions and subjected them to analysis only to find them breaking up (disjunctively) into more regular and theoretically tractable subcomponents.

The best way to proceed is probably the third. We could first try to state the form–function–fit correlations in as surfacey a way as possible, if only to (a) avoid unnecessary theoretic syntactic commitments; and (b) remain as close as possible to a left-to-right comprehension model. Second, we could try to state (linguistic) generalizations of the sort found in current grammars as meta-principles over form–function–fit correlations. Third, we could try to reconstruct the traditional notion of mood in terms of *central* form–function–fit pairings, plus variation. The basic idea would be to say that there is a central *illocutionary* connection between a small set of forms and a function, or a small set of functions and a form, and in addition there are syntactic variants of these forms which correlate not with *illocutionary* variants of their respective functions, but with variations in *conditions of appropriate use.* Thus, topicalized sentences have constative illocutionary function, but have different conditions of appropriate use, each of which is related to the details of the syntactic variation. Under this conception,

Mood

A mood is a collection of form–function pairings satisfying one of the following conditions: (a) a central form is correlated with a central illocutionary function, and stylistic variations are correlated with variations in appropriateness conditions; (b) a small set of forms have a single force or a small set of forces are expressed by a single form.

Whether or not this conception of mood will play a role in the best account of communication will have to await that account.

The topics of intonation, parentheticals and stylistic variation do press home the need to eventually give a more precise characterization of the concept of mood. Since it is partially theoretical, the notion should be characterized, in part, by the best theory it has a role in. On the other hand, its role in that theory will be determined in part by the characteristics we demand of it. Hence, we must juggle intuitive appropriateness and theoretical simplicity. The form this potential tradeoff takes in the present case can be seen by inspecting again the structural characterizations of mood. Note that in some cases (for example, the interrogative) the structural descriptions are disjunctive. Suppose that at the level of function, some of the specifications are disjunctive. How then should we count moods; or more specifically, how many interrogative moods are there? Fortunately, if we get the form–function–fit correlations right it may not matter how we count the moods, since no generalizations stated *over* the concept of a mood yet play a descriptive role in the theory. Perhaps only after we have completed the inferential chain to include illocutionary functions can we attempt to reconstruct the pretheoretic notion of mood.

Declaratives

There are sentences which have the form of declaratives, but have been claimed not to have the usual constative force of declaratives – the so-called 'explicit performatives'. John Austin (1961) introduced *performative* as a 'new and ugly word' into philosophy and linguistics. Here is part of what he said:

> I want to discuss a kind of utterance which looks like a statement ... and yet is not true or false ... in the first person singular present indicative active ... if a person makes an utterance of this sort we would say that he is *doing* something rather than merely *saying* something.
>
> (ibid.: 220)

What kind of utterance does he have in mind? Austin continues:

> When I say *I do* (take this woman to be my lawful wedded wife), I am not reporting on a marriage, I am indulging in it.

Typical examples of performatives include:

> (32) (a) I (hereby) order you to leave.
> (b) I (hereby) promise to pay you five dollars.
> (c) I (hereby) declare this meeting adjourned.

The problem performative utterances pose for our analysis of mood is that they are constative in their form, but frequently non-constative in their force. Bach and Harnish (1979: ch. 10.1) reconciled these properties by treating them as standardized indirect speech acts.[50]

Imperatives

From the foregoing characterization in (Mood-Structure) (p. 414) we have identified the imperative mood with a certain syntactic (and predictable phonological) structure. The strongest claim would be that all and only imperatives are structures with the force of expressions of desires that H do some specified act.

However, not all intuitively imperatival sentences fit (Mood-Structure). Some are *emphatic*:

> (33) (a) Do take out the garbage!
> (b) Do you take out the garbage!
> (c) Do someone take out the garbage!

Again, some are *negative*:

(34) (a) Don't take out the garbage!
     (b) Don't you take out the garbage!
     (c) Don't anyone take out the garbage!

How are we to incorporate these facts within our account of mood? Are there three moods lurking beneath the surface or really only one or two – with variations?[51]

The (F–L–F) compatibility condition (and inference rule) for (!) also requires some elaboration. The problem is specifying, in general, what counts as a *compliance condition.* It is not complying with the imperative 'Destroy the bathroom of my house!' to destroy the whole house. Thus, if H brings about q and q entails p, it does not follow that H complied with the imperative requesting H to bring it about that p; there is some notion of doing the minimal act(s) sufficient for p, operative. This aspect of fit needs further work.[52]

Third, consider the (F–EA) compatibility condition (and inference rule) for (!). As noted earlier, literal and direct utterances of strings analysable superficially as having the structure of imperatives can be acts other than directives. Consider:

(35) (a) S: What did he ask you to do?
          H: (He asked me to) Leave the room.
     (b) S: What do you want me to do?
          H: (I want you to) Leave the room.
     (c) S: What are you asking me to do?
          H: (I'm asking you to) Leave the room.
          S': (You are asking me to) Leave the room?

These cases should probably be handled differently. In case (35a) the preferred inference from H's remark is that in uttering 'Leave the room', H is answering S's question. Without special information to the contrary S will assume the Conversational Presumptions are in effect (in particular, the Presumptions of Sequencing[53] for questions), and so will favour that hypothesis.[54] Since answers to questions are usually characterized as being constative,[55] the utterance of 'Leave the room' in (35a) must be construed as contributing to the inference:

(36) (a) H uttered 'Leave the room' as an answer to the question 'What did John ask you to do?'
     (b) So, H constated that John asked H to leave the room.

But did H also *say* that John asked H to leave the room? Intuitions vary here, so without further evidence I will leave the matter open.
    Unfortunately, this indecision infects cases (35b) and (35c). In (35b), H

is constating that H wants S to leave the room, and so may be *indirectly* requesting S to leave. Likewise with case (35c), except that the inference from H's remark looks very much like the inference from explicit performatives. In neither case is it clear how to report what was *said*. Lastly, the utterance of 'Leave the room' by S' in (35c) appears to be a case of asking H a yes/no question, and as such would fail (*mutatis mutandis*) under a theory of that type of phenomena.

Fourth, various authors have pointed out that imperative forms have uses that do not seem to accord with the compatibility conditions (and inferences) we have characterized.

Schmerling (1982: 210–11) lists the following as exceptions to the stereotypical 'command' analysis of imperatives in the literature (her numbering):

[(24)]   *Plea*: (Please) let me go!

This is only a counter-example to imperatives as commands, not as directives in general – i.e. as expressions of the desire or intention that H do A.

[(25)]   *Offer*: Have some meatloaf.
[(26)]   *Permission*: Help yourself.

These too seem to be counter-examples only to the stronger 'command' analysis of imperatives. Also, it is puzzling why these examples are so categorized. Is [(26)] not also an offer? The problem comes from the fact that in general, offering something entails giving permission to have it, and vice versa.

[(27)]   *Warning*: Don't trip on that cord.

This too seems to be a counter-example only to the stronger conception of imperatives, not ours.

[(28)]   *Exhortations of varying directness*
         (a) Run!!
         (b) Save 10 cents.
         (c) Make me proud of you.
         (d) Be big and strong.

These are more complicated. [(28a)] seems like a normal imperative. However [(28b)] and [(28c)] have the feature that what H is to do is not mentioned in the sentence. Schmerling sees the problem as 'talk about events that are presented as inevitable consequences of some more primary action' (ibid.: 211). Yet this is not a problem for our analysis, which says that H is to make it the case that p. The analysis does not say *how* H is to bring about p. In some cases there is a normal natural way of doing it, and so that way could reasonably be intended or expected by the speaker, but in other cases not. Even a request to 'Close the door!' could be carried out in many ways, and the speaker might be leaving these up to the discretion of the doer. [(28b)] also has the force of information or advice, and so would be viewed as a kind of ellipsis. Construed as a sign on a counter display, it has the force of: if you buy this you will save 10 cents. [(28d)] has two occurrences. One is in contexts such as going to the dentist, where the mother might be urging the child to be grown up (act like a grown up). The other is in the context of doing something which will eventuate in being big and strong: eat your vitamins, spinach, etc., and be big and strong! The first seems mildly figurative, the second conforms to our analysis.

[(29)]   *Wishes*
      (a) Sleep well.
      (b) Have a good time.
      (c) Don't get the flu.

Here Schmerling's worry is that there is not anything specific that has to be done to satisfy the condition laid down by the content of the sentence. But this is no problem on our theory, because we do not say that the imperative mood must specify how p is to be brought about. (Of course it can, but it need not.) [(29)] should be read as: H is to do what H can to, for example, sleep well, etc.

[(30)]   *Healing*
      (a) Walk!
      (b) Hear!

These are supposed to be a problem because they cannot be complied with prior to the utterance (Schmerling 1982: 211). But our analysis of imperatives does not require that they be. It only says that H is to make it the case that p at some time after (and partly because of) the utterance. The real problem with such cases is determining the content of the imperative. Some people feel that they are genuine directives which are issued with the belief that by issuing them, the speaker is enabling the hearer to carry them out. Others feel that they are supernatural declarations (such as 'Let there be light!') whose primary purpose is to create the capacity for, for example, walking, and only incidently are they directives that the recipient demonstrate that newly acquired capacity. The first is compatible without analysis, the second would force us to take [(30)] as elliptical.

[(31)]   *Hocus-pocus*
      (a) Stay!
      (b) Start (dammit)!
      (c) Please don't rain.

These are a problem because the 'hearer' is inanimate (and so, presumably, cannot 'comply' with the directive). The main worry here is whether these utterances are serious and literal. Surely the speaker *wants* these states of affairs, and perhaps these utterances should be analysed as the expression of such desires. Notice that our analysis is that imperatives are used to express a desire or intention that H make p the case. Does this induce an ambiguity? This is a tricky problem. We do not say that the word 'grand-father' is ambiguous just because it can apply to either one's maternal grandfather or one's paternal grandfather. Why should we say that impera-tives are ambiguous just because they can express either desires or intentions that H make p the case? Wilson and Sperber (1988: 80–1) suggest in addition:

Advice
[(1)]   (a) Peter: Excuse me, I want to get to the station.
       (b) Mary: Take a number 3 bus.

Wilson and Sperber take it that this shows the utterance cannot be a direc-tive because 'there is no reason to think she [Mary] cares whether Peter follows her advice, and hence no reason to analyse her utterance as an attempt to get Peter to take a number 3 bus' (ibid.: 80).

In reply we might say first, that one can express the intention that H do something even if one 'doesn't care' whether or not they do it. Indeed, a sergeant might order a private to do something and not want them to do it so that they can be legitimately punished. Second, it also may be that the form [(1b)] is misleading; perhaps it is a case of discourse ellipsis: 'to get to the station I advise you to ...' where the fragment is just an infinitive, not an imperative at all.

Threats and dares
[(3)]   Go on. Throw it. Just you dare.

Here Mary's utterance is not an attempt to get H to do A, just the opposite (ibid.: 80). But if it is just the opposite maybe this is not a case of uttering the sentence seriously and literally. If not, it is not a counter-example to our analysis.

Predetermined cases
[(7)]   Please be out. (said to self by a child sent to apologize to someone)

Here there is no hearer intended to make p the case. Again, this is an expression of a desire or wish, and we need a reason to suppose this forces ambiguity on the form.

To these we might add:

(37)   Look before you leap. (proverb)

The function of such sayings is to express insights and guide action, much as a fable, or parable is intended to do. As such it is no counter-example to our analysis.[56]

As represented in (Mood-Structure) (p. 414), the distinctive features of the imperative are the absence of an auxiliary constituent (containing such things as tense and modals), and the optionality of subject noun phrases. It is sometimes said that the subject of imperatives must be 'you', which is optionally deleted:

(38) (a) You (will) take out the garbage!
    (b) Take out the garbage!

Considerable data appears to support this view. For instance, given an independently motivatable account of reflexives and object-linked pronouns it is possible to argue from the following data to the conclusion that (38a) is the source of (38b):

(39) (a) *I
    (b) You } take out the garbage!
    (c) *He

(40) Shave { (a) *my
           (b) your } self!
           (c) *him

(41) Nod { (a) *my
         (b) your } (own) head!
         (c) *his

(42) Shave { (a) me
         (b) *you } !
         (c) him

It is our position that the above data can be handled without postulating an underlying 'you'; that it is possible to account for the acceptability and oddity of the above sentences on independent grounds (see Harnish in preparation). Other things being equal this is the position one ought to opt for, since it seems to be the case that intuitively imperatival sentences need not have 'you' as possible subjects:

(43) (a) Nobody (no one) move!
    (b) Don't anyone take out the trash!
    (c) Someone take out the trash!
    (d) Everyone take their positions!
    (e) Some girls take out the trash, and some boys fix the faucets!
    (f) The man in the pork-pie hat come over here!
    (g) John take out the trash and Mary the books!

Thus, although no *pronoun* but 'you' will go as subject of imperatives, it does seem that a variety of noun phrases can take that position. However, the position is not free for noun phrases; indefinites and demonstratives seem odd:

(44) (a) ?A boy open the window!

     (b) ?That boy over there leave the room!
     (c) ?Several people leave the room!

An adequate general theory of imperatives should account for these various restrictions on subject. Harnish in preparation offers an account of the first batch of data, that tending to support the derivation of (38b) from (38a), and a first pass at an account of these last two batches of data.

Interrogatives

There are a number of sentences that *appear* to constitute counter-examples to the above account of the interrogative mood. Some of these, we suggest, are what we have called 'minor moods' and they include:

Alternative questions
(45) (a) Does John resemble his /father/, or his \mother\?
     (b) Who does John resemble, his /father/ or his \mother\?
Exclamatives
(46) Isn't that nice!

As distinct moods, the above will be given their own form–function–fit correlations, and so are not in that way problems for the account of the major moods.

There are others that cannot be handled in this way, or not obviously so. Bell (1975: 208–9) proposes that the following interrogatives are not used to solicit information (his numbering):

    [(46)] Which hand is it in? (request to choose, guess said to a child)

Bell says that 'the parent requests the child to guess which hand it is in, but not to inform or tell him anything' (ibid.: 208). It is true that the speaker is not trying to gain any new information, since S already knows which hand it is in, and S is trying to get H to pick a hand – this is the primary point of the utterance. But is it false that H is to tell S (say to S) which hand it is in? It would seem not, just as in the case of exam questions (to which we will return) we have interrogatives in the service of institutional practice (here a game), but they are still questions.[57]

    [(47)] What should I do now? (request for advice)

Bell says that 'here the answer will itself be a variety of command' (ibid.: 208). However, this is not so; the primary force of advice is informative; to say what someone should do to secure the ends at issue. This question has a straightforward answer (see also Harnish in preparation).

    [(56)] Was Kant an idealist? (exam question)

Bell says 'the question requests the candidate to tell him (*not* inform him of) the answer, and by convention, to do a lot more besides' (ibid.: 209). We can agree with Bell that the practice or institution of examining and answering 'has to be taught, and is not understood simply through one's grasp of the sense of the question' (ibid.: 209). What this shows is that the added behaviour is not a part of the interrogative, and that the real problem with exam questions is the same as with choice questions: the speaker already knows the answer. On our analysis of interrogative mood, S is saying that H is to tell H something, and this is not contradicted by the fact that S's primary purpose in uttering the interrogative is to find out if S knows the answer.

[(57)]   O Death, where is thy sting? (poetic rhetorical)
[(59)]   Am I not an apostle? Am I not free? ... (rhetorical)

The point of these utterances is not to question, but to assert: 'I take St Paul here to assert that he is an apostle, is free ...' (ibid.: 209). This can be handled as a species of indirect speech act; in questioning one is asserting. The assertoric force is not a part of the literal and direct force potential and so is not a threat to the analysis.

Wilson and Sperber (1988) give in addition:

Rhetorical questions
[(12)]   What was your New Year's resolution? (used to remind)

Wilson and Sperber say 'her utterance is not a request for information. Intuitively such rhetorical questions function as reminders, and do not call for any overt response' (ibid.: 92). Here we want to question whether 'reminding' is a speech act of the relevant sort. If it is analysed as 'calling something to mind' it is perlocutionary, not illocutionary, and could have been achieved by just saying, in the context 'New Year's resolution!' The fact that S can utter those words in the form of a question without meaning all of it does not show that those words are not in the interrogative mood.

Surprise question
[(14)]   (a) Peter: The president has resigned.
          (b) Mary: Good heavens. Has he?

Wilson and Sperber say 'It seems inappropriate to describe Mary's utterance as a request for information, which she was given only a few seconds ago. Intuitively [(14b)] expresses Mary's surprise or incredulity at the information she has been given' (ibid.: 92–3). This description seems right, but that makes the form-function very much like a tag: 'He hasn't resigned, has he?' It has an element of soliciting *confirmation*, not information.

Self-addressed questions
(47) 'Now why did I say that?' (said to oneself)
Speculative questions
(48) 'What is the best analysis of interrogative sentences?' (said idly to someone else)

In neither of these cases is one attempting to get an answer or intending someone to say anything. So they seem to be counter-examples to the analysis of mood. There is some point to distinguishing uses from meaning even here in the analysis of mood. Perhaps what should be said is that these are other uses of the interrogative form, but these uses do not induce new meanings on to these forms, because in part these are not illocutionary uses. Think again of reminding.

There are some technical problems with (Mood-Structure) as well. For instance, there is the problem of how to formally pick out the *wh*-element in the sentence, since it can be a constituent of indeterminate length:

    (49) *Whose wife's psychiatrist's . . . bill* did John refuse to pay?

Also there is the problem of multiple *wh*-elements in a single interrogative. However, multiple *wh*-questions are a predictable syntactic extension of simple *wh*-questions, in the sense that they must be generated by the syntax if the syntax freely generates noun phrases and other *wh*-phrases. It would seem desirable, therefore that the mood for such multiple *wh*-questions be an extension of (Wh?). In fact, it appears that this is possible. Notice that the main difference between simple and multiple *wh*-questions is that the latter have an unfronted *wh*-phrase. But both have a fronted *wh*-phrase. Therefore, we can use (Wh?) for multiple *wh*-questions as long as we make the appropriate revision in the rule that relates the mood to the locutionary act. Essentially, such a revision must involve the inclusion of a clause to the effect that all unfronted *wh*s are to be extracted from their syntactic positions and concatenated with the fronted *wh* in the specification of the logical form of the sentence, from which the locutionary act will be determined. Thus, for a sentence like:

    (50) Who put which books in which briefcase?

the locutionary act must be of the form 'S says that H is to tell S which people x, which books y and which briefcase z are such that x put y in z'.

As characterized in (Mood-Structure), *wh*-interrogatives have two forms, one where the *wh*-element is fronted and one where it is not fronted, but is highly stressed. The first is a normal *wh*-interrogative, the second is sometimes called an 'echo question'. Normal questions ('What do you see?') are used to solicit *new information*, or on occasion they are used when H did not hear what was said and S wants to repeat the remark.[58] Echo questions ('You saw *what*?' 'John likes *beans*?') express surprise at what was said (and hence imply understanding), but also solicit confirmation – usually by way of repetition.

    It is possible that the stressed forms of questions are stylistic (emphatic) variants of unstressed forms, and so should be handled not as a variant *within* a mood, but as a stylistic variant *of* a mood. Since changes in stylistic variation do not change communicative force and content, there should be unstressed versions of these sentences. Echo questions may constitute such a case for *wh*-questions, but there seem to be no hosts for the yes/no inter-rogatives; the sentence: 'John likes \beans\' is not used to ask a question at all. One way we could go here is to acknowledge the yes/no variant form in the mood for questions, but not the *wh*-version. It would be a stressed variant of the echo question. What could emphatic stress contribute that would make up for the difference in use between echo questions and stressed *wh*-questions? The most obvious suggestion is that emphatic final stress expresses *surprise*, related to what the stressed constituent is about; the sentence,

(51) You saw *Bob Dylan* (at the supermarket)

expresses surprise relative to seeing Bob Dylan.[59] Applied to echo ques-tions this would amount to expressing surprise relative to the *wh* consti-tuent. But what are *wh* constituents about? Since they do not refer to anything, what could they be about other than what they are being used to ask about? Now, to express surprise at what one is asking about implies having acquired the requested information and this seems to give us the use we wanted:

Form: NP + Aux + /wh/
Expressed Attitude: (a) surprise that NP + Aux + *wh*-answer;
                      (b) desire that H confirm that NP + Aux + answer.

But we still do not know how the echo question *loses* the previously mentioned contextual appropriateness conditions.

There is also a third type of interrogative with its distinctive flat or falling intonation contour, sometimes called a 'prompting question':

Prompting question
(52) (a) (And John,) you saw \what\?
     (b) (And then), you said \what\?

It is not clear whether these differences are differences in mood or not, though they do involve differences in conditions of appropriateness. Prompting questions such as (52a, b) above are, like normal questions, used to solicit information for the first time. But they also have some restrictive conditions on their appropriate use, in particular, they seem to involve items in a series. Such questions appear to be most appropriate when the speaker expected the hearer to spontaneously provide the answer, but the hearer did not. They can also be used in a classroom situ-ation, where the teacher is leading the students through a series of steps in an argument or through a list of related topics. And they appear not to be normally used upon encountering someone new:[60]

(53) (a) Excuse me, in /which aisle/ can I find the carrots?

454 Foundations of speech act theory

    (b) ?Excuse me, I can find in the carrots in \which aisle\.

Perhaps the absence of *Wh*-Fronting and Inversion in prompting questions constitutes a difference of emphasis rather than a difference of function.

Another problem about (Mood-Structure) for *wh*-interrogatives is that some declaratives such as (54) meet the structural description, but do not have the force of questions:

    (54) What is bothering John is bothering me.

Note that the initial sequence 'What is bothering John' could be a well formed *wh*-interrogative; this might effect the performance of a left-to-right comprehender.

Another class of apparent exceptions to the above account of mood are numerous (interrogative) pragmatic idioms:

    (55) (a) Where does he get off VP-ing?
        (b) What (do you) say we VP?
        (c) How are things (going)?
        (d) How's things?

Since these are not productive, we do not consider them to be even minor moods. In fact, each idiom must be learned individually, and this suggests that each idiom will require its own inference rule(s).[61]

According to the (F–L–F, CC) for interrogatives, the appropriate conditions of satisfaction are 'answerhood conditions'.[62] But the notion of an answer to a question requires more work. For instance, what counts as *directly answering* a certain question is determined in part by the form of the original interrogative:

    (56) Did you get up late?
        (a) Yes (I got up late)
        (b) No (I did not get up late)
        (c) *John (got up late)
    (57) Who got up late?
        (a) John (got up late)
        (b) *Yes, *No

There are also ways of *indirectly* answering a question.[63] Further, we must be able to distinguish possible and appropriate *answers* to questions from possible and appropriate *responses* to questions. The following are all possible appropriate responses to (Y/N?) or (Wh ?), but are not *answers* to either:

    (58) (a) It's none of your business.
        (b) Why do you ask?

    (c) Nosey, aren't you?

Finally, there are some borderline cases; should we say that the following are possible *answers*, or only possible *appropriate responses*?

(59) (a) Y/N: H nods his head
      (b) Wh?: H gestures towards John

There are fragments of complete questions that still seem to function as questions, though the material that is left out would determine specific aspects of interpretation. In rich enough contexts, this information seems to be recoverable. Consider:[64]

(60) (a) Last night's party *go* well?
      (b) She *likes* her new house?
      (c) *Have* any ideas about what to do?
      (d) *Meet* any new people?

So called 'pseudo-questions', such as the following, seem sometimes not to be used to request information:

(61) (a) (Question) Did you like the movie?
      (b) (Response) Is the pope Polish? (Yes)
      (c) (Response) Do pigs fly? (No)

Although such sentences can be used, in appropriate circumstances, to ask questions, in the above contexts they are appropriately used to do something else, what?

    Roughly, the speaker intends the hearer (the questioner) to infer that the answer to the speaker's question is the *same as* the answer to the response. Assuming that such 'answers' are not genuine requests for information, what should we say they are; are they types of indirect or non-literal language use?

CONCLUSION

The main purpose of this paper has been to outline a theory of mood for English meeting certain intuitive conditions of adequacy. In doing so we distinguished verbal from sentential mood and major moods from minor moods. We have given a preliminary formulation of form, force, fit compatibility conditions for each major mood. Then, for each mood, we stated inference rules which if followed under appropriate circumstances could eventuate in the performance of an illocutionary act within the (literal and direct) illocutionary act potential of that sentence. If the force and content is recognized by the hearer, the act is communicatively successful. Our proposal opened up a number of further issues that remain to be resolved. Some of these are taken up elsewhere (see Harnish in preparation). Perhaps the reader will be provoked by these reflections to join in the fun.

NOTES

1 There are about two dozen minor moods, which, compared to major moods, (a) are highly restricted in their productivity; (b) are peripheral to communication; (c) are probably low in their relative frequency of occurrence; and (d) vary widely across languages. We argue that minor moods cannot be analysed as compositional compounds of the major moods, and must be taken on their own, as form, force, fit correlations. See Harnish in preparation for more discussion.

2 Lyons says that this traditional terminology has the advantage that it

> enables us to draw a distinction, not only between utterances and sentences ... but also between sentences that are subclassified as declarative, interrogative, jussive, etc., in terms of their characteristic use and sentences that are subclassified as indicative, dubitive, imperative, etc., in terms of the mood of the main verb.
>
> (1977: 848)

But the Jespersen notion of mood also allows us to draw the first distinction, and it is just the utility of this second distinction that is at issue.

3 It is not clear what the theoretical payoff of these limitations is; by limiting the system to verbal inflections one loses generalizations of use over forms, and by limiting the function to speech acts one loses generalizations of forms over function.

4 'The imperative indicates the speaker's desire to influence future events' (Sadock and Zwicky 1985: 160). We discuss this and others on pp. 417 ff.

5 It is not clear what (b) above amounts to.

6 Davidson adds the condition '(3) Finally, the theory should be semantically tractable' (1979: 14–15). We assimilate this to compositionality.

7 The terminology 'major' and 'minor' moods was introduced in Harnish 1983. It also is used in Sadock and Zwicky 1985.

8 For further discussion see Akmajian, Steele and Wasow 1979: 4.4. Any descriptively adequate syntactic characterization of these classes of sentences would do for our present (pragmatic) purposes. See for instance McCawley 1988 for one alternative.

9 Notice that this correlation says nothing as to how speakers and hearers decide what mood an incoming sentence is to be assigned. For that we would need a theory of left-to-right sentence comprehension at the syntactic and pragmatic level; unfortunately we do not have such a theory even at the phonological level. All we are claiming now is that if a sentence can be analysed as having a certain structure, then it is a candidate for the indicated mood. How this might take place is presently a much more obscure problem.

10 Hare (1989) argues for two additional components: a sign of subscription or commitment, and a sign of completion.

11 Searle (1969) calls (C) the 'propositional content indicator', but Belnap (1990: 4) objects that non-declaratives do not have propositions as contents. This seems to be mainly terminological, since Searle's 'propositions' are not invariably bearers of truth value – only when they are asserted.

12 For a discussion of each of these conditions in turn see: Davidson 1967, Hamblin 1987 and Hamblin 1958. Belnap (1990) surveys some of these issues.

13 See also Anscombe 1957; and Searle 1975, reprinted in Searle 1979.

14 For a critique of the Higher Performative Analysis in general see Gazdar 1979: ch. 2; and Berckmans 1988.

15 Analogous points hold for Searle 1969. See Harnish 1979.

16 Perhaps, following Frege on indicatives, we might say that for non-indicatives,

the force is coded into the form of the sentence.

17 Notice that McGinn is not claiming that declaratives occur in the analysis of non-declaratives *simpliciter*, only in their paraphrases.

18 Davidson's version differs by displaying the indicative core.

19 McGinn intentionally leaves this broad enough to cover unintentional compliance by anyone; it is not clear why.

20 See Segal (1991: sect. III) for a first approximation.

21 See definition D4′ (Grice 1968: 63) for a more elaborate and qualified rendition.

22 See Bach and Harnish 1979: 25, 287. Here the ellipses around 'p' simply indicate that the value of 'p' is being fixed in part by meaning, and so what is said is always 'literal'.

23 See Bach and Harnish 1979: 34.

24 We ignore Lappin's qualification that it is (really) the utterance of a sentence that has a mood. We will take Lappin's proposal as a semantics for (types of) sentences.

25 Primed numbers preface applications of Lappin's principles to the analysis of specific examples.

26 Note that we do distinguish these; ordinarily we say that someone *obeys* an order, not a request, but that they *fulfil* a request but not an order.

27 The numbering in brackets is Pendlebury's.

28 As Pendlebury notes, (K?) does not require that a know that (:Q) answers a question (?P) (1986: 366).

29 'When we subtract this commitment from an act of ordering what we are left with is not a proposition, but *the mere expression of an order*' (1986: 368).

30 'As stage thunder is only apparent thunder and a stage fight is only an apparent fight, so stage assertion is only apparent assertion ... Therefore it must still always be asked, about what is presented in the form of an indicative sentence, whether it really contains an assertion. And this question must be answered in the negative if the requisite seriousness is missing' (Frege 1918a/1967: 22).

31 Hare (1989) suggests a sign of subscription is necessary to indicate the undertaking of commitment associated with the moods, though he notes, with Davidson, that it could not be relied on *by an audience* (ibid.: 28).

32 See Searle (1979: ch. 2); Bach and Harnish (1979: ch. 4).

33 To say nothing of the minor moods.

34 We distinguish a question's *being* answered from a question *having* an answer. Questions clearly can have answers no one ever gives as answers.

35 As Frege (1918a/1967: 22) noted, 'we have no particular clause in the indicative sentence which corresponds to the assertion, that something is being asserted lies rather in the form of the indicative'.

36 As Frege (1918a/1967: 21) said, 'I am not using the word "sentence" here in a purely grammatical sense where it also includes subordinate clauses. An isolated subordinate clause does not always have a sense about which the question of truth can arise, whereas the complex sentence to which it belongs has such a sense.'

37 Note that embeddings do not always de-force an utterance: 'You can count on me since I (hereby) promise to be there.'

38 See Akmajian, Demers and Harnish 1981; Sperber and Wilson 1986.

39 Notice that the definition of literality crucially involves the analysis of illocutionary acts given in the theory – it is not a *theory-neutral* analysis of the notion. Rather, it is more like the base clauses of a recursive definition of literality on the complexity of what is uttered (and so what is said), given the analyses in the taxonomy.

40 Occasionally present tense has the force of future time reference – or at least it

does not have the force of present time reference:

  (a) I leave tomorrow.
  (b) I jog often.
  (c) Anyone moves a muscle and I shoot.

41 For *wh*-interrogatives, the symbol 'Wh-x' next to 'p(x)' schematizes the identity of the x being questioned and which satisfies 'p(x)'. Thus 'Who discovered calculus?' becomes: S is asking the identity of the person x such that x discovered the calculus.

42 For the sake of simplicity I have avoided the necessary relativization of these conditions to speakers, hearers, times, occasions of utterances, etc. A significant amount of philosophy of language and linguistics will go into making these respectable.

43 Proper names, natural kind terms and indexicals come immediately to mind. However, the semantics of these terms is still too unresolved to know whether this is true or not.

44 For more detailed discussion see Harnish 1983; and Harnish in preparation.

45 See Harnish in preparation for further discussion.

46 Many of the following points are due to discussions with Peter Culicover.

47 By using the traditional labels for these structures we do not intend to subscribe to the traditional analysis of them as involving rules (transformations) of movement or deletion; perhaps rules of interpretation are the appropriate mechanism for correctly pairing sound and meaning in these cases. See e.g. Williams 1977 and references therein for more discussion.

48 Numbers in brackets are the author's original.

49 Interestingly, we do not have to give the mapping from Surface Form to Underlying Form independently. A serviceable notion of Underlying Form might be the level of S-structure of Chomsky and Lasnik 1977. The mapping is given by the stylistic transformations of the grammar, which need not be redundantly specified in our characterization of form–function. They, of course, play a role in the characterization of form, but not a redundant one.

50 See Searle 1989 for a critique of that view; and Harnish 1992a, and Bach and Harnish 1992 for an elaboration and defence.

51 See McCawley 1988: vol. I, 710, for more discussion.

52 See Holdcroft 1978, for further discussion.

53 See Bach and Harnish 1979: ch. 4.1, for a further discussion.

54 Of course tone of voice or special contextual beliefs can override these presumptions. Thus, a particularly loud/intense utterance of 'Leave the room!' (perhaps accompanied by appropriate gestures and facial expressions) along with some faint contextual justification for such a directive could promote the directive hypothesis over the constative one. Or imagine that it is mutually believed that H is expecting John to enter and H does not want to be seen with him. Just as S asks the question H sees John entering and says 'Leave the room (at once)!' Under these conditions it would be hard not to take the utterance as a directive.

55 Note again that not all contextually appropriate *responses* to questions are (direct) *answers* to questions; a 'return question', for instance, is not. The case of rhetorical questions is complicated by the fact that the force of H's remark below may be constative, but it is probably a standardized form of indirection:

  S: Have you read Aristotle's *De Anima*?
  H: Who reads Aristotle anymore?

56 See Harnish 1992b for more discussion.

57 Consider the following continuation:

(b) Child: I don't know.
(c) Parent: Well, go ahead, guess.

If this is OK it is some evidence that [(46a)] is still a question.

58 Or provide enough information for H to infer what was said.

59 Emphatic stress can also be used to express joy at something just found out about. Here there is no concomittant solicitation of confirmation: 'You saw *Bob Dylan* – great!'

60 Perhaps it is possible to render examples like (53b) appropriate by imagining that the hearer is a stock person. But if H was another shopper, (53b) would not be most appropriate.

61 See Harnish 1983 and in preparation for further discussion.

62 See Katz 1977, for further discussion.

63 See Belnap and Steele 1976: ch. 1, for further discussion.

64 See Harnish in preparation, for further discussion.

22 Speech act classification, language typology and cognition

William Croft

INTRODUCTION

A central concept to pragmatics is that of the speech act, or more specifically, the illocutionary act – what the speaker actually does in uttering a
sentence. The concept as found in contemporary linguistic theory was
originally developed in philosophy by Austin (1962) and Searle (1969,
1979). The most widely accepted speech act classification is that of Searle,
outlined briefly here (for a survey of prior classifications, see Hancher
1979: 1–4):

Representative: an assertion of a proposition, e.g. *It's cold here.*
Directive: a request that the addressee do something, such as produce an
    utterance (*Who just came in?*) or perform an action (*Please give that to
    me*).
Commissive: a commitment by the speaker to perform an action, e.g. *I
    promise to return by 5.*
Declaration: a speech act which by virtue of being uttered causes a change
    in the world, e.g. *I now declare you man and wife* (uttered in the
    appropriate context).
Expressive: an expression of speaker attitude towards a state of affairs, as
    in *I'm sorry to hear that.*

The philosophers who have proposed classifications of speech acts such
as Searle's above have concentrated their efforts on an a priori intuitive
analysis without much direct reference to the linguistic expression of illocutionary acts (let alone speech acts in actual conversational usage). For
example, the traditional distinction of interrogative and imperative speech
act types has no place in the philosophical classification of illocutionary
acts, since both are directives. From a philosophical point of view, there is
no real reason to take the linguistic form of speech acts into consideration,
since philosophers are exclusively concerned with the function of utterances.

From the linguist's point of view, on the other hand, the grammatical
expression of speech acts is a matter of greater concern; and from the

functionally oriented typologist's point of view, it is a source of hypotheses about human conceptual structures. A functionally oriented typologist uses the common or universal grammatical distinctions in the world's languages as the basis for the model of linguistic function. It is assumed that what is universal in the grammatical structure of languages is probably of quite basic human origin, since it is present (or potentially present) in all cultures. This origin is cognitive or interactional – though to put it in this way erects an artificial barrier between the two, since cognition is partly constructed socially, and interaction is the interaction of minds. It is further assumed that grammatical structure reflects the structure of the experience encoded by the grammatical structure; this is the principle of iconic motivation (Haiman 1983, 1985). Grammatical constructions represent the conventionalization of particularly salient distinctions found in language meaning and use, achieved through the mental internalization of patterns of conversational interaction itself (see Hopper's (1987) 'emergent grammar'). Thus, we can use cross-linguistically universal or common distinctions as empirical evidence for these ultimately internalized mental models of the experience encoded in language. This is true even when the experience is conversational interaction itself, or rather one important element of it, namely 'speech acts', or something similar to speech acts as the case may be.

The method of using cross-linguistically universal or widespread distinctions to uncover cognitively basic structures has been applied to a number of semantic domains, such as noun classes (Craig 1986), tense-aspect-modality (Anderson 1982, 1986), and verbal semantics (Croft 1990, 1991b). This same method can also be fruitfully applied to pragmatic domains, such as the domain of speech acts. This chapter will survey the empirical data for major sentence types, based on Sadock and Zwicky 1985 and other sources, and argue for a cognitive model of conversational interaction that respects the typologically most common or universal grammatical distinctions.

SPEECH ACTS AND MAJOR SENTENCE TYPES

The grammatical manifestation of speech acts in human languages is the concept of 'major sentence type'.[1] Since illocutionary acts are associated with speech events as a whole, they should be manifested by major distinctions between sentence types. While this is a priori not a necessary correlation, it follows from the principle of iconic motivation. In order to see the plausibility of applying this principle, it is worth considering first a simpler example.

In the sentence *Martin brought a pitcher of water to the table*, the major constituents of the clause correspond to the major perceptual–cognitive distinctions in the event: each participant corresponds to a noun phrase, and the main verb indicates the action that links the participants together.

Likewise, the syntactic structure of the clause reflects the semantic relations of the entities involved: 'Every relation of words rests genetically upon a relation of non-verbal fact' (Gardiner 1951: 154). The action that links the participants together is expressed by the main verb whose subcategorization and grammatical relations link the subject, object and oblique noun phrases together. Also, since the pitcher contains the water and defines the unit of that liquid being referred to by the speaker, *a pitcher of water* is a single constituent.

The reflection of fundamental semantic categories and relations in grammatical categories and relations pervades grammar so much that it is virtually taken for granted. The fact that it must be explicitly provided for in linguistic theory is demonstrated by the possibility of constructing a language in which such principles are violated, for instance, a language in which each word simultaneously describes parts of the semantic structures of agent, event and patient at once, such as words meaning 'a higher mammal transporting a liquid to a four-legged object' or 'something named "Martin" lifted a pitcher', which then must be combined in the proper fashion to create a meaningful sentence. The absurdity, or rather, extreme inefficiency and impracticality of a language that violates such basic principles of iconicity is quite obvious.

It is to be expected, then, that the grammatical typology of major sentence types can provide insight into the conceptual distinctions made by speakers on the nature of the utterances they produce. Thus, we must provide a definition of 'major sentence type' that can be used to determine which speech act related distinctions are manifested by major grammatical distinctions. Sadock and Zwicky propose that major sentence types can be identified by grammatical features – special particles or affixes, word order, intonation, or missing elements (Sadock and Zwicky 1985: 155). The sentence constructions with these special features must form a paradigmatic set – that is, they cannot occur in combination with each other, since a sentence cannot have two (literal) illocutionary forces at once (ibid.: 158–9). Sadock and Zwicky also argue that the primary conventional literal meaning of the construction must be some illocutionary force; this is to avoid the problem of indirect speech acts. If there are other meanings associated with a construction in addition to its primary illocutionary meaning, Sadock and Zwicky call these 'minor sentence types' (ibid.: 156).

Sadock and Zwicky's definition of 'major sentence type', while intuitively satisfying, has certain problems. In order to separate consideration of form – what we are treating as the dependent variable – from function, it is necessary to define what sort of grammatical features of sentences are 'major' distinctions as independent of their function as possible. Presumably, alteration of the form of an oblique noun phrase is not 'major' enough to constitute a major sentence type. It would be desirable to find criteria conforming to the principle of iconicity and relevant principles of perceptual salience to establish a definition of 'major sentence type'. The remainder of this section is devoted to arguing for a particular set of formal criteria for major sentence types, or rather for high degree of salience of differences in sentence type, since no sharp dividing line can be provided.

The best candidates for the most salient characteristics of a sentence are those properties that characterize the sentence as a whole rather than just one of its parts. Intonation is one such property; it is associated with the sentence (utterance) as a whole.[2] Beyond intonation we must turn to sentence structure. Here the most salient properties, that is, those that define the sentence as a whole, are its head and its immediate constituents. Thus major sentence types are most likely to be defined in terms of major alterations of the head and the immediate constituents of the sentence, that is, the main verb and its arguments.

Perhaps one of the most salient characteristics of the immediate constituents of a sentence, and a property that can be defined only over the sentence as a whole, is their order. This is manifested in two ways. First, in a language with relatively rigid word order such as English, reordering of the immediate constituents, in particular the main verb (that is, the head), is highly salient. In English, subject–verb or subject–auxiliary inversion signals speech act distinctions such as that between interrogatives and declaratives (*He is leaving* vs *Is he leaving?*), as well as other types (such as the exclamation *Is he smart!*). Of course, in a language with very free word order, reordering of constituents is presumably not as salient, though if a particular construction is found in only one order, its inflexibility is probably sufficiently salient to flag it as a relatively major sentence type.

The other respect in which word order of immediate constituents of the sentence is salient regards their relative position in the sentence. (This is also definable only at the sentence level.) A substantial psychological literature has convincingly demonstrated that initial position is the most salient position in the perception of a word, and in linear sequences in general (the 'serial position effect'; see e.g. Crowder 1976: 445–63). Hawkins and Cutler (1988: 295–301) review psycholinguistic evidence demonstrating that word recognition and lexical access begins with the initial portion of a word. It has also been demonstrated that final position is the next most salient position, with the 'interior' of a sequence being least salient (Hawkins and Cutler 1988: 300–1). Thus, the presence of a particle or other element in initial and final position, or the 'movement' of an immediate constituent into one of those positions, would be relatively highly salient and therefore indicative of a major sentence type. It should be pointed out here that second position in a sentence has also been found to be very relevant to sentence-level syntactic-semantic elements, such as auxiliaries (Steele 1975). Although I am not aware of any psychological evidence supporting the relatively high salience of second position, there are at least two possible explanations for its significant status. First, it may be thought of as a second element competing for first position. One frequently finds that a speech act or modal element is cliticized on to an initial element which occupies first position for reason of its own salience (for example, focus, new topic, grammatical subject), as in Makah (Anderson 1985: 155–8) and even English with its subject–auxiliary contracted forms (*I'll be back soon*). Second, if the initial position is treated as a special topic/focus position, the 'second-position' element may be thought of as the first element in the 'interior' of the linear sequence and hence is the next most salient element after absolute first and last position. Whatever explanation is correct, the typological evidence certainly indicates that elements that are associated with second position are the same ones associated with first and last position.[3]

Another significant property of the immediate constituents of a sentence is their presence or absence, for example the near-obligatory absence of the subject in English imperatives. Again, this property will be more salient for languages that do not freely allow null arguments, like English. As with word order, though, if a construction obligatorily requires the absence (or presence) of an immediate constituent in a language that otherwise freely allows that constituent to be present or absent, that will be a salient property possibly meriting categorization as a major sentence type.

Finally, alteration of the grammatical head of the sentence will be more salient than alteration (as opposed to deletion or reordering) of one of its dependents. This last criterion is probably the 'least major' alteration of the sentence. As with the other major properties of sentences, this is a matter of degree. Drastic alterations such as the elimination of all affixes in bare stem imperative forms are more likely major sentence types than the simple substitution of an affix to indicate a category (for example, mood). An intermediate case would be the introduction of an additional particle that is associated with the verb, such as the auxiliary *do* in simple English interrogatives (*I sing* vs *Do you sing?*).

In sum, we have identified the following as the most salient structural characteristics for distinguishing major sentence types:

1   A difference in intonation contour.
2   Change of the word order of immediate constituents of a sentence.
3   The positioning of an element in one of the salient positions of a sentence: first, last and second position.
4   Deletion or insertion of an immediate constituent.
5   Major alteration of the head of the sentence, namely the main verb.

Our definition is somewhat narrower than Sadock and Zwicky's in this respect, since it specifies that the special particles or affixes ought to be in a salient sentence position (or associated with the verb), and that word order and missing elements should refer to immediate constituents of the sentence, not any other elements. In fact all the examples that Sadock and Zwicky give in their paper fit with the above criteria for major sentence type; they are presumably relying on the same intuitions that yield the salient distinctions I have explicitly described here.

In another respect, our definition is broader than Sadock and Zwicky's. Our definition of 'major sentence type' is based on form independent of function, and therefore prevents us from excluding a priori any non-illocutionary-force major sentence type. Sadock and Zwicky's definition by contrast restricts 'major sentence types' to those which encode illocutionary force primarily and uniquely. In other words, Sadock and Zwicky's definition of 'major sentence type' is exclusive rather than inclusive. By requiring unique primary illocutionary force meaning and mutual exclusivity of forms, Sadock and Zwicky exclude sentence types that satisfy the structural criteria of 'major sentence type' but also encode other categories, such as modality and politeness. By taking this narrower approach, relationships between illocutionary force and other semantically closely related categories cannot be explored. Nevertheless, Sadock and Zwicky's study is a good starting point for the survey of the functional (semantic as well as pragmatic) distinctions encoded by the major sentence types of the languages of the world, and will be used here; it will, however, be supplemented with other studies. Needless to say, a fuller investigation would require the construction of a large sample for the specific purposes of this investigation, and for this reason the results in the following section are only preliminary. However, they accord with widespread observation to such an extent that it is likely that a new cross-linguistic study would produce the same results, though more fine-grained generalizations would also be discovered.

THE TYPOLOGY OF MAJOR SENTENCE TYPES

Sadock and Zwicky surveyed twenty-three languages in their study. They find that the traditional sentence types declarative, interrogative and imperative, clearly distinguished in European languages, are widely encoded by grammatical features that distinguish major sentence types across the languages in their sample. In order to make this tripartite distinction universal, the definition of 'imperative' must be loosened to include any one of the following: requests, commands, orders, suggestions, instructions, entreaties (Sadock and Zwicky 1985: 170). All of these have in common that they are directives to which the hearer is supposed to respond by performing some action. Interrogatives, on the other hand, represent directives to which the hearer is supposed to respond by communicating some information (i.e. an answer to the question).

The tripartite distinction between major sentence types does not correspond closely with Searle's five-way classification. Declaratives do correspond to Searle's representative class. However, languages make a major distinction between two speech act types, interrogative and imperative, that are subsumed under one type, directive, in Searle's classification. And Searle's commissives, expressives and declarations are not represented as major speech act types. Turning to 'minor sentence types' as defined by

Sadock and Zwicky,[4] we find that Searle's commissives and declarations do not make the grade even there. Instead, one finds still further distinctions among the three major speech act types as well as a small number of other types.

Sadock and Zwicky also note that there is a typologically very wide-spread distinction between positive imperatives and negative imperatives (also called *prohibitives*; ibid.: 175). Sadock and Zwicky call this a distinct sentence type because it does not involve the simple combination of the (declarative) negative construction with the imperative, but instead is formally distinct from both. These generalizations are confirmed in a slightly larger sample of thirty-five languages used for an unrelated study of negation (Croft 1991a: 14). Given this analysis of prohibitives, with which we concur, it is worth noting that negative *declaratives* also generally involve significant structural changes from the positive type in the world's languages. English is a good example, with the insertion of the sentence-level constituents, auxiliary *do* plus the negative clitic -*n't*, in second position in indicative declarative sentences. In general, one finds the declarative negative marker either associated with the verb, with a 'finite element' in salient sentential position, or standing alone in salient sentential position (Dahl 1979; Dryer 1988; Clausner 1991). (Negation in interrogatives will be dealt with below.) Thus, the positive/negative parameter, which we will call *polarity*, is comparable in typological significance to the declarative–interrogative–imperative speech act distinction. Again, polarity distinctions are not given this importance in Searle's classification.

Another typologically significant subtype of imperatives found by Sadock and Zwicky are hortatives, along with the closely related optatives. These involve the expression of a desire on the part of the speaker for action to be performed by the speaker, the addressee, both (as in English *Let's go!*), or by some other person; or simply for the action to occur. In addition to being more diffuse as to whom (if anyone) the directive is 'directed' to,[5] hortatives appear to impose a less strong obligation on the part of the addressee or third party (Sadock and Zwicky are unclear as to which of these is meant). In this case, the relevant additional parameter appears to be the nature of the expected response to the speaker's utterance by the addressee. This is a parameter not included by Searle in his five-way classification, but in his original discussion of illocutionary acts, Searle proposes just this parameter ('force or strength with which the illocutionary point is presented' (Searle 1979: 5)), but then dismisses it as a less significant criterion for defining speech acts. It appears instead to be typologically – and presumably, cognitively – *more* important than those which define commissives and declarations. Sadock and Zwicky note also the existence of distinct negative counterparts, namely, admonitives, further support for the importance of the polarity parameter.

Sadock and Zwicky note that interrogative sentences actually do not make up a single structurally coherent major sentence type, but fall into two broad categories, polarity (yes/no) questions (including here the closely related alternative questions) and information (*wh*) questions. I suggest that this distinction illustrates the grammatical importance of the parameter of polarity in interrogatives, just as we observed its importance in imperatives and declaratives. Polarity questions, since they question polarity, generally do not have distinct positive and negative forms – or rather, positive and negative polarity question forms (including positive and negative tags (Ultan 1978: 223–4; Sadock and Zwicky 1985: 180)) are used to express bias towards an expected response by the addressee. Information questions usually have negative markers that are identical to declarative negators, and for this reason Sadock and Zwicky do not consider interrogative negation a distinct sentence type. However, the form and function of biased questions suggest that the relationship between declarative and interrogative may be even closer than indicated above.

Biased questions often take the form of a declarative plus a tag particle or phrase (Ultan 1978: 224).[6] In many languages, unbiased interrogatives take the form of a declarative plus an interrogative particle, often sentence-final. Thus, interrogatives, biased and unbiased, are structurally often quite similar to declaratives, which are distinguished because they are unmarked. On the function side, biased questions are as much hedged assertions as questions: mutual agreement on the truth of the proposition is hedged until the addressee provides confirmation. In other words, functionally there is a continuum between declaratives, which firmly assert the speaker's belief and expect assent (or at least acknowledgement) from the addressee in response; biased questions, which more weakly assert the speaker's belief and invite explicit assent from the addressee; and neutral questions, which do not assert a speaker's belief and expect a 'filling' in of the indeterminate information from the addressee. This continuum can be illustrated by the following English sentences:

(1) (a) He's going to come.   (unhedged assertion)
    (b) He's going to còme, is hé?   (same-polarity tag, expecting confirmation)
    (c) He's going to come, isn't he?   (reverse-polarity tag, requesting confirmation)
    (d) Isn't he going to come?   (positive-biased polarity question)
    (e) Is he going to come?   (unbiased polarity question)

Thus the employment of the same negative marker for both declaratives and interrogatives may represent the grammatical manifestation of a continuum between assertion and request of information. Moreover, the continuum described here – degree of expected response from the addressee – is, I argue, the same as the continuum between imperatives and hortatives. In the latter case, the expected response is one of action, not information.

The parameter of degree of response raises the issue of the grammatical character of responses. Sadock and Zwicky treats these too as minor sentence types, at least in some languages. The most obvious case is the response to polarity questions. The yes/no response is a minor sentence type, indicated by lack of internal propositional structure and distinct behaviour as an interjection, not an adverb (Sadock and Zwicky 1985: 189; we will return to interjections below). The negative interjection is often distinct from both the negative declarative and the prohibitive forms (also confirmed in the aforementioned cross-linguistic study of negation (Croft 1991a)), which gives additional support to the hypothesis that polarity is a significant parameter. Responses as speech acts have been noted in other speech act types which are more obviously co-operative, such as invitations, bets and offers (Hancher 1979). Hancher argues that with invitations, bets and offers, the speech act is 'incomplete' until the addressee acknowledges and accepts the speaker's offer. As we have indicated above, and will further elaborate below, however, all speech acts involve a response of some kind, although the response may be only the minimal acknowledgement of the speaker's utterance. As the existence of the category of interjections and of response types indicates, responses make up a structurally and typologically significant class of utterances.

Thus, the major sentence types and a substantial number of the minor sentence types can be categorized in terms of the polarity of the proposition, the degree of expected response of the addressee to the content of the proposition, and the nature of the response if any (information or action). Both initial utterance and response are represented by sentence types. Before turning to the as yet unaccounted-for minor types discussed by Sadock and Zwicky, we will examine the other semantic categories with which 'illocutionary force' markers are lumped together in the grammar of human languages.

The semantic categories most likely to be associated with illocutionary force markers are modality, emphasis (these two mentioned in Sadock and Zwicky 1985: 158), attitude (ibid.: 161–2) and politeness (social status; see below pp. 470–1). Modality is quite commonly found in the same grammatical category as illocutionary force markers, as Palmer (1986: 78) has noted, mentioning Luiseño (ibid.: 44), Imbabura Quechua (ibid.: 69), Menomini (ibid.: 2), Serrano (ibid.: 55), Mandarin Chinese (ibid.: 88), Cashibo (ibid.: 89–90) and Hixkaryana (ibid.: 54).[7] For example, Luiseño second-position particles include tense markers, 'should', an interrogative marker, and a quotative – i.e. deontic modality, illocutionary force and epistemic modality (ibid.: 44). Imbabura Quechua has a grammatical category that includes three evidential markers, one emphatic evidential marker, and the polarity question/negative marker (ibid.: 69). In a number of European languages, the subjunctive form used in a main clause is an imperative or an optative, and in other languages, such as Quiché Mayan, an imperative or hortative inflection (used for first, second and third person) is in the same affix position as the declarative tense/aspect markers. In fact, because of this Sadock and Zwicky (1985: 177) and Palmer (1986: 110–11) suggest that such languages have no imperatives and 'directive' inflections. We would rather say that there is a continuum here, this time between forms of deontic modality which impose some obligation on the addressee to perform an action and an imperative in which specifically the speaker imposes a strong requirement that the addressee act (or at least voice his or her refusal to act). Likewise, the greater the epistemic or evidential uncertainty that is expressed by the speaker, the more likely it is that the speaker is expecting the addressee to respond by clarifying the uncertainty (or at least concurring with it). Typologically, this is manifested in part by the extremely widespread identity of indefinite and interrogative pronouns. For example, in Lakhota the only difference between a 'declarative' with an indefinite pronominal noun phrase and an interrogative is the presence of a sentence-final question particle:[8]

(2a) Mniluzahe   Othųwahe   ekta   tuwa   ya
     Rapid   City   to   who   go.3sg
     'Someone went to Rapid City.'

(2b) Mniluzahe   Othųwahe   ekta   tuwa   ya   he
     Rapid   City   to   who   go.3sg   Q
     'Who went to Rapid City?'

This is of course a significant source of indirect speech acts: the re-interpretation of apparently 'declarative' epistemic and deontic modals as interrogative and imperative constructions. In both cases, there is a shift in the degree of expected response from the addressee. But it is an error to consider modal declarative utterances as implying no expectations, since they do not occur in isolation; they always occur as part of a communicative interaction. One does not say to his or her addressee something like *You have to send it back* without expecting some sort of response, even if it is only an explanation why he or she will not follow the obligation that is expressed.[9] It is a short step to saying that these interpersonal expectations have become part of the 'meaning' of the sentence type, as is claimed for 'true' interrogatives and imperatives.

Conversely, the more emphatically the speaker expresses the certainty of the proposition, the more likely it is that the speaker is expecting explicit assent from the addressee; and the more emphatically the speaker expresses an obligation, the more likely it is that the speaker is expecting the addressee to respond. Presumably, this is the reason for the inclusion of emphatic particles in the same grammatical category as illocutionary force markers.

Attitude markers, semantically closely related to emphatic markers since they both express the speaker's evaluation of the propositional content of the utterance, are related in a similar fashion to expressive speech acts. Searle defines expressives as expressing the speaker's psychological state with respect to a proposition without asserting the proposition (Searle 1979: 15). Sentences with attitude markers, on the other hand, do the same thing but also assert the proposition. However, Sadock and Zwicky characterize exclamations, the sentence types that function as expressives, as emphasizing the speaker's emotional reaction, not necessarily to the exclusion of asserting the proposition; and their examples (such as English *Wow, can he knit!* or *How tacky that is!*) do both at once (Sadock and Zwicky 1985: 162). Thus, the difference between a declarative sentence with an attitude marker and an expressive is one of degree of emphasis on the emotional reaction of the speaker relative to the assertion of the propositional content of the utterance.

Figure 22.1:   Continua of sentence types

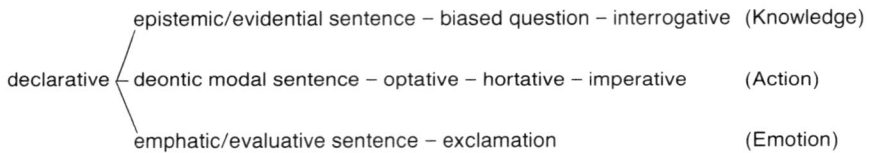

epistemic/evidential sentence – biased question – interrogative (Knowledge)

declarative   deontic modal sentence – optative – hortative – imperative   (Action)

emphatic/evaluative sentence – exclamation   (Emotion)

The cross-linguistic generalizations presented so far suggest that there are continua linking 'declarative' sentences on the one hand to 'imperative', 'interrogative' and 'exclamative' sentences on the other (see Figure 22.1). These continua demonstrate that attempts to draw a sharp distinction between declaratives on the one hand, especially declaratives combined with evidential, deontic or attitude markers, and interrogatives, imperatives and exclamations on the other hand are pointless from a formal grammatical point of view, which suggests that it should not be done in the functional (pragmatic) analysis either.

Finally, markers of politeness are frequently found in the same grammatical category as illocutionary force markers, and in fact can be fused with them, so that they will constitute a major sentence type in Sadock and Zwicky's sense. For example, in Lakhota one finds five different, mutually exclusive sentence-final particles used for imperatives. 'Normal' commands are expressed by *yo/wo* (used by men) and *ye/we* (used by women); 'softened, familiar' commands are expressed by *yethó* (men) and *nithó* (women), and an 'entreaty' is expressed by *ye* (both men and women) (Rood and Taylor 1976: 7–11, 7–13). The reason for this is that degree of solicited addressee response, which is a significant parameter for major sentence types, is influenced (or can be manipulated) by the social status of speaker and addressee and their relation in a particular speech situation. In fact, modal sentence types are often employed to indicate degrees of politeness by virtue of the fact that they do not impose as high an expectation of addressee response as imperatives and hortatives (if such exist as distinct sentence types). As Brown and Levinson would put it, the speaker goes 'off record' by not overly expressing the conventionalized speech act (Brown and Levinson 1987: 69).[10]

TOWARDS AN EMPIRICALLY-BASED COGNITIVE MODEL OF SPEECH ACTS

This brief discussion of the typology of major sentence types and their relationship to speech acts suffices to demonstrate that the structure of major sentence types does not reflect some inventory of primitive speech acts by speakers, but instead reflects a conceptualization of a more complex system of speaker–addressee interaction. The typologically most common distinctions among sentence types provide us with an empirical base for constructing the common-sense or cognitive model[11] of speech acts. The empirical evidence requires that the following parameters play a significant role in such a model:

1   Linguistic vs non-linguistic response (information vs action, and also emotion)
2   Polarity (positive vs negative)
3   Degree of expected response (ranging from acknowledgement to concurrence to reaction, linguistic or non-linguistic)
4   Explicitness of the solicitation of a response (a factor sensitive to status and interpersonal relations).[12]

This interpretation of the empirical work done by Sadock and Zwicky, Palmer, Dahl, and others will allow us to move beyond traditional speech act theory to a general model of the speech acts performed by speakers (and hearers).

By paying closer attention to the cross-linguistically valid distinctions between sentence types, we can construct a more adequate model of speech acts, but it has certain limitations which must be respected. First, it will only provide a very general framework for the description of speech acts. Nevertheless, it is a first step, and it is to be hoped that it will be a better first step than the philosophical taxonomy of illocutionary acts. Second, it is relevant only to the particular level of conversational interaction concerning speech acts (to be defined shortly). It will not be able to contribute to many other aspects of turn construction by interlocutors that have been the domain of study of conversational analysis. For that reason, there is some degree of complementarity in the subject area of conversational analysis and speech act analysis, although they must be integrated at some point. However, the revised view of speech acts to be proposed here is more congenial to the hypotheses of conversational analysis than those of the philosophical taxonomy of illocutionary acts.

Sentence types categorize sentences, that is, linguistic units bearing what is generally called 'propositional content'. Hence, the sort of interactive level being encoded by distinctions in sentence type must centrally involve the propositional content that has been constructed and thereby presented to the speaker, but probably not the co-operative process that led to the construction (involving, for example, the attention, interest and prior knowledge of the addressee). This is the level that Clark and Carlson (1982) describe as the 'informative act', which is essentially the minimal presentation of propositional content in an interaction. Hence, what is to be described here is what speakers and hearers are doing with propositional content; this is an appropriate definition of 'speech act' which gives it a place in the description of conversational interaction but distinguishes it from the other concerns of conversational analysis at both lower and higher levels of conversational organization.

The cross-linguistic generalizations presented in the previous section suggest that the basic properties of a typologically-based model of speech acts are as follows. Speech acts involve interaction of the speaker and addressee, not simply the execution of an utterance by the speaker; Connor-Linton (1991: 96–7) argues that the criteria for defining speech acts in context should be the likelihood of success in obtaining the desired response from the addressee, not just the felicitous execution of the utterance by the speaker, as Searle originally had it. This has been ignored or de-emphasized in most speech act analyses, which is exclusively speaker-based (Hancher 1979; and Clark and Carlson 1982 being the most notable exceptions), but is one of the foundation stones of conversational analysis (see for example Goffman 1976; Goodwin 1981).[13] However, the existence of responses as a sentence type, and the continua based on solicited/expected addressee response require speaker–hearer interaction as a central part of the model.[14] The model of interaction must include a gradable scale of 'strength' (Connor-Linton 1991) or some similar property that models the continua in Figure 22.1. There must be a principled basis for a primary division between knowledge, action and emotion (the three different continua beyond the declarative). Finally, polarity must be a central distinction falling out of the interactive model. These are properties of the use of propositional content as it has been conceptualized by language users; this is the reason that it is encoded into grammatical structures of languages. In this view, an explanation of the cross-linguistic taxonomy of sentence types is to be found in 'common-sense', 'folk' or 'cognitive' models of what speakers are doing with propositional content. In fact, cognitive models of the mind and of force-dynamic interaction cast up the same primary distinctions that are found in sentence types in the world's languages.

Let us begin with the least interactive aspect of the cognitive or 'folk' model of speech acts that is described above, the tripartite division between knowledge, action and emotion that is most directly manifested in the three right-hand endpoints of the sentence-type continua. The basic distinction corresponds to the basic components of the 'belief, desire, intention' (cf. knowledge, emotion, action) model found in philosophy, psychology and artificial intelligence.[15] This model is intended to be a folk model of human psychology, used by human beings in their common-sense reasoning about people. It assumes that human behaviour is a result of the internal relationships between these three distinct types of mental structures. Since linguistic communication employs the mind, this model suggests that this distinction will be reasonably well respected in the structure of language used to perform speech acts.

This hypothesis is borne out by the sentence types that are found. A declarative that is uttered and accepted is added to the shared knowledge of the interlocutors; one that is incomplete and completed by the addressee – i.e. question and answer – is a joint effort towards the same goal. An utterance can be challenged or denied, of course, in which case it is not considered to be mutual knowledge after the interchange. But the interchange itself is (in part) the negotiation of what will be mutual knowledge. The continuum from declarative to interrogative reflects the degree of overt hearer involvement in the goal of adding to shared knowledge, but our concern here is merely with what that goal is. This of course does not deny that the negotiation of mutual knowledge itself does not serve other, higher interactional goals; it is just to say that at a level of conversation relevant to sentence types, this is a primary low-level goal. This sort of model has been proposed by Gazdar (1979), Fauconnier (1985), and others with respect to epistemic modality and presuppositions, in which speech acts change the context of mutual knowledge (see Levinson 1983: 276–8). Artificial intelligence models of planning represent goals of action encoded by propositional content. Again, goals of action are always being negotiated, as offers, bets, requests, commands, and their acceptance, refusal and modification demonstrate; but our point here is that they are linguistically distinguished from the process of the flow of information in communicative interactions. Here the belief–desire–intention model would require some extension to account for the sentence-type data: it is a psychological model concerned largely with one's own actions, not attempts to influence the actions of others. Less examined by philosophers and artificial intelligence researchers, but recognized by them as a significant third component, is the role of emotion. The emotions expressed by expressive sentences tend to be evaluative rather than the emotion of desire focused on by belief–desire–intention psychology, which is primarily concerned with how volitional acts originate. As with action, a more elaborate model is necessary to account for the linguistic pattern, covering emotion in general rather than just desire. In sum, it appears that although the belief–desire–intention cognitive model of the mind is more narrowly focused than the knowledge–action–emotion division underlying the cross-linguistic pattern of sentence types, it provides a foundation for the basic tripartite distinction given in Figure 22.1.

The scalar, interactive character of speech acts and the significance of the positive–negative polarity distinction is also captured by another cognitive model, Talmy's model of force dynamics (Talmy 1988a, b), which he argues is applicable to the physical, psychological and social realms (see also Sweetser 1990). The force-dynamic model is a model of the interaction of two forces, which Talmy calls the Agonist and the Antagonist. This is an improvement over other causal models used in linguistic semantics, in which an agent acts on a patient but the patient is not thought of as having any power in his own right. More recent models of semantic relations among participants in events emphasize the degree of control that an agent may or may not have (for example, DeLancey 1984), but few emphasize the degree of control (or lack thereof) that the patient also has.[16] Since both speaker and addressee quite clearly have power or force, albeit with greater control in the hands (or rather voice) of the speaker, Talmy's force-dynamic model is more suitable than the traditional models of causation for representing speaker–addressee interactions.

Talmy considers two other parameters to be primary: whether the Agonist is inclined towards action or toward stasis; and whether or not the Antagonist can overcome the Agonist's 'momentum'. Applying the force-dynamic model to conversational interaction in the simplest (i.e. over-simplified) fashion, the Agonist is the addressee and the Antagonist is the speaker whose utterance affects the Agonist's knowledge and behaviour. If the Agonist is inclined towards stasis, then the Antagonist's force is towards action – this is the positive speech act which will add information (declarative) or a goal to be achieved (imperative). If the Agonist is inclined towards action, then the Antagonist's force is towards stasis – this is the negative speech act which will deny the addition of information (negative declarative) or remove a goal to be achieved (negative imperative). Hence, the positive–negative polarity parameter can be modelled by force dynamics.[17] (As conversational analysts have noted, this is a more passive description of the Agonist's role in the construction of an utterance by the speaker/Antagonist; but the attractiveness of Talmy's model is that since the Agonist is a force in his or her own right, this can ultimately be accommodated in the force-dynamic model.)

Our examples have assumed that the speaker/Antagonist has overcome the addressee/Agonist's momentum. Of course, this need not be the case in either speech acts or force dynamics: mutual knowledge and mutual goals have to be negotiated and agreed upon; success or failure is encoded in the addressee's positive or negative responses. The outcome of a conversational interaction is determined in part by the inherent influence or power that the speaker and addressee have on each other based on their relative social status and the status relations conferred on them by the particular speech situation, which determines their interaction in part.

Force dynamics can represent this straightforwardly by the inherent 'force' that the Agonist and Antagonist each have. And inherent force also determines at least in part the strength of the utterance (in Connor-Linton's sense), that is, the degree of expected response that is explicitly expressed.

CONCLUSION

A force-dynamic model of interpersonal relations, combined with a belief–desire–intention model of human behaviour, produces a cognitive model of interpersonal interaction that is reflected in the grammatical distinctions among major sentence types ('speech act' types) found in the world's languages. The distinction between knowledge, action and emotion found in the interrogative, imperative and exclamation continua is derived from the mental division of human states and actions in the common-sense model of belief–desire–intention psychology. The force-dynamic model applied to interpersonal relations yields the positive–negative distinction in the clash of forces between Antagonist (speaker) and Agonist (addressee), and degrees of expected response and their explicitness in terms of inherent forces associated with the interlocutors.

It is worth examining Levinson's comments on the viability of speech act theory (1983: 278–83) in the context of these observations. Levinson argues that the variability of speaker intention and hearer interpretation of that intention in the context of actual conversations is tremendous. He suggests that it is so great, in fact, that it is virtually impossible to claim that there is a speech act theory, by which he means a theory that claims certain linguistic forms correlate to certain illocutionary forces. The analysis presented herein supports a position like Levinson's. The linguistic form of sentences encodes several different aspects of speaker–addressee interactions, some of which are gradient and therefore pragmatically flexible, and no one of which can be identified as the 'illocutionary force' as defined in the philosophical tradition. There is no literal force – another central aspect of classical speech act theory – because illocutionary force itself is an emergent, context-sensitive effect. Nevertheless, linguistic form does appear to reflect linguistic function, in terms of the cognitive model of the manipulation of the propositional content of sentences in interaction presented here.

The limitations of these observations as well as their possibilities have to be emphasized. The typological evidence presumably reveals basic properties of the concepts being expressed, as hypothesized in the introduction; it does not provide a full-blown model of conversational interaction. Nevertheless, it lays down certain basic distinctions that should fall out naturally from any full-blown model of speech acts. It applies only to the linguistic level from which the typological evidence is drawn, namely the level at which the propositional content of whole sentences is manipulated by speaker and addressee. Thus, it does not have anything direct to contribute to many aspects of the construction of conversation that have been studied by conversational analysts. Finally, this is a speaker's idealized cognitive model (see note 11) of human interaction, which may not be the same as an analyst's real empirical model. Nevertheless, the cross-linguistic data point to a model of speech acts whose foundations are more in harmony with the principles and results of conversational analysis than the traditional philosophical classification of speech acts, in particular the essentially co-operative nature of speech acts, the continua between traditional 'speech act types', and the relevance of interlocutor status and situation type.

The major difference between what is proposed here and conversation analysis is the prominent role assigned to the cognitive models of the communicative interaction possessed by speaker and addressee. There is an unfortunate gap between researchers in language from the anthropological and sociological side, who focus on the social, interactive nature of linguistic communication, and researchers in language from the philosophical, psychological and artificial intelligence tradition, who speak of linguistic communication in terms of interacting agent's goals, mutual knowledge states, etc. Let us hope that an empirically grounded cross-linguistic study of speech acts will provide a meeting place where psychological and social approaches to language can construct common models.[18]

NOTES

1   There is an apparent mismatch between form and function in indirect speech acts; this problem will be addressed later.
2   However, Bolinger (1986, 1989) has argued that intonation expresses an emotive value that is logically independent of illocutionary force, although there is a strong correlation between certain intonation patterns and certain speech acts, for example, a rising intonation contour and polarity questions.
3   A caveat must be given here: the psycholinguistic experiments cited here have been applied only to words or strings of numbers or letters. The perception of sentences rather than words, in ordinary conversation rather than an experimental situation, may differ in relevant ways. However, I will follow psycholinguistic practice in assuming that experimental results, properly interpreted, can tell us something about how people perceive and behave in ordinary situations.
4   For Sadock and Zwicky, a 'minor' sentence type has significant structural differences but is also used for functions other than indicating speech act type. These qualify here as 'major' sentence types, for reasons discussed in the preceding section.
5   Searle's definition of a directive (1979: 13–14) is too restrictive, since it specifies that the addressee rather than any individual, must or should perform the action.
6   Ultan notes that tags generally take the intonation of polarity questions, which further links them to 'true' (unbiased) polarity questions.
7   Even when modality is not in the same category as illocution markers, modal markers are found in the most salient sentence positions (Steele 1975; Clausner 1991).
8   In this situation, one might expect the question particle(s) to be identical to the

imperative particles, since all the question particle does is change an assertion of incomplete knowledge to a request to fill in the missing information. But they are not, and in fact I am not aware of a language in which interrogatives and imperatives are marked identically in this fashion, despite the fact that they are both directives in Searle's classification.

9 If someone other than the addressee is the subject of the deontic modal sentence, then there cannot be a direct response, of course. Deontic modal sentences involving the addressee are obviously closer to imperatives than other deontic modal sentences.

10 Note that going off record possesses the highest degree of politeness short of not issuing a request, command, etc. at all; hence the appearance of a gap in the scale of degree of addressee response between a modal sentence and an outright imperative/interrogative etc.

11 In the sense of Lakoff's 'idealized cognitive model' (Lakoff 1987).

12 This parameter is identical to the (formal expression of the) parameter of 'strength' in Connor-Linton 1991.

13 As Goodwin (1981) points out, co-operation is pervasive in all aspects and all levels of the construction of a linguistic turn in conversation; this is simply another example.

14 Responses as distinct sentence types brings to mind the notion of an adjacency pair in conversational analysis. However, adjacency pairs are both more general and less general than the type of response intended here. A taxonomy of adjacency pairs will be more fine-grained than a typical taxonomy of sentence types, although sentence types will probably define superordinate categories of adjacency pairs. On the other hand, adjacency pairs are usually defined as pairings of linguistic turns, which is narrower than the class of responses suggested by the distinctions above. The division between linguistic and non-linguistic responses (such as performing a task requested by the speaker) implies that non-linguistic responses are part of the definition of interaction at the level of propositional content. The continua described in Figure 22.1 also suggest that responses range from the overt response, including a linguistic response at the next turn, which is implied by the right-hand extreme of the continua, to more subtle interactive cues that are not properly called the second parts of adjacency pairs, such as acknowledgement of an utterance or back-channeling (Goffman 1976).

15 An excellent summary of this model can be found in Wellman 1990: ch. 4.

16 Cole (1983) demonstrates that degree of control on the part of the causee in causative constructions (the participant that is made to perform an action by another agent, almost always a human being) has grammatical consequences in the choice of case marking for the causee in various languages. Since the causee is acted upon by the causer, he or she is like a patient in that regard. Consider also the interpretations of *Randy was willingly taught to play the violin*, in which Randy is interpreted to be willing, and *We persuaded Randy to be examined by the doctor*. These sentences are acceptable to the degree that we are able to attribute some control over the patient-subject of the passive constructions.

17 Both positive and negative acts are 'face-threatening acts' (FTAs) (Brown and Levinson 1987: 65–8), or rather can be, depending on the degree of expected response. A simple declarative may not be an FTA unless its propositional content inherently threatens face, as with expressions of envy (ibid.: 66, (iii)(c)) or of bad news about the addressee (ibid.: 67, (ii)(c)).

18 An earlier version of this paper was presented at the International Pragmatics Conference in Barcelona in July 1990. I wish to give my thanks to Dan Slobin and Sandra Thompson for their extremely helpful comments; they have no responsibility, of course, for what use I have made of them.

Bibliography

Akmajian, A., Demers, R. and Harnish, R. (1981) 'Overcoming inadequacies of the message model of linguistic communication', *Communication and Cognition* 12: 317–36.

Akmajian, A., Steele, S. and Wasow, T. (1979) 'The category AUX in Universal Grammar', *Linguistic Inquiry* 10: 1–64.

Aldrich, V. C. (1966) 'Telling, acknowledging, and asserting', *Analysis* 27: 53–6.

Alston, W.P. (1963) 'Meaning and use', *Philosophical Quarterly* 13: 107–24.

—— (1964a) 'Linguistic acts', *American Philosophical Quarterly* 1: 1–9.

—— (1964b) *Philosophy of Language*, Englewood Cliffs, NJ: Prentice-Hall, Inc.

—— (1974) 'Semantic rules', in M. Munitz and P. Unger (eds) *Semantics and Philosophy*, New York: New York University Press.

—— (1977) 'Sentence meaning and illocutionary act potential', *Philosophic Exchange* 2: 17–35.

—— (1987) 'Matching illocutionary act types', in J. J. Thomson (ed.) *On Being and Saying*, Cambridge, MA: MIT Press.

—— (1991) 'Searle on illocutionary acts', in E. Lepore and R. Van Gulick (eds) *John Searle and his Critics*, Oxford: Basil Blackwell.

Anderson, A. R. (1956) 'The formal analysis of normative systems', repr. in N. Rescher (ed.) *The Logic of Decision and Action*, Pittsburgh: Pittsburgh University Press, 1968.

Anderson, L. B. (1982) 'The "perfect" as a universal and as a language-particular category', in P. Hooper (ed.) *Tense-Aspect: Between Semantics and Pragmatics*, Amsterdam: John Benjamins.

—— (1986) 'Evidentials, paths of change, and mental maps: typologically regular asymmetries', in W. Chafe and J. Nichols (eds) *Evidentiality: The Linguistic Coding of Epistemology*, Norwood, NJ: Ablex Publishing Corporation.

Anderson, S. R. (1985) 'Inflectional morphology', in T. Shopen (ed.) *Language Typology and Syntactic Description*, vol. 3: *Grammatical Categories and the Lexicon*, Cambridge: Cambridge University Press.

Anscombe, G. E. M. (1957) *Intention*, Oxford: Basil Blackwell.

Anscombre, J. C. and Ducrot, O. (1981) 'Interrogation et argumentation', *Langue française* 52: 5–22.

Apel, K. O. (1991) 'Is intentionality more basic than linguistic meaning?', in E. Lepore and R. Van Gulick (eds) *John Searle and his Critics*, Oxford: Basil Blackwell.

Atlas, J. D. (1977) 'Negation, ambiguity, and presupposition', *Linguistics and Philosophy* 1: 321–36.

—— (1989) *Philosophy without Ambiguity*, Oxford: Oxford University Press.

Austin, J. L. (1950) 'Truth', repr. in Austin (1979).

—— (1953) 'How to talk: some simple ways', repr. in Austin (1979).

—— (1961) 'Performative utterances', repr. in Austin (1979).

—— (1962) *How to do Things with Words*, Oxford: Oxford University Press.

—— (1979) *Philosophical Papers*, 3rd edn, Oxford: Oxford University Press.

Bach, K. (1975) 'Performatives are statements too', *Philosophical Studies* 28: 229–36.

—— (1982) 'Semantic nonspecificity and mixed quantifiers', *Linguistics and Philosophy* 4: 593–605.

—— (1987) *Thought and Reference*, Oxford: Oxford University Press.

Bach, K. and Harnish, R. (1979) *Linguistic Communication and Speech Acts*, Cambridge, MA: MIT Press.

—— (1987) 'Relevant questions', *The Behavioral and Brain Sciences* 10: 711–12.

—— (1992) 'How performatives really work: a reply to Searle', *Linguistics and Philosophy* 15: 93–110.

Ballmer, T. T. and Brennenstuhl, W. (1981) *Speech Act Classification: A Study in the Lexical Analysis of English Speech Activity Verbs*, Berlin: Springer.

Bar-Hillel, Y. (1954) 'Indexical expressions', *Mind* 63: 359–79.

Barton, E. (1990) *Non-Sentential Constituents*, Amsterdam: John Benjamins.

Barwise, J. and Cooper, R. (1981) 'Generalized quantifiers and natural language', *Linguistics and Philosophy* 4: 159–219.

Barwise, J. and Perry, J. (1983) *Situations and Attitudes*, Cambridge, MA: MIT Press.

Bell, M. (1975) 'Questioning', *Philosophical Quarterly* 25: 193–211.

Belnap, N. D. (1977) 'A useful four-valued logic', in G. Epstein and M. Dunn (eds) *Modern Uses of Multiple Valued Logic*, Dordrecht: Reidel.

—— (1990) 'Declaratives are not enough', *Philosophical Studies* 59: 1–30.

Belnap, N. D. and Steel, T. (1976) *The Logic of Questions and Answers*, New Haven, CT: Yale University Press.

Bennett, J. (1976) *Linguistic Behaviour*, Cambridge: Cambridge University Press.

—— (1991) 'How do gestures succeed?', in E. Lepore and R. Van Gulick (eds) *John Searle and his Critics*, Oxford: Basil Blackwell.

Berckmans, P. (1988) 'Recent work on the performative hypothesis', *Communication and Cognition* 21: 29–65.

Bertolet, R. (1990) *What is Said*, Dordrecht: Kluwer Academic Publishers.

Bing, J. (1980) *Aspects of English Prosody*, Bloomington, IN: Indiana University Linguistics Club.

Bird, G. H. (1974) 'Confusing the audience', *Analysis* 35: 135–9.

—— (1979) 'Speech acts and conversation', *Philosophical Quarterly* 29: 142–52.

—— (1981a) 'Austin's theory of illocutionary force', *Midwest Studies in Philosophy* 6: 345–71.

—— (1981b) 'Warning', *Proceedings of the Aristotelian Society*, Supplementary Volume 55: 1–17.

Blackburn, S. (1971) 'Moral realism', in J. Casey (ed.) *Morality and Moral Reasoning*, London: Methuen.

—— (1984) *Spreading the Word: Groundings in the Philosophy of Language*, Oxford: Oxford University Press.

—— (1988) 'Attitudes and contents', *Ethics* 98: 501–17.

Bloomfield, L. (1933) *Language*, New York: Holt, Rinehart & Winston.

Boghossian, P. (1990) 'The status of content', *Philosophical Review* 89: 157–84.

Bolinger, D. (1986) *Intonation and its Parts*, Stanford, CA: Stanford University Press.

—— (1989) *Intonation and its Uses*, Stanford, CA: Stanford University Press.

Brandl, J. and Gombocz, W. L. (eds) (1989) *The Philosophy of Donald Davidson*, Amsterdam: Rodopi.

Brown, P. and Levinson, S. C. (1978) 'Universals in language usage: politeness phenomena', in E. N. Goody (ed.) *Questions and Politeness*, Cambridge: Cambridge University Press.

—— (1987) *Politeness*, Cambridge: Cambridge University Press.

Brown, R. and Gilman, A. (1960) 'The pronouns of power and solidarity', in T. A. Sebeok (ed.) *Style in Language*, Cambridge, MA: MIT Press.

Burge, T. (1979) 'Individualism and the mental', *Midwest Studies in Philosophy* 4: 73–121.

—— (1982a) 'Other bodies', in A. Woodfield (ed.) *Thought and Object*, Oxford: Oxford University Press.

—— (1982b) 'Two thought experiments revisited', *Notre Dame Journal of Formal Logic* 22: 284–93.

—— (1986a) 'Individualism and psychology', *Philosophical Review* 45: 3–45.

—— (1986b) 'Intellectual norms and foundations of mind' *Journal of Philosophy* 83: 697–720.

Bybee, J. (1985) *Morphology*, Amsterdam: John Benjamins.

Carnap, R. (1956) *Meaning and Necessity*, Chicago, IL: University of Chicago Press.

Carston, R. (1988) 'Implicature, explicature, and truth-conditional semantics', in R. Kempson (ed.) *Mental Representations*, Cambridge: Cambridge University Press; repr. in Davis 1991.

Cherniak, C. (1986) *Minimal Rationality*, Cambridge, MA: Bradford Books/MIT Press.

Chomsky, N. (1980) *Rules and Representations*, Oxford: Basil Blackwell.

—— (1981) *Lectures on Government and Binding*, Dordrecht: Foris.

—— (1982) *The Generative Enterprise* (with R. Huybregts and H. van Riemsdijk), Dordrecht: Foris.

—— (1984) *Modular Approaches to the Study of the Mind*, San Diego, CA: San Diego State University Press.

—— (1986) *Knowledge of Language*, New York: Praeger.

—— (1988) *Language and Problems of Knowledge*, Cambridge, MA: MIT Press.

Chomsky, N. and Lasnik, H. (1977) 'Filters and control', *Linguistic Inquiry* 8: 425–504.

Church, A. (1951) 'A formulation of the logic of sense and denotation', in P. Henle, H. Kallan and S. Langer (eds) *Structure, Method, and Meaning*, New York: Liberal Arts Press.

Clark, H. (1978) 'Inferring what is meant', in W. J. M. Levelt and G. B. Flores d'Arcais (eds) *Studies in the Peception of Language*, New York: John Wiley & Sons.

—— (1979) 'Responding to indirect speech acts', *Cognitive Psychology* 11: 430–477; repr. in Davis 1991.

Clark, H. and Carlson, T.B. (1982) 'Hearers and speech acts', *Language* 58: 332–73.

Clark, H. and Lucy, P. (1975) 'Understanding what is meant from what is said: a study in conversationally conveyed requests', *Journal of Verbal Learning and Verbal Behavior* 14: 56–72.

Clausner, T.C. (1991) 'Sentence types and salience', in W. Croft (ed.) *University of Michigan Working Papers in Linguistics*, Ann Arbor, MI: Program in Linguistics, University of Michigan.

Cohen, L. J. (1974) 'Speech acts', in T. A. Sebeok (ed.) *Current Trends in Linguistics, Vol. 12*, The Hague: Mouton.

—— (1977) *The Probable and the Provable*, Oxford: Oxford University Press.

—— (1979) 'The semantics of metaphor', in A. Ortony (ed.) *Metaphor and Thought*, Cambridge: Cambridge University Press.

—— (1980) 'The individuation of proper names', in Z. van Straaten (ed.) *Philosophical Subjects: Essays Presented to P. F. Strawson*, Oxford: Oxford Univesity Press.

Cohen, P.R. and Levesque, H. (1990) 'Rational interaction as the basis for communication', in P. R. Cohen, J. Morgan and M. Pollack (eds) *Intentions in Communication*, Cambridge, MA: MIT Press.

Cole, P. (1983) 'The grammatical role of the causee in universal grammar', *International Journal of American Linguistics* 49: 115–33.

Connor-Linton, J. (1991) 'A sociolinguistic model of successful speech act construction', in J. Verschueren (ed.) *Pragmatics at Issue*, Amsterdam: John Benjamins.

Cooper, D. E. (1986) *Metaphor*, Oxford: Basil Blackwell.

Craig, C. (ed.) (1986) *Noun Classes and Categorization*, Amsterdam: John Benjamins.

Cresswell, M. J. (1975) 'Hyperintensional logic', *Studia Logica* 34: 25–38.

Croft, W. (1990) 'Possible verbs and the structure of events', in S. L. Tsohatzidis (ed.) *Meanings and Prototypes: Studies in Linguistic Categorization*, London: Routledge.

—— (1991a) 'The evolution of negation', *Journal of Linguistics* 27: 1–27.

—— (1991b) *Syntactic Categories and Grammatical Relations: The Cognitive Organization of Information*, Chicago, IL: University of Chicago Press.

Crowder, R. G. (1976) *Principles of Learning and Memory*, Hillsdale, NJ: Lawrence Erlbaum Associates.

Dahl, O. (1979) 'Typology of sentence negation', *Linguistics* 17: 79–106.

Danto, A. C. (1965) 'Basic actions', *American Philosophical Quarterly* 2: 108–25.

Dascal, M. (1983) *Pragmatics and the Philosophy of Mind, Vol. 1*, Amsterdam: John Benjamins.

—— (1992) 'On the pragmatic structure of conversation', in H. Parret and J. Verschueren (eds) *(On) Searle on Conversation*, Amsterdam: John Benjamins.

Davidson, D. (1971) 'Agency', repr. in Davidson 1980.

—— (1972) 'Truth and meaning', *Synthese* 17: 304–23.

—— (1978) 'What metaphors mean', repr. in Davidson 1984.

—— (1979) 'Moods and performances', in A. Margalit (ed.) *Meaning and Use*, Dordrecht: Reidel.

—— (1980) *Essays on Actions and Events*, Oxford: Clarendon Press.

—— (1984) *Inquiries into Truth and Interpretation*, Oxford: Clarendon Press.

Davies, J. and Isard, S. D. (1972) 'Utterances as programs', in B. Meltzer and D. Michie (eds) *Machine Intelligence, 7*, Edinburgh: Edinburgh University Press.

Davis, S. (1979) 'Perlocutions', *Linguistics and Philosophy* 3: 225–43.

—— (ed.) (1991) *Pragmatics: A Reader*, Oxford: Oxford University Press.

Descartes, R. (1641) 'Meditations on First Philosophy, Meditation VI', in *The Philosophical Works of Descartes*, ed. and trans. E. S. Haldane and G. R. T. Ross, New York: Dover, 1931.

DeLancey, S. (1984) 'Notes on agentivity and causation', *Studies in Language* 8: 181–214.

Dennett, D. C. (1990) 'The myth of original intentionality', in K. A. Mohyeldin Said, W. H. Newton-Smith, R. Viale and K. V. Wilkes (eds) *Modelling the Mind*, Oxford: Oxford University Press.

Devitt, M. (1990) 'Meanings just ain't in the head', in G. Boolos (ed.) *Meaning and Method: Essays in Honor of Hilary Putnam*, Cambridge: Cambridge University Press.

Diffloth, G. (1972) 'Notes on expressive meaning', *Papers from the Eighth Regional Meeting of the Chicago Linguistic Society*, Chicago, IL: Chicago Linguistic Society.

—— (1976) 'Expressives in Semai', in L. C. Thompson, S. Starosta and P. N. Jenner (eds) *Austroasiatic Studies*, Honolulu: University of Hawaii Press.

Donnellan, K. (1966) 'Reference and definite descriptions', *Philosphical Review* 75: 281–304.

Dryer, M. (1988) 'Universals of negation position', in M. Hammond, E. A. Moravcsik and J. R. Wirth (eds) *Studies in Syntactic Typology*, Amsterdam: John Benjamins.

Ducrot, O. (1973) *La Preuve et le dire*, Paris: Mame.

Dummett, M. (1959) 'Truth', repr. in M. Dummett, *Truth and Other Enigmas*, London: Duckworth, 1978.

—— (1973) *Frege: Philosophy of Language*, London: Duckworth.

—— (1981) *The Interpretation of Frege's Philosophy*, London: Duckworth.

—— (1991) *The Logical Basis of Metaphysics*, London: Duckworth.

Dworkin, R. (1991) 'Two concepts of liberty', in E. and A. Margalit (eds) *Isaiah Berlin: A Celebration*, London: Hogarth Press.

Eilfort, W. and Schiller, E. (1990) 'Pragmatics and grammar: cross-modular relations in autolexical syntax', *Papers from the Twenty Sixth Regional Meeting of the Chicago Linguistic Society*, Chicago, IL: Chicago Linguistic Society.

Ervin-Tripp, S. (1976) 'Is Sybil there?: the structure of American English directives', *Language in Society* 5: 25–66.

Evans, G. (1982) *The Varieties of Reference*, Oxford: Oxford University Press.

Fauconnier, G. (1985) *Mental Spaces: Aspects of Meaning Construction in Natural Language*, Cambridge, MA: Bradford Books/MIT Press.

Fodor, J.A. (1983) *The Modularity of Mind*, Cambridge, MA: Bradford Books/MIT Press.

—— (1987) *Psychosemantics: The Problem of Meaning in the Philosophy of Mind*, Cambridge, MA: Bradford Books/MIT Press.

Fogelin, R. (1989) *Figuratively Speaking*, New Haven, CT: Yale University Press.

Fraser, B. (1987) 'Pragmatic formatives', in J. Verschueren and M. Bertuccelli-Papi (eds) *The Pragmatic Perspective*, Amsterdam: John Benjamins.

Frazier, L. (1988) 'Grammar and language processing', in F. J. Newmeyer (ed.) *Linguistics: The Cambridge Survey*, vol. 2, *Linguistic Theory: Extensions and Implications*, Cambridge: Cambridge University Press.

Frege, G. (1879) Selections from *Begriffsschrift*, in *Translations from the Philosophical Writings of Gottlob Frege*, ed. and trans. P. Geach and M. Black, Oxford: Basil Blackwell, 1952.

—— (1892) 'Uber Sinn und Bedeutung', *Zeitschrift für Philosophie und philosophische Kritik* 100: 25–50; transl. as 'On sense and reference', in *Translations from the Philosophical Writings of Gottlob Frege*, ed. and trans. P. Geach and M. Black, Oxford: Basil Blackwell, 1952.

—— (1918a) 'Der Gedanke, Eine logische Untersuchung', *Beiträge zur Philosophie des duetschen Idealismus* 1: 58–77, transl. as 'The Thought: a logical inquiry', in P. F. Strawson (ed.) *Philosophical Logic*. Oxford: Oxford University Press, 1967.

—— (1918b) 'Die Verneinung. Eine logische Undersuchung', *Beiträge zur Philosophie des deutschen Idealismus* 1: 143–57, transl. as 'Negation', in *Translations from the Philosophical Writings of Gottlob Frege*, ed. and trans. P. Geach and M. Black, Oxford: Basil Blackwell, 1952.

—— (1923) 'Logische Untersuchungen, Dritter Teil: Gedankengefüge', *Beiträge zur Philosophie des deutschen Idealismus* 3: 36–51.

Gamut, L. T. F. (1991) *Logic, Language, and Meaning*, 2 vols, Chicago, IL: University of Chicago Press.

Gardiner, A. (1951) *The Theory of Speech and Language*, 2nd edn, Oxford: Oxford University Press.

Gardner, H. (1985) *The Minds's New Science*, 2nd edn, New York: Basic Books.

Garfield, J. (ed.) (1987) *Modularity in Knowledge Representation and Natural Language Understanding*, Cambridge, MA: Bradford Books/MIT Press.

Gazdar, G. (1979) *Pragmatics*, New York: Academic Press.

—— (1980) 'Pragmatic constraints on linguistic production', in B. Butterworth (ed.) *Language Production*. vol. 1, *Speech and Talk*, New York: Academic Press.

—— (1981) 'Speech act assignment', in A. Joshi, B. Webber and I. Sag (eds) *Elements of Discourse Understanding*, Cambridge: Cambridge University Press.

Geach, P. (1960) 'Ascriptivism', *Philosophical Review* 69: 221–25.

—— (1965) 'Assertion', *Philosophical Review* 74: 449–65.

Goffman, E. (1976) 'Replies and responses', *Language in Society* 5: 257–313.

Goldman, A. (1970) *A Theory of Human Action*, Princeton, NJ: Princeton University Press.

Goodwin, C. (1981) *Conversational Organization*, New York: Academic Press.

Gordon, D. and Lakoff, G. (1971) 'Conversational postulates', repr. in P. Cole, and J. L. Morgan (eds) *Syntax and Semantics*, vol. 3 *Speech Acts*, New York: Academic Press, 1975.

Grice, H. P. (1957) 'Meaning', *Philosophical Review* 66: 377–88; repr. in Grice 1989.

—— (1961) 'The causal theory of perception', *Proceedings of the Aristotelian Society*, Supplementary Volume 35: 121–52; repr. in Grice 1989.

—— (1968) 'Utterer's meaning, sentence meaning, and word-meaning', *Foundations of Language* 4: 225–48; repr. in Grice 1989.

—— (1969) 'Utterer's meaning and intentions', *Philosophical Review* 78: 144–77; repr. in Grice 1989.

—— (1975) 'Logic and conversation', in P. Cole and J.L. Morgan (eds) *Syntax and Semantics*, vol. 3, *Speech Acts*, New York: Academic Press; repr. in Grice 1989.

—— (1978) 'Further notes on logic and conversation', in P. Cole (ed.) *Syntax and Semantics*, vol. 9, *Pragmatics*, New York: Academic Press; repr. in Grice 1989.

—— (1981) 'Presupposition and conversational implicature', in P. Cole (ed.) *Radical Pragmatics*, New York: Academic Press; repr. in Grice 1989.

—— (1989) *Studies in the Way of Words*, Cambridge, MA: Harvard University Press.

Haiman, J. (1983) 'Iconic and economic motivation', *Language* 59: 781–819.

—— (1985) *Natural Syntax: Iconicity and Erosion*, Cambridge: Cambridge University Press.

Hamblin, C. L. (1958) 'Questions', *Australasian Journal of Philosophy* 36: 159–68.

—— (1971) 'Mathematical models of dialogue', *Theoria* 37: 133–55.

—— (1987) *Imperatives*, Oxford: Basil Blackwell.

Hancher, M. (1979) 'The classification of cooperative illocutionary acts', *Language in Society* 8: 1–14.

Hare, R.M. (1971) *Practical Inferences*, London: Macmillan.

—— (1976) 'Some confusions about subjectivity', in J. Bricke (ed.) *Freedom and Morality: The Lindley Lectures Delivered at the University of Kansas*, Lawrence, KS: University of Kansas.

—— (1989) 'Some sub-atomic particles of logic', *Mind* 98: 23–37.

Harnish, R. (1976a) 'Logical form and implicature', in T. B. Bever, J. J. Katz and D. T. Langendoen (eds) *An Integrated Theory of Linguistic Ability*, New York: Thomas Y. Crowell; repr. in Davis 1991.

—— (1976b) 'Two consequences of transparent subject position', *Philosophical Studies* 30: 11–18.

—— (1979) 'A projection problem for pragmatics', in F. Heny and H. Schnelle (eds) *Syntax and Semantics.* vol. 10, *Selections from the Third Groningen Round Table,* New York: Academic Press.

—— (1983) 'Pragmatic derivations', *Synthese* 54: 325–73.

—— (1986) 'Pragmatics and modularity', in F. Récanati (ed.) *Communication et cognition,* Paris: CNRS.

—— (1990) 'Speech acts and intentionality', in A. Burkhardt (ed.) *Speech Acts, Meaning and Intentions: Critical Approaches to the Philosophy of John R. Searle,* Berlin: Walter de Gruyter.

—— (1992a) 'Performatives are default reflexive standardized indirect acts', *Acta Linguistica* 40: 1–24.

—— (1992b) 'Communicating with proverbs', MS.

—— (in preparation) 'Mood, meaning and speech acts'.

Harnish, R. and Farmer, A. (1984) 'Pragmatics and the modularity of the linguistic system', *Lingua* 63: 255–77.

Harrah, D. (1985) 'A logic of message and reply', *Synthese* 65: 275–94.

—— (1986) 'Message semantics', *Notre Dame Journal of Formal Logic* 27: 339–48.

Hartmanis, J. and Stearns, R. E. (1966) *Algebraic Structure Theory of Sequential Machines,* Englewood Cliffs, NJ: Prentice-Hall.

Hawkins, J. A. and Cutler, A. (1988) 'Psycholinguistic factors in morphological asymmetry', in J. A. Hawkins (ed.) *Explaining Language Universals,* Oxford: Basil Blackwell.

Heath, J. (1984) *Functional Grammar of Nunggubuyu,* Canberra: Australian Institute of Aboriginal Studies.

Helbig, G. (1990) *Lexicon deutscher Partikeln,* Leipzig: Verlag Enzyklopädie.

Heringer, J. T. (1972) 'Some grammatical correlates of felicity conditions and presuppositions', *Ohio State University Working Papers in Linguistics* 11: 1–110.

Holdcroft, D. (1978) *Words and Deeds: Problems in the Theory of Speech Acts,* Oxford: Oxford University Press.

—— (1992) 'Searle on conversation and structure', in H. Parrett and J. Verschueren (eds) *(On) Searle on Conversation,* Amsterdam: John Benjamins.

Holdcroft, D. and Smith, P. (1992) 'Speech acts and computation', in R. Spencer-Smith and S. Torrance (eds) *Machinations: Computational Studies of Logic, Language and Cognition,* Norwood, NJ: Ablex Publishing Corporation.

Hopper, P. (1987) 'Emergent grammar', *Proceedings of the Thirteenth Annual Meeting of the Berkeley Linguistics Society,* Berkeley, CA: Berkeley Linguistics Society.

Horn, L. R. (1972) *On the Semantic Properties of Logical Operators in English,* Bloomington, IN: Indiana University Linguistics Club, 1976.

—— (1978) 'Remarks on Neg-raising', in P. Cole (ed.) *Syntax and Semantics,* vol. 9, *Pragmatics,* New York: Academic Press.

—— (1989) *A Natural History of Negation,* Chicago, IL: University of Chicago Press.

Hornsby, J. (1986) 'A note on non-indicatives', *Mind* 95: 92–9.

—— (1988) 'Things done with words', in J. Dancy, J. M. E. Moravcsik and C. C. W. Taylor (eds) *Human Agency: Language, Duty, and Value,* Stanford, CA: Stanford University Press.

Horwich, P. (1990) *Truth,* Oxford: Basil Blackwell.

Humberstone, L. (1992) 'Direction of fit', *Mind* 101: 59–83.

Hyman, A. and Walsh, J. J. (eds) (1973) *Philosophy in the Middle Ages,* Indianapolis, IN: Hackett.

Jespersen, O. (1917) 'Negation in English and other languages', repr. in *Selected Writings,* London: Allen & Unwin (n. d.).

—— (1924) *The Philosophy of Grammar*, London: Allen & Unwin.

Johnson, M. (1987) *The Body in the Mind: The Bodily Basis of Meaning, Reason, and Imagination*, Chicago, IL: University of Chicago Press.

Kamp, H. (1979) 'Semantics versus pragmatics', in F. Guenthner and S. J. Schmidt (eds) *Formal Semantics and Pragmatics for Natural Languages*, Dordrecht: Reidel.

—— (1981) 'A theory of truth and semantic represenation', in G. Groenendijk, T. Janssen and M. Stokhof (eds) *Formal Methods in the Study of Language*, Amsterdam: Mathematical Centre Tracts.

Karttunen, L. and Peters, S. (1979) 'Conventional implicature', in C.-K. Oh and D. A. Dinneen (eds) *Syntax and Semantics*, vol. 11, *Presupposition*, New York: Academic Press.

Kasher, A. (1976) 'Conversational maxims and rationality', in A. Kasher (ed.) *Language in Focus: Foundations, Methods and Systems*, Dordrecht: Reidel.

—— (1977) 'What is a theory of use?', *Journal of Pragmatics* 1: 105–20.

—— (1980) 'The institutional man: beyond religion and language', *Diotima* 8: 54–9.

—— (1981) 'Minimal speakers and necessary speech acts', in F. Coulmas (ed.) *Festschrift for Native Speaker*, The Hague: Mouton.

—— (1982) 'Gricean inference reconsidered', *Philosophica* (Ghent) 29: 25–44.

—— (1984) 'On the psychological reality of pragmatics', *Journal of Pragmatics* 8: 539–57.

—— (1989) 'On art circularity: logical notes on the institutional theory of art', in *Du vrai, du beau, du bien*, Paris: Librairie Philosophique J. Vrin.

—— (1991a) 'Pragmatics and Chomsky's research program', in A. Kasher (ed.) *The Chomskyan Turn*, Oxford: Basil Blackwell.

—— (1991b) 'On the pragmatic modules: a lecture', *Journal of Pragmatics* 16: 381–97.

—— (1991c) 'Pragmatics and the modularity of mind', in S. Davis (ed.) *Pragmatics: A Reader*, Oxford: Oxford University Press.

Kasher, N. (1978) 'Deontology and Kant', *Revue internationale de philosophie* 126: 551–8.

Katz, J. (1977) *Propositional Structure and Illocutionary Force*, New York: Thomas Y. Crowell.

Katz, J. and Fodor, J. (1963) 'The structure of a semantic theory', *Language* 39: 170–210.

Katz, J. and Postal, P. (1964) *An Integrated Theory of Linguistic Description*, Cambridge, MA: MIT Press.

Kearns, J. T. (1984) *Using Language: The Structures of Speech Acts*, Albany, NY: State University of New York Press.

Kripke, S. A. (1963) 'Semantical considerations on modal logic', *Acta Philosophica Fennica* 16: 83–94.

—— (1982) *Wittgenstein on Rules and Private Language*, Oxford: Basil Blackwell.

Ladusaw, W. (1979) *Polarity Sensitivity as Inherent Scope Relations*, New York: Garland.

Lakoff, G. (1972) 'Linguistics and natural logic', in D. Davidson and G. Harman (eds) *Semantics of Natural Language*, Dordrecht: Reidel.

—— (1977) 'Pragmatics in natural logic', in A. Rogers, B. Wall and J. P. Murphy (eds) *Proceedings of the Texas Conference on Performatives, Presuppositions, and Implicatures*, Arlington, VA: Center for Applied Linguistics.

—— (1987) *Women, Fire and Dangerous Things: What Categories Reveal about the Mind*, Chicago, IL: University of Chicago Press.

Lakoff, G. and Johnson, M. (1980) *Metaphors We Live By*, Chicago, IL: University of Chicago Press.

Lakoff, G. and Turner, M. (1989) *More Than Cool Reason: A Field Guide to Poetic Metaphor*, Chicago, IL: University of Chicago Press.

Lakoff, R. (1971) 'Some reasons why there can't be any "some–any" rule', *Language* 45: 608–15.

Langton, R. (1993), 'Speech acts and unspeakable acts', *Philosophy and Public Affairs* 22: 293–330.

Lappin, S. (1982) 'On the pragmatics of mood', *Linguistics and Philosophy* 4: 559–78.

Leech, G. N. (1983) *Principles of Pragmatics*, London: Longman.

Levinson, S. C. (1983) *Pragmatics*, Cambridge: Cambridge University Press.

Lewis, C. I. (1918) *A Survey of Symbolic Logic*, Berkeley and Los Angeles, CA: University of California Press.

Lewis, D. (1972) 'General semantics', in D. Davidson and G. Harman (eds) *Semantics of Natural Language*, Dordrecht: Reidel.

—— (1979) 'Scorekeeping in a language game', *Journal of Philosophical Logic* 8: 339–59.

—— (1986) *On the Plurality of Worlds*, Oxford: Basil Blackwell.

Liberman, M. (1978) *The Intonational System of English*, Bloomington, IN: Indiana University Linguistics Club.

Liedtke, F. W. (1990) 'Representational semantics and illocutionary acts', in A. Burkhardt (ed.) *Speech Acts, Meaning and Intentions: Critical Approaches to the Philosophy of John R. Searle*, Berlin: Walter de Gruyter.

Linebarger, M. (1987) 'Negative polarity and grammatical representation', *Linguistics and Philosophy* 10: 325–87.

Loar, B. (1981) *Mind and Meaning*, Cambridge: Cambridge University Press.

Locke, J. (1690) *An Essay Concerning Human Understanding*, ed. P. H. Nidditch, Oxford: Oxford University Press, 1975.

Lyons, J. (1968) *Introduction to Theoretical Linguistics*, Cambridge: Cambridge University Press.

—— (1977) *Semantics*, 2 vols, Cambridge: Cambridge University Press.

McCawley, J. (1988) *The Syntactic Phenomena of English*, 2 vols, Chicago, IL: University of Chicago Press.

McCawley, N. (1973) 'Boy! Is syntax easy!', *Papers from the Ninth Regional Meeting of the Chicago Linguistic Society*, Chicago, IL: Chicago Linguistic Society.

McDowell, J. (1976) 'Truth conditions, bivalence, and verificationism', in G. Evans and J. McDowell (eds) *Truth and Meaning*, Oxford: Oxford University Press.

—— (1977) 'On the sense and reference of a proper name', *Mind* 86: 159–85.

—— (1980) 'Meaning, communication, and knowledge', in Z. van Straaten (ed.) *Philosophical Subjects: Essays Presented to P. F. Strawson*, Oxford: Oxford University Press.

—— (1981) 'Anti-realism and the epistemology of understanding', in J. Bouveresse and H. Parret (eds) *Meaning and Understanding*, Berlin: Walter de Gruyter.

—— (1986) 'Singular thought and the extent of inner space', in P. Pettit and J. McDowell (eds) *Subject, Thought, and Context*, Oxford: Oxford University Press.

McGinn, C. (1977) 'Semantics for nonindicatives', *Philosophical Studies* 32: 301–11.

Malcolm, N. (1991) ' "I believe that p" ', in E. Lepore and R. Van Gulick (eds) *John Searle and his Critics*, Oxford: Basil Blackwell.

Matisoff, J. A. (1979) *Blessings, Curses, Hopes, and Fears: Psycho-Ostensive Expressions in Yiddish*, Philadelphia, PA: Institute for the Study of Human Issues.

Mead, G. H. (1934) *Mind, Self, and Society*, ed. C. W. Morris, Chicago, IL: University of Chicago Press.
Merin, A. (1991) 'Imperatives: linguistics vs. philosophy', *Linguistics* 29: 669–702.
—— (1992) 'Permission sentences stand in the way of boolean and other lattice-theoretic semantics', *Journal of Semantics* 9: 95–162.
Mittwoch, A. (1976) 'Grammar and illocutionary force', *Lingua* 40: 21–42.
Montague, R. (1974) *Formal Philosophy*, ed. R. Thomason, New Haven, CT: Yale University Press.
Morgan, J. L. (1978) 'Two types of convention in indirect speech acts', in P. Cole (ed.) *Syntax and Semantics*, vol. 9, *Pragmatics*, New York: Academic Press.
Morris, C. W. (1938) *Foundations of the Theory of Signs*, Chicago, IL: University of Chicago Press.
Nash, J. F. (1953) 'Two-person cooperative games', *Econometrica* 21: 140–52.
Olsen, T. (1978) *Silences*, New York: Delacorte Press.
Palmer, F. R. (1986) *Mood and Modality*, Cambridge: Cambridge University Press.
Parry, W. T. (1933) 'Ein Axiomsystem fur eine neue Art von Implikation (analytische Implikation)', *Ergebnisse eines Mathematisches Colloquiums, Vol. 4.*
Pendelbury, M. (1986) 'Against the power of force: reflections on the meaning of mood', *Mind* 95: 361–72.
Perry, J. (1986) 'Thought without represenation', *Proceedings of the Aristotelian Society*, Supplementary Volume 60: 137–51.
Pope, E. (1973) 'Question-answering systems', *Papers from the Ninth Regional Meeting of the Chicago Linguistic Society*, Chicago, IL: Chicago Linguistic Society.
Price, H. (1986) 'Conditional credence', *Mind* 95: 18–36.
—— (1988) *Facts and the Function of Truth*, Oxford: Basil Blackwell.
—— (1990) 'Why "not"?', *Mind* 99: 221–38.
—— (1992) 'Metaphysical pluralism', *Journal of Philosophy* 89: 387–409.
Prior, A. N. (1967) *Past, Present, and Future*, Oxford: Clarendon Press.
Putnam, H. (1975) 'The meaning of "meaning"', in K. Gunderson (ed.) *Minnesota Studies in the Philosophy of Science*, vol. 9, *Language, Mind and Knowledge*, Minneapolis, MN: University of Minnesota Press.
Quine, W. (1953) *From a Logical Point of View*, Cambridge, MA: Harvard University Press.
Radford, C. (1969) 'Knowing and telling', *Philosophical Review* 78: 326–36.
Récanati, F. (1987) 'Contextual dependence and definite descriptions', *Proceedings of the Aristotelian Society* 87: 57–73.
—— (1989) 'The pragmatics of what is said', *Mind and Language* 4: 295–329; repr. in Davis 1991.
—— (1993) *Direct Reference: From Language to Thought*, Oxford: Basil Blackwell.
Rood, D. and Taylor, A. R. (1976) *Beginning Lakhota*, vol. 1. Boulder, Colorado: University of Colorado Lakhota Project.
Sacks, H., Schegloff, E. A. and Jefferson, G. (1974) 'A simplest systematics for the organization of turn-taking in conversation', *Language* 50: 696–735.
Sadock, J. (1974) *Toward a Linguistic Theory of Speech Acts*, New York: Academic Press.
—— (1990) 'Comments on Vanderveken and on Cohen and Levesque', in P. R. Cohen, J. L. Morgan and M. Pollack (eds) *Intentions in Communication*, Cambridge, MA: MIT Press.
Sadock, J. and Zwicky, A. M. (1985) 'Speech act distinctions in syntax', in T. Shopen (ed.) *Language Typology and Syntactic Description*, vol. 1, *Clause Structure*, Cambridge: Cambridge University Press.

Salkie, R. (1990) *The Chomsky Update*, London: Unwin Hyman.

Schiffer, S. (1972) *Meaning*, Oxford: Oxford University Press.

—— (1982) 'Intention-based semantics', *Notre Dame Journal of Formal Logic* 23: 119–56.

Schiller, E. (1991) 'Autolexical solutions to the problem of parts of speech', in M. Ratiff and E. Schiller (eds) *Papers from the First Meeting of the Southeast Asian Linguistics Society*, Tucson, AZ: University of Arizona Press.

Schmerling, S. (1982) 'How imperatives are special, and how they aren't', *Papers from the Parasession on Nondeclaratives*, Chicago, IL: Chicago Linguistics Society.

Scott, D. and Strachey, C. (1971) *Towards a Mathematical Semantics for Computer Languages*, Technical Monograph PRG-6, Oxford University.

Searle, J. R. (1962) 'Meaning and speech acts', *Philosophical Review* 71: 423–32.

—— (1965) 'What is a speech act?', in M. Black (ed.) *Philosophy in America*, Ithaca, NY: Cornell University Press.

—— (1968) 'Austin on locutionary and illocutionary acts', *Philosophical Review* 77: 405–24.

—— (1969) *Speech Acts: An Essay in the Philosophy of Language*. Cambridge: Cambridge University Press.

—— (1975) 'A taxonomy of speech acts', in K. Gunderson (ed.) *Minnesota Studies in the Philosophy of Science*, vol. 9, *Language, Mind and Knowledge*, Minneapolis, MN: University of Minnesota Press.

—— (1978) 'Literal meaning', *Erkenntnis* 13: 207–24.

—— (1979) *Expression and Meaning: Studies in the Theory of Speech Acts*, Cambridge: Cambridge University Press.

—— (1980) 'The background of meaning', in J. R. Searle, F. Kiefer and M. Bierwisch (eds) *Speech Act Theory and Pragmatics*, Dordrecht: Reidel.

—— (1983) *Intentionality: An Essay in the Philosophy of Mind*, Cambridge: Cambridge University Press.

—— (1986) 'Meaning, communication, and representation', in R. Grandy and R. Warner (eds) *Philosophical Grounds of Rationality: Intentions, Categories, Ends*, Oxford: Oxford University Press.

—— (1989) 'How performatives work', *Linguistics and Philosophy* 12: 535–58.

—— (1991a) 'Response: meaning, intentionality, and speech acts', in E. Lepore and R. Van Gulick (eds) *John Searle and his Critics*, Oxford: Basil Blackwell.

—— (1991b) 'Response: perception and the satisfactions of intentionality', in E. Lepore and R. Van Gulick (eds) *John Searle and his Critics*, Oxford: Basil Blackwell.

—— (1992a) 'Conversation', in H. Parret and J. Verschueren (eds) *(On) Searle on Conversation*, Amsterdam: John Benjamins.

—— (1992b) 'Conversation reconsidered', in H. Parret and J. Verschueren (eds) *(On) Searle on Conversation*, Amsterdam: John Benjamins.

Searle, J. R. and Vanderveken, D. (1985) *Foundations of Illocutionary Logic*, Cambridge: Cambridge University Press.

Segal, G. (1991) 'In the mood for semantic theory', *Proceedings of the Aristotelian Society* 91: 103–18.

Seuren, P. A. M. (1988) Review of Sperber and Wilson 1986, *Journal of Semantics* 5: 123–43.

Shwayder, D. S. (1976) 'On the determination of reference by sense', in M. Schirn (ed) *Studies on Frege, III*, Stuttgart: Friedrich Frommann Verlag.

—— (1977) 'A semantics of utterance', *Midwest Studies in Philosophy* 2: 104–19.

—— (1992) *Statement and Referent*, Dordrecht: Kluwer Academic Publishers.

Smith, A. (1776) *An Inquiry into the Nature and Causes of the Wealth of Nations*; repr. London: Ward, Lock & Tyler (n. d.).

Sperber, D. and Wilson, D. (1985–6) 'Loose talk', *Proceedings of the Aristotelian Society* 86: 153–71.

—— (1986) *Relevance: Communication and Cognition*, Oxford: Basil Blackwell.

—— (1987) 'Précis of *Relevance: Communication and Cognition*' and 'Authors' response', *The Behavioral and Brain Sciences* 10: 697–710, 736–54.

—— (1988) 'Representation and relevance', in R. Kempson (ed.) *Mental Representations*, Cambridge: Cambridge University Press.

Stalnaker, R. C. (1978) 'Assertion', in P. Cole (ed.) *Syntax and Semantics*, vol. 9, *Pragmatics*, New York: Academic Press.

Stampe, D. W. (1975) 'Meaning and truth in the theory of speech acts', in P. Cole and J. L. Morgan (eds) *Syntax and Semantics*, vol. 3, *Speech Acts*, New York: Academic Press.

Steele, S. (1975) 'On some facts that affect and effect word order', in C. Li (ed.) *Word Order and Word Order Change*, Austin, Texas: University of Texas Press.

Stenius, E. (1967) 'Mood and language-game', *Synthese* 17: 254–74.

Stevenson, C. L. (1944) *Ethics and Language*, New Haven, CT: Yale University Press.

Strawson, P. F. (1952) *Introduction to Logical Theory*, London: Methuen.

—— (1964) 'Intention and convention in speech acts', *Philosophical Review* 73: 439–60.

Sweetser, E. (1990) *From Etymology to Pragmatics*, Cambridge: Cambridge University Press.

Talmy, L. (1985) 'Force dynamics in language and thought', *Papers from the Parasession on Causatives and Agentivity*, Chicago, IL: Chicago Linguistic Society.

—— (1988a) 'The relation of grammar to cognition', in B. Rudzka-Ostyn (ed.) *Topics in Cognitive Linguistics*, Amsterdam: John Benjamins.

—— (1988b) 'Force dynamics in language and cognition', *Cognitive Science* 12: 49–100.

Tarski, A. (1935) 'Der Warheitsbegriff in dem formalizierten Sprachen', *Studia Philosophica* 1: 261–405.

Travis, C. (1975) *Saying and Understanding: A Generative Theory of Illocutions*, Oxford: Basil Blackwell.

—— (1981) *The True and the False: The Domain of the Pragmatic*, Amsterdam: John Benajmins.

—— (1985) 'On what is strictly speaking true', *Canadian Journal of Philosophy* 15: 187–229.

—— (1989) *The Uses of Sense: Wittgenstein's Philosophy of Language*, Oxford: Clarendon Press.

Tsohatzidis, S. L. (1986) 'Four types of counterexample to the latest test for perlocutionary act names', *Linguistics and Philosophy* 9: 219–25.

—— (1987a) 'Deontic trouble in speech act botany', *Analysis* 47: 80–3.

—— (1987b) 'An episode from the emergence of the Gricean paradigm', *Word* 38: 288–93.

—— (1989) 'Explicit performatives not derivable from Bach-derivations for explicit performatives', *Linguistische Berichte* 120: 154–62.

—— (1990) 'A few untruths about "lie"', in S. L. Tsohatzidis (ed.) *Meanings and Prototypes: Studies in Linguistic Categorization*, London: Routledge.

—— (1992) 'Pronouns of address and truth conditions', *Linguistics* 30: 569–75.

—— (1993a) 'A paradox of cooperation in the conversational calculus', *Language and Communication* 13: 305–9.

—— (1993b) 'Emotional states and linguistic events: a study of conceptual misconnections', *Pragmatics and Cognition* 1: 229–42.

—— (1993c) 'Scenes and frames for orders and threats', in R. A. Geiger and B.

Rudzka-Ostyn (eds) *Conceptualizations and Mental Processing in Language*, Berlin and New York: Mouton de Gruyter.
—— (1993d) 'Speaking of truth-telling: the view from *wh*-complements', *Journal of Pragmatics* 19: 271–9.
Ultan, R. (1978) 'Some general characteristics of interrogative systems', in J.H. Greenberg, C. A. Ferguson and E. A. Moravcsik (eds) *Universals of Human Language*, vol. 4, *Syntax*, Stanford, CA: Stanford University Press.
Urmson, J. O. (1952) 'Parenthetical verbs', *Mind* 61: 480–96.
—— (1977) 'Performative utterances', *Midwest Studies in Philosophy* 2: 120–7.
van der Sandt, R. A. (1991) 'Denial', *Papers from the Parasession on Negation*, Chicago, IL: Chicago Linguistic Society.
Vanderveken, D. (1985) 'What is an illocutinary force?', in M. Dascal (ed.) *Dialogue: An Interdisciplinary Approach*, Amsterdam: John Benjamins.
—— (1990) 'On the unification of speech act theory and formal semantics', in P. R. Cohen, J. L. Morgan and M. Pollack (eds) *Intentions in Communication*, Cambridge, MA: MIT Press.
—— (1990–1) *Meaning and Speech Acts*, vols. 1 and 2, Cambridge: Cambridge University Press.
—— (1991) 'Non-literal speech facts and conversational maxims', in E. Lepore and R. Van Gulick (eds) *John Searle and his Critics*, Oxford: Basil Blackwell.
—— (1993) 'What is a proposition?', in M. Marion (ed.) *Logic and Philosophy of Science in Quebec*, Dordrecht: Kluwer Academic Publishers.
Waismann, F. (1951) 'Verifiability', in A. Flew (ed.) *Logic and Language*, 1st Series, Oxford: Basil Blackwell.
Warnock, G. J. (1973) 'Some types of performative utterance', in I. Berlin (ed.) *Essays on J. L. Austin*, Oxford: Oxford University Press.
—— (1989) *J. L. Austin*, London: Routledge.
Wellman, H. (1990) *The Child's Theory of Mind*, Cambridge, MA: MIT Press.
Wiggins, D. (1976) 'Truth, invention and the meaning of life', *Proceedings of the British Academy* 62: 331–78.
Williams, E. (1977) 'Discourse and logical form', *Linguistic Inquiry* 8: 101–39.
Williamson, T. (1992) 'Vagueness and ignorance', *Proceedings of the Aristotelian Society*, Supplementary Volume 66: 145–62.
Wilson, D. and Sperber, D. (1988) 'Mood and the analysis of non-declarative sentences', in J. Dancy, J. M. E. Moravcsik and C. C. W. Taylor (eds), *Human Agency: Language, Duty, and Value*, Stanford, CA: Stanford University Press.
Wittgenstein, L. (1921) *Tractatus Logico-Philosophicus*, London: Routledge, 1961.
—— (1953) *Philosophical Investigations*, Oxford: Basil Blackwell.
Wright, C. (1988) 'Realism, antirealism, irrealism, quasi-realism', *Midwest Studies in Philosophy* 12: 25–49.
—— (1993) 'Realism – the contemporary debate: whither now?', in J. Haldane and C. Wright (eds) *Reality, Representation and Projection*, Oxford: Oxford University Press.
Yanofsky, N. (1978) 'NP utterances', *Papers from the Fourteenth Regional Meeting of the Chicago Linguistic Society*, Chicago, IL: Chicago Linguistic Society.
Zwicky, A. (1974) 'Hey, whatsyourname', *Papers from the Tenth Regional Meeting of the Chicago Linguistic Society*, Chicago, IL: Chicago Linguistic Society.

Index